A Handbook of Information and Opportunities
for Disabled and Handicapped People

DIRECTORY FOR DISABLED PEOPLE

FIFTH EDITION

Compiled by
ANN DARNBROUGH AND DEREK KINRADE
Foreword by
KEN DAVIS

**Published in association with
The Royal Association for
Disability and Rehabilitation**

WOODHEAD-FAULKNER
New York   London   Toronto   Sydney   Tokyo

**Member: Association of
British Directory Publishers**

Published by Woodhead-Faulkner Limited,
Simon & Schuster International Group,
Fitzwilliam House, 32 Trumpington Street,
Cambridge CB2 1QY, England

First edition 1977
Second edition 1979
Third edition 1981
Fourth edition 1985
Second impression 1986
Third impression 1987
Fifth edition 1988

ISSN 0309-4413

British Library Cataloguing in Publication Data
Darnbrough, Ann
    Directory for disabled people: a handbook
    of information and opportunities for
    disabled and handicapped people.—5th ed.
    1. Great Britain. Facilities for physically
    handicapped persons. Information sources –
    Directories
    I. Title   II. Kinrade, Derek
362.4

ISBN 0-85941-449-3

Designed by Ron Jones
Typeset by Pentacor Ltd., High Wycombe, Bucks
Printed and bound in Great Britain at
the University Press, Cambridge

DIRECTORY FOR DISABLED PEOPLE

Member of

Association of British Directory Publishers

The best in British directory publishing

Registered Office:
Imperial House, 17 Kingsway, London WC2B 6UN
Telephone: 01-650 7745
Registered in England No: 1838313

CONTENTS

CONTENTS

FOREWORD

Ken Davis

This, the fifth edition of the *Directory for Disabled People*, is as much a record of change as it is an extremely useful source book. Since it was first published in 1977, successive volumes reveal increases in the range of information of value to disabled people. In turn, this growth of information reflects significant changes in the aspirations and expectations of disabled people themselves. Disabled people in the 1980s are becoming active and organised in what is now an international movement. The British Council of Organisations of Disabled People (BCODP), recognised as the representative voice of disabled people in Britain with some 60 member organisations – all controlled by disabled people themselves – was little more than a twinkle in the eye of a few disabled activists when the first edition of this Directory was published. Now it is Britain's national assembly on the Disabled Peoples' International (DPI), currently made up of representatives from 70 member nations.

It is helpful to see the Directory in the context of these changes to fully appreciate its role. First and foremost, however, it is a practical handbook of great value to any individual seeking information about a particular aspect of disability. Should it not provide all the answers, somewhere within its pages it will certainly point the enquirer in the right direction. In this way it becomes a powerful tool, reconciling the problems of range, depth and selectivity in one compact volume.

At the same time it is a book which can help to raise the awareness of disabled individuals in a number of ways. Simply by browsing through its pages, a reader's horizons can be extended. Newly disabled people struggling to make their way in an ablebodied world often have difficulty in knowing exactly what questions they need to ask. The Directory can help someone in this position to see the nature of their problems and formulate their enquiries more clearly. However, although the book addresses itself primarily to individuals, it also has an implicit consciousness-raising role in relation to disabled people collectively.

In this latter respect, it may perhaps seem ironical that the increasing amount of information available for inclusion in the Directory simply reveals how much more remains to be done to achieve the IYDP (International Year of Disabled People) aim of *full participation and equality* for all disabled people. The authors are committed to the liberating potential of open and accessible information. However, that potential is only fully realised when it leads to practical action in the real world. The disabled peoples' movement is the proper vehicle for this and, although the Directory does not set out to become a tool for disability action, it does lend itself incidentally to this purpose. This fifth edition comes at a time when much of the individual and social wellbeing of disabled people is being threatened by hostile political forces, and the need for a strong and united movement has never been more obvious.

Ann Darnbrough and Derek Kinrade have always recognised the importance of disabled people becoming organised and active in their own affairs. This new edition carries even more information about aspects of the work of the movement in Britain, particularly the growth of Centres for Independent or Integrated Living (CILs). New material is, of course, included from many other sources and where this is progressive and positive its inclusion is very much to be welcomed. However, as pressure continues to grow from disabled people themselves, we should expect more information to flow from improvements in the provision of appropriate housing, technical aids, personal assistance, transport and environmental access. This infrastructure of facilities is the key to our participation in education, employment and other social activities.

Whatever future changes occur however, the need for up to date, accurate information about them will remain constant. Such information is the basis of all considered decisions and this pre-eminence requires that it is communicated in ways which are accessible to all disabled people. There are, of course, two messages here: one for the authors and publishers, about versions of or inclusions in the Directory which make it more accessible and valuable to more disabled people, and one for disabled people themselves, who may be excluded from its contents because of its emphasis on the printed word. Having worked for some time in coalitions between people with visual, hearing and other impairments, I am only too aware of the difficulties involved. However, I know the authors are equally aware and willing to consider any suggestions which might make any future edition even more useful and more widely accessible.

Ken Davis
Secretary, Derbyshire Centre for Integrated Living
Member of Derbyshire County Council
Member of the British Council of Organisations of
Disabled People (BCODP)

INTRODUCTION

It is now 11 years since the first edition of this Directory was published in 1977. We believe that it has come to be relied upon as a basic information source for disabled people. In each new edition, there is a temptation to try to say something new by way of introduction, but the fact is that our aims and objectives remain the same: to provide, primarily for disabled people, signpost information to sources of help and opportunity. The fact that the Directory has grown in size, edition on edition, is an indication that there has been some development in what is available. Particularly welcome – though there is a long way to go – is the growing recognition of disabled people as consumers with rights: people who have identifiable interests which are not necessarily the same as those identified by service providers; and of the fact that services should be responsive to consumer need rather than what it is convenient to provide.

But in a number of key areas – employment, education and social services – progress has been largely cosmetic; indeed, in many basic respects provision and opportunity have actually regressed.

Nor has there been any perceptible movement towards reducing discrimination against disabled people. To enact legislation to that end would involve treating disabled people fairly, with resource implications which appear to be politically unacceptable. Even more deplorable is the fact that many disabled people reliant upon state benefits are now even worse off. The benefits system remains massively inadequate and blatantly unfair, and it is not encouraging to see an increasing tendency to shift responsibility onto the charities. Apart from the fact that such provision is undignified, subject to whim, and fragmented, some of the major charities concerned with disability are still run by able-bodied worthies who remain obdurately concerned to hold onto power and patronising in their attitudes. Charitable trusts can never be an adequate substitute for comprehensive statutory provision; in the present case, for a proper disability income.

Ann Darnbrough and Derek Kinrade
July 1988

NOTE: We learnt as we were going to press that the DHSS was being split into two departments – the Department of Health and the Department of Social Security. There has unfortunately not been time to incorporate this change in the Directory.

ACKNOWLEDGEMENTS

We can never thank enough all those people and organisations who regularly provide us with information by newsletters, leaflets, books, notices or personal contact, or indeed the hundreds of correspondents who responded to our questionnaire. As always, all of our information has been checked at source: this Directory owes its accuracy and breadth to the co-operation of so many others.

We cannot mention all their names here, but particular thanks are due to Richard Stowell whose advice and unstinting help on further education was invaluable; and to Department of Employment officials who took a good deal of trouble to set out the information on a scene which continued to change even as we wrote.

Finally, we are indebted to each other.

LIST OF ADVERTISERS

SECTION 1

STATUTORY SERVICES

Local Authority Services

GENERAL PROVISIONS

Under a number of Acts of Parliament (for which *see* Section 13), local authorities are concerned in meeting the needs of disabled people resident in their areas in a variety of ways. The broad areas of responsibility are set out below. In some of these, authorities are under a duty to make appropriate provision, in others (indicated by the use of italics), they are empowered to make provision with the approval of the Secretary of State and to such extent as he/she may direct.

1. Provision of residential accommodation for the aged and infirm.
2. *Making arrangements for promoting the welfare of disabled people.*
3. *Provision of facilities to enable disabled people to be employed or work under special conditions.*
4. Specified responsibility for the welfare and accommodation of people with mental disorders.
5. Provision of home-help and laundry facilities.
6. *Promotion of the welfare of old people.*
7. Provision of information and welfare services for disabled people (partly discretionary, see below).
8. Regard, in considering housing conditions and provision, to the special needs of chronically sick or disabled people.

The starting point for making arrangements for promoting the welfare of disabled residents is the National Assistance Act 1948 (*see* page 262). Provision may include the following:

1. *Advice on available services.*
2. *Instruction in ways of overcoming the effects of disabilities.*
3. *Provision of recreational facilities.*
4. *Compilation and maintenance of a register of handicapped persons.*

In making such arrangements, local authorities can (and, of course, do) use voluntary organisations as their agents. But the bedrock of provision

is the Chronically Sick and Disabled Persons Act 1970 (*see* page 263), which has recently been reinforced so that a disabled person or a carer of that person can now require a local authority to decide whether the disabled person's needs are such as to call for the provision of such welfare services (*see* Section 4 of the Disabled Persons (Services, Consultation and Representation) Act 1986, page 267).

Under the 1970 Act, local authorities must (this is a duty) first take steps to inform themselves of the numbers and needs of disabled people in their areas. They must also publish information as to the services they provide under Section 29 of the National Assistance Act 1948, but only 'from time to time and at such times and in such manner as they consider appropriate'. They must, however, ensure that disabled people who use any of these services are informed of any other service provided by the authority which in the opinion of the authority is relevant to their needs, and (by the 1986 Act) of any service provided by any other authority or organisation which in the opinion of the authority is so relevant and of which particulars are in the authority's possession. These are particularly important provisions and it is imperative that, if necessary, 'opinion' should be suitably influenced and action taken to ensure that local authorities do have all relevant information. There can then be no excuse for failing to provide information about both local and national services.

Section 2 of the 1970 Act is concerned with meeting the practical needs of disabled residents. This is subject to the authority being 'satisfied' that in order to meet the needs of a disabled resident it must make arrangements for any or all of the following kinds of provision. When it is so satisfied, however, then it is under a duty, under the general guidance of the Secretary of State, to make those arrangements.

1. The provision of practical assistance in the home.
2. The provision of, or assistance in obtaining,

wireless, television, library or similar recreational facilities.

3. The provision of lectures, games, outings or other outdoor recreational facilities, or assistance in taking advantage of available educational facilities.

4. The provision of facilities for, or assistance in, travelling to and from home for the purpose of participating in any services provided under arrangements made with the approval of the authority, or in any similar services which are otherwise provided and which could be provided under such approved arrangements.

5. The provision of assistance in arranging for works of home adaptations, or the provision of any additional facilities designed to secure the disabled person's greater safety, comfort or convenience.

6. Facilitating the taking of holidays (whether or not provided under arrangements made by the authority).

7. The provision of meals whether at home or elsewhere.

8. The provision of, or assistance in obtaining, a telephone and any special equipment needed to enable the disabled person to use it.

HOUSING

As well as the provision in respect of home adaptations at (5) above, Section 3 of the 1970 Act requires a local housing authority in discharging its general duty under Section 10 of the Housing Act 1985 (to consider housing conditions and the need for further housing accommodation in its district) to have regard for the special needs of chronically sick and disabled people (*see* Section 4 of this Directory).

ACCESS

Sections 4, 5, 6, 7, 8, 8A, 8B of the 1970 Act (as amended by the Disabled Persons Act 1981) impose access requirements not only on local authorities but on others (*see* page 264 and Section 16 of this Directory).

PARKING CONCESSIONS

These too are the responsibility of local authorities, under Section 21 of the 1970 Act (*see* Section 8 of this Directory).

DISABLED SCHOOL LEAVERS

Since February 1988, local authorities have also been required, in respect of children over 14 who have been the subject of a statement under the Education Act 1981 (*see* pages 246–9) and who are leaving special education, to decide whether or not any such child is a disabled person and if so to make an assessment of his/her needs (Sections 5/6 of the Disabled Persons (Services, Consultation and Representation) Act 1986).

CARERS

Social services departments, when assessing the needs of a disabled person who is cared for by another person (who is not an employee of the statutory services), must have regard to the carer's ability to provide that care on a regular basis (Section 8(1) of the Disabled Persons (Services, Consultation and Representation) Act 1986).

NOTE: Not all local authority services are free, and the amount an individual is expected to contribute varies in different localities. People dependent on state benefits should not normally have to pay anything (*see* Health and Social Services and Social Security Adjudication Act 1983 and Housing Act 1985 in Section 13).

SOCIAL WORKERS

Many of the local authority services described above are laid to social services authorities (by the Local Authority Social Services Act 1970 – *see* page 265). Social workers play a vital role in providing support in the community, while remaining the focal point for the essential communication between the various welfare services. They give personal help to disabled people on a visiting basis, especially when difficulties arise through illness, stress or other domestic problems. They will advise how the best use can be made of statutory and voluntary services available in their locality.

If you have cause to feel dissatisfied about, or have relationship difficulties with, a particular social worker, you are entitled to seek a change. The first point of contact is the manager of your area social work team, but if this is unproductive you may have to use the formal complaints procedure (*see* page 3).

BOOKS AND PUBLICATIONS

Guide to the Social Services (Family Welfare Association, 1988), price £7.65 including postage and packing. Distributed by Bailey Bros & Swinfen Ltd., Warner House, Folkestone, Kent CT19 6PH. This guide is published annually and provides a concise source of reference for all those working in and alongside the social services and for interested members of the general public.

Social Services Year Book (Longman Group UK Ltd., 6th Floor, Westgate House, The High, Harlow, Essex CM20 1NE, 1987/8), price £42.50. A reference directory of the individuals and organisations involved in social services in the United Kingdom. Its 806 pages contain information on national and local government provision, children's rights, health authorities, advice and counselling, voluntary service, elderly people's welfare organisations, professional bodies, research and development, and travel.

REGISTRATION

People who come within the definition set out in Section 29 of the National Assistance Act 1948 – i.e. who are blind, deaf or dumb, or substantially and permanently handicapped by illness, injury or congenital deformity – can apply to their local authority (social services) to be registered as disabled. This is a different kind of registration than that available for employment purposes (*see* Section 7). If your disability is such that you obviously qualify, no medical evidence should be necessary; otherwise a statement from your GP will be required. You don't have to apply for registration, but a number of state benefits depend on it, and some local authorities make it a pre-condition for the supply of services such as those under the Chronically Sick and Disabled Persons Act 1970. Other authorities will extend help equally to registered disabled people and to those who are entitled to be registered.

Some local authorities or local borough associations for disabled people have already produced guides to local services and it is well worth asking about these.

POSTAL VOTING

Physically handicapped people
If you cannot go personally to the polling station, or are unlikely to be able to do so, because of physical incapacity or blindness, or if, though able to go, you cannot vote unaided, you can apply to be treated as an absent voter and to vote by post. The application should be made on form RPF7, available from local council offices, and sent to the electoral registration officer responsible for the area where you live. The officer will allow the application if you have been registered as a blind person by your local authority or if your application has been certified by a medical or Christian Science practitioner (the officer can accept a certificate by someone else, e.g. a district nurse, but this is a matter for his/her discretion). Once an application has been approved, it is valid for an indefinite period. Postal voting is available at all parliamentary and local government elections except those for parish and community councils.

Voluntary mental patients
Special provision is made under the Representation of the People Act 1983 (*see* Section 13) for the registration of electors who are patients in mental hospitals. The provision does not, however, include patients who are detained compulsorily by the order of a court, nor to voluntary mental patients whose stay in hospital is only short term and who are registered for their home address in the normal way. If, on the qualifying date for electoral registration (10 October in Great Britain), you are a voluntary mental patient and not resident anywhere other than in a mental hospital, you are entitled to be registered as an elector under a 'patient's declaration'.

The 'patient's declaration' should be made on form RPF35, stocks of which are held in mental hospitals. You are entitled to make this declaration as a voluntary mental patient only if you are able to do so without assistance (in this context, 'assistance' does not include help necessitated by blindness or other physical incapacity). The declaration must be made in the presence of an authorised member of the hospital staff who must attest the declaration and the fact that it was made without assistance other than assistance needed because of blindness or physical incapacity. The declaration must also provide an address at which the voluntary mental patient would be resident if not in hospital, or an address at which he/she has lived in the United Kingdom. The patient will be treated as registered at this address and, since it may well be at some distance from the mental hospital, will be allowed to vote by post. Application to vote by post in these circumstances should be made on form RPF36; approval, if given, will be valid for only one particular election.

COMPLAINTS ABOUT LOCAL AUTHORITY SERVICES

In practice, the level and standard of assistance available to disabled people varies considerably from place to place. Some authorities appear to lack a genuine commitment to the needs of disabled people, while all have found recent economic constraints a considerable problem. Where both these drawbacks apply, the results can be disastrous. It is essential, therefore, that together with their carers, disabled people are aware of their rights to services and are persistent and forceful in pressing for necessary help. In particular, they should be aware of Section 4 of the Disabled Persons (Services, Consultation and

Representation) Act 1986 (*see* page 267) and be prepared to exercise the right which it confers. If that fails, or if there is unjustified delay, it may be necessary to turn to the complaints procedures. If local authorities – or, indeed, local authority officials – are slow and unconcerned, then they need to be made to jump. For too long disabled people, generally, have been passive and grateful for small mercies.

Complaints against local authorities should first be raised with the department concerned or with the Chief Executive of the authority. If the complaint is not resolved, ask a member of the authority – a councillor, not one of the paid officials of the council – to help you. If the complaint is still not resolved, ask the councillor to send the written complaint to the Local Ombudsman. If the councillor fails or refuses to refer the complaint, you can send it direct to the Local Ombudsman.

A free booklet, *Your Local Ombudsman*, is available from council offices, citizens' advice bureaux or from the Local Ombudsman at 21 Queen Anne's Gate, London SW1H 9BU (Tel: 01–222 5622).

The Local Ombudsman can investigate complaints only if:
(a) the complaint has previously been brought to the attention of the authority, and the authority has had reasonable time to reply;
(b) personal injustice has been caused as a result of administrative fault, e.g. unjustifiable delay, bias, incompetence, neglect, etc.

There are three Local Ombudsmen for England, two of whom work from the London office at Queen Anne's Gate, the other from 29 Castlegate, York YO1 1RN (Tel: York (0904) 30151). Similar arrangements exist for Wales, Scotland and Northern Ireland. The relevant addresses are as follows:

Commissioner for Local Administration in Wales
Derwen House, Court Road, Bridgend, Mid-Glamorgan CF31 1BN9 (Tel: Bridgend (0656) 61325).

Commissioner for Local Administration in Scotland
5 Shandwick Place, Edinburgh EH2 4RG (Tel: 031–229 4472).

Commissioner for Complaints in Northern Ireland
Progressive House, 33 Wellington Place, Belfast BT1 6HN (Tel: Belfast (0232) 3821).

Health Services

The full range of health and community health services is, of course, available to disabled and able-bodied people alike. Facilities which are of particular benefit to handicapped people include the provision of aids and equipment (*see* Section 3), child health clinics, chiropody clinics, remedial therapy, help and advice from health visitors and home nursing by district nurses. In all cases, the primary contact is your family doctor.

Financial help with fares is given to people on low incomes who have to attend hospital as a patient (for details, *see* DHSS Leaflet H11). If, because of disability, you cannot use public transport to get to hospital for treatment, or if no public transport is available, special transport arrangements can be made by the hospital concerned. Disabled people can sometimes be admitted to hospital for short periods to give their relatives a break.

If you are worried about the possibility that a disabling condition might be passed on if you or your partner were to have children, your local doctor can refer you, if necessary, to a Genetic Counselling Centre. There is a useful free DHSS booklet on genetic conditions, *Human Genetics*, available from CMP 3C, DHSS, Hannibal House, Elephant and Castle, London SE1 6BY.

In-patient services in hospitals sometimes include purpose-built units for the care of physically disabled people, as well as facilities for reassessment and rehabilitation back into normal life. Medical rehabilitation (as distinct from rehabilitation for employment) may involve, as well as normal medical and nursing care, the specialist help of remedial therapists. This can continue on an out-patient basis after discharge.

HEALTH PERSONNEL

Chiropodists
Disabled people, among others, are entitled to free chiropody, but this must be arranged through your GP. Some chiropodists will treat disabled people at home if they cannot easily visit a clinic. Some Health Authorities operate a visiting community service.

Dentists
There is a Community Dental Service in every Health Authority. It has responsibility for providing dental services to people who because of disability cannot visit a dentist in the ordinary way. Some dentists will treat disabled people at home in these circumstances. *See also* DLF Notes, *Dentistry and Disability* (Disabled Living Foundation Information Service, 380–384 Harrow Road, London W9 2HU), price £1.20.

Dieticians
Dieticians can advise on specialist diets. They may be seen at local hospitals, normally on the recommendation of a doctor.

District nurses
District nurses are employed by district health authorities and provide help with domestic nursing care on a visiting basis. Anyone needing their services should contact their doctor.

Family doctors
The key person and the primary contact for help and advice about health and related services is the family doctor. You can choose your own doctor, providing he/she does NHS work and will accept you. Your local Community Health Council, post offices, libraries and Citizens' Advice Bureau should each have a list of doctors in your area. In any case of difficulty, your local Family Practitioner Committee (*see* telephone directory) should be able to help. All you have to do is to take your medical card on your first visit to the doctor of your choice. You can change your doctor at any time without giving a reason, though you would be wise to make sure you have been accepted by your chosen new doctor before asking to be withdrawn from your present doctor's list. Normally, each doctor simply signs your medical card and the changeover is immediately effective. In case of difficulties, or if you feel embarrassed about it, you can effect a change of doctor by sending a letter to the Family Practitioner Committee, advising your wish to transfer, and enclosing your medical card. The Committee will return the card with a slip attached showing the earliest date on which a transfer can be made (normally 14 days after receipt of your letter). This can then be taken to your new doctor. If the change is caused by a move to a new district, it is necessary only to take your medical card to the new doctor of your choice.

In an emergency, you can ask any NHS doctor for treatment, but it is for the doctor to decide if it is a genuine emergency. Similarly, your own doctor has discretion as to whether a visit to your home is necessary.

Health visitors
These people are trained nurses employed by district health authorities. They can give advice and assistance on all family health and associated welfare problems.

Medical social workers
Medical social workers are hospital based and are able to play a key role if you need help to sort out social problems, e.g. advising you on your entitlement to benefits, arranging for you to receive help on such as meals-on-wheels and home-help on your discharge from hospital. (It is important that, where necessary, there is full liaison between medical and local authority social workers before you are due to be discharged from hospital.) Medical social workers can also help you and your family to work through the emotional and social conflicts which may arise because of your disability. If necessary, they will help you to register as a disabled person.

Occupational therapists
These people assess the practical needs of disabled people to live and work as normally as possible. Their help should be sought through a doctor or social worker. In most areas, OTs operate on a visiting basis to advise you on any equipment, adaptations or structural alterations which may be necessary to your home. They can also instruct you in techniques for overcoming physical handicaps and to encourage maximum possible dexterity through the performance of congenial tasks. Information can be obtained from District Occupational Therapists in Health Authorities and Principal Occupational Therapists in social services departments. (*See also*, *Occupational Therapy in the Community* edited by Eileen E. Bumphrey (Woodhead-Faulkner (Publishers) Ltd., Fitzwilliam House, 32 Trumpington Street, Cambridge CB2 1QY, 1988, price £12.50 paper, £19.95 cased, plus postage and packing.)

Physiotherapists
They help to maintain bodily movements, as far as possible, by means of physical techniques. These include massage, electro-therapy and treatment by infra-red and ultra-violet light. Their services must normally be sought through a doctor, but some operate on a private professional basis.

Psychiatric social workers
Their work is particularly concerned with people who are mentally ill, helping both patients and their families to work through their problems towards the achievement of maximum potential. In some cases, practical help is given on discharge from hospital, e.g. in arranging hostel accommodation and places in day centres.

Remedial gymnasts
They are attached to rehabilitation centres in some localities and can help you to achieve greater mobility by exercises and recreational activities.

5

Speech therapists
Specialists in helping with speech difficulties of all kinds. Serious cases will normally be referred by a doctor acting on his/her own initiative, but help is also available to improve or remove even minor impediments. (The College of Speech Therapists, Harold Poster House, 6 Lechmere Road, London NW2 5BU, Tel: 01–459 8521, maintains lists of speech therapists within the National Health Authorities, of specialist advisers and of speech therapists prepared to treat privately.)

COMMUNITY HEALTH COUNCILS
These work to improve the services provided by the district health authority – hospitals, health centres, clinics and community health services, and in this role represent a bridge between the public and those who administer the NHS.

Community health councils have a major part to play in informing members of the public about local health services, on such things as how to change your GP, or how to register a complaint about a local service. They will guide you from the initial lodging of a complaint right through, if necessary, to accompanying you to a tribunal. Addresses appear in telephone directories under Community Health Council.

REHABILITATION CENTRES
In addition to the rehabilitation work done in hospitals, sometimes in special units, there are a number of purpose-built or specially adapted rehabilitation centres throughout Great Britain. They provide facilities for the rehabilitation of patients, on referral, who are suffering serious handicap as a result of injury, disease or, in some cases, age. Some, such as Mary Marlborough Lodge at Oxford and the Wolfson Centre at Wimbledon, are famous for their work with patients who have very severe physical/neurological impairments.

Rehabilitation centres offer expert assessment and testing of functional abilities, intensive treatment, training for coping with disability in everyday activities and the provision of any necessary aids.

DISABLEMENT SERVICES CENTRES
Formally known as Artificial Limb and Appliance Centres, DSCs are strategically placed throughout the United Kingdom. They are responsible for the provision of artificial limbs, wheelchairs, and for the supply of surgical appliances and other services to war pensioners. Apart from the Artificial Eye

Service and the Invalid Vehicle Service, which will continue to operate from these centres under DHSS control, responsibility for DSC services has passed to a new Disablement Services Authority. This authority will oversee the reorganisation of the Service into regions with boundaries that are co-terminous with those of the National Health Service. It is envisaged that management responsibility will pass to Regional and District Health Authorities on 1 April 1991.

These changes follow the highly critical report of a working party chaired by Professor Ian McColl. Improvements in the training and status of prosthetists are planned, and it is hoped that the reorganised management structure will facilitate stronger links with occupational therapy, physiotherapy and rehabilitation services already operating within the NHS.

As recommended by the McColl report, the 27 existing centres will be supplemented by more small 'satellite' centres over the next two or three years. Improvements in transport facilities to bring disabled people to the centres are also being made, and the first steps have already been taken to separate the fitting service from the supply of limb hardware, to increase the number of prosthetics companies, and to introduce competitive tendering (after a reference by the Office of Fair Trading to the Monopolies and Mergers Commission to investigate the supply of artificial lower limbs in the United Kingdom). The intention is to encourage a quicker and more flexible service for disabled people. Should this not be achieved in practice or in every case, a formal complaints procedure now exists.

The Wheelchair Service, which has often been found slow and unresponsive, will eventually be provided mainly at a more local level, away from the DSCs, probably in hospitals on referral from GPs. District Health Authorities will have the benefit of therapists to prescribe the wheelchairs, and these arrangements are already being introduced at some DSCs, in advance of transfer to the NHS. Three wheelchairs will be available: a low-performance, occasional-use wheelchair, a children's wheelchair and a sports wheelchair. Professor McColl, we are told, is still very keen to see an indoor/outdoor occupant controlled wheelchair introduced, one of the main recommendations of his report which has not, presumably on grounds of cost, been acted upon.

NOTE: In Northern Ireland, the National Health Service took over Artificial Limb and Appliance Centres in 1980. There is an integrated rehabilitation service which, according to Professor McColl, is 'better by far than the English set-up', and has been described by *Disability Now* (February 1988) as 'a service to be proud of'. For those in Great Britain, comfort can perhaps be taken from the fact that Professor McColl is vice-chairperson of the new Disablement Services Authority. We await future developments with interest.

BOOKS AND PUBLICATIONS

The Health Information Handbook. See Appendix A.

Patients' Association Leaflets. The Patients' Association, Room 33, 18 Charing Cross Road, London WC2H 0HR (Tel: 01–240 0671), makes available a number of helpful publications: *Rights of the Patient*, price 20p; *Changing your Doctor*, price 20p; *Going into Hospital*, price 40p; *Using the NHS*, price 40p; *Can I Insist?*, price 40p. (This booklet poses such questions as 'I'm being treated by my GP, but I'm not getting any better. I'd really really like to see a specialist. How can I arrange it?'; 'I've been in hospital for tests but they won't tell me what the matter is or what the tests showed. Haven't I a right to know what's wrong with me?' Helpful and informative answers are provided to these and other questions about visits by children in hospitals, dental treatment, donating your body or particular organs, home and hospital confinement, and pregnancy tests and abortions); *Self-help and the Patient*, price £2.95 (*see* Appendix A); and *Patient Voice*, quarterly, £5.00 per annum.

A Patient's Guide to the NHS (Consumers' Association with Hodder and Stoughton, available from PO Box 44, Hertford SG14 1SH, 1983), price £5.95. A joint production of the Patients' Association and the Consumers' Association.

Patients' Rights: a guide for NHS patients and doctors (HMSO, 1983), price £1.50. Produced by the National Consumer Council, this is an admirable publication in all respects: concise and to the point yet crammed with relevant, factual information of a kind which we all need from time to time, and organised in a way which makes it easy to access. Entries include such matters as abortion, changing/choosing/finding a GP, complaints, confidentiality, death (the right to die; use of your body), drugs (addiction; consent to treatment); osteopathy and second opinion. The only regret is the lack of an index.

HELPFUL ORGANISATIONS

As well as statutory services, a number of voluntary organisations have been formed which are specially concerned with health services and the welfare of patients generally. They are ready to help people who may encounter difficulties or who are worried about illness, diagnosis, treatment and related problems. Details of some of these are given in Section 15, Helpful Organisations, under the heading 'Health'.

COMPLAINTS ABOUT HEALTH SERVICES

The first thing to be said about complaints procedures in the health sector is that they have worked very badly. *Disability Now* (January 1988) reported the view that the present system is 'defensive, slow, bureaucratic, impersonal and soft on follow-up'. More and more people are necessarily having recourse to legal remedies.

With that proviso, however, your Community Health Council (address in telephone directory) will always give guidance on making a formal complaint about the health service, assisting through all stages which may be necessary to resolve the problem.

Should you wish, at least at first, to pursue the matter yourself, formal complaints about family doctors, opticians, dentists or chemists should be made to your local Family Practitioner Committee. Formal complaints about hospitals or community health services should be referred to the district administrator of the NHS district management team (ask the CHC for the address). It is good practice always to put a formal complaint in writing and to retain a copy.

If you are dissatisfied with the result, the Health Service Commissioner may be able to carry out an investigation. His terms of reference are, however, strictly limited by Act of Parliament, and he is precluded from investigating certain matters, for instance complaints which have been taken to a tribunal or a court of law or which involve clinical judgements. Further details are given in leaflets available from the following addresses, to which complaints should also be addressed:

The Health Service Commissioner for England
Church House, Great Smith Street, London SW1P 3BW.

The Health Service Commissioner for Scotland
2nd Floor, 11 Melville Crescent, Edinburgh EH3 7LU.

The Health Service Commissioner for Wales
4th Floor, Pearl Assurance House, Greyfriars Road, Cardiff CF1 3AG.

Complaints which may call into question the clinical judgement of a doctor may well involve legal action if they are of a serious nature. In less serious cases, when you are dissatisfied with an initial response, you can renew your complaint. If the matter cannot then be resolved, e.g. by discussion with you, there is an established procedure which provides for a review of the medical matters involved by two independent consultants who, by discussion of the whole issue with you and the medical staff concerned (possibly combined with a physical examination if you wish and if it seems appropriate), will seek to determine whether the care provided was fully appropriate to your condition and performed to a proper standard. The discussion with you will be private and completely confidential, but, if you wish, you may bring a relative or personal friend with you to the meeting. The independent consultants will then report on a confidential basis to the Regional Medical Officer, with any recommendations they wish to make, e.g. on matters requiring action by the health authority. The administrator for the authority concerned will then write to you, explaining where appropriate any action it has taken as a result of your complaint.

Where to Find Local Sources of Help

Consult the telephone directory under the following headings:

Citizens' Advice Bureaux	Listed as such
Community Health Councils	Listed as such
Disablement Services Centres (formerly Artificial limb and Appliance Centres)	Health and Social Security, Department of (Disablement Services Centres or Appliance Centres)
Disablement Resettlement Officers	Employment, Department of (Job Centres)
Education Authorities	The relevant county, district or London borough council (Education Authority)
Family Planning	Listed as such
Income Tax	Inland Revenue
Rent and Rates	The relevant county, district or London borough council (Housing Department)
Social Security	Health and Social Security, Department of (Local Social Security Offices)
Voluntary Organisations	The name of the organisation (or see Section 15, Helpful Organisations)
Welfare Rights Officers (in some areas only)	The relevant county, district or London borough council (Welfare Rights Offices)

SECTION 2
FINANCIAL BENEFITS AND ALLOWANCES

Introduction

In our previous edition, we criticised the state benefits system for its complexity, inadequacy and inequality, and suggested that it was time for reform. Some, perhaps, felt that we were unduly harsh: after all, much progress had been made. A number of benefits for disabled people had come into being which at one time simply did not exist at all. However flawed, however bewildering, the welfare net was securely in place. There was a base on which to build, scope for improvement. The mobility allowance might, in time, be extended to elderly people; the rules for attendance allowance might be relaxed; the severe disablement allowance might be extended to cover more disabled people; and the invalid care allowance might be increased to compensate carers more realistically for loss of earnings.

In practice, of course, nothing of the sort has happened. Far from making progress, the much publicised 'reform' of the social security system has taken us backwards. This is not surprising, given that the primary motivation for change (and this has not really been disguised) has not been a desire for greater social justice, but rather to keep the lid on expenditure and, in particular, to reduce the administrative burden imposed by the supplementary benefit additional allowances and discretionary single payments. The stringency which has for many years conditioned the whole approach to welfare benefits has become a strait-jacket, and provision is guided not by what is needed or what is fair, but by the credo of cash limits.

Not only have we had no improvements. We have in place of supplementary benefit an income support scheme which will leave many disabled people substantially worse off, and instead of single payments we have the Social Fund, a resource which seems to take us back towards the worst Victorian values, and one in which, for the most part, money for essential needs will be available only to a limited extent and only as a loan. With local and national cash limits, it is inevitable that many people will be turned away. Budgetary loans will be refused if it appears that you won't be be able to pay the money back, thus pushing the least able into the jaws of the loan sharks. The 'lucky' ones who are seen as meriting a loan will have to pay it back from resources already stretched to the limit.

The philosophy used as an apology for this latest round of social injustice runs along the lines of people taking personal responsibility for their lives and not being encouraged in dependency, a notion which is completely out of touch with the problems of poverty and which conveniently overlooks the fact that better-off people are themselves heavily dependent on tax allowances, company 'perks' and, not infrequently, a privileged upbringing, comfortable family circumstances and inherited wealth. Disabled people would prefer not to be dependent. But those that are, need and deserve decent help. The case for a comprehensive disability income is stronger than ever and will not be effectively met by piecemeal grants from charitable trusts.

These are our views, and we feel that we must state them unequivocally. For the purpose of providing information, however, we can only report things as they are, not as we would like them to be. We have not attempted to bring out every detail of the benefits and allowances which are available. This would require a book in itself, and there are already a number of excellent guides devoted to this purpose (*see* pages 39–40). Our objective is to bring the central facts to your attention, to give you enough guidance to decide that a particular scheme may be appropriate to your circumstances, and to trigger you to seek further guidance. Such is the difficulty of the system that you may well need advice on a one-to-one basis from someone who is expert and who can look at your circumstances in the round. We mention some helpful sources of such help on page 39.

Complaints Procedures

It is important that unsatisfactory standards in the way that you or your affairs are dealt with by civil servants should not be allowed to pass without challenge. Hopefully, cause for complaint is rare, but there are some grounds for concern that in certain places services to the public are so inadequate that dissatisfaction is almost inevitable. In the ordinary way, complaints about the actions of a government department should first be taken up with the department concerned at a suitably high level, and preferably in writing. Sometimes you may find it useful to seek the help of a local organisation, e.g. your Citizens' Advice Bureau or Association for Disabled People, which can support your complaint. If the matter is really serious, you may feel it necessary to take legal advice or to seek the help of your Member of Parliament, either in writing (keep a copy) or at one of his/her local 'surgeries'.

In the most serious cases – where it is claimed that injustice has been sustained through maladministration – your MP can be asked to refer the matter to the Parliamentary Commissioner for Administration, Church House, Great Smith Street, London SW1P 3BW. The scope of the Commissioner's powers excludes the investigation of certain matters – for instance, complaints which have already been taken to a tribunal or a court of law, or which involve local authorities, the police, nationalised industries or the Post Office. Nor can he accept a complaint direct from a member of the public. It must be referred through an MP, and include a statement that the complainant consents to the matter being put to the Commissioner. Further details are given in a leaflet available from the Great Smith Street address.

Capital Taxes

CAPITAL GAINS TAX

This is a tax on the gain made when you give away, exchange or sell something you own, which has increased in value since you acquired it. For example, if you sell shares you may have to pay CGT. However, any increase in value which is attributable to inflation after March 1982 is discounted in calculating your net gain, and there is an exemption limit for each tax year (1988/9: £5,000 for individuals).

If you sell your house but do not buy another there is, of course, a capital gain, but if the house was your only or main residence, you may not have to pay CGT. Leaflet CGT4 *Capital Gains Tax – Owner-occupied Houses* explains the rules.

You may be exempt from CGT if you sell your business or shares in a family-owned company because you are retiring at age 60 or over, or because you are ill. Leaflet CGT6 *Retirement – disposal of a business* will tell you more.

INHERITANCE TAX

This tax applies to estates above a prescribed exemption limit at death. It may also apply to transfers of possessions which would reduce the value of your estate when you die, for example if you gave your house to a daughter or son as a present. The rules are complex, so if you are thinking of transferring your home or business to your children or otherwise giving away capital, you would be well advised to seek professional advice. Transfers between husband and wife are exempt. A helpful booklet IHT1, *Inheritance Tax* is available from the Capital Taxes Office at: Minford House, Rockley Road, London W14 0DF, or 16 Picardy Place, Edinburgh EH1 3NB, or Law Courts Building, Chichester Street, Belfast BT1 3NU.

Income Tax

When you are worried about your health, or how you can cope with a partner who is ill, income tax may not be very high on your order of priorities. But it is important to tell your tax office if there is a change in your circumstances which could affect your tax position. For example, you may have to give up work or you may start to get a taxable state benefit. By letting your tax office know promptly you can be sure that you pay the right amount of tax from the outset and that you will not be faced by a bill for arrears at some later date.

Look at leaflet IR52 *Your Tax Office* if you are in any doubt about which tax office to contact.

ARE ALL STATE BENEFITS TAXABLE?

No. Some are and some are not. There have been several changes in recent years, so if you are in doubt about past years, check with your tax office.

As at April 1988, the position is as follows:

Taxable
    retirement pension including any invalidity addition;
    widow's pension, widow's allowance and widowed mother's allowance;
    unemployment benefit;

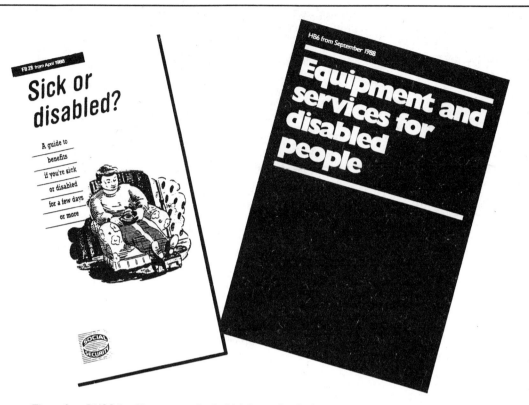

These free DHSS booklets are packed with information for long-term sick and disabled people.

So if you're disabled, or if you look after someone who is, send for them now — simply fill in the coupon below. Or you can get them from your Social Security office.

Organisations requiring supplies of the booklets should write to the address on the coupon saying how many copies they need.

Please send me booklets FB28 Sick or disabled? ☐

(tick boxes   HB6   Equipment and services for ☐
as required)   disabled people

Name_____

Address_____

_____

_____ Postcode_____

Post coupon to DHSS Leaflets Unit, PO Box 21, Stanmore, Middx. HA7 1AY.

income support paid to those who are unemployed, on strike or involved in a trade dispute;

invalid care allowance;

industrial death benefit

Not taxable

sickness benefit;

invalidity benefit, including invalidity allowance;

severe disablement allowance;

industrial disablement benefit;

attendance allowance;

housing benefit;

maternity allowance;

child benefit and one-parent benefit;

income support paid to those who are not unemployed, on strike or involved in a trade dispute;

family credit;

Christmas payment to pensioners;

guardian's allowance;

child's special allowance;

war widow's pension;

mobility allowance;

Social Fund payments.

SICK PAY AND MATERNITY PAY

Statutory sick pay and statutory maternity pay are paid to you by your employer and taxed as if they were part of your pay. If sick pay is paid out of an employer's sick pay scheme, the amount the employer has contributed to it is taxable.

TAX ALLOWANCES

Personal allowances

A guide to all the income tax personal allowances (Leaflet IR22) can be obtained free from any office of HM Inspector of Taxes or from PAYE Enquiry Offices, where information and help on specific problems can be obtained. Except where married couples opt for their earnings to be taxed separately (an option which is advantageous only where the joint earnings are high) a wife's income is aggregated with her husband's for income tax purposes. If the husband's income falls below the amount of his allowances (even to nil) his full allowances may nevertheless be set against the joint income of himself and his wife. If his wife works she is entitled to an 'earned income allowance' (1988/ 9: £2,605).

In the following notes on those allowances most likely to be of special interest to disabled people it has been assumed that married couples have *not* elected to be taxed separately, and that they are living together.

Additional personal allowance

The allowance for 1988/9 is £1,490. It may be available provided that:

(a) the taxpayer has a child living with him or her and is either:
  (i) entitled to the single person's allowance as a single-parent, widow or widower; or
  (ii) a married man whose wife is totally incapacitated by physical or mental infirmity throughout the whole of the relevant tax year; and

(b) the child is either a child of the taxpayer (including a step-child or a legally adopted child) or any other child maintained at the taxpayer's own expense. Two people living together but not married can only claim one additional personal allowance between them.

Blind person's allowance

A taxpayer who is a registered blind person is entitled to an allowance of £540 (1988/9). This means a person who is so blind as to be unable to do any work for which eyesight is essential. A married man may claim in respect of himself or his wife. Where both husband and wife are registered blind, the allowance is £540 each (1988/9). A registered blind person may claim the full allowance even where he or she has been registered for only part of the tax year.

One-parent families

Leaflets IR29 and IR77 give details of the special tax position of lone parents.

PENSIONERS

Leaflet IR4 *Income Tax and Pensioners* answers many of the questions pensioners ask about their income tax. First, it gives some general explanation on matters which often cause misunderstandings. It goes on to describe some of the tax allowances which may be claimed and the way in which National Insurance pensions and other pensions are taxed. Finally, it deals with the taxation of other kinds of income. Leaflet IR4A *Income Tax Age Allowance* should be read in conjunction with IR4.

WIDOWS

Leaflet IR23 *Income Tax and Widows* explains how income tax affects widows, especially those recently bereaved.

TAX RELIEF FOR EXPENSES INCURRED BY SELF-EMPLOYED PEOPLE

In calculating the profits of a trade, profession or vocation which fall to be taxed under Schedule D, the extent to which expenses may be deducted is governed by section 130 of the Income and Corporation Taxes Act 1970 (as amended). The rules are of great complexity, and in practice each case is judged on its merits, but the underlying principle is to limit relief to expenses 'wholly and exclusively' for the purposes of the trade. In general, an expense whose purpose is to overcome a physical disability of the trader does not meet this condition. However, individual circumstances may sometimes produce a different result. For example, a shopkeeper who was fit might be able to cope single-handed with the number of customers patronising his or her shop. If some disability reduced his or her mobility, s/he might find it necessary to engage an assistant to do some of the work. The direct and exclusive purposes of paying wages to the assistant would then be a trade purpose, even though in the absence of the disability the necessity would not have arisen.

A similar distinction is to be found in the case of medical expenses. If a trader has to have medical attention, its cost is not exclusively for the purposes of his trade and is not allowable as tax relief. But if s/he has to engage a *locum tenens* to run the business during his/her absence owing to illness, the fee payable to the *locum* is allowable as being exclusively for the purposes of the trade.

RELIEF FOR EXPENSES INCURRED BY EMPLOYEES

To qualify for this relief, the expenses must be incurred 'wholly, exclusively and necessarily' in the performance of the duties of the employment. Expenses incurred in order to put a person in a position to do his/her job do not, unfortunately, qualify for a tax allowance; neither do expenses arising from his/her personal circumstances as distinct from those which are inherent in his duties. On these criteria (which have been upheld by the courts in a number of cases) expenditure arising from a person's disability is not within the admissible category and cannot, therefore, be allowed.

HOME TO WORK TRAVEL OF SEVERELY DISABLED EMPLOYEES

A person who is severely and permanently disabled and incapable of using public transport because of his/her disability may be provided with alternative means of transport or receive financial assistance with the cost of journeys between his/her home and place of employment. Normally such assistance would come from the Department of Employment under their Assistance with Fares to Work Scheme for Severely Disabled People or from local authorities in respect of those employed in sheltered workshops.

By concession, income tax is not charged under any of the provisions of Schedule E on the amount received or benefit provided.

PENSIONS

Pensions are normally taxable, but the amount by which the pension awarded on retirement through disability caused by injury on duty or by a work-related illness (e.g. pneumoconiosis, asbestosis, etc.) or by war wounds, exceeds the pension which would have been awarded if retirement had been on ordinary ill-health grounds is not treated as income for income tax purposes. Similarly, a pension awarded solely on account of such retirement is not treated as income.

IF YOU HAVE TO STOP WORK BECAUSE OF AN ILLNESS OR DISABILITY

If you are an employee, make sure you get a form P45 from your employer. It shows your pay and tax to date in the tax year. You will need it if you want to claim unemployment benefit or a tax refund.

LUMP SUMS ON LEAVING EMPLOYMENT

Liability to tax depends on why the payment was made. Special rules apply if your contract of employment gives you the right to receive the lump sum. The following payments are not usually taxed if they are under £30,000:

redundancy payments;
payments for loss of office;
payments in lieu of notice;
ex-gratia payments.

If your employer pays you a lump sum because your illness means that you cannot continue in your job, it may be completely free of tax even if it is more than £30,000, but your employer should seek prior authorisation from the tax office.

Lump sums paid under the rules of most pension schemes are free of tax whatever the amount.

Attendance Allowance

WHO?

Adults and children aged 2 or more who are severely disabled, physically or mentally, and who will need a great deal of looking after for at least six months are eligible for attendance allowance. This is tax free, non-means-tested and non-contributory.

HOW MUCH? (APRIL 1988)

The allowance is paid at one of two rates – the higher rate is paid to those who require attendance both by day *and* by night; the lower rate is payable to those needing attendance either by day *or* by night.

Higher rate	£32.95 a week
Lower rate	£22.00 a week.

MEDICAL CONDITIONS

The disability must be so severe that for six months you have needed:

(a) **during the day**: frequent attention throughout the day in connection with your bodily functions; or continual supervision throughout the day in order to avoid substantial danger to yourself or others;

(b) **or at night**: prolonged or repeated attention in connection with your bodily functions; or another person to be awake for a prolonged period or at frequent intervals for the purpose of watching over you to avoid substantial danger to yourself or others. (This condition reflects an amendment made by the Social Security Act 1987 to limit the effect of the Court of Appeal decision in the *Moran* case: this upheld a claim for attendance allowance by an epileptic who, while she did not need her husband to be awake all the time, did need him to be there on standby in case she had a fit.)

Bodily functions, for the purpose of the allowance, include walking and getting about; eating or drinking; using the lavatory; washing, bathing, or undressing; shaving; using a kidney machine at home or in a hospital self-care unit with assistance from someone who is not employed by the hospital.

A child of two or over, but under 16, must satisfy a further requirement that the attention or supervision required must be substantially in excess of that normally required by a child of the same age and sex.

You should claim if you need a lot of looking after, even if you don't get as much attention or supervision as you need, e.g. because you live alone.

There is no provision for the allowance to be back-dated, so it is important to claim as soon as possible. You can claim three months in advance of satisfying the six-month rule (in the case of a child under two, at the age of 21 months).

RESIDENCE CONDITIONS

You must be living in the United Kingdom or the Isle of Man when you claim, and normally you must have been living here for six out of the past 12 months. (*See* DHSS leaflet NI38 if you have recently lived outside the United Kingdom or are temporarily abroad. *See* DHSS leaflet FB5 if you are a member of an HM service family.)

LIVING AWAY FROM HOME

You can apply for attendance allowance, but it cannot be paid to you while you are living in a place which is provided or helped by public money, e.g.:

(a) a home run by a local authority;

(b) a hospital, unless you are a private patient paying all your costs except treatment (but *see* below);

(c) a boarding school paid for by a local authority;

(d) a special college or training centre for disabled people; or

(e) a private or voluntary home where some or all of your costs are paid by a local authority.

But the allowance is still paid for:

(a) the first four weeks after admission to hospital (this allows payment to continue through short periods of respite care, but if you have been in hospital within the previous 28 days and are being readmitted, the two periods will normally be linked);

(b) a child who lives with foster parents, whether or not the local authority pays a boarding out allowance;

(c) a child in a home or school not paid for by a local authority, but whose parents pay an amount towards the child's keep;

(d) a person living in local authority rented accommodation such as a council house, or temporary housing for homeless people; or

(e) a person during those times he or she is away from residential home, hospital or school, e.g. weekends at home.

WHO CAN CLAIM?

It is the disabled person concerned, if meeting the conditions, who is entitled to benefit, not the attendant or supervisor. In the case of an adult, the disabled person should normally make the claim, but someone can complete the form if they declare that they have done so. If, through illness or a mental condition, a disabled person is unable to manage his/her own affairs, the DHSS will appoint someone to act (this may be a legal representative). In the case of a disabled child, the person who has care of that child should normally claim. If the child lives with both parents, the mother should claim; if with one parent, that parent should claim; if with neither parent, the person whose name appears on the order book for child benefit for that child. If, however, the child lives with foster parents who receive a boarding-out allowance, then the foster mother should claim.

RELATIONSHIP TO OTHER BENEFITS

Attendance allowance stands on its own. It is normally paid in full and in addition to other benefits. An exception is where constant attendance allowance is being paid with an industrial, war or service pension, when, if the CAA is the lesser, the difference between the two will be paid.

Income support is not normally affected, except where you are being paid on an 'urgent needs' basis and sometimes in the case of boarders .

Attendance allowance does not count as income when claiming means-tested benefits, e.g. housing benefit or income support, and is not affected by any earnings you may receive. If, however, you start work while receiving the allowance, this is likely to be regarded as a change of circumstances, and may prompt a review of your entitlement. But provided that your need for attention or supervision remains unchanged, the allowance should not be affected.

NOTE: The rules governing attendance allowance are extremely restrictive and tend to be rigidly applied. It is therefore important that applications (which must be made in writing) are accurate and clear, and give a full and proper picture of the facts. You would be well advised to get the Disability Alliance checklist (see below) and to seek expert help in completing the form.

The attendance allowance may be a vital factor in determining a carer's entitlement to invalid care allowance (see page 25).

FURTHER INFORMATION

Read DHSS leaflet NI205 which includes details of how to claim.

Get *Attendance Allowance – Going for a Review* (Disability Alliance ERA, 25 Denmark Street, London WC2H 8NJ), price £1.50 to advisers, 75p to claimants (both including postage). This includes a 'Checklist' which sets out the practical circumstances which can give rise to the need for attention and supervision; the 'Review Procedure' section is specifically intended for people who have had their first claim for attendance allowance turned down.

Telephone the free DHSS telephone enquiry service: 0800–666 555.

Contact one of the organisations listed on page 39.

Read one of the guides listed on pages 39–40.

Employment Training Grants

See Section 7, Employment.

Family Credit

WHO?

Family credit is tax free, means-tested and non-contributory. Working people (employed or self-employed) who have at least one child and whose total family income falls below levels prescribed by law are eligible. You can claim family credit if you are a single parent, or married, or living with someone as if you are married to them.

HOW MUCH? (APRIL 1988)

If your income is not more than £51.45 a week, you are entitled to the full amount of family credit set out below as appropriate to your family circumstances.

If, however, your income exceeds £51.45 your family credit will be reduced by 70 per cent of the extra income. Income includes money which either adults or children have coming in regularly, but some items are disregarded (*see* below).

The maximum weekly amounts of family credit are as follows:

Adult credit (lone parent *or* couple)	£32.10
Child credit (unless the child has savings over £3,000)	
under 11 years old	£6.05
11 to 15 years old	£11.40
16 to 17 years old	£14.70
18 years old	£21.35

The income taken into account is net of income tax and National Insurance contributions, and some items are disregarded, e.g.:
(a) attendance allowance;
(b) mobility allowance;
(c) certain other benefit income – child benefit, one parent benefit and housing benefit;
(d) the first £5 a week of a war pension;
(e) the first £5 a week of voluntary and charitable payments.

Savings up to £3,000 are also disregarded, but after that, up to £6,000, each £250 or part of £250 will be treated as an income of £1 a week. So if you have savings of, say, £4,100, they will be treated as equivalent to £5 weekly income. If your savings exceed £6,000 you will not be entitled to family credit. (If you have a partner, to whom you are married or with whom you live as if you were married, your partner's savings are added in.)

BASIC CONDITIONS

You must be present and ordinarily resident in Great Britain (there is separate legislation for Northern Ireland).

Your savings must not exceed £6,000.

You must be working at least 24 hours a week and supporting at least one child who normally lives with you.

NOTES:

1. Family credit replaced family income supplement on 11 April 1988.
2. In two parent families, the woman should normally claim.
3. The Social Security Act 1988 provides a new statutory framework for the Welfare Foods Scheme to bring it into line with the provisions of the Social Security Act 1986, so that from April 1988 families qualifying for family credit will receive a cash allowance instead of welfare foods.

FURTHER INFORMATION

Read DHSS leaflet NI 261 *A Guide to Family Credit* (leaflets FB4 and FB27 may also be helpful).

Telephone the free DHSS telephone enquiry service: 0800–666 555.

Contact one of the organisations listed on page 39.

Read one of the guides listed on pages 39–40.

The Family Fund

PO Box 50, York YO1 1UY.

Financed by the Government and independently administered by the Joseph Rowntree Memorial Trust, the Fund helps families caring for a very severely physically and/or mentally handicapped child under 16 years, living in the United Kingdom. Decisions and policy rest with the staff at York, but the Fund's own visiting social workers may call on families to discuss their needs, and to obtain the information necessary to establish eligibility and, if possible, to make a grant. Grants given by the Fund do not affect entitlement to social security or other benefits.

For a successful application it must be shown that:

(a) the child's handicaps are very severe within the definition laid down by the Fund's medical advisers;
(b) the family's social and economic circumstances justify help from the Fund; and
(c) the application is within the scope of the Fund's guidelines.

Decisions about severity of handicap are based on a detailed description of the child's functioning in all areas, and if necessary a report from the doctor most familiar with the child's problems. A statement of income is *not* requested, but each grant has to be justified in the light of the family's economic circumstances. The Fund would not help parents whose income could reasonably be expected to cover the modest needs with which the Fund is concerned. The help given relates to the basic needs posed by the child's handicap, and not available from existing services: laundry equipment to cope with incontinence; family holidays to relieve the stress; outings when holidays prove too difficult to face; driving lessons if the caring parent would then have access to a car; clothing and bedding when the handicap causes extra wear and tear; recreational equipment if justified by the handicap; a fridge/freezer to cope with shopping or diet problems arising from the disability, and many other items. Help takes the form of goods or a grant for a specific purpose. Each application is considered on its own merits in the light of the Fund's criteria. It is not possible to help with general needs which would arise irrespective of the presence of the handicapped child. Nor does the Fund help with private education, nor private medical treatment, nor private housing. It cannot be used as an alternative for items which are the responsibility of the statutory services, although there are times when the Fund complements such provision.

Application can be made directly by parents, or from professionals who have sought the parents' consent. Write to the Fund at the above address, giving the child's full name and address, details of the disability and the nature of the request being made.

Further Education Grants

See Section 6, Further Education and Training.

Home Responsibilities Protection

WHO?

This is not a direct benefit, but a scheme designed to protect your pension rights if you are unable to keep up your normal National Insurance contributions because you have to look after someone at home, and you do not get invalid care allowance (which would credit you with contributions).

Any full tax year (6 April to the following 5 April) in which you qualify for HRP on the grounds set out below will be regarded as a year of 'home responsibility' and deducted from the number of qualifying years of National Insurance contributions you would otherwise need for a full pension or for a wife's benefit as a widow (though, in either case, a prescribed minimum number of qualifying years is nevertheless required).

CONDITIONS

HRP can cover any tax year after 6 April 1978 in which either you do no work at all or, though you do some work, your contributions are insufficient to count for pension purposes, provided that, for the whole tax year, you have been:
(a) getting child benefit for a child under 16; or
(b) looking after someone regularly (for at least 35 hours every week) who has been in receipt of attendance allowance or constant attendance allowance paid with a war or service pension or industrial injuries benefit; or
(c) getting income support to enable you to stay home to look after an elderly or sick person; or
(d) any combination of these conditions.
A married woman or widow paying reduced NI contributions cannot qualify for HRP.

Hospital In-Patients

Most social security benefits are paid to help with your ordinary needs at home, or the special needs caused by your disability. When you, or your partner or child, are in hospital, some of these needs are met by the National Health Service, so your benefit may go down or stop. But if you are paying the whole cost of accommodation and non-medical services in hospital, your social security benefits will not be affected (except for invalid care allowance and income support).

FURTHER INFORMATION

Read DHSS leaflet NI9 *Going Into Hospital*.
Telephone the free DHSS telephone enquiry service: 0800–666 555.
Contact one of the organisations listed on page 39.
Read one of the guides listed on pages 39–40.

Hospital Travelling Costs

If you have to travel to hospital, either as an out-patient or an in-patient, you may be able to get help with your normal public transport fares (including, in some special circumstances, taxi fares), or reasonable petrol costs. You can also get help with travel when you come out of hospital. If you need someone to go with you, you may get help with their fares too. If you visit hospital to see a patient who is a close relative, you may be able to get help with travelling costs if you are getting income support.

FURTHER INFORMATION

Read DHSS leaflet H11 *NHS Hospital Travelling Costs*.
Telephone the free DHSS telephone enquiry service: 0800–666 555.
Contact one of the organisations listed on page 39.
Read one of the guides listed on pages 39–40.

Housing Benefit

WHO?

People on low incomes who need help to pay their rent and/or rates are eligible. Housing benefit is tax free, means-tested and non-contributory and can be claimed whether you own your own home or live in rented accommodation, whether council or private housing. Nor do you have to be getting other social security benefits. While the amount you get is affected by income, you are not ruled out because you are working.

Most people who get income support are automatically entitled to housing benefit if they pay rent or rates (but have to claim). If you stop getting income support, you may still be entitled to housing benefit, but would need to make a new claim.

People living in board and lodging, hostels, residential care or nursing homes cannot get housing benefit in addition to income support.

WHAT DOES HOUSING BENEFIT COVER?

Housing benefit can cover some or all of your rent and up to 80 per cent of the rates you pay just to live in your home. They are called your 'eligible rent' and 'eligible rates', and may not be the same as you pay to your landlord. Among other things, authorities have discretion to make reductions if they consider the accommodation to be unreasonably large, unreasonably expensive (private sector rents only) or in an unreasonably expensive area, provided always that there is suitable and cheaper accommodation available. However, reductions on this account should not be made if your personal circumstances are such that it would be unreasonable to expect you to move. Such circumstances include age, health, disability and special accommodation needs.

If you rent your home, or if you own the lease on your home and the lease was originally made for 21 years or less, your eligible rent may include some service charges that you have to pay for things like children's play areas, cleaning shared areas, and lifts.

Housing benefit cannot be given for:

mortgage interest repayments;
the cost of fuel for heating, lighting and cooking;
the cost of meals included in the rent;
water charges;
some service charges for things like personal laundry and household cleaning;
ground rent and service charges for your home if the lease was originally for more than 21 years;
rates for business premises.

HOW MUCH? (APRIL 1988)

All claims are worked out by your local council.

If you are getting income support and pay rent or rates, you will get housing benefit up to a maximum entitlement. This will be all of your eligible rent (if any) and 80 per cent of your eligible rates, but if you have other people living with you who do not depend on you to support them, your housing benefit will normally be reduced.

If you don't get income support, the above entitlement to housing benefit will be reduced by a fixed percentage (65 per cent for purposes of the rent element; 20 per cent for purposes of the rates element) of the amount by which your net income exceeds an amount (called the applicable amount and made up of personal allowances and premiums as set out below) prescribed by law on which you are expected to live.

NET INCOME

This is the amount of money you have coming in apart from certain 'disregards'. It includes both earnings (but *after* tax, National Insurance and related pension contributions) and any unearned income you may receive (including some social security benefits, but *not* mobility allowance or supplement, nor attendance allowance).

The main items of income which are disregarded are:
(a) the first £5 a week of your earnings (if any);
(b) the first £5 a week of your partner's earnings (if any) (for some people £15 of their earnings will not be counted, e.g.: lone parents; those getting a disability premium; couples under 60 who have been out of work and getting supplementary benefit (before 11 April 1988) or income support for two years or more);
(c) the first £5 a week of a war pension; and
(d) the first £5 a week of voluntary and charitable payments.

Savings up to £3,000 are also disregarded, but after that, up to £8,000, each £250 or part of £250 will be treated as an income of £1 a week. So if you have savings of, say, £4,100, they will be treated as equivalent to £5 weekly income. If your savings exceed £8,000 you will not be entitled to income support. (If you have a partner, to whom you are married or with whom you live as if you were married, your partner's savings are added in.)

ALLOWANCES AND PREMIUMS

Single people	Weekly rate
16 and 17 years old	£19.40
18 to 24 years old	£26.05
25 years old and over	£33.40
18 years old and over and bringing up a child on your own	£33.40
Couples	
both under 18	£38.80
with at least one of the couple aged 18 or over	£51.45
For each child in the family (unless the child has savings over £3,000)	
under 11 years old	£10.75
11 to 15 years old	£16.10
16 to 17 years old and doing a full-time course that is not above A level or OND standard	£19.40
18 years old and doing a full-time course that is not above A level or OND standard	£26.05

In addition, some people may be entitled to a premium to meet special needs as set out below. If you qualify in more than one category, you will nevertheless normally get only one premium – that which gives you the most money, but the family premium, disabled child's premium and severe disability premium can be paid on top of other premiums.

For people with children
If you have at least one child you qualify for *family premium* £6.15
If you have a child who is getting attendance allowance or mobility allowance or who is registered as blind you qualify for *disabled child's premium* £6.15
If you are bringing up one or more children on your own you qualify for the *lone parent premium* £3.70

For long-term sick or disabled people	Single person	Couples
If you or your partner is getting a benefit such as invalidity benefit, severe disablement allowance, mobility allowance or attendance allowance, or is registered as blind you qualify for the *disability premium*	£13.05	£18.60
If you are sick and cannot work and have been submitting doctor's statements about this to the DHSS for at least 28 weeks you qualify for the *disability premium*	£13.05	£18.60
If you (or a person with whom you live) is getting attendance allowance, and no one is getting invalid care allowance for looking after you (or a person with whom you live) you qualify for the *severe disability premium*	£24.75	£24.75
If you both qualify as above (severe disability premium is paid as well as the disability premium described above or the higher pensioner premium described below)		£49.50

For people aged 60 or over

If you or your partner is 60 to 79 years old you qualify for the *pensioner premium*	£10.65	£16.25
If you or your partner is 60 to 79 years old and getting attendance allowance, invalidity benefit, severe disablement allowance, or is registered as blind you qualify for the *higher pensioner premium*	£13.05	£18.60
If you or your partner is 80 or over you qualify for the *higher pensioner premium*	£13.05	£18.60

FURTHER INFORMATION

Read DHSS leaflet RR1 which includes details of how to claim, or the more detailed RR2.

Contact a local Housing Aid Centre.

Telephone the free DHSS telephone enquiry service: 0800–666 555.

Contact one of the organisations listed on page 39.

Read one of the guides listed on pages 39–40.

Anyone requiring a really detailed knowledge of the legislation may wish to obtain *Annotated Housing Benefit Legislation: A Guide through the* *Labyrinth* (Child Poverty Action Group Ltd., 1–5 Bath Street, London EC1V 9PY, 1988), price £14.95.

Housing Grants for Improvements, Repairs, Provision of Standard Amenities

See Section 4, House and Home.

Income Support

WHO?

People whose total family income falls below amounts prescribed by law, and who are:
(a) unemployed, or
(b) aged 60 or more; or
(c) bringing up children on their own; or
(d) too sick or disabled to work, or only able to work part-time; or
(e) staying at home to look after a disabled relative

are eligible for income support which is tax free, means-tested and non-contributory.

HOW MUCH? (APRIL 1988)

This is a prescribed amount (called the *applicable amount* and set by law at what it is considered you need to live on) less your income. There are special systems for working out income support if you live in board and lodging, a hostel, residential care or a nursing home which are not dealt with here.

The applicable amount depends on your circumstances, as follows:

	Weekly rate
Single people	
16 and 17 years old (on a very restricted basis)	£19.40
18 to 24 years old	£26.05
25 years old and over	£33.40
18 years old and over and bringing up a child on your own	£33.40
Couples	
both under 18	£38.80
with at least one of the couple aged 18 or over	£51.45
For each child in the family (unless the child has savings over £3,000)	
under 11 years old	£10.75
11 to 15 years old	£16.10
16 to 17 years old and doing a full-time course that is not above A level or OND standard	£19.40
18 years old and doing a full-time course that is not above A level or OND standard	£26.05

In addition, some people may be entitled to a premium to meet special needs as set out below. If you qualify in more than one category, you will nevertheless normally get only one premium – that which gives you the most money, but the family premium, disabled child's premium and severe disability premium can be paid on top of other premiums.

For people with children

If you have at least one child you qualify for *family premium* £6.15

If you have a child who is getting attendance allowance or mobility allowance or who is registered as blind you qualify for *disabled child's premium* £6.15

If you are bringing up one or more children on your own you qualify for the *lone parent premium* £3.70

For long-term sick or disabled people

	Single person	Couple
If you or your partner is getting a benefit such as invalidity benefit, severe disablement allowance, mobility allowance or attendance allowance, or is registered as blind you qualify for the *disability premium*	£13.05	£18.60
If you are sick and cannot work and have been submitting doctor's statements about this to the DHSS for a least 28 weeks you qualify for the *disability premium*	£13.05	£18.60
If you (or a person with whom you live) is getting attendance allowance, and no one is getting invalid care allowance for looking after you (or a person with whom you live) you qualify for the *severe disability premium*	£24.75	£24.75
If you both qualify as above (severe disability premium is paid as well as the disability premium described above or the higher pensioner premium described below)		£49.50

For people aged 60 or over

If you or your partner is 60 to 79 years old you qualify for the *pensioner premium* £10.65 £16.25

If you or your partner is 60 to 79 years old and getting attendance allowance, invalidity benefit, severe disablement allowance, or is registered as blind you qualify for the *higher pensioner premium* £13.05 £18.60

If you or your partner is 80 or over you qualify for the *higher pensioner premium* £13.05 £18.60

You can also have help to pay the interest on mortgages or home loans. The amount will depend on your age. If both the person getting income support and his/her partner are under 60, an amount will be added to cover half the interest for the first 16 weeks of entitlement to benefit; after this an amount to cover all the interest will normally be added. If, however, the person getting income support, or his/her partner, is 60 or over an amount to cover all the interest will normally be added on from the outset. Extra money for any ground rent that has to be paid can also be added to income support.

Any income you have (apart from a few exceptions) is deducted from your 'needs allowances' to arrive at the amount of income support payable. The main items of income which are disregarded are:

(a) the first £5 a week of your earnings (if any);
(b) the first £5 a week of your partner's earnings (if any) (for some people £15 of their earnings will not be counted; e.g.: lone parents; those getting a disability premium; couples under 60 who have been out of work and getting supplementary benefit (before 11 April 1988) or income support for two years or more);
(c) the first £5 a week of a war pension;
(d) the first £5 a week of voluntary and charitable payments.

Savings up to £3,000 are also disregarded, but after that, up to £6,000, each £250 or part of £250 will be treated as an income of £1 a week. So if you have savings of, say, £4,100, they will be treated as equivalent to £5 weekly income. If your savings exceed £6,000 you will not be entitled to income support. (If you have a partner, to whom you are married or with whom you live as if you were married, your partner's savings are added in.)

BASIC CONDITIONS

You must live in Great Britain.

You must be aged 16 or more (after September 1988, with some exceptions, the starting age for income support is 18).

Your savings must not exceed £6,000.

You must not be working for 24 hours or more a week, unless:

(a) you work at home as a childminder, or

(b) you are so disabled that you cannot earn much money.

(If the work condition rules you out of income support, you may nevertheless be entitled to claim family credit – *see* page 15).

You must not be in full-time, non-advanced education.

You must, with some exceptions, be 'available for work'.

AVAILABILITY FOR WORK

It is a normal requirement that claimants should be signing on as available for work. Certain groups are, however, exempt from this requirement. These include:

(a) people aged 60 or more;
(b) people who, on the evidence of a current doctor's statement, are incapable of work;
(c) people registered as blind;
(d) people who are mentally or physically disabled and whose earning capacity is reduced to 75 per cent or less of what they would, but for that disability, be reasonably expected to earn;
(e) students who are severely mentally or physically handicapped and because of that would be unlikely, even if they were available for work, to obtain work within the next 12 months;
(f) students who, because of a mental or physical disability, would, in comparison with other students, be unlikely to obtain work within a reasonable period of time;
(g) people getting a training allowance;
(h) people attending an Open University required residential course; and
(i) people regularly and substantially engaged in caring for another person who gets or has claimed attendance allowance, or who themselves get invalid care allowance.

OTHER HELP YOU CAN GET WHILE YOU ARE GETTING INCOME SUPPORT

1. Housing benefit (from your local authority) to help you to pay your rent and rates. But you will have to pay your water charges and part of your rates.
2. For yourself, your partner or your children:
   (a) free NHS prescriptions;
   (b) free NHS dental treatment;
   (c) free travel to hospital for NHS treatment;
   (d) help with the cost of spectacles.

Exceptional expenses payments formerly paid with supplementary benefit are no longer available, but you may be able to get help from the Social Fund if you are faced with exceptional expenses that you cannot afford to pay (*see* page 34).

NOTES

1. Income support replaced supplementary benefit on 11 April 1988. The higher long-term rates and weekly additions have been abolished. Weekly additions have been replaced by flat rate premiums, but access to these is defined and restricted and the amount may be less than some people were receiving when individually assessed. Some transitional protection has been provided, but this is short term (*see* below).
2. If both partners in a couple might be entitled to income support, either one of them can claim the benefit. If one of them cannot work because of illness, they may get more income support after 28 weeks if the person who is ill claims.
3. By the Social Security Act 1988, young people under 18 will not qualify for income support except in circumstances and for periods to be prescribed in regulations. At the time of writing (April 1988), this section of the Act had not yet been brought into force. When it is, it will also provide the Secretary of State with a discretionary power to treat a young person as entitled to income support in circumstances where severe hardship would otherwise result, and we can only hope that the position of disabled teenagers will be appropriately protected.

TRANSITIONAL ARRANGEMENTS

The transitional rules are complex, but the basic principle is that if you were receiving supplementary benefit in the week before 11 April 1988, and your total benefit entitlement then was higher than under the new rules in the week 11 to 17 April 1988, you will receive a transitional addition equal to the difference between your benefit income for the two weeks. The addition will still be paid even if you have no entitlement to income support because your income is too high. But it will not be paid if you cease to qualify for income support under the new rules. The effect of this is that if your circumstances remain unchanged you should normally receive the same total benefit after 11 April as before. But the bad news is that the transitional addition will be reduced progressively as your entitlement to income support increases through annual upratings; this means that your benefit entitlement is frozen until the level of income support due catches up with your protected benefit. There is one exception: those previously entitled to a supplementary benefit additional requirement payment for domestic assistance of £10 or more may qualify for a *special* transitional addition. This is dealt with separately from the calculation of total benefit income described above. If you qualify for income support severe disability premium, you will get a special transitional addition only if the previous domestic assistance allowance was higher – the amount will be the difference between the two. If you do not qualify for the severe disability premium, the special transitional addition will be the whole of your domestic assistance allowance. This special addition is not normally affected by changes in your circumstances, but it will end if you lose entitlement to income support, or if you are in hospital longer than six weeks (though it may be re-awarded when you come out), or if you go permanently into a residential care or nursing home.

FURTHER INFORMATION

Read DHSS leaflet SB20 *A Guide to Income Support* (also leaflets FB6 *Retiring?*, FB9 *Unemployed?*, FB23 *Young People's Guide to Social Security*, FB27 *Bringing up Children?*, FB28 *Sick or Disabled?*).

Telephone the free DHSS telephone enquiry service: 0800–666 555.

Contact one of the organisations listed on page 39.

Read one of the guides listed on pages 39–40.

The Independent Living Fund

Room 520, New Court, Carey Street, London WC2A 2LS.

WHO?

Very severely disabled people who need to pay someone for personal care and help with domestic duties are eligible.

HOW MUCH? (APRIL 1988)

The Fund is financed by the Government which has made up to £5 million available. Unless this provision is increased, the scope for grants would appear to be extremely limited and likely to benefit only a very small number of people. Applicants must usually be already getting attendance allowance (though some discretion is allowed) and must have less than £6,000 in savings. It is not necessary to be on income support. The main object is to permit very severely disabled people to live independently in their own homes rather than in residential care. As well as regular cash payments towards regular care and domestic help, one-off grants to buy equipment which might assist a person to live independently (e.g. environmental control equipment) are a possibility. Applicants who appear to qualify will be visited to discuss what help they need. There is no right of appeal.

Industrial Injuries Benefit

WHO?

Employees (other than members of HM Forces) who remain disabled or unable to work because of an accident arising out of and in the course of work or a prescribed disease contracted while working after 15 weeks (90 days, excluding Sundays) has passed since the date of the accident or onset of the disease are eligible for this tax free, non-means-tested and non-contributory benefit.

HOW MUCH? (APRIL 1988)

Disablement benefit is now paid as a weekly pension in addition to any sickness benefit, invalidity benefit or retirement pension you may be getting. The amount depends on the degree to which you have suffered a loss of physical or mental faculty causing impairment of your power to enjoy a normal life (this can include disfigurement). The loss of faculty is assessed by comparing your condition as a result of the accident or disease with the condition of a normal healthy person of the same age and sex. The assessment is expressed as a percentage up to a maximum of 100 per cent. Assessments for more than one qualifying accident or disease can be added, subject to the 100 per cent maximum. No disablement benefit is now payable where the loss of faculty is assessed at less than 14 per cent, unless it is due to one of three progressive chest diseases: pneumoconiosis, byssinosis and diffuse mesothelioma, but you may be able to get reduced earnings allowance (*see* below) if your disability or loss of faculty is 1 per cent or more.

BASIC RATES
Weekly Pension

		18 and over and under 18 with dependants	under 18
14 to 24%	(counts as 20%)	£13.44	£8.23
25 to 34%	(counts as 30%)	£20.16	£12.35
35 to 44%	(counts as 40%)	£26.88	£16.46
45 to 54%	(counts as 50%)	£33.60	£20.58
55 to 64%	(counts as 60%)	£40.32	£24.69
65 to 74%	(counts as 70%)	£47.04	£28.81
75 to 84%	(counts as 80%)	£53.76	£32.92
85 to 94%	(counts as 90%)	£60.48	£37.04
95 to 100%	(counts as 100%)	£67.20	£41.15

SPECIAL INCREASES

Unemployability supplement, although not available to people claiming after 6 April 1987, continues to be paid if you were already a beneficiary before that date and you are likely to be permanently unable to work or unable to earn more than a limited prescribed amount in a year. This can, however, affect other benefits. The normal rate is £41.15, but this can be increased for early incapacity at one of three rates: £2.75, £5.50, £8.65.

Reduced earnings allowance (previously called special hardship allowance) can be paid if you are unable to return to your normal job or to do work with the same pay because of the accident or disease. The amount is the difference between how much you earned in your main job and how much you earn in a suitable job that you can do now, subject to a maximum of £26.88.

REA is separate from disablement benefit and can be paid as well as a 100 per cent assessment.

If you are receiving reduced earnings allowance and you are over pension age and retired for National Insurance purposes at or after 6 April 1987, your payments of the allowance will not be increased at any uprating after that date. By the Social Security Act 1988, a new benefit, retirement allowance, will replace (at a date to be announced) reduced earnings allowance after retirement. The rate of REA will be frozen for those who retire before the new benefit comes into force.

Constant attendance allowance (not to be confused with the higher rate of attendance allowance described on page 13) can be paid if the disease or accident has caused disablement so serious that you receive the 100 per cent rate of disablement benefit and need daily attendance which you are likely to need for a long time, e.g. if you are bedridden or paralysed. The attendance need not last throughout the day, and the allowance can be claimed whether or not it is a relative who provides the attendance, and whether or not it is on a paid basis. How much you get depends on how much looking after you need. There are four rates: £13.45, £26.90, £40.35 and £53.80. The normal maximum is £26.90.

Exceptionally severe disablement allowance can be paid if the disease or accident has caused disablement which is exceptionally severe, the need for attendance is likely to be permanent, and you are already entitled to the constant attendance allowance described above at a rate above the normal maxiumum of £26.90. The amount is £26.90.

BASIC CONDITIONS

Benefit is limited to employed people, but this includes office holders such as company directors who have to pay income tax under Schedule E on their salary, wages or fees. Since October 1986, the scheme has extended to all countries, and all workers liable to pay Class 1 National Insurance contributions while abroad are covered. Volunteer development workers can also be covered if they choose to pay a special rate of contribution.

In the case of an accident at work, you can get benefit only if it occurred on or after 5 July 1948 and resulted in personal injury, but the effects of the injury need not have been immediate, and the definition of an accident at work is quite widely drawn (*see* DHSS leaflet NI6 for examples).

In the case of the prescribed diseases, it must normally be established not only that you suffer from the disease, but that you have been employed in the relevant prescribed occupation after 4 July 1948, e.g. sufferers from cadmium poisoning must have worked in an occupation involving exposure to cadmium dust or fumes. The prescribed diseases are listed in DHSS leaflet NI2 and may be added to by new regulations from time to time.

In the case of occupational deafness, benefit is payable for deafness resulting from noise at work. You must have been employed for a total of not less than ten years in one or more of a number of prescribed occupations, and must be suffering from substantial permanent hearing loss as legally defined.

NOTES
1. By the Social Security Act 1988, industrial death benefit has been abolished, except for existing cases, from 11 April 1988.
2. If you were injured at work through the fault of your employer, you may well be entitled to cash compensation from your employer. The amount you can get depends, of course, on how badly you are injured or disabled. Your employer has to display a certificate of insurance covering liability for this compensation. If you need more information about this ask a solicitor or your trade union. Libraries and Citizens Advice Bureaux keep lists of local solicitors.

ACCIDENTS AND DISEASES BEFORE 1948

Although you can't get disablement benefit, you may be able to get an allowance under the Workmen's Compensation (Supplementation) Scheme (DHSS leaflet WS1) or the Pneumoconiosis, Byssinosis and Miscellaneous Diseases Benefit Scheme (DHSS leaflet PN1).

FURTHER INFORMATION

Read DHSS leaflets NI2, *If you have an industrial disease*; NI3, *If you have pneumoconiosis or byssinosis*; NI6, *Industrial Injuries Disablement Benefit*; NI207, *If your job has made you deaf*; NI237,

If you have asthma because of your job, or *Compensation for Personal Injury* by R. Lewis (Professional Books Ltd., 1987), price £24.50.

Telephone the free DHSS telephone enquiry service: 0800–666 555.

Contact one of the organisations listed on page 39.

Read one of the guides listed on pages 39–40.

Invalidity Benefit

WHO?

Invalidity benefit is available for people who have been getting sickness benefit or statutory sick pay and remain incapable of work after 28 weeks. It is non-taxable, non-means-tested and contributory.

HOW MUCH? (APRIL 1988)

Invalidity benefit is made up of several parts, the most important of which is invalidity pension. You can't get any other kind of invalidity benefit if you don't qualify for the invalidity pension.

The different parts of invalidity benefit are:
(a) basic invalidity pension;
(b) additional invalidity pension;
(c) invalidity allowance; and
(d) additions for dependants.

Your basic invalidity pension may be reduced, or not paid at all, if you are getting another National Insurance benefit, a non-contributory benefit, industrial injuries disablement benefit, an unemployability supplement of any kind, or a training allowance. The weekly payment for the different parts of invalidity benefit is as follows:

Invalidity pension	£41.15

Additional invalidity pension is earnings-related, and depends on your earnings since April 1978 on which you have paid Class 1 National Insurance contributions (for further details see DHSS leaflet NI16A).

Invalidity allowance:	
higher rate (aged under 40)	£8.65
middle rate (aged 40–49)	£5.50
lower rate (aged 50–54 women; 50–59 men)	£2.75
Dependency additions:	
for spouse or person looking after children	up to £24.75
for each child	up to £8.40

BASIC CONDITIONS

For many people, entitlement will be straightforward, but where interruption of employment has not been continuous, the rules are quite complex and you will need to seek further information.

To qualify for invalidity pension you must have been entitled to, or be treated as entitled to, 28 weeks of sickness benefit in a period of interruption of employment. Entitlement to maternity allowance can count too. If you are an employee who was entitled to get statutory sick pay for 28 weeks, you can be treated as having been entitled to sickness benefit, provided you have satisfied the contribution conditions for that benefit. If you got less than 28 weeks statutory sick pay you will have to receive sickness benefit until you reach a total of 28 weeks. Your periods of statutory sick pay entitlement will be treated as periods of sickness benefit entitlement.

The 28 weeks of entitlement do not have to be all in a row. Periods of interruption of employment which are not more than eight weeks apart count as one period. This is called linking.

If you qualify for the basic invalidity pension, you will continue to get it for as long as your incapacity in that period of interruption of employment lasts, up to 65 (men) or 60 (women). There are special arrangements for people over those ages who decide not to retire. If your incapacity for work is due to an industrial accident or disease, you may be able to get sickness benefit followed by invalidity benefit even if you haven't paid enough National Insurance contributions, so long as your incapacity remains due to the industrial accident or disease. (*See* DHSS leaflet NI16, *Sickness Benefit*.

If you are a widow or a widower and have been incapable of work for 28 weeks, you may be able to get basic invalidity pension, even if you didn't qualify for sickness benefit.

To qualify for invalidity allowance as well as invalidity pension, you must be under 60 (men) or 55 (women) on the first day of your incapacity for work in the period of interruption of employment.

When you finally retire or reach 70 (men) or 65 (women), your retirement pension will be increased permanently by the amount of the invalidity allowance if:
(a) you were getting invalidity allowance on a day not more than eight weeks before you reached 65 (men) or 60 (women), and
(b) you are entitled to a retirement pension based on your own contributions, or your retirement pension has replaced an invalidity pension you got under the special rules for some widows and widowers.

NOTE: If you don't qualify for invalidity pension, you may be able to get severe disablement allowance (see page 31).

Claimants may, in certain circumstances, derive earnings from work without affecting their entitlement to sickness or invalidity benefit. Your local social security office will advise whether the work concerned falls within this concession. Full details must be given, including whether your doctor approves the work. For this purpose, earnings must not exceed £27 a week (April 1988), after deduction of allowable expenses.

FURTHER INFORMATION

Read DHSS leaflet NI16A, *Invalidity Benefit*, which includes details of how to claim.

Telephone the free DHSS telephone enquiry service: 0800–666 555.

Contact one of the organisations listed on page 39.

Read one of the guides listed on pages 39–40.

Invalid Care Allowance

WHO?

Invalid care allowance is taxable, non-means-tested and non-contributory. People under pension age (60, women; 65, men) who are unable to work because they have to stay at home to look after a disabled person are eligible. In order for the carer to qualify for invalid care allowance, the person being cared for must be receiving, and therefore have satisfied the stringent qualification rules of, either attendance allowance at either the lower or the higher rate, or constant attendance allowance at the maximum rate (paid in association with a war or service pension, industrial disablement pension, workmen's compensation, or an allowance under the Pneumoconiosis, Byssinosis and Miscellaneous Diseases Benefit Scheme).

You can get ICA irrespective of your sex or whether you are married, and whether or not you are related to the disabled person or live at the same address.

HOW MUCH? (APRIL 1988)

Claimant	£24.75 a week
Increase for spouse or person looking after children	£14.80 a week
Increase for each dependent child	£8.40 a week

The above dependency additions are subject to detailed conditions (*see* DHSS leaflet NI212).

CONDITIONS

To be eligible the following conditions apply.

1. You must be spending at least 35 hours a week (Sunday to Saturday) caring for a disabled person as described above. If, however, you stop looking after the disabled person for a short time you may still be able to get ICA for weeks when, for example:
   (a) you need a short holiday, or
   (b) the disabled person is in hospital (and still getting attendance allowance), or
   (c) you are in hospital.
   You can take a total of 12 weeks' break in any six-month period but no more than four can be 'holiday' weeks. And you must tell the ICA Unit about any short breaks (*see* Further Information below for address).
2. You must be aged between 16 and 60 (women) or 16 and 65 (men).
3. You must not be earning (nor expecting to earn) more than £12 a week. (As to what counts as earnings see DHSS leaflet NI212.)
4. You must not be attending a full-time course of education.
5. You must be resident in the United Kingdom, and have been resident here for 26 weeks out of the 52 preceding your claim.

RELATIONSHIP TO OTHER BENEFITS

You cannot get invalid care allowance if you are already in receipt of the same amount or more from one of the following benefits for yourself:
(a) sickness or invalidity benefit;
(b) unemployment benefit;
(c) unemployability supplement (paid with an industrial disablement or war pension);
(d) a training allowance or grant paid out of government funds;
(e) industrial death benefit;
(f) maternity allowance;
(g) widow's benefit (including industrial or war widow's pension);
(h) a state retirement pension;
(i) severe disablement allowance.
If the amount received from the above benefits is less than the invalid care allowance, you can claim the difference.

If you cannot get ICA because the weekly amount you get from one of the above benefits is the same as or more than you would get on ICA, it might still be worth applying for ICA so that you can get credits for National Insurance purposes. But this would not be worthwhile if you already get the maximum amount of widow's pension (£41.15

a week) because the credits would not make any difference. You will also need to take account of the fact that ICA is taxable, but severe disablement allowance is not and is therefore to be preferred if you have that option. If you are getting income support you can claim invalidity care allowance, but if this is granted the allowance will be deducted from the income support. It is obviously to your advantage to claim invalid care allowance if it will exceed your income support, but even where the invalid care allowance is slightly less than your income support it may be preferable to claim it because it is non-means-tested and gives credits for National Insurance contributions.

Benefits received by the person being cared for are not affected.

NOTE: From April 1988, ICA can, subject of course to entitlement, be backdated up to 12 months.

FURTHER INFORMATION

Read DHSS leaflet NI212, which includes details of how to claim.

Contact the ICA Unit, DHSS, Palatine House, Lancaster Road, Preston, Lancashire PR1 1NS.

Telephone the free DHSS telephone enquiry service: 0800–666 555.

Contact one of the organisations listed on page 39.

Read one of the guides listed on pages 39–40.

Mobility Allowance

WHO?

Mobility allowance is tax free, non-means-tested and non-contributory and available to all severely disabled people who are unable or virtually unable to walk, and who are aged five or over and under 66. If you are already 65, you will have to show that you could have qualified for the allowance before you were 65. If the allowance is awarded, it will be for a stated period, at most until you are 75. The allowance stops when you reach 75, or after the stated number of years, or when you cease to qualify for any reason.

HOW MUCH? (APRIL 1988)

£23.05 per week.

BASIC CONDITIONS

Residence condition

You must be living in the United Kingdom, and must have been living there for at least 12 months in the 18 months preceding the date of claim.

Medical conditions

1. You must be suffering from physical disablement such that you are either unable to walk or virtually unable to do so. This requirement will be regarded as satisfied if your physical condition *as a whole* (without special factors peculiar to where you live or work or the nature of your work) is such that:
    (a) you are unable to walk; or
    (b) your ability to walk out of doors is so limited, as regards the distance over which or the speed at which or the length of time for which or the manner in which you can make progress on foot without severe discomfort, that you are virtually unable to walk; or
    (c) the exertion required to walk would constitute a danger to your life or would be likely to lead to a serious deterioration in your health.

    If, however, the habitual use of a suitable artificial aid or prosthesis overcomes or would overcome your inability or virtual inability to walk, then you may not qualify.
2. You must be likely to remain unable or virtually unable to walk for at least a year.
3. You must be able to make use of the allowance, i.e. you must be able to be moved without danger to your life and must be capable of appreciating your surroundings.

NOTES:

1. Past experience has indicated that some people are either reluctant to claim or fail to present a fully accurate picture of their condition when they do. By their sheer determination to cope with a disability, they present a more favourable impression of their difficulties than is justified by the facts. Certainly the view of the doctor carrying out the first examination can be wrong. *A significant percentage of applicants* who are turned down are awarded the allowance after a Medical Board or Appeal Tribunal.
2. Mentally handicapped people may qualify for mobility allowance if it is accepted that their handicap has a physical cause (e.g. genetic or brain damage) and that any interruptions in their walking are part and parcel of this physical disablement and not under their conscious control. But these interruptions (stopping, sitting down, etc.) must happen often enough, or soon enough, to allow them to pass the test of being 'virtually unable to walk'. This is a difficult area. We would refer anyone who may be affected by this to pages 106–7 of the 1988/9 edition of the *Disability Rights Handbook* (see page 40).
3. Mobility allowance does not affect entitlement to other social security benefits. It can, in fact, help you in obtaining other concessions; some suppliers of goods and services accept entitlement to mobility allowance in allowing special

terms. You cannot, however, normally have both mobility allowance and a travel to work grant under the Department of Employment scheme, though there are some exceptions to this rule (*see* page 37). No check is made on how mobility allowance is spent unless the beneficiary is a child. Then the person who looks after the child has to sign an undertaking to apply the allowance for the benefit of the disabled child.

4. Mobility allowance continues to be paid to eligible disabled people who enter hospital or residential accommodation whatever the length of stay, provided that you still benefit from it.

BENEFICIARIES UNDER EARLIER SCHEMES

Certain disabled drivers, who were beneficiaries under the pre-1976 vehicle scheme, have a right to switch to mobility allowance, regardless of their age and without any automatic cut-off at age 75. This special option applies to:

(a) those who currently have a car, 'trike' or private car allowance provided under the pre-1976 vehicle scheme (i.e. in response to an application made up to 1 January 1976);

(b) those who had a provided car, 'trike' or private car allowance on 1 January 1976 and, although they do not have one now, remain medically eligible; and

(c) those who were beneficiaries under the invalid vehicle scheme both before and after 1 January 1976 who have already switched to mobility allowance under the normal arrangements.

The main medical conditions for the mobility allowance will be deemed to be satisfied and medical examinations will not normally be required. The allowance will normally be payable throughout the rest of the person's lifetime. It will cease only if his or her condition improves to such an extent that he or she no longer meets the old vehicle scheme medical conditions, or if the condition deteriorates to the extent that he or she is unable to benefit from outdoor mobility.

Details and application form are contained in DHSS leaflet NI 225 (*not* NI 211) available as follows:

England and Wales: DHSS, N9C (IVS), Warbreck Hill Road, Blackpool FY2 0UZ.

Scotland: Scottish Home and Health Department, St. Andrews House, Edinburgh EH1 3DE.

Northern Ireland: DHSS, Castle Grounds, Stormont, Belfast BT4 3SG.

A special provision (The Mobility Allowance (Amendment) Regulations 1981) allows certain disabled people to keep their 'trikes' for a period not usually exceeding six months while first claiming mobility allowance. This overlap applies to people who need mobility allowance to buy a car

and need to learn to drive. It is intended to enable anyone in this position to retain independent mobility while they are learning to drive a standard car and while they are taking the driving test.

A small number of people received 'trikes' in response to applications made after 1 January 1976. Though they can retain the vehicle after retirement age, they do not enjoy the special option described above and do not have reserved rights to further mobility help when their vehicles wear out. Thus by retaining the vehicle after the age of 64 they would find themselves debarred from applying for mobility allowance under the ordinary conditions because of the age qualification. The mobility allowance scheme does not affect the continued issue of wheelchairs nor does the free issue of wheelchairs affect the allowance.

TEMPORARY MOBILITY ALLOWANCE

Disabled people who still have a vehicle issued by the DHSS may be able to get mobility allowance on a temporary basis during any period when they lose the use of the vehicle and a replacement cannot be immediately provided. This includes periods when the vehicle is off the road for repairs, and unavoidable delay in its return can be foreseen. The allowance can be paid in addition to a travel to work grant in these circumstances. If you find yourself immobilised and your local approved repairer cannot help, you should get in touch at once with your local Disablement Services Centre, who should advise you about what can be done to assist you.

WAR PENSIONERS

A special allowance, war pensioners' mobility supplement, paid at a higher rate, is available to disabled war pensioners (*see* DHSS leaflet MPL153).

FURTHER INFORMATION

Read DHSS leaflets NI211, which includes details of how to claim, and NI225, which describes the special option for vehicle scheme beneficiaries.

Mobility Allowance – Guide and Checklist (Disability Alliance ERA, 25 Denmark Street, London WC2H 8NJ, 1987), price £2 for advisers; £1 for claimants (both including postage). Gives advice on how to present your case, what to expect at the different stages, and how to appeal if you consider a refusal to be wrong.

Telephone the free DHSS telephone enquiry service: 0800–666 555.

Contact one of the organisations listed on page 39.

Read one of the guides listed on pages 39–40.

NHS Dental Treatment Charges – Concessions

WHO?

Special arrangements apply if you are:

(a) under 18 (except that you have to pay for dentures and bridges if you are over 16 and not in full-time education);
(b) under 19 and still in full-time education;
(c) an expectant mother who is pregnant at the start of the treatment, or have had a baby within the last 12 months;
(d) getting income support or family credit (in which case the arrangements extend to dependants);
(e) receiving free milk and vitamins and/or free prescriptions because you are on a low income;
(f) on a low income not much above income support level (for details see DHSS leaflet D11). If you are aged 16 or over, you can claim on grounds of *your own* low income, even if you are still living with your parents.

If you are a war or service pensioner you may, of course, qualify under the normal rules summarised above. If not, you will have to pay the basic charges for dental treatment unless it is needed because of your war or service disablement.

HOW MUCH? (APRIL 1988)

If you qualify under one of the categories (a) to (e) above, treatment is free. If you qualify under (f) on grounds of low income, treatment may be free or at a reduced charge.

Everyone is entitled to the following NHS dental treatment free of charge:

(a) check-ups;
(b) stopping bleeding;
(c) repairs to dentures;
(d) calling a dentist out to his/her surgery in an emergency or for a necessary home visit (but in either of these circumstances you will have to pay for the treatment itself (if any) unless you qualify for free treatment).

Outside these concessions, the following charges apply:

Dentures

Metal-based dentures having:	
1–3 teeth	£64
4–8 teeth	£69
more than 8 teeth	£71

Synthetic resin-based dentures having:	
1–3 teeth	£26
4–8 teeth	£34
more than 8 teeth	£40

Maximum charges for more than one synthetic resin denture

Synthetic resin based full upper and full lower dentures	£59
Any other combination of synthetic resin-based dentures	£62

Bridges

An acid-etched retained bridge	£65
Any other bridge	£150

Crowns

High gold alloy	£51 to £55
Other alloy	£26 to £42
Other treatment	75% of cost
Maximum charge for a course of treatment	£150

REFUNDS

If you qualify for free or reduced charge treatment but do not realise this until after you have paid your dentist, you may be able to get a refund. See DHSS leaflet D11 for details.

FURTHER INFORMATION

Read DHSS leaflet D11 which includes details of how to claim.

Telephone the free DHSS telephone enquiry service: 0800–666 555.

Contact one of the organisations listed on page 39.

Read one of the guides listed on pages 39–40.

NHS Glasses; Voucher Scheme

WHO?

You qualify for vouchers towards the cost of glasses if you are:

(a) under 16; or
(b) under 19 and in full time education; or
(c) getting income support or family credit; or
(d) in receipt of free milk and vitamins and/or free prescriptions because you have a low income; or
(e) on a low income, not much above income support level (for details see DHSS leaflet G11). If you are 16 or over, you can claim on grounds of *your own* low income, even if you are still living with your parents;
(f) prescribed complex/powerful lenses with at least one lens which has a power in any one

meridian of plus or minus 10 or more dioptres, or is made in lenticular form (your optician will advise in such cases).

If you are a war or service pensioner, you may, of course, qualify under one of the above categories. If not, you will have to pay the basic charges for NHS glasses unless they are needed because of your war or service disablement.

HOW MUCH? (APRIL 1988)

This varies according to the prescription and whether you are entitled to all or part of the maximum voucher value. If you qualify under (a) to (d) above, you will be entitled to the full voucher value, if under (e) to a proportion of the full voucher value (depending on your income), and if under (f) alone to the amounts shown below under the heading 'Complex lens vouchers'.

Your optician will complete a voucher form with a code letter covering your prescription. Each code letter carries a maximum voucher value as follows:

Single-vision glasses		Bifocal glasses	
A	£15.50	D	£29.50
B	£25.50	E	£50.00
C	£42.00	F	£85.00
plus, where clinically necessary:			
P (prism)	£3.50 per lens	P	£4.50 per lens
T (tint)	£3.50 per lens	T	£4.50 per lens

Complex lens vouchers (for those not entitled to standard vouchers (i.e. group (f) above):

£3.00   £17.00

Children needing very small glasses qualify for a supplement of £30.

HOSPITAL EYE SERVICE ONLY

If you are referred to the Hospital Eye Service, and are prescribed glasses as part of your treatment, there are two special vouchers in addition to those available from opticians, and some special supplements as set out below. Some hospitals have their own arrangements for supplying glasses, and there are special arrangements for maximum charges if the glasses prescribed are very expensive:

Any glasses other than single-vision or bifocal	£85 (voucher code G)
Contact lens	£25 (voucher code H)
Supplement if you need specially made frames	£30
Supplement if you are prescribed photochromatic lenses for clinical reasons	£3 (single-vision)
	£4 (complex lenses)

Maximum charges:

Single-vision glasses	£32
Complex lens glasses	£52
Contact lenses (per lens)	£25

REFUNDS

If you pay for your glasses yourself, you cannot get a refund afterwards even if you were entitled to a voucher. Make sure you have your voucher *before* you buy.

FURTHER INFORMATION

Read DHSS leaflet G11 which includes details of how to claim.

Telephone the free DHSS telephone enquiry service: 0800–666 555.

Contact one of the organisations listed on page 39.

Read one of the guides listed on pages 39–40.

NHS Prescription Charges

WHO?

The following categories of people are exempt from prescription charges.

(a) Men aged 65 or over or women aged 60 or over.

(b) Children under 16.

(c) Pregnant women or women who have had a baby within the last 12 months.

(d) People getting income support or family credit.

(e) War or service pensioners needing prescriptions for an accepted disablement.

(f) Those suffering from one of the following conditions:

permanent fistula (including caecostomy, colostomy, laryngostomy or ileostomy) requiring continuous surgical dressing or an appliance; or

the following disorders for which specific substitution therapy is essential:

Addison's disease and other forms of hypo-adrenalism;

diabetes insipidus and other forms of hypo-pituitarism;

diabetes mellitus;

hypoparathyroidism;

myasthenia gravis;

myxoedema (hypothyroidism); or

epilepsy requiring continuous anti-convulsive therapy; or

a continuing physical disability which prevents them leaving home without the help of another person (temporary disabilities, even if they last a few months, do not count).

(g) People on a low income, not much above income support level (see DHSS leaflet P11 for details) (if you are 16 or over, you can claim on grounds of *your own* low income, even if you are still living with your parents).

Prescription charges do not apply to items which are supplied and personally administered by either prescribing or dispensing doctors.

HOW MUCH? (APRIL 1988)

If you qualify, the whole of the prescription charge (£2.60 per item) is waived.

If you do not qualify for exemption, but need a lot of prescriptions, you can buy a prepaid 'season ticket' covering any number of prescriptions in a given period. This may cost you less than paying per prescription. The current prices of season tickets are:

£13.50 for 4 months (you will save money if you need more than 5 items in this period)

£37.50 for a year (you will save money if you need more than 14 items in this period).

REFUNDS

If you realise that you qualify for free prescriptions only after paying the charge, there is a procedure for reclaiming the amount provided you do so within three months (see DHSS leaflet P11 for details).

FURTHER INFORMATION

Read DHSS leaflet P11 which includes details of how to claim.

Telephone the free DHSS telephone enquiry service: 0800–666 555.

Contact one of the organisations listed on page 39.

Read one of the guides listed on pages 39–40.

Postal Concessions

ARTICLES FOR BLIND PEOPLE

Packets containing the articles described at (A) below, which have been specially produced or adapted for use by blind people, are transmitted by first class letter post free of charge subject to the conditions at (C) below.

(A) Permissible articles
1. Books, papers and letters to or from a blind person, impressed or otherwise prepared for use by blind people.
2. Paper sent to any person for impressing or otherwise preparing for that purpose.

And the following articles which have been specially designed or adapted for use by blind people:
3. Relief maps.
4. Machines, frames and attachments for making impressions for use by blind people.
5. Writing frames and attachments.
6. Braillette boards and pegs.
7. De Braille instructional devices.

The following articles may be sent only to blind persons by organisations or institutions which have entered into special arrangements with the Post Office for sending these articles, or to such organisations by blind people.
8. Games (including card games).
9. Mathematical appliances and attachments.
10. Metal plates impressed or sent for impressing for use by blind people.
11. Supplies of wrappers, envelopes and labels for sending articles for use by blind people.
12. Watches, clocks, timers, tools, aids, precision instruments, rules and measures designed or adapted for use by blind people.
13. Sectional or collapsible walking sticks.
14. Harness for guide dogs.
15. Talking Books and Talking Newspapers, i.e. voice records on tape, disc, film or wire of either:
    (a) readings from printed books, journals, newspapers, periodicals or similar publications; or
    (b) material which, though not necessarily printed, is *of the nature of* a book, journal, newspaper, etc., but which stops short of general *entertainment* programmes available on radio or recordings.

NOTE: Examples of acceptable material under (b) are: short stories; live reports of news events; commentaries on news and other events; listeners' views on the recordings themselves, or on any general topic; advice and guidance on any subject; travel details; details of welfare facilities and assistance available to blind people; guides to and reports and reviews on broadcast programmes, sporting events, concert and theatre performances, etc.; live interviews of general interest to blind people; 'letters to the editor' on topics of general interest, not constituting personal messages.

Apparatus designed to play such recordings may also be sent free of charge.

(B) Inadmissible articles
1. Personal messages between blind people, or to or from blind people and organisations or institutions.
2. Music or other entertainment, except:
   (a) an introductory and closing jingle of one

or two bars, and similar interludes between sections of the recording; and

(b) a recording with a musical or entertainment feature (e.g. a feature on a local orchestra) may be illustrated by a selection of relevant music or other entertainment. This may not exceed 10 per cent of the total duration of the tape.

(C) Conditions

1. The maximum weight is 7 kg.
2. The limits of size are 610 mm (2 ft) in length, 460 mm (1 ft 6 in) in width and in depth. If made up in the form of a roll, length plus twice the diameter must not exceed 1.040 m (3 ft 5 in) and the greatest dimension must not exceed 900 mm (2 ft 11 in).
3. A packet may consist only of the articles described at (A) above for use by blind people, and may not contain any communication in writing or printing in ordinary type, except:

   a title, date of publication, serial number, name and address of printer, publisher or manufacturer, price and table of contents of a book or paper, or any key or instructions for the use of the enclosed article, and a printed label for return of the packet.

4. A packet must be posted either without a cover or in a cover easily removed for examination. Where, however, recording equipment or other fragile equipment is sent, the packet may be fully sealed by permission of the posting office.
5. Packets must bear on the outside the words 'ARTICLES FOR THE BLIND' and the written or printed name and address of the sender. The use of a white label bearing green printing is recommended.
6. The service is restricted to (a) registered blind people, and (b) other visually handicapped people who are able to produce a certificate signed by an ophthalmologist, doctor or ophthalmic optician stating that their close-up vision, with spectacles, is N12 or less.

If the above conditions are not fulfilled, the packet will be charged as an unpaid letter, or transferred to the parcel post and charged as an unpaid parcel.

Severe Disablement Allowance

WHO?

People aged 16 or more who are unable to work because of long-term sickness or severe mental or physical disablement are eligible. You may be able to get severe disablement allowance if you cannot get invalidity benefit because you have not paid enough National Insurance contributions. It is tax free, non-means-tested and non-contributory.

HOW MUCH? (APRIL 1988)

The basic rate is £24.75 a week with additions for spouse or an adult who looks after your children (up to £14.80), and for your children (up to £8.40 for each child).

BASIC CONDITIONS

You must be aged 16 or over (but *see* Note 2).

You must be incapable of work because of sickness or disability (doctor must certify), *and* either:

(a) have been so incapable for 28 weeks continuously, or
(b) getting severe disablement allowance at any time in the last 8 weeks, or
(c) getting severe disablement allowance previously with no gap of more than 8 weeks between getting SDA, signing on as unemployed (or getting an MSC training allowance) and your new claim for SDA.

Unless excepted (*see* Note 3), you must be assessed by a doctor as at least 80 per cent disabled (in practice 75 per cent or more qualifies).

RESIDENCE CONDITIONS

You must:

(a) be living in the United Kingdom when you apply for severe disablement allowance; and
(b) have been in the UK for at least 24 weeks of the 28 weeks when you have been incapable of work; and
(c) have lived in the UK for at least 10 of the last 20 years (if you are under 20, for at least 10 years).

RELATIONSHIP TO OTHER BENEFITS

You won't normally get severe disablement allowance if you are already getting one of the following benefits, unless the SDA would be higher:

(a) sickness or invalidity benefit;
(b) maternity allowance;
(c) retirement pension;
(d) widow's benefit of any kind;
(e) invalid care allowance;
(f) unemployability supplement paid with industrial injuries disablement benefit or a war or service pension;

(g) Training allowance from the Department of Employment, the Manpower Services Commission or the Ministry of Agriculture.

If you are getting income support, it will be reduced by any amount of severe disablement allowance you get, so there may be no net gain, but it is still worth claiming SDA because there are usually long-term advantages.

Severe disablement allowance is reduced if you are in hospital for longer than six weeks.

NOTES

1. Severe disablement allowance has replaced non-contributory invalidity pension (NCIP) and non-contributory invalidity pension for married women (HNCIP).

2. If you are under 19 you can normally get severe disablement allowance only if any supervised education you get is for less than 21 hours a week. But any time spent in special education that would be unsuitable for someone of the same age who doesn't have a physical or mental disability is ignored, e.g. learning to do things that other young people of your own age can do easily.

     If you are at retirement age or over (65 for men, 60 for women at the time of writing), you can get SDA only if you were entitled to it on the day before you reached retirement age.

3. You will be treated as being 80 per cent disabled if any of the following circumstances apply:

    (a) you get attendance allowance;
    (b) you get mobility allowance;
    (c) you get war pensioners' mobility supplement;
    (d) you have received a vaccine damage payment;
    (e) you have an invalid tricycle or invalid car or private car allowance from the DHSS;
    (f) you are registered with your local authority as blind or partially-sighted; or
    (g) you have already been found to be 80 per cent disabled for the purpose of industrial injuries disablement benefit or for war disablement pension.

You do not need to have your disablement assessed if any of the following circumstances apply:

    (a) your incapacity for work started on or before your 20th birthday;
    (b) your first period of incapacity for work started on or before your 20th birthday and lasted for at least 28 weeks, and you have not been capable of work for more than 26 weeks since that period of incapacity;
    (c) there have been no gaps of more than 8 weeks in between you getting non-contributory invalidity pension or non-contributory invalidity pension for married women, signing on as unemployed (or getting an MSC training allowance), and your new claim for severe disablement allowance;
    (d) you have been getting severe disablement allowance at any time in the last 8 weeks without having had to show 80 per cent disablement; or
    (e) there have been no gaps of more than 8 weeks in between you getting severe disablement allowance without having had to show 80 per cent disablement,

signing on as unemployed (or getting an MSC training allowance), and your new claim for severe disablement allowance.

FURTHER INFORMATION

Read DHSS leaflet NI 252 (with claim form).

Telephone the free DHSS telephone enquiry service: 0800–666 555.

Contact one of the organisations listed on page 39.

Read one of the guides listed on pages 39–40.

Sickness Benefit

WHO?

Sickness benefit is tax free, non-means-tested and contributory and is available to people who are incapable of work for at least four days in a row (excluding Sunday) because of sickness or disablement, who satisfy prescribed National Insurance contribution conditions, *and* who are either:

(a) employed people who have run out of entitlement to statutory sick pay (*see* page 35), or who are excluded from that scheme, or whose sickness or disability is the result of an industrial accident or a prescribed disease; or

(b) people who are self-employed, unemployed or non-employed.

Periods for which you claim sickness benefit (or invalidity benefit, but not statutory sick pay), which are not more than eight weeks apart, are said to be linked and are treated as one period. This can include a period for which you claimed but did not get benefit because you had not made enough contributions.

HOW MUCH? (APRIL 1988)

Benefit is not normally paid for absences which last less than four days (excluding Sunday), and the first three days in any qualifying period (linked or unlinked) are treated as 'waiting days'. There are, however, some exceptions to these rules:

(a) waiting days will not be attributed to you if you were due statutory sick pay at any time in the eight weeks prior to your claim to sickness benefit;

(b) benefit can be claimed for a period of less than four days if you cease to be entitled to statutory sick pay just before you are due to return to work; and

(c) benefit may be allowed for regular weekly absences of two or three days which occur because you need treatment by dialysis, radiotherapy, chemotherapy with cytotoxic drugs, or plasmapheresis (this concession does not apply to statutory sick pay).

Sickness benefit is paid for a maximum of 28 weeks (168 days excluding Sundays). Thereafter, if your incapacity continues, invalidity benefit (*see* page 24) is paid instead. This may be after the maximum 28 weeks or after only 20 weeks if you have exhausted your entitlement to eight weeks statutory sick pay, and that happened eight weeks or less before your sickness benefit started.

Increases for dependants are payable, but are subject to detailed conditions (*see* DHSS leaflet NI16)

The weekly rates are as follows:

Claimant under pension age	£31.30
Increase for spouse or an adult who looks after your children	£19.40
(No increases for children)	
Claimant over pension age	£39.45
Increase for spouse or an adult who looks after your children	£23.65
Increase for each child	£8.40

CONTRIBUTION CONDITIONS

Cover for sickness benefit is provided only by Class 1 contributions (paid by those who work for an employer) or Class 2 contributions (paid by the self-employed). There is a weekly lower earnings limit at which contributions become due (1981/2: £27; 1982/3: £29.50; 1983/4: £32.50; 1984/5: £34; 1985/6: £35.50; 1986/7: £38; 1987/8: £39; 1988/9: £41) and the rate of contribution varies with your earnings up to a prescribed maximum.

There are two contribution conditions:

(a) that in any one tax year since 6 April 1975, Class 1 and/or Class 2 contributions have been paid which amount to at least 25 times the contributions payable on earnings at the lower earnings limit for that year, *or* you have paid 26 flat-rate contributions before 6 April 1975.

(b) that in the tax year relevant to the claim (see note below) Class 1 and/or Class 2 contributions have been paid or credited amounting to at least 50 times the contributions payable on earnings at the lower earnings limit for that year (if you have less than 50 but more than 25 times the contributions, you may be entitled to a reduced rate of benefit).

NOTE: National Insurance credits do not count for condition (a). The relevant tax year (b) is the last complete tax year before the start of your 'benefit year'. Your 'benefit year' (which commences on the first Sunday in January) is the year in which the first day of your period of interruption of employment (linked or unlinked) occurs.

By the Social Security Act 1988, from October 1988, the second condition is changed so that contributions on earnings of at least 50 times the lower earnings limit must have been paid or credited in both of the last two tax years before the year in which the claim starts (instead of in only the preceding year).

The reduced rate on National Insurance contributions paid by some married women and widows does not qualify them for benefit.

If you are sick or disabled because of an accident at work or an industrial disease, you will be treated as having satisfied the contribution conditions.

OTHER CONDITIONS

1. You must not do anything which might stop you getting better as soon as possible.
2. You should leave word where you can be found if you go away from the address you have previously given.
3. You must not work, unless the work is of a therapeutic nature and done with your doctor's approval and advised to the DHSS (*see* 'Therapeutic earnings' below).
4. You must, if asked, see a Regional Medical Service doctor for an examination under the normal sickness and invalidity benefit rules.
5. You will not get benefit if you earn more than a set limit after deduction of allowances (£27 at April 1988).
6. With some exceptions, you cannot get sickness benefit for any period outside Great Britain, Northern Ireland or the Isle of Man.
7. You cannot usually get benefit if you are in prison or detained by the police in legal custody.

THERAPEUTIC EARNINGS

Claimants may, in certain circumstances, derive earnings from work without affecting their entitlement to sickness or invalidity benefit. Your local social security office will advise whether the work concerned falls within this concession. Full details must be given, including whether your doctor approves the work. For this purpose, earnings must not exceed £27 a week (April 1988), after deduction of allowable expenses.

RELATIONSHIP TO OTHER BENEFITS

You cannot be paid sickness benefit at the same time as:

(a) other weekly National Insurance benefits such as unemployment benefit, retirement pension, widow's benefit or maternity allowance;
(b) an unemployability supplement of any kind; or

(c) a training allowance from public funds;

(d) statutory sick pay or statutory maternity pay. If you are entitled to more than one state benefit at the same time, you will normally get an amout equal to the greater, or greatest, of them (but *see* 'Mobility Allowance'). Attendance allowance for severely disabled people, or basic war or industrial disablement pension or gratuity do not affect benefit.

A widow, getting a war widow's pension, or an industrial death benefit, may in some circumstances get full sickness benefit on the basis of her own Class 1 contributions paid. You cannot get sickness benefit for any period for which you are covered by the SSP scheme. But sickness benefit is not affected if you get salary, wages or occupational sick pay from your employer or benefit from a friendly society or trade union while you are sick.

If, notwithstanding sickness benefit, you don't have enough money to live on, or if payment of sickness benefit is delayed, you may be entitled to income support (*see* page 19).

PAYMENT WHILE IN HOSPITAL

If you are admitted to a hospital where you receive treatment and your keep free of charge, sickness benefit is unaffected for six weeks, but thereafter will be reduced. Increases for dependants may also be affected if they go into hospital.

FURTHER INFORMATION

Read DHSS leaflet NI16, which includes details of how to claim.

Telephone the free DHSS telephone enquiry service: 0800–666 555.

Contact one of the organisations listed on page 39.

Read one of the guides listed on pages 39–40.

The Social Fund

WHO?

People with exceptional expenses which are difficult for them to meet from their regular income are eligible. The Social Fund is tax free, means-tested and non-contributory.

HOW MUCH?

Only a limited amount of money has been allocated to the Social Fund, much less than was paid by way of supplementary benefit single payments. Given this constraint, Social Fund officers will have to look at the needs of all applicants and decide which needs can be met and to what extent.

There are three types of discretionary payment:

(a) budgeting loans (minimum £30; maximum £1,000);

(b) crisis loans (maximum £1,000, except for living expenses);

(c) community care grants (minimum £30, except in respect of travelling expenses).

GENERAL EXCLUSIONS

The following needs cannot be met from the Social Fund:

(a) any need occurring outside the United Kingdom;

(b) educational or training needs;

(c) school uniform or sports gear;

(d) school travelling expenses;

(e) school meals;

(f) expenses arising from a court appearance;

(g) removal charges if you are being rehoused under legislation concerned with homelessness or following a compulsory purchase order, a redevelopment or closing order, or a compulsory exchange of tenancies;

(h) domestic assistance and respite care provided by a local authority;

(i) repairs to property of public sector housing bodies;

(j) medical or other health expenses;

(k) returnable accommodation deposits;

(l) work related expenses;

(m) debts to government departments;

(n) investments; and

(o) expenses for which an award has been made or refused within the previous 26 weeks (unless there has been a change in your circumstances).

BUDGETING LOANS

These are for people getting income support. The applicant or his/her partner, must have been receiving income support for the last 26 weeks with no more than one break not exceeding 14 days. The Social Fund Officer must be sure that you can afford to repay the money, usually by weekly deductions from benefit. If you stop getting benefit, e.g. because you start work, you still have to repay the loan. You can't get a budgeting loan if you or your partner are involved in a trade dispute.

In addition to the general exclusions shown above, you cannot get a budgeting loan for:

(a) mains fuel bills and standing charges;

(b) housing costs (other than intermittent costs not met by housing benefit or income support, and rent in advance where the landlord is not a local authority).

CRISIS LOANS

These are for people who are faced with expenses arising from an emergency or a disaster, and whose resources are insufficient to meet the short-term needs of themselves or their families. They can be claimed whether or not you are in receipt of a social security benefit. Crisis loans will, however, be approved only if there is no other way of preventing a serious risk to your or your family's health or safety. The loan must be repaid, either by weekly deductions from benefit or in some other way.

The following categories of people are not eligible for crisis loans:

residents of Part III accommodation, a nursing home or residential care home;
prisoners or anyone lawfully detained;
members of a religious order who are maintained by it;
people in full-time education;
hospital in-patients (unless they are to be discharged within the next two weeks); and
people involved in a trade dispute (unless the expenses are the result of a disaster).

In addition to the general exclusions shown above, you cannot get a crisis loan for:

telephone installation, rental or call charges;
mobility needs;
holidays;
televisions and radios;
motor vehicle costs (except for emergency travelling expenses); or
housing costs (other than intermittent costs not met by housing benefit or income support, rent in advance where the landlord is not a local authority, and boarding charges).

COMMUNITY CARE GRANTS

These are for people who are getting income support, or who expect to get income support when they move into the community. They are intended to help you:
(a) return to the community rather than having to be in care, i.e. in places like hospitals, nursing homes, old people's homes and residential care homes;
(b) return to the community from places like hostels for homeless people, detention centres, or local authority care for young people;
(c) stay in the community rather than having to be in care;
(d) cope with very difficult problems in your family, such as disability, long-term illness or family breakdown; or
(e) pay fares to visit someone who is ill or for another urgent reason.

If you get income support you won't have to repay a community care grant. If, however, you don't get income support when you move into the community, you will have to pay the grant back.

In addition to the general exclusions shown above, you can't get a community care grant for:
(a) telephone installation, rental or call charges;
(b) any expenses your local authority has a statutory duty to meet;
(c) fuel costs and standing charges;
(d) housing costs.

NOTE: The Social Fund legislation also provides for maternity and funeral grants, which are not dealt with here. The Social Security Act 1988 provides a power to continue a regulated scheme to make payments in respect of extra heating costs attributable to cold weather.

FURTHER INFORMATION

Read DHSS leaflet SB16 *A Guide to the Social Fund*.

The Social Fund Manual (DHSS, November 1987), price £9.50 and available from HMSO bookshops or the DHSS Leaflet Unit, PO Box 21, Stanmore, Middlesex HA7 1AY, contains official guidance and directives issued to Social Fund officers, and sets out the basic rules about eligibility, maximum amounts, and exclusions.

Social Fund Chart (Community Care, 28 January 1988). A limited number of copies are available from Simmonds Postal Publicity, 82–84 Peckham Rye, London SE15 4HB, price £2 including postage. A very useful wallchart guide.

Telephone the free DHSS telephone enquiry service: 0800–666 555.

Contact one of the organisations listed on page 39.

Read one of the guides listed on pages 39–40.

Statutory Sick Pay

WHO?

Most people aged 16 or over who work for an employer whose place of business is in Great Britain, who have earned enough to have paid National Insurance contributions, and who are off sick for at least four days in a row (all days count for this purpose, including weekends and holidays) are eligible for statutory sick pay which is taxable and earnings related.

EXCLUSIONS

1. You are not treated as an employee if you are:
   (a) unemployed (but *see* Sickness Benefit, page 32)
   (b) self-employed and not also working for an employer (but *see* Sickness Benefit, page 32)
   (c) a foreign-going mariner or a serving member of HM Forces.
2. You cannot get SSP if, when your spell of sickness begins, you are an employee in one of the following groups:
   (a) you have had 28 weeks of SSP and you stopped getting SSP less than eight weeks ago;
   (b) you have had a spell of sickness while with the same employer which lasted three years and finished less than eight weeks ago (for SSP, all spells of sickness of four days or more with eight weeks or less between them are 'linked' and treated as one spell);
   (c) you are a woman over 60 or a man over 65 and your spell of sickness does not link with a spell that began before you reached that age;
   (d) your average total pay (before any deductions) during the eight weeks before your spell of sickness was less than the amount on which you have to pay National Insurance contributions;
   (e) you were claiming sickness benefit, invalidity benefit, maternity allowance or severe disablement allowance eight weeks ago or less (at the end of a claim for one of these benefits, your social security office gives you a form telling you when you can next qualify for SSP);
   (f) you were taken on by your employer for three months or less (if you have worked for the same employer before, and the gap between the jobs is eight weeks or less, your employer should count the jobs together. If the length of time you worked in the earlier job, and the length of time s/he has now taken you on for total 13 weeks or less, you do not qualify for SSP);
   (g) your first day of sickness is during a work stoppage at your place of work which is due to a trade dispute in which you are taking part or which affects you;
   (h) you have not yet done any work for your new employer;
   (i) you become sick while you are entitled to maternity allowance or statutory maternity pay or you are sick at the start of the sixth week before the week in which your baby is due. In each of these cases you cannot get SSP for at least 18 weeks (see DHSS leaflet FB8 *Babies and Benefits*;
   (j) you fall sick outside the European Community, unless you are aircrew based in the United Kingdom, or work on the continental shelf;
   (k) you are in legal custody.

HOW MUCH? (APRIL 1988)

You get SSP from your employer for 'qualifying days'. These are usually the days in the week when you are required to work under your contract of employment (for most people Monday to Friday). The first three qualifying days in a spell of sickness which lasts four or more days are called 'waiting days' and carry no entitlement to SSP, but if you have more than one period of sickness of four or more days within the same employment and the interval between the end of one period and the start of the next is less than eight weeks, they are treated as 'linked', and the number of waiting days is limited to three in relation to the periods taken together. Thereafter, your employer will pay you SSP for up to 28 weeks in any spell of sickness (linked or not), after which, if you remain or again become unable to work through sickness or disability, you may qualify for sickness benefit (*see* page 32) or, in the case of long-term incapacity, invalidity benefit (*see* page 24).

There are two rates of SSP as set out below, depending on how much you earned before you were sick.

1. £49.20 if your average earnings were £79.50 a week or more
2. £34.25 if your average earnings were £41.00 to £79.49 a week.

You will not get SSP if your average earnings were less than £41 a week.

There are no additions for children or other dependants, but you may qualify for income support (*see* page 19).

Many employers operate their own sick pay schemes and pay their employees for some or all of a spell of sickness. If your employer is one of these, and you qualify for SSP, the amount that you receive must be as least as much as SSP.

FURTHER INFORMATION

Read DHSS leaflets NI244 and NI16 (NI227 for employers).

Telephone the free DHSS telephone enquiry service: 0800–666 555.

Contact one of the organisations listed on page 39.

Read one of the guides listed on pages 39–40.

Therapeutic Earnings Rule

Claimants may, in certain circumstances, derive earnings from work without affecting their entitlement to sickness, injury, or invalidity benefit. Your local social security office will advise whether the work concerned falls within this concession. Full details must be given, including whether your doctor approves the work. For this purpose, earnings must not exceed £27 a week (April 1988), after deduction of allowable expenses.

Travel to Work Grants

WHO?

Disabled people who are registered under the Disabled Persons (Employment) Act 1944 who incur extra costs in travelling to and from work, who find it impossible to use public transport for all or part of their journey as a result of their disability. If public transport would not be available anyway, you must have higher travelling costs because of your disability.

HOW MUCH? (APRIL 1988)

Grants are usually paid towards the cost of taxi fares, but may also be paid if your family or friends drive you to and from work.

For taxi fares, the grant is three-quarters of the total cost, up to a maximum of £69.25 a week. This applies to people working a five-day week. If you work more or less than five days a week, the amount is adjusted in proportion. If you are driven to and from work, the grant is based on the extra mileage your driver travels.

If you own your own car and use it to drive to work, you cannot get a grant. However, if your car cannot be used because of a breakdown, you can claim for a temporary period while it is being repaired.

PEOPLE GETTING MOBILITY ALLOWANCE

If you are getting mobility allowance, you cannot also claim a travel to work grant unless:
(a) you are legally barred from driving because of your age or disability; or
(b) your doctor has advised you not to drive or you are unable to drive because of your disability; or

(c) you are making arrangements to buy your own car; or
(d) your own car cannot be used temporarily because of a breakdown; or
(e) you are learning to drive.
In these exceptional circumstances, your travel to work grant can be granted but may be reduced if you also receive a mobility allowance.

FURTHER INFORMATION

If you think you may be entitled to a grant, you should contact the Disablement Resettlement Officer at your local Jobcentre straight away (grants cannot be back dated). Further details in The Employment Service leaflet PWD1.

Underpayments arising from official mistakes

Full payment of arrears of a social security benefit where there had been a previous underpayment due to an official error which was not the fault of the beneficiary used to be limited to a period of 52 weeks. Now, arrears which are properly due can be paid in full. Where, however, the underpayment arises because of reinterpretation of the law by a social security commissioner or other superior appellate body, payment beyond 52 weeks is a matter for consideration and is possible only on an extra-statutory basis.

Vaccine Damage Payments Scheme

WHO?

These tax free non-means-tested and non-contributory payments are available to people who have suffered severe disablement as a result of vaccination. A claim should be made if someone is thought to be severely disabled:
(a) as a result of having been vaccinated against one of the following diseases – diphtheria, tetanus, whooping cough, tuberculosis (BCG), poliomyelitis, measles, rubella (German measles); or
(b) because they have been in close personal contact with a person who has been vaccinated against one of the above diseases; or
(c) because their mother was vaccinated against one of the above diseases while she was pregnant.
To qualify, you must be aged 2 or more and have been vaccinated in the United Kingdom or the Isle of Man (except as described below). Unless the vaccination was against polio or rubella during an outbreak of the disease within the United Kingdom or the Isle of Man, the vaccination must have taken place before your 18th birthday.

A claim can be made if you were vaccinated outside the United Kingdom, if you or someone in your family were in the armed forces and the vaccination was given as part of the armed services medical facilities.

HOW MUCH?

A one-off payment of £20,000 (claims prior to 18 June 1985: £10,000). Disablement is worked out as a percentage, and severe disablement means at least 80 per cent disabled. This could be a mental or physical disablement. For example, total loss of sight or hearing is usually 100 per cent.

TIME LIMIT

A claim must be made within six years of the latest of the following dates:
(a) the date of vaccination; or
(b) the date on which the disabled child reached 2 years of age.

FURTHER INFORMATION

DHSS leaflet HB3 and a claim form can be obtained from: The Vaccine Damage Payments Unit, Department of Health and Social Security, North Fylde Central Offices, Norcross, Blackpool FY5 3TA.

War Disablement Pension

WHO?

You may be able to get a tax free non-means-tested and non-contributory war disablement pension if your disablement was because of, or made worse by, service during the 1914–18 war, or at any time since 2 September 1939. The following groups qualify:
(a) members of the armed forces, merchant navy or nursing staff between 4 August 1914 and 30 September 1921, and members of the armed forces who served after 2 September 1939 (note that the service need not have been during wartime); or
(b) a merchant seaman disabled as a result of a wound or disease received during time of war, or due to the effects of detention by the enemy after 2 September 1939.
Civilians injured in the Second World War (2 September 1939 to 19 March 1946) may also qualify, but not in respect of the worsening of a pre-existing disability. You may qualify if you:
(a) are seriously disabled, or likely to be disabled for a long time, as a result of a war injury; or
(b) were a civil defence worker and were seriously disabled, or disabled over a long period, as a result of war service.

Widows, widowers or dependent relatives of someone who has died as a result of injury or disablement in the circumstances set out above may also qualify for a war pension.

NOTE: The above pensions are the responsibity of the Department of Health and Social Security, North Fylde Central Office, Norcross, Blackpool FY5 3TA. Pensions for disablement or death arising solely from service in HM Forces between 1 October 1921 and 2 September 1939 are dealt with by the Ministry of Defence.

HOW MUCH? (APRIL 1988)

The scheme is similar to that for industrial injuries, with a basic disablement pension (which is related to the severity of disablement and your rank during service) and a number of special allowances. The basic pension for 100 per cent disablement for a private, for example, is £67.20. Less than total disablement is expressed as a percentage depending on the severity, and the basic entitlement is calculated *pro rata*. If the disablement is assessed as less than 20 per cent, the pension takes the form of a lump-sum gratuity.

If you were an officer, you may get war disablement pension as either disability retired pay or pension, *or* a service retired pay award with a disablement addition, whichever is the greater.

RELATIONSHIP TO OTHER BENEFITS

Basic war disablement pension does not affect the payment of National Insurance benefits. But some of the additional allowances can affect other benefits (*see* DHSS leaflet NI50 for details). If you claim income support, £4 of your war disablement pension is disregarded.

FURTHER INFORMATION

Read DHSS leaflets MPL153 (which includes details of how to claim), MPL154 (rates), FB16 (a brief guide), and MPL152 (for war widows).

Contact DHSS, North Fylde Central Office, Norcross, Blackpool FY5 3TA.

Telephone the free DHSS telephone enquiry service: 0800–666 555.

Contact one of the organisations listed on page 39.

Read one of the guides listed on pages 39–40.

War Pensioners' Mobility Supplement

WHO?

The tax-free, non-means-tested and non-contributory supplement is available only to people who are receiving a war pension for disablement arising from service in the forces, either in the 1914 war or at any time after 3 September 1939 (this includes civilian, Polish, and some Mercantile Marine Scheme war pensioners), whose walking problems are caused wholly or mainly by the pensioned disablement, and who either:

(a) have double leg amputations, one above or through the knee; or

(b) to all intents and purposes are unable to walk.

Those covered by (a) above qualify automatically without medical examination. For qualification under (b), if you have some ability to walk, the DHSS may require a medical examination and will take into account the way, how far, how fast and the length of time for which you can walk without feeling severe discomfort, and whether the exertion needed to walk would put your life at risk or be likely to lead to a serious deterioration in your health. Where appropriate, account will be taken of your walking ability with aids you can use, such as an artificial limb or a walking stick. Your problems must be such that you are likely to remain unable, or for all practical purposes unable, to walk for at least a year.

NOTE: Though similar to mobility allowance (*see* page 26), mobility supplement is paid at a higher rate and without age limitation. Subject to qualification the supplement can be claimed by war pensioners who are currently receiving mobility allowance or who have a DHSS vehicle on loan, but it cannot, of course, be paid as well at the same time. (Vehicles are no longer issued, and the supplement will, in any event, progressively replace existing vehicles supplied under the War Pensioners' Vehicle Scheme.)

HOW MUCH? (APRIL 1988)

£25.60 a week.

PAYMENT WHILE IN HOSPITAL

The supplement will continue to be paid if you go into hospital (or, indeed, if you go abroad).

RELATIONSHIP TO OTHER BENEFITS

Neither National Insurance benefits, nor industrial injury benefits are affected by payment of the mobility supplement.

If notwithstanding your war pension and mobility supplement you haven't enough money to live on, you may be entitled to income support (*see* page 19).

FURTHER INFORMATION

Read DHSS leaflet MPL155 which includes details of how to claim.

Contact DHSS, North Fylde Central Office, Norcross, Blackpool FY5 3TA.

Telephone the free DHSS telephone enquiry service: 0800–666 555.

Contact one of the organisations listed on page 39.

Read one of the guides listed on pages 39–40.

Helpful Organisations

Advice about benefits is normally best sought locally, where you can meet the adviser and explain and discuss your individual circumstances. In some places there are Welfare Rights officers, often employed by the local authority, specialising in this field, and in most parts of the country an excellent service on benefits as well as many other matters is provided by Citizens Advice Bureaux. Another important service is provided in various locations by DIAL UK (*see* page 296) or by an affiliated information service. DIALs are particularly useful because they are intended specifically for disabled people and are mostly run by disabled people who themselves have a particular understanding of the kind of difficulties which disability can cause. Social workers (*see* page 2) ought, in theory, to be a prime source of information, but in practice they tend to be greatly overstretched and are not always able to keep up to date with the complexities of the welfare benefits system.

Many of the disability organisations featured in Section 15 run information services and some have specialist advisers on benefits. If you are otherwise in touch with such an organisation, you may find that they can offer particularly personal and sensitive guidance.

Should you be concerned on a point of detail, you will find the DHSS freephone service on 0800 666 555 very helpful and, of course, expert.

Further Information

BOOKS AND PUBLICATIONS

The Adjudicating Officers' Guide (AOG) (HMSO, 1988). This is for those who need a very detailed knowledge of the benefits system. Legislation in 1983 established the post of Chief Adjudication Officer (CAO) whose statutory duties include the provision of advice and guidance to adjudicating officers in the field. This guidance is now for the first time published in its entirety, with the CAO's interpretation of social security legislation for almost all relevant benefits. It replaces two unpublished guides and the published guidance on supplementary benefits in the S Manual.

The new Guide is in 10 volumes:

1. Adjudication	£13.75
2. Subjects common to all benefits	£21.00

3. Income support, Social Fund
   maternity and funeral expenses   £32.00
4. Family credit   £15.50
5. Child benefit, child benefit
   increases, guardian's allowance   £12.25
6. Subjects common to benefits other
   than child benefit and income-
   related benefits   £20.00
7. Benefits for incapacity, invalidity,
   severe disablement and maternity   £17.75
8. Industrial injuries benefits   £21.00
9. Widow's benefits and retirement
   pension   £11.75
10. Unemployment benefit   £22.00

The complete set of ten volumes is priced at £160 and is available from HMSO bookshops and their agents. The AOG will be kept up to date with regular supplements.

Disability Rights Handbook (Disability Alliance ERA, 25 Denmark Street, London WC2H 8NJ, 13th edition, April 1988 to April 1989), price £3.50 including postage, reduced rates for bulk orders from voluntary organisations and trade unions. A low priced guide, published annually, which will be invaluable to claimants and advisers alike. Certainly no member of the caring professions or voluntary organisation should be without a copy. It is expertly written with disabled people in mind and is both clearly set out and wide ranging, going into the kind of detail and explanation which is not possible in this Directory.

Disability Rights Bulletin (Disability Alliance ERA, 25 Denmark Street, London WC2H 8NJ), price £2.00 per bulletin. Issued quarterly to update the Disability Rights Handbook. The Handbook and Bulletins can be ordered as an inclusive package at a subscription of £6.75.

Explanatory Booklets (Board of Inland Revenue). A free guide to Inland Revenue booklets offering guidance on income tax, corporation tax, capital gains tax, inheritance tax and extra statutory concessions. Updated regularly.

Extra-Statutory Concessions Supplement (Board of Inland Revenue, 1987). A free booklet supplementing the main listing of extra-statutory concessions, IR1.

Guide to Benefits for Hospital Patients by Clive Martin (Disability Alliance ERA, 25 Denmark Street, London WC2H 8NJ, 1988), price £3.30 to advisers; £1.80 to claimants, including postage and packing.

How to Claim State Benefits by Martin Rathfelder (Northcote House Publishers Ltd., Harper & Row House, Estover Road, Plymouth PL6 7PZ, April 1988), price £6.95. An A – Z guide which contains all April 1988 up-dating. The author, an adviser at the Manchester Welfare Rights Unit brings to notice many of the details of which the general public may be unaware.

National Welfare Benefits Handbook (Child Poverty Action Group Ltd., 1–5 Bath Street, London EC1V 9PY, 1988), price £5.50 including postage and packing, £2.50 to individual claimants. Written by experienced advisers who have worked at CPAG Citizens' Rights Office. Detailed coverage of means-tested benefits.

Non-contributory Benefits for Disabled People (DHSS, 1988). A free guide.

Reviews and Appeals (DHSS, 1988). A free guide.

Rights Guide to Non-Means-Tested Social Security Benefits (Child Poverty Action Group Ltd, 1–5 Bath Street, London EC1V 9PY, 1988), price £4.50 including postage and packing, £2.00 to individual claimants. Provides expert coverage of benefits for unemployment. sickness, maternity, widowhood, disablement and caring, and pensions.

SECTION 3
AIDS AND EQUIPMENT

All of us use aids and equipment every day of our lives, either to extend the range of our activities or to compensate for some limitation. If it is necessary to overcome a physical or sensory handicap, the aid is sometimes bespoke to our needs – for example, spectacles, which are individually prescribed – or it may be highly specialised, as in the case of some communication aids for people who cannot speak.

Quite often, people with disabilities, who may not find it easy to be up and about searching for information, are unaware of aids and equipment relevant to their particular needs which would make life much easier for them, or are uncertain as to what they do need. They may need both information and guidance. Indeed, apart from the simple, general-purpose aids, careful consideration of individual requirements, and detailed enquiries are absolutely essential. If there is one thing worse than an unmet need, it is a need which is met inappropriately. Unfortunately, in practice, many aids are acquired which are found to be unsuitable, ineffective, inoperative, non-durable or unacceptable to the user. It is important to recognise that, even if you can be satisfied about the quality of a product, aids which are made to a standard design may suit one individual but not another.

Wherever possible, it will be helpful if you can visit one of the increasing number of disabled living centres (*see* page 48), communication aids centres (*see* page 50), resource centres for blind people (*see* page 50) or an information centre for hearing-impaired people (*see* page 53) to see a range of aids and to enlist the advice of a trained adviser. If this is impracticable, much helpful guidance as to what is available and the application of the various items of equipment and clothing can be gained from one of the information services which specialise in aids and equipment (*see* page 46), occasionally from a travelling exhibition (*see* page 50), from books (*see* from page 54 onwards), from your doctor, from social service departments or from voluntary organisations concerned with particular disabilities.

It is quite impracticable in this short section to list and describe all the special equipment which is available. What we seek to do is to advise you where you can seek help and further information, and to draw attention to the broad categories of aids, including purpose-made, 'one-off' aids, which are available.

Statutory Provision of Aids by Local Authorities

Under the Chronically Sick and Disabled Persons Act 1970, local authorities are required to acquaint themselves with the numbers and needs of people in their areas who are 'blind, deaf or dumb, and other persons who are substantially and permanently handicapped by illness, injury or congenital deformity or such other disabilities as may be prescribed by the Secretary of State', and to meet those needs.

Various kinds of help available to a disabled person are set out in Section 2 of the Act and these include: 'assistance . . . in arranging for the carrying out of any works of adaptation in his home or . . . any additional facilities designed to secure his greater safety, comfort or convenience'. Local authorities also have the power to provide, or help to obtain, special aids to hearing for deaf people. These are known as environmental aids, e.g. flashing doorbells, vibrator pillows and induction loop systems.

There are similar requirements to provide a disabled person with, or to help him or her to obtain, 'wireless, television, library or similar recreational facilities' and a 'telephone and any special equipment necessary to enable him to use a telephone'. Whenever a real need is felt for help with aids or adaptations to assist daily living, an approach should be made through a doctor or social worker for the help of an occupational therapist or social worker in your local social services department. A home visit may then be arranged to make practical suggestions about ways of doing things, about aids and equipment, and, if necessary, about alterations to your house.

Unfortunately, the provisions of the Chronically Sick and Disabled Persons Act apply only where the local authority is 'satisfied' that such action is 'necessary' to meet the needs of the disabled person, subject to the general guidance of the Secretary of State. In practice, local authorities vary considerably in the extent to which they provide aids and assistance, and in their interpretation of the Act, which may be affected by political attitudes. As well as disparities in provision and unmet needs, there are alarming examples up and down the country of inordinate delays in the process of assessment and supply, and in the care which is taken to ensure that such equipment as is supplied is appropriate to need.

Economic constraints placed upon local authorities by central government suggest that provision is likely to deteriorate rather than improve. This means that there will be a greater need than ever for disabled consumers and their relatives, friends and advisers to be knowledgeable about special needs and appropriate solutions, and to press for those needs to be met. The 'cap in hand', 'grateful for small mercies' approach is out of date. Disabled people have a right to demand, and society has a duty to supply efficiently, whatever is required to redress, as far as it is possible, the disadvantages imposed by disability.

Statutory Provision of Aids by the National Health Service

In general, aids and equipment required in connection with medical and nursing care at home are supplied through the NHS. These can include ripple beds, cushions, hoists and aids for incontinence. General practitioners have lists of aids which may be prescribed where necessary. They can also recommend to the Department of Health and Social Security that large items be prescribed, even though they may not be on the regular list.

In the case of hearing aids, doctors can refer their patients to a special clinic at a local hospital for examination. If a hearing aid is found to be necessary, patients are then referred to a hearing aid centre, where the appliance will be fitted and supplied. Hearing aids are also available on free loan. NHS hearing aids are serviced, maintained and supplied with batteries free of charge.

If a person is attending a rehabilitation department of a local hospital, the occupational therapist will assess the patient and prescribe whatever aids are needed. A number of rehabilitation centres, both NHS and voluntary, offer highly specialised programmes of rehabilitation, with assessment and training to maximise the individual's ability to cope with everyday activities at home and elsewhere, and provide expert advice on aids. Whether or not you are under medical care, it may be possible to secure a referral to such a centre from your doctor or therapist.

A wide range of body-worn surgical appliances can be obtained on the recommendation of a hospital consultant. These include surgical footwear, colostomy and ileostomy appliances, and arm, neck and head appliances.

Artificial limbs are supplied, maintained and, if necessary, replaced under the NHS free of charge. NHS hospitals will arrange for a patient to visit a centre to make the necessary arrangements (a list of centres is given in DHSS leaflet HB2). As is well known, this service has been the subject of some criticism. At the time of writing, the arrangements for provision and supply are under scrutiny, and changes are taking place which hopefully may considerably improve the service.

Not all aids supplied under prescription are free, but where they are for the personal or domestic use of a disabled person, they normally carry the zero rate of value added tax, though it may be necessary to make sure that the entitlement is taken up (for details of VAT zero rating, *see* page 43).

Advice on the problems of incontinence should be sought from health visitors, district nurses or social workers. Both district health authorities and local authority social services departments can supply incontinence pads to people who live in their own homes. However, while DHAs may not charge for them, local authorities may do so, according to local policy. They cannot be prescribed by GPs, nor dispensed by chemists under the NHS, and it is left to the discretion of the supplying authority to decide the type of pad to be provided, to whom they will be supplied, and how they are delivered.

Statutory Provision of Aids by Local Education Authorities

Aids connected with education may be supplied by local education authorities for use in schools and colleges.

Statutory Provision of Aids for Employment

The Department of Employment can provide, on free permanent loan, any aids necessary, because of disability, to enable employees to perform their particular duties. These include modifications to machines, purpose-built desks and seating, counter-balanced drawing boards, electric typewriters, keyboard guards, telephone aids and accessories, reading and writing aids, and Braille measuring devices.

Grants can also be made up to a maximum of £6,000 to help employers who need to make essential adaptations to premises in order to take on, or retain in employment, a disabled person. The adaptation must relate to the needs of a specific employee, and the employer is then expected to keep the disabled person concerned in the job as long as he or she is capable of doing it satisfactorily.

Disabled employees or those seeking work may well wish to bring these opportunities to the notice of employers/potential employers, who can get further information from leaflet EPL 71 or by contacting their local Job Centre's Disablement Resettlement Officer.

Provision of Aids by Voluntary Organisations

Given the present severe restraints on public expenditure and the financial constraints imposed on local authorities, the statutory provision of aids is increasingly limited. It may be necessary to seek help in the voluntary sector. Many of the organisations listed in Section 15 of this Directory, especially those concerned with particular disabilities, provide this sort of practical help for their members. Other charities may be prepared to make grants for necessary aids and equipment which cannot be obtained from other sources. A recent book, *A Guide to Grants for Individuals in Need* (Directory of Social Change, Radius Works, Back Lane, London NW3 1EL, 1987), price £9.95, has a section devoted to charities for sick and disabled people, and should be available, if necessary by special request, from your local library.

Reliefs from VAT and Car Tax

VALUE ADDED TAX

The reliefs on aids, equipment and services for disabled people are not simple and we have therefore set them out in some detail. In essence, the zero rate applies provided that the goods or services are designed solely for use by a handicapped person and they are supplied to such a person or to a charity for the use of handicapped people. Some goods qualify because they are of a description such as to be invariably for use only by handicapped people; in other cases it will be a matter for consideration whether they can be said to be 'designed solely' for handicapped people. The

goods must have specialised design features which make them clearly belong to the category in question; the relief does not apply to general purpose goods which are used by disabled people. For example, an ordinary walking stick is not entitled to relief, since it is sometimes used by able-bodied people, whereas crutches and walking frames would obviously qualify.

Sometimes, there is doubt. Incontinence pads, for example, were not, until 1984, regarded as 'designed solely for use by a handicapped person', but in April of that year it was accepted on review that they could be zero rated.

The reliefs are set out in Group 14 of the Zero Rate Schedule as consolidated in the Value Added Tax Act 1983, Schedule 5 (as amended). We apologise in advance for some of the now inappropriate language which is a feature of the law. In addition to medical prescriptions, the reliefs are as follows:

Item 2

The supply (including supply by letting on hire) to a handicapped person (defined in law as someone who is 'chronically sick or disabled') for domestic or his/her personal use, or to a charity for making available to handicapped persons (whether by sale or otherwise) for domestic or their personal use, of the following goods:

(a) medical or surgical appliances designed solely for the relief of a severe abnormality or severe injury;
(b) electrically or mechanically adjustable beds designed for invalids;
(c) commode chairs, commode stools, devices incorporating a bidet jet and warm air drier and frames or other devices for sitting over or rising from a sanitary appliance;
(d) chair lifts or stair lifts designed for use in connection with invalid wheelchairs;
(e) hoists and lifters designed for use by invalids;
(f) motor vehicles designed or substantially and permanently adapted for the carriage of a person in a wheelchair or on a stretcher and of no more than five other persons;
(g) equipment and appliances not included in paragraphs (a) to (f) above designed solely for use by a handicapped person;
(h) parts and accessories designed solely for use in or with goods described in paragraphs (a) to (g) above.

NOTES: Item 2 is deemed to *include*, so far as they relieve a severe abnormality or severe injury or are otherwise designed solely for the use of a handicapped person, the following:
(i) clothing, footwear and wigs;

(ii)   invalid wheelchairs and invalid carriages other than mechanically propelled vehicles intended for use on roads (but see page 45); and

(iii) renal haemodialysis units, oxygen concentrators, artificial respirators and other similar apparatus.

Item 2, however, is deemed to *exclude*:

(i)   hearing aids (except those designed for the auditory training of deaf children);

(ii)   dentures;

(iii) spectacles;

(iv) contact lenses.

(But these items are normally eligible for exemption (different from zero rating but also carrying no tax) under item 1 or item 2 of Group 7 of the VAT Exemption Schedule.)

Item 3

The supply to a handicapped person of services of adapting goods to suit his/her condition.

Item 4

The supply to a charity of services of adapting goods to suit the condition of a handicapped person to whom the goods are to be made available, by sale or otherwise by the charity.

Item 5

The supply to a handicapped person of a service of repair or maintenance of any goods which were supplied to him/her, or to a charity, where the supply was of a description specified in item 2 or item 6.

Item 6

The supply of goods in connection with a supply described in item 3, item 4 or item 5.

Item 7

The supply to a handicapped person or to a charity of services necessarily performed in the installation of equipment or appliances (including parts and accessories therefor) specified in item 2 and supplied as described in that item.

Item 8

The supply to a handicapped person of a supply of constructing ramps or widening doorways or passages for the purpose of facilitating his/her entry to or movement within his/her private residence.

Item 9

The supply to a charity of a service described in item 8 for the purpose of facilitating a handicapped person's entry to or movement within any building.

Item 10

The supply to a handicapped person of the services of providing, extending or adapting a bathroom, washroom or lavatory in his/her private residence where this is necessary to suit his/her condition.

Item 10A

The supply to a charity of a service of providing, extending or adapting a bathroom, washroom or lavatory for use by handicapped persons in a residential home where such provision, extension or adaptation is necessary by reason of the condition of the handicapped persons.

Item 11

The supply of goods in connection with a supply described in item 8, item 9, item 10 or item 10A.

Item 12

The letting on hire of a motor vehicle for a period of not less than three years to a handicapped person in receipt of a mobility allowance or mobility supplement where the lessor's business consists predominantly of the provision of motor vehicles to such persons. (Effectively, this relates to the Motability Scheme (*see* page 125). The vehicle must be new at the start of the hire, the payments under the hire must consist wholly or partly of sums paid to the lessor by the DHSS on behalf of the lessee in respect of the mobility allowance or mobility supplement to which the lessee is entitled, and the zero rating applies only to leasing contracts entered into on or after 1 September 1984.)

Item 13

The supply to a handicapped person of services necessarily performed in the installation of a lift for the purpose of facilitating his/her movement between floors within his/her private residence.

Item 14

The supply to a charity providing a permanent or temporary residence or day-centre for handicapped persons of services necessarily performed in the installation of a lift for the purpose of facilitating the movement of handicapped persons between floors within that building.

Item 15

The supply of goods in connection with a supply described in item 13 or item 14.

Item 16

The supply to a handicapped person for domestic or his/her personal use, or to a charity for making available to handicapped persons by sale or otherwise for domestic or their personal use, of an alarm system designed to be capable of operation by a handicapped person, and to enable him/her to alert directly a specified person or a control centre (these expressions refer to a person or centre which is appointed to receive directly calls activated by an alarm system as described, and which retains information about the handicapped person to assist him/her in the event of illness, injury or similar emergency).

Item 17
The supply of services necessarily performed by a control centre (as described above) in receiving and responding to calls from an alarm system specified in item 16.

Comment: The liability of vehicles needs some further explanation. Item 2(f) is limited. It covers only cars or vans which have both permanent fittings to load and secure a wheelchair or stretcher, and seating accommodation for up to five other persons.

In the case of a vehicle designed or adapted to carry a disabled person sitting in a wheelchair, there must be a permanently fitted hoist or ramp and suitable clamps to secure the wheelchair.

In the case of a vehicle designed or adapted to carry a disabled person on a stretcher, there must be adequate means of access to the space within the vehicle for the stretcher, as well as suitable fixtures to secure it.

There is advantage in the case of such vehicles in making sure that any necessary conversion is carried out before the vehicle is supplied. Provided that a single payment covering the whole cost of the vehicle as converted is made, the supplier can zero rate the whole transaction. If, however, you were to buy a standard production vehicle and subsequently arrange for it to be converted in the ways described above, only the charge for the conversion could be zero rated. You would not be able to recover the VAT originally paid on the vehicle itself.

Other services of adapting cars or vans to make them more suitable for use by a disabled person qualify for relief when supplied to that person, under item 3 (labour) and item 6 (parts) even though the vehicle itself does not then qualify under item 2(f). We are advised that this includes adaptations such as the fitting not only of hand controls, but such facilities as automatic transmission, power assisted steering, swivel seats, cruise control, central locking and electric windows if they are essential requirements because of your disability.

Equipment which you fit yourself qualifies for zero rating under item 2(g) provided that it is designed solely for use by a disabled person (e.g. hand controls in kit form), and associated parts

and accessories would then qualify under item 2(h).

HOW TO OBTAIN ZERO RATED SUPPLIES
A supplier who is registered under VAT law is liable for tax on his supplies if the conditions for relief are not fulfilled, and there is a danger that if there is any doubt, or if the supplier is unaware of the provisions of Group 14, he will charge tax. It may be necessary for the customer to point out that the supply is entitled to zero rating. The supplier will, in any event, require a declaration from the customer. The declaration is not supplied as an official form, but models are printed in the Customs and Excise leaflet *Aids for Handicapped Persons* of which most suppliers are aware. This leaflet also gives further details of the reliefs available, and the procedures for obtaining relief on goods which are eligible for zero rating under Group 14 when they are imported.

OTHER RELIEFS
Goods which are eligible for relief under Group 14, and certain other goods, are eligible for zero rating under certain conditions when they are donated or, in some cases, sold to certain institutions. For details *see* Customs and Excise leaflet, *Donated Medical and Scientific Equipment, etc.* Leaflets can be obtained from any local VAT office (*see* telephone directory under Customs and Excise) who will also advise or refer for Head Office advice any questions of doubt concerning eligibility.

CAR TAX
Relief for 'private ambulances' from car tax (not to be confused with vehicle excise duty, sometimes called road tax) is in line with the zero rating described in item 2 of Group 14 of the VAT Zero Rate Schedule (*see* above). The relevant legislation is the Car Tax Act 1983, section 2(2)(c) as amended. This relieves, among other things, 'ambulances and vehicles designed or substantially and permanently adapted for the carriage of a chronically sick or disabled person in a wheelchair or on a stretcher and of no more than five other persons'. Further details are contained in Customs and Excise Notice No. 670. Anyone contemplating the adaptation of a vehicle which has not previously borne car tax would be well advised to contact his/her local Customs and Excise office (*not* VAT office) in advance.

Relief from Import Duty for Articles Imported for Blind and Other Handicapped People

Certain articles can be imported free of customs duty by blind or other handicapped people for their own use or by or on behalf of approved organisations concerned with the advancement of such people. Relief is subject to the following conditions:

(a) that the goods must be used only to give educational, scientific or cultural help to blind or other handicapped people;

(b) that goods imported by blind or other handicapped people for their own use must not be lent, hired out or transferred unless the importer first obtains the agreement of his/her local Customs and Excise office;

(c) that organisations wishing to import goods under these arrangements have prior approval from the Department of Trade and Industry. (Goods imported by such approved organisations may be lent, hired out or transferred on a non-profit-making basis to blind or other handicapped people or, subject to prior permission from the DoTI and notification to Customs & Excise, to another approved organisation.)

The goods concerned are:

Braille paper;

white canes;

typewriters adapted for use by blind or partially sighted people;

equipment for the mechanical production of Braille and recorded material;

television enlargers for blind and partially sighted people;

electronic orientator and obstacle detector appliances;

teaching aids and apparatus specifically designed for use by blind or partially sighted people;

Braille watches with cases not made of precious metals;

record players and cassette players specially designed or adapted for blind or partially sighted people;

talking books, magnetic tapes and cassettes for the production of Braille and talking books;

electronic reading machines;

table games and accessories specially adapted or designed for blind and partially sighted people;

all other articles specially designed to be of educational, scientific or cultural help to blind and partially sighted people;

spare parts, components, tools and accessories specially or recognisably intended for any of the above goods;

any goods specially designed to give educational, employment or social help to physically or mentally handicapped people, and spare parts, components, tools and accessories specifically or recognisably intended for such goods.

NOTE: This last item is subject to the special condition that relief will not prejudice the production of equivalent goods in the European Community, unless the goods are sent as a gift without any commercial consideration on the part of the donor.

HOW TO CLAIM RELIEF

Relief from duty is given by HM Customs and Excise, against certificates issued by the Department of Trade, to whom application should be made on special forms (DFA(BW) for goods for blind and partially sighted people; DFA(H) for goods for other handicapped people), obtainable from the Department of Trade and Industry, International Trade Policy Division, Room 429, 1 Victoria Street, London SW1H 0ET (Tel: 01–215 4705). There is no need for organisations to apply for prior registration as an approved body: each application for relief will be considered on its merit at the time. In no circumstances can applications be accepted from agents, distributors or other commercial organisations.

NOTE: Fuller details of conditions and procedures are given in Notice 371, obtainable from the above address or from any local Customs and Excise office (but *not* VAT office).

Information Services on Aids and Equipment

General information services are included in Section 15, Helpful Organisations. In addition, many organisations listed in that section and concerned to meet the needs of people affected by particular disabilities will be able to give advice on aids and equipment, as can any of the centres listed on pages 48–50. The following services are those which specialise in the provision of information about aids and equipment.

British Database on Research into Aids for the Disabled (BARD)
Handicapped Persons Research Unit, Newcastle upon Tyne Polytechnic, 1 Coach Lane, Coach Lane Campus, Newcastle upon Tyne NE7 7TW (Tel: Newcastle upon Tyne (091) 2358211).
This is a computerised register of 'non-manufactured' aids and related research projects. It contains descriptions of current design and development projects, prototypes, one-offs, latest

developments, as well as surveys, evaluations and research in the use of aids. The database complements information provided by other organisations whose emphases lie in manufactured and commercially available aids.

The aim of BARD is to facilitate the exchange of ideas, a process which is central to the research and development stage of producing aids for handicapped people. Each entry in the database contains a description of the project together with the name and address of maker, aid function and type of handicap. Information is supplied through print-outs in response to specific enquiries, and through reports on particular descriptions of aids, *viz.* therapy and training; prosthetics and orthotics; personal care; mobility; household and daily living; furniture and fixtures; communication and environmental control; aids for handling other projects; leisure and sports; building/environmental design; education; workplace; communication and education.

BARD is keen to hear from those working in this field, with specific details of their work.

A second database, BARDSOFT, contains information on a wide range of computer software for special needs. At the time of writing, it consists of 1,700 entries each occupying an A4 sheet when printed. These relate to over 40 types of microcomputer and are keyworded under ten main subject descriptors and about 200 sub-descriptors. The ten main descriptors are: assessment, cognition, employment, language, numeracy, perception/motor, recreation, teaching, training/therapy, general. This database is intended for information providers, software developers, teachers, occupational therapists, and other care workers.

Disabled Living Foundation Information Service
380–384 Harrow Road, London W9 2HU (Tel: 01–289 6111; also available on Telecom Gold 84; DD P002).

A national information service and database offering a comprehensive service to disabled people and those professionally concerned with care provision including voluntary organisations and other groups requiring information on technical aids, equipment and services. Information is supplied free to disabled people and by subscription to all others. Subscribers receive a pack of 24 publications, each of which deals with a particular subject area, giving details of the type of equipment, a product description, price and address and telephone number of the supplier. There is also an index to the complete package.

The great advantage of this service is that each publication is completely revised annually, and regular mailings include amendments between editions. The service is essential for any organisation involved in supplying information and/or equipment to disabled people, and overcomes the difficulties and expense of maintaining an independent information collection. Subscribers also have access to the DLF specialist advice service by telephone and letter.

Additional publications include resource papers and advice notes on a wide range of topics. A list of second-hand equipment is also maintained.

DLF-DATA, the computerised database of products, technical aids and associated advice notes is now available on-line at DLF, and it is anticipated that on-line access will be extended to remote users during 1988. The system is the most advanced in Europe and compares favourably with any other in this subject area world-wide. Benefits include fast accurate recall of information by almost any search term, and a comprehensive range of on-line help screens and search prompts. At the time of writing, there are 12,000 entries and these are being added to all the time.

The DLF also provides advisory services on clothing, footwear, incontinence, music, and visual impairment. All these advisory services can give information and guidance in response to enquiries from people with disabilities, their families and all those professionally concerned with these particular subjects. Lectures and demonstrations can be arranged and publications and some training kits are available.

The Information Service is open 9.30am to 5.00pm, Monday to Friday.

Northern Ireland Information Service for Disabled People
2 Annadale Avenue, Belfast BT7 3JR (Tel: Belfast (0232) 491011).
This comprehensive information service includes aids and equipment, with a particular interest in the role of occupational therapists in housing adaptations. A subscription service based on the Disabled Living Foundation service is available, with regular despatch of updating materials, and is used by professionals. libraries and others working with people with disabilities.

Scottish Council on Disability Information Department
5 Shandwick Place, Edinburgh EH2 4RG (Tel: 031–229 8632).

The Information Department answers queries on all aspects of disabled living, except the purely medical. It offers the most comprehensive information service in Scotland on aids, equipment, services and facilities connected with disability. From an extensive information bank, 24 different information lists are compiled and regularly updated. The lists can be obtained through subscription.

Disabled Living Centres

These used to be called Aids Centres, but have been renamed to avoid confusion with AIDS, the Acquired Immune Deficiency Syndrome. They offer information and advice about aids and equipment and display a range of aids, which you can see and try out. A visit to such a centre is very useful in helping you to sort out what is available and what best meets your needs. Invariably it is necessary to make an appointment before you visit. As the size and scope of the centres vary considerably, it is a good idea to check that the purpose of your visit can be fulfilled.

ENGLAND

BUCKINGHAMSHIRE

Aylesbury
Dial and Smile, (South Corridor), Stoke Mandeville Hospital, Mandeville Road, Aylesbury, Buckinghamshire HP21 8AL (Tel: Aylesbury (0296) 84111, ext. 3114); limited service only.

CHESHIRE

Macclesfield
Centre for Disabled Living, Macclesfield District General Hospital, Macclesfield, Cheshire SK10 3BL (Tel: Macclesfield (0625) 21000, ext. 2759); limited service only.

Stockport
Disabled Living Centre, St Thomas' Hospital, Shawheath, Stockport, Cheshire SK3 8BL (Tel: 061–419 4476).

CLEVELAND

Middlesbrough
Department of Rehabilitation, Middlesbrough General Hospital, Ayresome Green Lane, Middlesbrough, Cleveland TS5 5AZ (Tel: Middlesbrough (0642) 813133, ext.158); limited service only.

ESSEX

Colchester
Disabled Living Centre, Occupational Therapy Department, Colchester General Hospital, Colchester, Essex (Tel: Colchester (0206) 853535); limited service only.

GREATER LONDON

London
The Disabled Living Foundation, Equipment Centre, 380–384 Harrow Road, London W9 2HU (Tel: 01–289 6111).
The Spastics Society Aid and Equipment Exhibition, 16 Fitzroy Square, London W1P 5HQ (Tel: 01–387 9571).

GREATER MANCHESTER

Manchester
Disabled Living Services, Diasabled Living Centre, Redbank House, 4 St Chad's Street, Cheetham, Manchester M8 8QA (Tel: 061–832 3678).

HAMPSHIRE

Portsmouth
Disabled Living Centre, Prince Albert Road, Eastney, Portsmouth PO4 9HR (Tel: Portsmouth (0705) 737174); limited service only.

Southampton
Southampton Aid and Equipment Centre, Southampton General Hospital, Tremona Road, Southampton SO9 4XY (Tel: Southampton (0703) 777222, ext. 3414 or 3233).

LANCASHIRE

Blackpool
Disabled Living Centre, 8 Queen Street, Blackpool, Lancashire FY1 1PD (Tel: Blackpool (0253) 21084, ext. 1 or 4); limited service only.

LEICESTERSHIRE

Leicester
Trent Region Aids, Information and Demonstration Service, (TRAIDS), 76 Clarendon Park Road, Leicester LE2 3AD (Tel: Leicester (0533) 700747/8).

LONDON *see* GREATER LONDON

MANCHESTER *see* GREATER MANCHESTER

MERSEYSIDE

Liverpool
Merseyside Centre for Independent Living,

Youens Way, East Prescot Road, Liverpool L14 2EP (Tel: 051–228 9221).

STAFFORDSHIRE

Newcastle-under-Lyme
The Independent Living Centre, The Arts Centre, Brampton Park, Newcastle-under-Lyme, Staffordshire ST5 0QP (Tel: Newcastle-under-Lyme (0782) 634949); limited service only.

TYNE AND WEAR

Newcastle upon Tyne
The Dene Centre, Castles Farm Road, Newcastle upon Tyne NE3 1PH (Tel: 091– 284 0480).

YORKSHIRE – SOUTH

Sheffield
Sheffield Independent Living Centre, 108 The Moor, Sheffield S1 4DP (Tel: Sheffield (0742) 737025).

YORKSHIRE – WEST

Huddersfield
Disabled Living Centre, Kirklees Social Services, Unit 6, Silvercourt Trading Estate, Silver Street, Huddersfield, West Yorkshire (Huddersfield (0484) 5118809); limited service only,

Leeds
The William Merritt Disabled Living Centre, St Mary's Hospital, Greenhill Road, Armley, Leeds LS12 3QE (Tel: Leeds (0532) 793140).

Wakefield
National Demonstration Centre, Pinderfields General Hospital, Wakefield, West Yorkshire WF1 4DG (Tel: Wakefield (0924) 375217, ext. 2510 or 2263).

WEST MIDLANDS

Birmingham
The Disabled Living Centre, 260 Broad Street, Birmingham B1 2HF (Tel: 021– 643 0980)

Dudley
Disabled Living Centre, 1 St Giles Street, Nethertyn, Dudley, West Midlands (Tel: Dudley (0384) 55433, ext. 5839); limited service only.

WILTSHIRE

Swindon
Swindon Centre for Disabled Living, The Hawthorn Centre, Cricklade Road, Swindon SN2 1AF (Tel: Swindon (0793) 643966).

NORTHERN IRELAND

Belfast
Disabled Living Centre, Musgrave Park Hospital, Stockman's Lane, Belfast BT9 7JB (Tel: Belfast (0232) 669501, ext.565 or 609.

SCOTLAND

LOTHIAN

Edinburgh
Disabled Living Centre, Astley Ainslie Hospital, Grange Loan, Edinburgh EH9 2HL (Tel: 031–447 6271, ext.5635).

STRATHCLYDE

Paisley
Disability Centre for Independent Living, Community Services Centre, Queen Street, Paisley (Tel: 041–887 0597); limited service only.

WALES

GLAMORGAN – MID

Caerphilly
Resources (Aids and Equipment) Centre, Wales Council for the Disabled, Caerbragdy Industrial Estate, Bedwas Road, Caerphilly, Mid Glamorgan CF8 3SL (Tel: Caerphilly (0222) 887325/6/7).

GLAMORGAN – SOUTH

Cardiff
The Demonstration Aids Centre, The Lodge, Rookwood Hospital, Llandaff, Cardiff, South Glamorgan (Tel: Cardiff (0222) 566281, ext.51 or 66).

Mobile Advice Centre (MAC)

The Scottish Council on Disability run a travelling exhibition of aids and information for disabled people which tours Scotland visiting various sites including shopping centres, colleges and health centres. MAC also attends conferences and exhibitions and may be available for request visits. Contact The Secretary, Mobile Advice Centre, SCOD, 5 Shandwick Place, Edinburgh EH2 4RG (Tel: 031–229 8632).

Communication Aids Centres

Communication Aids Centres offer assessment, advice and training in the use of communication aids. They have a wide range of such aids for demonstration. Assessment is by appointment only.

AIDS AND EQUIPMENT

ENGLAND

AVON

Bristol
Mrs Jayne Easton. Assistive Communication Aids Centre, Speech Therapy Department, Frenchay Hospital, Bristol BS16 1LE (Tel: Bristol (0272) 701212, ext. 2151).

GREATER LONDON

London
Communication Aids Centre, Charing Cross Hospital, Fulham Palace Road, Hammersmith, London W6 8RF (Tel: 01–748 2040, ext. 3064).

London
Nicola Jolleff (Children), Communication Aids Centre, The Wolfson Centre, Mecklenburgh Square, London WC1N 2AP (Tel: 01–837 7618, ext. 9).

TYNE AND WEAR

Newcastle upon Tyne
Communication Aids Centre, Castle Farm Road, Newcastle upon Tyne NE3 1PH (Tel: 091–2840480).

WEST MIDLANDS

West Bromwich
Sandwell Health Authority, Communication Aids Centre, Boulton Road, West Bromwich, West Midlands B70 6NN (Tel: 021–553 0908).

NORTHERN IRELAND

Belfast
Mrs H.Robinson, Speech Therapist, Musgrave Park Hospital, Stockmans Lane, Belfast 9 (Tel: Belfast (0232) 669501).

SCOTLAND

STRATHCLYDE

Glasgow
Ms Janet Scott, Scottish Centre of Technology for the Communication Impaired, Victoria Infirmary, Langside Road, Glasgow G42 9TY (Tel: 041–649 4545, ext. 5579/5580).

WALES

GLAMORGAN – SOUTH

Cardiff
Communication Aids Centre, Rookwood Hospital, Fairwater Road, Cardiff CF5 2YN (Tel: Cardiff (0222) 566281, ext. 51).

Centres for Blind and Partially Sighted People

The Disabled Living Centres and Communication Aids Centres listed above have a range of aids for blind and partially sighted people (though this may be limited at the DLCs). In addition, the Royal National Institute for the Blind (*see* GREATER LONDON below) displays and sells a wide range of equipment both sophisticated and simple, to help visually handicapped people in their everyday lives. Many games such as chess, backgammon and ludo have also been specially adapted. This and other resource centres for visually handicapped people have been advised by the RNIB, as follows:

ENGLAND

AVON

Bristol
Maytrees Resource Centre, East Park, Fishponds Road, Fishponds, Bristol BS5 6YA (Tel: Bristol (0272) 510215).

Weston-super-Mare
Woodspring Association for the Blind, Roselawn, Walliscote Grove Road, Weston-super-Mare, Avon BS22 1LT (Tel: Weston-super-Mare (0934) 419393).

BEDFORDSHIRE

Luton
Enterprises by the Blind (Bedfordshire), 93a Marsh Road, Luton, Bedfordshire LU3 2OG (Tel: Luton (0582) 583996).

BERKSHIRE

Reading
Berkshire County and Blind Society, Middleton House, 5 Erleigh Road, Reading, Berkshire RG1 5LR.

CAMBRIDGESHIRE

Cambridge
Cambridgeshire Society for the Blind, Resource Centre, 28 Glisson Road, Cambridgeshire CB1 2HF (Tel: Cambridge (0223) 352728).

Huntingdon
Huntingdon Society for the Blind, The Resource Centre, 8 St Mary's Street, Huntingdon, Cambridgeshire PE18 6PE (Tel: Huntingdon (0480) 53438).

Peterborough
The National Deaf/Blind Helpers League, 18 Rainbow Court, Paston Ridings, Peterborough,

Cambridgeshire PE4 6UP (Tel: Peterborough (0733) 73511).

CHESHIRE

Chester

Chester Blind Welfare Society, The Resource Centre, 67 Liverpool Road, Chester, Cheshire CH2 1AP (Tel: Chester (0244) 382222).

CLEVELAND

Middlesbrough

The Cleveland, Dasham and North Yorkshire District Society for the Blind, The Resource Centre, Station Road, Middlesbrough, Cleveland.

CORNWALL

Truro

Cornwall County Association for the Blind and Partially Sighted, The Resource Centre, 1/2 Victoria Square, Truro, Cornwall TR1 2RS (Tel: Truro (0872) 73952).

DEVON

Exeter

Partially Sighted Society, 3 Colleton Crescent, Exeter, Devon EX2 4DG (Tel: Exeter (0392) 210656).

Devon Association for the Blind, The Resource Centre, 16 York Road, Exeter, Devon EX4 6BA (Tel: Exeter (0392) 77196).

DORSET

Blandford Forum

Dorset Association for the Blind, The Resource Centre, 8 Thornicombe Road, Blandford Forum, Dorset.

Bournemouth

Bournemouth Blind Aid Society, The Resource Centre, Hammington Hall, Hammington, Bournemouth, Dorset.

ESSEX

Brentwood

Brentwood Visually Handicapped Club, The Aids Centre, Brentwood, Essex.

Southend-on-Sea

Southend Social Services, Joint Aids Store, 4th Floor, Queensway House, Southend-on-Sea, Essex SS2 5TB (Tel: Southend-on-Sea (0702) 616311, ext 362/3).

GREATER LONDON

Centre for Visually Handicapped People in Haringey, Room 9, Tottenham Town Hall, Town Hall Approach Road, London N15 4RY (Tel: 01–808 1000, ext. 261).

Enfield Geranium Club for the Blind, Blind Aids Centre, 111 Carvanon Avenue, Enfield, Middlesex.

London Association, The Jewish Blind Society, 221 Golders Green Road, London W2 (Tel: 01–458 3111).

Merton Voluntary Association for the Welfare of the Blind, The Centre for the Blind, 65 Clarendon Road, Colliers Wood, London SW19 (Tel: 01–947 2854).

Royal National Institute for the Blind, 224 Great Portland Street, London W1N 6AA (Tel: 01–366 1288, ext. 356) (*see* note above).

GREATER MANCHESTER

Dunkinfield

Tameside Blind Association, The Resource Centre, 4 Wellington Parade, Dunkinfield.

Manchester

Henshaw's Society for the Blind, The Resource Centre, Warwick Road, Old Trafford, Manchester M16 0GS (Tel: 061–872 1234).

HAMPSHIRE

Eastleigh

Hampshire Association for the Care of the Blind, Eric Heys House, 48 Leigh Road, Eastleigh, Hampshire SO5 4DT (Tel: Eastleigh (0703) 641244).

HERTFORDSHIRE

Hertford

The Hertfordshire Society for the Blind, Blind Aids Centre, Room 1, Leahoe House, County Hall, Hertford, Hertfordshire SG13 8EP (Tel: Hertford (0992) 556272).

KENT

Maidstone

Kent Association for the Blind, 15 Ashford Road, Maidstone, Kent ME14 5DB.

LEICESTERSHIRE

Leicester

The Royal Leicestershire, Rutland & Wycliffe Society for the Blind, Margaret Road, Leicester, Leicestershire LE5 5FU (Tel: Leicester (0533) 736562).

LONDON *see* GREATER LONDON.

MANCHESTER *see* GREATER MANCHESTER.

MERSEYSIDE

Liverpool
Christopher Grange Day Rehabilitation Centre, Catholic Blind Institute, Youens Way, East Prescot Road, Liverpool L14 2EW (Tel: 051–220 2525).

NORFOLK

Norwich
Norwich Institution for the Blind, Magpie Road, Norwich, Norfolk NR3 1JH (Tel: Norwich (0603) 629558).

OXFORDSHIRE

Charlbury
Oxfordshire Association for the Blind, 3 Enstone Road, Charlbury, Oxfordshire OX7 3QR (Tel: Charlbury (0608) 810329).

SOMERSET

Highbridge
The Sight and Sound Centre, The Morland Hall, off Morland Road, Highbridge, near Burnham-on-Sea, Somerset.

STAFFORDSHIRE

Stafford
Staffordshire Association for the Welfare of the Blind, Centre for the Blind, North Walls, Stafford, Staffordshire ST16 3AD (Tel: Stafford (0785) 54572).

Stoke-on-Trent
Stoke-on-Trent Blind Welfare Voluntary Association, Elsing Street, off City Road, Fenton, Stoke-on-Trent, Staffordshire ST4 2PR (Tel: Stoke-on-Trent (0782) 46194).

SURREY

Leatherhead
Surrey Voluntary Association for the Blind, 'Redwood', OT Unit, School Lane, Fetcham, Leatherhead, Surrey (Tel: Leatherhead (0372) 377701).

SUSSEX – EAST

Eastbourne
Eastbourne Blind Society, Blind Centre, Eastbourne, East Sussex (Tel: Eastbourne (0323) 29511).

TYNE AND WEAR

Newcastle upon Tyne
Newcastle upon Tyne Voluntary Society for the Blind, Disabled Aids Centre, MEA House, Ellison Place, Newcastle upon Tyne NE1 8XS.
Newcastle Council of Voluntary Service, Blind Aids Centre, The Arts Centre, Brampton, Newcastle.

WARWICKSHIRE

Warwick
Warwickshire Association for the Blind, The George Marshall Centre, Blind Aids Centre, Puckering's Lane, Warwick, Warwickshire CV34 4UH (Tel: Warwick (0926) 494129).

WEST MIDLANDS

Birmingham
Birmingham Royal Institute for the Blind, Resource Centre, 49 Court Oak Road, Harborne, Birmingham B17 9TG (Tel: 021–427 2248).
Duchess Road Rehabilitation Unit for the Visually Handicapped, 79/81 Duchess Road, Edgbaston, Birmingham B16.
Day Centre for the Visually Handicapped, The Resource Centre, Wolverhampton Road East, Sedgley, Birmingham.

Sheffield
City of Sheffield Family and Community Services Department, Sheffield Independent Living Centre, Unit 1, MSC Building, Moorfoot, Sheffield S1 (Tel: Sheffield (0742) 737025).

YORKSHIRE – WEST

Leeds
North Regional Association for the Blind, Headingley Castle, Headingley Lane, Leeds, West Yorkshire LS6 2DQ (Tel: Leeds (0532) 752666).

NORTHERN IRELAND

Belfast
The Blind Centre for Northern Ireland, 70 North Road, Belfast BT5 5NJ (Tel: Belfast (0232) 654366). Also has special information units in Belfast, Dungannon, Londonderry and Newry.

SCOTLAND

CENTRAL

Stirling
RNIB Scottish Branch, 9 Viewfield Place, Stirling FK8 1NL (Tel: Stirling (0786) 3652).

STRATHCLYDE

Glasgow
Glasgow Resource Centre for the Blind, 174 St Vincent's Street, Glasgow (Tel: 041–248 5811).

TAYSIDE

Perth
Perthshire and Kinross-shire Society for the Blind, The Blind Aids Centre, 8 St Leonards Bank, Perth.

WALES

GLAMORGAN – SOUTH

Cardiff
Cardiff Institute for the Blind, 20 Newport Road, Cardiff, South Glamorgan F2 1YB.

GWYNEDD

Bangor
North Wales Society for the Blind, The Resource Centre, 325 High Street, Bangor, Gwynedd (Tel: Bangor (0248) 353604).

Centres for Deaf and Hearing Impaired People

See also Communication Aids Centres above.

ENGLAND

GREATER LONDON

Redbridge South Woodford
The Further Education Department, Sir Winston Churchill Schools for the Deaf, 10 Churchfields, South Woodford, London E18. (Open Thursdays, 1 to 4 p.m.; closed during school holidays).
Has a working display of environmental aids for the telephone, television, loop system, doorbells, etc. and relevant information.

WEST MIDLANDS

Birmingham
National Deaf Children's Society, Technology Information Centre, 4 Church Road, Birmingham B15 3TD (Tel: voice 021–454 5151; Vistel 021–454 9795).
The Centre provides information on hearing aids and other equipment for deaf people. Also operates a loan service of equipment to parents of deaf children.
Breakthrough Trust Deaf/Hearing Integration, Charles W.Gillett Centre, Selly Oak Colleges, Birmingham B29 6LE (Tel: voice 021–472 6447; Vistel 021–471 1001).
The Link Room at the above address provides a wide range of information for hearing impaired

people and those concerned with deafness. This includes an extensive library of literature, books and a working display of special equipment concerned with deafness. A Public Sector Telephone is also available.

British Standards

British Standards Institution, BSI Sales, Linford Wood, Milton Keynes MK14 6LE. (Tel: Milton Keynes (0905) 221166).
British Standards apply to a wide variety of goods. The following standards (the list may not be comprehensive) have so far been established for aids and appliances for people with disabilities:

BS 2655 Lifts, escalators, passenger conveyors and paternosters;
BS 4922 Metal tripod and tetrapod walking sticks;
BS 5043 Book holders, magnifiers and prismatic spectacles for use as reading aids in hospitals and the home;
BS 5104 Adjustable height walking frames;
BS 5181 Wooden walking sticks;
BS 5205 Adjustable metal walking sticks;
BS 5655 Lifts and service lifts;
BS 5776 Powered stairlifts;
BS 5900 Powered homelifts;
BS 5965 Manually driven balanced personal homelifts;
BS 6083 Hearing aids.

See also Section 4 for British Standards covering housing, and Section 16 for British Standards covering access.

Complaining About Aids and Equipment

Your consumer rights are protected in law in respect of aids, equipment and related services as for any goods and services. This is a complex area, but you can readily obtain advice and help. Contact either your local Trading Standards Department (in some areas called the Consumer Protection Department) which is a service run by your local authority, or your local Citizens Advice Bureau. If possible, it is better to be wise before things go wrong and you will find the following books particularly helpful:

A Handbook of Consumer Law, by the National Federation of Consumer Groups (Consumers' Association with Hodder and Stoughton, 2nd edition, 1986).

How Not to Get Ripped off, by Barbara Lantin

(Unwin Paperbacks, 37/39 Queen Elizabeth Street, London SE1 2QB, 1987), price £3.95.

Making a Complaint (Disabled Living Foundation, 380–384 Harrow Road, London W9 2HU), price £1.00.

In addition, a number of concise, authoritative free leaflets are available from the Office of Fair Trading, Field House, 15–25 Bream's Buildings, London EC4A 1PR (Tel: 01–242 2858).

Further Information

GENERAL PUBLICATIONS

The problem with books about aids and equipment is that they rapidly become out of date. This is true even of the series, *Equipment for the Disabled*, which is divided into 13 volumes, each of which is periodically updated. Our own *Directory of Aids for Disabled and Elderly People* (Woodhead-Faulkner Ltd, Fitzwilliam House, 32 Trumpington Street, Cambridge CB2 1QY, 1986), price £14.95 is, we think, the most recent one volume book on the subject, and you may find it useful in obtaining an overview of the range and kinds of aids which are available. But if you need really up-to-date information on aids and equipment you would, we believe, do best to use the information services of the Disabled Living Foundation, the Northern Ireland Information Service for Disabled People, or the Scottish Council on Disability Information Department as appropriate (*see* page 47).

Further Information about Particular Kinds of Aids

We have divided this sub-section up into the following headings (page numbers are indicated between brackets):

Beds and Bedding	(54)
Chairs	(54)
Children	(54)
Clothing and Footwear	(55)
Communication	(55)
Continence Management	(56)
Do-it-Yourself	(57)
Eating and Drinking	(57)
Hoists and Lifting Equipment	(57)
Household	(57)
Leisure	(58)
Office	(58)
Personal	(58)
Pressure Relief	(58)
Purpose-made	(58)
Transport (personal)	(59)
Visual Handicap	(59)
Walking Aids	(60)
Wheelchairs	(60)

Under these headings, we will frequently refer to publications available from the following organisations:

1. Disabled Living Foundation Information Service, 380–384 Harrow Road, London W9 2HU (Tel: 01–289 6111).
   DLF Information Lists cost £1.20 each and are also available as a complete set (24 lists) with bi-monthly updatings on subscription. Similar lists are available from the Northern Ireland Information Service for Disabled People and The Scottish Council on Disability Information Department (*see* page 47).
2. Disabled Living Foundation (Sales), c/o Haigh and Hochland Ltd, International University Booksellers, The Precinct Centre, Oxford Road, Manchester M13 9QA (Tel: 061–273 4156).
3. Equipment for the Disabled, Mary Marlborough Lodge, Nuffield Orthopaedic Centre, Headington, Oxford OX3 7LD (Tel: Oxford (0865) 64811, ext. 272). Each book in this series costs £3.95 plus postage and packing. A binder is available at £3.95.

Beds and Bedding

Includes beds and accessories, mattresses, bedding, waterproof bed protection, self-lifting aids, bed and cantilever tables, enuresis alarms.

BOOKS AND PUBLICATIONS

DLF Information List No 1A (from address 1 above).

Chairs

Includes high seat (including adjustable) chairs, self-lift seats, raising blocks, reclining chairs, sag bags, footstools, cushions.

BOOKS AND PUBLICATIONS

DLF Information List No 2 (from address 1 above).

DLF Advice Notes, Choosing a Chair (April, 1987), price 80 pence, (from address 1 above).

Housing and Furniture (Equipment for the Disabled, 1986) (from address 3 above).

Children's Aids

Includes eating and drinking aids, balance and exercise equipment, personal toilet, personal care, protective equipment, toys and play equipment, mobility aids.

BOOKS AND PUBLICATIONS

DLF Information List No 15 (general) and *15A (mobility)* (from address 1 on page 54).

Disabled Child (Equipment for the Disabled, 1986, from address 3 on page 54).

Clothing and footwear

Includes daywear. nightwear, underwear, swimwear, hosiery, warm and heated garments, dressing aids; odd, extra-large and small sized footwear, shoe conversions, shoes suitable for use with calipers etc., footwear accessories.

BOOKS AND PUBLICATIONS

DLF Information Lists No 13 (Clothing) and *14 (Footwear)* (from address 1 on page 54).

Clothes for Disabled People, by Maureen Goldsworthy (Batsford, 1981), price £8.95.

Clothing and Dressing for Adults (Equipment for the Disabled, 1981), from address 3 on page 54).

The Disabled Living Foundation has a large range of books on clothing and footwear (and has a specialist adviser). The Scottish Council on Disability also runs a clothing advisory service.

Communication Aids and Environmental Control Systems
(*see also* Visual Handicap Aids on page 59)

Includes reading aids, page turners, writing aids, tape recorders, speech replacement aids, communication aids for deaf and visually handicapped people, remote control apparatus, alarms and emergency call systems, intercoms and telephone aids, environmental control systems.

SPECIALIST ADVISER ON ELECTRONIC AIDS

Roger M. Jefcoate
Willowbrook, Swanbourne Road, Mursley, Buckinghamshire MK17 0JA (Tel: Mursley (029) 672533).
Roger Jefcoate is adviser on electronic aids to many organisations concerned with disability in Britain and overseas. His work is free of any vested interest and almost completely charitably sponsored.

As well as helping individuals, Roger has established several projects which provide technical help on a wider scale, helping to set up information and equipment centres in Britain, USA and Israel, both national and regional.

He travels throughout the United Kingdom and widely overseas visiting severely disabled people

at school, home or work giving advice and help on the practical application of electronic technology to increase independence. This service is free to disabled people. He is often able to obtain financial help towards the cost of appropriate equipment through various charities with which he is associated – most notably the Aidis Trust. He specialises in electronic environmental controls, reading aids, writing aids, communication aids and computers.

The more significant aids projects with which he is associated are:

ACTIVE
See page 57.

Electronic Equipment Loan Service
Free loans of used electronic equipment including typewriters, page turners, communicators and computers. Send 9in × 4in s.a.e. for latest list.

The Aidis Trust
Long term loans of sophisticated electronic aids, especially computers.

HELPFUL ORGANISATION

Electronic Aids for the Blind
28 Crofton Avenue, Orpington, Kent BR6 8DU (Tel: 01–709 1186).
As far as funds allow, provides advanced equipment which is not ordinarily available from social services departments or other charities to visually handicapped people who will be able to use and exploit it. For further details, *see* Section 15, Helpful Organisations.

INSURANCE OF ELECTRONIC AIDS

Sun Alliance Insurance Group at its Aylesbury office (12 Rickford's Hill, Aylesbury, Buckinghamshire HP20 2RX) operates a *Special Aids Scheme for Disabled People* which covers electronic aids used by disabled people (whether or not owned by them) at home, school or work. The scheme is also open to organisations, special schools etc. It offers protection against fire, theft and accidental damage (including in transit) anywhere in Britain. The premium will vary according to the total value and type of equipment to be insured, and quotations will be provided on request.

BOOKS AND PUBLICATIONS

DLF Information Lists Nos 3A and *3B* (from address 1 on page 54) (3A includes advisory organisations).

Alarm Systems (DLF, Feb. 1987), price 80 pence (from address 2 on page 54).

British Telecom's Guide to Equipment and Services for Disabled Customers (British Telecom, Action for Disabled Customers, 1988), free on request.

Calling for Help: a guide to emergency alarm systems Age Concern/Anchor/Research Institute for Consumer Affairs (RICA, 2 Marylebone Road, London NW1 4DX, 1987), price £2.95. Like all RICA publications, this is a thorough and clear treatment of the subject, with details of manufacturers and organisations which supply alarms or monitoring services. It examines: how emergency alarms work; how to get an alarm; buying guidelines; what to take into account in choosing an alarm; details and the main pros and cons of each model; how to get the best out of your alarm and test results.

Communication (Equipment for the Disabled, 1987) (from address 3 on page 54).

Communication Systems, by Clare Latham, a tape/slide set (59 slides) available from Graves Medical Audiovisual Library, Holly House, 220 New London Road, Chelmsford, Essex CM2 9BJ, 1980). An introduction to the commonest systems used in the United Kingdom. (A booklet summarising the main points is available.)

Computers and Accessories for People with Disabilities (DLF), price £1.00 (from address 1 on page 54).

Computer Help for Disabled People, by Lorna Ridgway and Stuart McKears (Souvenir Press, 43 Great Russell Street, London WC1B 3PA, 1985), price £5.95. Intended for more severely disabled people, this book explains for the lay-person how computer technology can help.

Electronic Communication Aids: Selection and Use, by Iris R.Fishman (Taylor and Francis Ltd., Rankine Road, Basingstoke, Hampshire RG24 0PR, March 1987), price £13.50. A very thorough treatment of the subject which looks at the assessment of needs, the various selection and scanning techniques, symbol/vocabulary capabilities, and output systems. It discusses common mistakes in the selection of electronic communication aids, the factors to be considered when comparing one type with another and strategies for their effective use. It looks particularly at computer-based aids, both dedicated and adapted, and is helpful in considering both consumer resistance to (fear of?) elec-

tronic aids and the opposite extreme of unrealistic expectations. The text is clear and well illustrated, and the terms and guidelines are carefully defined and backed up by examples.

Hearing Impairment, by Kenneth Lysons (Woodhead-Faulkner Ltd, Fitzwilliam House, 32 Trumpington Street, Cambridge CB2 1QY, 1984), price £14.95.

The Royal National Institute for the Deaf 105 Gower Street, London WC1E 6AH, publishes a wide range of leaflets describing aids which assist with hearing problems:
Aids to Daily Living is a basic leaflet describing aids such as doorbells, alarm clocks, sound activated visual alarms, TV listening devices, telephone bells and amplifiers, and telephone keyboard communication.
Hearing Aids: Questions and Answers
List of Hearing Aids
NHS Hearing Aids
Help with TV
Induction Loops in Public Places
Radiomicrophone and Infra-red Hearing Aid Systems
Visual doorbell systems.

Telephone Communication and Hearing Impairment, by Norman P. Erber (Taylor and Francis Ltd., Rankine Road, Basingstoke, Hampshire RG24 0PR, 1985), price £18.50.

See also the entry on page 46 relating to the BARDSOFT database of software information held at the Handicapped Persons Research Unit at Newcastle-upon-Tyne.

Continence Management

Includes equipment, deodorants and neutralisers.

BOOKS AND PUBLICATIONS

Childhood Incontinence, by Roger Morgan (Heinemann Medical Books, 23 Bedford Square, London WC1B 3HH, 1981), price £3.50.

Directories published by and available from the Association of Continence Advisors, c/o Disabled Living Foundation, 380–384 Harrow Road, London W9 2HU:
Directory of Continence and Toiletting Aids (1988), price £17.00.
Directory of Educational Resources for Continence (1986), price £4.00.
ACA is a multidisciplinary group of health care

professionals with a special interest in the promotion of continence and the management of incontinence. It is closely linked with the Continence Advisory Service at the Disabled Living Foundation which has a range of modestly priced literature for both lay people and professionals (details on written request, but please send an s.a.e. if asking for literature).

DLF Information List No 12
(from address 1 on page 54).
Contains notes on continence management. In addition, the DLF has a large range of books on continence management (and a specialist adviser). A bibliography is published, price £7.00 (all from address 2 on page 54).

Incontinence, by R. C. L. Feneley (Churchill Livingstone, Robert Stevenson House, 1–3 Baxter's Place, Leith Walk, Edinburgh EH1 3AF, 1984), price £1.85.

Incontinence Explained by Eve McLaughlin (Ian Henry Publications Ltd, 20 Park Drive, Romford RM1 4LH, 1981), price £4.95.

Incontinence and Stoma Care (Equipment for the Disabled, 1984) (from address 3 on page 54).

The Management of Incontinence, by Dorothy A. Mandelstam. A two-part tape/slide set produced and distributed by Camera Talks Ltd, 197 Botley Road, Oxford OX2 0HE.

Portable Urinals and Related Appliances, by Eric Ryckmans. A tape/slide presentation available from Graves Medical Audio-visual Library, Holly House, 220 New London Road, Chelmsford, Essex CM2 9BJ. Descriptive lists (DLF, 1975) are separately available (from address 2 on page 54), offer price 60p.

Do-it-yourself Aids

Includes simple aids which can be made by a semi-skilled lay person.

HELPFUL ORGANISATION
ACTIVE
c/o Play Matters, 68 Churchway, London NW1 1LT (Tel: 01–387 9592).
This organisation collects practical information about adaptations to and designs for toys, games, equipment and communication aids, and encourages their development and use.
ACTIVE's approach is one of 'do-it-yourself' with help, ensuring that individual needs are met appropriately, quickly and at minimum cost. Good

ideas are passed on through *Ark*, the journal of Play Matters, through conferences and courses, and through an emerging network of local groups.

BOOKS AND PUBLICATIONS
ACTIVE Worksheets (ACTIVE, c/o Play Matters, 68 Churchway, London NW1 1LT).
These give instructions for making a wide range of play, leisure and communication aids for severely disabled children and adults. The designs are submitted by ACTIVE members, parents, therapists, teachers etc., and they are tested and drawn up in worksheet format by the ACTIVE design team, so that the aid can be made up for individual needs. The worksheets are categorised according to the skills and facilities needed. They range from simple 'kitchen table' woodwork to sophisticated electronic, woodwork, or metalwork designs.

Easy to Make Aids for Your Handicapped Child, by Don Caston (Souvenir Press, 43 Great Russell Street, London WC1B 3PA) price £4.95.
Includes 60 aids often needed at home or in school, which can be made to individual requirements using simple, cheap equipment. Some of the aids have particular relevance to third-world needs.

I Can Do It Myself, by Wouter Van Leeuwen and Hans Elzenger (Spindlewood, 70 Lynhurst Avenue, Barnstaple, Devon EX31 2HY, 1986), price £6.95. A lovely little book describing a range of D-I-Y aids promoting independence at home. Well and wittily illustrated, it shows how to solve day-to-day practical problems in an imaginative way.

Eating and Drinking Aids

Includes cutlery, plates, trays, egg-cups, non-slip materials, drinking aids and bibs.

BOOKS AND PUBLICATIONS
DLF Information List No 4
(from address 1 on page 54).

Hoists and Lifting Equipment

Includes mobile, fixed and electric hoists, manual lifting aids, lifts and stairlifts.

BOOKS AND PUBLICATIONS
DLF Information List No 5 (from address 1 on page 54).

Choosing a Hoist (DLF). Advice notes (from address 1 on page 54), price 80p.

Hoists and Lifts (Equipment for the Disabled, 1985) (from address 3 on page 54).

Household Aids

Includes all kinds of household equipment, kitchen/storage units, sinks, taps, flooring, doors and door furniture, wall protection, windows, electrical switches.

BOOKS AND PUBLICATIONS

Aids and Adaptations in the Home. A two-part tape/slide set produced and distributed by Camera Talks Ltd., 197 Botley Road, Oxford OX2 0HE.

DLF Information Lists Nos 11A and *11B* (from address 1 on page 54).

Gas Aids for Disabled People (British Gas, 1981), free leaflet available from RADAR, 25 Mortimer Street, London W1N 8AB.

Home Management (Equipment for the Disabled, 1987) (from address 3 on page 54).

Housing and Furniture (Equipment for the Disabled, 1986) (from address 3 on page 54).

In Touch at Home (Isis Large Print, 55 St Thomas' Street, Oxford OX1 1JG), price £5.95. This is a 100 page illustrated book in large print. It deals with adaptations in the home to meet the needs of visually handicapped people.

Kitchen Sense for Disabled People, edited by Gwen Conacher (Croom Helm for DLF, revised 1986), price £8.95 (from address 2 on page 54). This freshly researched and completely revised edition reflects the wider choice of equipment, appliances and aids. Problems facing visually handicapped people and those with chronic skin conditions are now included. It contains practical, detailed advice on planning and equipping a kitchen, on the aids to making life easier for disabled people, on short cuts in cooking and on shopping.

Making Life Easier for Disabled People (Electricity Council, 1981), free leaflet available from RADAR, 25 Mortimer Street, London W1N 8AB.

Notes on Cookers and Cooking Appliances for Disabled People (DLF, Jan.1987) (from address 1 on page 54).

Leisure Aids

Includes aids to the enjoyment of music, drama, gardening, holidays, libraries, hobbies, clubs.

BOOKS AND PUBLICATIONS

DLF Information List No 6 (from address 1 on page 54)

Gardening (Equipment for the Disabled, 1987) (from address 3 on page 54).

Office Aids and Equipment

Includes furniture and accessories (except computer equipment).

BOOKS AND PUBLICATIONS

DLF Information List No 16 (from address 1 on page 54). Includes notes on office layout, organisations concerned with career advice, job opportunities and training.

Personal Aids

Includes lavatory aids and aids for personal care: washing, dressing, cosmetic and personal hygiene aids, rails, baths, bath aids (including bath hoists), showers, wash basins, hairwashing units.

BOOKS AND PUBLICATIONS

DLF Information Lists Nos 7A (Toilet) and *7B (Care)* (from address 1 on page 54).

Disabled Eve: Aids in Menstruation, by Brenda McCarthy (DLF, 1981) (from address 2 on page 54).

Personal Care (Equipment for the Disabled, 1985) (from address 3 on page 54).

Showers for Use by Disabled People (DLF, 1987), price 80p (from address 1 on page 54).

Pressure Relief

Includes beds and cushions designed for pressure relief, sheepskins, inflatable/foam rings.

BOOKS AND PUBLICATIONS

DLF Information List No 1B (from address 1 on page 54). Includes advice notes.

Purpose-made Aids

Includes any type of aid which needs to be made to a person's individual requirements. Sometimes, however, although these start as 'one-offs', they are found to be useful to other people and are replicated.

HELPFUL ORGANISATIONS

Chailey Heritage Rehabilitation Engineering Unit Chailey Heritage Hospital and School, North Chailey, Lewes, East Sussex BN8 4EF (Tel: Newick (082 572) 2112, ext 210).
As well as marketing a range of aids developed at the Unit, it is possible to respond to requests for one-off aids or personalised equipment for chil-

dren, adolescents and some adults. However, it is imperative in such cases that a member of the medical or therapy staff, responsible for treatment, accompanies the client on appropriate appointments.

Rehabilitation Engineering Movement Advisory Panels (REMAP)
25 Mortimer Street, London W1N 8AB.
REMAP offers engineering help, advice and research on aids for disabled people. It brings together engineers who, advised appropriately by members of the medical and paramedical professions, design and make items of equipment to suit the special needs of handicapped individuals.

REMAP operates through over 90 local panels which will make every attempt to solve problems which have not been overcome by standard equipment. By taking a fresh look at difficult problems, these panels are often able to devise ingenious solutions. The number of panels continues to grow.

Its work is voluntary, though a charge may need to be passed on if raw materials, usually donated, have to be bought. Such charges may be borne by the local social services department.

Details of local REMAPs available from above address.

BOOKS AND PUBLICATIONS

Aids for Independence. An information and sales catalogue of aids produced at the Rehabilitation Engineering Unit, Chailey Heritage Hospital and School, North Chailey, Lewes, Sussex BN8 4EF. The aids were designed to overcome some of the problems experienced by children and adolescents at Chailey Heritage Hospital and School, but are likely to have a wider application. In some instances, the designs have been taken up by recognised manufacturing and marketing outlets, but the majority are available only from the Chailey Unit. The catalogue illustrates both batch-produced and one-off designs.

The REMAP Yearbook (REMAP, 25 Mortimer Street, London W1N 8AB), price £2.00. This yearbook is one of the best of its kind – inspiring, encouraging and worth every penny of its cover price. It gives examples of all kinds of equipment, shows exactly what REMAP is about and how others can help its work.

Transport (Personal)

Includes bicycles and tricycles, cars, van conversions, car hoists, accessories.

BOOKS AND PUBLICATIONS

DLF Information List No 8 (from address 1 on page 54) includes information on vehicle hire and tuition.

Motoring and Mobility for Disabled People, by Ann Darnbrough and Derek Kinrade (RADAR, 25 Mortimer Street, London W1N 8AB, 1988), price £3.00 (plus p & p). Covers all aspects of the subject, including special purpose vehicles, control conversions, access and storage of wheelchairs, and accessories.

Outdoor Transport (Equipment for the Disabled, 1987) (from address 3 on page 54).

Visual Handicap

Aids designed or adapted for use by blind and partially sighted people (*see also* 'Communication aids' in this Section, and Section 14, Contact and Communication Organisations).

BOOKS AND PUBLICATIONS

Articles Specially Designed or Adapted for Blind People and sold by RNIB (Royal National Institute for the Blind, 224 Great Portland Street, London W1N 6AA).

Can't See to Read: Resources for Visually Handicapped People (Library Services Trust, 7 Ridgmount Street, London WC1E 7AE, 4th edition 1987). A brief guide to large print literature, reading aids, talking books and newspapers, tape services and organisations. Single copies available free of charge in response to an s.a.e. 9in × 12in.

The Disabled Living Foundation Visual Handicap Advisory Service has a wide range of literature. Details on request to address 1 on page 54; please send s.a.e. if asking for literature. The DLF also publishes a bibliography of information on partial sight, price £7 (from address 2 on page 54).

In Touch Handbook, by Thena Heshel and Margaret Ford (Broadcasting Support Services). A comprehensive guide to aids and services for blind and partially sighted people. The print, tape and Moon versions cost £4.95 inclusive, and can be obtained only by post from In Touch Handbook, PO Box 7, London W3 6XJ. Cheques should be made out to Broadcasting Support Services. The braille version, published by Scottish Braille Press, costs £3 (concession price) and can be ordered direct from them at Craigmillar Park, Edinburgh EH1 5NB.

In Touch at Home. See 'Household aids' on page 57.

So You're Partially Sighted (Optical Information Council, Temple Chambers, Temple Avenue, London EC4Y 0DT). A free leaflet detailing the help available for the visual problems of partially sighted people. It includes information on low-vision magnifying aids.

Walking Aids

Includes frames and trolleys, sticks and seat sticks, crutches, standing aids.

BOOKS AND PUBLICATIONS

DLF Information List No 9 (from address 1 on page 54)

The Use of Walking Aids (DLF, Nov.1987). Advice notes (from address 1 on page 54), price £1.

Walking Aids (Equipment for the Disabled, 1985) (from address 3 on page 54).

Wheelchairs and Accessories

Includes manual wheelchairs and electric wheelchairs and accessories for both.

BOOKS AND PUBLICATIONS

Choosing the Best Wheelchair Cushion for your Needs, your Chair, and your Lifestyle, by Peggy Jay (RADAR, 1984), price £4.85 including postage and packing.

DLF Information Lists Nos 10A(Manual) and *10B(Electric)* (from address 1 on page 54). Also includes ramps and information about hire and insurance.

DLF Advice Notes, Choosing an Electric Wheel-chair (DLF, April 1987), price 80 pence (from address 1 on page 54).

DLF Advice Notes, Choosing a Wheelchair (DLF, March 1987), price 80 pence (from address 1 on page 54).

DLF Library Resource List, Wheelchairs (DLF), price £1.00 (from address 1 on page 54) gives details of publications.

Manual Wheelchairs – a Guide (ICTA Information Centre, Box 303, S–161 26 BROMMA, Sweden, 1986), price SEK 45. Although a Swedish publication, this is not a guide to Swedish wheelchairs, but describes rather the various types of manual wheelchairs – with rearwheel versus frontwheel drive, fixed versus folding frame, wheelchairs for children, and accessories. It covers wheelchair design, wheelchair practice, maintenance, wheelchair manufacture using intermediate technology, and advice on how to adapt your home for wheelchair use.

Powered Wheelchairs: A guide to help you choose (RICA, 2 Marylebone Road, London NW1 4DX, 1984). Because the detailed brand information is now out of date, there is no charge for this booklet: but please enclose a 24 pence stamp to cover postage.

Wheelchairs (Equipment for the Disabled, 1982) (from address 3 on page 54)

Wheelchairs and their Use: A Guide to Choosing a Wheelchair, by Janet Weyers (RADAR, 25 Mortimer Street, London W1N 8AB, Nov.1986), price £2.00 including postage and packing.

SECTION 4
HOUSE AND HOME

Housing Standards

Mobility housing

This is built to 'normal' space standards, but includes such features as a ramped entrance and wide doors; it may be provided for those who can walk a little and do not need to use a wheelchair all the time or at all.

The important feature of mobility housing is that it can be lived in without the need to cope with steps or stairs. 'No steps or stairs' mobility housing can be achieved with: bungalows; ground-floor flats in low-rise blocks; flats with lifts to upper levels; two-storey houses with a bathroom and bedroom at ground level; and two-storey houses with a suitable staircase, enabling a stairlift to be installed so that upper rooms can be reached without climbing the stairs.

Wheelchair housing

This housing is specially planned for people who use wheelchairs. Important design considerations are: a level or slightly ramped approach to the entrance with no threshold obstruction; internal planning for wheelchair manoeuvre, with passageways 1,200 mm wide and suitable doors – either 900 mm doorsets or sliding doors with a 775 mm opening; a kitchen planned for wheelchair manoeuvre, with space to turn the wheelchair and access to equipment and storage; a bathroom planned for use from a wheelchair, with a shower or bath allowing a person to transfer from a wheelchair; a lavatory planned for transfer from a wheelchair; switches, window controls, door furniture and other fittings placed so as to be comfortably reached from a wheelchair; windows placed to give views out for wheelchair users; a garage or carport (if provided) with undercover access to the dwelling; a flexible and economic central heating system.

Sheltered housing

This can be built to the standards of 'wheelchair' or 'mobility' housing as above, but will also have the advantage of being 'warden assisted' either by having a warden on site, or available from a central point via an intercom or alarm system.

Some 'special housing' is available through local authorities or through housing associations *see* page 73), but some privately rented and owner-occupied schemes are now being built. Information can be obtained from your local Housing Advice Centre or from the Citizens Advice Bureau.

British Standards Institution codes of practice.

Design of housing for the convenience of disabled people – the British Standards Institution's Code of Practice BS 5619: 1978 (price £11 to non-members). The principle behind this Code of Practice is that whenever practicable, ordinary housing should be convenient for disabled occupants or visitors. Three main areas are considered. First are design recommendations for the approach to a dwelling (including ramps, lifts, parking, garden paths, and entrance doors). Second are recommendations for interior features such as circulation spaces and internal doors, floors, windows, kitchens, bedrooms, WCs, bathrooms, and stairs. Finally, the code deals with the design of services; electricity, heating, controls, and refuse disposal.

The level of disablement considered is that of people using wheelchairs who are not so disabled that they need special housing. The guidelines set down in the code are to encourage good practice. The recommendations are to be regarded as a list of desirable provisions, which, according to circumstances, should be observed wherever practicable. The code, drawn up by experts in the field of building together with government and voluntary organisations is a landmark in the campaign for integrated housing. It goes a long way to establishing that housing built to such standards need not be considered exclusive but is more comfortable and convenient for a very wide range of people. Now it is essential that we all continue to press these standards on all those responsible for building our houses.

Other British Standard codes include:

Powered stairlifts BS 5776:1979. Price to non-members £19.10.
Powered homelifts BS 5900:1980. Price to non-members £25.60.
Manually driven balanced personal homelifts BS 5965:1980. Price to non- members £19.10.
Access for the Disabled to Buildings BS 5810: 1979. Price to non-members £19.10. For details see Section 16.

Copies of British Standards Codes may be obtained from: BSI Sales, Linford Wood, Milton Keynes MK14 6LE (Tel: Milton Keynes (0908) 221166).

Statutory Provisions

Under the provisions of the Chronically Sick and Disabled Persons Act 1970, local social service authorities are required to consider housing needs in their areas in respect of the special requirements of registered disabled people, and to provide assistance to such persons to adapt their homes and to provide any necessary extra facilities to secure their greater safety, comfort or convenience.

The powers that local housing authorities have to assist with adaptations derive principally from the Housing Acts 1957, 1974 and 1980. These and other pieces of housing legislation have been consolidated in the Housing Act 1985. (For details *see* Section 13.)

While wide powers are available to both housing and social services authorities to undertake or to provide assistance with adaptations, it has to be emphasised that local authorities vary widely in their interpretation of the needs of disabled people. There has been in the past a confusion of responsibilities between the housing and the social services departments. In order to make matters clearer a government circular defined the responsibility.

Housing authorities should be responsible for structural modifications to dwellings owned or managed by them. These modifications include extensions or alterations to provide a bathroom, WC or bedroom, etc., with level or suitable ramped access, replacement of steps with ramps, widening or rehanging of doors, alterations to electrical and heating systems, and alterations to bathroom and WC fixtures. These responsibilities lie alongside the housing authorities' role in the provision of mobility and wheelchair housing.

Social Services should be responsible for non-structural features and the provision of aids and equipment. In addition, social services are responsible for identifying, assessing and advising on the needs of disabled people, including the need for adaptations to their homes.

Advice should be sought from the local social services department, or housing department.

OWNER-OCCUPIERS AND PRIVATE TENANTS

Alternatively, under the Housing Act 1974 (as amended by Housing Rents and Subsidies Act 1975) home improvement grants (i.e. improvement and intermediate grants) may be available to disabled people to meet their special needs. Owner-occupiers who qualify (*see* Section 13) may find it advantageous to choose this method of securing adaptations and financial help rather than the less well-defined arrangements operated by the social services authority, as described above. The decision will, of course, hinge upon the relative cost of the alternative schemes to the person concerned: the cost under social services arrangements will depend to a large extent on the financial circumstances of the applicant, whereas in the case of grants there is a prescribed percentage to be paid by the applicant (though in certain circumstances the social services department may help with this cost).

COMPULSORY PURCHASE

If a dwelling which has been constructed or adapted to meet the needs of a disabled person is compulsorily purchased, compensation may be based on the reasonable cost of equivalent reinstatement (Land Compensation Act 1973: *see* Section 13).

HOUSE RENOVATION GRANTS

There are four separate kinds of grant for which you can apply and, in the case of disabled applicants, these qualify for the higher eligible expense limits and rates of grant which apply in priority cases. These grants are: Improvement grants; Intermediate grants; Repairs grants; and Special grants (not available to tenants). We describe them below.

More information is contained in the booklet Home Improvement Grants – A guide for home-owners, landlords and tenants.
Who can apply?
The applicant must be the freeholder or leaseholder (including both owner-occupiers and landlords), or a regulated or secure tenant.

Are conditions attached to the grants?
Owner-occupiers and landlords have to supply a

certificate of future occupation and conditions are attached to the grants to ensure broadly that for a period (normally five years) the dwelling is used in the manner described in the certificate. Tenants cannot be asked to repay, but the local authority may require an undertaking from the landlord that he/she will continue to let the dwelling, before approving an application from a tenant.

HOME IMPROVEMENT GRANTS

These are made at the discretion of the local authority and they are intended to help improve homes to a good standard. For disabled people, improvement grants are available for work to adapt a house for the accommodation, welfare or employment of a disabled occupant, who may be yourself or another person who is disabled and is living in your home. While these grants are generally not intended to help with improvements to modern houses, nevertheless, they may be used to install standard amenities for the convenience of a disabled person where these amenities are otherwise inaccessible whether the property is modern or not.

Disabled people qualify for the higher eligible expense limits and rates of grant which apply in priority cases. The current (1987) eligible expense limits for improvement grants are £13,800 in Greater London and £10,200 elsewhere.

Intermediate grants
These are available as of right for the provision of missing standard amenities so long as the basic condition, that the dwelling shall be fit for human habitation, is met. Application may also be made to provide extra standard amenities for a disabled occupant to whom existing amenities may be inaccessible. For instance if a lavatory upstairs is out of reach you can claim an intermediate grant to put in a downstairs lavatory. Intermediate grants are available at 75 per cent of the eligible expense or 90 per cent if the local authority considers that the applicant could not meet his/her share of the expense without undue hardship. The eligible expense limits are:

	In Greater London £	Elsewhere £
Fixed bath or shower	450	340
Wash-hand basin	175	130
Sink	450	340
Hot and cold water supply at		
bath or shower	570	430
wash-hand basin	300	230
sink	450	340
Water closet	680	515
Total	3,075	2,325

Value added tax
For zero-rated alterations for disabled people *see* page 44.

Repairs grants
These are now available generally and are made for substantial and structural repairs to pre–1919 dwellings within specified rateable value limits and at the discretion of local authorities. The eligible expense limit is £4,800 outside London and £6,600 in Greater London.

Special grants
These are for the provision of standard amenities and means of escape from fire, together with repairs, in houses in multiple occupation. Landlords can apply, but not tenants. The eligible expense limits are the amounts per standard amenity to be provided, as set out above; for means of escape £8,100 outside London and £10,800 in Greater London; and for repairs £3,000 outside London and £4,200 in Greater London.

Insulation grants
If your home was built before 1976, and has no loft insulation, or none over 30mm thick, you could get a grant towards the cost. For elderly or severely disabled people the grant can be 90 per cent of the cost up to a maximum of £95. More details are available in the booklet *Save money on loft insulation*.

DIALYSIS ADAPTATIONS

District health authorities are responsible for any necessary adaptations directly related to the installation of home dialysis equipment, as advised in paragraph 21 of DOE Circular 59/78. In exceptional circumstances a local authority may use their discretion to approve an improvement grant for work required to adapt or provide a room housing home dialysis equipment where they consider that such an adaptation is needed to make the house suitable for the accommodation or welfare of a disabled person.

THE RIGHT TO BUY

Unfortunately the right to buy does not arise if the 'dwelling house has features which are substantially different from those of ordinary dwelling-houses and are designed to make it suitable for occupation by physically disabled persons'. For details see Section 13.

A voluntary scheme agreed between most public housing authorities in the UK, i.e. local councils, new towns, the Development Board for Rural Wales, and the Northern Ireland Housing Executive, to help their existing tenants, those high on housing waiting lists and other people with pressing needs, to move to a different area. As well as needing to move for job or social reasons, the scheme may be able to help those who need to move to be near a relative for care or support. For further information, if you are a tenant of one of the above authorities you should go to the offices of your own housing authority, if you are the tenant of a housing association, you should go to the local office of the association.

RELIEF FROM RATES IN RESPECT OF SPECIAL FACILITIES FOR DISABLED PEOPLE

The Rating (Disabled Persons) Act 1978 clarifies the circumstances in which rate relief is available to disabled people on the extra rates they might otherwise be expected to pay on any extra facilities needed expressly as a result of disability. This might happen if you have made alterations to your home because of the disability, or if you have moved into a house or flat with special features needed because of your disability, or it could happen simply because your home already has some special feature needed because of the disability. For details of the provisions of the Rating (Disabled Persons) Act 1978 *see* Section 13.

HOUSING BENEFIT

For details of housing benefits *see* Section 2.

Planning Permission

So long as the overall use of the house is not changed planning permission is not required for internal modifications designed to assist disabled people. Adaptations or extensions affecting the external appearance of a house will mostly amount to development requiring planning permission, but the Town and Country Planning General Development Order 1977 (as amended) grants a general permission for a wide range of such works and these can therefore be undertaken without the need to make a planning application. A free booklet prepared by the Department of the Environment: *Planning Permission, A guide for Householders* (*see* below) sets out the permitted development tolerances. It will very often be possible to build an extension to provide ground floor sleeping accommodation, to install a hardstanding

for a car and a porch or carport to provide protection from the weather, or to erect a shed or outhouse in the garden to accommodate essential medical equipment without the specific permission of the local planning authority. Permitted development rights are occasionally withdrawn however, and it is therefore worth checking the position with the planning officer of the local district council before starting work.

The booklet mentioned above is obtainable free of charge from local planning authorities or direct from the Department of the Environment, Distribution Section, Building 3, Victoria Road, South Ruislip HA4 ON2.

Home Adaptations and Equipment

There are many aids and a wide range of useful equipment to enable disabled people to adapt the environment of their home to their own special needs and requirements. By the addition of a lift or stair-climbing apparatus it may be possible to continue to live in a house which has become unsuitable or to buy a house in an area where a single-storey building is not available. It would obviously be necessary to ensure that there was a suitable position for the lift or that the stairs were suitable to take the stair-climbing apparatus. There are also a number of prefabricated rooms available such as purpose-built bathrooms and lavatories, which from a practical point of view are relatively easy to install, and provide the necessary amenities with the minimum of fuss. Adaptation of existing accommodation has an important part to play in the provision of housing suitable for the needs of disabled people. It has the advantage, not always possible with new housing, of enabling people to remain close to friends and relations, and in familiar surroundings. For details of aids and equipment see Section 2.

GAS AND ELECTRICITY IN THE HOME

Free gas safety checks
On request British Gas will carry out a free gas safety check on your appliances and installation if you live alone and:
(a) are over 60 years of age; or
(b) a registered disabled person of any age; or
(c) receive a disability benefit.
The check will show whether your gas appliances and installation are safe to use and includes the cost of any necessary adjustments up to £2.50 plus VAT. One free check is available in any period of 12 months. If any additional work needs to be done an official estimate can be given.

British Gas Home Service Advisers will give advice on the choice or use of a gas appliance and will visit at home where necessary. Their advice is free of charge. They can also advise on the special adaptors available for cookers, fires and wall heaters which can be supplied at £2.20 plus VAT per appliance. Studded and braille controls are available for visually handicapped people and information on gas services and the use of a gas oven is available on tape cassette.

To enable blind persons to check the identity of meter readers, advisers and slot meter cash collectors, most British Gas Regions operate a special password scheme.

A useful directory of services, information, and advice to domestic consumers is available: *GAS Can We Help?* This directory is obtainable from British Gas showrooms or service centres. Regions of British Gas also have their own information leaflets which are available from the Public Relations Department in each region. In case of difficulties in getting the directory locally, contact: British Gas Department, KPA Direct, The Posting House, Uxbridge Road, London W3 9RT.

Gas accounts
Savings schemes are available and monthly pay-ments may be made based on estimated consumption. Prepayment meters can be repositioned at a more convenient height for a disabled person. There is a standard charge of £3.30 plus VAT for this service.

Electricity accounts
All electricity boards offer monthly budget payment schemes by cash, bank Giro, or monthly standing order. A settlement is made annually and then the level of monthly payments is also reviewed. Quarterly accounts advise the consumer of the amount of electricity that has been used enabling the consumer to check that all payments have been credited to the account. Interim payment schemes are similar but settlement is made quarterly.

Most boards also offer payment schemes at their shops where the customer can pay an amount and collect a personal card or book of payment receipts. All boards offer a savings stamp scheme with stamps of various denominations available from their shops. In cases of hardship a code of practice is available from Electricity Board Shops which gives details of how to get help in paying electricity bills.

HOW BRITISH GAS HELPS ELDERLY AND DISABLED PEOPLE

British Gas has a long-standing and continuing commitment to caring. That's why we offer a variety of services for elderly and disabled people.

WE CAN GIVE ADVICE ON:-

1 Free gas safety checks for elderly and disabled people who live alone. ☐

2 Special help for physically and visually handicapped people. ☐

3 Fuel saving. ☐

4 Paying for gas. ☐

5 Gas safety. ☐

6 Appliance servicing. ☐

Tick the subjects which interest you and send this advertisement to FREEPOST, British Gas, P.O. Box No. 82, Chesterfield, Derbyshire S41 8UT and we'll send you our helpful leaflets.

Name_____

Address_____

_____

_____

_____

I am a member of the caring professions ☐

British Gas
ENERGY IS OUR BUSINESS

Free gas booklets
Advice for Disabled People, *Advice for Senior Citizens*, and *Help Yourself to Gas Safety* are available through Home Service.

Free electricity booklet
Making Life Easier for Disabled People Gives brief advice on heaters, cookers, mixers, clothes, and dish-washing appliances, refrigerators and freezers. Also included are details of some of the special controls which can be fitted to appliances such as cookers. Available from Electricity Board showrooms.

Free booklet – gas and electricity combined
Paying Electricity and Gas Bills – How to get help if you can't pay your bill – A Code of Practice for Domestic Customers issued by the Electricity and Gas Industries.

Water bills
Special payment arrangements for water bills may be arranged for those who are blind, severely sick or disabled.

Independent Living

Many more disabled people are choosing to live independently including those who are severely disabled who need help for most of their daily living activities. The institutional style of life is being positively rejected and individuals are gaining strength from banding together with other disabled people to plan ways in which an acceptable and independent style of life can be managed without depending, more than is absolutely necessary, on relatives. These include single people with disabilities and couples where both partners are disabled. *The Source Book* (see page 77) has been produced by a group of disabled people from the Hampshire Centre for Independent Living, and provides a lot of useful information.

We describe below some of the projects and support services which very often, in combination, can make a home of one's own a practical possibility. Section 2 in this Directory describes the financial benefits which may be juggled around to offset the not inconsiderable cost of living independently.

There are also details of specialist housing associations who, in addition to building appropriate

accommodation, may provide wardens on their estates who are on call for emergencies, and, in the case of Habinteg, a resident Community Assistant who provides personal care and support. *See* page 74.

SOCIAL SERVICES

Home helps
Domestic and other help, where this is needed to relieve the domestic situation in the home when someone in the household is sick or handicapped, may be provided by a local authority. Most local authorities make a charge for this service, and this is often based on the means of the household and the number of hours the home help is in attendance.

The service, on its own, is intended to provide back-up help and cannot usually be stretched enough to enable a severely disabled person to live independently.

Laundry service
Where there is a laundry service in a particular area for those having incontinence problems or for those too ill or handicapped to manage laundry it will more usually be run by the local social services department (possibly through the Home Help service). However, in some areas the service may be run by the District Health Authority. Where a laundry service does not exist as such, extra practical help may be given through the Home Help service. Enquiries about a laundry service should be made to your local social services department or to the District Health Authority.

Disposing of waste
Soiled incontinence pads, dressings and other nursing waste which cannot be disposed of normally and which arises from the care of a sick and handicapped person at home should be collected by the local authority refuse disposal service.

This service is sometimes provided by the District Health Authority, but is generally provided by the Environmental Health Department which is listed in the telephone book under the name of your local council.

Meals-on-wheels
These are administered by local authorities and may be delivered by volunteers. There may be a charge.

HEALTH SERVICE

District nurses
Are employed by District Health Authorities and provide help with domestic nursing care on a visiting basis. They may help with getting up and going to bed, and with bathing among their general duties. Anyone needing their services should contact their doctor.

CENTRES FOR INDEPENDENT LIVING
CILs are essentially local, non-residential centres of enablement under the direct control of disabled people themselves. They aim to provide the necessary support and services disabled people require in order for them to lead fully independent lives and become fully participating members of an integrated community. CILs have been described as resource centres in which disabled people can work together in order to overcome the many social and economic problems with which they are usually confronted by everyday living. CILs also take on the role of lobbying to influence and co-ordinate existing services and provisions.

The CIL movement was started in the USA in the early 1960s by a group of severely disabled students who were determined to maintain maximum control over their lives. Their success has been a source of inspiration to disabled people in this country who espouse similar principles of independence.

A number of projects, run by disabled people, are now providing services while others are being planned. These are described below.

Derbyshire Centre for Integrated Living (DCIL)
Long Close, Cemetery Lane, Ripley, Derbyshire DE5 3HY (Tel: Ripley (0773) 40246).
DCIL was set up as a result of initiatives taken by the campaigning Derbyshire Coalition of Disabled People, with the aim of enabling disabled people to join the rest of society as equals. DCIL provides a comprehensive information and advice centre.

The 50/50 mix of disabled and able-bodied people at Long Close is a model for DCIL's pioneering policy that as far as possible services should be planned and designed by disabled people with direct experience of the problems.

DCIL not only provides a direct service at the especially adapted centre, but is also able to take its service throughout Derbyshire through the work of ten community link workers. Based in the area they cover and including a high proportion of disabled people, link workers give top priority to helping disabled people with their problems in their own homes. DCIL offers help and advice on the following: housing, transport, access, employment, personal assistance, local community facilities, technical aids, disability benefits. DCIL also provides a counselling service and information service. The latter is run by disabled people through a telephone advice line from the centre as well as by working on information desks in local hospitals and community centres.

ExCIL (Exeter Council for Independent Living)
Ashclyst Centre, Hospital Lane, Whipton, Exeter, Devon EX1 3RB (Tel: Exeter (0392) 61989).

ExCIL was established in 1983 and it was decided at the outset that it should act as a link between the voluntary and statutory sectors. It would provide consumers to advise those who planned and implemented services on how new and existing services might best meet real need. ExCIL monitors developments around the country where new services are concerned and assists in bringing about similar services in Exeter. ExCIL is closely involved in health and social service planning and brings together the local groups of and for disabled people to establish a 'consumer voice'. The services (some of which existed prior to ExCIL) include: information – a DIAL type service responding to individual consumers personal needs for information; transport – Dial-a-Ride service where all drivers and office staff are volunteers; access – a committee monitors plans and advises on access issues; care attendant scheme – a Crossroads style scheme serves the Exeter area and provides help for carers to have time off; and meetings – a meeting room is available free of charge to disability related groups.

It is hoped that plans for an Active Intervention Team will be developed. It is intended that this team will assist disabled people in special need.

Greater Manchester Coalition of Disabled People
11 Anson Road, Manchester M14 5BY (Tel: 061 224 2722).
The Coalition, controlled by disabled people, has as its aim the integration and participation of disabled people in all areas of society. It has policies on housing, transport, employment, care in the community, and education. Coalition members receive a fortnightly information sheet and a quarterly magazine.

The Coalition hopes to be able to work towards establishing a centre for independent/integrated living sometime in the future.

Hampshire Centre for Independent Living
Richard Rowe, 39 Queens Road, Petersfield,

Hampshire GU32 3BB (Tel: Petersfield (0730) 68208).

> HCIL is concerned with people who want to run their own lives, choose their own choices, bedtimes, friends and daily round in a place of their own.
>
> (Quote from an HCIL leaflet)

In the late 1970s a few young, severely disabled people living in a residential home in Hampshire formed a group with the aim of moving into their own homes with suitable care support, out of the institution into the community. By the early '80s most of the group had reached their goal and had started to assist other disabled people along the same path. Together with other disabled people in Hampshire they formed the Hampshire Centre for Independent Living.

HCIL aims to assist disabled people: by fostering a public image which expresses their true value and potential as equal members of society; by promoting the philosophy of *Independent Living* and helping to plan and implement the decisions which affect their lives; and by providing practical peer advice and support for those wishing to live independently in the community. With the support of like-minded disabled people in the community, HCIL has grown and become more representative over the years. (Using finance jointly provided by local Health Authorities and Hampshire Social Services, the group attempts to operate throughout the county. HCIL's ultimate goal is true integration throughout all facets of society and full participation by disabled people in everything that affects them. A quarterly newsletter is produced.

Activities include working with locally-based people to encourage them to become active and involved in their area and establishing an effective and distinctive, organised voice as a balance to orthodox agencies as well as acting as spokesperson for like-thinking people.

Programmes seek to advance the education of the public about the needs and potential of disabled people and the part that such people can play in society generally. Also to protect and promote the physical, mental and psychological health of disabled people through peer support and advice by peer models and to provide assistance with care support and housing matters.

HCIL's aim is to promote independent/integrated living through CILs strategically located in the county of Hampshire. They say: '*We are keen to see disabled people meeting, talking about and contributing to such developments*'.

Management is by a committee of dedicated voluntary workers (all disabled people) who meet on a monthly basis to decide policy.
(See details of HCIL publications page 77.)

Your Move Centre for Independent Living (Nottinghamshire)
Alpine Street, Basford, Nottingham NG6 OHS (Tel: Nottingham (0602) 422236).
Your Move, Notts CIL is a consumer based voluntary organisation with 60 per cent of its management committee as well as its Chairperson having to be disabled people.

Your Move has three main functions.
1. To educate disabled people, families/friends and professionals about independent living, the services which are available and those which could be developed or made available.
2. To negotiate with statutory and other voluntary bodies (e.g. social services and housing associations) in order to secure resources in the field of independent living.
3. To assist individuals interested in independent living to achieve a satisfactory level of support and accommodation.

The CIL is also keen to encourage peer counselling as they believe that many of the problems faced by disabled people starting to live independent lives can best be helped by those who have been in similar circumstances.

At present they are concentrating on the sphere of housing and support, while acknowledging that other issues (access, transport, education, employment etc.) all have to be dealt with in order that disabled people can live as full and active members of the community.

Southampton Centre for Independent Living Ltd.
Disability Resource Centre, 4 Canute Road, Southampton SO1 1FH (Tel: Southampton (0703) 330982).
The SCIL is a voluntary organisation of disabled people who have set up an information, support and advice service for disabled people. This service is based on their own practical experience. The Centre campaigns for the right of disabled people to live independently in the community and in this respect are involved in community education.

HELPFUL ORGANISATIONS

British Council of Organisations of Disabled People (BCODP)
St. Mary's Church, Greenlaw Street, Woolwich, London SE18 5AR (Tel: 01–854 7289).

BCODP (for fuller details *see* Section 15) has a clearing house on housing issues for disabled people and has a standing committee to progress and monitor developments in this area.

Centre on Environment for the Handicapped
35 Great Smith Street, London SW1P 3BJ (Tel: 01–222 7980).
CEH provides a specialist information and advisory service on the environmental needs of all disabled and elderly people. It is committed to the shaping of environments which enable people with disabilities to achieve their potential and to contribute to the social, cultural, and economic life of the community. CEH services are used by architects, occupational therapists, health and social services, housing authorities, housing associations, voluntary organisations, and individual people.

While CEH's principal focus is on the built environment, and it is therefore primarily concerned with the contribution made by architects, it recognises that the provision of good environments which cater for everybody is not simply a matter of buildings but also one of attitudes and relationships, and policies and controls exercised by local authorities and central government.

CEH's accessible new offices, with their central location in Westminster, include a library room which is open to visitors by appointment.

CEH publications are informative and imaginative, and include *Reading Plans – a layman's guide to the interpretation of architects' drawings* (price £3.50), and *Living Independently* (*see* page 78) a paperback which describes the lives of nine severely disabled people who are living in their own homes.

The Architectural Advisory Service is a national register of architects with experience of designing for disabled people, broken down into regional lists. It is available free of charge to enquirers.

CEH members receive discounts on all CEH services. Corporate membership is £40 pa. Individual membership £20 pa.

CEH services include the following:

Information and consultancy service
Library and current awareness service
Seminars on topics of current concern
Publications (list available)
CEH journal *Design for Special Needs*. Annual subscription UK and overseas surface mail £10, overseas mail £12
Architectural Advisory Service.

Community Service Volunteers – Independent Living Scheme
237 Pentonville Road, London N1 9NJ (Tel: 01–278 6601). For further details of CSV *see* page 114.
The Independent Living Scheme is a flexible and broadly applicable form of non-professional care which seeks to match volunteers with individuals and families who need a particularly high and concentrated level of support to enable them to remain within the community and live as independent a life as possible. Some 'projects' work on a contractual basis, running for a specified period of time. Others are long-term, and as one volunteer completes his/her period of service, arrangements are made for another to take his/her place.

Families and individuals in all sorts of difficult situations can find the scheme useful. Some of these may be disabled people wanting to live independently in their own homes; disabled people needing help to complete courses in further education; mentally handicapped people needing special care within day centres or hostels, or in the community; people disabled through injury who need support to create new lifestyles.

CSVs are young, untrained people, committed to helping where they can. Their role is to enable, not to impose care. They can undertake physical care and offer genuine support, but they need expert direction from the individual or family with whom they are working.

Projects are expected to be organised through and supported by the local social services, health authority or other statutory or voluntary agency. Potential users are asked to consider how much care is required, then to judge the number of volunteers needed. An external project supervisor with an overall view of the project is nominated to offer regular support for the CSV before any placement can begin. The CSV's pocket money (at £15.25 a week), board (or food allowance of up to £18.50 a week), lodging and travelling expenses and the placement fee (£50 a month) must be met by the appropriate agency and/or the CSV user.

Crossroads Care Attendant Scheme
See page 284.

Disabled Living Centres
These centres provide professional practical help and advice on all aspects of living with a disability, including housing and help in the home. For details *see* Section 3.

Housing Debtline
The Birmingham Settlement, 318 Summer Lane, Birmingham B19 3RL (Tel: 021– 359 8501).
This is a national advice service to which anyone in England and Wales with mortgage arrears, rent arrears, rates arrears and other debt problems can turn to for advice. Every caller is given expert advice on the telephone, and this is backed-up by a self-help information pack consisting of three A4 size booklets packed with information on the steps you can take, how to decide priority debts and how to deal with these, how to cope with court orders and so on. The writing is clear and concise and the advice is very practical and comforting in its concern for a reader's problems. The booklets are entitled: *Dealing with Your Debts; Mortgage, Rates and Water Rates Arrears; Rent, Rates and Water Rates Arrears.*

Housing Debtline recommends that after having worked through the information pack you again contact them so that they can give specific advice as the situation develops.

Housing Debtline is a registered charity. Their telephone lines are open on Monday and Thursday 10 a.m. to 4 p.m. and Tuesday and Wednesday 2 to 7 p.m.

SHAD (Sheltered Housing Assistance for the Disabled)
13 – 15 Stockwell Road, London SW9 (Tel: 01–737 6748/801 2227).
SHAD was established so that severely disabled people could have the opportunity to live in their own houses, enabling them to lead independent and full lives, working or studying, as members of the community.

Projects exist in Haringey, Islington, Lambeth, and Wandsworth where SHAD aims to establish homes for severely disabled women and men. Priority is given to local people. Prospective tenants must be severely physically dependent and intellectually and emotionally independent. Each house is in a different area of each of the boroughs concerned and like any other in its street, except for the special conversions to meet the needs of the disabled occupant.

A vitally important area of SHAD's work is the provision and co-ordination of volunteers who assist the disabled tenants. SHAD has therefore appointed a Tenant Support Worker in each of the boroughs named to co-ordinate the recruitment and placement of the volunteers, to liaise with them on their projects in the community and to act as their supervisor, available for support.

Spinal Injuries Association
76 St James's Lane, London N10 3DF (Tel: 01–444 2121).
The SIA aims to help all those who are spinally injured and to enable them, wherever possible, to live independent lives in the community in a home of their own. The SIA Welfare Officer will support, encourage, advise and put members in touch with others who have experience of managing their own lives. SIA maintains up-to-date information on all aspects of independent living.

SIA has a Care Attendant Agency for full members. This provides helpers for people in five categories: for respite care; for short periods in emergencies; to enable someone to attend a conference, for example; for holidays; to help members find long-term care assistance.

Further Helpful Organisations

Carematch – Residential Care Consortium Computer Project
286 Camden Road, London N7 OBJ (Tel: 01–609 9966).
This computer-based service aims to help physically disabled people (below retirement age) who are looking for suitable residential care. Carematch maintains a database register of homes in the UK with details about them, and in response to an application and following a completed questionnaire, will send information about a number of homes which may match the requirements as described by the enquirer. It is up to the client to approach the homes and any arrangements must be made directly between the applicant and the home.

Carematch will also provide a counselling service where it is possible to discuss options including alternatives to residential care.

Caresearch
1 Thorpe Close, Portobello Green, London W10 (Tel: 01–960 5666).
The Caresearch database contains information on residential care throughout Britain for mentally handicapped people. The clients' needs are matched with the database and the appropriate residential establishments are produced by the computer and sent to the enquirer. The fee for a search is £5.

Family Fund
Information on the Fund's help for families with a disabled child is given on page 16. We would just mention here that help can sometimes be made available to aid with the installation of a telephone where the social services cannot help. Grants sometimes include an amount for the first year's rental of the telephone, but no help is given towards the cost of calls. Help with furniture, furnishings and floor coverings can sometimes be given.

Family Investment for the Handicapped
51 Old Dover Road, Canterbury, Kent CT1 3DE (Tel: Canterbury (0227) 456963).
Family Investment has been formed by a group of professional people to offer families with a mentally handicapped member a future for their relative.

It is a private limited company which joins together groups of families to meet this need. A place in a home for a named person is secured by an investment in a share in the company which owns the particular home. Family Investment acts as a management company administering the needs of each group home formed.

Because property has always been considered a good investment families can be assured that their money will not be lost.

The scheme provides for the return of the investment whenever a place in a home is no longer required. Conversely the future of a resident is secured even after the lifetime of the parents as a share can be transferred within the family.

The residents are selected from applicants of 19 years and over. They must be capable of: dealing with their own basic needs; participating in an active working day; benefiting from a social and community based lifestyle – but be in need of support to enable them to live a life of fulfilment.

Family Investment aims to offer a worthwhile job to each individual in its own sheltered workshops.

Home Assessment and Advisory Services
Woodcock Hill, Durrants Land, Berkhamsted, Hertfordshire HP4 3TR (Tel: Berkhamsted (04427) 5407).
State registered occupational therapists provide a service of independent assessment and individually designed programmes for people with physical disabilities. Work includes major adaptations to housing, court reports, training programmes, and care associated projects.

Leonard Cheshire Foundation
26–29 Maunsell Street, London SW1P 2QN (Tel: 01–828 1822).
The Foundation has set up 23 Family Support Services around the country. In these a network of

carers is available to respond to requests for help. Each Service aims to provide practical help where this is needed. For further details of the services and the areas covered contact the above address.

MENCAP – the Royal Society for Mentally Handicapped Children and Adults
MENCAP National Centre, 123 Golden Lane, London EC1Y ORT (Tel: 01–253 9433).
One of the greatest worries of the parents of a mentally handicapped child is what will happen to him or her when they have died, or are too old to provide care. In response to this concern the MENCAP Homes Foundation aims to provide small, family-sized homes in ordinary houses in the community, where mentally handicapped adults can live as independently as possible, but still receive any help they may need to cope with life. Its purpose is to establish homes now, to enable mentally handicapped people to live independently of their parents.

The residents get as much help as they need to live safely, happily and comfortably. If they need constant care, they can live in a house which has full time staff. If they are very independent, they can live in an unstaffed house, but they will have someone to turn to in case of problems.

The Homes Foundation will make sure *all* the needs of its residents are taken care of, either by the Foundation itself, or by the authorities responsible.

The addresses of Local Societies and Regional Offices may be obtained from MENCAP National Centre as above.

Royal Association for Disability and Rehabilitation (RADAR)
25 Mortimer Street, London W1N 8AB (Tel: 01–637 5400).
RADAR is able to offer advice and guidance on housing. It also adopts a research policy to appraise in depth all aspects of housing for disabled people and then to bring pressure to bear on the various authorities and organisations to build more accommodation of the type and standard required. (*see also* Books and Publications in this section).

Royal Institute of British Architects – RIBA
66 Portland Place, London W1 (Tel: 01–580 5533 ext. 4739).
The RIBA Client Advisory Service may be able to put you in touch with architects in your area having a particular knowledge of the needs of disabled people. Not all of these are registered with the

Centre on Environment for the Handicapped (*see* page 70) whom it might be wise to approach in the first instance.

SHAC (The London Housing Centre)
189a Old Brompton Road, London SW5 OAR (Tel: 01–373 7276).
A housing aid centre for people living in the Greater London area, SHAC offers information, advice and help to those who are homeless, threatened with eviction, living in bad conditions or needing general advice on housing. SHAC advises on landlord/tenant and public health law, financial problems including rent and mortgage arrears, and on options for rehousing through councils, house purchase or housing associations. SHAC has no accommodation of its own.

Shelter, National Campaign for the Homeless
88 Old Street, London EC1V 9HU (Tel: 01–253 0202).
Scotland: 103 Morrison Street, Edinburgh EH3 8BX (Tel: 031-229 8771).

Housing Associations

Housing Associations are non-profit-making organisations which provide accommodation, generally to rent. Under the arrangements of the Housing Act 1974 registered housing associations may be funded by the Housing Corporation or local authorities to provide housing facilities for special needs groups. Unfortunately, at the time of writing, the principles of housing associations are under threat and their public funding may be severely curtailed. If they have to borrow most of their money from private sources, they will have to pay high interest rates and this will have to be passed on in the form of higher rents. If present legislation goes through it will end the current charter of rights for housing association tenants and the present 'fair rent' system. The National Federation of Housing Associations is seeking to convince the government of the need to set limits on rent levels. The Federation is also seeking to convince the government that housing should not simply be divided up between private and public sectors (council housing), but that there should be a separate third sector where Housing Associations would provide housing for specialist groups at affordable rents.

We suggest you contact your local housing department or housing aid centre to ask about Housing Associations in the area who include specialist housing in their developments.

Often the associations work in co-operation

with specific voluntary organisations. Some of the
housing associations cater for both able-bodied
and disabled people on an integrated basis. Most
of them require an interview and assessment after
the initial application forms have been completed.
The great advantage that housing associations
have over local authorities is flexibility. They do
not have to be tied to strict allocation procedures
and restrictive residential requirements. Local
authorities have a responsibility to provide accommodation for a wide cross-section of the community. Housing associations, on the other hand,
can choose either to concentrate on certain specialist fields or to provide more general family
accommodation, or, indeed, to combine the two.
As a flexible alternative to local authority housing
they are in a position to complement provision
made by the authorities, and also to provide
housing for those who, for one reason or another,
are not or cannot be provided for by the authorities
to any extent. Among these special need groups
who can benefit from the voluntary housing
movement are one-parent families, and elderly
and disabled people. Some social services departments refer applicants to these associations on
recommendation. It is the specialist housing associations which have led the way in developing
housing alternatives to institutions for disabled
people.

Anchor Housing Association
Oxenford House, 13–15 Magdalen Street, Oxford
OX1 3BP (Tel: Oxford (0865) 722261).
Warden-supported housing in the form of self-
contained flats for those of retirement age and
over. Each person has their own front door and
privacy, but is helped with meals and everyday
tasks. Priority is given to those in poor housing
conditions, in distress through loneliness and of
limited income. Most schemes are designed to full
mobility housing standards and some include a
specially designed flat for a disabled elderly person. Specialist schemes are in Altrincham, Bradford, Newcastle upon Tyne, Birmingham, Guiseley, Halifax, Ilkeston, Morecambe, Leeds. Flats
throughout the country are also available in sheltered housing schemes.

Disabled Housing Trust
Ernest Kleinwort Court, Oakenfield, Burgess
Hill, West Sussex RH15 8SJ (Tel: Burgess Hill
(04446) 47892).
The Trust provides purpose-built hostels and shel-
tered accommodation for physically disabled

adults. In Burgess Hill there are 17 bungalows and
a hostel with 23 residents. At Eastbourne the Trust
is now (1988) building a hostel of similar size and
15 flats. Full care services are available to residents
in the Trust's sheltered housing as well as the
hostels.

John Grooms Housing Association
10 Gloucester Drive, Finsbury Park, London N4
2LP (Tel: 01–800 9245).
Specialises in wheelchair housing. Nineteen developments are now in operation or planned for the
near future – with or without warden care –
situated in southern England and Wales.

Habinteg Housing Association Ltd
10 Nottingham Place, London W1M 3FL (Tel: 01–
935 6931/3004).
Sister Association in Northern Ireland: Habinteg
(Ulster) Ltd, 12 Sullivan Close, Holywood,
County Down BT18 9HZ (Tel: (02317) 7211).
Habinteg is a charity and specialist housing association. Its philosophy is to provide housing for
disabled people and families in an ordinary setting
to enable them to live independently with freedom
of choice and the right to make their own decisions.
   This is achieved by good design within their
accommodation, coupled with an accessible environment which encourages social integration,
and locally based management. Habinteg's first
scheme was in Haringey in 1973. Now there are
1,100 homes in management across the country,
with a further 300 homes under construction or
being designed. Each scheme differs according to
local preferences and need, but the following
broad principles are followed.
1. A quarter of all dwellings are designed to full
    wheelchair standard. These are of all sizes
    from one-bedroom flats to four-bedroom
    houses, to suit single people, couples, families
    and single people sharing. These homes are
    interspersed through the scheme to avoid se-
    gregation.
2. The balance is designed to mobility standards
    with wider doors and level access. These
    homes are let to non-handicapped people and
    families in housing need. The mobility stan-
    dard enables wheelchair users to visit their
    neighbours, but also benefits elderly frail
    people and families with young children.
3. Special care is taken in the selection of sites, so
    that both wheelchair and non-wheelchair

users can have easy access to local shops and other facilities.

4. Internal design enables unhampered movement around the dwelling. Bathrooms and kitchens are flexibly planned so that adjustments can be easily made to suit the specific needs of the wheelchair users. This includes the height of work-tops and sink units, the provision of showers where preferred to baths, and the location of switches and handles. Specialist fittings such as hoists or grab-rails are fitted to suit individual requirements.

All schemes have a resident Community Assistant who is linked to an emergency call system and supports the disabled and elderly tenants. The Community Assistant is the local day-to-day manager, arranging repairs, ensuring that all tenants get a proper management service, working with the Tenants Association and housing management staff.

Key Housing Association Ltd

1 James Watt Street, Glasgow G2 8NS (Tel: 041–226 4868).
Key Housing Association has a range of accommodation for mentally handicapped people throughout central and west Scotland. This consists of various types of housing, including hostels, sheltered housing with warden support, self-contained bed-sits, flats and houses. Most developments provide for both mentally handicapped and non-handicapped tenants.

Margaret Blackwood Housing Association.

(Sister charity – Margaret Blackwood Foundation In association with the Scottish Trust for the Physically Disabled.)
Pritchard House, 32 Inglis Green Road, Edinburgh EH14 2ER (Tel: 031–443 7239).
These three charities share premises and staff. MBHA provides specially designed houses and flats for disabled people in most districts of mainland Scotland. It also manages hostels for severely disabled people in Aberdeen and Stirling. MBF raises and distributes funds for the benefit of MBHA tenants and runs a transport service in Stirling and Alloa. STPD raises and disburses funds for the benefit of physically disabled people. Its principal activities at present are related to the provision of accommodation.

Raglan Housing Association

Jolliffe House, West Street, Poole, Dorset BH15 1LA (Tel: Poole (0202) 678731).

Housing for disabled people in the east Midlands and southern England. In some a warden service is provided.

The Royal British Legion Housing Association Ltd

PO Box 32, Unit 2, St John's Industrial Estate, St John's Road, Penn, High Wycombe, Buckinghamshire HP10 8JF (Tel: Penn (049 481) 3771).
Provides housing for elderly ex-service personnel or their elderly dependants in 300 schemes in England, Scotland and Wales. Although not specifically designed for disabled people there are built-in bathroom aids which make the accommodation suitable for those elderly people having a need for such aids. Applications through the local Branch Service Committee of the Royal British Legion or, if there is no local branch, enquiries should be made direct.

Shaftesbury Housing Association

2a Amity Grove, London SW20 0LJ (Tel: 01–946 6634).
This Association provides blocks of flatlets for elderly and disabled people throughout the country. All tenants must be able to look after themselves, but within the schemes there are wardens who answer to a call alarm system which is installed in every flat and who help out in emergencies. In each scheme one or two flats are provided which are designed for wheelchair users. Communal facilities are always available including lounge, television room, guest bedroom, and laundry.

Hostels for those who are frail and elderly have recently been added to the Association's work, together with those for mentally or physically handicapped people. Care and dining facilities are provided.

Sutton Housing Trust

Sutton Court, Tring, Hertfordshire HP23 5BB (Tel: Tring (044 282) 4921).
The Trust is a charitable housing association providing rented accommodation for people on low incomes who are in housing need.

The Trust has accommodation especially designed for physically disabled people on Trust estates in Birmingham, Bolton, Bradford, Hemel Hempstead, Hull, Leeds, Leicester, London, Manchester, Middlesbrough, Newton-le-Willows, Plymouth, Salford, South Shields, Stoke-on-Trent, Tamworth, Warrington, and Widnes. Additionally many ground floor flats and bungalows on all but the oldest of the Trust's estates have been built to 'mobility standard' and are accessible to wheelchair users.

Books and Publications

Are You Cooking Comfortably by Ann Macfarlane. A British Gas publication for Arthritis Care. This is a practical cook book which encourages the user to be flexible in choosing and preparing meals. The recipes, including convenience foods, are designed to bridge the gap between dependence and independence.

The book is physically easy to use being ring-bound on wipe-clean pages with an easel-type cover to enable it to stand upright. Available at leading booksellers for £2.95, it can also be ordered from: Biblios Publishers Distribution Services Ltd, Glenside Industrial Estate, Partridge Green, Horsham, West Sussex RH13 8LD (Tel: Partridge Green (0403) 710971) for the same price.

Cookery for Handicapped People by James Hargreaves. Published by Souvenir Press, 43 Great Russell Street, London WC1B 3PA (Tel: 01–580 9307). Price: £8.95 plus £1.10 postage and packing. An illustrated guide for teaching children with limited reading and numerical ability how to cook independently from recipes. These recipes were developed as the result of much trial and error in a school kitchen, using the minimum of words and requiring only a rudimentary knowledge of figures. The range of recipes, from cakes and main dishes to puddings and salads are all illustrated with diagrams.

Department of the Environment publications publish *Housing for the Handicapped*. The housing problems of handicapped children and disabled people are examined in two reports, *Handicapped Children: their homes and lifestyles,* HDD Occasional Paper 4/78 (price £1.40), and *Housing Services for Disabled People,* HDD Occasional Paper 3/78 (price: £1.10). Both are available from The Department of the Environment and Transport, Publications Sales Unit, Building 1, Victoria Road, South Ruislip, HA4 ONZ.

Designing for the Disabled by Selwyn Goldsmith. This is still the most comprehensive guide yet produced about the planning and design of buildings for disabled people. The author sees this publication as a consultancy service for the practising architect informing her/him on every aspect of designing for disabled people from anthropometrics and wheelchair circulation spaces, through ramps, doors, lifts, kitchens, bathrooms and lavatories, to provision in public buildings such as cinemas, theatres, hotels, swimming pools, and libraries, to employment, transport, and educational buildings, and on to the planning of housing, residential homes and hospital accommodation. It gives straightforward practical recommendations and comment. Available from RIBA Bookshop, 66 Portland Place, London W1N 4AD for personal callers only. Correspondence to Finsbury Mission, Moreland Street, London EC1V 8VB (Tel: 01–251 0791). Price: £28.50.

The Directory of Residential Accommodation for the Mentally Handicapped in England, Wales, and Northern Ireland (1982). Available from MENCAP, The Bookshop, 123 Golden Lane, London EC1Y 0RT. Price: £5.95 plus £1.25 postage and packing.

Disabled Living Foundation publications are available from: Haigh & Hochland Ltd, International University Booksellers, The Precinct Centre, Oxford Road, Manchester M13 9QA (Tel: 061–273 4156).

Books include:

(a) *Kitchen Sense for Disabled People* by Gwen Conacher, Jean Symons, Creina Murland and Marian Lane. This freshly researched and completely revised edition includes a wider choice of kitchen furniture, appliances and aids which are now available. Problems are tackled facing visually handicapped people as well as those with chronic skin conditions. The book gives practical detailed advice on planning and equipping a kitchen, on the numerous aids and methods which make life easier for disabled people, and includes hints on short cuts in cooking, and on shopping. There are easy-to-remember guidelines on healthy eating and how to overcome difficulties of eating in company or outside the home. The appendices provide information on sources of further advice, and the addresses of suppliers of equipment. Brenda Naylor's line drawings illustrate points of design, method and equipment throughout the book. Price: £8.95 plus 50p postage and packing.

(b) *Handicapped at Home* by Sydney Foott, published by the Design Council. This book, fully illustrated by photographs and line drawings, suggests ways in which a home may be shared by able and disabled people, whatever the age or disability. It is aimed at maximum independence and sharing of enjoyment and responsibilities. Price: £3.20.

The following publications are also available direct from the Disabled Living Foundation, 380–384 Harrow Road, London W9 2HU (Tel: 01–289 6111):

A bibliography of publications relevant to the design of housing for disabled people.

Accommodation for Disabled People of All Ages Including Those with Special Needs providing general notes, as well as lists of sources of help, residential accommodation for all ages, community villages, independent/integrated living, short term accommodation, and legislation. Price: £1.20.

Notes on Cookers and Cooking Appliances for Disabled People Price: £1.20.

Independent Living a 4-page Library Resource List available free with a SAE.

Equipment for the Disabled Mary Marlborough Lodge, Nuffield Orthopaedic Centre, Headington, Oxford OX3 7LD (Tel: Oxford (0865) 750103). Five of the books in this series are described below. Each book contains a wealth of precise information (regularly updated) regarding the aids and equipment described, all of which are illustrated. Each is priced at £3.95 plus 80p postage. Cheques should be made payable to Oxfordshire Health Authority. For further details of this series *see* Section 3.

(a) *Housing and Furniture*: Relevant legislation; funding of house adaptations; special design needs; fire and safety; heating and insulation; refuse disposal; electrical fittings; environmental controls; garages; ramps; external steps; powered lifting platforms; handrails and grab-rails; stairlifts and home lifts; flooring; doors and door furniture; protective finishes; windows; sanitary wear; adjustable beds; pillows; back-rests; boards; cradles; mirrors; lifting aids; chairs: high seat, reclining, self-rise, special; raising units; foot-stools; lumbar cushions; work chairs and stools; tables; select bibliography.

(b) *Home Management*: General information; kitchen design and furniture; sinks; cookers; refrigerators and freezers; dishwashers; refuse disposal; table-top appliances; kettles and teapots; table-ware; special feeding aids; cutlery; drinking utensils; feeding trays; stools; picking-up aids; trays and trolleys; knives; scissors; graters; food choppers; vegetable peelers; scales; mixers; food processors; can openers; jar openers; packet openers; cooking and serving utensils; bedmaking; laundering safety.

(c) *Disabled Mother*: Cots; carrycots; bedding; nightwear; feeding bottles, sterilizing units, baby foods; bibs; cups and plates; multi-purpose chairs; nappy changing; potties; trainer seats; bathing; baby baths, dressing; slings; harnesses; carriers; prams and pushchairs; play; playpens; bouncing cradles; safety precautions; guards; fire, cooker, iron, socket; thermometers; gates; baby alarms, visual and vibrating indicators; car safety; select bibliography.

(d) *Disabled Child*: Chairs; corner seats; tables; wedges; side-lying boards; standing boxes; prone boards; standing frames; trolleys; Go-karts; hand/foot propelled tricycles; car safety seats; push-chairs; walking aids; wheelchairs; bath and toilet aids; incontinence appliances and protective pants; feeding bottles, cups, mugs, plates, and cutlery; boots and shoes; protective helmets; play; swimming aids; select list of organisations; select bibliography.

(e) *Personal Care*: Bathroom layout; grab-rails; grooming; care of hair, nails, teeth, make-up, shaving; washbasins and fittings, tap turners; washing aids; baths: standard, walk-in, adjustable, with built-in seats; bath inserts, accessories, seats, boards, lifts, rails; showering: shower valves, cubicles, seats and stools; bidets; toileting: WCs, raised and special seats, rails, frame supports, chemical toilets, cleaning and personal aids; menstruation; commodes and sani-chairs; urinals and bed-pans; select bibliography.

Hampshire Centre for Independent Living publications available from: HCIL, c/o Mark Walsh, 31 Churchfield, Headley, Bordon, Hampshire GU35 8PF. The following two books are priced at £4 each, but if you order both together the price is £7 + £1 postage and packing for each copy and/or pack (the two books together) ordered.

(a) *Source Book Toward Independent Living*. This book contains a collection of advice, suggestions, references, and helpful hints and comments provided for disabled people by a group of disabled people from the HCIL.

The text is based on the premise that, given the necessary opportunities, disabled people can be in control of their own lives and that the ability to direct personal care staff is a skill which can be learnt. This book is designed to help disabled people to assess their needs for care support and to approach agencies for the finance with which to pay for the amount of care support needed. Then advice is given on how to find, employ and work with a personal care worker.

(b) *One Step On*. This book is the story of three young disabled people who, while living in a residential home decided to work together to each find personal homes of their own. The ways they achieved this are carefully described.

A Handbook of Housing for Disabled People by John Penton. A reference book for the designer who is faced with the challenge of producing housing for disabled people. It includes a section on adaptations. Published by the London Housing Consortium and available from RADAR, 25 Mortimer Street, London W1N 8AB (Tel: 01–637 5400). Price: £4.50.

Housing the Disabled by John Hunt and Lesley Hoyes. Published by Torfaen Borough Council. A report of a project carried out to identify and meet the housing needs of disabled people living in the borough of Torfaen. While this nicely illustrated book is principally of interest and encouragement to planners and architects, its practicality makes it of use to disabled people who may want to impress local authorities with their understanding of the problems and the ways in which their housing needs can be met. For instance, Part II is entitled 'Providing Solutions' and has a section on 'Making the Policies Effective'. Available from Torfaen Borough Council *(Housing the Disabled)*, Gwent House, Town Centre, Cwmbran, Gwent. Price: £3.95 plus 95p postage.

Housing Year Book. A reference directory of the bodies and organisations involved in housing in the United Kingdom. Its pages contain information on local authorities, housing advisory bodies and pressure groups, housing aid and building centres, major home builders, the media and research, and training organisations. Price: £42.50 (1988 edition). Available from public libraries or from the Sales Promotion Department, Longman Group Ltd, Freepost, Harlow, Essex CM20 1YQ. (Tel: Harlow (0279) 29655).

Living Independently by Ann Shearer. This book looks at the lives of nine severely disabled people who, seemingly against all the odds, have established homes of their own in the community in a

way and a place which they have chosen and for which they are responsible. Descriptions of their daily lives show the variety of help they have drawn on and the difficulties they encountered in finding what was possible.

The book is very practical in that it clearly describes how each person manages their daily routine and does not gloss over the difficulties they encountered. Each story includes a plan of the living accommodation, not only showing the layout but also giving details of the fittings. The knotty problems of finance are clearly described. One of the householders reckoned that it took her five years to work out the benefits and allowances due to her. Published by and available from: Centre on Environment for the Handicapped, 35 Great Smith Street, London SW1P 3BJ (Tel: 01–222 7980). Price: £5 including postage and packing.

New Rights for Tenants. A guide to the Housing Act 1980 for council, housing asssociation and new town tenants. Published by the National Consumer Council, 20 Grosvenor Gardens, London SW1W ODH. Available free.

Royal National Institute for the Blind, 224 Great Portland Street, London W1N 6AA (Tel: 01–388 1266).
The following material is available free from the Residential Services Department of the RNIB:
Lists of Homes for the Visually Handicapped. These are provided on a regional basis giving brief details of each home.
RNIB Homes brochures describing individual RNIB residential homes in Westgate-on-Sea, Harrogate, Burnham-on-Sea, and Hove.
Available free from the RNIB Public Affairs Dept: *Designing Buildings for Blind People*. This illustrated booklet aims to help those responsible for the design, planning and maintenance of accommodation for visually handicapped people.

SHAC 189a Old Brompton Road, London SW5 OAR (Tel: 01–370 6203).
SHAC produces the following guides: *Buying a Home,* price: £1.70; *Rights Guide for Home Owners* price: £3.50; *Your Rights to Repairs* (two volumes,one for council tenants and the other for private and housing association tenants), each £1.95; *Homeless, Know Your Rights*, price: 50p; *A Guide to Housing Benefits*, price: £4.95 (a very detailed guide aimed principally at people advising claimants).

Wheelchairs – no handicap in housing. Published by the National Federation of Housing Associations, 175 Gray's Inn Road, London WC1X 8UP (Tel: 01–278 6571).

This booklet gives advice on design and management issues on housing for disabled people using wheelchairs. Written in a light-hearted style it is intended to help those who have little specialist experience – whether associations, co-operatives, local authorities, developers or architects – to accommodate wheelchair users in their housing programmes. It would also be useful for disabled clients to have at hand to bring out at the appropriate moment.

EDUCATION

The law governing the provision of special education to children with special educational needs in England and Wales is contained in the Education Act 1981, which came into force on 1 April 1983, and the Regulations made under that Act *(see* Section 13 for a detailed summary). This Act was based on the recommendations of the 1978 Warnock Report *Special Educational Needs* and promotes the concept of the special educational needs of the individual child.

Special educational needs may arise from a variety of causes. The concept embraces a wider group of pupils than those 'ascertained' as handicapped under the previous arrangements (approximately 2 per cent of the school population). As an indication of scale, the Warnock Committee estimated that nationally about 20 per cent of pupils might have special educational needs at some time during their school careers. The proportion of children with such needs will, however, vary from area to area and from school to school.

Under the 1981 Act, Local Education Authorities have a duty to identify those children in their area with special educational needs. Where, at first sight, there are grounds to suggest that a child's needs are such as to require provision additional to, or different from, the facilities and resources generally available in ordinary schools in the area, they will be required to conduct a multi-professional assessment of all such children, taking medical, educational, psychological and other factors (including the views of parents) into account. If the assessment confirms that the child's needs should be 'determined' by the Local Education Authority, that authority is required to maintain a statement of those needs. The statement must also specify the special educational provision which should be made to meet those needs.

Special education provision may be made in various forms, such as in special schools, special units attached to primary or secondary schools, in special classes, in day and boarding special schools, in hospital or even in a child's own home.

The 1981 Act, however, gives impetus to educating children with special educational needs in ordinary schools where possible. Local Education Authorities may use special schools run by voluntary bodies and independent schools where they cannot make suitable special educational provision themselves.

The impetus towards integration contained in the 1981 Act has been seen as a break with the past. If we look back to 1944, to the Education Act of that year, the thinking of Parliament was that special education should, as far as possible, be provided for seriously disabled pupils in appropriate special schools. Only if this was impracticable, or if the disability was not serious, might education be provided in an ordinary school. It could be said that special schools were regarded as the normal solution to significant handicap, and integration in ordinary schools exceptional.

In recent years, and in reaction against this trend, a powerful movement, not limited to this country and certainly not confined to education, has urged that disabled people are not to be treated as 'different'; that facilities should be provided so as to allow them to join in the mainstream of life alongside their able-bodied peers. Thus, in education it is argued that handicapped children should not be separated off from other children, but should be educated in a common setting towards the day when they may take their place in ordinary society and share the opportunities enjoyed by able-bodied people.

Not everyone, in fact, is fully convinced of the merits of the case for integration. Teachers warn of the harm which can be done if integration is 'forced' without adequate support services. There are also those, including some parents, who believe that there will always be children who will benefit from the specialised facilities and care a special school is built, staffed and equipped to offer, and who will develop better in a somewhat protected environment. They see a danger, particularly if facilities – including those of time and

patience – are not fully adequate, that handicapped children will suffer in a system based on competition and meritocracy, and will find the experience extremely stressful.

Warnock, while looking forward to a shift of emphasis towards greater integration and improved provision for special education in ordinary schools, at least in England and Wales, cautions that the interests of those whose needs cannot be so met must be safeguarded, and this caution is reflected in the 1981 legislation.

The reality of what has happened since the 1981 Act is something else again. If we look at pupil statistics from 1961 to 1981, we see that while the total school population rose by 20 per cent, the number of pupils in full-time education in special schools went up by 90 per cent. It is true that since 1981 this trend has been halted, but there has been no dramatic reversal. Between 1981 and 1986, the total school population fell by 10 per cent. The comparative decrease for special schools was only slightly higher at 13 per cent. So that falling rolls have had relatively little effect and some would say that an opportunity has been lost. Although the 1981 Act was important in providing the ground rules for the assessment of special educational needs on an individual, rather than a categorised basis, and in establishing formal rights for parents to be involved (for which we urge those concerned to see Section 13, pages 246–9), there has been a wide gulf between legislation and practice. According to the Muscular Dystrophy Society (*The Search,* Summer 1987), 'What happens to a particular child depends to a large extent not only on his or her disabilities but on the view of the local education authority in his or her area and on the education facilities it has available. Both vary substantially from place to place.'

The legislative impetus towards integration was anyway decidedly muted, being subject to a number of provisos which included compatability with the 'efficient use of resources'. This, together with the fact that the legislation was not backed up by the considerable resource input needed if integration was to be achieved on any scale, ensured that local education authorities needed, in practice, to do little or nothing. Certainly, some progress has been made in some places, and there are a number of mainstream schools which have successfully demonstrated that children with difficulties severe enough to be the subject of a statement under the Act can be educated alongside and in harmony with their able-bodied peers, given careful initial placement, necessary equipment, and, perhaps above all, an adequate number of trained and committed teachers.

Department of Education statistics in 1985 showed Cornwall as having 73 per cent of children who had been the subject of a statement in ordinary schools, with Oxfordshire and Avon close behind. But at the other end of the scale, Wakefield, Wigan and Barnsley scored only 1 per cent, 4 per cent and 4 per cent respectively.

According to Giles Radice MP, questioned before the 1987 General Election, statements are often not prepared early enough, and take too long to prepare, while some local education authorities seem to tailor-make the statements in line with what provision they have available. Mr. Radice quotes shortages of educational psychologists and special therapists as examples of the way in which lack of money has impeded progress and notices that the number of non-teaching assistants has actually *decreased* since the introduction of the 1981 Act. Even the Conservative-dominated Education, Science and Arts Committee, in its third report *Special Educational Needs: Implementation of the Education Act 1981*, published in June 1987, comments on a general shortage of resources for schools as well as the lack of money for special education. It says: 'The two are related in that pressure on schools' and LEAs' resources had made it difficult for them to make proper general provision for children in a way which would minimise the numbers needing special educational provision.' The Committee points to confusion in defining 'learning difficulties' and in the criteria used in deciding whether to issue a statement, so that the proportions of children receiving statements across the various local education authorities varied from as little as 0.04 per cent to as much as 4.2 per cent.

Generally, the response to the intention and spirit of the 1981 Act has been inadequate and variable, and parents have found pursuit of their statutory rights to be an uphill struggle (presupposing, of course, that they are aware of their rights).

A survey by the Centre for Studies on Integration in Education published the following statistics in 1986. Only half of the 63 per cent of local education authorities which bothered to respond to its enquiries gave parents a proper background to the assessment of, and provision for, special educational needs; only a third told parents that they have a right to be fully consulted and to receive all relevant information; only 14 per cent referred to the concept of parents as partners in the assessment process (which only 8 per cent properly explained); and, most shocking of all, only one authority (of 64) referred to the need to take account of the feelings and perceptions of the children.

It is a depressing picture. In many areas, there is a genuine lack of money; in more there is a lack of will. If the present Government's proposals to loosen the control of local authorities is realised, the tide towards integration, such as it is, may ebb altogether. The Education Reform Bill, introduced in November 1987, gives rise to particular concern. The provisions for schools to 'opt out' of local education authorities and assume a grant-maintained status has serious implications for children with special educational needs. Schools which choose to opt out of local education authorities completely will not, as things stand at the time of writing, be under any duty to admit such children. If such schools rely on grants on a 'per head' basis, they are likely to be reluctant to admit children with special educational needs whose education will almost certainly be more costly than that of their peers.

Further Information

STATUTORY

Scottish legislation (*see* page 249) imposes a duty on education authorities to disseminate information in their areas as to the importance of the early discovery of special educational needs and the statutory opportunities for assessment. There is no such general requirement in the law as it relates to England and Wales. However, under the Education (School Information) Regulations (made under section 8 of the Education Act 1980), local education authorities are required to publish information concerning the arrangements to identify and assess children with special educational needs; the special educational provision made available in ordinary schools, special schools, or otherwise than in a school; and the arrangements to enable parents to obtain advice and further information. Reference copies should be available at local education authority offices, schools and public libraries. Personal copies can be obtained by parents free of charge from local education authority offices. General information about special education can be found in the Department of Education and Science/Welsh Office publication, *The Educational System of England and*

Wales (September 1985) which can be obtained free of charge from either DES, Publications Despatch Centre, Honeypot Lane, Stanmore, Middlesex HA7 1AZ or from Welsh Office Education Office, Crown Buildings, Cathays Park, CF1 3NQ. A free booklet, *List of addresses of LEAs in England and Wales* can also be obtained from those two sources.

Booklists about children with particular handicaps or learning difficulties can be supplied on written request to the DES Library, Elizabeth House, York Road, London, SE1 7PH. The following further publications are available from Her Majesty's Stationery Office:
The Warnock Report Special Educational Needs (1978), £14.75
Meeting Special Educational Needs (a shortened version of the Warnock Report). £1.75.
Guides to the 1981 Education Act (*see* Section 13, Legislation, page 246).

Reference Books

Education Year Book (Longman Group, 1988 edition, price £42.50). A reference directory of the individuals and organisations involved in education in the United Kingdom. Its 708 pages contain information which includes government and local education authority provision including that for special educational needs; independent and non-maintained special schools and special further education establishments; employment and careers; teachers' organisations; physical education and sport including sport for disabled people.
The Educational Grants Directory (Directory of Social Change, 1988, price £12.50) A comprehensive listing of educational charities for children and students in need. It covers over 1,000 sources of help, including both national and local charities, in relation to a variety of specific needs.

Guidance for Parents

The Advisory Centre for Education (ACE) Ltd (*see* page 85) publishes a wide range of information relating to education law and provision. As well as its detailed explanation of the 1981 Education Act (*see* Section 13, Legislation page 246) parents may find the following information sheets (50p each) helpful:
Children with Special Needs: sources of help
The '81 Act: safeguarding your rights
Summary of the Warnock Report
Education to 19: your rights.
The Centre for Studies on Integration in Educ-

ation (*see* page 86) have numerous relevant publications.

(a) *Educating Special Children in Ordinary Schools* (free). What is integration? What does the centre for Studies on Integration in Education do and how does the Centre work? This is a short guide to the work of CSIE and the principles of the philosophy behind the issue of integration.

(b) *Education: New Deal For Children With Special Needs* (free). The main changes brought about by the 1981 Education Act are listed point by point in an easily-readable style.

(c) *Integration: The Main Arguments* (free). This outlines the arguments supporting integration of children with special needs in ordinary schools, The Spastic Society's position and brief details of the work of the Centre (CSIE).

(d) *Education Act 1981: Where To Get Help And Advice* (free). This factsheet lists organisations and people able to help and gives information and advice to parents of children with Special Education Needs in relation to the operation of the new law.

(e) *16–19: Students With Special Needs – The Right To Further Education* (free). The Spastics Society's statement on 16–19 provision. It outlines the basic local education authority duty to provide full-time education up to 19 for all who request it; discusses payment of fees, puts the society's position and tells parents what to do if they are refused education for their 16-year-olds.

(f) *Selected Reading List* (20p). This contains a listening and viewing list as well as book and magazine articles grouped under eight main headings on special education, with particular reference to integration. Details of the Open University Course Special Needs in Education (E241). Reading books and course units are also given.

GCSE: Arrangements for Candidates with a Disability. These are comprehensive guidance notes prepared by the six GCSE examining groups which explain arrangements for candidates whose disability is likely to handicap them in GCSE examinations. The purpose of the arrangements is to compensate for the limitations imposed by the handicap, but not otherwise to advantage the student. The guidance notes will be incorporated in documents issued by all examining groups. Candidates or their parents who would like information about provision for candidates with special needs should contact the examining group conducting the examination concerned.

The Rathbone Society (*see* page 89) has published a series of leaflets concerning the rights and responsibilities of parents who have children with special educational needs. The series is produced as a complete pack consisting of 15 factsheets.

The Royal National Institute for the Blind (see page 89) publishes a range of leaflets and books for parents and teachers on all aspects of the education of visually handicapped children.

Further relevant books, publications and video films are available from the organisations listed below.

Conductive Education (CE)

CE is an education system for those who have problems of controlling bodily movements (motor disorders) caused by certain conditions of the brain or spine (e.g. cerebral palsy and spina bifida, or, in adults, strokes, multiple sclerosis or Parkinson's Disease). It involves an integrated programme of physical and intellectual education, with intensive stimulation and encouragement of correct movement, and a determination to achieve vital developmental goals such as walking, using and eventually abandoning the simplest of aids. Highly-trained 'conductors' (movement educators) guide their pupils through regimes of daily living, movement, games, song, ceremony and formal education towards all-round personal and social advancement. As far as possible, pupils are given responsibility for their own progress, but they also encourage each other in group practice.

The system was developed in Hungary from 1945 by its originator, Andras Peto. Since his death in 1967, the development of CE has been the required educational provision for Hungarian children suffering from motor disorders. Official statistics indicate that around two-thirds to three-quarters of the children who leave the Peto Institute each year have reached the goal of being 'orthofunctional', that is to say, able to function independently, without a wheelchair or other special aids or appliances, and without welfare assistance. Such children use the normal furniture, tools and implements of everyday life. In adults, orthofunction is the ability to work or look after oneself at home.

In the United Kingdom, some schools have offered CE, usually under the auspices of The Spastics Society, but the authenticity of such teaching in relation to the Peto model is disputed.

CE became a major issue in 1986, as parents of motor-disordered children and those who work with them became widely aware that the approach developed in Hungary might hold out new hope for their children's development. This has led to the setting up of The Foundation for Conductive Education (*see* page 87).

Not all children or adults can benefit from CE, but, in general terms, this is not because of the severity of the motor disorder, but rather that there are other complications. Chief amongst these appear to be mental limitation: profound mental handicap or autistic behaviour which cut the child off completely from the social world.

A review of the subject is available in the book, *Conductive Education*, edited by Phillipa Cottam and Andrew Sutton (Croom Helm Ltd., Provident House, Burrell Row, Beckenham, Kent BR3 1AT, 1985), price £9.95, also available from the Foundation (add £1 for postage and packing).

Helpful Organisations

81 Action
52 Magnaville Road, Bishops Stortford, Hertfordshire, CM23 4DW
This is a national network of parents of children with special educational needs. It is concerned that many parents, faced with the fact that many local education authorities fail to provide adequate information and support, cannot cope with the procedures they have to follow to obtain their rights. 81 Action therefore has the following aims:

(a) to offer information, guidance, help and advice on the workings of the 1981 Education Act and other legislation and administrative practices concerned with special educational provision;

(b) to link up and support groups and individual parents of children with special educational needs;

(c) to raise awareness of the issues of integration;

(d) to promote equality of opportunity in education for *all* children;

(e) to encourage parents to take their rightful place in the education policy-making process, including equal access to information;

(f) to encourage education, health and social services to fulfil their duties and responsibilities in making provision for children with special needs and integrating them; and

(g) to promote the concept of parent-professional partnership.

Membership costs £1. Affiliation: £10 for groups, £5 for professionals.

Advisory Centre for Education (ACE) Ltd
18 Victoria Park Square, London E2 9BP (Tel: 01–980 4596, afternoons only).

The Centre provides information and advice for all those involved in the education service through its magazine *ACE Bulletin*. It aims to help people to become more involved in education and to make more effective choices. It encourages closer home–school relations and urges greater consideration of the views of parents and students in educational decisions, as well as seeking a generally more open and responsive system. As well as its many advisory publications, ACE runs conferences on topical issues for parents, students, teachers and administrators. ACE also runs a free telephone advice line between 2.00 and 5.30 every afternoon. Publications include the following.
ACE BULLETIN, a magazine on education. Published six times a year, £7.50 per annum (£7 by banker's order).
Where to look things up (third edition, 1983), an A-Z of the sources of all major educational topics, £4.50.
Ace also publish booklets for school governors:
Special Education Handbook the 1981 Education Act explained for parents of children with special needs; £3
Special Choice Appeals; £2
Choosing a School; £2
Many other booklets and information sheets are available. Free publications list on request.

Association for All Speech Impaired Children (AFASIC)
347 Central Markets, Smithfield, London, EC1A 9NH (Tel: 01–236 3632/6487).
For a general note *see* Section 15.
The following AFASIC booklets are available.
Educational Facilities for Speech and Language Impaired Children.
The Assessment and Diagnosis of Children with Speech and Language Disorders – Notes for Parents.
Children with Speech and Language Disorders – A Brief Guide to the Law concerning their Education.
These booklets are free to members, prices on application to non-members.

Association for Spina Bifida and Hydrocephalus
22 Upper Woburn Place, London WC1H 0EP (Tel: 01–388 1382).
A general note on the Association is given in Section 15.
The Association is always willing to give advice

on all aspects of education. It publishes the following booklets on aspects of educating children with spina bifida and hydrocephalus:
The Handwriting of Spina Bifida Children
Children With Spina Bifida at School
Young People With Spina Bifida and/or Hydrocephalus – Learning and Development Problems.
Further publications deal with other aspects of the disabilities, and the Association provides a list of suggested reading on the subject.

Blissymbolics Communication Resource Centre (UK)
c/o The Spastics Society, 382–384 Newport Road, Cardiff CF3 7YU (Tel: Cardiff (0222) 496240).
Blissymbols Communication provides an alternative or augmentative to speech for non-speaking children and adults. It is estimated that there are 3,500 individuals in the United Kingdom who use symbols as an expressive medium. The UK Resource Centre provides a service to professionals, parents and users of Blissymbols by disseminating information, providing training, co-ordinating research, developing materials and maintaining standardisation.

The British Association for Early Childhood Education
Studio 3:2, 140 Tabernacle Street, London, EC2A 4SD (Tel: 01–250 1768).
The Association is concerned with all aspects of children's development and learning from birth to the age of about 8 to 9 years. It believes that education in the early years is vital, and presses for the provision of adequate facilities of high standard. It recognises a need for team work in terms of closer collaboration with parents and a wider interdisciplinary concept of education.

It recognises that a disturbing number of children are disadvantaged through poor housing, overcrowding, isolation, poverty, ill-health and other handicapping conditions, and is concerned to ensure that the health, education and well-being of all young children are advanced wherever they may be. The teacher in the nursery class often has the opportunity to help with the early diagnosis of a disability.

BAECE publishes inexpensive leaflets on child care and child development, and welcomes enquiries from parents, either by telephone or letter. Please send an s.a.e. for reply.

British Dyslexia Association
See Section 15.

British Epilepsy Association
Anstey House, 40 Hanover Square, Leeds LS3 1BE (Tel: Leeds (0532) 439393).
For a general note, *see* Section 15. The Association stages conferences, seminars and lectures to both professional and lay audiences, and has produced a *Teachers' Package* for use in schools.
A leaflet guide, *Schools and Centres for Epilepsy* is available, price 25p, and a literature list and film guide will be sent on request.

British Institute of Mental Handicap
Wolverhampton Road, Kidderminster, Worcestershire DY10 3PP (Tel: Kidderminster (0562) 850251).
For a general note, *see* Section 15. There are a number of publications including the following book.
Curriculum Planning for the ESN (S) Child, Skills Analysis Model. An effective curriculum for children with severe learning difficulties.

The Campaign for Mentally Handicapped People
12A Maddox Street, London, W1R 9PL (Tel: 01–491 0727).
CMH publications, available from: 5 Kentings, Comberton, Cambridgeshire CB3 7DT, include a range of relevant books and leaflets.

Centre for Studies on Integration in Education (CSIE)
1st floor, 840 Brighton Road, Purley, Croydon CR2 2BH (Tel: 01–660 8552).
The Spastics Society set up this Centre in July 1981 to raise public, professional and political awareness of the issue of integration and to promote good practice. It aims to encourage local education authorities, individual schools, parents, governors and others to establish effective and successful integration schemes for children with special needs, and to ensure that any re-evaluation of policy will be considered an integral part of a whole education service.

A central theme of CSIE's work is the exchange of information relating to integration. This includes:

(a) publicising and promoting the principle of integration of children of all disabilities as widely as possible;
(b) establishing a national register of integration schemes;
(c) helping to develop a framework of support for parents of children with special educational needs;
(d) pressing for resources and careful planning to implement schemes;

(e) arranging national and regional conferences on different aspects of integration;
(f) helping to link up those running successful schemes with those who wish to do the same, and giving advice; and
(g) producing factsheets, leaflets, case-studies and other publications relating to the 1981 Education Act.
For free leaflets and a publications list, write to the above address.

Children's Legal Centre
20 Compton Terrace, London N1 2UN (Tel: 01–359 6251)
This is an independent national organisation concerned with law and policy affecting children and young people in England and Wales. It aims to promote the recognition of children and individuals participating fully in the decisions which affect their lives.

The core activities of the Centre include running a free advice and information service by letter and telephone (2 p.m. to 5 p.m. weekdays), pursuing selected cases, initiating research, running courses and conferences, and monitoring and responding to policies and proposals which affect children and young people. The Centre's free and confidential advice and information service covers all aspects of law and policy affecting children and young people in England and Wales, and as such can be of great benefit to parents battling with local education authorities over the implementation of the 1981 Education Act. Among the aims of the Centre is the elimination of diversification by sex, race, colour, class and disability.

A monthly bulletin, *Childright*, is available on subscription of £18.50 a year (unwaged £10).

The Children's Society
Edward Rudolf House, Margery Street, London WC1X 0JL (Tel: 01–837 4299).
For a general note *see* Section 15.
The Society has Community Living Units at Palmers Green and Hornsey in north London, where physically handicapped young people work towards independent living within the community.

Concord Video and Film Council Ltd
201 Felixstowe Road, Ipswich, Suffolk IP3 9BJ (Tel: Ipswich (0473) 726012).
For a general note on this company *see* Appendix A. Programmes available for hire include a considerable range and number of educational documentaries. There are many helpful films concerning the special problems of blind, deaf, mentally

handicapped and disabled children. There are 16mm films, and VHS, Betamax and V-matic cassettes for hire and sale.

Dr Barnado's
Tanners Lane, Barkingside, Ilford, Essex IG6 1QG (Tel: 01–550 8822).
Dr Barnado's is organised in divisions, *viz:*

London (above address, Tel: 01–551 0011): three residential special schools.
Yorkshire (Four Gables, Clarence Road, Horsforth, Leeds LS18 4LB, Tel: Leeds (0532) 582115): two residential special schools;
South Wales and South West (177 Newport Road, Cardiff CF2 1UD, Tel: Cardiff (0222) 485592): one residential special school; and
Scotland (235 Corstorphine Road, Edinburgh EH12 7AR, Tel: 031–334 9893): two residential special schools.

Dyslexia Institute
133 Gresham Road, Staines TW18 2AJ (Tel: Staines (0784) 59498).
A non-profit-making organisation providing professional assessment and teaching for dyslexic children and adults, an advisory service for parents and teachers and training for teachers of dyslexic children and adults. Centres have been established throughout England and in Glasgow. Write to the above address for a list of centres and services.

The Foundation for Conductive Education
University of Birmingham, PO Box 363, Birmingham B15 2TT (Tel: 021–472 1301).
This is a national charity formed at the end of 1986 to establish conductive education (CE) (*see* page 84) in the United Kingdom. Its first task is to train British 'conductors', specialist educators of motor-disordered children, to bring the science and skills of CE out of Hungary. The Foundation has signed a four-year agreement with the Peto Institute by which this training will be carried out under Hungarian direction to the same high standard as is expected of Hungarian student-conductors.

The development of CE in this country has only just begun, but the Foundation has taken the first step in setting up the *Birmingham Institute for Conductive Education*. This is situated at Bell Hill, Northfield, Birmingham B31 1LD (Tel: 021–477 0801). A group of young British teachers will undergo training to become 'conductors'. It is expected that about 30 children will attend the Institute and they will be of pre-school and primary school age, suffering from cerebral palsy, and living in the Midlands area. Teaching of adults

with Parkinson's Disease will also be undertaken. Conductor training and conductor groups will be run in close collaboration with the Peto Institute in Budapest.

Membership of The Foundation is open to parents, professionals and anyone else concerned to see CE effectively established in the United Kingdom, at £10 a year.

Home and School Council
81 Rustlings Road, Sheffield S11 7AB (Tel: Sheffield (0742) 662467).
For a general note *see* Section 15. Publications include the following books:

The Child with a Medical Problem in the Ordinary School, price 80p including postage and packing. This covers a wide range of problems, such as asthma, eczema, loss of limbs, spina bifida, partial deafness and diabetes, which may be met in an ordinary classroom situation, and offers guidance to teachers.

Children with Special Needs: a Guide for Parents, price 80p including postage and packing. This covers help for child and parents, assessment, integration, special schools, hospitals and home tuition, after 16, list of organisations and further reading.

Invalid Children's Aid Nationwide (ICAN)
Allen Graham House, 198 City Road, London EC1V 2PH (Tel: 01–608 2462).
This organisation's work (*see* Section 15) includes the provision and running of four schools:

Dawn House, Helmsley Road, Rainworth, Nottinghamshire (speech and language disorders);
John Horniman, 2 Park Road, Worthing, Sussex (speech and language disorders);
Meath, Brox Road, Ottershaw, Surrey (speech and language disorders); and
Pilgrims, Firle Road, Seaford, Sussex (seniors with severe asthma, asthma/eczema).

Children are taken from all over the United Kingdom on referral from local education authorities.
A publications list is available on request.

The Makaton Vocabulary Development Project
31 Firwood Drive, Camberley, Surrey GU15 3QD.
The Makaton Vocabulary is a language programme which provides a basic means of communication and encourages language development in children and adults who are mentally

handicapped, autistic, physically handicapped or have other communication difficulties.

Speech and signs are combined to teach the Makaton Vocabulary and, if required, symbols may also be used. The signs used in the United Kingdom are from British Sign Language. Training is given at workshops and courses throughout the United Kingdom and abroad. This provides signing instruction, background information on the Makaton Vocabulary structure and training in the specific teaching procedures which are recommended.

Professional workers are in post throughout the United Kingdom. They are available to give advice on implementation and training at a local level. A wide variety of teaching materials is available from the above address. These include: language programme manuals, line drawing illustrations, record sheets, video tapes, and picture cards. A Research Information Service is available to keep workers informed of current research in the field, and contact is maintained with researchers.

MENCAP – The Royal Society for Mentally Handicapped Children and Adults
123 Golden Lane, London EC1Y 0RT (Tel: 01–253 9433).
For a general note on the society *see* Section 15.

MIND (National Association for Mental Health)
22 Harley Street, London W1N 2ED (Tel: 01–637 0741).
For a general note *see* Section 15. MIND is active in the field of education in several ways.
(a) It does continuous campaigning work aimed at improving the educational services for both mentally ill and mentally handicapped children and adults.
(b) It has regular training courses, workshops and conferences for mental health professionals. MIND's training programmes aim to give mental health workers access to specialist skills.
(c) It runs a pioneering residential school for children with emotional problems, Feversham School, near Newcastle.

The National Autistic Society
276 Willesden Lane, London NW2 5RB (Tel: 01–451 3844).
For a general note *see* Section 15. One of the Society's primary functions is the field of education. It aims to provide and promote day and residential centres for the care and education of autistic children and adults, and to help their parents.

The Society's advisory service for parents specifically offers help with educational placement, and its information service provides a resource for professional workers on the nature of childhood autism and the type of service and teaching methods needed. It also publishes and distributes literature on the management and education of autistic children.

The Society runs six schools:

Radlett, Harper Lane, Radlett, Hertfordshire;
Dedisham, Slinfold, Horsham, Sussex;
Gulworthy, The Old Rectory, Gulworthy, nr. Tavistock, Devon;
Helen Allison, 29 The Overcliffe, Gravesend, Kent;
Storm House, 134 Barnsley Road, Wath-on-Dearne, Rotherham, South Yorkshire;
Sybil Elgar, 10 Florence Road, Ealing, London W5.

All offer residential facilities.

In addition, NAS local societies run eight schools at Nottingham, Colchester, Southampton, Southport, Sunderland, Christchurch, Alloa and Newton-le-Willows. A list of all these schools together with local authority and other independent schools for autistic children is available from the Society, price 50p.

The National Centre for Cued Speech
29/30 Watling Street, Canterbury, Kent CT1 2UD (Tel: Canterbury (0227) 450757).
Cued speech is a language tool designed for use with and amongst the deaf. It is also used to reach hearing-dyslexic children. Eight hand-shapes, used in close proximity to the lips, reflect the elements of spoken language in such a way that the observer is forced to watch the lips, thus developing oral language, clarifying lip reading and assisting speech production.

The National Centre for Cued Speech exists to advise schools, clinics, local education authorities, voluntary organisations, individuals and government on the method. It provides lectures, literature, films, visual aids and lesson materials, and organises regional conferences. It offers courses of instruction for parents, teachers and any other interested people, and group instruction to parents and staff of any school wishing to adopt cued speech techniques. A certificate of proficiency in cueing is offered in conjunction with the City Literary Institute Centre for the Deaf.

National Children's Bureau
8 Wakley Street, London EC1V 7QE (Tel: 01–278 9441).
For a general note *see* Section 15. The Bureau stocks bibliographies covering the educational implications of various forms of handicap, asthma, cerebral palsy, cardiac disorders, diabetes, haemophilia, spina bifida, orthopaedic handicaps; and Ronald Gulliford's *Helping the Handicapped Child at School* (NFER Publishing Company, 1975, price £2.25). All books can be consulted in the Bureau's library.

National Children's Home
Highbury Park, London N5 1UD (Tel: 01–226 2033).
Provides non-maintained residential schools; some with extended education units:

Crowthorn, nr. Bolton, Lancashire;
Ryalls Court, Seaton, Devon;
Bourne Place, Hildenborough, Kent;
Hilton Grange, Bramhope, Leeds;
Penhurst, Chipping Norton, Oxfordshire; and
Headlands, Penarth, South Glamorgan.

NCH operates projects for mentally handicapped children of various kinds and intermediate treatment facilities in addition to a wide range of other projects.
For further information contact Director of Social Work.

National Council for Special Education
1 Wood Street, Stratford-upon-Avon CV37 6JE (Tel: Stratford-upon-Avon (0789) 205332).
An organisation formed from the Association for Special Education, the College of Special Education, and the Guild of Teachers of Backward Children. The Council exists to further the education and welfare of all who are in any way handicapped, whether in ordinary or special schools, and whether the handicap is mental, physical, emotional or environmental. Membership consists mostly of specialist teachers in the field, but administrators, medical personnel, social workers, psychologists and therapists are also welcome. There are some 50 branches with a membership of over 4,500.
A variety of books and pamphlets is available, though these are aimed at the professional worker rather than parents.

National Deaf Children's Society
45 Hereford Road, London W2 5AH (Tel: 01–229 9272/4 – voice; 01–229 1891 – Vistel).

For a general note *see* Section 15. The Society's activities in the education field are:
(a) to provide information and advice to parents regarding educational provision in the United Kingdom;
(b) to liaise and co-ordinate with schools, special schools and units and local authorities;
(c) to provide information to general enquirers about education facilities and methods for hearing impaired children;
(d) to campaign for improvements in services, the need for which is brought to light by parents and/or education committees.

The Rathbone Society
1st Floor, Princess House, 105/107 Princess Street, Manchester M1 6DD (Tel: 061–236 5358).
For a general note *see* Section 15.
This organisation, originally founded by Elfrida Rathbone 70 years ago to help backward children in North London, is now a national society with a wide range of functions throughout the UK.
It still concentrates its support on those who are slow learners and educationally retarded, but now includes community projects, hostels and parental guidance in addition to workshop and training facilities at 17 locations in London, the Midlands, Bristol, the North West and North East regions. These concentrate on training 'slow learners' of both sexes and are having considerable success under YTS schemes in placing a high proportion of trainees in jobs that develop into regular employment.

Royal National Institute for the Blind
224–228 Great Portland Street, London W1N 6AA (Tel: 01–388 1266).
For a general note, *see* Section 15.
RNIB Education Advisers are all qualified teachers of blind children. They are based round the country and on request they will visit parents, teachers and others concerned with blind children and give practical help and advice about the future. The service covers the whole of the United Kingdom. Some young blind children, especially those with other handicaps, may need to be educated away from home. At RNIB's three Sunshine Nursery Schools the children can develop their independence and begin the first stages of their early education. They may go on to Rushton Hall (primary) near Kettering, or Condover Hall (secondary) near Shrewsbury, or RNIB schools for blind children with other physical, mental or emotional handicaps.

At RNIB's Worcester College for blind boys and girls, students study for GCSEs or 'A' levels. Most leavers go on to university, college or other professional training, for instance at RNIB's North London School of Physiotherapy. Pupils who are unsure what to do next can go to Hethersett College in Surrey, where staff will assess their aptitude and interests and suggest useful training and employment.

RNIB also provides financial help in the form of grants for purchase of books and equipment or payment of readers for students doing a higher education or degree course.

For details, contact the Education Department at the above address.

Royal National Institute for the Deaf
105 Gower Street, London WC1E 6AH (Tel: 01–387 8033).
For a general note *see* Section 15. RNID's technical departmemt has produced a variety of aids to assist the education of deaf children. These aids are marketed commercially, but details are available from RNID.

Royal Schools for the Deaf
Stanley Road, Cheadle Hulme, Cheadle, Cheshire SK8 6RF (Tel: 061–437 5951).
A non-maintained school with 52-week residential facilities for hearing impaired children with multiple handicaps, learning difficulties and behaviour problems. The school assessment centre provides an assessment and advisory service (no charge). Further education courses cover a large range of disabilities with on-site facilities for vocational training (City and Guilds courses in catering and bakery).

Scottish Epilepsy Association
48 Govan Road, Glasgow G51 1JL (Tel: 041–427 4911).
The Association's Education Department employs full-time training officers who provide training in relation to epilepsy for students and professional personnel in the fields of health, education, social work and the employment services.

Seminars, talks, film shows and discussion groups can be arranged. The Association's headquarters in Glasgow have been developed as a national resource centre for epilepsy. A wide range of educational materials is available.

Shaftesbury Society
For a general note *see* Section 15.

The Spastics Society
Education Division, 840 Brighton Road, Purley, Surrey CR2 2BH (Tel: 01–660 8552).
The Society runs eight residential schools for children of differing abilities from the ages of 5 to 8.

Rutland House, Nottingham, for severely mentally and physically disabled children who, because of the multiplicity of their disabilities, are not being provided for elsewhere.
Ingfield Manor School, Five Oaks, Billinghurst, Sussex. The school is for slow- learning children. An additional wing carries out 'conductive education' (Peto method) for 12 severely disabled children from 3 to 7 years of age. There is also a Mother and Baby Unit.
Meldreth Manor School, Meldreth, Royston, Hertfordshire, for children who are severely physically and intellectually disabled.
Beech Tree School, Preston, Lancashire, for behaviourally disturbed children.
Craig-Y-Parc, Pentyrch, Cardiff CF4 8NB. This school is for handicapped children of average intelligence.
Thomas Delarue School, Tonbridge, Kent. Handicapped pupils at this school are in the average ability range. Comprehensive education is provided and courses offered may lead to GCSE.
Hawksworth Hall, Hawksworth, Guiseley, Leeds, which has exceptional facilities for the long-term assessment of children who are so severely disabled that the level of their ability cannot be clearly determined.
Trengweath School, Plymouth, Devon, which provides education for children of differing intellectual abilities. Those within the average ability range may transfer to other schools, but secondary education for the mentally handicapped is provided here until the age of 16.

Voluntary Council for Handicapped Children
National Children's Bureau, 8 Wakley Street, London EC1V 7QE (Tel: 01–278 9441).
For a general note *see* Section 15. The Council's information services range over mental, physical, sensory and social handicap and include expert advice on educational matters. The Council's Principal Officer, Mrs. Philippa Russell, is author of *The Wheelchair Child* (revised edition, 1983), one of the most comprehensive and up-to-date works on the subject of handicapped children.

SECTION 6

FURTHER EDUCATION AND TRAINING

Not so many years ago, most disabled young people left school at 16, either to get a job, or to sit at home or in a centre, with little chance of continuing their education. Even fewer adults got a second chance to study or retrain.

Nowadays, the chances of any disabled young person getting a job straight from school are considerably lessened, but so too are the many barriers to full participation in further education and training. A survey, published in 1987 by the National Bureau for Handicapped Students (now the National Bureau for Students with Disabilities) showed that in that year as many as 55,000 disabled young people and adults benefited from opportunities in further and higher education. The courses attended covered a very wide range indeed, and two-thirds of all colleges had disabled students enrolled.

The survey also unfortunately showed that, despite the rapid advances made, very few colleges could offer a *full* range of courses to all disabled people, and in many parts of the country there were still colleges who were unwilling or unable to help. Our advice to any disabled person thinking of going to college is ask, and don't take 'no' for an answer too readily.

Training Commission

The government training and employment services, formerly under the Manpower Services Commission, are now separated. Jobcentres and their related services became part of the Department of Employment in October 1987. In 1988, the national training authority became known as the Training Commission (TC).

Opportunities available

Below we describe some of the opportunities available, and also some of the sources of help and advice if you come up against any difficulties. We hope that the information provided in this section of the Directory will help young people and their parents to take advantage of the further education and also higher education opportunities which

may suit their own individual needs and aspirations.

Where to study or train?

Just as any other student, disabled people – young and those who are older – are to be found in a wide variety of education and training establishments.

Schools

Most schools offer the chance to stay on until 18 or 19 years of age, particularly if the young person is sitting examinations. Many special schools also let their pupils remain beyond 16, especially when they feel they will benefit from the opportunity to catch up on education missed, although many now see a benefit in their senior pupils leaving for the more adult atmosphere of a further education college. Often schools and colleges work together to develop a *link course*, which allows pupils to attend college one day a week to try out college subjects. While at school the statement of special educational need (see Section 5) has to be maintained by the local education authority who should, in any event, have reviewed and updated the statement when the young person reached 14½ years old. From 1990 onwards the education authority will also have the duty of informing the local social services department when a disabled person is about to leave full-time education. Even before 1990, many education authorities may want to help in this way.

Further Education Colleges

There are more than 400 further education colleges throughout the country, often called colleges of technology or 'tech' colleges. Most disabled students are to be found in these colleges, some on special courses, others studying and training alongside the 1 million or so 'able-bodied' students. Among the different types of course that may be on offer are the following.

Full-time special courses

The majority of further education or tech colleges

now put on special courses, mainly designed for young people with moderate or severe learning difficulties, which emphasise building up confidence, basic skills, and perhaps also some vocational skills. Some specially designed courses may also be found for young people who are deaf, or have a visual or physical handicap, and who need a period on a special course catching up on education missed.

Part-time special courses
In addition to full-time courses (which are mainly, though not exclusively for 16–19 year olds), many local colleges also put on a variety of part-time special courses. We have already mentioned the link courses some colleges have developed with local schools. Some colleges have also built up links with local day centres or social education centres. In some instances 'residents' visit the college once or twice a week; in other instances teaching staff from the college travel to the centre. These link courses, and other part-time courses, can offer anything from pottery to cookery, from computing or adult literacy to special courses in lip-reading or use of Braille. No college will offer the full range of all courses, but most will offer some.

'Ordinary courses'
Further education colleges have traditionally offered a range of 'vocational' courses such as hairdressing, engineering, business and office studies, horticulture, catering etc. To this list of courses (which often depends on local employment needs), and a range of GCSE courses, further education colleges have recently added a number of more general 'pre-vocational' courses. These latter courses, which have names such as the 'Certificate of Pre-Vocational Initiative (CPVE), or the Technical and Vocational Education Initiative (TVEI), offer the opportunity to young people who have not yet decided on a career, a chance to try out a number of different skills, while also improving their basic skills of literacy, communication etc. Disabled people are to be found on all of these courses, though again the willingness and ability of a college to accept a disabled person will vary from town to town.

In their report on college provision, the National Bureau for Handicapped Students record the provision available at one college of further education (Tameside College of Technology). Unfortunately, the survey also shows that, as yet, very few other colleges have the same level of provision. None the less, it does show what colleges may provide both in specialised courses and in help to disabled students on ordinary courses.

Specialist course provision includes:
1. Education for Work course – designed to help school leavers from special schools and remedial classes who would find it difficult to obtain and keep their first jobs because their literacy and numeracy skills are not good enough for them to cope. This is a 2-year course.
2. Education for Work – follow-on programme.
3. Education for Living Course – intended for those with severe physical handicaps with delayed learning/maturity.
4. Springboard link course – for young people from schools for moderate learning difficulties and remedial departments.
5. Learning for Living course – for students with more severe learning difficulties.
6. Department of Adult Education classes include: Braille course; typing for blind people; cookery for blind people; sign language course; crafts for blind people; computing for blind people; crafts for physically handicapped people; improving English for people who are partially hearing; and crafts for mentally handicapped people.
7. 'Special' Pre-retirement courses.
8. Literacy and numeracy classes at a 'MIND' centre.
9. Training workshop and other special YTS courses.

It should be remembered that this is only one example of a local college. Information on what is available in your local college is usually available from the college 'special needs co-ordinator', specialist careers officer or from the National Bureau for Students with Disabilities (*see* page 101).

Residential Colleges

Long before most further education colleges made any provision for disabled people, a number of residential special colleges were set up – often by voluntary organisations like MENCAP or The Spastics Society. Still today they offer an opportunity to study or train away from home and chances for many, particularly severely disabled people, not available in their local college. Some particularly emphasise vocational training and are described in more detail below under the heading 'Residential Training Colleges'. Others offer a more general education, often coupled with a period of assessment to determine future goals, and an emphasis on encouraging personal independence. Fees at all of these colleges are high, and almost all students are sponsored by their local authorities. More than 100 such residential colleges are listed in *COPE – A Compendium of Post–16 Residential Establishments*, published by and available from Wiltshire Careers Service, (*see* page 104). The advice of a specialist careers officer (see below) should be sought if a residential college place is being considered.

Residential training colleges

As is the case with further education, *most* disabled people undergo training in ordinary training establishments (see below). However, for those who, for one reason or another, require special provision, four residential training establishments have been set up by the Manpower Services Commission (now Training Commission) which cater for people with all types of disabilities except blindness in the 16–58 age range. These are independent voluntary organisations and are located in rural surroundings at Durham, Mansfield, Leatherhead, and Exeter. Courses are aimed at preparing disabled people for ordinary employment in industry or commerce. Courses can last from 8–52 weeks and subjects are similar to those in non-residential establishments. Training is based on a normal five day working week. Each college has residential nursing staff. The cost of training and accommodation is met by the TC. In addition, students receive a training allowance and free travel warrants are issued for certain journeys to and from home. Further information is contained in leaflet ATL64 *Willing and Able*, obtainable from Jobcentres.

Training for blind people

Residential courses for computer programmers and for commercial employment in shorthand and typing, audio typing and telephony are available at the Royal National Institute for the Blind Commercial College in London. Similar course facilities, excluding computer programming, exist for people living in Scotland at the Royal Blind School, Edinburgh. The RNIB North London School of Physiotherapy has a three-year residential course leading to the qualifying examinations of the Chartered Society of Physiotherapy. Training of piano tuners, on courses lasting two years or more, is available at the London College of Furniture and the Royal National College for the Blind.

Queen Alexandra College in Birmingham runs a two-year course in machine operating and inspection, and one on bicycle repair. The Letchworth Skillcentre (Employment Service) provides introductory courses in light engineering, machine operating, repetitive assembly and inspection training for blind people. Hostel accommodation is provided. The Employment Service also works with the Royal National Institute for the Blind.

Training opportunities

Apart from the residential training opportunities listed above, there are other training schemes available – in most cases locally – which may suit the needs of many disabled people. These, together with many of the employment schemes (*see* Section 7) are organised by the Department of Employment.

YOUTH TRAINING SCHEME

The YTS is a programme of vocational training, education and work experience intended to bridge the gap betwen school or further education and the world of work. It offers all eligible young people an integrated programme of training and planned work experience with the opportunity to gain vocational qualifications or a credit towards one. For young people with disabilities, including moderate or severe learning difficulties, a range of special help is available to enable them to take advantage of the opportunities offered.

1. Eligibility criteria have been relaxed to enable these young people to remain in full-time education up to the age of 21 without losing entitlement to two years of training.
2. There is an extension of training by up to 6 months if necessary to enhance employment prospects.
3. Assessment courses lasting up to 13 weeks (included in the 6 month extension of training) are placed either before or during a programme.
4. There is additional 'premium' funding to finance higher staffing ratios for tuition/supervision/counselling.
5. Permanent Additional Funding for the Disabled (PAFD) covers the extra costs of providing individualised training programmes for young disabled people.
6. An Adaptation to Premises and Equipment scheme (APE), provides a contribution towards the cost of alterations to accommodate young disabled people.

7. A Special Aids to Employment scheme (SAE), provides long-term loans of specialised equipment.

8. A Personal Reader Service is available for the Blind (PRSB).

9. There is a Communications Service for the Deaf (CSD).

10. A Residential Training Allowance covers the additional costs of specialised accommodation and medical supervision if young people need this extra care during training.

For young people unable to join ordinary schemes, places are available on schemes specialising in training people with disabilities.

Trainees on YTS receive a training allowance of £28.50 in the first year and £35 in the second year of YTS. Travel costs over £3 per week are paid. Young people with disabilities may also claim the cost of taxi fares. Further details of the Scheme can be obtained from any Careers Office and from Specialist Careers Officers in particular. The National Bureau for Students with Disabilities can also offer advice.

INFORMATION TECHNOLOGY CENTRES

ITeCs, part of YTS, offer basic training in electronics, microcomputing and the electronic office. The same eligibility rules apply as in YTS, including the special help offered to disabled young people. Details of these centres are available as for YTS above.

JOB TRAINING SCHEME

This Scheme, introduced in 1985 to replace the old Training Opportunities Scheme, offers opportunities for unemployed adults – including disabled adults – to update their existing skills or learn new ones leading to a recognised qualification or a credit towards one. It is open to people aged 18 and over signing as unemployed at an Unemployment Benefit Office for at least the last six months, with priority given to those under 25. Courses are run throughout the country in a wide range of skills including office or craft skills, computing, and basic skills training for a large range of industries. Trainees receive a training allowance equivalent to their benefit entitlement (plus travelling expenses) and continue to receive linked benefits such as free dental and optical treatment and housing benefit. There is also provision for aids to employment, adaptations to premises, a communicator service for deaf people and a personal reader service for those who are visually impaired. Further information about the scheme is in the leaflet *The New*

Job Training Scheme: How it can work for you (JTL5) available from your local Jobcentre or Restart Counsellor.

ADULT TRAINING

The TC provides occupational training for people with disabilities on a wide range of courses. These are held at local colleges, TC's own skillcentres, private training establishments, universities, and polytechnics throughout Great Britain and may last up to 12 months. Courses are free and training allowances may be payable. Details of all aspects of occupational training can be obtained from the Disablement Resettlement Officer at the local Jobcentre.

The Community Programme

This new government programme is to operate from September 1988. It is intended to provide training and practical experience with employers and on projects for people who are unemployed. The emphasis is on practical learning to help people to get back into employment. Accordingly the training will range from basic working skills, including numeracy and literacy, to training at craft and technician level. It is for those people between 18 and 24 who have been unemployed for more than six months and for those people under 50 who have been unemployed for longer than two years. However, disabled people will be eligible to join whatever their length of time of unemployment.

Each individual will have a personal action plan either from the Approved Training Agent or the Training Manager. Each action plan will contain objectives for the individual covering, for example, basic skills or generic competencies, development of motivation and personal effectiveness, training in occupational skills and training in job search. Each individual will be entitled, if he or she wishes, to stay up to 12 months in the programme.

Disabled people will be encouraged to work alongside able bodied people and will be given a range of special help. Aids and equipment for themselves and the employer will be available as described in Section 7. The services of a communicator will be available to those who are hearing impaired, and readers will be available to those who are visually impaired.

Every trainee in the programme will receive a payment of £10 more than his or her weekly benefit entitlement except for those on Income Support who will be entitled to a higher payment. It remains to be seen how the programme works out in practice.

For further details contact your local Disablement Resettlement Officer at the Jobcentre.

Under the TC's Old Job Training Scheme (OJTS) and Wider Opportunities Training Programme (WOTP) eligibility rules may be relaxed for people with disabilities. This means that among other concessions, people with disabilities may be eligible for more than a year's training in a 3-year period. The following specialist provision is available to people with disabilities in OJTS.

Individual Training Throughout with an Employer (ITTWE)
This scheme allows people with disabilities to retrain on an individual basis with an employer and aims to provide training skill or semi-skill which is transferable from one place of employment to another. The training programme normally lasts from four weeks to twelve months, but longer periods can be considered. An employer must undertake to employ a trainee for a period of at least six months after the training period. Whilst training, the trainee receives either wages or JTS allowance.

Release for Training (RFT)
Under RFT, TC support can be provided for disabled people who are already in employment but who are experiencing difficulties which can only be resolved by a period of essential training. Throughout the training period, the employer must continue to pay wages to the employee.

Professional Training Scheme (PTS)
People with disabilities and of suitable ability may receive help under the PTS to meet the cost of courses of higher level study, including university degree courses, for employment at a professional level. The scheme is meant as a back up provision for people with disabilities unable to get a local education authority (LEA) grant. One of the criteria for support under PTS is that applicants have a letter of rejection from their LEA. Under PTS, TC pays a grant based on the rate laid down by the Department of Education and Science. Part funding can be considered. Applications are taken by Disablement Resettlement Officers in Jobcentres.

Higher education

With a few notable exceptions universities, poly-technics and institutes of higher education have not managed to increase their numbers of disabled students over the years, in part perhaps because few are willing to depart very far from entry requirements which stress past achievement in formal examinations rather than a person's potential. Having said that, most higher education establishments are much more attuned to the needs of students with disabilities, and provide some services. A few provide specialist accommodation (*see* Accommodation below); others have their own or share services for deaf people; still others have available a stock of specialist equipment. The National Bureau for Students with Disabilities keeps information on all higher education establishments, and also runs 'Transition to higher education' short courses for people hoping to go on to university or polytechnic.

Adult education

Adult education is provided from a number of different sources, and varies from area to area. Further education colleges, adult education institutes, university extra-mural departments, the Open University and the Open College, and local voluntary organisations are all potential providers in the field, offering a wide range of subjects for study or recreation.

Provision is patchy, but in many parts of the country there are innovative schemes to encourage participation in adult education by adults with disabilities, and some local education authorities and colleges have appointed a member of staff to the role of adult education special needs co-ordinator.

For further information contact your local education authority (LEA) adult education service, or the advisor for adult education special needs in the LEA or college for initial advice about courses, access to buildings, transport, etc.
There are four types of provision:
1. Mainstream
   Many adults with disabilities will be able to participate in mainstream classes if access is suitable. Potential students are advised to contact their local college or adult education institute, or their local education authority, to discuss any special needs they may have.
2. Special courses
   Some adult education providers offer courses specifically with disabled people in mind, often across a wide range of courses, e.g. special computing courses, pottery, art or dressmaking, drama, etc. Sometimes college

lecturers will hold these classes also in day centres, or adult training centres.

3. Integrated

In some areas schemes exist to aid the integration of disabled and able-bodied students. Some local education authorities, for example, operate a scheme pairing a student with a learning difficulty with a volunteer who attends an adult education class alongside, on a regular basis, to provide support.

4. Home Study

Home study is an option for disabled people for whom travel into an adult education centre is difficult or impossible. Several alternatives exist including: Flexi–study: whereby learning takes place at the student's own pace, and at times negotiated between the student and tutor; and Distance learning – some colleges operate distance learning schemes which allow students to study principally at home, with the possibility of tutorials and peer-group meetings at the local college or study centre. Many of these now run in conjunction with the Open College. *See* information on the Open College and the Open University below.

Home study

The Open University

Open University courses are specifically designed for home-based study. Courses are offered in arts, educational studies, mathematics, science, social sciences and technology. No entry qualifications are required and the University is open to all over the age of 18 who are resident in Britain. Entry is on a 'first come first served' basis; hence early application is advisable, but applications from disabled people may receive special consideration.

The main element of study is the specially written course material. In addition, courses may utilise television and radio, records and tape cassettes, slides and home experiment kits. Though study at home is the basis of Open University study there are opportunities for tuition and group discussions at local study centres. Tuition and counselling are also carried out by telephone or letter. Many courses run week-long residential summer schools at conventional university campuses. If need demands, disabled people may take a personal assistant, or the summer school's office will find such a helper. This will incur no extra cost for the student. In certain circumstances students may be excused summer school attendance.

The United Kingdom is divided into 13 regions, and within these regions there is a member of staff with an interest in and responsibility for disabled students. All students are appointed a tutor counsellor in their first year of study, who also remains a contact person in subsequent years of study. Tuition at higher course levels is undertaken by course tutors.

The Open University provides certain advice and services specifically to meet the needs of disabled students. These include: assistance at summer schools; cassette tapes of course material for those unable to deal with written text; transcripts of broadcasts; study weekends for persons with particular handicaps; advice on the accessibility of courses to those with specific disabilities and advice on study techniques. These services come from different areas within the University and there is an Adviser on the Education of Disabled Students to advise and liaise with these departments and outside bodies.

If you would like further information about admission and registration for undergraduate courses write to: The Undergraduate Admissions Officer, the Open University, PO Box 48, Milton Keynes MK7 6AB. For further information on admission and registration for associate student courses write to the Open University, PO Box 76, Milton Keynes MK7 6AN. You can contact The Open University Adviser to Disabled Students at: the Open University, Walton Hall, Milton Keynes MK7 6AA (Tel: Milton Keynes (0908) 653442).

OU financial help – grants and awards

In the first instance, local authorities' social services departments or local education authorities should be approached for financial assistance relating to: preparatory studies; tuition fees; kit deposits; set books; summer school attendance; summer school assistant's travelling expenses; or travel to tutorials.

Those handicapped students who belong to an organisation related to a particular disability may find they can apply for assistance with fees. In the event of an undergraduate being unsuccessful with an application for funds from the local education authority then he or she may apply to the Open University Financial Assistance Fund for a grant or a loan.

The Open University Students' Association (OUSA)

PO Box 397, Walton Hall, Milton Keynes MK7 6BE (Tel: Milton Keynes (0908) 653351).
The Association offers many facilities and a back-up service for disabled students, including recruit-

ing helpers for those who need assistance at summer schools.

There is a regionally operated welfare scheme with a representative in each region who will be available for anyone (disabled or able-bodied) with problems, to contact.

In addition, the Open University Students' Association has a Trust Fund, which is designed to assist disadvantaged students of the University. Applications for aid should be addressed to the Secretary for the Trust, at the central office address given above.

Among the many societies organised by OU students, there is OUMPAS (the OU Mixed Physical Ability Society). This society is made up of about half handicapped students and half able-bodied students. They organise social events, visits to museums and study weekends in different parts of the country.

The Open College
Freepost, PO Box 35, Abingdon, OX14 3BR (Tel: Abingdon (0235) 555444).
The Open College represents a new national approach to skills training with the emphasis on learning rather than teaching. It increases opportunities for vocational education and training by making open learning readily available. Courses are made up of television and radio programmes, videos, audio tapes, workbooks and other learning materials with advice and tutorial support available if required through a network of local centres. The training aims to be responsive and flexible, designed to meet the needs of employers and individuals.

More detailed information about how the College operates is contained in its prospectus *The Open Book*. As well as describing the courses available *The Open Book* offers guidance on prices, where help can be obtained and which qualifications or credits courses lead to.

National Extension College, Cambridge (NEC)
This is a non-profit-making educational trust founded to provide adults with high-quality home study courses. It provides correspondence courses for Open University preparatory and GCSE and 'A' levels, as well as special interest courses. It also provides a correspondence tuition service for London University external degrees and diplomas and for certain professional examinations. For further information apply to National Extension College, 18 Brooklands Avenue, Cambridge CB2 2HN (Tel: Cambridge (0223) 316644).

Grants for NEC courses
Most handicapped students studying with NEC get grants from their local education authorities. Before applying for a grant for an NEC course it is advisable to contact the Head of Student Services at NEC for advice on how to phrase the application.

Education and Training Bureau
RADAR, 25 Mortimer Street, London W1N 8AB (Tel: 01–637 5400).
The aim of the Bureau is to provide education and training opportunities for people who, because of their disabilities, are unable to take advantage of the normal further education facilities. The Bureau can provide financial assistance for correspondence courses (from colleges which are approved by the Council for the Accreditation of Correspondence Colleges) and also arranges home tuition for people living in the Inner London Education Authority area. Similar services are administered by the Midlands Council for the Preparatory Training of the Disabled and the Scottish Council for the Tuition of the Disabled in their regions. Anyone who is physically handicapped and over the age of 16 is eligible to apply for assistance from the Bureau. Courses are generally in basic English and mathematics but a wide range of other subjects can be studied. In some instances courses are taken with the view to assisting people to find employment; others are taken for their therapeutic value. A Disablement Resettlement Officer (DRO) or other professional is usually required to support applications.

Further details and application forms may be obtained from RADAR. Enquiries from the Midlands should be sent to Mrs R. Wolf, The Midlands Council for Preparatory Training of the Disabled, 14 Barlows Road, Edgbaston, Birmingham B15 2PL, and enquiries from Scotland should be sent to The Scottish Council for the Tuition of the Disabled, Edinburgh University Settlement, Student Centre, Bristo Street, Edinburgh EH8 9AL.

Scottish Centre for the Tuition of the Disabled
Queen Margaret College, Clerwood Terrace, Edinburgh EH12 8TS (Tel: 031–339 5408).
The SCTD is a voluntary organisation which provides information and advice about educational opportunities to adults with disabilities. It also provides a home teaching service using volunteers.

The aim of the Centre is to encourage and enable the integration of adults with disabilities into existing educational provision. However, the Centre recognises that this is not always possible or appropriate and that many disabled adults are cut off for various reasons from education and leisure facilities. For these students the Centre's volunteer organisers, based in the regions, find voluntary tutors to work on a one-to-one basis, usually in the student's home.

Help is given in a wide variety of activities: academic studies, learning new skills or crafts, developing new interests together. In particular, students who are actually following a course of study at an educational institution by part- or full-time attendance or through open learning schemes can receive additional support from a voluntary tutor if they need it. The help given is free and can be for a short or a long time depending on the student's needs and the volunteer's commitment.

Tape and Braille courses

A wide variety of correspondence courses is offered on cassette or in Braille by a correspondence school for the blind in the United States. Courses are free of charge to blind students all over the world. Details from the Hadley School for the Blind, 700 Elm Street, Winnetka, Illinois 60093, USA.

Financial Help Available

GRANTS

Certain awards are mandatory, that is they are made under statutory regulations and, provided certain conditions are met, an award is automatic. The following courses attract mandatory awards: degree and courses prescribed as equivalent to degree; initial teacher training; Diploma in Higher Education; the Higher National Diploma or the Higher National Diploma of the Business and Technician. To be eligible for these awards students must have been ordinarily resident in the United Kingdom for the three years before 1 September of the year their course begins. In addition, students must not have attended certain courses in the past.

The main rate of grant (1987/8) for students living away from home in London is £2,330, for students living away from home other than in London £1,972 and for students living at home £1,567. Additional allowances may be paid in respect of travel (some disabled students have heavy travel costs which can be met in this way), additional weeks of study, dependants and, in the case of students aged 26 or over, a mature student's allowance. These awards are normally means-tested on parental income unless the stu-

dent is independent, i.e. over 25 or has supported her/himself out of earnings.

Special Allowance for Disabled Students
The extra allowance for disabled students in 1987/8 is a maximum of £700 per annum and Local Education Authorities are empowered by the Secretary of State for Education and Science to pay up to this amount to any of their award-holding students who are disabled. The statutory instrument relating to this provision reads: 'In the case of a disabled student where the authority are satisfied that by reason of her/his disability s/he is obliged to incur additional expenditure in respect of her/his attendance at the course . . . such expenditure shall be such amount as the authority considers appropriate not exceeding £700.' It is a disabled student's right to claim this grant if s/he incurs extra financial costs as a result of disability. These costs may relate to such items as tape recorders for blind students, extra heating and dietary needs in certain circumstances, use of readers and amanuenses and other extra aids.

Income Support
See Section 2.

RNIB grants
The RNIB will make grants for students taking O and A level courses. Grants are also available for full-time degree, OND, HND, and teacher training courses as well as for those taking higher degrees, PGCE and post-graduate qualifications. The RNIB will also make grants to students taking OU degree courses.

Further information from RNIB Education Department, 224 Great Portland Street, London W1N 6AA (Tel: 01–388 1266).

Educational Grants Advisory Service
Family Welfare Asssociation, 501–505 Kingsland Road, London E8 4AU.
EGAS endeavours to put students in touch with sources of charitable and other help. Where required and possible, it also advises students in their negotiations with local education authorities and other official bodies. Enquiries should be in writing. Priority is given to referrals from members of the service.

Snowdon Award Scheme
The awards are designed to help physically disabled young people (this includes deafness and blindness) take up the offer of a course of further education or training.

Each award is for a period of one or two years,

and awards are not normally more than £1,500 a year in value. To be eligible, you should be at least 17 and preferably under 25, although somewhat older applicants may be considered under special circumstances. You must have been offered further education or training, and be able to show that financial difficulties and the problems of disability mean you will have difficulty taking advantage of the offer of a place.

The Snowdon Award Scheme is not designed to be a replacement for grants which should be claimed from Local Education Authorities. It is a scheme of 'last resort' for students who have tried everywhere else for help but have been unsuccessful.

Application forms are available from: The Snowdon Award Secretary, The National Fund for Research into Crippling Diseases, Vincent House, North Parade, Horsham, West Sussex RH12 2DA Tel: Horsham (0403) 64101.

Concerned Micros in Education and Training (COMET)
This scheme, administered by the National Bureau for Students with Disabilities, offers bursaries to people undergoing a course of further education or training, to enable them to purchase micro-computing equipment. Further details are available from the Bureau.

Professional training scheme for disabled people
Disabled people with the necessary educational qualifications but unable to obtain a local education authority grant (or an appropriate award if at post-graduate level) may be eligible for a grant from the Training Commission for an approved course which is likely to lead to professional work. Further details on this scheme are available from Jobcentres or the National Bureau for Students with Disabilities.

TRAVEL COSTS
It may be possible to receive an award from the local education authority, but such awards are discretionary in the light of all relevant circumstances. However, all necessary costs must be reimbursed. In the case of a disabled student, it may be possible for a claim to be supported by a social worker, and the National Bureau for Students with Disabilities (*see* below) may also make representations on a student's behalf. In some areas, the social services department of the local authority may be prepared to help.

Railcards
Anyone who is under 24 years of age at the time of purchase of the Young Person's Railcard or a student of any age who is in full-time education for over 15 hours weekly and for at least 20 weeks in a year, can buy this Railcard costing £12 and covering a 12 months period.

Severely disabled people may qualify for the Disabled Person's Railcard for the same price. For those who do qualify, the Disabled Person's Railcard can be a better buy because it also allows an accompanying adult to travel at the same reduced fare. For further details see page 149.

Accommodation

As a rule most students in further education and technical colleges live at home, while most students in higher education (universities, polytechnics, institutes of higher education), live away from home. Consequently, accommodation is much more easily found in higher education, and many establishments have accommodation specifically reserved and sometimes adapted for disabled students. At university level, for example, the universities of Essex, Sussex, and Southampton have purpose-built units. The Oxford Hostel for Disabled Students (Taylor House, 16 Osler Road, Headington, Oxford (Tel: Oxford (0865) 66322)), offers accommodation, domestic and medical assistance to students with severe physical disabilities enrolled at any of Oxford's many places of further or higher education.

Bridgend College of Technology also has a residential unit catering for up to 28 physically handicapped students, in order that they may attend an appropriate course of further education. The hostel is fully staffed and supplemented by specialist support services. Elsewhere about another two dozen further education colleges have some residential accommodation specially adapted for disabled students. Further information on accommodation is available from the National Bureau for Students with Disabilities.

Help with personal care

District nurse
Some students manage by arranging for the district nursing service to come in on a regular basis. A nurse may help, for instance, with taking baths, with getting up or going to bed, or with any medical requirements. District nurses will also be able to advise on borrowing equipment such as ripple mattresses, incontinence aids, etc. They could provide details of possible help with laundry.

It would be important to discuss your needs with the college medical staff to see whether this form of help would be sufficient to help you study independently.

Living-in helper
This degree of help may be provided by a Community Service Volunteer or by a private-care helper. We give details of the CSV Independent Living Scheme in Section 4.

Some students may have sufficient funds to employ a private-care helper. This option can be very expensive indeed and involves the student in finding and appointing the helper and being completely responsible for all the arrangements surrounding the appointment.

Examination arrangements

Arrangements may be made for disabled students taking examinations on the understanding that they compensate for the purely practical restrictions imposed by a handicap. Additional time may be needed. You may require an amanuensis to copy what you dictate which will also necessitate a separate room in which to take the examination plus an extra invigilator. If you are unsure of the practical arrangements needed, it would be useful to have a trial run using an old examination paper. This would also provide very practical guidance for your tutors.

The National Bureau for Students with Disabilities would be glad to advise. For those who are visually impaired, the Bureau together with the RNIB have produced guidance notes for students and staff entitled *Blind and Partially Sighted Students in College*, including information on examination concessions (details on page 106).

For those who are hearing impaired the National Association for Tertiary Education for the Deaf produces information on examination concessions made by the various examining boards for the pre-lingually hearing impaired. For details *see* page 101.

Helpful Services

College 'special needs co-ordinator'
Most colleges of further education, universities, polytechnics and institutes of higher education now have a staff member designated as 'special needs co-ordinator' or 'adviser to disabled students'. This person should not only be able to advise on services available in their college, but should also know of other local courses.

Specialist careers officers for the handicapped
These officers can provide a valuable link between a student seeking to continue her/his education and all the various bodies who can help in these endeavours. They may often help by advising on any grants available and how to approach social services with requests for financial help, say to fund the costs of having a personal care helper.

Disablement resettlement officers
For details *see* Section 7.

NBSD regional organisers
The National Bureau for Students with Disabilities has a network of regional groups, each with a designated honorary regional organiser who should be able to help with local information and contacts. For local addresses contact the Bureau's national office – *see* page 101.

Helpful Organisations and Services

Students are recommended to contact any organisation which exists specifically to cater for their particular handicap. As well as advising, such bodies may be able to help with fees and the cost of necessary special equipment. For tape-recording equipment and services *see* Section 14.

The Armchair Book Service
The Cleuch, Twynholm, Kirkcudbright, Scotland DG6 4SD (Tel: Twynholm (055 76) 215).
This is a personal book service for customers in the United Kingdom and overseas who do not have access to a good bookshop. The main business is in new rather than second-hand books, but any available book can be supplied to order. The service operates six days a week by mail order only. Telephone enquiries are welcome at any reasonable hour, including the cheap period after 6 p.m. Monday to Friday and all day on Saturday.

Association of Disabled Professionals
The Stables, 73 Pound Road, Banstead, Surrey SM7 2HU (Tel: Burgh Heath (0737) 352366. The Association exists to secure improvements and to provide advice on educational and employment opportunities for disabled people. Membership fee is £6 per annum and £2 for disabled students. There is an occasional newsletter and a quarterly house bulletin.

CRYPT
The CRYPT Foundation, Forum Workspace, Stirling Road, Chichester, West Sussex PO19 2EN (Tel: Bracklesham Bay (0243) 786064/670000). Creative Young People Together (CRYPT) is a

charitable trust which sets out to help young people with disabilities develop their creative talents. The Trust aims to equip group homes for young people and helpers will be appointed for the special needs arising from disability. Tutors to further the creative work may visit but students will be encouraged to join ongoing classes in the community. Currently there are three projects in Bracklesham, West Sussex; Newham, London; and Nottingham.

Detaf – Disabled People's Employment and Training Action Fund

The National Council for Voluntary Organisations has launched a fund to help disabled people to take action to promote employment and training opportunities. Grants are made to groups promoted and managed by disabled people to enable them to initiate local action in this area. All project budgets must fall within an upper cash limit of £1,000 as far as the bid to the Fund is concerned. Details are available from Detaf, Employment Unit, NCVO, 16 Bedford Square, London WC1B 3HU.

Disabled Living Foundation

380–384 Harrow Road, London W9 2HU (Tel: 01–289 6111).
Provides a general information service on aids and equipment for disabled people (*see* Section 3). Details of specific aids will be supplied on request. The Foundation also publishes an information leaflet on tertiary education for people with physical disabilities.

The Library Association

7 Ridgmount Street, London WC1E 7AE (Tel: 01–636 7543).
A leaflet *Can't See To Read?* has been prepared for visually handicapped people and others with reading problems. It provides information on the publishers of large print books, talking newspapers, and reading aids of all kinds. For a free copy send s.a.e. (minimum 9 in × 12½ in) to Ann Hobart at the above address.

National Association for Tertiary Education for the Deaf

c/o Rene Zannetlou, NATED Secretary, Shirecliffe College, Shirecliffe Road, Sheffield S5 8XZ.
NATED exists to promote post–16 education of all kinds for hearing-impaired people. This may be on full-time or part-time courses in further education colleges, in institutes of higher education, within adult education, on extended education and bridging courses, on YTS courses, or on other similar schemes.

NATED has a range of publications including details of examination concessions, information of educational provision, as well as advisory notes for hearing-impaired students and for lecturers.

NATSPEC

Derwen College for the Disabled, Oswestry SY11 3JA (Tel: Oswestry (0691) 661234).
NATSPEC is an Association of National Residential Specialist Colleges formed in 1983 in an attempt to bring together many of the problems that relate to individual colleges and to be able to deal with those problems that it was considered should be dealt with as a body rather than individually.

NATSPEC is very happy to consider applications from prospective students through local authorities, and the colleges pass on information between themselves where they feel that the specific college approached is not the ideal one for that particular individual. However, NATSPEC does not have a common 'sorting house' because they feel it is better for individual colleges to be approached direct.

National Bureau for Students with Disabilities

336 Brixton Road, London SW9 7AA (Tel: 01–274 0565).
NBSD is a national voluntary organisation developing opportunities in further, higher, and adult education and training throughout the United Kingdom. It is concerned with the special educational needs of students who have physical and sensory disabilities, learning difficulties or emotional problems.

NBSD offers the following services:
(a) information service for students, staff, and parents;
(b) publications on aspects of provision;
(c) research on a range of topics;
(d) monitoring local and national provision through working parties;
(e) staff development through advice and training opportunities such as conferences, workshops, and services.

A network of 14 regional groups support members in all areas of the United Kingdom through meetings, newsletters, and other locally directed activities.

Membership to NBSD is open to: local authorities; education and training bodies; student unions; professional and voluntary bodies; and individuals who have an interest in the work of NBSD.

The Bureau publishes a journal *Educare* which aims to cover any subject which facilitates and enhances the teaching, learning, and work experience of students with special educational needs.

Rehabilitation – Great Britain (The Rehabilitation Trust of Great Britain)
PO Box 23, Hailsham, Sussex.
Rehab's objectives are to advance study, teaching and research in the rehabilitation of disabled people. They operate a personal tuition service to help individuals who need extra coaching in academic or vocational training subjects, particularly where such help should lead to employment opportunities.

Rehab (GB) has founded the Institute of Agricultural Medicine and Rehabilitation in order to concentrate more fully upon the needs of the rural worker.

Disabled Students' Committee
National Union of Students, Nelson Mandela House, 461 Holloway Road, London N7 6LJ (Tel: 01–272 8900).
Publishes a *Disabilities Pack: It's Our College Too!* (jointly with Student Community Action) with sections on positive images, awareness training, accessibility campaigns, disabled students and financial benefits, and legislation. Price: £1.50 including postage and packing.

Also publishes the annual *Welfare Manual*, with a chapter on disabled students, covering grants, allowances for disabled students, charitable trusts and training opportunities. Price: £10 including postage and packing.

Royal National Institute for the Deaf
105 Gower Street, London WC1E 6AH (Tel: 01–387 8033).
RNID has a list of further education courses for deaf people.

The Spastics Society – Careers Advisory Service
The White Building, Fitzalan Square, Sheffield S1 2AY (Tel: Sheffield (0742) 753411).
A small team of careers advisory officers, working in liaison with local authority careers officers, helps many adolescents with cerebral palsy to plan their future after leaving school, giving advice and information about further education, training and employment. The careers advisory officers also organise residential vocational assessment courses where young people can test out their abilities and interests in a relaxed friendly setting over a period of five days. Enquiries should be made to the Senior Careers Advisory Officer.

Services for blind people

RNIB
Braille House, 338/346 Goswell Road, London EC1V 7JE (Tel: 01–837 9921/278 9611 and 24-hour direct order line 01–278 9615).
If you use tape or braille, it is useful to know about RNIB's Customer Service department. They will provide material for your studies as well as for work, hobbies or general reading.

RNIB offer the following services:
(a) Full up-to-date details of what is available covering not only RNIB but also other UK producers and overseas sources.
(b) Tape recording and Braille transcription services to produce for you items which are not already available. There are no restrictions on the requests you can make – any kind or quantity of material is accepted subject to availability of resources.
(c) Mini-catalogues covering popular topics such as cookery, hymn books, computers and health. All are free in Braille or print.
(d) A 24-hour, direct order telephone service.

Can I Get It On Tape or In Braille at College. Students will find this RNIB leaflet useful; it suggests ways in which RNIB can help with your reading list. As a student you can borrow as many books from RNIB libraries as you need, and keep them as long as necessary. They will record or braille as much material for you as possible – there is no rationing system, each request is dealt with according to capacity available at the time, not the number of requests you have previously made.

RNIB can also arrange to borrow books for you from overseas libraries. This is particularly useful for language students.

If you need something urgently, but are able to wait a couple of weeks, you can use RNIB's Express Reading Service which offers a guaranteed minimum of one hour a day of recorded material to all clients. Often it is possible to do more. The service is directly tailored to the needs of the individual. You describe how you want diagrams treated, for example, or whether you require 2- or 4-track. Once you are accepted as a client, the service follows your instructions every time.

Examination papers RNIB offers a secure, confidential service for the brailling of examination papers. You should make sure your examination office knows you need this service and tell them to contact *Customer Services*. RNIB requires a minimum of six weeks' notice.

National Library for the Blind

Cromwell Road, Bredbury, Stockport SK6 2SG (Tel: 061–494 0217 (24-hour answerphone).

The Library is a charity and provides reading of all kinds, free, in Braille (including music), Moon and large print. Braille and Moon are lent post free to individual readers; large print through public libraries.

Public Libraries

These provide commercial recordings on disc and tape.

Tape Organisations and Services

See Section 14.

Large Print Books

See Section 14.

OTHER RESOURCES FOR BLIND AND PARTIALLY SIGHTED STUDENTS

Learning to type

In some areas, typing is taught to newly blind people either at home or in a local rehabilitation centre. Where these facilities are not provided by the social services it may not be too difficult for a blind person to follow instruction at an ordinary sighted typing class, as all students are taught to type by touch alone. Braille versions of typewriting manuals are available from the RNIB, 224 Great Portland Street, London W1N 6AA (Tel: 01–388 1266).

In addition, some blind people may be prepared to teach themselves with the aid of a cassette typing course. Available free of charge, but requests must be accompanied by four blank C60 cassettes and a self-addressed label from Charles Cadwell, Tape Recording Service for the Blind, 48 Fairfax Road, Farnborough, Hampshire GU14 8JP (Tel: Farnborough (0252) 547943).

Talking calculators and other aids

The RNIB has a series of leaflets which have been compiled into a pack to give starter information on commonly used aids and apparatus for work. Obviously much of this information would be useful to students. Leaflets are available separately or as a pack in Braille or in large print from: RNIB (Employment Development Unit), 224 Great Portland Street, London W1N 6AA (Tel: 01–388 1266). This information is also available on cassette. Requests should be sent to: RNIB Express Recording Centre, 79 High Street, Tarporley, Cheshire. Leaflets are available on the following topics: Braille embossers; the use of the BBC microcomputer; *Can I get it in Braille or on tape?*; calculators; electronic reading aids; large character displays; large print typewriters; paperless Braille devices; Personal Reader Service; recorders; speech devices; note-taking.

Services for People Who are Hearing Impaired

Deaf students have successfully completed many courses offered in further education colleges, on training schemes, and in higher education. Some may be specially structured for their needs e.g. to improve communication skills, or to give an opportunity to mature, and 'catch up' on education they need. Many deaf students, however, follow ordinary courses, with extra tutorial support. *See* page 105 for details of the booklet *After School* published by the National Deaf Children's Society.

The availability of support services varies widely from one part of the country to another. Information on what is available can be obtained from the National Association for Tertiary Education for the Deaf – details from the NATED Secretary, Shirecliffe College, Shirecliffe Road, Sheffield S5 8XZ.

Among the support services that may be available, to support students in further and higher education, are support tutors, support from teachers of the deaf, help from an interpreter for the deaf, and note-takers, and various technical resources such as radio microphone and induction loop systems. A description of these services is to be found in the useful publication *Deaf Students in College*. For details *see* page 106.

Organisations Providing Directories of Educational Opportunities

Association of British Correspondence Colleges

6 Francis Grove, London SW19 4DT.

The Association aims to safeguard the interests of all students taking correspondence courses and to ensure that its members provide a high standard of tuition and an efficient service. It also operates an advice and information centre on matters pertaining to correspondence education, in which context it offers, free on request, a broadsheet that details its member-colleges and lists the subjects and examinations for which correspondence instruction is available from them.

COPE – the Compendium of Post–16 Education and Training in Residential Training Establishments for Handicapped Young People
COPE provides detailed information on residential establishments (or establishments with residential facilities) offering further education and/or training to young people with handicaps or special needs.

A full page of information is provided for the majority of establishments, including: general description of each college or centre; its stated aims; categories of handicaps accepted; details of courses and training programmes; intake dates, waiting lists and fees; method of application and selection; staffing and care provision; and links with local further education colleges and the community.

Establishments are classified in a simple alphabetical sequence. Indexes allow readers to find establishments according to type of handicap or special need catered for, by geographical location, and by controlling body. Price: £6.85 (including postage and packing) from: Wiltshire Careers Service, Support Services Unit, Room 341, County Hall, Trowbridge BA14 8JB.

Council for the Accreditation of Correspondence Colleges
27 Marylebone Road, London NW1 5JS (Tel: 01–935 5391).
The Council is the only organisation in the United Kingdom officially recognised as responsible for the award of accreditation to correspondence colleges.
The principal objects of the Council are:
(a) to promote education by setting standards for all aspects of tuition, education or training conducted wholly or in part by post, to investigate the manner in which such activities are carried out and to grant, where appropriate, the award of accreditation stating that the activities of the college conform to such standards; and
(b) to protect the educational interests and progress of students and to ensure that a satisfactory and responsible service is provided by accredited correspondence colleges, having regard to the distinctive characteristics, traditions and needs of both.
A list of accredited correspondence colleges is available from the Council's offices.

The National Institute of Adult Continuing Education (England and Wales)

19b De Montfort Street, Leicester LE1 7GE (Tel: Leicester (0533) 551451).
Acts as a co-ordinator for local authorities, universities, voluntary organisations, and other agencies, including broadcasting and television. NIACE publishes details of a wide range of short courses in its booklet *Residential Short Courses*. Details are given of those having facilities for disabled people. For further details *see* Section 9.

In 1983, NIACE established a Special Needs Advisory Group and this has formed the basis of an expanding network. The Group commissioned a survey (undertaken by Dr Alan Charnley) which looks at educational provision for adults with special needs living in the community. The research report is available entitled *Care in the Community: Adult Continuing Education and Joint Finance*. The report is described as optimistic in that it finds willingness among Health Authorities to involve Local Education Authorities in making educational provision for adults with special needs. Price: £2.

Regional Advisory Councils for the Organisation of Further Education – Guides for Handicapped Students
These guides provide useful information covering all colleges of further and higher education in each of the regions, with the names of co-ordinators to whom enquiries about opportunities for handicapped students should be directed. Details of specialist teaching staff as well as other relevant details are included. Unfortunately, since the last edition of this Directory, guides for London and South Eastern Region and for the West Midlands are now out of print and there was doubt when they would be reprinted. Enquiries about information to these two regions should be made to: Regional Advisory Council for Further Education, London and South Eastern Region, Tavistock House South, Tavistock Square, London WC1H 9LR (Tel: 01–388 0027); and West Midlands Council for the Disabled, Moseley Hall Hospital, Birmingham B13 8JZ.

Details of remaining guides are as follows:

East Midlands – Further Education and Special Needs 1987–88 Available from: The Secretary, East Midland Further Education Council, Robins Wood House, Robins Wood Road, Aspley, Nottingham NG8 3NH. (Tel: Nottingham (0602) 293291). Free but please enclose a 12 in × 9 in addressed envelope, stamped for 3 oz per copy.

Yorkshire and Humberside – Further Education for the Handicapped in Yorkshire and Humberside Available from Chief Officer, Yorkshire and Humberside Association for Further and Higher Education, Bowling Green Terrace, Leeds LS11 9SX. (Tel: Leeds (0532) 440751). Price: £1.
See also *A Directory of Open Learning Opportunities in Scotland* (page 106).

Travelling Fellowship

The Winston Churchill Memorial Trust offers Churchill Travelling Fellowships for people to make studies overseas related to their trade, profession or interests, in order that they might bring back knowledge and experience for the benefit of the community. Each year applications are sought from UK citizens, with no age limits and no special qualifications required. Categories of subject change each year. A number of disabled people are now Fellows having successfully completed their travelling fellowships. For further information apply to: The Winston Churchill Memorial Trust, 15 Queen's Gate Terrace, London SW7 5PR (Tel: 01–584 9315).

Vocational Guidance and Training

LOCAL EDUCATION AUTHORITY CAREERS SERVICE
See Section 7.

VOCATIONAL TRAINING FOR BLIND PEOPLE
Courses are available at the Royal National Institute for the Blind Commercial College in London for computer programmers and for those interested in commercial employment. Subjects include shorthand and typing, audio typing, and use of Optacon. There are also short courses in word processing. Similar course facilities, excluding computer programming, exist for people living in Scotland at the Royal Blind School, Edinburgh. The RNIB North London School of Physiotherapy has a three-year residential course leading to the qualifying examinations of the Chartered Society of Physiotherapy. Training as piano tuners, on courses lasting two years or more, is available at the London College of Furniture and Royal National College for the Blind.

Queen Alexandra College in Birmingham runs a two-year course in machine operating and inspection, and one on bicycle repair.

The Letchworth Skillcentre (TC) provides introductory courses in light engineering, machine operating, repetitive assembly and inspection training for blind people. Hostel accommodation is provided.

DAY AND EVENING CLASSES
Local education authorities publish each year a full prospectus of all local part-time, day and evening classes. Where a particular subject is not covered, if a number of people get together and make a request a class can usually be arranged. Handicapped students can nearly always be accommodated, if necessary by making special arrangements.

Holiday Courses

See Section 9.

Books and Publications

A-Z of First Degrees, Diplomas and Certificates. A Guide to Qualifications Awarded by Universities and Polytechnics in the UK. Published by Kogan Page Ltd, 120 Pentonville Road, London N1 9JN (Tel: 01–278 0433). Price: £6.95 + 70p postage and packing.
This book is a quick reference source for school-leavers and their advisers, who will be able to look up a particular subject, see immediately where the course can be studied and then contact the relevant institution for further details. Each entry is listed by subject in alphabetical order, specifies the universities and polytechnics where a specific course is offered and gives the title of the qualification gained. The names, addresses and telephone numbers of the universities and polytechnics are also provided.

A College Guide: Meeting Special Educational Needs. Published on behalf of the Further Education Unit by Longman Group. Available from Longman Group Resources Unit, 62 Hallfield Road, York YO3 7XQ. Price: £4.50.
This book aims to satisfy the pressing need for detailed background information and practical advice for those wanting to make better provision for students with a wide range of special needs. Following a general overview of practical matters related to starting a college course, the book gives specialist advice about individual needs stemming from a range of physical impairments as well as learning, emotional, and behavioural difficulties. Each section includes case studies as well as books and helpful organisations.

After School. This is a parent's guide to further education for deaf students available from the National Deaf Children's Society, 45 Hereford Road, London W2 5AH (Tel: 01–229 9272). Price: 50p. For further information on the work of the Society *see* Section 15.

Directory of Educational Courses for Mentally Handicapped Adults. 1982 edited by Victoria Shennan. Available from MENCAP, The Bookshop, 123 Golden Lane, London EC1Y ORT. Price: £3.95 plus 75p postage and packing.

A Directory of Open Learning Opportunities in Scotland. Each year The Scottish Council for Educational Technology publishes this directory which is available free of charge. It contains nearly 700 different Open Learning courses. Open Learning delivers education and training to adults in a flexible way to suit their particular circumstances. Open Learning helps the student study at a time, in a place, and at a pace that is most convenient.

Examples of subjects covered include: adult basic education; business studies; computing; engineering; management; technology; education; and personal and caring services.

Copies of the Directory are obtainable from: The Learning Systems Unit, Scottish Council for Educational Technology, Dowanhill, 74 Victoria Crescent Road, Glasgow G12 9JN (Tel: 041–334 9314).

Directory of Opportunities for School Leavers with Disabilities. Produced by Queen Elizabeth's Foundation for the Disabled, Leatherhead, Surrey KT22 OBN Tel: Oxshott (037 284) 2204).

The Directory gives information about facilities in all parts of the United Kingdom which are available for school leavers with disabilities. The Directory provides brief details of organisations and other places providing assessment, vocational training, open and sheltered employment, hostels and residential homes, and younger disabled units.

The Directory, with amendment sheets, is available at £4 including postage and packing. An alphabetical list is available at 75p.

Directory of Technical and Further Education. Available from Longman Group UK Ltd, 6th Floor, Westgate House, The High, Harlow, Essex CM20 1NE. Price: £44.

A reference directory of organisations providing technical and further education in the United Kingdom. Its 375 pages contain information on government and local education authority provision of technical and further education, listing individual colleges, both local education authorities and non-maintained, with their departments and courses including adult education, health studies, nursing, social care, social sciences, YTS, special needs, adult literacy.

The Educational Grants Directory – Voluntary and Charitable Help for Children and Students in Need This Directory gives details of sources of help for 'students who are handicapped or disabled and also for mature students'. For further details see page 83.

Have Wheels: Will Travel. A first study tour of Rome by Open University disabled students. The aim of the tour was to extend to OU disabled students parity of educational opportunities – in this instance to join fellow humanities students for course studies in Italy. The reporting, by the students themselves, is both frank and informed, and there is sound advice for future disabled travellers – what to take, how to cope with incontinence and other practical problems, and guidance on accessibility difficulties in Rome. Available from the OUSA office, PO Box 397, Walton Hall, Milton Keynes MK7 6BE.

NATED Publications – *National Association for Tertiary Education for the Deaf* produces a range of literature including details of examination concessions and information on further educational provision for those who are hearing impaired. Also available advisory notes for hearing impaired students and for lecturers. For further information contact: Rene Zannetlou, NATED Secretary, Shirecliffe College, Shirecliffe Road, Sheffield S5 8XZ.

National Bureau for Students with Disabilities 336 Brixton Road, London SW9 7AA (Tel: 01–274 0565).
The Bureau has a range of publications including:
(a) *After 16: what next?* Published by the Family Fund and available from the Bureau; price: £2 including postage. A general guide for young people with disabilities as they reach their 16th birthday. Also helpful to parents and advisers. Information is included on: further education, employment, benefits, aids and adaptations, holidays, independent living and mobility.
(b) *Applying to Higher Education.* Some notes for disabled students, their parents and advisers. Answers many of the questions disabled people seeking entry to higher education have brought to the Bureau's information service over the years in a simple 'question and answer' format. Price: 50p – single copies free to students with disabilities.
(c) *Deaf Students in College.* This has been prepared in conjunction with the National Association for Tertiary Education of the Deaf.

Provides guidance and support – both tutorial and technical – which can enable a deaf student to complete a college course with confidence. Price: £1.00 – single copies free to students with disabilities.

(d) *Blind and Partially Sighted Students in College*. This was prepared in conjunction with the Royal National Institute for the Blind. This sheet offers a wide range of information on aids and equipment and on support available for visually handicapped students. It is intended for college staff with little experience of visually handicapped students' study needs and for students themselves. Price: 50p. Single copies free to students with disabilities.

National Union of Students publications. See page 102.

Never Too Late To Learn by Judith Bell and Gordon Roderick. Published by Longman Group Ltd, Retail Services Department, 4th Avenue, Harlow, Essex (Tel: Harlow (0279) 29655).

A well-indexed guide to adult education. Details of courses, grants and sponsorships are well covered. Guidance is also given on job prospects and there is a list of books on how to study.

Typewriting Exercises for One-Handed People by Jean Kempthorne. The author is a qualified typing teacher with a special interest in the difficulties of handicapped students. While this book is published primarily for the teacher's use, there are sufficient explanatory notes for the student working alone. Available from St Albans College Library, 29 Hatfield Road, St. Albans, Hertfordshire AL1 3RJ. Price: £3 including postage and packing.

SECTION 7
EMPLOYMENT

Earning a living may often not be all it's cracked up to be, but it's what most of us want to do. As well as the first and obvious reason, we gain pleasure from the company of colleagues and we feel we are part of the world. Some jobs also provide profound satisfaction when we can readily identify with the aims of the organisation or company. However in the present climate jobs can be hard to find, and for disabled people doubly so.

Perhaps the most difficult part of finding a job is the interview itself and the best way of learning the techniques is through experience. Even attending interviews when you are not sure you want the job, can provide the extra confidence needed. This can be like trial through fire, but it's a useful way to gain the necessary confidence and expertise in handling leading questions. Preparatory courses in job-seeking, preparing your *curriculum vitae* and taking part in mock interviews can all be useful. Such courses are sometimes available locally and it would be worth asking at your nearest Jobcentre.

Unless you have very specialised qualifications, it is probably a good idea to be fairly flexible about the kind of work you are prepared to do, particularly where really suitable posts do not appear to be available at the time. All work experience can be valuable, and you are in a much stronger position applying for jobs when you are already employed.

This section attempts to set out the statutory assistance there is available and also to provide some general ideas. It definitely helps to be talented, but those of us who cannot aspire to creative writing or painting should not despair; persistence and determination are also talents and they can be cultivated. There are a good many aids available, including an increasing range of sophisticated electronic equipment, which, for many disabled people, can provide the means to earn a living.

This section should be read in conjunction with Section 6 on Further Education, for who knows where a few acquired skills may lead, certainly to greater opportunities and to a confidence which in itself is likely to produce opportunities.

Statutory Services

Statutory provision for the employment and training for employment of disabled people is based on the Disabled Persons (Employment) Acts 1944 and 1958. These Acts are summarised in Section 13 on Legislation. Training is dealt with in Section 6 on Further Education. The following paragraphs describe in broad outline the practical employment services which are now available.

THE EMPLOYMENT REHABILITATION SERVICE

The Training Commission (TC) runs a network of 26 Employment Rehabilitation Centres (ERCs) and four ASSET (Assistance Toward Employment) Centres. They offer courses of assessment and rehabilitation for people who, through illness or injury, are having difficulty obtaining or retaining a job. Three ERCs have residential provision for clients who cannot travel daily to their local centre.

The assessment courses aim to identify clients' needs and capabilities and help produce a plan for future action. These courses are carried out either on-site at a client's local centre, or by a mobile assessment team who will visit arranged sites to meet demand from people who are unable to travel daily to a centre. They will normally last for two days.

Following the assessment, a client's rehabilitation needs are considered and a rehabilitation course will be structured to meet the individual's requirements. This may involve any combination of elements such as a period of work in an ERC workshop or with a local employer to give work experience and restore confidence; help with literacy and numeracy; physiotherapy and ergonomic advice; training in jobsearch techniques (interview skills, self-presentation, letter writing, etc.). The length of these rehabilitation courses will be flexible (up to 26 weeks in exceptional cases) according to the content required, although the average length will be four to six weeks.

The TC also helps fund a number of agency

108

centres run by local authorities and voluntary bodies providing rehabilitation courses for special client groups such as blind people, those who are cerebrally palsied, and those who are mentally ill. An extension of this form of rehabilitation is proposed.

People are generally referred to ERCs and ASSET centres by the Disablement Resettlement Officer (DRO) or Employment Adviser at their local Jobcentre. However direct references by doctors and employers are encouraged. (For further information see leaflet EPL86.) Whilst attending courses clients will be paid allowances and given assistance with fares and, where necessary, the expenses involved in being away from home.

THE EMPLOYMENT SERVICE

The Department of Employment runs the network of local Jobcentres; in addition, it offers some specialist services for particular groups of employees and for particular industries. The services include the Disablement Resettlement Officer Service, the Disablement Advisory Service, and Professional and Executive Recruitment (PER). Included in these services is the administration of sheltered employment for disabled people and advice about employment rehabilitation for those who have suffered illness or injury.

THE LOCAL AUTHORITY CAREERS SERVICE

The Employment and Training Act 1973 also places a legal obligation on each local authority to provide a vocational guidance and employment placement service, known as the Careers Service, for young people leaving school. Under these arrangements all Careers Officers have a duty to assist young disabled people, and most local education authorities have appointed Careers Officers to specialise in this field. As a normal feature of the work Careers Officers maintain close co-operation with Jobcentres, local authority social workers and specialist voluntary organisations, as appropriate.

REGISTRATION

Disabled people over the statutory school-leaving age (at present 16 years) may apply to their local Jobcentre for registration under the Disabled Persons (Employment) Act 1944 (see Section 13). A Disablement Resettlement Officer will arrange, in suitable cases, for medical certification of this disablement before finding the person eligible. Registration in this way may, in some cases, be an aid to employment because large firms are re-

quired by law to employ a certain quota of people on the register. Certain other facilities also, in particular sheltered employment, are limited to those who are registered. The three main conditions of registration are:

(a) that the applicant is substantially handicapped in finding and keeping suitable employment;
(b) that the disability is likely to last for at least 12 months;
(c) that the applicant wants a job and has a reasonable prospect of obtaining and keeping one.

Full details from any Jobcentre (leaflet DPL 1).

NOTE: Registration as described above should not be confused with registration under Section 29 of the National Assistance Act 1948.

COMPANIES' DIRECTORS' REPORTS

Many companies now have to state their policies in the annual reports regarding their employment of disabled people. For further information see page 251.

PROFESSIONAL AND EXECUTIVE RECRUITMENT (PER)

PER is the specialist branch of the Employment Service which provides a recruitment service for employers who wish to engage professional, executive, managerial, scientific and technical staff, and assists people seeking employment at this level. PER operates nationally through a network of offices and offers a comprehensive recruitment service which includes selection, interviewing and advertising. The service is free to job-seekers while employers are charged a fee based on the type of service used.

When a disabled person enrols, he or she is invited to contact the Disablement Resettlement Officer (DRO) by the PER Candidate Consultant.

EMPLOYMENT SERVICES FOR DISABLED PEOPLE

Wherever possible disabled people make use of existing Jobcentre provision, including the self-service vacancy displays. However, for those with more complex employment problems related to disability, Disablement Resettlement Officers (DROs) provide advice and guidance through counselling on suitable job opportunities and the special facilities available.

Jobcentres will give advice to people with disabilities about facilities for assessment, guidance and further training, including, where necessary, residential courses. They can also advise on special aids and equipment needed to help a disabled person at work, and can make arrangements for financial help with the cost of travel to work in certain cases.

Blind Persons Resettlement Officers (BPROs), as the title implies, help blind and some partially sighted people. There are Blind Persons Training Officers (BPTOs) who carry out initial training on the job and advise on technical matters and aids for blind people in employment. They also visit employers' premises in an attempt to identify suitable work for blind and partially sighted people.

The Employment Service also operates the quota scheme whereby employers with 20 or more employees have a duty to employ a quota of registered disabled people (at present 3 per cent of their total staffs).

The Employment Service's Disablement Advisory Service, comprises 65 small specialist teams at local level to encourage and give practical advice to employers about the adoption of progressive personnel practices for people with disabilities and the retention of those employees who become disabled. DAS teams can be contacted through the Jobcentre.

SHELTERED EMPLOYMENT

The minority of people who are so severely disabled as to be unable to cope with employment under ordinary conditions, but who are nevertheless able to carry out productive work, may benefit from suitable 'sheltered' work. Advice and information can be obtained from Disablement Resettlement Officers at Department of Employment (DE) Jobcentres.

Sheltered employment is provided at workshops run by:
(a) Remploy;
(b) local authorities or;
(c) voluntary organisations.

REMPLOY

Remploy is a government-supported company set up under the provisions of the Disabled Persons (Employment) Act 1944 to provide employment for severely disabled men and women in England, Scotland and Wales who are unable to obtain or retain work in open industry.

The Secretary of State for Employment appoints the 15 men and women who sit on the Board of Directors. Its turnover is in the region of £70 million and it employs nearly 9,000 severely disabled people in 94 production units. Many disabled people are employed in supervisory, managerial or administrative positions. Remploy

has three trade groups, namely: Furniture and Medical Equipment; Leather and Textile Products; and Packaging and Assembly.

A disabled person seeking employment with Remploy must be registered with the Department of Employment. S/he will then be referred, at the discretion of the Disablement Resettlement Officer, to the nearest Remploy factory. Part-time medical officers assist Remploy factory managers in assessing the work capabilities and functional limitations of potential employees, and the candidate will undergo a three-month trial period during which s/he will receive training and further assessment as to the job most suitable for him/her. Emphasis in Remploy factories is on meaningful employment under industrial conditions as near normal as possible. Conditions are very similar to those in any other industrial concern, while the industrial environment is designed to meet the employment needs of disabled people. The 39-hour working week compares with the normal basic working hours of other British companies.

LOCAL AUTHORITY AND VOLUNTARY BODY WORKSHOPS

Employees in sheltered workshops are engaged in a wide range of activities and are employed under contracts of service, receiving the rate for the job, and paying income tax and National Insurance contributions. The Department of Employment provides financial assistance to the employment providers in the form of capital grants towards expenditure on land, building and equipment and capitation grants to help meet actual workshop running costs. For further information contact your local DRO.

SHELTERED PLACEMENT SCHEME

The Sheltered Placement Scheme aims to provide integrated employment opportunities for severely disabled people who, when given the opportunity to work within their own capacity, have the ability to do a useful job of work. The people concerned undertake normal work, receive the full wage for the job and are no different from their able-bodied colleagues, except for their lower output.

The mechanics of the scheme involve a sponsor (a local authority, voluntary body or Remploy) which employs the disabled person and a host firm which provides the work and workplace. There is a contract between the sponsor and the host firm whereby the services of the disabled person are made available to the host firm in return for an agreed payment based on the disabled person's output, which must be at least one third that of an able-bodied person. The sponsor then makes up the disabled person's wage to that of an able-bodied employee in the host firm and claims a grant towards the costs from the Employment Service of the Department of Employment, up to a stipulated maximum which may vary from year to year.

The Sheltered Placement Scheme is nationwide, operating across a wide range of industries and has the advantage of providing employment for severely disabled people in those areas of the country which do not have either a Sheltered Workshop or a Remploy factory. (See leaflets SPSL1 and SPSL5.)

GRANTS, ALLOWANCES AND AIDS

Assistance to look for work away from home
There is a scheme to assist people in finding a new job. An unemployed person who is looking for work beyond daily travelling distance may be helped with fares through the Travel to Interview Scheme. The scheme is run through Jobcentres. There are several qualifying rules to be satisfied before assistance can be given. One of these rules is that all applications for assistance must be made at a Jobcentre before travelling to the interview. (See leaflet EPL 150.)

Travel to work grants
These are available to registered disabled people who, because of their disability, are unable to use public transport for all or part of their journey to and from work and therefore incur travelling costs over and above those of an able-bodied person making the same journey. The financial assistance provided is normally in respect of taxi fares, at a rate of three-quarters of the total cost, and is normally subject to a maximum weekly amount of £69.25 for five-day-week workers. Applications by disabled people for assistance with extra costs, other than taxi fares, will be considered.

People in receipt of a mobility allowance may be included if they are permanently or temporarily unable to drive. People in sheltered employment may also be eligible.

Applications for assistance under this scheme should be made in the first instance to local Disablement Resettlement Officers, who can be contacted through any local Jobcentre. (See also Leaflet DPL 13.)

Aids to employment
These may be supplied on free permanent loan; the scheme covers any aids necessary to enable disabled people to perform their particular duties but which they would not need if they were not disabled. Examples of the type of aid that can be issued are: special purpose jigs and fixtures; modifications to machines; special fitments for tools; purpose-built desks; seats and benches, including counter-balanced drawing boards and tilting stands and tables; electric typewriters; telephone aids and accessories; reading and writing aids; and Braille measuring devices such as Braille rulers and micrometers. Application in the first instance should be made to the local DRO who can be contacted through any Jobcentre. (See also Leaflet EPL 71.)

ADAPTATIONS TO PREMISES AND EQUIPMENT
Grants of up to £6,000 can be made by the ED to employers towards the costs of adaptations to their premises and equipment. The adaptations, such as installations of ramps and special toilet facilities, must be for the benefit of a specific disabled employee. Application should be made in the first instance to the local DRO who can be contacted through any Jobcentre.

SOCIAL SECURITY ADVICE LINE FOR EMPLOYERS
If you are an employer yourself you will find this service useful. However, if you are an employee you might find it helpful to draw the service to the attention of your employer.

A new free social security telephone advice service for employers is now available to provide expert advice on national insurance contributions and the payment of statutory sick pay and statutory maternity pay. Employers from all over Great Britain can telephone the Social Security Advice Line for Employers free of charge by dialling 0800 393539.

PERSONAL READER SERVICE
To help you handle your immediate reading needs, the Employment Service operates *The Personal Reader Service*. This scheme is administered by the RNIB. Through it you can get a regular sum of money which you can use to pay someone to read to you at times which you arrange. The maximum allowance covers 15 hours of reading per week. If you would like further information contact the RNIB Employment Department, 224 Great Portland Street, London W1N 6AA (Tel: 01–388 1266).

JOB INTRODUCTION SCHEME
This scheme enables the Employment Service to make a grant of £45 per week to employers who

engage a selected person for a trial period of usually six weeks but up to a maximum of 13 weeks. It operates at the discretion of the DRO and is designed to encourage employers to allow disabled people the opportunity of proving their ability to perform a particular job, where doubts are expressed by the employer.

THERAPEUTIC EARNINGS RULE

Disabled persons may, in certain circumstances, derive earnings from casual work without affecting their entitlement to sickness, injury or invalidity benefit. (For further details *see* Section 2, pages 9–40.)

COMMITTEES FOR EMPLOYMENT OF DISABLED PEOPLE

There are 86 Committees for Employment of Disabled People (CEDPs) established under the Disabled Persons (Employment) Act 1944 to advise on matters relating to the employment, or undertaking of work on their own account, of disabled people in their area. In practice, they work largely with the Employment Service staff on the following functions: marketing, such as 'Fit For Work' presentations to employers; surveying disabled people's employment and training needs; stimulating improvements in services to meet those needs; and quota and registration functions under the 1944 Act. CEDP membership brings together high-level representation from both sides of industry and other people, including doctors, with practical experience of resettlement.

CEDPs are complemented at a very local level by members of the local community, called Recognised Local Contacts (RLCs),who give the Employment Service staff practical help in their work of assisting disabled people obtain and retain employment.

Aids and Equipment

Disabled Living Foundation
380–384 Harrow Road, London W9 2HU (Tel: 01–289 6111).
Aids can be vital to employment. The DLF Information Service and Equipment Centre offers useful advice on the range of equipment which may be necessary in the workplace. This includes ranges of wheelchairs and some office furniture. (*See* Section 3 for further details.)
DLF publications include:

Office Furniture and Equipment – List 16 has notes on general office layout, specific furniture and accessories; organisations concerned with career

advice, job opportunities, and training. Price: £1.20.

Computers and Accessories for People with Disabilities (advice paper). Covers inputs, outputs, computer equipment for blind and visually handicapped people and for those who are deaf and hard of hearing; key guards, key locks, and accessories; useful contacts and relevant publications. Price: £1.20.

Royal National Institute for the Blind
224 Great Portland Street, London W1N 6AA (Tel: 01–388 1266).
The Employment Development Unit has produced a series of fact sheets to give you starter information on commonly used aids and apparatus for work. Braille and large print fact sheets are available on the following topics:

Braille embossers
The use of the BBC microcomputer
Can I get it in Braille or on tape?
Calculators
Electronic reading aids
Large character displays
Paperless Braille devices
Personal Reader Service
Recorders
Speech devices
Note-taking

There is a reference guide available to the suppliers of the above equipment contained in each fact sheet.

This information is also available on cassette. Requests for any or all of the fact sheets should be sent together with a C90 cassette to: RNIB Express Reading Service, Tarporley Recording Centre, 79 High Street, Tarporley, Cheshire.

NOTE: Some aids and equipment for employment may be supplied on free permanent loan by the Department of Employment – for details see page 111.

Self-employment

Self-employment can be a most satisfying way to earn a living and many independently minded people would rather accept a lower income and be their own boss than sell themselves to the vagaries of employers. However, working for yourself usually means working harder and for longer hours than those who suffer the 9 to 5 routine. For disabled people self-employment may very well be the answer to a number of problems and, when all is said and done, there is a marvellous satisfaction at the end of the day, when the work produced is all of your own making. There is no room in this section to outline all the possibilities and opportunities. We have merely provided a few pointers, but there is also valuable information in the books we describe at the end of this section.

Income tax allowances – self-employed
Self-employed people may claim tax relief for expenses they incur wholly and exclusively in connection with their trade or profession. This, in practice, may include a wide range of expenses which the new 'tycoon' may not have anticipated – for instance, business travel expenses including the cost of hiring a car, some subscriptions to magazines and professional or trade associations, use of home as an office, where a proportion of heating, lighting, rent, rates, cleaning, and insurance may be offset against tax. Much useful information is given in the Inland Revenue booklet IR28 *Starting in Business*, which is available free of charge from the office of any HM Inspector of Taxes or from PAYE Enquiry Offices.

People setting up on their own should consider engaging an accountant, not just for dealing with tax matters but also for general advice about running a business and keeping records. Her or his fee may also be included in the deductible expenses. When starting a business even while self-employed, it is essential to inform the local Inspector of Taxes, whose address appears in the local telephone directory under Inland Revenue. (*See also* 'Tax Relief for Expenses Incurred by Self-Employed People' under Income Tax in Section 2.)

VAT
Value added tax is chargeable on a wide range of goods and services in the United Kingdom and is therefore of significance to anyone who contemplates starting a business. Registration is obligatory for anyone whose taxable turnover exceeds, or is likely to exceed, £22,100 a year, but voluntary registration can be sought by smaller traders if this would be to their advantage. However, you would need to show that you have a compelling and continuing business need for registration.

A registered trader must charge VAT on sales and account for this to Customs and Excise, but is allowed to offset VAT paid on purchases (with certain exceptions). A trader not registered pays VAT on purchases (as part of the price paid to suppliers), but does not have to add a further VAT charge or to account for VAT on sales.

Customs and Excise publish a useful booklet *Should I be Registered for VAT?* This leaflet and others are available from local VAT offices, which are listed in your local telephone directory under Customs and Excise.

National Insurance contributions – self-employed
As a self-employed person you must pay Class 2 National Insurance contributions (Leaflet NI 41) unless you have applied for and been granted exception because your earnings are below the exception limit for Class 2 contributions.

It is important to note that sickness and invalidity benefit is only awarded to those who pay Class 1 (employed) or Class 2 (self-employed) contributions.

GOVERNMENT SERVICES

The present government is committed to the encouragement of small business enterprise, and a wide range of services has been established to encourage the setting up of new initiatives. While these are not intended particularly for disabled people, they present an opportunity for those who, notwithstanding physical limitations, are imaginative and enterprising. Skilled counsellors, working at local level, can bring the necessary expertise.

Small Firms Service
This is an information and counselling service provided by the Department of Employment to help owners and managers of small businesses with their plans and problems. The service also offers advice to those thinking of starting their own business, as well as a specialist counselling service, called the Business Development Service for established businesses who are considering expansion.

The Small Firms Service operates through 10 centres in England, and a similar service is provided by the Development Agencies in Wales and Scotland. In Northern Ireland, an information service is provided by the Department of Economic Development. (These agencies are described in this Section.)

The Small Firms Service offers free information on any business problem from finance, diversification and industrial training to exporting, planning, use of high tech, industrial relations, marketing and exporting.

The first three sessions with a Small Firms Service counsellor are free; a modest charge is made for any further sessions needed.

To contact your nearest Small Firms Centre dial 100 and ask the operator for FREEFONE ENTERPRISE.

Enterprise Allowance Scheme

This Department of Employment scheme can be very helpful in assisting unemployed persons who wish to start up in business but are deterred from doing so because they would lose their entitlement to unemployment or other benefits. EAS was introduced to help overcome this problem, compensating for the loss of benefit by paying £40 a week for up to 52 weeks – to supplement the income from your business whilst it strives to become established. In order to qualify you must show you have £1,000 that can be put into the business during the first year and you must agree to work full-time (at least 36 hours per week) in the business. Details are available from your local Jobcentre.

The Business On Own Account Scheme

Another scheme of possible interest to disabled people, but one which is very strictly limited, is the Business on Own Account Scheme. Through this scheme limited facilities are occasionally provided under Section 15 of the Disabled Persons (Employment) Act 1944 to enable severely disabled people to work on their own account from home if all other possibilities of employment have been found unsuitable and where the suggested business seems a viable economic proposition. Each case is considered on its merits and the scheme is likely to be recommended only if no other option for employment seems possible.

Volunteering

Community Service Volunteers (CSV)

237 Pentonville Road, London N1 9NJ (Tel: 01–278 6601).

CSV places volunteers in a large number of projects each year, and each project is different. CSV accepts every volunteer between 16 and 35 and positively encourages physically, socially or culturally disadvantaged people who wish to offer their services. CSV take pride in pointing out that a good deal of their effort goes in matching the volunteer to the project: in fact they would see this as their main skill as an organisation.

The CSV Able-to-Help Scheme is designed specifically to offer the opportunity of volunteering to people with physical disabilities. All volunteers involved on the Scheme serve under the same terms and conditions as all other CSVs, but a special effort is made to secure uniquely appropriate project settings. The Scheme employs a specialist worker who, through close consultation with individual physically handicapped volunteers, attempts to find and design a project which suits their physical limitations and abilities as well as capitalising on their individual strengths, positive interests and skills. The Scheme is a specialist service, dealing with a relatively small number of volunteers and offering a high degree of support to participants. Projects are available in a volunteer's home area or away from home, with or without residential board provided. The Able-to-Help Scheme offers a flexible programme to potential volunteers and attempts to start positive work from what they can do. The normal full range of types of project and settings available to all CSV volunteers is offered on the Able-to-Help Scheme. No one is rejected, whatever their handicap. Enquiries should be made to the Able-to-Help Scheme worker at the above address.

For details of the Independent Living Scheme *see* page 22.

The Association of Blind Piano Tuners

The Secretary, 24 Fairlawn Grove, Chiswick, London W4 5EH (Tel: 01–995 0295 (day), 01–994 7592 (24 hours)).

Recognised and known by many people in the piano and music trade, the ABPT is a nationwide organisation of highly trained, qualified people with branches where members can meet to discuss new ideas in the piano world, ways of improving the service which members offer to clients, and any problems which they may encounter.

Association of Disabled Professionals

The Stables, 73 Pound Road, Banstead, Surrey SM7 2HU (Tel: Burgh Heath (0737) 352366).

The ADP was formed because it was felt that very little of the statutory provision for the rehabilitation, training, and employment of disabled people was geared to the particular needs of professional people, disabled in childhood or adult life.

The Association is concerned, among other issues, with:

(a) improving the rehabilitation, education and training facilities and opportunities of disabled people, assisting them by encouragement and example of its disabled members to develop their physical and mental capacities to the full and promoting their entry into the professions and their full participation to society;

(b) improving the employment opportunities and

career prospects of disabled people, and assisting them by encouragement and example in finding and retaining employment commensurate with their abilities and qualifications; and

(c) educating the public regarding the problems, needs and capabilities of disabled people and how to assist in compensating disabled people for their physical, mental or financial handicaps in relation to education, employment and recreation.

Some 90 per cent of the members are disabled (about one-tenth of these are students). The other 10 per cent of non-disabled members are qualified professionals working in the field of disablement or having an interest in this area. The Association has disabled members from both Houses of Parliament and also includes amongst its members solicitors, barristers, engineers, computer programmers, dentists, actuaries, writers, editors, librarians, social workers, economists, statisticians, doctors, university lecturers, psychologists, scientists, educational technologists, accountants, teachers, graphic designers, hospital administrators, and civil servants.

The ADP has a growing Register of Professional Advisers: members qualified and practising in professions, who have volunteered their help to those who need advice on employment prospects in particular fields. A large proportion of the work of the Association is concerned with educational and employment problems and members are frequently in touch with organisations and individuals who might be able to help them. In many cases the ADP will take up issues with outside organisations on members' behalf.

The ADP submits evidence regularly to the appropriate government departments who in turn consult the Association in its specific areas of interest. It is a fundamental aim of the Association that a battle fought successfully by one disabled person shall be a victory for all, and that those who follow in the successful path of existing members shall encounter fewer obstacles and far more encouragement and help on the journey. Membership fee is £6 a year and £2 for disabled students, but if there are financial difficulties the subscription may be deferred. There is an occasional newsletter and a quarterly house bulletin.

Association for Spina Bifida and Hydrocephalus
22 Upper Woburn Place, London WC1H OEP (Tel: 01–388 1382).
The national office is always willing to support and advise individuals on aspects of training and employment. There is close liaison with further education establishments, Careers Officers, DROs, and employers. Work experience placements can be arranged at the national office. ASBAH is also involved with sponsoring people in employment under the Department of Employment Sheltered Placement Scheme.

AVHOW – Association of Visually Handicapped Office Workers
Secretary: Ms K. Shelley, Flat 5, 43 Avenue Gardens, London W3 8HB (Tel: 01–992 9921).
AVHOW aims to work for the benefit of blind and partially sighted office workers. It offers membership to all visually handicapped people in office occupations. It also organises training schools and exhibitions, and publishes a yearbook and also a quarterly magazine on compact cassette.

Business in the Community (BIC)
227a City Road, London EC1V 1LX (Tel: 01–253 3716).
BIC publishes a Directory of Local Enterprise Agencies throughout the UK at £3.50 including p&p. The LEA in your area would be able to advise you about any business enterprise you had in mind.

CoSIRA – Council for Small Industries in Rural Areas
141 Castle Street, Salisbury, Wiltshire SP1 3TP (Tel: Salisbury (0722) 6255).
CoSIRA is responsible for improving the prosperity of small businesses in English country areas, by providing a local source of advice backed up by technical and management services, supervised training and loans. CoSIRA has representatives (known as small industries organisers) who are stationed in every English county. In addition to their own knowledge of small rural businesses they can call upon the experience and support of a local voluntary committee and thus can provide assistance with a wide variety of problems affecting the small firm. They also have regular contacts with Disablement Resettlement Officers in the counties for whom they are responsible. CoSIRA operates only in the rural parts of England. Similar services to small businesses are offered in other parts of the UK.

CoSIRA has some very interesting publications which are most encouraging in the support being offered – these include: *Publications for Small Rural Businesses; Training – Technical and Business Management* describing a broad range of courses on such subjects as thatching, furniture and antique furniture restoration, forgework, farriery; *Are you in the Tourist and Leisure Business – Would you like to join it?*; *Rural Transport*; *Village Shops – Do you own one? Would you like to own one?*; *Redundant Building Grants* describing how old buildings can be converted to house an appropriate business.

Welsh Development Agency – Awdurdod Datblygu Cymru
Business Development Centre, Treforest Industrial Estate, Pontypridd, Mid-Glamorgan CF37 5UT (Tel: (0443) 853021).
The Business Development Centre has been set up to provide practical opportunities for those intending to start in business and for developing companies. There are workshop facilities available covering metalworking, woodworking and joinery, garment manufacture and sewing which can be used by individuals seeking to set up in business and small companies wishing to expand prior to possible investment in machinery and premises.

The facilities can be used over a period of months while individuals develop their ideas and products. They may, on the other hand, be used for as little as half a day per week to help small companies widen their product range and to decide, for example, whether additional equipment should be purchased to assist in gaining new orders.

There is also a range of support services available. Experienced, professionally qualified engineers are able to provide guidance on production management and technical aspects of business. The group has at its disposal an extensive computer system for design and manufacture (CAD/CAM). They can also assist with prototype manufacture, the design and manufacture of tooling, and workshop layouts.

Charges for the facilities outlined above are made on the basis of facilities used, and the time involved.

As well as a Marketing Advisory Service advice can also be given in such areas as preparation of business plans and on obtaining finance. 'Skill into Business' and other practical courses are also run from the Centre.

For further information or an appointment to visit, contact the Centre Administrator.

Scottish Development Agency
120 Bothwell Street, Glasgow G2 7JP (Tel: 041–248 2700).

Small Business Division, 102 Telford Road, Edinburgh EH4 2HP (Tel: 031–343 1911).
The Scottish Development Agency offers a wide range of assistance to people wishing to start up or develop a business in Scotland. Assistance is available through the Agency's Small Business Division, with headquarters in Edinburgh and area offices in Aberdeen, Dumfries, Dundee, Glasgow, and Edinburgh. The following services are offered.
(a) A counselling service covering management, finance and investment.
(b) An information service to put small businesses in touch with the right person to help with any business problem.
(c) A marketing service to advise companies on market research, marketing problems and exporting. The service also organises a programme of trade visits and exhibitions in the United Kingdom and abroad to promote the goods of small Scottish companies.
(d) A range of technical advisory services including instruction in various trades, contacts with customers for sub-contract work and assistance with production problems.
(e) Financial assistance in the form of loans of up to £150,000 to assist companies to develop their products or services. These can be made in respect of buildings, equipment, and working capital.
(f) Advice in all aspects of financial management.
(g) An advisory and information service on all matters relating to crafts including publications, exhibitions, advice on conservation.
(h) Grants for craftspeople towards setting up in business, equipment, work-shop and exhibition costs and a crafts fellowship scheme for research.
(i) Training schemes for established and trainee craftspeople and those involved in conservation work.

Northern Ireland Department of Economic Development
Netherleigh Massey Avenue, Belfast BT4 2JP (Tel: Belfast (0232) 63244 ext. 443).
The Department will provide information on schemes to help people setting up their own business, as well as helping those running small businesses. They have a range of brochures and other publications including *Action for Jobs in Northern Ireland* describing training and employment programmes as well as grants and other help at hand. The Department can also give you details of the

Local Enterprise Development Unit (LEDU), the small firms agency for businesses with not more than 50 employees, and area offices based in Londonderry, Newry, Belfast, and Omagh.

The Crafts Council
12 Waterloo Place, London SW1Y 4AU. (Tel: 01–930 4811).
Open Tuesday–Saturday 10 a.m.–5 p.m.; Sunday 2 p.m.–5 p.m.
The Crafts Council is a government funded body which supports crafts in England and Wales, and promotes the work of artist–craftspeople. The Gallery presents a variety of changing crafts exhibitions and has special facilities for wheelchairs – a ramp, a lift and lavatory facilities.

In the Information Centre, visitors may consult the slide library containing the work by makers on the Selected Index, which may be hired by lecturers or organisations. Also available is the non-selected Register in which any craftsperson may be listed. There is a helpful information service covering craft courses, craft shops, galleries, exhibitions, supplies of materials and equipment, magazines featuring crafts and crafts publications.

The Council publishes a bi-monthly magazine, Crafts, with features on crafts activities in the UK and overseas.

A range of grants and loan schemes has been designed to help the artist–craftsperson at various stages in his/her career. Further information is available from the Grants and Services section. The Council's Education Section runs a 'Craftspeople in Schools' scheme and a gallery programme for schools, and regular lectures for the public.

The Welsh Arts Council
9 Museum Place, Cardiff CF1 3NX (Tel: Cardiff (0222) 394711).
With financial support from the Crafts Council (*see* above) the Welsh Arts Council gives grants and itself organises projects of particular interest to Wales and Welsh craftspeople. The scheme does not duplicate those of the Crafts Council and individual craftspeople working in Wales can apply for any of the Crafts Council schemes already described. Details of the Welsh scheme are available from the Crafts and Design Department of the Welsh Arts Council.

Disabled Graduates Careers Information Service
Careers Advisory Service, University of Nottingham, University Park, Nottingham NG7 2RD (Tel: Nottingham (0602) 506101 ext. 2947).

This service (incorporating The Disabled Graduates Data Bank) contains over six hundred case histories of disabled graduates and of members of the Association of Disabled Professionals showing how various hurdles have been overcome in the pursuit of a wide range of careers. More case studies would be welcome from Directory readers, and questionnaires are available – all information is held in confidence.

The service aims to educate employers by showing what disabled workers have achieved; and to encourage and advise disabled students and graduate job seekers by providing relevant comparative information and examples of strategies that have proved useful.

Enquiries are welcomed from disabled students or graduate job seekers and their advisers.

Employment Medical Advisory Service
Magdalen House, Stanley Precinct, Bootle, Merseyside L20 3AZ (Tel: 051–951 4000).
This is a national government service of doctors and nurses trained in occupational health, whose main functions are to help to prevent ill health caused by work and to advise on medical aspects for fitness for training or employment in relation to both mental and physical disabilities. Employers may wish to consult the service about the ability of individuals to cope with a particular type of work, or the health pattern of certain disabilities. The EMAS will also advise disabled people on suitable employment, and works closely with DROs. Enquiries should be made to local offices of the service which are listed under Health and Safety Executive in the telephone directory.

Mouth and Foot Painting Artists
9 Inverness Place, London W2 3JG (Tel: 01–229 4491).
Any person without the use of hands who paints by holding the brush in the mouth or with the feet and who is seriously interested in art as a way of earning a living should apply in writing, giving biographical details, disability, any art training, etc. Examples of work will be requested and assessed by the Association.

MENCAP – The Royal Society for Mentally Handicapped Children and Adults
MENCAP Centre, 123 Golden Lane, London EC1Y ORT (Tel:01–253 9433).
MENCAP has a number of schemes to help mentally handicapped people integrate into a normal working life. It advocates and encourages local adult training centres to include such subjects

as horticulture in their training programmes and to be more adventurous in their plans for more services for mentally handicapped people. In addition, MENCAP has a unique work training scheme known as Pathway. The scheme revolves around the MENCAP Pathway placement officer, who is based at the Society's divisional office. An individual social education and training programme is worked out for every Pathway trainee, based on a panel of experts' assessment of his/her abilities and potential. Once the trainee has successfully completed his or her pre-work preparation courses the placement officer co-operates with the local Disablement Resettlement Officer and careers specialists to find the trainee a suitable job with a sympathetic employer.

Outset
Drake House, 18 Creekside, London SE8 3DZ (Tel: 01–692 7141)
The Employment Development Unit of Outset (action on disability) has set up six training and employment projects in the field of information new technology. The EDU offers a wide range of advice, development, and research skills to assist trainers and employers interested in similar or new initiatives. The Unit can conduct feasibility studies and can help the development of projects while providing a wide range of advice and support services before and after. Outset itself has over 60 per cent disabled people on its staff.

Royal National Institute for the Blind
224 Great Portland Street, London W1N 6AA (Tel: 01–388 1266).
For details of Braille and Tape libraries and of the RNIB's Express Reading Service *see* page 102.

The RNIB's Employment Officers and Careers Advisers offer a service to all visually handicapped people in the UK seeking employment in professional or commercial fields. This includes introducing them to potential employers and advising on equipment and methods for a particular job.

The Personal Reader Service will help you handle your immediate reading needs. Through the Department of Employment you can get a regular sum of money which you can use to pay someone to read to you at times which you arrange. The maximum allowance covers 15 hours of reading per week. For further information, contact the RNIB's Customer Service department and they will be glad to advise you (24-hour direct order line 01–278 9615). Details of these services are briefly described in the RNIB leaflet *Can I Get It on Tape on in Braille at Work?*

The Spastics Society
16 Fitzroy Square, London W1P 5HQ (Tel: 01–387 9571).
The Society operates eight skills development centres which aim to enable people with cerebral palsy to fulfil their potential. A variety of local group centres also provide employment. Other employment services include centres in Welwyn, Hertfordshire; Birmingham, and Milton Keynes.

Earning Opportunities
WORKING WITH COMPUTERS

The British Computer Society – Disabled Specialist Group
13 Mansfield Street, London W1M OBP (Tel: 01–637 0471).
The principal objectives of the Group are:
(a) to secure the increasing involvement of severely disabled computer people with all sections of the computing community;
(b) to study and publicise the special needs of severely disabled people in computing;
(c) to draw the attention of other severely disabled persons to the possibilities of engaging in computer practice.

British Printing Society (Disabled Printers)
The Secretary, 34 Chinnor Road, Thame, Oxfordshire OX9 3LW (Tel: Thame (084 421) 2485).
The Society will advise disabled people regarding printing opportunities and will assist them to overcome problems perhaps by advising on the use of special tools or techniques.

Countrywide Workshops Charitable Trust
177 Drury Lane, London WC2B 5QF (Tel: 01–405 7417).
This organisation is aimed at promoting quality goods produced by blind, partially sighted, and physically or mentally handicapped people. The emphasis is on employment rather than fund raising. The catalogue (£1.50) underlines the quality of the products which range from stylish and attractive garments, knitted sweaters and socks, men's hats and ties, engraved glass, goods in leather, wood, china, wax and much more. A small shop at the above address shows a sample selection of goods in the catalogue, plus items not suitable for mail order. Any disabled producer of quality goods looking for further outlets should contact Valerie Wood-Gaiger at the above address.

Mail Order Firms
These can always be approached through their advertisements in the national press to ask if there

is scope for an agent in the relevant area. Through showing the catalogue to friends and acquaintances a small remunerative hobby can be built up.

Opportunities for the Disabled
1 Bank Buildings, Princes Street, London EC2R 8EU (Tel: 01–726 4961).
This is an employers' organisation providing a link between employers and employees. They have recognised the need for co-ordinated action to ensure that disabled job seekers receive a fair chance in the competitive field of open employment.

Two main services are provided, both of which are completely free of charge.
1. To improve the employment prospects for people with disabilities by helping them to get real jobs.
2. To provide a service to employers which includes advice and guidance on special equipment and financial assistance available.
In addition, Opportunities aims to encourage employers to consider more disabled people to fill their job vacancies.

There are regional offices in: Bristol, London, Leicester, Studley, Hull, Sheffield, Aylesford, Manchester, Birmingham, Gatwick, Merseyside, Hove. Key staff are seconded from both the private and public sectors.

Women's Institutes
39 Eccleston Street, London SW1W 9NT (Tel: 01–730 7212).
The movement offers to its members the opportunity of extending their horizons in all directions by making new friends, becoming involved in public questions and learning or improving skills in cooking, crafts, the arts and sport.

WI markets are held usually once a week in towns and villages easily accessible to rural producers. Home-grown and home-made produce of good quality, and crafts are sold direct to the general public. The WI markets are subject to the usual trading regulations and goods are sold at reasonable prices according to the locality. They are registered under the Industrial and Provident Act and are run by committees elected by shareholders. Men and women who are not WI members may apply to become shareholders and sell their produce through the markets, provided it comes up to the standard required. The money from the sale of goods (less a small commission deducted for overhead expenses) goes back to the producers. Produce which may be sold at a market includes vegetables, flowers and plants, fruit,

herbs, preserves, fruit syrups, cakes, cookies, breads, savouries, sweets, eggs, and craftwork. New producers should consult the controller of their nearest market to find out what can be sold locally and how and when to bring it in.

Wherever possible producers help in running the market. For a complete, free list of markets in England, Wales, and the Channel Islands, for marketing details and for a copy of *Marketing for Pleasure and Profit* (£1.70) apply to WI Books Ltd at the address above. For free literature please send an s.a.e. If you would like information on how to join the Women's Institutes write to the Administrative Secretary, Organisation Department.

Books and Publications

Consumers' Association books
Available from: Subscription Department, Consumers' Association, PO Box 44, Hertford SG14 1SH; also from bookshops.
Amongst the broad range of books produced by the Consumers' Association the two following may be of interest to those starting their own business.
(a) *Starting Your Own Business* sub-titled *How to make a success of going it alone* Price: £6.95 including postage. The latest edition of this handbook, first published in 1983, gives an easy-to-read, practical guide to everything the budding entrepreneur needs to know: from how to approach the bank for start-up and working capital to protecting your business ideas. It outlines the up-to-date position on tax and concessions for small businesses, explains the mysteries of VAT, and gives helpful hints on keeping detailed financial records.

If you are going into manufacturing or retailing you can find out all about choosing the right premises, buying stock, and your obligations towards any employees. There is advice on pricing the product and marketing it at home and abroad.

The book includes information about possible sources of capital, both government and private. It is unfortunate that such a useful book should apparently be aimed largely at men.
(b) *Earning Money at Home* Price: £6.95 including postage. Like its earlier editions, this book provides a broad range of information and clear advice whether you are brushing up on previous job experience or starting from scratch. It points out how your house insurance might be affected, whether you need to

get planning permission, and warns what the neighbours might object to. It covers all the financial aspects of working from home – dealing with tax and business expenses, costing your work and, most difficult for beginners, your time. It gives advice on selling yourself and charging your customers, and suggests potential outlets for your work. As before, colleges running appropriate courses are listed, and other sources of specialist help and advice given.

Employment for Handicapped People: Bibliography. Compiled by Struan Simpson it covers such subjects as architecture and design, community and group work, employment, epilepsy, history, income and earnings, job classification, legislation, mental handicap and mental illness, rehabilitation and sheltered employment. Published by Reedbooks, Chertsey and available from Disabled Living Foundation, Haigh and Hochland Ltd, International University Booksellers, The Precinct Centre, Oxford Road, Manchester M13 9QA (Tel: 061–273 4156).

Employment Service leaflets available from Jobcentres:

Employment Rehabilitation Centres – EPL 86.
The Disabled Person's Register – DPL 1.
Employment in Sheltered Workshops – DPL 11.
Assistance with Fares to Work Scheme for Severely Disabled People – DPL 13.
Aids and Adaptations for Disabled Employees – EPL 71.
Job Introduction for Disabled People – DPL 15.
The Sheltered Placement Scheme – SPSL 1 & 2.
The Travel to Interview Scheme – EPL 150.
Employing Someone who is Deaf or Hard of Hearing – EPL 38.
Employing Someone with Epilepsy – EPL 40.
Employing Someone who is Mentally Handicapped – EPL 44.
Employing Someone who is Blind or Partially Sighted – EPL 63.
Employing People who have had a Mental Illness – EPL 93.
Employing Someone with Haemophilia – EPL 98.
Employing Disabled People – EPL 147.
Employing Someone with Multiple Sclerosis – EPL 102.

Employers' Guide to Disabilities by Bert Massie and Melvyn Kettle. Published by Woodhead-Faulkner. Available from RADAR, 25 Mor-timer Street, London W1N 8AB. Price: £19 including postage.

This slim book aims to help employers realise what disabled people can do and to consider their suitability for employment on the strength of their abilities and not their disabilities. Emphasis is on how handicaps associated with particular disabilities can be minimised. In the first chapter thirty disabilities are covered with descriptions of each in non-medical terms. Details are provided on the nature of the disability, the extent of any handicap, the implications for employment, various considerations for health and safety and sources of further specific information on that particular disability.

The rest of the book deals with the wider issues connected with disability. It includes chapters on statutory services, legislation, access and safety and the importance of a formal employment policy. Information is also provided on the help that is available for disabled people in terms of grants and the provision of practical aids.

Epilepsy and Getting a Job. A leaflet available from the British Epilepsy Association, Anstey House, 40 Hanover Square, Leeds, LS3 1BE (Tel: Leeds (0532) 439393). It briefly discusses whether to tell prospective employers about having epilepsy, the sort of jobs best avoided, and ways of countering objections. These leaflets are available from regional offices or from the address above. They are free but a donation of 10p is suggested. An s.a.e. would be welcome.

Getting to Work by Edward Whelan and Barbara Speake. The authors of this book set out to identify and develop the knowledge, attitudes and abilities necessary for the young handicapped person seeking employment. It is intended to help instructors, teachers, counsellors and parents, and draws on the experience of workers in the field, as well as that of employers. The importance of 'job satisfaction' is discussed, as well as the range of jobs open to such youngsters and the necessity of helping them to make their own choices. There are sections on pre-vocational training and on the facilities available for learning specific skills. The authors include advice on applying for a job, creating a favourable impression at the interview, job-rehearsal and starting work. Published by Souvenir Press as one of the 'Human Horizons Series', price £6.95 hardback; £4.95 paperback.

How to Start, Run and Succeed in Your Own Business by Derek Jones and W. H. Perry. Published by Wheatsheaf Books Ltd, 16 Ship Street, Brighton, Sussex BN1 1AD (Tel: Brighton (0273) 723031). This is a practical and realistic book. The authors aim to make your aspirations attainable and successful.

Into Work – A Guide for Disabled People. Produced by RADAR, 25 Mortimer Street, London W1N 8AB. Available free, although an s.a.e. (10in × 7in) is requested. This loose-leaf information pack provides brief information and advice on some of the matters connected with seeking employment, from the first stages of training to the rights a disabled person has when he or she has obtained a job. Part-time employment and sheltered employment are also covered.

Kogan Page Limited

120 Pentonville Road, London N1 9JN (Tel: 01–278 0433).

This company publishes a number of books concerned with self-employment, and small businesses, careers and personal finance. We recommend you send for their catalogue which also includes other titles. To give you the flavour we describe some of the books:

(a) *An A-Z of Careers and Jobs*, edited by Diane Burston. Price: £5.95 plus £1 p&p. Alphabetically arranged for easy reference, each entry has a standard format and gives details of:

More than 350 jobs and careers – from accountant to zoologist
Qualifications and training
Personal qualities needed
Starting salary
Sources of further advice and information.

(b) *Be Your Own Boss at 16* by Alan Watts. Price: £3.95 plus 50p p&p. For those school-leavers who wish to set up in business for themselves or work as freelances, this book gives practical advice and guidance. It outlines both the advantages and disadvantages of being self-employed and gives ideas on how to find work. Illustrated with case-studies, it details the areas to be exploited, such as: window-cleaning; portrait painting; designing; running a sandwich counter; stamp dealing; fashion knitting; toymaking; doing repairs.

Advice on how to avoid possible difficulties and stay on the right side of the law is included together with suggestions on how to manage the financial aspects of your business, covering everything from getting a loan to paying tax.

(c) *Employment for Disabled People* by Mary

Thompson. Price: £4.95 plus 75p p&p. A good variety of courses, careers, self-employment ideas and opportunities for disabled people are explored throughout this book. It will help disabled people to make the most of their own abilities and the help that is available. The book discusses the current employment situation including: policies; legislation; benefits; professional advice services. Details are provided on education and training opportunities and specific schemes such as sheltered employment and community programmes. It encourages disabled people to consider options such as starting a business and making the best use of information technology, mobility and equipment for living.

(d) *Raising Finance: the Guardian Guide for the Small Business* by Clive Woodcock. Price: £5.95 plus £1 p&p. A guide to the wide range of sources of finance now available to the small business. From starting up to expansion, development and eventually to the public issue of shares, case studies illustrate the various ways in which these sources of finance can best be used. It shows you how to go about getting finance, what the advantages and disadvantages of each type of finance are and who is involved in providing it. It also considers important facts such as interest rates and how to benefit from the tax system. Finally, for easy reference, there are directories of names and addresses of all the various sources together with an index and section on further information.

(e) *Working for Yourself: The Daily Telegraph Guide to Self-Employment* by Godfrey Golzen, ninth edition. Price: £5.95 plus £1 p&p. Sets out clearly basic techniques required for setting up your business and lists some 35 different opportunities in self-employment. It provides a crash course in planning cash flow, raising money, keeping records and pricing the product or service on offer.

Re-Hab Network Published by the Rehabilitation Resource Centre, Department of Systems Science, The City University, Northampton Square, London EC1V OHB. Editor John Fordree (Tel: 01–353 0186). This is a quarterly magazine which aims to help all those concerned with rehabilitation and employment issues in the field of disability and in closely related fields. Single issues: £2.50; annual subscription: £9.50 including postage.

Royal National Institute for the Blind
224 Great Portland Street, London W1N 6AA.
The RNIB has a range of publications on employment; these include three leaflets: *Looking for
Work; Blind People at Work;* and *Working with
Computers.* The first of these is for blind job-
hunters; the second describes for employers the
sort of jobs blind people do and the aids and
support services available; and the third explains
how blind people train and work in data processing.

Also available from the RNIB Employment
Development Unit, a series of fact sheets which
gives starter information on commonly used aids
and apparatus. These are described on page 112.

Most RNIB publications are available in large
print, in Braille and on tape.

Working from Home (1982) by Marianne Gray.
Published by Judy Piatkus (Publishers) Ltd, 5
Windmill Street, London W1P 1HF (Tel: 01–631
0710).
Price: £4.95 plus 75p postage. This is a useful
practical book for men and women who wish to
earn money from their homes either to supplement
their income or as their major source of revenue.

The book is divided into two sections. The first
deals with the factors involved in setting up a
business, where to work, how much capital is
required, how the home can be organised and how
to assess what can be done in the time available.
The second section contains over two hundred
ideas for ways of earning money from home including: agencies which can be set up; pet-care;
working with children; crafts which can be made
and sold; repair work which can be done; services
which can be provided; food which can be prepared at home and sold; fruit and vegetables which
can be grown; and qualifications which can be
easily acquired.

SECTION 8
MOBILITY AND MOTORING

The car, because it is a machine, is capable of having an infinite variety of mechanical alterations made to its various parts to make it drivable by people who have limited movement and powers of control. Engineers have been most ingenious in the various adaptations they have made available to disabled motorists. In addition to adaptations to the mechanics of driving, a variety of swivel seats and mobile hoists have made the tricky business of getting in and out of the car an altogether easier task.

From cars to ships, planes and trains, increasingly, handicapped people are proving that obstacles are to be overcome and that travel is not only possible but actively to be pursued. Airports have led the way in providing helpful facilities, now planes themselves are becoming more accessible and providing better facilities. Railways are improving their services and hopefully there will be fewer and fewer guards' van travellers tumbling about among the baggage.

It is sadly true that public transport in this country so often lags behind the best in modern design thus making its use difficult even for nimble travellers and impossible for many disabled people. Trying to board a pay-as-you-enter bus – up the steep steps, through the narrow entrance, while fumbling for change and clutching children, parcels, walking stick, crutches requires the agility of a mountain goat. It is interesting to note that in the United States, bus companies are substantially adapting parts of their fleets to take into account the needs of disabled travellers. In England we have the splendid example of the Tyne and Wear Metro which is accessible and usable by people in wheelchairs and those with sight difficulties, not to mention parents with prams or pushchairs.

The biggest obstacle to acquiring the freedom of mobility is, of course, finance, and the mobility allowance is the statutory answer. With some extra outlay it is now possible to use the mobility allowance to help in the hiring or hire-purchase of a car at fairly reasonable terms through Motability. For many people the ownership of a car is impossible and for these the growing number of Dial-a-Rides provides a welcome opportunity to get out and about. However, many of these are very limited in the number of rides they can offer to an individual and the distance they will travel.

Integration is a meaningless concept without mobility, and for mobility to become a reality depends on cash, imagination and determination: cash to cater for individual needs, imagination to see past steps and other artificial barriers, and determination to continue to press for much needed action to overcome the difficulties. As we move into the 1990s, with all the technical innovations at our service, it is ridiculous and totally unjust that disabled people still have very serious mobility problems. It can only be a lack of will on the part of government and other decision-making bodies.

Mobility by Car

THE MOBILITY ALLOWANCE
For details *see* page 26.

VEHICLE EXCISE DUTY
Exemption from paying VED is available to people with severe mobility problems in the following two categories.

1. *Those receiving mobility allowance* – since 1 December 1978 a person receiving mobility allowance (or a person appointed to act for her/him) with a car of his/her own has been eligible for exemption from vehicle excise duty (sometimes called road tax). If s/he does not have a car of his/her own, s/he may nominate someone else for exemption. The vehicle to be exempted must be used by, or for the purpose of, the person receiving the mobility allowance. The DHSS automatically sends an application form for a VED exemption certificate to all those receiving the mobility allowance certificate issued in response to a valid application which may then be used as proof

123

when applying for a 'tax-exempt' disc at the local vehicle licensing office of the Department of Transport.

2. *Those* not *receiving mobility allowance* – exemption from VED extends to disabled people (including children between the ages of two years and four years nine months) who do not already enjoy exemption as mobility allowance beneficiaries, if they:
   (a) are unable or virtually unable to walk; and
   (b) need to be driven; and
   (c) need to be cared for by a constant attendant (this condition is satisfied if attendance allowance at either the higher or lower rate is in payment); and
   (d) have a vehicle that is registered in their name and is suitable for their use (special arrangements about registration apply in the case of children).

How to claim
First, ask for form MHS 564 from Disablement Services Branch, Department of Health and Social Security, Block 1, Government Buildings, Warbreck Hill Road, Blackpool FY2 OUZ. Complete and return it to the same address. If satisfied, the DHSS will issue certificate MHS 330 which constitutes the required evidence of disability. Next, complete form V10 (application for a vehicle licence), obtainable from any local vehicle licensing office or main post office, and send or take it to the LVLO with the vehicle registration document, insurance certificate or cover note, the certificate MHS 330 and the MOT certificate if appropriate. If satisfied, the LVLO will issue a 12-month exempt licence and exempt licence disc. The licence disc must be displayed in the vehicle and renewed on expiry like the ordinary tax disc.

Provided that the vehicle is registered in the disabled person's name, and is used for his/her purposes, a refund of duty may be claimed on a normal licence in the same way as for those receiving mobility allowance.

MOBILITY SUPPLEMENT FOR DISABLED WAR PENSIONERS
The vehicle scheme for severely disabled war pensioners is being progressively phased out. No cars have been issued since 21 November 1983. Eligible war pensioners now have the choice of claiming the mobility supplement (*see* page 38) and giving up their present car, or waiting until their car becomes unroadworthy. The supplement is not taxable and will be paid for life. It is set at a rate above that of the civilian mobility allowance.

VEHICLE LICENSING REGULATIONS

When applying for a driving licence, the nature of any disability must be declared in the appropriate section of the application form. The licensing authority may then ask the applicant to consent to his/her doctor being contacted for further details. The term of licence to be issued is dependent on the medical facts, i.e. one year, two years, three years, etc. It is important to bear in mind that where there are no indications to the contrary, i.e. that the disability is not recurring nor likely to be progressive, the new long-term licence may be issued, that is up to the age of 70. After considerable pressure by members of disabled groups, the Department of Transport decided in 1978 that drivers paralysed by spinal cord injuries may be granted driving licences valid until the age of 70. It was finally accepted that provided medical investigation shows that the condition of drivers injured in this way has stabilised, and that they are not suffering from secondary complications, the period of the licence should not be restricted. They are, of course, under the same obligation as all licence holders to notify the Licensing Centre of the onset of a disability or the worsening of an existing condition. Licences may be renewed after age 70 but will run for three years or less, depending on the circumstances – though with the possibility of further renewals.

Those people who hold a full licence which only authorises them to drive an invalid carriage or restricts them to a vehicle of special construction or design do not have provisional entitlement to drive any other type of vehicle. If they wish to drive a vehicle of a type not covered by the full licence, they must first apply for the appropriate provisional entitlement to be added to the licence. After the initial cost of a licence has been paid, there are no further charges for those who have to reapply having only been granted a restricted-term licence.

Drivers who become disabled must inform the Licensing Centre without delay regarding any disability which is likely to last more than three months and which is or may become likely to affect the ability to drive, whereupon the same procedure will be followed as above. Regulations are variable to take into account the different circumstances of an individual's disability. Should a retest be necessary, there will be no charge and test centres will automatically give priority to disabled applicants.

Licences are issued by the Driver and Vehicle Licensing Centre, Swansea SA6 7JL. Application forms for driving licences are obtainable at main post offices.

DRIVING AND EPILEPSY

People who have epilepsy may be issued with a licence to drive if they fulfil the following conditions:

(a) s/he has been free from any epileptic attack during the period of two years immediately preceding the date when the licence is to have effect (or, if not, that s/he has had such attacks only whilst asleep during a period of three years immediately preceding the date when the licence is to have effect); and

(b) the driving of a vehicle is not likely to be a source of danger to the public.

BUYING A CAR

Assistance and Independence for Disabled People (AID)
AID Centre, 182 Brighton Road, Coulsdon Road, Surrey CR8 2NF (Tel: 01–645 9014).
This company offers finance on a commercial basis and on commercial terms, but has shown a particular interest in needs of disabled people. A deposit is required (depending on the particular transaction, but never less than 10 per cent). Disabled purchasers, up to age 65, enjoy insurance against the risk of death during the repayment period without extra charge. It is a condition of finance that the vehicle is covered by fully comprehensive insurance for the duration of the agreement.

The company can also offer a selection of used cars, including automatics, some with power assisted steering. AID say that all used cars are prepared to the very highest standard, and are supplied with a warranty covering parts and labour for a period of three months or 3,000 miles.

AID can also arrange the supply and fitting of most types of adaptations. Free delivery to the customer's home is offered within the UK mainland.

The Motability schemes
Motability, 2nd floor, Gate House, West Gate, The High, Harlow, Essex CM20 1HR (Tel: Harlow (0279) 635666).
Motability is an independent charitable organisation whose main objective is to enable people who receive mobility allowance (drivers and passengers including children) to use this to hire a new standard production car or to hire-purchase a new or secondhand production car which may be,

where necessary, adapted for special needs. In order to provide favourable terms, Motability has negotiated discounts with motor manufacturers, insurance brokers and others. Motability has also arranged favourable hire-purchase terms for certain wheelchairs and pavement vehicles from a range of companies.

Before coming to a decision, you need to look at the schemes very thoroughly, first of all to decide which Motability option may be the most useful to you (hire or hire-purchase, new or secondhand), or indeed whether there may be another source of funding which may suit you better. In our book *Motoring and Mobility for Disabled People* (1988) (*see* page 151) the subjects of choosing a car on the open market as well as alternative means of finance are fully discussed.

Extra help available from Motability
Charitable funds are available to help people who find difficulty in paying for those extras not covered by the leasing or hire purchase arrangements. For instance, the cost of adaptation or the deposit on hire-purchase or extra rental on a lease. However, as funds are limited, it will be necessary to show you need what you have asked for, whether it is a more expensive car, an automatic gearbox or adaptation, and also to show you cannot pay for these items yourself. Charitable funds are very limited and even when they are available there is a ceiling of £1,000 on any grant made.

Bank loans
Personal loans offer a popular alternative way to finance car purchase. The principal advantage is that you are not tied down to the credit terms offered by any particular dealer (or by Motability). You have an unlimited choice of suppliers and the opportunity to look for a bargain. It is important to remember for those who are nervous about approaching banks for cash, seeing themselves, perhaps, as not very creditworthy, that a mobility allowance can change all that. Bank managers are inclined to look very favourably on those receiving a nice predictable and regular source of income like mobility allowance. Normally you will approach your own bank, but it is worth knowing that some banks will lend money to applicants who do not have an account with them. You can generally vary the repayment period, up to a specified maximum, to suit your own financial circumstances. Details of bank lending policies are given in *Motoring and Mobility for Disabled People (see* page 151).

Hire purchase with dealers
Many garages are able to make arrangements with finance companies to provide hire-purchase facilities for their customers. It is worth asking and worth shopping around for the most favourable terms.

CAR PURCHASE DISCOUNTS AND OTHER CONCESSIONS
A number of the leading car manufacturers have discount schemes, over and above those offered to the general market, which allow special terms to disabled drivers or to the immediate family of those qualifying disabled people who do not drive.

Most of these schemes rely on the goodwill of dealers who are encouraged to sell certain models at reduced prices, but for whom there is no overall ruling. Dealers will, in any case, not usually consider offering special discounts in trade-in situations, so intending customers who wish to take advantage of any discount scheme may be better advised to sell their existing cars privately rather than seeking a part-exchange deal.

TYRE, BATTERY, AND EXHAUST SYSTEM CONCESSIONS
Motorway Tyres and Accessories Limited
43 Bartholomew Street, Newbury, Berkshire RG14 5QA (Tel: Newbury (0635) 32375).
This company is offering discounts to disabled people on tyres, remoulds, and batteries. Special discount cards are available on application and these will enable the driver/passenger to receive an additional 5 per cent discount over and above any special price offers which may normally be available. The cards may be obtained from the above address and when writing you should quote the number of your mobility allowance *or*, if you drive a trike, of your vehicle registration document.

Alternatively, any of the above documents will be accepted as entitlement for these special terms at any of the 200 Motorway branches throughout the UK and Ireland. For details see your local telephone directory.

National Tyre Service Ltd
Retail Marketing Department, 80–82 Wellington Road North, Stockport SK4 1HR (Tel: 061–480 7461).
National Tyre Service Motorist Discount Cards are available to all who receive mobility allowance, and can be obtained from the above address. Please enclose an s.a.e.

This card entitles the holder to a further 5 per cent discount on all retail prices at just over 400 depots spread nationwide. The range of services available includes new and remould tyres (fitted free), a range of 'Monarch' batteries to fit most makes of British and foreign cars and, at selected depots, large discounts off retail prices on complete and part exhaust systems, fitted free of charge.

TOLL CONCESSIONS

A number of tunnel and bridge authorities waive their charges for disabled travellers provided they meet certain requirements. For those holding Orange Badges these include the Severn Bridge, the Erskine Bridge, the Forth Road Bridge, the Tay Bridge, the Tamar Bridge, and Torpoint Ferry. For Tamar and Torpoint, vouchers must be obtained in advance on an application form available from: City of Plymouth, City Treasury, Civic Centre, Plymouth PL1 2AA.

For the Tyne and Dartford tunnels, exemption may be obtained for any disabled person whose vehicle is exempt from Vehicle Excise Duty. Vouchers to be completed will be issued at the barriers. In the case of the Mersey Tunnel, Express Cards will be issued to people in the following categories: disabled drivers who hold Orange Badges and who own their own vehicles, or who hire their vehicles through the Motability scheme; disabled drivers who use a DHSS trike; war disabled drivers in receipt of mobility allowance; individuals who have been issued with an Orange Badge but who are dependent on the vehicle owner/driver and who need to be driven for reasons of disability (both Orange Badge holder and vehicle owner/driver must reside at the same address); and registered blind persons who are Orange Badge holders and vehicle owners. Applicants must produce appropriate documentation to claim entitlement. Applications for Express Cards should be made to the Mersey Tunnels, George's Dock Building, George's Dock Way, Pier Head, Liverpool L3 1DD (Tel: 051–227 5234).

For the Humber Bridge, exemption is granted to a disabled driver in possession of either a tax exemption certificate MY 182 or a MHS 330 or a MPB 1266 following the completion of an application form available from: The Bridgemaster, Humber Bridge Board, Administration Building, Ferriby Road, Hessle, North Humberside HU13 OJG.

It is always worth enquiring about possible concessions which may be available if you are likely to be travelling regularly where there is a toll charge, since it is not possible to list all the concessions, and regulations are liable to change.

FERRY CONCESSIONS
See Section 10.

ORANGE BADGE PARKING SCHEME

This scheme is designed to help severely disabled and blind people with mobility and parking problems by allowing them special privileges in the form of parking concessions. Present regulations allow badge holders to leave their vehicles, without charge or time limit, at parking meters and restricted parking spaces. Drivers with blind passengers may also benefit from the concessions. Badge holders in England, Wales, and Northern Ireland may park for up to two hours on yellow lines except where there is a ban on loading and unloading in force at the time; in Scotland they may park on yellow lines without time limit where there is no ban on loading or unloading. To control this entitlement, a special orange parking time disc (provided by the issuing authority) must be displayed and set to show the time of arrival. In the case of broken yellow lines the parking disc need be displayed only when the restrictions are for more than two hours and are in operation when the period of parking begins. Vehicles may also park free of charge at certain ancient monuments and sites of historic buildings.

Who is eligible?
The badge, which may be used on any motor vehicle (including taxis or hired cars) driven by or carrying a badge holder, is now available only to disabled people over two years of age who are either:
(a) recipients of mobility allowance; or
(b) blind; or
(c) using vehicles supplied by government departments or receiving grants towards their own vehicle; or
(d) have a permanent and substantial disability which makes them unable to walk or to have very considerable difficulty in doing so.

Orange badges are issued by local authorities and are universally recognised except within certain areas of central London as follows: City of London, City of Westminster, Royal Borough of Kensington and Chelsea, and part of the London Borough of Camden south of, and including, the Euston Road, where authorities issue their own parking badges for the use of disabled people resident or working in their respective districts. Wardens are generally sympathetic to disabled people visiting these areas, and by exercising tact and discretion Orange Badge holders will often be

The Royal Association for Disability and Rehabilitation (RADAR) is concerned with all aspects of physical disability and believes that disabled people should be part of the community and share in all its activities. To achieve this RADAR campaigns vigorously for the recognition of the needs and rights of disabled people.

RADAR provides information and advice to disabled people, their friends and relatives and others in the field of disability. Last year it dealt with over 200,000 enquiries. It is particularly active in the following areas:— employment, education, access, housing, holidays, social services provision, social security, mobility and general welfare. In addition to this it ensures information is available to disabled people by publishing newsletters, journals, access guides and other publications. The Research and Intelligence Unit monitors legislation of interest to disabled people and offers advice on proposed legislation.

RADAR also co-ordinates the efforts of voluntary and statutory bodies working for the welfare and rehabilitation of disabled people. More than 350 of these bodies are members of RADAR and to ensure close contact RADAR has development officers in various parts of the country.

RADAR needs funds to continue its work. Please help disabled people through a bequest or donation.

Registered Charity No. 273150

RADAR HELPS

THE ROYAL ASSOCIATION FOR DISABILITY AND REHABILITATION
25 MORTIMER STREET, LONDON W1N 8AB·Tel: 01·637 5400

treated generously. (Nine designated parking places with 20 spaces are now available in the City of Westminster in Duke Street, Orchard Street, Marylebone Lane, Vere Street, Leicester Square, Howick Street, Chapel Street, and Avery Row.) Able-bodied people who try to pass themselves off as badge holders are liable to a maximum fine of £200.

Badges are issued by local authorities (normally the Social Services Department) for a period of three years from the date of issue. They remain the property of the authority which is entitled to charge a fee, but this may not exceed £2. Applicants within categories (a), (b), and (c) will need to prove their entitlement, but this should be possible with the minimum of formality, e.g. by producing an official letter confirming award of mobility allowance, the payment book or a vehicle excise duty exemption certificate (MHS 330). In the case of applicants under category (d), the decision rests with the local authority, but it may wish to have medical advice in reaching that decision. This is likely to be sought in the form of a standard medical certificate, on a confidential basis.

'Orange Badges' in other European countries
For reciprocal 'Orange Badge' concessions with other European countries see page 198.

MOTORING INSURANCE
As any disabled driver knows, securing motor insurance at an affordable price can be a thorny problem; it is always best to 'shop around' and to beware of possible dangers hidden away in the small print. It is not unusual for a quotation to include a premium loading, even for a mild disability which is easily overcome by adaptation of the vehicle. If this happens to you, you would be well advised to take your custom elsewhere. There should be no real difficulty in a disabled driver obtaining 'fair' insurance, but there are no hard and fast rules and many insurers insist on treating each case on what they see as its merits. Those who automatically regard disability as a risk are unlikely to be sympathetic or even reasonable and are best avoided.

Equally, of course, you have a responsibility to declare the full facts about your disability, and failure to do so could well invalidate any future claim. You must also be sure to inform your insurers about *all* alterations made to the insured vehicle. The cost of motor insurance depends on many variable factors, principally the scope of the policy, your age, whether you enjoy 'no claims'

discount, the area in which you live, and the type of car you drive.

Specialist insurance services
The following insurance brokers have recognised the reliability of the average disabled driver and accordingly provide reasonable insurance cover. You would be wise always to seek a number of quotations before signing on the dotted line, and to consider carefully whether the cover offered is adequate, should you be unfortunate enough to be involved in an accident.

Boncaster Limited
54 High Street, Brentwood, Essex CM14 4AN (Tel: Brentwood (0277) 262626).
This firm has a special motor scheme for people with epilepsy. It does not extend this scheme to people with any other disability.

Disabled Drivers' Insurance Bureau
(a subsidiary of Chartwell Insurance Brokers)
292 Hale Lane, Edgware, Middlesex HA8 8NP (Tel: 01–958 3135).
This broker has specialised in insurance for disabled people for over 20 years. They 'fully appreciate the need for competitive premium levels', and use a panel of underwriters to obtain a wider choice of rates. All of the insurers provide normal terms regardless of the nature of the disability or of adaptations to the vehicle. Disabled clients in fact receive the benefit of a priority claims service to minimise the difficulties that can arise when a disabled person is without transport. Also, no claims discount can be offered in respect of claim-free driving experience gained in Motability hired cars or with DHSS trikes subject to a letter of confirmation from the appropriate body.

Amicable Insurance Consultants
40 The Broadway, Crawley, West Sussex RH10 1HG (Tel: Crawley (0293) 546666/31082).
This company offers an insurance scheme at basic rates for disabled drivers. Cover for wheelchairs up to £250 is included under the contents cover of the vehicle without further charge.

Consumer Insurance Services
Osborn House, 20a High Street South, Olney, Buckinghamshire MK46 4AA (Tel: (0234) 713535).
This brokerage firm has designed a 'vehicle-related' insurance package in consultation with various organisations and individuals representing disabled drivers. It combines (a) motor insurance (b) legal advisory and motoring prosecution de-

fence, and (c) vehicle accident/breakdown recovery services.

Gibbs Hartley Cooper Ltd
(incorporating Duveen and Walker), Chartist Tower, Dock Street, Newport, Gwent NP9 1DW (Tel: Newport (0633) 50222) or Freephone Gibbs Hartley Cooper.
This firm are the brokers to the Department of Health and Social Security in connection with vehicles on loan to disabled people. They have also arranged a special motor insurance scheme for privately owned vehicles. The company states that disabled people are treated no differently from any other member of the public and in fact enjoy a particularly attractive discount on their premium.

M. J. Fish & Co.
1–3 Slater Lane, Leyland, Preston, Lancashire PR5 3AL (Tel: Preston (0772) 45111).
This firm has arranged a special scheme of motor insurance for disabled drivers details of which are given very fully in a helpful booklet *Independent Insurance and Investment Advice for Disabled People*.

L. Hughes & Co
Insurance Brokers, 40 Frances Street, Newtownards, Co. Down, Northern Ireland BT23 3DN (Tel: Newtownards (0247) 817375).
This company has arranged a special Motor Insurance Scheme with Paladin Motor Policies at Lloyds. This scheme is exclusive to disabled drivers in Northern Ireland. The premiums offer a 10 per cent reduction off Paladin's normal Northern Ireland rates. There are no premium loadings or exclusions on the policy.

STANDARD PRODUCTION CARS
It can be very difficult to buy just the right car taking into account personal taste, family requirements, and personal needs where these relate to disability. It is obviously important to think very carefully before making an expensive mistake. If your limbs are stiff is there enough enough room for comfort? If a wheelchair has to be stowed is there room for this? Do you really need to buy an automatic rather than a manual car? Many disabled people do need to buy larger cars than they might otherwise choose – so perhaps a good sized second-hand car might fit the bill taking all due precaution in that situation. It is certainly worth consulting those who have experience in these matters. The three disabled driving organisations are always ready to help and may have members

local to you. The Mobility Information Service is always ready to give advice and will provide you with details of makes and models which interest you. Details of these organisations are given in this Section.

We would recommend you consult our book *Motoring and Mobility for Disabled People* (*see* page 151) where we examine the general considerations governing the choice of a car in some detail and give the vital specifications of a wide range of cars.

CAR HIRE
Cars for hire by disabled people in Europe, including the UK, are few and far between; hopefully the situation will improve. Hertz have a useful scheme using Alfred Bekker hand controls and Practical Car Hire tell us they are ready and waiting for disabled drivers, but so far there has been no demand. Perhaps readers of this book will alter all that by showing there is a demand. In the United States it is relatively easy to hire cars with hand controls at no extra charge.

Avis Rent a Car Ltd
Trident House, Station Road, Hayes, Middlesex (Tel: 01–848 8765).
In the United States, Avis are able to offer cars with hand controls for hire. We understand there is no extra charge for this facility. For further details contact Avis (as above Tel: 01–848 8733. Toll-free number for international reservations (for use only in USA): 800–331 2112.) Locations available: all major US cities. Cars with hand controls: any available car. Advance notice 14 days.

Hertz Rent a Car
UK and International Reservations Centre, Radnor House, 1272 London Road, Norbury, London SW16 (Tel: 01–679 1799).
Hand controls are available in the UK (at no extra charge) for drivers with lower limb disabilities only. The car is available at all UK locations with the exception of Northern Ireland. Reservations on request with minimum seven days' advance notice.

Hertz Reservations Centres: Manchester – (Tel: 061–437 8321); Glasgow – (Tel: 041–248 7733); London as above.
In the United States, Hertz are able to offer cars for hire which are fitted with hand controls: over 40 cities and virtually all locations in Florida. Available on all cars and vans. Reservations on request with five days' advance notice. Right- or left-hand

controls available. Cars have to be returned to specific renting locations, although there are exceptions. Cash renters are asked to leave an additional deposit of $25. Handicapped Identification Dash Board Cards are provided.

Inter Touring Service
117 Boulevard Auguste-Blanqui, 75013 Paris, France (Tel: 45 88 52 37).
This firm provides a Renault 18 automatic and a Peugeot 205 automatic for self-drive hire equipped with hand controls. They will be glad to send you details and a tourist tariff.

Kenning Car and Van Hire
Central Reservations Office, Manor Offices, Old Road, Chesterfield, Derbyshire (Tel: (0246) 77241).
This company have been providing automatic cars equipped with full hand controls for several years and has a good deal of experience in this field. Depots in London (01–882 3576), Sheffield (0742 71141), and Edinburgh (031–343 3377) specialise in cars for disabled drivers so contact ought to be made to the one nearest to your home. Kennings has a nationwide spread of depots to ensure a full back-up service. Hires are normally a week minimum and a week's prior notice of reservation but other enquiries, we are assured, will be assisted where possible.

Perry's of Edgware
51–55 High Street, Edgware, Middlesex (Tel: 01–952 2353).
This garage provides a good and friendly service for disabled drivers. There is no charge for fitting hand controls on hire cars. In fact they work out cheaper with hand controls than without. For instance, in 1987, an Escort 1600 – Estate or Saloon – the price charged was £31.91 per day (usually £43.70); £191.46 per week. Any car can be converted at a customer's request, with rentals varying depending on size of car. Prices include VAT, insurance, and unlimited mileage. Delivery and collection is free to customers in London and nearby. Prices for further afield can be negotiated but will, in any case, be kept to a minimum. We recommend you speak direct to Mr Gittens who is very ready to help.

Practical Used Car Rental
137/145 High Street, Bordesley, Birmingham B12 0JU (Tel: 021–771 4524).
This firm has 32 locations throughout Great Britain. Cars are available from £5.95 per day and 5p per mile. Cars are also available for hire by the hour (minimum 3 hours) at £2.50 per hour. Vans can be hired from £10.95 per day and 5p per mile. A car fitted for use by disabled drivers is available at no extra cost.

If there is shown to be a demand for cars with hand controls more will be made available.

Wadham Stringer (Southsea) Ltd
Granada Road, Southsea, Hampshire PO4 0RF (Tel: Portsmouth (0705) 735311).
This firm is offering a 10 per cent discount on the hire of their cars to anyone in receipt of the mobility allowance or to anyone who is a member of the DDA, DDMC or DMF.

GARAGE RATES EXEMPTION

Garages, carports, and car spaces accommodating a vehicle needed by a disabled person may attract rate relief. In England and Wales the amount of relief is calculated in one of two ways, which the claimant can elect:
either
1. (a) £25 for a garage;
    (b) £15 for a carport;
    (c) £5 for land;
or
2. So much of the rateable value of the property as a whole as is attributable to the garage, carport or land as certified by a Valuation Officer. (If the accommodation for the vehicle is rated in its own right, the rebate would be equal to the rates chargeable for the period of relief.) Where the facility is also used for other purposes, the rating authority can reduce the rebate under this option.

In Scotland, relief is that part of the rates chargeable on the property for the rebate period which is attributable to the special facility, as certified by the Assessor. Application should be made to your local rating authority.

For further information on rates relief (including Scottish regulations) *see* Section 13.

CONVERSION OF A VEHICLE – RELIEF FROM VAT

The VAT position on 'personal' ambulances, specialised vehicles, conversions to suit the condition of a handicapped person, goods supplied for such conversions, and the repair or maintenance of such goods is described in Section 3.

MOTORING CONTROL CONVERSION COMPANIES

It would be impossible to give a comprehensive list of firms who specialise in this type of equipment; however, the following are leaders in this field. The conversions and adaptations can very often be specially tailored to suit the driver's own particular needs.

Further information may be obtained from the specialist motoring organisations, or from the assessment agencies mentioned later in this Section. See also our book *Motoring and Mobility for Disabled People,* referred to on page 151.

Adaptacar
Cooks Cross, South Molton, North Devon EX36 4AW (Tel: South Molton (076 95) 2785).
Provides a variety of different types of hand controls. In addition the firm will carry out many other minor adaptations as required including a swivel seat for passenger or driver, power lifts, and portable ramps. They will also install power assisted steering. They cover Cornwall, Devon, parts of Dorset and Somerset, collecting and delivering cars at a cost a little over the expenses involved.

Ashley Mobility
Hay Road, Hay Mills, Birmingham B25 8HY (Tel: 021–772 5364). Also at: Derwent Close Industrial Estate, Langdale Drive, Warnden, Worcester (Tel: Worcester (0905) 28575); and 45 Swiss Road, Weston-super-Mare (Tel: Weston-super-Mare (0934) 26011).
Provides a range of conversion services to cover any degree of leg disability for most types of cars, automatic or manual gearbox models. Conversions are undertaken in the firm's workshops in Birmingham, but a nationwide collection and delivery service is available. This firm has a Mini 1000 converted to hand controls which is available to enquirers in the West Midlands area for demonstration and assessment services.

Automobile & Industrial Developments Ltd
Queensdale Works, Queensthorpe Road, Sydenham, London SE26 4JP (Tel: 01–778 7055/698 3451).
Provides hand controls for most makes of cars. A.I.D. will fit these controls themselves or will supply them in kit form with instructions for fitting at a local garage. A.I.D. say servicing is seldom required.

Alfred Bekker
'The Green', Langtoft, Nr. Driffield, North Humberside YO25 0TF (Tel: Driffield (0377) 87276).
Makes and markets hand controls for any make and model of car, either in kit form for the local garage to fit (he also has a nationwide network of fitters – many of them disabled) or for fitting at his workshops while you wait, for a small extra charge.

Alfred Bekker provides an assessment service (around his own equipment) and will also make available overnight accommodation in specially adapted rooms with every facility.

Brig-Ayd Controls
Warrengate, Tewin, Welwyn, Hertfordshire AL6 0JD (Tel: Welwyn (043 871) 4206).
Provides various hand control systems and will also install special conversions for drivers with severe disabilities.

Cowal Mobility Aids Ltd
32 New Pond Road, Holmer Green, nr. High Wycombe, Buckinghamshire HP15 6SU (Tel: High Wycombe (0494) 714400).
This firm specialises in conversions to a range of vehicles; also supplying hand control kits.

Derby Disabled Driving Centre
Southern Derbyshire Health Authority, Kingsway Hospital, Kingsway, Derby DE3 3LZ (Tel: Derby (0332) 371929).
This Centre will convert cars to disabled people's individual needs. Included in their service is the making of individual grips for steering and braking controls for customers with arthritis. These are one off grips made to a cast of the person's grip then superimposed on the controls to make long distance driving more safe and comfortable.

The Centre has a test track and two test vehicles; it also has a considerable technical and legal library to deal with queries over the telephone.

Assessments and conversions can be referred from any area.

Easydrive Systems
John Player Building, Stirling Enterprise Park, Stirling (Tel: Stirling (0786) 51077).
Easydrive is agent for Guidosimplex who produce hand controls as well as an automatic clutch. This fits most production cars. The hand control system allows not only steering by both hands but also operation of the accelerator by both hands. There is a locking switch on the brake lever for hill starts, etc. Throttle control on Easydrive is by an inner rim on the steering wheel.

Eurostag (Leeds) Ltd
Wellbridge Industrial Estate, Wellington Bridge, Leeds 12 (Tel: Leeds (0532) 444765).
Hand controls and other conversions for all types of cars to suit individual requirements. All conversions made in Leeds. No kits supplied.

Feeny & Johnson (Components) Ltd
Alperton Lane, Wembley, Middlesex HA0 1JJ (Tel: 01–998 4458).
This firm provides a variety of conversions to suit individual needs. All controls apart from one to control the throttle only must be fitted by Feeny & Johnson or their accredited agents.

D. G. Hodge and Son Limited
Feathers Lane, Wraysbury, Staines, Middlesex (Tel: Wraysbury (078 481) 3580).
This firm has a reputation for providing very helpful service, innovative ideas and a degree of personal assessment. They specialise in providing a wide range of driving controls to suit an individual person's needs including foot steering. They do not supply controls in kit form. A demonstration car is available to show customers an example of hand controls; it is also fitted with a sliding, swivelling seat and a wheelchair lifting winch.

Interbility Ltd
5 Badminton Close, Bragbury End, Stevenage, Hertfordshire SG2 8SR (Tel: Stevenage (0438) 813365).
This firm will fit hand controls and special seating. It also adapts vehicles for wheelchair use.

Midland Cylinder Rebores
Torrington Avenue, Coventry CV4 9BL (Tel: Coventry (0203) 462424).
Provides a one-handle kit of brake and accelerator designed to fit any car. A throttle conversion kit is available for most makes of car, also brake and throttle conversion.

Motor Services (Manchester) Ltd
Royal Works, Canal Side, Edge Lane, Stretford, Nr. Manchester M32 8HS (Tel: 061–865 6922).
Provides a range of conversions and adaptations including Feeny and Johnson and BRIG-AYD equipment for cars having automatic and manual transmission, also Alfred Bekker brake and accelerator controls.

Brian Page
18 Pooley Green Road, Egham, Surrey TW20 8AF (Tel: Egham (0784) 35850).
Brian Page is the Southern Distributor for Alfred Bekker hand controls. In addition to fitting the controls at their works in Egham there is also a mobile fitting service for southern England.

Brian Page also fits an infra-red switching device to allow functions such as indicators, horn, main/dip beam, wipers/washers, etc, to be switched without removing the hand from the steering wheel. The device is mounted on the steering wheel and revolves with the steering knob to which it is attached. In addition, Brian Page will now fit an automatic clutch. This can be added to the factory-installed engine and gear box without change. It can be installed in any car – new or secondhand.

Poynting Conversions
Faraday Road, Churchfields Industrial Estate, Salisbury, Wiltshire SP2 7NR (Tel: Salisbury (0722) 336048).
Hand controls and various driving control modifications are fitted to most automatic and some manual cars.

Reselco Engineering Ltd
Kew Bridge Pumping Station, Green Dragon Lane, Brentford, Middlesex TW8 0EF (Tel: 01–847 4509).
Provides a variety of special controls for most makes of car whether automatic or with a manual gearbox and offers a free consultation service at the premises for people who are undecided on the type of controls suited to their disability.

Ross Auto Engineering
2–3 Westfield Road, Wallasey, Cheshire L44 7HX.
Also at Banastre Road, Southport, and Athlone Road, Warrington. (Tel: Wallasey 051–653 6000; Southport (0704) 35757; Warrington (0925) 34289).
This firm provides a range of services for disabled people including adaptations to cars, hand-control conversions, and wheelchair sales, service and hire.

In the Wallasey works there is also a static Chevette Automatic transmission-type car (less engine and wheels). It is adapted for hand controls which provide for simulated speed and braking. To test physical ability to brake, servo-assisted brakes and hydraulic pressure read-out are installed. Over-cam park braking, twin-pedal acceleration and other aids are also shown.

Steering Developments Ltd
Unit 3, Eastman Way, Hemel Hempstead, Hertfordshire HP2 7HF (Tel: Hemel Hempstead (0442) 212918).
This firm specialises in converting manual steer cars to power assisted steering for mainly small engined vehicles, both automatic and manual transmission. Included in their service is an electronic assessment facility, whereby any strength in

the driver's arms can be precisely measured to provide the necessary information for the manufacture of a power steer system to suit that individual's requirements.

A new development is the remote control steering which enables those who cannot manage a steering wheel to operate the steering via a lever/tiller and this system comes complete with a back-up steering system in the event of a failure of the primary circuit.

S.W.S Motor Bodies
Unit 9, Hartford House, Newport Road, Weston Street, Bolton, Lancashire (Tel: Bolton (0204) 395660).
In addition to converting Fiat Fiorino vans into purpose-built vehicles to take wheelchair passengers, this firm also fits cars with hand controls and undertakes a range of other modifications where necessary.

Wards Mobility Services Ltd
Ware Works, Bells Yew Green, Tunbridge Wells TN3 9BD (Tel: Tunbridge Wells (0892) 75686).
This firm manufactures and fits its own throttle and brake conversions for automatic cars as well as carrying out other modifications to individual requirements including power steering. Wards have a demonstration vehicle. It is an automatic version of the Austin Mini Metro which has had hand controls fitted together with a power steering conversion. It enables the firm to test a driver's brake reaction times and steering strength ability on an individual basis.

SEAT CONVERSIONS
Elap Engineering
43 King Street, Accrington, Lancashire BB5 1QE (Tel: Accrington (0254) 36042).
Manufactures a conversion kit consisting of a swivel mechanism which can be fitted to the basic frame of many car seats enabling the seat to rotate around and beyond the doorway of the vehicle at a right angle. Occasionally, it is not possible to supply the kit alone and a complete seat is provided.

Neill & Bennett
7 Wyngate Road, Cheadle Hulme, Cheadle, Cheshire SK8 6ER (Tel: 061–485 3149).
This firm makes a swivel seat base. This eases the transfer from wheelchair to driver or passenger seat. When used with the original seat base and seat it adds only 5/8 in to the seat height.

Remploys Autobility System
11 Nunnery Drive, Sheffield S2 1TA (Tel: Sheffield (0742) 757631).
This firm has a range of seat conversions; these include: the *flipseat* adaptation which allows the seat to tilt fully forward at the release of a catch. Fitted to the passenger side of a five-door car, this allows a person in a wheelchair to transfer into the passenger seat, fold their wheelchair, transfer into the driver's seat, tilt the passenger seat forward, and pull their chair into the car. The *swivel seat* adaptation, which can be fitted to either front seat, allows the seat, at the release of a catch to swivel around facing outwards. The *seat height adjuster* is an electrically operated device for disabled people who have height problems. Once in the car, the seat can be raised to the desired driving position at the press of a rocker switch on the car fascia. *Extended seat slides* allow the front seat of the car to travel back to the rear seat, if necessary, giving plenty of room to manoeuvre into the car when the seat can be returned to the driving position.

A number of conversion firms provide special seating arrangements, including Ashley Repairs, Cowal Mobility Aids Ltd, and D. G. Hodge & Son Ltd.

CONVERSIONS AND SPECIALISED VEHICLES WHICH CAN BE DRIVEN FROM A WHEELCHAIR
Carchair Ltd
Unit 69, Station Road Industrial Estate, Hailsham, Sussex BN27 2ES (Tel: Hailsham (0323) 840283).
This consists of a special wheelchair and lift/transfer mechanism, which together eliminate the need for the difficult transfer between wheelchair and car seat as well as the problem of wheelchair stowage. The wheelchair user remains in the Carchair throughout. The system is suitable for both passengers and drivers (who drive from the chair). It can be fitted to operate on either side of most two-door family saloons. The mechanism can be removed and transferred to your next car, without affecting the resale value of the first vehicle. New vehicles fitted with a Carchair system prior to registration will be exempt from both VAT and car tax. The wheelchair is designed for ordinary use both indoors and outdoors.

Gowrings Mobility International
18–21 Church Gate, Thatcham, Berkshire RG13 4PH (Tel: Thatcham (0635) 64464 or dial 100 and ask for Freephone Gowrings).

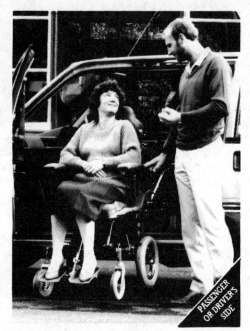
Gowrings build the Chairman range of cars specifically designed for motorists using wheelchairs. Most of the models are intended for wheelchair passengers but the Chairman Astra, with a conversion on the Vauxhall Astramax van, with simple modifications, can be driven by a disabled driver from a wheelchair. Each car offers easy access at the rear and ample headroom.

Poynting Conversions
Faraday Road, Churchfields Industrial Estate, Salisbury, Wiltshire SP2 7NR (Tel: Salisbury (0722) 336048).
A conversion of the Ford Transit van is available to enable a disabled person to drive from a wheelchair. This consists of a van with automatic transmission, a self-stowing hydraulic side lift, power operated side door, wheelchair locking device and suitable hand controls. Power steering is available. The interior is fitted to customer requirements, and side windows are fitted. This conversion also exempts the vehicle from liability to VAT and car tax.

Special Vehicle Designs Limited
Ravenstone Road Industrial Estate, Coalville, Leicestershire LE2 2NB (Tel: Coalville (0530) 810440).
The NIPPI is a useful little vehicle for local journeys which can be entered from the rear and driven without leaving your wheelchair. Built for road use, it is not restricted to the very low speeds of pavement vehicles. A two stroke petrol engine provides, in the least powerful model, a top speed of 25 mph. The design is simple but functionally well suited to its purpose. Well-established and reliable scooter components have been adapted to form a motor tricycle combining a rugged frame with attractive bodywork. Entry is made by a ramp/tailgate at the rear, and the chair locks securely into place in a simple clamp. While you can remain open to the weather, with a protective windscreen and an enveloping cape, there is now also a Surrey type roof.

Stratford Specialist Vehicles Ltd
Unit A, Altbarn Industrial Estate, Revenge Road, Lordswood, Chatham, Kent ME5 8UD (Tel: Medway (0634) 684465).
In developing the Crusader as a maxi-estate car, Stratford has retained the essential design features which make the vehicle suitable for use by both wheelchair passengers and drivers.
The Crusader is a 'six-wheeler' with the twin rear car axles giving the load carrying capacity

required – but with a low platform height – just 11 inches from the ground. The interior headroom is 60 inches. While the vehicle is fitted with four conventional doors, the wheelchair riders can enter via an electrically operated low gradient ramp in place of the tailgate. This is easily replaced by a standard rear tailgate for resale purposes. With a flat floor throughout, the wheelchair driver can readily move into position behind the steering wheel, and secure the wheelchair into position as the driver's seat. A second wheelchair can be similarly accommodated in the front passenger position; alternatively a conventional front passenger seat can be fitted. Price: from £8,000 on the road.

CONVERSIONS WHICH ALLOW ACCESS AND TRAVEL IN THE REAR SECTION WITHOUT LEAVING A WHEELCHAIR

There is an increasingly wide range of vehicles which lend themselves to conversion for carrying people who use wheelchairs – for family use as opposed to institutional use. The converters listed below are no more than a selection. We are aware that there are quite a number of local converting firms who will do one-off jobs for particular disabled clients while not holding themselves out as specialists in this field.

In certain circumstances (*see* Section 3) converted vehicles may qualify for VAT zero-rating and exemption from car tax.

Atlas Conversions
128 Milton Road, Portsmouth PO4 8PW (Tel: Portsmouth (0705) 815151).
This firm provides conversions based on the Fiat Fiorino and the Renault Trafic. The Fiorino can accommodate one person in a wheelchair while the Renault Trafic will take up to three passengers in wheelchairs. Wheelchair access is by a folding lightweight ramp via the rear doors (hydraulic lift option) to a reinforced floor with Unwin lock fixings. The layout is variable according to individual requirements.

Brotherwood Conversions (Yetminster) Ltd
Station Garage, Yetminster, Sherborne, Dorset, DT9 6LH (Tel: Yetminster (0935) 872603).
The Brotherwood conversion of the Nissan Prairie allows easy access for a wheelchair passenger with two simple operations: lifting the hydraulically assisted rear door; and lowering the short ramp.

Galway Smith of Huddersfield Ltd
4 Queensgate, Huddersfield HD1 2UW (Tel: Huddersfield (0484) 48111).
This firm makes available the Fiat HI-Fiorino (a

development from the small Fiat van) wheelchair transporter which it maintains is as cheap to run as a standard car and which blends easily with surrounding traffic.

Gowrings Mobility
See above.

Life-Line Conversions
Lifeline House, Lynmouth Avenue, Reddish, Stockport SK5 7AL (Tel: 061–431 4255).
This firm produces conversions of the VW Caddy and the Renault Extra van for wheelchair travellers. These conversions can also be fitted with tail lifts or ramps together with wheelchair restraint systems.

Mellor Coachcraft
Bodybuilding Division, Durham Street, Rochdale OL11 1BY (Tel: Rochdale (0706) 355355).
Included in Mellor's product range of converted vehicles is a conversion of the Ford Escort van to accommodate one or two wheelchairs.

Neill & Bennett
7 Wyngate Road, Cheadle Hulme, Cheshire SK8 6ER (Tel: 061–485 3149).
This firm provides a range of conversions. One of these is based on the Renault Trafic van. It is available in long or short wheelbase versions, with high or standard roof, and a choice of petrol or diesel engine. A 34½in wide side door combined with a low-level uninterrupted floor allows easy wheelchair access by a self-stowing ramp. The standard seating arrangement is for five seated passengers plus one in a wheelchair; however, the total of six passengers can include up to three in wheelchairs.

There is also a motor caravan conversion with elevating roof which comes fully equipped for up to four people including a wheelchair user, with flushing toilet, sink, and cooker.

Poynting Conversions
Faraday Road, Churchfields Industrial Estate, Salisbury, Wiltshire SP2 7NR (Tel: Salisbury (0722) 336048).
This coachbuilder provides conversions based on the Austin Metro, Austin Maestro van and the Ford Escort van. These are designed to allow access to, and to accommodate a wheelchair seated passenger. The conversion can be carried out on your own vehicle (in which case only the conversion qualifies for VAT zero rating) or you

can purchase a new converted vehicle fully relieved of both VAT and car tax subject to the conditions set out in Section 3.

SWS Motor Bodies
Unit 9, Hartford House, Newport Road, Weston Street, Bolton, Lancashire (Tel: Bolton (0204) 395660).
This company provides a conversion based on the Fiat Fiorino van which allows access for a disabled person in a wheelchair through the rear doors, and travel in the rear without leaving the wheelchair.

Wessex Garages
Feeder Road, St. Philips, Bristol (Tel: Bristol (0272) 716181).
The Wessex Chairliner is based on the Nissan Prairie. The inside has been extended upward and a tailgate has been fitted. There is a backward facing seat alongside the wheelchair area.

William Towns Ltd
Park Farm, Compton Verney, Warwick CV35 9HJ (Tel: Warwick (0926) 640241).
This company's normal production is of bodyshells for customers' own Mini, Metro, or Morris 1100 subframes. One of these, the Hustler Harrier can be built to order as a complete car. Ramped access for entry through the rear door (aperture 29½ in × 50 in) can be provided, and a high roof and/or long wheelbase can be incorporated to special order. The Harrier is very attractive, and comes in black and white as standard, with customer's choice of alternative colours as an optional extra.

DEVICES TO ASSIST ACCESS TO A CAR WITH SEPARATE WHEELCHAIR LOADING
It is not always necessary to have a device to help you lift a wheelchair into a car but it can be helpful to have a few tips. The Disabled Living Foundation have produced a useful leaflet *A Method of Loading a Wheelchair into a Two-Door Car*. They would be glad to send you this if you send a large stamped addressed envelope with your request. The DLF also produce details of *Wheelchair Lifting Systems* in their List 8 – Transport. Available from them at 380–384 Harrow Road, London W9 2HU.

Autochair
Millford Lane, Bakewell, Derbyshire DE4 1DX (Tel: Bakewell (062 981) 3493).
The Autochair wheelchair carrier/winch will collect your wheelchair from beside your car, and stow it in a fibreglass housing on top of the car (or vice versa) in 90 seconds. It is powered from the car battery and is controlled by simple switches on a mobile control box. The housing can be fitted to any car which will accept a roof rack. It measures 13 in deep × 33 in long × 35 in wide, sufficiently large for most modern foldable chairs with removable footplates. The cost of transferring it to your next car would be for only a few hours' labour – no components are built into the car. This firm has an agency network and will be glad to provide details.

Autosteer Controls Ltd
Moorfield Industrial Estate, Yeadon, Leeds LS19 7BN West Yorkshire (Tel: Rawdon (0532) 504642).
This firm produces small electric winches suitable for fitment in the rear of small cars and vans to pull wheelchairs up ramps. A large number of these have been fitted to Fiat Fiorino vans that have been converted to high roof units as well as to a range of individuals' vehicles. They can be fitted to a 12v or 24v electric system on a vehicle.

Cowal (Mobility Aids) Limited
32 New Pond Road, Holmer Green, nr. High Wycombe, Buckinghamshire HP15 6SU (Tel: High Wycombe (0494) 714400).
The GZ–91 roof rack provides automatic wheelchair storage. It is designed to fit any car and the device automatically raises and lowers the wheelchair to and from the covered roof rack from either side of the car.

D. G. Hodge & Son Ltd
Feathers Lane, Wraysbury, Staines, Middlesex (Tel: Wraysbury (078 481) 3580).
This firm produces a wheelchair winch and a traversing seat. The winch is powered by a low consumption motor which runs off the car battery. It will lift your wheelchair into the car in any one of several ways at the press of a button. When fitted to either side door pillar, you can stow the chair behind the front seats, or if used in conjunction with the traversing seat, the chair can be brought into the space between the seat and the door (two door cars are, of course, most suitable). It can be fitted to the back of an estate car or hatch-back to lift the chair over the rear panel.

The Hodge thighlift will lift people from the sitting position to standing position at the touch of a switch.

ASSESSMENT CENTRES
Learning to drive can be a daunting business to anybody. However for anybody with a disability or for anyone who has driven before but has acquired

a disability it may be useful and helpful to have an assessment, first of ability to drive, and second of the sort of controls and equipment you will need to help overcome any physical limitations. Advice of this sort is still in fairly short supply but things are improving and we are delighted to be able to give details of assessment centres which are now able to provide tailor-made individual assessment and advice services.

We are, of course, not forgetting that disabled drivers themselves have always been the greatest source of help to fellow aspiring drivers. Through the various disabled driver organisations a 'matching' process has long been in action, when by way of network schemes of members a would-be driver is put in touch with an established driver with a similar disability who is able to guide and help through his/her own personal experience. Very often this means having the opportunity to try out vehicles with the special controls needed to compensate for certain specific physical difficulties. The DDMC have Area Representatives who seek to 'match' in this way, while the DDA and DMF perform a similar service through their clubs.

Banstead Place Mobility Centre
Park Road, Banstead, Surrey SM7 3EE (Tel: Burgh Heath (073 73) 56222/51674).
The Centre, which is available to members of the general public, is equipped:
(a) To provide a free Information Service to disabled people, their families or professional workers on any aspect of outdoor mobility;
(b) To demonstrate and assess from the wide range of powered outdoor wheelchairs and 4 mph pavement vehicles, the best vehicle for a particular client;
(c) For assessment and recommendation on car adaptations;
(d) For a comprehensive examination for suitability to apply or re-apply for a driving licence;
(e) To provide training courses for therapists and driving instructors;
(f) To provide driving tuition on modified cars; and
(g) To carry out research concerning disabled drivers and pavement vehicle users.
There are three types of assessment.
1. Demonstration – clients can try out models from the range of equipment available in simulated road conditions. Qualified therapists consider the medical aspects of posture, controls and transfers so they may offer suit-

able advice. Instruction on use and maintenance of the vehicle selected is included in this type of assessment, which usually lasts two to three hours.
2. Car adaptations – the need for suitable adaptations to standard production vehicles can be investigated and recommendations made. Clients are assessed on a car assessment unit incorporating fully adjustable seating, reaction timing equipment and a variety of controls which help to assess strength, co-ordination and joint range in each limb. Access seat and controls are investigated by a therapist and a disability driving consultant. A full written report is sent to the client and his/her general practitioner.
3. Driving ability – this type of assessment is recommended for those individuals whose disability involves neurological damage. Many of these applicants have the basic ability to use modified car controls but possible impairment of their speed reaction, perceptual, visual and reasoning skills suggest that further investigation is necessary. At the conclusion of the assessment they exchange findings and a written report is sent to the client and his/her general practitioner.
Clients are welcome to refer themselves to this Centre. While an appointment must be made before a visit can be made to the Mobility Centre, anyone may contact Banstead Place by telephone or in writing for general information.

Fees: the information service is free but fees are charged for the assessments as described above. In certain circumstances fees are recoverable from other agencies and further advice on this is available on application. Details of fees and services will be sent on request.

Barnsley Disabled Drivers Centre
37 Cross Lane, Royston, Barnsley S71 4AT (Tel: (0226) 723742).
The assessments at the Centre include hand controls, specially adapted vehicles as well as electronic equipment. Advice can also be given on the choice of car and a typed report on the capabilities of the driver will also be given,

Derby Disabled Driving Centre
Kingsway Hospital, Kingsway, Derby DE3 3LZ (Tel: Derby (0332) 371929).
This centre for disabled drivers and would-be drivers provides an enthusiastic and flexible assessment service. The assessment facilities are backed up by two workshops where disabled drivers can

have their vehicles (car, vans, farm vehicles, etc.) converted – often paying only for the cost of components. Driving assessment is provided on a module with interchangeable hand controls and a variety of seats and hand brakes. There is also a computer link-up to the module to enable range, strength, and speed of movement on arms and legs to be measured. Also available a mobile electronic assessor which can be fitted to the driver's own car to test braking pressures and steering strength. A test track is available for motorists to try out a vehicle which has already been made available. There are also two test vehicles available.

Individual disabled people are welcome to telephone with queries or to make an appointment. Assessments and conversions can be referred from any area.

Mobility Advice and Vehicle Information Service (MAVIS)
Department of Transport, TRRL, Crowthorne, Berkshire RG11 6AU (Tel: Crowthorne (0344) 770456).
This has been set up by the Department of Transport and is based at the Transport and Road Research Laboratory at Crowthorne. The service offers:
(a) assessment and advice on driving ability and car adaptation;
(b) consultation and advice on car adaptations;
(c) vehicle familiarisation session; and
(d) information on all aspects of transport (public and private) and outdoor mobility.
Charges are made for the first three services.

People visiting the Centre for consultation and advice will have the opportunity of looking at a wide range of adapted vehicles, equipment and accessories and to take a test drive on the road system. This is a reconstruction of an urban road network, complete with pedestrian crossings, roundabouts and road signs.

There is a static rig at the Centre which is used to assess and measure strength, grip, correct seating position and other factors which are important when assessing driving ability and when advising on appropriate car choice and adaptations.

Anyone with a disability who has a full or provisional driving licence can arrange an appointment. You should take your licence with you when you visit.

Mobility Information Service
Unit 2a, Atcham Estate, Upton Magna, Shrewsbury SY4 4UG (Tel: Shrewsbury (0743) 77489).
This specialist assessment and information service

offers guidance and advice on mobility problems including wheelchairs, choice of vehicles, mobility allowance, hiring, parking privileges, and financial/tax concessions. There is no charge for the information service.

The information officers are themselves disabled drivers and wheelchair users, and they have extensive experience of many kinds of disabilities. They are able to deal with enquiries in a very personal way, gearing their advice to particular needs. They often go to considerable lengths to solve individual problems in the appropriate way, believing that there is no one answer to meet the vast spectrum of disabling conditions. They understand that those with slender resources need advice as to how they can meet their needs in the most economical way.

The MIS offers an assessment service, advising disabled drivers on individual needs, costing £20. Included in this service is the opportunity to see and try a suitable car. A written report will be available which can be shown to the Driver Vehicle Licensing Centre, driving tutor or insurance company.

In addition, a specially designed driving simulator capable of assessing the needs of the majority of disabled people prior to trying an adapted car is operated at the Centre. The simulator is able to test reaction for braking by hand or foot and physical effort available. It is also equipped with a variable resistance steering mechanism and a wide range of adjustments.

Anyone wishing to visit the Centre needs to make an appointment in advance.

MIS publishes a complete information pack covering all aspects of the service and containing a wide selection of manufacturers' and other brochures. Price: £2.

Northern Ireland Council on Disability
2 Annadale Avenue, Belfast BT7 3JR (Tel: Belfast (0232) 640011).
NICD has a purpose-built assessment unit where guidance can be given to disabled motorists on any adaptations they may need. There is a qualified driving instructor in attendance.

Tehidy Friends' Mobility Centre
Tehidy Hospital, Camborne, Cornwall TR14 0SA (Tel: Camborne (0209) 710708).
The Mobility Centre offers driving and car adaptation assessments in suitably adapted cars. Two modified cars are being used to suit any type of disability. One car is equipped with a computer which records reaction time and measures muscle power. There is an off-road track for clients who

do not have a road licence. The Centre also offers driving tuition for people with provisional licences, for those who have not driven for a time due to illness or those who have had to have their car adapted to compensate for their recently acquired handicap.

There is a fortnightly Mobility Assessment Clinic at which the client is able to see the medical adviser to the centre as well as having a driving assessment/car adaptation assessment.

Clients can refer themselves to the Centre or they can be referred by their doctor. Driving and car adaptation assessments and driving tuition are all by appointment only. Clients receive a full report from the Mobility Centre manager following their appointment.

Vehicles (For the Disabled) Centre
Astley Ainslie Hospital, Grange Loan, Edinburgh EH9 2HB (Tel: 031–667 3398).
The Centre is able to offer advice to disabled people who wish to drive as well as assessment on fitness to drive where necessary. The full assessment involves:
(a) a standard medical history and examination;
(b) an evaluation on a test rig where lay-out of controls, reaction time, etc. are tested; and
(c) an assessment in one of two cars which have been fitted with the types of controls required most frequently.
The service is offered free of charge as a straightforward National Health Service consultative appointment and drivers wishing to be assessed must therefore be referred by their GP or hospital consultant to: Dr. John Hunter, Consultant in Rehabilitation Medicine at the above address.

The Centre does not undertake adaptations but will be able to advise where these may be undertaken. They will also advise where appropriate driving instruction may be obtained.

Wales Disabled Drivers Assessment and Mobility Information Centre
18 Plasnewydd, Whitchurch, Cardiff, South Glamorgan (Tel: Cardiff (0222) 615276).
Assessment is offered to disabled people living in Wales but, in addition, the Centre will not turn away applicants living elsewhere in the UK. The driving simulator used is computer controlled and is able to test reaction for braking by hand or foot and the physical strength available. It is also equipped with a variable resistance steering mechanism and a wide range of adjustments.

Applications are accepted from individuals as well as from hospitals, social work departments, colleges of further education, and special schools. Advice is given on choosing the most suitable make and model of car and on adaptations. Information is given on choosing sources of supply, fitters, etc, as well as support services. Information is readily available on all matters of mobility for disabled people.

MOTORING ASSOCIATIONS

Automobile Association
Membership Administration Division, PO Box 50, Basingstoke, Hampshire RG21 2ED or contact your nearest Service Centre. Benefits of membership include Roadside Service by AA patrols or AA appointed garages. Members must pay for any spare parts provided.

The AA Relay Service which operates in the UK is available to members at an extra annual fee of £16.75 and is used when a prompt local repair cannot be arranged following a roadside breakdown. Recovery is provided for cars, three-wheelers, motor caravans, and light commercial vehicles up to a maximum length of 18ft, maximum width of 7ft 6in and not more than three and a half tonnes gross laden weight. Caravans up to 23ft long may be towed behind the recovery vehicle and up to five persons conveyed in that vehicle.

Another option is Home Start Service which provides minor repairs at the member's home address or recovery to a garage of the member's choice within a reasonable distance. Fee: £9.25.

Annual subscriptions: £22 basic; £5.50 associate subscription for spouse. Enrolment fee: £5. Drivers of invalid tricycles pay a reduced subscription of £8.75 a year and enjoy the extra benefits of Relay Service and Home Start Service without additional charge.

All hiring and hire purchase arrangements through Motability automatically include AA membership.
See also the AA Travellers Guide for the Disabled in Section 10.

The British School of Motoring
The Disabled Driver Training Centre, BSM Specialist Services Ltd, 81–87 Hartfield Road, London SW19 3TJ (Tel: 01–540 8262).
The Centre provides an assessment service which includes use of a reaction test unit. Driving tuition can be arranged in the owner's specially converted car. Alternatively tuition can be given in an existing BSM converted car. Advice will also be given on types of conversion appropriate to overcome a particular disability.

If it is impossible to attend the Centre in Wimbledon for a detailed assessment, it is usually possible to arrange for a home appointment with a Driver Assessment Consultant.

In addition, a number of BSM branches have cars (all Metros with automatic transmission) with partial or full hand controls.

The British Wheelchair Motorcycle Association
16 Tippets Mead, Tawney Croft, Bracknell, Berkshire RG12 1FH (Tel: Bracknell (0344) 59796).
The BWMA is mostly for enthusiasts who want to keep on motorbike riding after becoming disabled. Members have a range of bikes, including the Suzuki ATI. They will be glad to advise on any adaptations necessary to enable a disabled person to drive – these may include hand controls, and footplates instead of pegs. Motorbikes will need to be balanced with a side car which can also carry the wheelchair. A number of members are enthusiastic racers.

Disabled Drivers' Association
Ashwellthorpe, Norwich NR16 1EX (Tel: Fundenhall (050 841) 449).
The DDA was founded in 1948 as the Invalid Tricycle Association, adopting its present name in 1963, and now has over 14,000 members. It aims to promote the welfare of disabled people and to assist and encourage them to achieve greater mobility.

The Association will help and advise physically disabled people, who are fully paid-up members, whether drivers or not, on all matters of mobility including vehicles and conversions, ferry concessions, insurance, legal requirements and government and local authority help.

A series of fact-sheets is made available to members only on car adaptations, ferry concessions, buying your car, and the Association's holiday hotel.

Members are organised into about 60 local groups in 14 'areas' and each group has a good deal of autonomy in the range of its activities. All receive the Association's quarterly magazine *The Magic Carpet* and enjoy a number of concessions such as cheap travel on certain ferries.

Subscriptions are currently £5 a year (£4 to receive the magazine).

Disabled Drivers' Motor Club Limited
Cottingham Way, Thrapston, Northamptonshire NN14 4PL (Tel: Thrapston (080 12) 4724).
This club, founded in 1922, has expanded very rapidly in recent years and now has over 15,500 members. It aims to protect the interests and welfare of physically disabled drivers and to help and encourage disabled people to achieve greater mobility.

Members can seek help and advice on motoring problems, ferry concessions, vehicles, conversions and statutory help either from their area representatives or from head office where there is a 24-hour answering service. Members are kept well-informed of significant developments through a bi-monthly newspaper *The Disabled Driver* and a year-book.

Members are also entitled to certain ferry concessions and other discounts. Social events are regularly arranged on a national basis, which encourage members to meet, exchange their views and pass on ideas.

There are two classes of membership: full (disabled people) and associate (those who are interested in promoting the welfare of disabled people and in furthering the aims of the Club). Subscriptions are currently £5 a year.

Disabled Motorists Federation
Unit 2a, Atcham Estate, Upton Magna SY4 4UG (Tel: Shrewsbury (0743) 77489).
The DMF was founded in 1973 by a group of experienced disabled motorists who believed that there was a need for an organisation to give representation to individual groups of disabled motorists without affecting their independence in any way.

Currently, 23 clubs are linked in this way, as far apart as Swansea and Huddersfield, and they have been active within their local areas in securing improvements in the arrangements for disabled motorists.

The main aims of the Federation are to promote joint action as may be necessary on important matters affecting disabled people, and to provide opportunities for joint activities and the exchange of information, ideas and visits between member organisations.

An excellent quarterly journal *Flying Mat* is published to members, keeping them up to date with technical and policy developments in the field of mobility, and providing a forum for passing on personal experience and solutions to motoring problems.

Motability
For details see page 125.

Mobility Information Service
For details see page 140.

Royal Automobile Club

RAC Motoring Services, RAC House, Lansdowne Road, Croydon CR9 2JA (Tel: 01–686 2525) or 17 area offices plus local sub-offices (see telephone books for addresses and telephone numbers).

Basic subscription for wife and husband of £22.50 plus a £5 enrolment fee. This subscription covers the rescue service and other benefits. The rescue service provides roadside repair or tow to the nearest garage and apart from breakdowns covers vandalism and accidents. Seventeen emergency controls provide reasonably fast emergency services. The optional extra service of 'At Home' extends the rescue service to breakdowns at or near a member's home and costs £9.50. The additional recovery service costs £16.50 and covers the transport of the car and up to five passengers anywhere in the UK (also Northern Ireland but excludes ferry fares). If there is only one driver, illness and injury are covered under the recovery service as are caravans and trailers.

Further savings and additional RAC benefits may be obtained by joining the RAC through the following associate clubs: the DDMC and DDA as described above.

Welsh Disabled Motorists Club

18 Plasnewydd, Whitchurch, Cardiff (Tel: Cardiff (0222) 615276)

The WDMC is a member of the Disabled Motorists Federation. The club operates over a wide area of Wales but concentrates its activities mainly in South Wales. It provides practical advice, services and information for individual disabled motorists and also seeks to improve conditions and services for disabled motorists generally. Details of the assessment services are given on page 141.

Help can also be given to potential drivers looking for suitable driving instructors. The Club has a list of instructors. Through the Institute of Advanced Motorists it may also be possible to arrange for extra driving practice. The Club organises annually a Disabled Driver of the Year competition and a Roadshow (exhibiting special vehicles and accessories) at RAF St. Athan, Barry, South Glamorgan. A similar event also takes place in Colwyn Bay, North Wales.

OTHER HELPFUL ORGANISATIONS

Association for Spina Bifida and Hydrocephalus

143

22 Upper Woburn Place, London WC1H OEP (Tel: 01–388 1382).

ASBAH has a mobility adviser who can be contacted through the address above.

The adviser will give information and advice about all kinds of mobility problems to people suffering from spina bifida and/or hydrocephalus. Some of the matters she can help with include: how to use the mobility allowance; Motability schemes for buying outdoor powered wheelchairs and for buying or hiring new or second-hand cars; how to apply for a driving licence; special facilities to provide assessment and help for young people who want to learn to drive; details of driving schools with motor cars fitted with hand controls; taking the driving test; choosing a car; adapting a car; and information about manufacturers providing special car controls, seats, powered wheelchairs, etc.

DIAL UK (National Association of Disablement Information and Advice Services)

DIAL House, 117 High Street, Clay Cross, Derbyshire (Tel: Chesterfield (0246) 250055).

DIAL is an organisation encompassing local groups who provide a free, impartial and confidential service of information, advice and, in some cases, practical help provided by people with direct personal experience of disability.

Local DIALs are able to help with queries surrounding every aspect of disability and will be particularly knowledgeable about local resources. Information naturally includes the subject of mobility and where specialist advice may be sought in the locality.

Disabled Living Foundation

380–384 Harrow Road, London W9 2HU (Tel: 01–289 6111).

The DLF operates a comprehensive information service (see Section 3) and also has a display centre which includes a range of electric wheelchairs and scooters. Here visitors can try, test and compare these products. There is also an informal second-hand list. Enquiries will be dealt with by telephone or letter. Before visiting the DLF equipment centre it is necessary to make an appointment when expert assistance will be given in discussing and assessing the individual needs of a disabled person.

The Family Fund

PO Box 50, York YO1 1UY.

The Fund tries to ensure that where a family is confined to the home because of a child's handicap help is given to ensure that they can at least get out for recreational purposes. Once a child is getting the mobility allowance the Fund would not help with transport costs as such, but might help with driving lessons to allow another to make use of the family car. For details of the Fund and how to apply see page 16.

Joint Committee on Mobility of Blind and Partially Sighted People

224 Great Portland Street, London W1N 6AA (Tel: 01–388 1266).

The Committee is concerned with the problems of the mobility of visually handicapped people and seeks to consider ways in which blind people may be enabled to move more safely and independently, including improvement of the environment. The Committee is also concerned to make the general public more aware of ways in which they can improve the quality of life for blind people in matters relating to mobility and to seek government support to achieve these aims.

Membership is open to representatives from designated national organisations concerned with visual impairment.

Joint Committe on Mobility for the Disabled

Hon. Sec. Tim Shapley, 9 Moss Close, Pinner, Middlesex HA5 3AY (Tel: 01–866 7884).

This national committee represents the mobility interests of disabled people who have 'motor' or 'locomotor' disabilities. Twenty-seven organisations are represented, joining together to examine and promote all relevant matters of concern to disabled people, and ensure that they are properly brought to the attention of local and central government and statutory and other organisations.

The Committee works primarily in the area of policy, seeking to establish principles and effective strategies through which the indoor and outdoor mobility needs of disabled people can be met. It seeks legislative changes where they are needed, and has influenced government policy on many important issues. Representatives of the Department of Transport and the Department of Health and Social Security attend its meetings.

The Committee lays great emphasis on taking account of the needs of both those who do not drive and those who do. In addition to dealing with personal transport, it works strenuously for improvements in public transport facilities.

London Regional Transport
Unit for Disabled Passengers, 55 Broadway, London SW1H OBD (Tel: 01–222 5600).

As well as co-ordinating developments in the transport facilities available to people with disabilities and mobility handicaps, the Unit provides information and advice about transport services for disabled and elderly people. This includes information about London buses and the underground.

Mobility Trust
4 Hughes Mews, 143A Chatham Road, London SW11 6HJ (Tel: 01-924 3597).

The Trust works in a variety of ways to help with the mobility needs of disabled people. It can purchase equipment such as motor cars, electric wheelchairs, computers, stairlifts, and special chairs for children which are supplied in perpetuity to applicants – also driving lessons can be arranged.

The information states that as an advisory service, the Trust is open seven days a week for personal callers, telephoned enquiries and letters.

Rehabilitation Engineering Movement Advisory Panels (REMAP)
25 Mortimer Street, London W1N 8AB (Tel: 01–637 5400).

The Panels are concerned with practical problems affecting every aspect of disabled living, naturally including hoists and lifting equipment, walking aids, wheelchairs, children's aids and equipment and also transport. Some devices created by Panels for transport needs include: driving mirror for a client with a locked neck; truck for amputee to use in garden; transferable car seat for disabled child; driving seat for very short person; Citroen car handbrake extension; and for a client with rheumatoid arthritis – help to open the car door and lift handbrake. For further details of REMAP *see* Section 3.

Royal Association for Disability and Rehabilitation
25 Mortimer Street, London W1N 8AB (Tel:01–637 5400).

RADAR will advise on aspects of mobility. Contact the Information Department.

Scottish Council on Disability
5 Shandwick Place, Edinburgh EH2 4RG (Tel: 031–229 8632).

The Council provides a means of consultation and joint action among voluntary and statutory organisations working for disabled people in Scotland. It operates an information service (*see* Section 3) and a mobile aids centre.

Spinal Injuries Association
76 St. James's Lane, London N10 3DF (Tel: 01–444 2121).

The SIA links paraplegics and tetraplegics, providing information on spinal cord injury and rehabilitation. The Association is expert in the problems of mobility and the needs of disabled drivers and outstanding in the provision of relevant and practical information.

Through their LINK scheme SIA are able to put members in touch with each other for mutual help and encouragement. In matters of mobility this can be particularly helpful, with some members being prepared to show the car adaptations which they have found useful whilst encouraging new drivers to try out the controls before committing themselves to inappropriate conversions. For further details of SIA *see* Section 15.

Help with Travel Costs

CONCESSIONARY FARES

Local authorities have powers to operate a concessionary fares scheme for travel on local buses – free or at reduced rates – and disabled people may benefit under these schemes. To find out what concessions you may be entitled to locally ask your social worker or enquire at the Town Hall.

FARES TO AND FROM HOSPITAL

If you are a patient and you need help with these fares you should ask at the hospital.

If you are not the patient, but you are a close relative of a patient who is in hospital and you need help with fares because you are on a low income and are receiving Income Support then you should apply to the DHSS for a Community Care grant.

EMPLOYMENT TRAVEL

Assistance with fares is available to severely disabled people in ordinary employment who, because of their disability, incur excessive costs in travelling to work, for example, by having to use taxis (*see* page 37).

Mobility Equipment

There is a wide range of aids to mobility available, including walking aids, grab rails, stair lifts (including a 'stair driver' for independent negotiation of stairs whilst in a wheelchair), hoists, ramps and wheelchairs. Detailed information on this equipment can be obtained from: Disabled Living

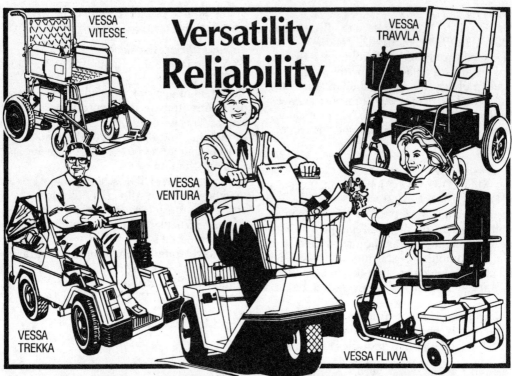

Foundation, 380–384 Harrow Road, London W9 2HU (Tel: 01–289 6111) (*see* also Section 3). Wheelchairs are normally obtained from Disablement Services Centres on prescription from your doctor, whereas walking aids are more generally arranged through the district nurse, health visitor or occupational therapist.

WHEELCHAIRS

If a wheelchair is needed for a short time – for example because someone has a broken leg – the hospital arranging for treatment will also arrange to provide a wheelchair. If a wheelchair is needed for long-term or permanent use, the Department of Health and Social Security (DHSS) supply and maintain it (through Disablement Services Centres (DSCs) – formerly Artificial Limb and Appliance Centres) on the recommendation of a hospital consultant or general practitioner. The first step, therefore, if a wheelchair is required, is to see your doctor. Ideally the doctor should arrange for a home visit by the local authority occupational therapist to assess the type of chair needed not only in relation to you as a person but also to the home environment. The doctor sends the recommendation to the local DSC of the DHSS who will arrange the supply. The hospital you attend or the Red Cross will sometimes loan wheelchairs to tide people over where there may be a gap in provision.

The non-powered wheelchairs supplied by the DHSS include not only the more conventional types but also hand and foot propelled tricycles. Their range covers the needs of all ages. More than one non-powered wheelchair may be supplied if these are really necessary – for example, one needed for home and the other for work or school use, or two different types required for differing uses, although the DHSS tries to provide one that will be suitable for all needs. Most wheelchairs can be equipped with accessories or alternative items, such as leg rests, backrest extensions and trays.

The DHSS does not provide powered outdoor wheelchairs for control by the occupant.

Leaflet HB2 *Help for Handicapped People* lists Disablement Services Centres (formerly Artificial Limb and Appliance Centres).

WHEELCHAIR HIRE PURCHASE

Motability (*see* page 125) will arrange favourable hire-purchase terms with a small deposit for certain electric vehicles. Send for their special leaflet.

REGULATIONS REGARDING THE USE OF POWERED WHEELCHAIRS ON PAVEMENTS

Since 1970 it has been legal to use certain powered wheelchairs on pavements, footpaths and footways, to cross roads in them and drive along where there are no pedestrian sidewalks. No driving test, licence or number plates are required. This concession applies whether vehicles are controlled by the occupant or by an attendant and to disabled adults or children using mechanically propelled tricycles, powered wheelchairs or powered 'Go-Karts'. However, if a qualifying vehicle is being used during the hours of darkness, on a road which has no pedestrian sidewalk, it must have a single white light in front and a single red light plus a red reflector at the back, and both lights and reflector must be in good working order. Otherwise lights need not be fitted and no lights are needed if the vehicle is being used during the hours of darkness on a pavement or crossing a road from one pavement to another.

To qualify for this concession the vehicle must be incapable of being driven faster than four miles per hour on level ground under its own power. Such a vehicle must have an efficient braking system in good working order, capable of bringing it to rest and holding it stationary on a gradient of 1 in 5. The vehicle's unladen weight must not be more than 250 lb.

Those vehicles which qualify are exempt from the compulsory insurance requirements of the Road Traffic Act 1972. However, the disabled person would do well to consider carefully the desirability of obtaining suitable insurance cover.

Mobility by Rail

SPECIAL FACILITIES – TRAINS

(*See under* country headings in Section 10 for special rail services in some European countries)

In recent years there has been considerable improvement in the design of trains, and British Rail have been at some pains to provide and incorporate reasonable facilities for disabled passengers. If you have particular complaints it would certainly be a good idea to write to British Rail who may then act to put forward ideas to overcome the difficulties for future travellers.

BRITISH RAIL

It is important that you give good notice to British Rail (or any other railway company) of any special help needed in transferring from your car on to a train and vice versa in order that they may be able to help where this is needed. For British Rail this would be the Area Manager at your departure station and the details most needed are:

(a) date and time of train;
(b) destination station and any intermediate changing points;
(c) nature of disablement (e.g. using a wheel-chair, can be transferred from wheelchair to seat, can walk with the aid of sticks, blind, etc.);
(d) any special need to be accommodated near a lavatory;
(e) if wheelchair is required at stations; and
(f) accompanied or travelling alone.

Motorail

The Motorail network criss-crosses the country, and terminals are located at Aberdeen, Bristol, Carlisle, Crewe, Edinburgh, Inverness, London, Penzance, and Stirling. However, it can be rather expensive where normal Motorail fares apply, but holders of Disabled Persons Railcard are now entitled to discounts on most Motorail routes – *see* the Motorail brochure for details.

The British Motorail system links up with similar rail systems throughout Europe. The Car Ferry Centre, Victoria Station, London SW1 (Tel: 01–730 3440) will advise on the Continental Motorail service.

A number of facilities and services are provided for disabled people travelling by train. At most Motorail terminals standard wheelchairs are available. However, people who remain in their wheelchairs should note that sleeper compartments and the saloons of coaches used on day services are not accessible.

Full details of Motorail services and routes and fares are contained in a special brochure obtainable from Travel Centres or stations or from British Rail appointed travel agents.

INTERCITY SERVICES

Wide access doors, automatic interior doors, grab-rails, a removable seat for wheelchair access, enabling the passenger in a wheelchair to stay in the chair in First Class compartments, removal of a table in Standard Class to allow more leg room and situated in a group of seats nearest the entrance and next to the accessible lavatory, and priority labelling of seats are now standard facilities. Vestibule doors and areas afford access from the platform by means of lightweight ramps kept at stations served by the trains. InterCity 125 High Speed Trains offer this facility.

Discounted Standard Class single and return fares are available to a disabled person travelling in a First Class compartment as described above. The same rate is charged for one travelling companion. Prior notice for this facility is needed.

On many other InterCity trains, coaches also have wide doors for easier access and handy grab-rails, but unfortunately it is not possible to travel while remaining in a wheelchair unless you are prepared to travel in the guard's van. For those people who can transfer to a seat, it is often possible for a wheelchair to be taken on board the train and positioned close to the train seat. Some British Rail stations also have special narrow chairs for carrying people aboard trains to transfer to a normal seat. Otherwise wheelchairs are carried free of charge in the guard's van.

INTERCITY SLEEPERS

Standard Class compartments have twin berths, one above the other, and if a disabled person is travelling alone the lower berth may be reserved.

First Class single-berth compartments have communicating doors with the adjacent compartment which may be convenient for a severely disabled traveller who needs to be in close contact with a companion. However, normal berth fees apply.

Guide dogs accompanying blind people may be taken into sleeper compartments if prior booking is made and suitable space is available. Normally the blind passenger and guide dog travel in a single berth compartment, but pay only a second class fare and berth fee.

Access to sleepers is not practicable for people using stretchers nor those remaining in wheelchairs.

TRAVELLING IN A GUARD'S VAN

A permit is no longer required for passengers in wheelchairs travelling in the guard's van. Thankfully some provisions are now being made such as lighting, heating, as well as seating for a companion.

LAVATORIES

Some mainline stations have lavatories which are accessible to wheelchair users. Unfortunately, they are usually kept locked – a notice will indicate where the key is kept. Also some of the lavatories are equipped with National Key Scheme locks. (See page 357 for details of this scheme.)

Lavatories accessible to travellers in wheelchairs are being introduced on some train services.

TRAVELLING REFRESHMENTS

Drinks and snacks are available on most long distance services and are progressively being served to passengers in their seats. Full meals are available on many InterCity services.

FARES FOR BLIND PEOPLE

When a registered blind or partially sighted person travels with a companion the following discounts apply:

(a) Standard Single – 34 per cent discount per person

(b) Standard Return – 34 per cent discount per person

(c) Standard Day Return – 50 per cent discount per person

(d) Season Tickets – 50 per cent discount per person.

DISABLED PERSON'S RAILCARD

This card is available to permanently and severely disabled people who are:

(a) registered as blind or partially sighted or are deaf with or without speech;

(b) entitled to attendance, mobility or severe disablement allowance or if someone is receiving these allowances on your behalf;

(c) receiving a war pensioner's mobility supplement or a DHSS car or if you are the driver of an invalid 3-wheeler, or you are buying or hiring a vehicle through the Motability scheme;

(d) entitled to industrial disablement benefit (where paid with constant attendance allowance) or if someone is receiving this benefit on your behalf; or

(e) receiving war or service disablement pension for 80 per cent or more disability.

Railcards cost £12 and are valid for 12 months from the date of purchase.

The following discounts are available to Railcard holders: one-third off Saver fares; half price Cheap Day Returns; one-third off Standard return tickets; one-third off Standard single tickets; half price Standard Day Returns.

Full details about the Railcard, including how to apply, are contained in a leaflet *Disabled Persons Railcard* available from stations, travel centres, and at Post Offices.

Books and Publications

AA Travellers' Guide for the Disabled: where to go, where to stay. As well as giving information on accommodation, this book also gives guidance on regulations affecting disabled drivers, available concessions, etc. Further details are given in Section 9.

British Rail and disabled travellers
BR provides two leaflets for disabled travellers which are available free at stations and travel centres.

The main leaflet gives a brief outline of special facilities and services provided for disabled travellers, including access to stations, InterCity services, seat reservations, travelling in the guard's van, sleeper services, Motorail services, lavatories, and concessions for blind travellers.

Disabled Person's Railcard. This describes the Railcard – who is entitled, when it may be used, and how to apply for one. This leaflet is also available in Post Offices.

Travelling with British Rail – A Guide for Disabled People. A guide to British Rail stations, describing access to buffets, lavatories, ticket offices, and platforms, with information on parking facilities. The guide also gives the telephone number which disabled people should use when wishing to make special arrangements for help or for having a seat removed on a Mark III coach, and describes very briefly some of the facilities available on trains.

Available from W.H. Smith price: £2 or from RADAR, 25 Mortimer Street, London W1N 8AB. Price: £2.70 inc. p&p.

Disabled Drivers' Motor Club Handbook. Produced by and available from the Disabled Drivers Motor Club, Cottingham Way, Thrapston, Northamptonshire NN14 4PL (Tel: Thrapston (08012) 4724) Price: £1.75 including postage (free to members on receipt of an sae – 10in × 7in with 37p stamps).

This publication contains a broad range of information presented in a succinct and logical way. It covers not only specific details on motoring information, but touches on wider issues such as benefits and allowances, and helpful organisations in the field of disability. The format does not permit much detail, but the basic clues are provided for you to follow up.

The 1987 edition includes sections on adaptations, ferries, tolls and tunnels, suppliers, accessories, insurance, and advice for newly disabled people.

Disabled People and the Tyne and Wear Metro – a Field Evaluation. The evaluation provided by the Handicapped Persons Research Unit, Newcastle upon Tyne Polytechnic, describes in detail this first rapid transit system designed and built within the United Kingdom which specifically includes provision for disabled and elderly people from the early planning stages. A description is given of the planning and design decisions that have made it accessible to people with a range of disabilities. Sketch layouts for each of the first 18 stations to be opened together with an outline of the ticketing system are provided. (A major project to evaluate 26 new stations was recently launched.) Available from the Handicapped Persons Research Unit, Newcastle upon Tyne Polytechnic, 1 Coach Lane, Coach Lane Campus, Newcastle upon Tyne NE7 7TW (Tel: Newcastle upon Tyne 091–235 8211). Price: £6 including postage and packing.

Door to Door, A Guide to Transport for Disabled People. This is a 96-page guide published in its second edition in 1986 by the Department of Transport. It is admirably laid out and remarkably wide ranging, covering benefits, mobility aids, personal and public transport (local, national, and international). Naturally, in a book of this relatively small size, the information is basic – a starting point – but its succinct style permits the inclusion of a huge amount of material, which is accurate and reliable. Appendices give details of organisations which can provide more detailed advice or help, both nationally and locally. Available from RADAR, 25 Mortimer Street, London W1N 8AB. The book is available free but please send 25p postage.

Equipment for the Disabled
A series of illustrated books compiled at Mary Marlborough Lodge, Nuffield Orthopaedic Centre, Headington, Oxford OX3 7LD (Tel: Oxford (0865) 750103).
Published by the Oxfordshire Health Authority on behalf of the DHSS. Four of the books in the series are listed below. Each book is priced at £3.95 plus 75p postage.
Wheelchairs. Information: obtaining a wheelchair, wheelchair assessment, wheelchair features, handling a wheelchair, simple home maintenance, methods of wheelchair propulsion, Mobility Allowance, VAT exemption, Motability; *DHSS Handbook on wheelchairs* (MHM 408); summary of *Notes on availability,* ALAC addresses (note – these are now termed Disability Services Centres), Approved Repairers' addresses, details of chairs supplied by DHSS; occupant controlled, push-chairs, indoor electric chairs, accessories, commercially available and self-propelling chairs, children's chairs, elevating chairs, sports chairs, electric chairs, cushioning support systems, chair accessories, movable and portable ramps; step lift; chair carrier; select bibliography.
Outdoor Transport. Information: mobility allowance, Motability, war pensioners' mobility supplement, assistance with fares to work, driving licences, tuition, tests, AID, exemption from VED, motor insurance, seat belt exemption, Orange Badge scheme, motoring regulations; discounts and concessions; Driving Assessment Centres; motoring organisations; public transport; community transport; escort services; rail, air and sea travel; taxis; choosing a car; car and van conversions; car control conversions; car seats and backrests; seat belts; child car safety; transfer equipment; wheelchair stowage; garages; vehicle conversions; passenger restraint harnesses; wheelchair restraint systems; tail lifts; fitted ramps; electric bicycles; tricycles; pavement vehicles; scooters, electric buggies, petrol powered vehicles, outdoor wheelchairs, indoor/outdoor wheelchairs, wheelchair accessories, protective clothing, travel chairs, portable ramps, stair climbers, select bibliography.
Hoists and Lifts. Includes information on car transfer as well as car hoists.
Walking Aids. Information: standing frames; parallel bars; stair aid; fixed and adjustable height folding walking frames; special frames and accessories; mobile walking frames; wooden and metal axillary crutches; Canadian crutches; forearm trough crutches; single and double adjustable elbow crutches; tetrapods; tripods, walking sticks; rest seats; accessories; foot rubbers, carrying bags, stick holders; select bibliography.

Esso Service Station Address List. Available free from: Esso Merchandising Service, P.O. Box 2, Feltham, Middlesex.
The booklet is a list of those Esso petrol stations whose operators have indicated their willingness to assist disabled drivers. In some cases the sites are totally attendant service anyway, and in others the sites are self-service, but there is someone available on site during certain hours who would be happy to serve disabled drivers. Both the site opening hours and the disability service hours are shown in this directory.

The Unit for Disabled Passengers
London Regional Transport, 55 Broadway, London SW1H OBD (Tel: 01–222 5600).
The Unit publishes a range of literature including: *Access to the Underground,* a 74-page handbook for elderly and disabled people, price: 70p including post; *Access to Central London*

Underground Stations, at-a-glance list of stations in the Central area, showing whether access is by stairs, escalator or lift; *Large Print Underground Map*, folds out to measure 23in × 16in; *A Talking Map of the London Underground*, cassette tape for visually handicapped people; *Tactile Central Underground Map* with stations shown in Braille (1988 – currently in course of preparation); *Large Print Central London Bus Map*; *Timetable Leaflets* for the wheelchair accessible buses in Waltham Forest, Newham, Hackney, Islington, Haringey, and Enfield; *Careline* leaflet about its wheelchair-accessible bus service linking the main line stations in London and Heathrow Airport; *A Conducted Tour of the London Transport Museum*, cassette tape which can be borrowed free by visually handicapped visitors to the LT museum at Covent Garden or purchased for listening to at home, price: £1; *Welcome Aboard* leaflet published jointly with Age Concern Greater London especially for the older passenger; *A Helping Hand Across London* leaflet published jointly with British Rail showing the easiest ways for disabled people to get between the main-line stations by bus and Underground.

Mobility Information Service publications
Unit 2a, Atcham Estate, Upton Magna, Shrewsbury SY4 4UG (Tel: Shrewsbury (0743) 77489).
The MIS has a range of useful publications including details of road tests of particular cars. Their Mobility Information Pack includes information on cars with automatic transmission, hand controls, insurance, manufacturers' discounts and concessions, special adaptations, road test reports on suitable cars. Price: £2 including p&p. Their Bumper Pack includes all the above plus manufacturers' literature on conversions, special vehicles, etc. Price: £3 including p&p.

Motoring and Mobility for Disabled People by Ann Darnbrough and Derek Kinrade. This book is the first and remains the only publication to cover the subject of motoring plus mobility generally in real depth. Every aspect of these subjects is covered in considerable detail. Subjects covered include: a run-down on standard cars giving all those measurements not included in the brochures but so

necessary to disabled motorists (both drivers and passengers); details of specialist controls including recent innovations; descriptions of assessment centres and the services they provide; holiday motoring; motoring accessories; financial allowances, financing the purchase of a car; exemption from VED; insurance; driving tests and lessons; orange badge scheme; problems of incontinence while travelling or simply of being 'caught short'; specialist organisations; useful books and publications. Price: £3 plus £2 postage and packing. (1988 edition)

RADAR
25 Mortimer Street, London W1N 8AB (Tel: 01–637 5400).
RADAR produces an invaluable publications list, free of charge, containing a number of books, pamphlets and other literature relating to mobility and travel, as well as the whole range of disability information. Send a large s.a.e. with your request.

REMAP Yearbook. This book of the Rehabilitation Engineering Movement Advisory Panels (*see* Section 3) reflects the ingenious work of the organisation in designing aids to meet individual needs, and includes examples from the REMAP case lists. These include a number of mobility aids, modifications, and adaptations with helpful illustrations. Most importantly, the yearbook contains details of local REMAP contacts, whose help can be sought where a practical problem arising from disability cannot be met by any standard aid.

Published by and available from RADAR, 25 Mortimer Street, London W1N 8AB (Tel: 01–637 5400). Price: £2 plus 30p postage.

ScotRail and the Disabled Traveller. This well-set-out guide gives details of access and facilities in 66 Scottish railway stations. It is available from stations.

INFORMATION SERVICES

For details of these services *see* Section 3 where their information on aids (including mobility aids) is listed.

In addition, the Northern Ireland Council on Disability has published *On the Move – Guide to Mobility in Northern Ireland*.

HOLIDAYS IN BRITAIN

Increasingly, standard tour operators, holiday organisers and others are accepting that disabled people prefer and have a right to take their holidays much as anyone else on an integrated basis. Similarly, many accommodation guides now use the access symbol to denote establishments with suitable access facilities. The golden rule is to contact the airline/railway/ferry/accommodation well in advance, mentioning any special requirements. Unfortunately, access symbols are often not all that they should be and do not reflect accessible places – even steps get completely forgotten in the sometimes misplaced enthusiasm to claim accessibility. It is, of course, essential that a disabled person provides him/herself with all necessary personal equipment and does not rely on hotels to provide these extras. For those who require personal help it is essential that they are accompanied by a friend, as staff in hotels, guest houses, and holiday camps cannot give this type of personal assistance. On the other hand, there are a number of group holidays for unaccompanied disabled people where there are voluntary helpers to provide the necessary help (*see* information on voluntary organisations on page 161).

See Section 8 for general travel advice and Section 10 for ferry concessions and information on air travel. Section 10 also has information on helpful travel agents, etc, some providing hotels in the UK as well as overseas.

Finance

Under the Chronically Sick and Disabled Persons Act 1970, the Social Services departments of the local authorities are empowered to assist financially registered disabled people to have a holiday and, where necessary, to suggest suitable locations and provide transport. However, the amount of help given varies greatly from area to area. Relevant charities and trade and professional organisations may also be approached for help and many of these bodies own holiday homes, bungalows, caravans, etc. which are available at very reasonable rates (*see* Voluntary Organisations on page 161).

The Family Fund may help with holidays for severely handicapped children, under 16, who normally live with their families. This Fund is at present administered by the Joseph Rowntree Memorial Trust, PO Box 50, York YO1 1UY.

Cancer Relief Macmillan Fund
Anchor House, 15–19 Britten Street, London SW3 3TY (Tel: 01–351 7811).
Unwaged cancer patients having only small savings can apply to the Fund for a grant to go on a UK holiday with their family. Patients can be recommended by their GP.

The Family Holiday Association
Hertford Lodge, East End Road, London N3 3QE (Tel: 01–349 4044).
The Family Holiday Association specialises in giving grants to underprivileged families, so that they can have a week away together as a family. Many of the families have handicapped children.

All applications on behalf of families have to be made by social workers, health visitors, family welfare organisations or similar agencies, to whom the grants are made. A Grant Allocation committee meets regularly to consider these applications. Grants vary in size according to the needs of each family but, in general, will cover the full cost of accommodation, travel and meals for a one-week break for the whole family. Families have complete choice of the type of holiday – caravan, guesthouse, holiday camp, visit to relatives etc.

A maximum grant is based on current prices at holiday camps and at present is in the region of £125 for an adult, with lesser sums for children according to age. It is unlikely that a family would receive a grant if they have had a holiday within the last four years.

For details of other holiday financial help *see* Section 10, page 173.

Insurance

For details of holiday insurance see Section 10.

Interest and Specialist Holidays

For all those people who get easily bored on holiday lying in the sun, there is a wide range of interest and specialist holidays to suit most tastes. We give details below.

Artventure Scotland

Art and activity holidays for children – for details *see* Holidays for Children page 159.

The Askrigg Foundation

Low Mill Youth Centre, Askrigg, Leyburn, North Yorkshire DL8 3HZ (Tel: Wensleydale (0969) 50432).

This residential youth centre is in the heart of Wensleydale, situated in the Dales National Park on the edge of the village. Low Mill offers outdoor activities for groups of young people spending a weekend or a midweek period at the Centre. A special feature of Low Mill is the new wing which is specially equipped for physically disabled visitors. The Centre is keen to include disabled people with those who are able-bodied.

Bookings must be made in groups – 20 is the minimum (26 maximum), and 10 in the new wing as a minimum (14 maximum).

The interest from a capital bursary account is used to provide some financial assistance for those who are described as 'particularly deserving' youngsters. The warden would be glad to advise.

Badaguish Centre

Aviemore, Inverness-shire PH22 1QU (Tel: Cairngorm (047 986) 285).

Badaguish provides fully serviced and equipped all season log cabin and summer camp accommodation. It provides countryside recreation for people with special needs and it caters for supervised groups of any size up to 50 and unaccompanied individuals on small group 'Open Camps'. Applications are welcomed from people with all degrees of handicap and care is taken to put together appropriate groups depending on age, severity of handicap and whether there is mental and/or physical handicap.

Although an outline programme is prepared for each camp in order to book instructors for certain activities, individual tastes are taken into account at the beginning of each camp. Activities include sailing, canoeing, pony trekking, a 'walk' up Cairngorm with the chairlift, and overnight 'bothy trips', walking, cycling and picnicking on the surrounding forest tracks, indoor and outdoor games. A week's programme will usually include visits to many of the local tourist facilities like Aviemore Centre, the Go-kart track, a nature reserve and the Highland wildlife park.

Bendrigg Lodge

Old Hutton, Kendal, Cumbria LA8 ONR (Tel: Kendal (0539) 23766).

The centre is open for use by a wide range of groups and organisations including mentally and physically disabled people and socially disadvantaged young people.

The building is a converted hunting lodge with 7 acres of land, fully equipped to take one or two mixed groups of up to 40 people for stays of two to ten days. The grounds consist of 4½ acres of woodland, a smallholding and a games field. The wood contains an adventure playground and campsite. There is a range of facilities and equipment for disabled people.

Groups using the centre are usually assisted with catering and have their own leaders who plan for their visit with the Bendrigg staff. A wide range of activities is available to groups, led by qualified staff. They include fell walking, rock climbing/abseiling, caving, canoeing, sailing, horse riding, archery, orienteering, swimming, camping, photography, painting, drawing, craftwork, drama, games, and living skills. Other options may be available.

Brecon Beacons National Park

National Park Office: 7 Glamorgan Street, Brecon, Powys LD3 7DP (Tel: Brecon (0874) 4437). This is the administrative headquarters and address for written enquiries about the National Park. The address of the Mountain Centre is: near Libanus, Brecon, Powys LD3 8ER (Tel: Brecon (0874) 3366).

A centre from which to enjoy the beauties of the National Park. Wheelchairs have access in all parts of the building. There is also a lavatory designed for wheelchair visitors. Suggestions for local walks with wheelchairs can be obtained from the information desk.

Calvert Trust Adventure Centre

Little Crosthwaite, Underskiddaw, Keswick, Cumbria CA12 4QD (Tel: Keswick (076 87) 72254).

The Trust was opened in 1978 to enable disabled people to enjoy the Lake District National Park in the same way as able-bodied people.

The Adventure Centre is situated near Keswick

in an area of outstanding natural beauty on the foothills of Skiddaw and overlooking Bassenthwaite Lake.

Comfortable accommodation is provided in a converted farmhouse and barns modified for the convenience of people with special needs. Facilities include heated indoor swimming pool, games room, TV lounge, library, and conservatory. There is easy access to these facilities and to the bedrooms which are single, twin, three- and four-bedded, each with wash basin. Bunkhouse accommodation is also available for self-programming, self-catering groups of up to 12 people.

The Centre is open from mid-January to mid-December and groups of up to 36 people can experience a variety of activities including riding, sailing, canoeing, hill walking, rock climbing, bird watching, with archery, angling, orienteering, nature trails, and camping as additional options.

Kielder Adventure Centre

Low Cranecleugh, Kielder Water, Falstone, Hexham, Northumberland NE48 1BS (Tel: (0660) 50232).

The Kielder Centre is part of the Calvert Trust and runs a similar programme for people with special needs. Activities include: riding, navigation and orienteering, canoeing, sailing, birdwatching and nature walks, camping and hill walking, cross-country skiing, fishing and pony driving.

Indoor games, art/craft and general recreation areas are available together with a library and lounge and bar facilities. The Centre is open from mid-January to late November.

Multi-Activity Adventure Centre

YMCA National Centre, Fairthorne Manor, Curdridge, Southampton SO3 2GH (Tel: Botley (048 92) 5228).

Fairthorne Manor offers good facilities on the 94 acre estate for integration of able-bodied and disabled youngsters in a varied programme of outdoor activities – canoeing, archery, climbing, horse riding, sailing, and environmental awareness.

There is accommodation for 160 in two and four bedded rooms plus 150 in tents. Facilities are for weekend or week stays.

Northlew Grange

Northlew, Okehampton, Devon EX20 3BR (Tel: Beaworthy (040 922) 765).

Provides a broad range of sporting activities and expeditions. Activities include: climbing/abseiling, riding, orienteering, canoeing, board-sailing, archery and there is also an assault course.

Disabled visitors are very welcome and we are informed that most activities can be adapted to suit an individual's needs. There are purpose-built bathroom and dormitory facilities. Individual requirements can be discussed with the administrator who has personal experience of disablement.

The Outward Bound Trust

Chestnut Field, Regent Place, Rugby CV21 2PJ (Tel: Rugby (0788) 60423).

Outward Bound courses are short and intensive, offering the opportunity for achievement through challenge and adventure. Outward Bound encourages young people with a disability or special needs to join its open courses.

Courses are held at centres in Wales, the Lake District, and Scotland throughout the year and can be tailored to suit any specific requirements.

The Pines Trust

The Bungalow, The Pines, Bishop's Castle, Shropshire (Tel: Bishop's Castle (0588) 638234).

The Pines house and grounds on the outskirts of the little town of Bishop's Castle in the heart of the border hill country of southern Shropshire provides opportunities for groups and individual disabled people, who must be accompanied, to enjoy weekends and holidays camping in the house and grounds. Visitors look after themselves with the help of a specially adapted kitchen, lavatory, and washing accommodation.

A range of other facilities is available in the surrounding area including fishing, riding, canoeing, and gliding.

Indoor and outdoor charges are £3 per person per night. These charges cover tent pitches and use of indoor washing/toilet/kitchen accommodation. A limited number of four berth tents is available.

Queen Elizabeth II Silver Jubilee Activities Centre

Upper Hamble Country Park, Pylands Lane, Bursledon, Hampshire (Tel: Bursledon (042 121) 4844).

The QE II Centre, situated in the attractive woodland setting of the Upper Hamble Country Park at Bursledon near Southampton, offers residential outdoor activity courses for persons of all ages who are mentally or physically disabled. The site is surrounded by a network of bridle paths for riding activities, and has its own jetty and boat compound on the Upper Hamble river.

Accommodation is in wooden frame cabins for

either six or ten people. Two cabins are wheelchair accessible.

A wide range of recreational activities is available at the Centre including: canoeing, riding, cycling, launch trips, sailing, jogging, and minigolf. The boats and equipment have been chosen for their suitability for use by disabled people and many who would not be able to participate using equipment at conventional centres, have been able to take part using the specialist equipment.

The Centre has a large indoor sports area which can be used for a variety of games and activities including unihoc, snooker, table football, skittles, table tennis, and darts.

Share

Share Centre, Smith's Strand, Shanaghy, nr Lisnaskea, Co. Fermanagh (Tel: Lisnaskea (036 57) 22122).

Share is a residential activity centre, situated on the shores of Upper Lough Erne. It is designed for use by both able-bodied and disabled people. It is open all year round and in the summer months it concentrates on organised activity holidays for both families and individuals. The Centre occupies a beautiful eight-acre site with direct access to the lake and to an adjacent beach. It has its own jetty from which to canoe, sail or windsurf, and the scores of wooded islands in the lake are ideal for picnics, barbecues, and overnight camps.

Stackpole Trust

Goldborough Farm, Hundleton, nr Pembroke, Dyfed SA71 5RF (Tel: Pembroke (0646) 685929). The Trust provides an adventure, holiday and studies centre for disabled people and their friends. The Centre is at Stackpole Home Farm, close to the village of Bosherston. It is surrounded by farmland and is very close to the Bosherston Lily Ponds in the South Pembrokeshire National Park. There are a number of beaches nearby, at least two of which are accessible to wheelchair users.

The self-catering accommodation, all of which is designed with the needs of wheelchair users in mind is in seven cottages and one group house.

The Trefoil Holiday and Adventure Centre for the Handicapped

Gogarbank, Edinburgh EH12 9DA (Tel: 031–339 3148 warden).

The Centre is set in the countryside seven miles from Edinburgh, and is specially designed to cater for up to 40 physically disabled people with their helpers, either in groups or as individuals. The

house is centrally heated throughout and has a bar, shop, TV room and three well-stocked games rooms; indoor heated pool; minicoach with lift. Rambler cars are available for guests to explore the grounds, gardens, and woods. Barbecues and discos are organised; advice is given on suitable outings and other activities.

Registered Guide, Lecturer, and Travel Consultant

William Forrester, 1 Belvedere Close, Guildford, Surrey GU2 6NP (Tel: Guildford (0483) 575401).

William Forrester is the first person in a wheelchair to succeed in becoming a London Tourist Board Registered Guide. He is also a fully qualified Round Britain Tour Guide. Having taught history for several years, he specialises in bringing English heritage to life. This combined with his accurate, up to the minute information on access makes for a unique service for disabled people – though William emphasises that he regularly works for able-bodied people as well.

He offers to:
(a) guide you or your party round London or the UK;
(b) tailor-make an itinerary to suit your needs, including where to stay and how to travel around (successful itineraries have been constructed for individuals, groups, and travel firms);
(c) visit you in your hotel to discuss and help you firm up your plans;
(d) arrange minibus or minicab guided tours of London, etc – particularly for wheelchair users;
(e) carry out research and consultancy work in the field of tourism and access for disabled people; and
(f) Give background lectures (illustrated by slides) on the heritage you will see on the topic of tourism for disabled people.

CAMPING AND CARAVANNING

Camping for the Disabled

David Griffiths is an enthusiastic camper with a great deal of experience (good and bad!) which he is prepared to share with other intrepid adventurers. He has camped extensively in the United Kingdom and on the Continent and never allows his wheelchair to stop him, although he admits he has never discovered anyone yet who has managed to erect a tent from a wheelchair! He points out that quite a proportion of Britain's camp sites have accessible washing and toilet facilities, and on the Continent there are few inaccessible camp sites.

David has compiled a number of guides to camp sites including Britain, West Germany, Switzerland, and Holland. The membership subscription to *Camping for the Disabled* is £2 covering a family of up to five members. It entitles you to receive all camp site lists published by them and a reduction in the camp site charges. Contact David at 20 Burton Close, Dawley, Telford, Shropshire TF4 2BX (Tel: Telford (0952) 507653 evenings; Shrewsbury (0743) 77489 daytime).

See also Forest School Camps for children under Holidays for Children in this Section of the Directory.

See also Stichting Vakantie en Handicap (Holiday and Handicap Association) page 189 in Section 10 for information on camping and caravanning holidays on the Cote d'Azur and in the Netherlands.

RAC Camping and Caravanning Guide – Great Britain and Ireland

In addition to details of the facilities and amenities of all the RAC Appointed and Listed sites, this annual guide includes information on sites with facilities for disabled people.

Available from the Publications Manager, RAC, RAC House, Lansdowne Road, Croydon CR9 2JA, from all RAC Offices or from bookshops. Price: £2.95 + 70p p&p.

The Scottish Council on Disability has a very full list on holidays which includes a good deal of information on camping and caravanning throughout the UK including a special section on Scotland. This list is available free from them at: Princes House, 5 Shandwick Place, Edinburgh EH2 4RG (Tel: 031–229 8632).

For further details of caravan holidays see under Voluntary and Specialist Organisations concerned with holidays.

CYCLING

See also Cycling in Section 11 – the *Tandem Club* arranges touring weekends.

Cyclorama – Lakes and Coastal Holidays

The Grange Hotel, Grange-over-Sands, Cumbria LA11 6EJ (Tel: Grange-over-Sands (044 84) 3666). Cycling holidays in Cumbria are planned for a carefree tour of the region. A support service carries any baggage to booked hotels and guest houses. Cyclorama do not have special bicycles, but anyone who can safely ride and control a bicycle, disabled or otherwise can be accommodated. They suggest that disabled people con-

templating a Cyclorama holiday should write to them and indicate any special needs.

Just Pedalling

9 Church Street, Coltishall, Norfolk NR12 7DW (Tel: Norwich (0603) 737201).

This is a family firm arranging cycling holidays in East Anglia. Itineraries are arranged and included in each cycling tour package is bed and breakfast accommodation at guest houses; a three-speed touring cycle with lights; large luggage panniers; wet weather gear; cycle lock, basic repair kit, and tools; brochures, booklets and maps; as well as descriptions and directions to your accommodation which may be in an Elizabethan Manor house, a flint cottage, a working farm or a real ale inn.

Any of the tours are available to blind or partially sighted holidaymakers by using tandems, provided a sighted companion can do the steering.

RIDING

See also Interest and Specialist Holidays in previous pages.

Riding for the Disabled Association

National Headquarters, Avenue R, National Agricultural Centre, Kenilworth, Warwickshire CV8 2LY (Tel: Coventry (0203) 56107).

Riding holidays for disabled children and adults are organised by headquarters and local groups of individuals. Priority is given to those who ride with an RDA member group.

SAILING AND CRUISING

See also Interest and Specialist Holidays in previous pages, and *see* page 166 the Spinal Injuries Association for details of their *Kingfisher* narrow boats).

See also the Holiday list from the Scottish Council on Disability. This has a section on sailing and boating holidays throughout the UK. It is available free from them at: Princes House, 5 Shandwick Place. Edinburgh EH2 4RG (Tel: 031–229 8632).

Jubilee Sailing Trust

PO Box 180, The Docks, Southampton SO9 7NF (Tel: Southampton (0703) 631388 or 631395 (voyage department)).

The Trust gives disabled people an opportunity to find fulfilment as working crew members and to share on an equal basis with their able-bodied counterparts the integrating and challenging experience of sailing an ocean-going square-rigged ship at sea. The Trust has built its own specially designed 141 ft barque, *STS Lord Nelson*. She has 50 berths of which 40 are for PH and AB crew on voyages from a weekend to two weeks' duration. The balance of berths is for a professional crew of eight including an SRN and two volunteer helpers. The challenge is open to all would-be sailors from 16–70 years old with or without experience.

Medina Valley Centre

Dodnor Lane, Newport, Isle of Wight PO30 5TE (Tel: Newport (0983) 522195).
We are informed that the Centre is designed in such a way that disabled people have few mobility difficulties. The staff are always glad to help organised group leaders.

Groups can use the Centre as a base for their own activities on the Isle of Wight, or they can join in with Centre organised activities which include sailing, art courses, wildlife and environmental studies. Sailing courses for disabled people are provided using purpose-designed single-seat Trimaran and Seastar dinghies.

The Centre is run as a Christian home and some time is given each day to examining Christian beliefs.

Ranch Adventure Complex

Llanbedr, Gwynedd LL45 2HU (Tel: Llanbedr (034 123) 358).
This is one of the Northamptonshire Association of Youth Clubs Action Centres and has special facilities for disabled people. The Complex is at Pensarn Harbour at the foot of the Rhinog Mountains in Wales. Sailing and canoeing courses are arranged.

Reach Out for Kids

Diocesan Education Centre, Hall Grove, Welwyn Garden City, Hertfordshire AL7 4PJ (Tel: Welwyn Garden (0707) 335968 – Monday, Wednesday, Friday 9.30 a.m.–noon, otherwise there is an answerphone).
The Albans fleet of traditional narrowboats include facilities making them accessible to people in wheelchairs. Some have wheelchair lifts or ramps. The *Fellowship of Waterford* features wide access, a wheelchair ramp, hydraulic/tilt bed, large purpose built shower and toilet area.

The base is situated on the Grand Union Canal close to Hemel Hempstead in Hertfordshire.

There are also two ocean-going sailing yachts based on the Hamble near Southampton. For disabled users access is provided within the constraints of a large yacht. Lifting gear enables good access to the cockpit and galley. Additional grab handles throughout give a reasonable measure of support. Cockpit facilities are an audio/Braille compass and a hand held VHF.

Staffordshire Narrowboats Ltd

The Wharf, Newcastle Road, Stone, Staffordshire ST15 8JW (Tel: Stone (0785) 816871).
Doubloon is a 'family' boat for those who want to take a cruising holiday while also having special facilities for a disabled family or group member. There is full access throughout for most wheelchairs plus other useful adaptations including a lift and special toilet facilities. *Doubloon* is centrally based at Stone on the Trent and Mersey Canal, giving access to the Cheshire Ring, the Four Counties Ring, and the Caldon Canal.

Peter Le Marchant

Colston Bassett House, Colston Bassett, Nottingham NG12 3FE (Tel: Kinoulton (0949) 81205).
The Trust arranges free day trips and short holiday trips for disabled people of all ages on their broadbeam boats *Symphony* and *Serenade*. *Symphony* is used for day trips and can take 28 people including helpers, while *Serenade* provides short holiday trips and can carry 12 disabled people, plus wheelchairs if necessary. Each boat is equipped with hydraulic lifts, large shower and toilet areas, resuscitation equipment and radio telephones. All trips take place between April and October from the Derby Road moorings at Loughborough. A new cruiser is available for the use of disabled people, particularly families, at a subsidised cost, and is based on the Norfolk Broads.

Port Edgar

South Queensferry, Edinburgh EH30 9SQ (Tel: 031–331 3330).
Lothian Regional Council Department of Planning arrange a watersports programme every year and disabled people are welcome on the courses, including canoeing and board-sailing. There are also courses arranged especially for disabled people. Most of the courses are for the novice, although there are some at intermediate and advanced levels for those who are more experienced.

Port Edgar is the base for a specially designed *Challenger* Trimaran which we understand can be sailed safely by those with restricted mobility. Lavatory facilities are available for disabled people.

Vale of Llangollen Canal Boat Trust

East Street, Llangollen, Clwyd (Tel: Llangollen (0978) 861450).

The canal boat *Myfanwy*, moored at Trevor basin during the summer, may be hired for day plus ½-day trips (up to 12 people) or for cruises (up to six people). A hydraulic lift is installed for the use of people in wheelchairs, and other facilities are available. There is no charge for the use of *Myfanwy*, but donations are appreciated.

SKIING

The British Ski Club for the Disabled

Corton House, Corton, nr. Warminster, Wiltshire (Tel: Warminster (0985) 50321). For further details *see* Section 11.

GENERAL STUDY COURSES

A wide range of educational courses is available, including some with facilities for disabled people, details of which are published every January and August by the National Institute of Adult Continuing Education, De Montfort House, 19B De Montford Street, Leicester LE1 7GE (Tel: Leicester (0533) 551451) in *Residential Short Courses*. Price: £1.05 inclusive of postage and packing.

The following colleges and course centres are among those which can accept some disabled students for suitable courses. In general, this does not mean that these centres are suitable for students who cannot walk at all, although there may be some facilities, e.g. ground-floor bedrooms and lifts.

Those who need personal help would need to be accompanied. However, Maryland College does have special facilities for non-ambulant students and its Principal will give further details. Intending students should give the nature of their disability and their special needs when applying for a place. Early application is strongly recommended since suitable accommodation is usually limited.

The Earnley Concourse

Earnley, Nr. Chichester, Sussex PO20 7JL (Tel: Bracklesham Bay (0243) 670392).

For those aged 16 plus. A variety of courses including painting, music, crafts, yoga, cookery, wine tasting, china restoration, sociology, realising self-esteem, caring for antiques, and modern languages (French, German, Spanish, and Italian).

Halsway Manor Society Ltd

Crowcombe, nr Taunton, Somerset TA4 4BD (Tel: Crowcombe (098 48) 274).

Folk holiday weeks.

The Hill Residential College

Pen-y-Pound, Abergavenny, Gwent NP7 7RP (Tel: Abergavenny (0873) 5221).

Courses include pottery, arts, crafts, history, social science, languages, flower arranging, music appreciation, and industrial archaeology courses. There is only very limited access for wheelchair users who would need to bring a companion. Bursaries are available to help with course fees for disabled people.

Knuston Hall

Irchester, Wellingborough, Northamptonshire (Tel: Rushden (0933) 312104).

Short residential courses all year. Subjects include arts, literature, music, archaeology, education, crafts, and languages. For those aged 18 plus.

Maryland College

Woburn, Milton Keynes MK17 9JD (Tel: Woburn (0525) 290688).

Gardening, architecture, photography, languages, nature studies, writing, lace making, painting and art, antiques, film making, crafts, and literature courses.

Millfield Village of Education

Millfield School, Street, Somerset (Tel: Street (0458) 45823).

In addition to 400 courses, and over 90 sports, cultural, and creative activities, there is also a communication course for young hearing impaired people and their families.

Westham Adult Residential College

Barford, Warwickshire CV35 8DP (Tel: Barford (0926) 624206).

Painting, literature, languages, music, and other courses.

FIELD STUDIES AND OUTDOOR PURSUITS

Churchtown Farm Field Studies Centre

Lanlivery, Bodmin, Cornwall (Tel: Bodmin (0208) 872148).

This Centre provides field study and linked education/adventure holiday courses for all types of handicapped children and adults. Accommodation is in a mixture of purpose-built residential blocks and converted, traditional stone barns. There is a well-equipped laboratory, library and photographic dark-room as well as a range of audio-visual aids. A feature of the development is an indoor heated swimming pool. All the buildings and facilities are linked by the imaginative use of ramps and a covered concourse. Churchtown Farm can accommodate 45 students plus the necessary visiting staff in small student and staff bedrooms. All the accommodation has been specifically designed for the disabled visitor.

Courses are provided in natural sciences, rural studies, adventure pursuits including sailing, canoeing, rock-climbing and a wide variety of leisure activities. The Centre is situated close to the coast, river and moor and has its own nature reserve and nature trail. There is an educational farm which includes animals, greenhouses, and a kitchen garden.

Groups may attend with their own teachers and/or care staff. The Centre is able to take single bookings but this will depend on the degree of care required by the individual.

Transport is available both for courses and to collect parties from the local railway station. Courses start and finish on Wednesdays.

Preston Montford Field Centre
Montford Bridge, Shrewsbury SY4 1DX (Tel: Shrewsbury (0743) 850380).
The centre provides courses in painting, design, flower illustration, creative writing, photography, local history, architecture, heraldry, and natural history.

The Scottish Field Studies Association Ltd
Kindrogan Field Centre, Enochdhu, Blairgowrie, Perthshire PH10 7PG (Tel: Strathardle (025 081) 286).
The Association is interested in encouraging disabled people to use the Centre. However, they point out that their facilities are somewhat limited especially access for wheelchairs. Notwithstanding these difficulties the Association is keen to arrange special courses for groups of disabled people. It would be possible to adapt courses like 'Natural History in the Highlands' and 'Exploring Tayside'. A wide range of environmental and countryside courses is arranged.

Quaker International Social Projects
Friends House, Euston Road, London NW1 2BJ (Tel: 01-387 3601).
A programme of about 15 international work-camps is arranged each year, in which a group of people come together for a couple of weeks to live and work together on socially useful projects. It is not necessary to have any connection with Quakers to take part. Disabled volunteers are welcome to apply and will be given advice as to the most suitable work-camp for each individual.

HOLIDAYS FOR CHILDREN

Artventure Scotland
Art and Activity holidays for children, c/o Blackshill Farm, Moscow, Ayrshire KA4 8PP (Tel: Moscow (056 07) 231).
Artventure Scotland is a new kind of activity holiday which introduces the arts to children in an adventure holiday atmosphere. During short stay residential courses Artventure provides a stimulating programme of art activities combined with excursions, outdoor recreational and social activities. Sculpture, painting, mosaic, tapestry, treasure hunts, fancy dress competitions, and mad-hatters tea parties are just a few of the things you might be involved in on an Artventure holiday. Artventure also has a particular interest in designing unique courses for children with special needs.

The emphasis is on fun but the experience of an Artventure holiday is considered to be of social and educational value for children. Artventure offers a specialised care service so children can come unaccompanied either independently, with a friend or with a group.

Artventure combines its aim to encourage youth enthusiasm in the arts with the following commitments:
(a) to cater for all groups of children, including those with a physical or sensory handicap and those who are sick with a long-term condition; and
(b) to integrate these children and able-bodied children wherever possible.
Details can be obtained from Jane Anderson, Bonsecours Cottage, Isar Lane, Mansionhouse Road, Langside, Glasgow.

Association for All Speech Impaired Children (AFASIC)
347 Central Markets, Smithfield, London EC1A 9NH (Tel: 01-236 3632/6487).
AFASIC organises activity week holidays every summer in which volunteers and children are linked on a one-to-one basis. Details from: Mr J. Richards, Chairperson, AFASIC Creative and Outdoor Activities subcommittee, 21 Rhos Avenue, Middleton, Manchester M24 1EG.

BREAK
20 Hook Hill Road, Sheringham, Norfolk NR26 8NL (Tel: Sheringham (0263) 823170/823025).
BREAK provides a wide range of short-stay residential care, designed to be very flexible and covering most needs from holidays to emergency

admissions. Individual and group placements of both mentally and physically disabled children (including pre-school ages), mentally- and multi-handicapped adults and families with special needs. In the case of groups, accompanying staff can be accommodated if required. There are two centres on the Norfolk coast open all the year round and placements can be from long weekends to several weeks.

A good ratio of experienced staff is provided giving both day and night cover. Parents are most welcome to accompany their child or children but should know that each centre is organised around the needs of its handicapped guests. However, there is plenty of opportunity for parents to follow an independent programme, leaving their children in the care of staff or alternatively they can join in the programme organised by the centres. A wide range of activities is provided in a holiday atmosphere and these include frequent outings in specially adapted transport. Independence training, counselling, observation, and assessments can be embraced if required. Both centres are furnished and decorated like family homes. Escort facilities are available from and to most parts of the country.

Buckets and Spades Charitable Trust
Lancaster Road, Hollington, St. Leonards-on-Sea, Sussex TN38 9LX (Tel: (0424) 52119).
A Jewish home for mentally handicapped children of any age or religion up to 18 years of age. However the first three months of the year and during other limited periods the home is reserved for mentally handicapped adults.

Forest School Camps
Details from the Secretary: Lorna English, 110 Burbage Road, London SE24 9HD (Tel: 01–274 7566).
Forest School Camps runs camping holidays for about a thousand children a year, mainly during the summer holidays but also over half terms and at other weekends throughout the year. It has over 35 years' experience of organising and running camps.

Both physically handicapped and able-bodied girls and boys are welcomed at the camps, many of them returning year after year. Its 'standing camps' take about 65 children of all ages though most activities take place in small groups.

Forest School Camps aims not only to give children a good time but also to enable them to experience living together in a community where everyone, staff and children, has a say in running the camp and takes their turn with the chores. They live outdoors mainly in small two person tents. Campers are encouraged and shown how to do everything for themselves from collecting and chopping wood for fires (under supervision) to preparing food and cooking it.

Other events during the camp may include swimming, exploring, night walks, country dancing, camp fires and games. Some of the camps are mobile and involve cycling or walking holidays.

Scripture Union in Schools
130 City Road, London EC1V 2NJ (Tel: 01–250 1966).
Organises holidays for disabled and able-bodied young people of 14 plus under expert supervision.

Holiday Care Service
The Service provides a number of information sheets on holidays for disabled children. These include: *Holidays for Mentally and/or Physically Handicapped Children and Young People; Special interest and Activity Holidays Suitable for Disabled Children and Young People; Other Holiday Ideas for Mentally or Physically Handicapped Children or Young People; Hotels where Parents with Handicapped Children are Welcome; Holidays for Unaccompanied Children and Young People; Outdoor Activity Holiday Centres Accepting Deaf Young People;* and *Activity Holidays for Sight Impaired Youngsters.* For further details of Holiday Care Service *see* page 163.

Jane Hodge Holiday Home
Trerhyngyll, Maendy, nr Cowbridge, South Glamorgan CF7 7TN (Tel: Cowbridge (044 63) 2608/2972).
Varied and interesting holidays are provided designed to improve the quality of life, broaden the outlook, strengthen the confidence and encourage the independence of handicapped children. The holidays provided include trips to places of interest e.g. beaches, bird and wildlife sanctuaries, zoos, museums, etc. Amenities include a hydrotherapy swimming pool with aqua roundabouts, a well-equipped playroom, music/television room, lake, roundabouts, putting green, and croquet lawn. A full leisure programme is organised under trained supervision. Every application is considered on its merits and there are no fixed age limits. Prices vary in seasons and for other reasons, but as a guide the total cost of a week's holiday for a child during the peak period could be £175.

Voluntary Council for Handicapped Children
National Children's Bureau, 8 Wakley Street,

London EC1V 7QE (Tel: 01–278 9441).
A free fact-sheet is available on holidays for handicapped children.

HOME EXCHANGE SCHEMES FOR HOLIDAYS

Homeshare Ltd
3 Main Street, New Elgin, Elgin, Moray, Scotland IV30 3BQ (Tel: Elgin (0343) 45738).
Home-owners can join in this scheme to exchange their homes with other compatible home-owners. Homeshare welcome disabled home-owners who may be able to swap with others having suitably equipped homes where they can enjoy a holiday in an environment specially suited to their needs. It is necessary first to inform Homeshare of your particular disability and requirements to enable a suitable exchange to be effected.

The cost of the service will be the same at £23 but, in addition, for disabled applicants there is an introductory offer whereby the registration fee of £5 is waived. The necessary proof of ownership and insurance along with a photograph will still be required. The service runs alongside the present service but forms a separate register.

Handihols
12 Ormonde Avenue, Rochford, Essex SS4 1QW (Tel: Southend-on-Sea (0702) 548257).
Joan Humphrey and Rhona Thring, realising the need, through personal experience, for disabled people to have homely facilities and where possible special adaptations when they are on holiday, have compiled a register of families who wish to exchange their homes for a break, be it a weekend, several days or one or more weeks. There is a registration fee plus £3 for each successful introduction. People and their houses are matched to similar accommodation catering for similar needs as far as possible, so that the disabled holiday maker may remain as independent as possible. Please send s.a.e. with enquiries.

Intervac
International Home Exchange Scheme, 6 Siddals Lane, Allestree, Derby DE3 2DY (Tel: Derby (0332) 558931).
As the brochure says Intervac unlocks the door to rent-free holidays worldwide. The application form seeks the sort of information which will help members to choose the sort of exchange best suited to their preferences. Included is a question about the suitability of a member's home for disabled visitors. It would then be up to an intending visitor to check that any facilities were in fact suitable for individual needs. Intervac were very positive that they wanted to encourage home exchanges which included those in wheelchairs or with mobility difficulties. All kinds of homes are offered, from modest bed-sitters to mansions.

Each year Intervac publishes three Holiday Directories. Your details are listed in one of these and you receive all three books as they are published. Those offering accommodation which may be suitable for disabled people are indicated by the use of the wheelchair symbol. Holidays are arranged by contacting other members by 'phone or letter. The international code helps to reduce language problems, and, in any case, most members speak English.

The annual membership fees £27.

VOLUNTARY AND SPECIALIST ORGANISATIONS CONCERNED WITH HOLIDAYS

Many of the organisations catering for people with specific disabilities or problems either run their own holiday facilities from caravans and chalets to bigger accommodation, or are able to advise prospective holidaymakers on the type of accommodation where they may enjoy a holiday suited to their needs and their tastes. Some are listed below, but this list is by no means exhaustive. We recommend you look through Section 15 on Helpful Organisations and make enquiries to the appropriate association or group.

Arthritis Care
6 Grosvenor Crescent, London SW1X 7ER (Tel: 01–235 0902).
The Association has four specially adapted holiday centres for the use of members, three in England (Lancashire, Devon, and Dorset) and one in Scotland (Nairn).

Breakthrough Trust – Deaf-Hearing Group
Charles W. Gillett Centre, Selly Oak Colleges, Birmingham B29 6LE (Tel: 021–472 6447 (voice only); 021–471 1001 (teleprinter only).
Adventure holidays are planned and the purpose of these projects is to provide children with an opportunity to gain a deeper understanding of each other by extending the integration programme of both deaf and hearing children beyond the local environment. Besides camping activities, there are visits to places of interest, canal trips, and outdoor pursuits.

The British Diabetic Association
10 Queen Anne Street, London W1M OBD (Tel:01–323 1531).
Education and activity holidays are run annually for people with diabetes of all ages, plus weekends for families with diabetic children.

British Kidney Patients Association
Bordon, Hampshire (Tel: Bordon (042 03) 2021).
The BKPA has three Holiday Dialysis Centres – two abroad (for details see Section 10) and one at the Sussex Beach Holiday Village near Chichester, West Sussex.
Dialysis is carried out Mondays, Wednesdays, and Fridays. The duration of the dialysis is five hours. Patients need to complete and return an application form, signed by their doctor, before treatment can be offered at the Centre.
Families have a choice of two-, four- or six-berth luxury holiday bungalows. Sussex Beach offers facilities for indoor and outdoor sports, including tennis, football, cricket, volleyball, crazy golf, croquet, bowls, archery, table tennis, billiards, snooker, darts, go-karts, and skateboards. There is also a children's own clubroom and playground, and nightly entertainment. In addition there is a heated outdoor swimming and paddling pool, and licensed bars.

It is essential to contact the British Kidney Patients Association first to see whether or not there is a dialysis vacancy at the time you want.
The address for the brochure about holiday facilities is Sussex Beach Holiday Village, Earnley, nr. Chichester, West Sussex (Tel: Chichester (0243) 671213).

British Polio Fellowship
Bell Close, West End Road, Ruislip, Middlesex HA4 6LP (Tel: Ruislip (0895) 675515).
The Fellowship runs a residential/holiday establishment as well as self-catering accommodation, i.e. a bungalow, holiday flats, and a holiday caravan.

British Red Cross Society
9 Grosvenor Crescent, London SW1X 7EJ (Tel: 01–235 5454).
The British Red Cross branches organise holidays for disabled people either open to general applicants or only to applicants from the area of the branch. Branches also provide information on holidays available through other organisations and it is usually possible to borrow equipment such as wheelchairs, commodes, etc. for use on holiday, but early application is advisable. In addition, holiday camps are organised through the Youth Red Cross where young members of the Society entertain disabled children. Red Cross branches will also help and advise disabled people concerning travel arrangements within this country. This may take the form of providing escorts to travel with disabled people on public transport, or the provision of private transport by car or ambulance. All enquiries should be made to the local branch of the British Red Cross (address in local telephone directory).

Care Home Holidays Ltd
Wern Manor, Porthmadog, Gwynedd LL49 9SH (Tel: Porthmadog (0766) 3322).
Care Home Holidays are able to offer a winter and summer holiday service in care homes throughout England and Wales – each one vetted and checked – which aim to give elderly and infirm people an enjoyable holiday.
The 'Rose Award' scheme enables the holiday maker to choose the home best suited to their pocket and personal requirements, similar to the familiar hotel star rating.
Specialist transport can be arranged, if necessary, by a network of private ambulances. Every holidaymaker will receive a call from the courier

service during their stay to make certain they are happy and contented.

Care Home Holidays are operated in consultation with Help the Aged.

Cystic Fibrosis Research Trust

Alexandra House, 5 Blyth Road, Bromley, Kent BR1 3RS (Tel: 01–464 7211).

The Trust manages, with the help of voluntary workers, several holiday caravans and chalets for use by those with CF and their immediate families. Caravans are sited around the country.

For further details of the Trust *see* Section 15.

Disabled Christians Fellowship

50 Clare Road, Kingswood, Bristol BS15 1PJ (Tel: Bristol (0272) 616141).

The DCF organises holidays throughout July and August and brochures are available from March each year.

The Disabled Drivers Association

Ashwellthorpe Hall, Ashwellthorpe, Norwich, Norfolk NR16 1EX (Tel: Fundenhall (050 841) 449; holiday enquiries: (050 841) 324).

The Association runs a moated Tudor country house holiday hotel in Norfolk offering excellent facilities in the midst of 22 acres of delightful grounds near the Norfolk Broads and Yarmouth.

In addition, local groups have funded the purchase of properties in Belfast, Bournemouth, Glasgow, and Llanelli, and some groups own holiday caravans.

For further details of the DDA *see* page 142.

Elizabeth FitzRoy Homes

Caxton House, Station Approach, Haslemere, Surrey GU27 2PE (Tel: Haslemere (0428) 52001).

Elizabeth FitzRoy Homes provide Christian residential care for mentally handicapped children and adults for life in small family units, enabling them to obtain their full potential development.

Long- and short-term care is offered in ten homes in Essex, Richmond-upon-Thames, Norfolk, Worcestershire, Birmingham, Manchester, Sussex and Hampshire (three homes). This Trust also organises summer holidays for physically handicapped boys and girls (8–18) in schools, etc. Those in wheelchairs and those who are incontinent are welcome.

The Farrell Trust

(Self-catering holidays for disabled people and their families.)

1 Hollyridge, Midhurst Road, Haslemere, Surrey GU27 2NQ (Tel: Haslemere (0428) 54845).

All of the holiday homes are specially designed for disabled people including those using wheelchairs, and are situated as follows:

Beach Lodge and 27 Nelson Road are modern houses in Bognor Regis; two caravans are installed at West Sands Leisure Centre, Selsey, nr. Chichester with two more at the AA 5-star Hoburne Holiday Park at Christchurch; chalets on the Naish Estate in New Milton in Hampshire (they are set on the cliff top with views across the Solent to the Needles and the Isle of Wight); and a holiday apartment and holiday bungalows in the King's Holiday Park in Eastbourne.

Gillmour Travel Services

Gillmour House, Blennerhasset, Carlisle CA5 3RE (Tel: Aspatria (0965) 21553).

They offer specially 'tailor made' holidays for families who have a disabled member. The holidays are personalised so that they fit the needs and interests of the family rather than the family having to fit into a pre-arranged package. The aim of the Service is to provide as normal a family holiday as possible which can be equally enjoyed by all the family.

Each family is sent a short questionnaire about their members and about their interests. From the answers, an itinerary will be worked out and suitably priced accommodation will be booked. The family is assured that they can have every confidence that everything concerning the needs of the disabled member will have been thoroughly checked out beforehand. This includes facilities such as bath and toilet arrangements, wheelchair access, special diets. If necessary, arrangements can be made for medical care such as conditions requiring dialysis.

Touring holidays can be arranged. The family will be driven in a Nissan Prairie which can accommodate a family of four – one of whom may be using a wheelchair.

Holiday prices vary according to the requirements of each family. However, as a rough guide a 14-day holiday for a family of four would cost approximately £2,000 plus hotel and meal costs.

Holiday Care Service

2 Old Bank Chambers, Station Road, Horley, Surrey RH6 9HW (Tel: Horley (0293) 774535).

The Service has established itself as a most valuable resource providing a wide range of information on holidays for several thousands of disabled people each year. While most of their enquiries are for holidays in the United Kingdom, they also help with details of places around the world.

The Service has an extensive range of leaflets available to enquirers. These include the following which deal with holidays in the UK: *Companies Involved in the Provision of Holidays in the UK and Ireland for Disabled People; Access Guides; Self Catering Accommodation for Disabled People; Special Interest Weaving, Pottery and Cooking Holidays; Painting Holidays and Courses for Disabled People; Farm Holiday Accommodation in England with Ground Floor Bedrooms; Hotels and Guest Houses* (sheets covering different areas of the United Kingdom); *Hotel Accommodation for Disabled People on a UK Tour; Hotels in the South East for Disabled People Suggested for Spending a Honeymoon; Access in London; Holiday Camps and Centres Suitable for Disabled People; Accommodation where Nursing or Personal Care is Provided; Beach Access for Disabled People; Bird Watching for Disabled People; Organisations or Companies Offering Specially Adapted Narrow Boats; Special Diets* (lists of hotels and guest houses in England and Scotland which are able to cater for special diets); *Hotels where Epileptic Guests are Accepted; Hotels and Guest Houses Accepting Mentally Handicapped or Ill Guests; Voluntary and Paid Escorts on Holidays for Disabled People; Holiday Information for Visually Handicapped People;* and *Holiday Facilities for Hearing Impaired People.* Additional sheets provide information on holidays for disabled children.

Holiday Care Service also has a book available free *Providing for Disabled Visitors.* This is published by the English Tourist Board and provides information for hotel and guest house proprietors on how to meet the needs of disabled visitors. You might find this helpful to discreetly pass on!

Holiday Helpers

This is a project run by the Holiday Care Service *(see above)* to help anyone seeking a companion or carer to accompany them on an independent holiday. Holiday Helpers knows of volunteers with a wide range of experience, and tries to introduce a volunteer from an enquirer's own area to enable them to meet and discuss a possible holiday. Contact the Holiday Care Service.

John Grooms Association for the Disabled

10 Gloucester Drive, Finsbury Park, London N4 2LP (Tel: 01–802 7272).
John Grooms has two hotels, one in Minehead, Somerset and the other in Llandudno, North Wales. These provide purpose-planned accommodation for wheelchair users and their families/

escorts. In addition, there are 13 self-catering holiday caravans, bungalows, a chalet, and a holiday flat in London N4. All are adapted for people in wheelchairs.

John Grooms also runs the London Visitors Club which reserves rooms at the 4-star Tara Hotel, where a number of rooms have been adapted for wheelchair users. Significant price reductions are available. A free brochure will be sent on request.

MENCAP – The Royal Society for Mentally Handicapped Children and Adults

123 Golden Lane, London EC1Y 0RT (Tel: 01–253 9433).
Holiday queries (enclosing large s.a.e.) to Holidays Officer, MENCAP, 119 Drake Street, Rochdale, Lancashire OL16 1PZ.

MENCAP publishes a *Holiday Accommodation Guide* showing independent hotels, boarding houses, self-catering flats, chalets, and caravans where families may be together. In addition, the Society arranges a variety of provisions for mentally handicapped children and adults. Adventure holidays can accommodate children with a quite severe degree of handicap. On special care holidays, priority is given to guests in wheelchairs and those with mobility difficulties. A qualified state registered nurse always accompanies each special care holiday.

The Multiple Sclerosis Society of Great Britain and Northern Ireland

25 Effie Road, London SW6 1EE (Tel: 01–736 6267).
Scotland: 27 Castle Street, Edinburgh EH2 3DN (Tel: 031–225 3600).
The Society has a number of holiday homes in Exeter, Worthing, Leamington Spa, North Berwick, Grantown on Spey, and Co. Antrim. In addition, local branches own bungalows, caravans, and chalets for the use of members at very reasonable rates. The Society will sometimes help with the cost of members' holidays where necessary.

Northern Ireland Council on Disability

2 Annadale Avenue, Belfast BT7 3JR (Tel: (0232) 491011).
The Council will be glad to advise about holidays and has a holiday leaflet.

PHAB (Physically Handicapped and Able-Bodied)

Tavistock House North, Tavistock Square, London WC1H 9HX (Tel: 01–388 1963).
Northern Ireland: Northern Ireland PHAB, 76

University Street, Belfast BT7 1HE (Tel: Belfast (0232) 325506).
Besides the 500 PHAB clubs throughout the United Kingdom, PHAB organises a full programme of residential courses catering for all ages and for families. The activities on the courses include: art, pottery and other crafts, music, drama, photography, sailing, riding, swimming, canoeing, outings to places of interest, visits to the theatre, discos, etc.

Royal Association for Disability and Rehabilitation
25 Mortimer Street, London W1N 8AB (Tel: 01–637 5400).
The Association has a Holidays Officer and publishes two annual guides, *Holidays for Disabled People* covering the UK, and *Holidays and Travel Abroad*, (for details *see* pages 168 and 192). RADAR also publishes a wide selection of Access Guides – for details *see* Section 16 on Access.

Royal National Institute for the Blind
224 Great Portland Street, London W1N 6AA (Tel: 01–388 1266).
The RNIB has four hotels, in Scarborough, Llandudno, Blackpool, and Eastbourne for which application should be made early in January direct to the manager of the selected hotel. Other holiday accommodation is available in Hove and Burnham-on-Sea. Christmas bookings begin in April. Further details are available from the Residential Department, RNIB.

Scottish Council on Disability
5 Shandwick Place, Edinburgh EH2 4RG (Tel: 031–229 8632).
Among its information lists is a very full and informative one (a book in itself) on holidays including sections on holiday places providing nursing assistance, hotels and guest houses providing specialised accommodation, group, and activity holidays, self-catering holidays, camping and caravanning holidays, sailing and boating holidays, holidays abroad, and other specialist information. List free to disabled people.

Scottish Epilepsy Association
48 Govan Road, Glasgow G51 1JL (Tel: 041–427 4911).
The Association has over 30 years' experience in providing group holidays for adults and children with epilepsy, both in Scotland and abroad. Several holidays are organised each year, some designed for the energetic and adventurous holidaymaker, and others for those who require less demanding timetables.

Application should be made early in the year through the Association's Social Work Department.
The Association also has an eight-berth caravan available to families or small groups.

Scout Holiday Homes Trust
Baden-Powell House, Queen's Gate, London SW7 5JS (Tel: 01–584 7030).
The Trust provides fully furnished six-berth caravans and chalets for any family with a handicapped member, all of which have specially constructed wheelchair ramps. They all have their own toilets and all sites have excellent facilities.
The trust has caravans at Exmouth, Devon; Paignton, Devon; Felixstowe, Suffolk; Berrow, Somerset; Seton Sands, Longniddry, Scotland. Chalets at Westward Ho!, Devon; Ferryside, Kidwelly, South Wales; New Milton, Hampshire.

Servas
77 Elm Park Mansions, Park Walk, London SW10 OAP (Tel: 01–352 0203).
An organisation concerned with promoting peace by encouraging people to travel in the cause of peace and to visit others in different countries with similar views. Travellers, unless invited to extend their visit, stay for two nights and are asked to rely on their various talents and to offer assistance where it is needed. Travellers must carry an approved Letter of Introduction, a current Servas list, a sheet sleeping bag or sleeping bag, and a towel. In addition they must have paid a registration fee of £5. The hosts, for their part, are not expected to go to a lot of trouble and expense to look after their Servas travellers.
Servas has contacts with many countries, and continues to encourage people to travel seriously and thoughtfully, rather than fast and far, and to turn their minds to building peace. Servas members are kept informed about the progress of the organisation by periodic issues of *Servas International News* and the national newsletter. These are sent free to all members. From time to time there are meetings in hosts' homes to which all members and interested friends are invited. We understand that the USA group already lists those hosts who are able to offer special provisions for members with various types of physical disability. Otherwise no mention is made of facilities for disabled travellers. However, it would be worth enquiring about the possibility of hosts meeting your particular needs. In return, you may be able to act as host to others in similar circumstances.

165

Tripscope

63 Esmond Road, London W4 1JE (Tel: 01–994 9294).

Tripscope is a new transport information service. It is so far unable to answer queries from individuals but will provide information to those organisations helping disabled or elderly people to plan journeys.

The Visitors Club

John Grooms Association for the Disabled, 10 Gloucester Drive, Finsbury Park, London N4 2LP (Tel: 01–802 7272).

The purpose of the Club is to be of help to disabled people wishing to stay away overnight (or longer) in London. Arrangements have been made for special facilities to be available at the London Tara Hotel, Scarsdale Place, London W8. Rooms have been specially adapted to meet the requirements of those in wheelchairs or otherwise disabled. Each room has a specially equipped bathroom. Adjoining rooms with communicating doors are available for able-bodied friends or members of the family.

Although these rooms are available to any disabled person, the London Tara Hotel has also agreed to make them available at a concessionary rate to anyone booking through this organisation. Room rates will inevitably vary from time to time but in 1988 the rate for bed and breakfast for a single room is £30 and the rate for a twin room is £22 per person per night. These prices are for members of the Visitors Club.

Membership subscription to the Visitors Club is £2. As well as its concern with the Tara Hotel, the Club aims to find property to build a hotel and also to encourage other hotels to adapt rooms.

Winged Fellowship Trust

Angel House, Pentonville Road, London N1 9XD (Tel: 01–833 2594).

The Trust povides holidays for severely physically disabled people and welcomes those who have additional problems such as incontinence and speech defects – people who have difficulty in finding holiday accommodation.

The Trust caters for over 100 holidays a fortnight in their three centres in Essex, Nottinghamshire, and Surrey which are staffed by qualified nurses and volunteers. They offer a varied programme of entertainment and a lively informal atmosphere.

The Trust also now provides holidays abroad and has opened a fourth centre, *Sandpipers* in Southport.

The Spinal Injuries Association

76 St. James's Lane, London N10 3DF (Tel: 01–444 2121).

SIA offers holidays afloat or by the sea. Their Kingfisher narrowboats, which they claim are the first such boats in the world which can be skippered from a wheelchair, are available for hire with reduced charges for members.

The narrowboats, based near Daventry and on the Llangollen canal sleep seven and five respectively. They have two hydraulic lifts, one in the bow to enable people to get their wheelchairs on and off and down to the galley, and the other at the stern to raise a wheelchair from the galley to the back deck level or up to a position where a clear view can be had over the top of the cabin while taking over the controls of the boat.

Prices per week including VAT are about £327 in the low season and £378 in the high season. You are also charged £10 for full tuition before you set off to adventure through the British canal system.

The SIA caravans are based at a holiday centre in Selsey on the Sussex coast and at the Ile d'Oleron in France and are also available for hire. Prices range from about £55 to £245 depending on the season.

Young Disabled on Holiday

c/o Rosemary Girdlestone, 6 Yewland Drive, Boothsmere, Knutsford, Cheshire WA16 8AP.

An organisation which provides holidays for physically handicapped young people between the ages of 18–30. Active holidays are arranged in this country and abroad. Please send an s.a.e. when applying for details.

Youth Hostels Association (England and Wales)

National office: Trevelyan House, 8 St Stephen's Hill, St Albans, Hertfordshire AL1 2DY (Tel: St Albans (0727) 55215).

Many YHA hostels are suitable for people with certain degrees of disability, but it is essential that intending hostellers enquire about possible facilities in advance. Broad Haven Youth Hostel, Haverfordwest, however, is the first hostel in the country to be specially designed to cater for people with physical disabilities. The whole building is on one level with easy routes to the sandy beach. Facilities for field work at Broad Haven are available for the study of marine biology, geography, geology, ornithology, geomorphology, etc. Address: YHA, Broad Haven, Haverfordwest, Dyfed SA62 3JH.

Information on hostels detailing the degrees of

accessibility is given in the relevant sections of the RADAR book described below.

GENERAL HOTELS

Best Western Hotels International
Vine House, 143 London Road, Kingston upon Thames, Surrey KT2 6NA (Tel: Reservations 01–541 0033); Groups 01–541 0050; Brochure requests 01–541 5767); and 90 Mitchell Street, Glasgow G1 3NQ (Tel: 041– 204 1794).

The hotels within the Best Western organisation are independently owned and run, and annually inspected by the AA to maintain their standards. There are nearly 200 in the UK and 3,200 world-wide in 36 countries. Their glossy brochures give information about the hotels and also use the access symbol (a) when accompanied by an able-bodied companion and (b) when unaccompanied.

Country Holidays: Self-Catering Northern England
Spring Mill, Earby, nr. Colne, Lancashire BB8 6RN (Tel: Colne (0282) 445566.
The brochure, giving details of a wide variety of properties, is a delight to browse through. The line drawings provide tempting glimpses of holiday residences. The facilities are well described and give a much better idea than having to plough through a sea of symbols. Included are details of those places considered accessible for people in wheelchairs. Country Holidays itself is a holiday booking organisation specialising in self-catering holidays in the Yorkshire Dales, the Lake District, and Northern England. The brochure costs 50p.

Holiday Inns
10–12 New College Parade, Finchley Road, London NW3 5EP (Tel: 01–722 7755) – central booking.
Each hotel in the United Kingdom has a room (if possible on the ground floor) with access facilities incorporating a bathroom, and including helpful details such as handrails, low mirrors, etc.

Novotel
Resinter, Hammersmith W6 8DR (Tel: 01–724 1000) – central booking.
This chain of hotels assures us that all their hotels have facilities for disabled visitors. Each hotel has two bedrooms with private bathrooms which are specially fitted out for people in wheelchairs to use. There are no steps up from the car park into the hotels.

Restaurants in London

Restaurant Switchboard
Association of Restaurant Diners, Restaurant Switchboard House, 108–114 Myddleton Road, London N22 4NQ (Tel: 01–888 8080 – 9 a.m. to 8 p.m. Monday to Saturday).

This is an information and booking service for London restaurants which will also give details on the accessibility of premises if you explain your particular requirements. It will suggest restaurants best suited to a particular occasion and will make free table reservations.

There is also a membership service for those who enjoy eating out regularly. Personal member-ship is £15 a year. As a member you will receive the Association of Restaurant Diners magazine and you will be entitled to a Menu Club privilege card.

Specialist Books and Publications

See also Access Guides in Section 16.
AA Travellers' Guide for the Disabled – where to go, where to stay. Annually updated, this Guide gives information on accommodation throughout the British Isles, which has been checked for accessibility and is considered suitable for disabled visitors using wheelchairs. Details are given of such features as steps, number of ground floor rooms, type of doors, turning space in toilets, and room service.

There is also guidance on regulations affecting disabled drivers, available concessions, picnic sites and, throughout the UK, country parks recom-mended for people in wheelchairs.

The section on travelling abroad has details of overseas organisations, and facilities for disabled people on French motorways. There are also six tours of Europe which have been specifically de-signed for accompanied disabled people who wish either to include a short tour of a specific area in their itinerary, or to use them as the basis for a motoring holiday. The section also includes details of recommended hotel accommodation. In addi-tion, there is now also a feature on travelling in the United States.

The guide is free to AA members, but otherwise costs £2.95. It is published by and available from the Automobile Association, Fanum House, Bas-ingstoke, Hampshire RG21 2EA (Tel: Basing-stoke (0256) 20123).

Also available from the AA: *Hotels and Res-taurants in Britain*, which identifies facilities for disabled people with the access symbol. Price: £9.95 plus 95p p&p.

Devon Holiday Accommodation Guide for the Disabled. Holiday Services, an organisation offering information and advice to disabled holidaymakers and their families taking a break in the Teignmouth area, issues the above guide. As well as listing hotels and self-catering properties that may be suitable for use by disabled guests, the guide also gives general access information on a range of West Country resorts.

Available from: Holiday Services, The Shop, 1 Orchard Gardens, Teignmouth, Devon TQ14 8DP (Tel: Teignmouth (062 67) 79424). Price: £1.

Get Away With Ye. Guide for holidays for disabled people, provided by voluntary organisations. In addition to details of provision by 27 voluntary organisations, there are sections on air travel, transport services, parking, toilets, and travel concessions. General holiday information covers finance, holidays for carers, insurance notes for organisations, travel agents, and guides and publications. Available from the Northern Ireland Council on Disability, 2 Annadale Avenue, Belfast BY7 3JR (Tel: Belfast (0232) 491011). Price: £1 plus 25p p&p.

Holidays for Disabled People. This guide includes a wealth of information on all kinds of holiday accommodation such as hotels, apartments, nursing homes, and holiday centres, and grades the extent of their suitability to match an individual's needs. It contains sections on accommodation with nursing care, accommodation for children and young people, and for groups. There are large sections on transportation and activity holidays, as well as details of voluntary and commercial organisations involved in holiday provision for people with disabilities.

This book can either be obtained from branches of W.H. Smith price £3, or from RADAR, 25 Mortimer Street, London W1N 8AB price £4.00 including p&p.

Holiday Care Service
This Service provides a wide range of very helpful leaflets on holidays in the UK (*see* page 163), also details of holidays for children (*see* page 160).

Motoring and Mobility for Disabled People (fourth edition) by Ann Darnbrough and Derek Kinrade. The book includes a chapter on holiday motoring, giving information on ferries, Motorail, toll concessions, etc. For full details of the book *see* page 151.

Northern Ireland Tourist Board
River House, 48 High Street, Belfast BT1 2DS (Tel: Belfast (0232) 231221.

The Board, in association with the Northern Ireland Council on Disability, publishes the following guide of interest to disabled people: *The Disabled Tourist in Northern Ireland – things to see, places to stay*. It includes information on accommodation, restaurants, concerts halls, places of interest, access to cinemas, and theatres. Information is also given on sporting activities – access, and provision of facilities. Details are given about shopping – description of town centre access in the main towns. Price: 50p.

GENERAL GUIDES
Now incorporating the wheelchair access symbol for those establishments having suitable facilities for disabled people.

The AA publish *Hotels and Restaurants in Britain* also *Britain: 2000 Places to Visit* price: £5.95 plus 95p p&p. For details of the *AA Travellers Guide for the Disabled see* page 149.

All the Places to Stay (Northern Ireland). Among the general accommodation listed there are plenty of hotels, guest houses, and farm and country houses which are suitable for disabled visitors. These are indicated by a symbol. Available, price £1.50 from Northern Ireland Tourist Board, River House, 48 High Street, Belfast BT1 2DS (Tel: Belfast (0232) 246609).

The Consumers Association
The CA publishes two guides in which they indicate those places which have facilities for disabled people.
(a) *The Good Food Guide*; and
(b) *The Good Hotel Guide* (UK and Western Europe).
Available from the Consumers Association, PO Box 44, Hertford SG14 1SH (Tel: Hertford (0992) 589031). Both price £10.95 each including postage.

The Cornwall Tourist Board
The Board produces a colour guide to Cornwall and a register of approved accommodation. Each of these contains a key to facilities indicating those properties which cater for disabled people. Both publications are available from the Cornwall Tourist Board, County Hall, Station Road, Truro, Cornwall (Tel: Truro (0872) 74282 ext. 3103).

Egon Ronay's guides.
Both the following guides are available from bookshops and from the AA, Mail Order Department, Fanum House, Basingstoke RG21 2EA (Tel: Basingstoke (0256) 20123).

The Cellnet Guide to Hotels and Restaurants by Egon Ronay. The guide contains many hotels and restaurants and includes the access symbol where the management say this is suitable. Price: £9.95 plus 95p postage.

Just a Bite by Egon Ronay. This is a guide to informal meals to be found in carefully selected places such as tea rooms, coffee shops, wine bars, cafés, and vegetarian restaurants. Those considered accessible by the management are marked with the access symbol. Price: £6.95 plus 95p postage.

Farm Holidays. This delightful guide, evocative of farm and countryside includes the access symbol for nearly 200 well described holidays which can accommodate disabled holiday makers. Those in wheelchairs are requested to make careful enquiries about the accessibility of a particular farm as the symbol can only be an indication of possible accessibility given the nature of farm buildings.

Produced and available from the Farm Holiday Bureau, National Agricultural Bureau, Stoneleigh, Kenilworth, Warwickshire CV8 2LZ (Tel: Royal Show (0203) 555100. Price: £2.99 plus 51p postage.

The Good Stay Guide. An interesting reference book for group leaders, teachers, students, community workers, and organisers of outdoor activities, leisure and study pursuits. Details of location, accommodation, prices and facilities for groups and families are accompanied by practical articles on planning, travel, safety, and opportunities for outdoor study. Particular attention has been paid to the needs of special interest groups including disabled people, making town and country more accessible to all.

Available from: The Council for Environmental Education, School of Education, University of Reading, London Road, Reading RG1 5AQ. Price: £6.95 plus £1 postage.

Hotels and Restaurants of Britain. This guide, as well as describing hotels and restaurants, also details motorway services, and has 64 pages of colour maps – each one of the 1,700 entries is map referenced. The access symbol shows where facilities for disabled people are provided. The publication is available from The British Hotels, Restaurants and Caterers Association, 40 Duke Street, London W1M 6HR (Tel: 01–499 6641).

The Good Value Guide. This Les Routiers guide contains the access symbol where appropriate in hotels, restaurants, guest houses and other eating and sleeping places. Available from Les Routiers, 354 Fulham Road, London SW10 9UH (Tel: 01–351 3522). Price: £6.95 plus £1 postage.

Isle of Man. This guide of places to stay and places to visit includes a few hotels which are considered suitable for wheelchair visitors. Available free from the Isle of Man Department of Tourism, 13 Victoria Street, Douglas, Isle of Man (Tel: Douglas (0624) 74323).

Isle of Wight. This guide indicates a fair proportion of hotels, guest houses, and other serviced accommodation, which has suitable amenities for disabled visitors. Available from the Isle of Wight Tourist Office, Quay Store, Town Quay, Newport, Isle of Wight PO30 2EF (Tel: Newport (0983) 524343).

Michelin Red Guides. Among the Red Guides there are two for the UK which use the access symbol for those establishments having access facilities; these are: *Great Britain and Ireland*, price: £7.50; and *London*, price: £2. Available in bookshops or direct (at no further charge) from: Michelin Tyre plc, Tourism Department, Davy House, Lyon Road, Harmondsworth, Middlesex HA1 2DQ (Tel: 01–861 2121).

RAC Guides
The RAC publish two guides which include details of facilities for disabled people:
(a) *RAC Hotel and Touring Guide*. This guide is published in December each year, price: £6 plus £1 postage.
(b) *RAC Camping and Caravanning Guide – Great Britain and Ireland*. In addition to details of the facilities and amenities of all the RAC appointed and listed sites, this annual guide includes information on sites with facilities for disabled people. Price: £2.95 plus 70p postage.
Both publications are available from the Publications Manager, RAC, RAC House, Lansdowne Road, Croydon CR9 2JA (Tel: 01–686 2525). Also available from all RAC offices or from bookshops.

The Scottish Tourist Board
23 Ravelston Terrace, Edinburgh EH4 3EU (Tel: 031–332 2433).
The Board publishes three *Where to Stay* guides which include access information: *Where to Stay, Self-Catering*, £3.95 plus 85p p&p; *Where to Stay, Bed & Breakfast*, £2.30 plus 80p p&p; *Where to Stay, Hotels & Guest Houses*, £3.95 plus 95p p&p.

Other guides using access symbols include: *1,001 Things to See* £3.20 plus 60p p&p; *Touring Map*, £2.75 plus 45p p&p; *Enjoy Scotland Pack – 1,001 Things to See and Touring Map*, £5.95 plus 95 p&p; *Events in Scotland*, free; *Scotland – Handling Agents, Specialist and Chauffeurs Drive Operators*, free.

Self-Catering Holidays. This is a useful guide for all those people who want to do their own thing in their own way. Ideal for those accompanied by children or dogs, the book provides scope for individual holidaymakers to indulge their own timetables and whims without upsetting the landlady or hotel manager. The guide covers UK and Ireland, and includes houses, chalets, flatlets, caravans, bungalows, cottages, farms and flats. A symbol shows where somebody considers the accommodation suitable for disabled guests. Published by Pastime Publications Ltd, 15 Dublin Street Lane South, Edinburgh EH1 3PX (Tel: 031–556 1105). Price: £1.50 plus 40p postage.

Staying off the Beaten Track by Elizabeth Gundrey, who has herself sampled all the places she describes. In fact, the whole book has a wonderful personal quality about it. Reading it is just like joining a club of people who like individual style holidays rather than the impersonal big hotel form of catering. In this edition there is more emphasis on imaginative breakfasts, vegetarian or wholefood options, cycle hire, no-smoking rooms, and extra-firm mattresses. The letter H denotes those places with facilities for visitors who have disabilities. Published by Arrow Books, price: £4.95.

English Tourist Board
The Board publishes three guides which have the access symbol where appropriate.
(a) *Hotels, Guest Houses and Universities*, price: £4.95 plus £1.25 postage.
(b) *Farmhouses and Bed and Breakfast*, price: £3.95 plus 95p postage.
(c) *Holiday Homes and Holiday Centres*, price: £3.95 plus 95p postage.
Available from: Department D, English Tourist Board, 4 Bromells Road, London SW4 OBJ.
English Tourist Board Regional Guides. A new national scheme of verified classification for hotels and other serviced accommodation was introduced during 1986 by the Tourist Boards for England, Scotland, and Wales. The scheme shows the overall classification of 'Listed' and one to five Crowns, according to the number of facilities offered.

London Tourist Board and Convention Bureau
26 Grosvenor Gardens, London SW1W ODU (Tel: 01–730 3450).
A specialist publication *London made easy for the over sixties* includes the access symbol and details of facilities for those who are hearing or sight impaired. A great deal of sightseeing and general information is packed into this guide together with brief information on places to stay. Price: £2.25 plus 35p postage.

Other publications using the access symbol include: *Children's London* price: £2.25 plus 35p postage; *Exploring Central London* price: £1.95 plus 50p postage; *Exploring Outer London* price: £1.75 plus 50p postage; *Where to Stay in London*, a guide to London hotels, guesthouses, and apartments. Price: £2.45.

Southern Tourist Board
(Covering Hampshire, Dorset, Isle of Wight, and South Wiltshire.)
Town Hall Centre, Leigh Road, Eastleigh, Hampshire SO5 4DE (Tel: Eastleigh (0703) 616027).
The STB has a number of free publications which include the access symbol for those places considered accessible for disabled people. These include:
(a) *Selected Places to Stay in Southern England*. The types of accommodation included in this publication are: hotels, motels, guest houses, pubs and bed and breakfast, camping, caravan and chalet parks, self-catering accommodation including holiday flats and flatlets, holiday centres plus a selection of specialist agencies and operators including activity and special interest holiday operators. The accommodation is grouped together into the various types and is listed by town in alphabetical order.
(b) *Travel Trade Information Manual for Southern England*. This guide has been put together to help the coach operator and tour organiser in arranging accommodation, transport and tours in Southern England.
(c) *Take a Break*. This guide covers not only Southern England as identified above but also East Anglia, Thames and Chilterns, and South East England. These are described as 'great value' breaks covering the winter season. They must be of two nights hotel or three nights self-catering accommodation.
(d) *The Best of Dorset*. This booklet describes, in the Board's own words, '28 memorable places to visit'. Details are given of accessibility.

(e) *The Best of Hampshire*. This booklet describes over 40 attractions to visit in Hampshire and gives details of accessibility.

The Heart of England Tourist Board
(Covering the Cotswolds, Staffordshire, Shakespeare's country, the Welsh Borderland, the West Midlands.)
Trinity Street, Worcester WR1 2PW (Tel: Worcester (0905) 613132).
Explore The Heart of England, price: £2.25 plus postage. The access symbol is used alongside accommodation information. In addition there is information on where to eat, and what to see and do.

East Midlands Tourist Board
(Covering Derbyshire, Leicestershire, Lincolnshire, Nottinghamshire, Northamptonshire.)
Exchequergate, Lincoln LN2 1PZ (Tel: Lincoln (0522) 31521).
Attractions and accommodation carry symbols to indicate their accessibility. The guide includes information on where to stay, and places to visit, price: 90p.

Northumbria Tourist Board
(Covering Cleveland, Durham, Northumberland, Tyne and Wear.
Aykley Heads, Durham DH1 5UX (Tel: Durham (0385) 46905).
The NTB produces separate sheets indicating accessibility to go alongside its tourist guide. Two lists are available, *Serviced Accommodation Accessible to the Disabled* and *Attractions Accessible to the Disabled*.

Thames and Chilterns Tourist Board
(Covering Bedfordshire, Berkshire, Buckinghamshire, Hertfordshire, and Oxfordshire.)
8 The Market Place, Abingdon, Oxfordshire OX14 3UD (Tel: Abingdon (0235) 22711).
Where to Go. Unfortunately, this guide does not carry the access symbol at all. However, this area is partly covered by the Southern Tourist Board publication *Take a Break* described above. Price: £1.50.

Yorkshire and Humberside Tourist Board
(Covering North Yorkshire coast and Humberside, Yorkshire Dales, Yorkshire Moors, West and South Yorkshire, Peaks and Pennines, and Broad Acres.)
312 Tadcaster Road, York YO2 2HF (Tel: York (0904) 707961.
The tourist guide for the area includes the access

symbol in the accommodation section. The guide also describes places of interest, sporting occasions and facilities, etc. This tourist board is also going to produce two smaller guides on Farm Holidays, and on Caravan/Camping Parks both of which will show the access symbol for disabled visitors, where appropriate. Price: 70p.

North West Tourist Board
(Covering Cheshire, Greater Manchester, Lancashire, Merseyside, and Derbyshire High Peak.)
The Last Drop Village, Bromley Cross, Bolton, Lancashire BL7 9PZ (Tel: Bolton (0204) 591511).
The free tourist guide for the area *England's North West* includes the access symbol for its accommodation.

Other guides using the access symbol, both of which are free, are: *Ideas for Party Visits*, which depicts a wide variety of places to visit and includes the access symbol to show which are considered manageable by disabled visitors; and *Discover England's North West*, a picturesque and useful map of the region which graphically pinpoints the local places of interest.

East Anglia Tourist Board
(Covering Essex, Suffolk, Norfolk, and Cambridge.)
Toppeshall Hall, Hadleigh, Suffolk IP7 5DN (Tel: Hadleigh (0473) 822922).
This Tourist Board publishes a supplement *Information for Physically Disabled Visitors to East Anglia*. It describes travel within the region as well as accommodation and places of interest and their degree of accessibility. The supplement is intended to be used alongside the two general guides, *East Anglia Touring Guide* which includes touring maps (price: £1.75); and *East Anglia: Hotels, Bed & Breakfast, Self-Catering, Camping & Caravanning* (price: 40p).

Cumbria Tourist Board
Ashleigh, Holly Road, Windermere, Cumbria LA23 2AQ (Tel: Windermere (096 62) 4444).
The Tourist Board publishes one free general guide which uses the access symbol, *Cumbria English Lake District: Where to Stay, What to See, What to Do*. It also publishes a specialist guide: *Freedom of Cumbria: Accommodation and Recreational Opportunities for the disabled visitor to Cumbria including the Lake District National Park*, price 50p.

South East England Tourist Board
(Covering East Sussex, Kent, Surrey, and West Sussex.)

1 Warwick Park, Tunbridge Wells, Kent TN2 5TA (Tel: Tunbridge Wells (0892) 40766).

The guide, *Hundreds of Places to Visit in South East England* includes the access symbol where there are special facilities for disabled people; price: £1 plus 35p postage. They also produce a much more detailed information sheet, *Places of Interest for Disabled Visitors*. This describes accessibility, whether there is level ground, how near it is possible to alight to the entrance, lavatory facilities, and whether there are seats at intervals, etc. For details of accommodation see the English Tourist Board guides above.

West Country Tourist Board
(Covering Avon, Cornwall, Devon, Somerset, Western Dorset, Wiltshire, and Isles of Scilly.) Trinity Court, 37 Southernhay East, Exeter EX1 1QS (Tel: Exeter (0392) 76351).

Where to Stay in the West Country. This guide mostly covers accommodation and includes the access symbol, price: £1.95 post free. *West Country Holidays* is a general information guide. It also includes the symbol and is available free.

VOLUNTARY WORK OPPORTUNITIES

Sparetime Sharetime: a guide to voluntary work opportunities in England and Wales. This guide lists over 110 projects which welcome young people as volunteers, for periods ranging from a day or two to a year or longer. A number of projects welcome disabled volunteers depending on the nature of the disability and on the work involved in the project. Copies of the guide are available free (but please send 50p to cover charges), from The Sales Department, National Youth Department, 17–23 Albion Street, Leicester LE1 6GD (Tel: Leicester (0533) 471200).

SECTION 10
HOLIDAYS ABROAD

For general guidance please see information in Section 9 on Holidays in Britain. The advice given there is doubly important to remember when planning a holiday abroad. In addition to taking all possible equipment that may be needed, it is essential to remember to take an adequate supply of any necessary medication.

Financial Help Available

Some local authorities' social services departments may be willing to consider giving financial support for a disabled person's holiday abroad, up to the amount they would allocate for a holiday in this country. Unfortunately, this is now a rare occurrence and holidays have become a low priority on stretched budgets.

Voluntary organisations are sometimes able to help their members to have a holiday abroad. In practice, this is likely to be as an organised group rather than helping an individual to pay for a self-planned holiday. Young people may choose to take part in an educational visit or exchange for which grants are sometimes available. The Youth Exchange Centre will advise groups on suitable contacts, also on sources of partial funding for specific projects (*see* page 188).

For information on motoring and mobility *see* Section 8.

Handicapped Aid Trust
21 Malden Hill, New Malden, Surrey KT3 4DS.

The Trust exists to provide towards the costs of helpers of severely disabled people on holidays abroad where these costs can be met by neither the helper nor the disabled person and where the disabled person would be unable to go on holiday without someone to help him or her with everyday needs.

The Trust was inaugurated in 1981 by the IYDP Working Group on Leisure. As a result, a scheme to collect small change in foreign currency from travellers returning from abroad has been put into operation by the International Association of Tour Managers, whose members change the donated currency into sterling. In order to get the scheme off the ground Thomson Holidays also donated a number of their own holidays together with a sum of money.

Funds are limited and applications can only be received from individual disabled people or from groups who plan to travel abroad but cannot afford to pay helpers' expenses. There are separate application forms for individuals and for groups. Individual applications must be supported by a bona fide organisation or doctor willing to verify that they meet the scheme's requirements. The minimum age for applicants is 17 years.

The closing date for applications for assistance towards holidays being taken between 1 October and 31 March is 1 August and for holidays being taken beween 1 April and 30 September the closing date is 1 February.

Ex-Royal Air Force and Dependants Severely Disabled Holiday Trust
Contact M. F. Sykes, 57 Junction Road, Ashford, Middlesex TW15 1NJ.

The Trust is able to offer holidays to severely disabled ex-RAF personnel (the disability need not be service related) and/or their severely disabled dependants. These holidays are available in Time Share developments. Accommodation is made accessible and functional for holidaymakers in wheelchairs.

For other holiday financial help available *see* Section 9, page 152.

Insurance

There are basically two types of policy – package and selective. A 'package' offers cover for a variety of events such as illness or accident, loss of baggage, costs arising from holiday cancellation and, possibly, personal liability. In almost every case, the client has to sign a form indicating that s/he is free from illness or disability, and, in principle, a disabled person cannot therefore make a claim under *any* section of the policy. However, most holiday firms now include details of insurance as part of their package deals and some of them offer policies without the exclusion clause relating to pre-existing disability. It is worth browsing through the brochures, not only for the best holiday, but also for the best insurance deal.

We would recommend you read the small print very carefully indeed. Some of the companies operating apparently helpful schemes are as follows.

Europ Assistance Ltd

252 High Street, Croydon CR0 1NF (Tel: 01–680 1234).

Europ Assistance offer two standard schemes. Their Personal Service applies worldwide, covering the full range of medical emergencies, providing comprehensive repatriation facilities and incorporating medical expenses insurance. Conventional travel insurance covering baggage, cancellation risks, personal accident and public liability is included in both motoring and personal services.

A Motoring Emergency Service caters for the special needs of the motorist abroad in addition to the medical protection outlined. Repatriation of vehicles, car hire benefits, location and transport of replacement parts, and assistance with roadside repairs are some of the features of this service.

Europ Assistance are, naturally, unable to cover anyone who is likely to be ill abroad, and they require of both individuals and groups that the nature of any disability is declared when the application is made. They will, however, give complete cover to many individuals who have previously been excluded, in particular, those who are disabled, but who are normally in good health. Their booklet *Assistance Advice Guide* provides useful information on services.

Extrasure Holdings Ltd

Lloyd's Avenue House, 6 Lloyd's Avenue, London EC3N 3AX (Tel: 01-480 6871/488 9341). This firm specialises in insurance for business and holiday trips worldwide. There are no exclusions for pre-existing medical conditions, unless travelling against a doctor's specific advice. A 24-hour emergency telephone service is operated for the benefit of insured persons, so that, in the event of an emergency, medical problems covered by the insurance and help and advice will be given. If necessary emergency repatriation will be arranged.

A. M. Marrs (P.G.) Ltd

54 Aldermans Hill, Palmers Green, London N13 4PQ (Tel: 01–882 4511).

The TravelMarrs Handicare Scheme offers cover while travelling abroad for personal accident, wheelchair indemnity, medical expenses, in addition to the normal baggage and cancellation cover. There is no age limit, nor any exclusion for pre-existing conditions. The policy will fully indemnify physically and mentally disabled people and able-bodied people accompanying them, provided that the applicant is not travelling against doctor's orders.

C. R. Toogood & Co. Ltd

Duncombe House, Ockham Road North, East Horsley, Leatherhead, Surrey KT24 6NX (Tel: East Horsley (048 65) 4181).

This company informs us that it has facilities for placing travel insurance on a worldwide basis, both at Lloyd's and in the company market, without exclusion of pre-existing medical conditions. Leaflets and details of cover and rates together with proposal forms are available on request. Cover includes sections for baggage and personal effects, personal liability, cancellation or curtailment, personal accident, and medical and other expenses. Under the Lloyd's contract, cover is also available for loss of or damage to wheelchairs up to £300 for a modest additional premium.

We are assured that the company is able to deal with all classes of insurance and is always pleased to discuss insurance arrangements with disabled individuals or with disability organisations.

Tyser (UK) Limited

Ellerman House, 12–20 Camomile Street, London EC3A 7PJ (Tel: 01–623 6262).

This firm provides a worldwide Holiday Travel Insurance package for people with epilepsy. In order to qualify for the insurance the person applying must sign a declaration that: 'They are in good health and free from any physical defect or infirmity apart from epilepsy as declared above [in the application form] at the inception of the insurance.' In respect of those who have epilepsy, the applicant must declare that the epilepsy is stabilised and that s/he is not travelling contrary to doctor's advice. A letter to that effect from the doctor would need to be sent with the application form.

Medical Treatment Overseas

SICKNESS BENEFIT DURING A TEMPORARY VISIT TO A MEMBER COUNTRY OF THE EEC

Most UK citizens covered by the UK National Insurance scheme, and their dependants, are entitled to immediately necessary medical treatment if they become ill while visiting another EEC country.

Persons covered by the regulations who are on holiday or otherwise staying temporarily in a Community country will be entitled to medical treatment for sickness or accidents which require urgent attention on the same basis as insured nationals of that country. It must be borne in mind, however, that treatment available in the Community countries is that provided under their own domestic legislation, and in some, but not all of them persons receiving medical treatment have to pay part of the cost. Medical benefits available under these schemes are dependent upon certain insurance conditions and *are available only on production of a certificate of entitlement to medical benefits* (form E111). To apply for this certificate (which is now valid during all short visits abroad as long as you continue to live in the UK) it is necessary to complete an application form at least a month in advance of your first visit. Form E111 is obtainable from social security offices or from DHSS Leaflets Unit, PO Box 21, Stanmore, Middlesex HA7 1AY. Leaflet SA41 (replaces leaflets SA30 and SA35) explains how to get emergency medical treatment as well as any entitlements (through reciprocal agreements).

Leaflet SA41, as well as providing brief details on travelling to EEC countries as a temporary visitor, also provides information on AIDS, malaria, and rabies. Some other countries outside the European Community also have reciprocal health agreements; these are: Anguilla, Australia, Austria, British Virgin Islands, Bulgaria, the Channel Islands, Czechoslovakia, Falkland Islands, Finland, East Germany, Hong Kong, Hungary, Iceland, Malta, Montserrat, New Zealand, Norway, Poland, Romania, St Helena, Sweden, Turks and Caicos Islands, USSR, and Yugoslavia. The leaflet is available from social security offices and most travel agents. We mention some entitlements under the countries concerned – where these are listed in this section. These apply if you fall ill or have an accident but don't apply if you go to a country to be treated for an illness which you already had when you left the United Kingdom.

Leaflet SA40 *The Traveller's Guide to Health* can be obtained by phoning (free of charge) 0800 555 777.

Vaccination Certificate Requirements for International Travel and Health Advice to Travellers is published annually by the World Health Organisation and available from HMSO Publications Centre, 51 Nine Elms Lane, London SW8 5DR (Tel: 01–211 5656).
Price: £5.75 including postage and packing.

This is an official handbook intended for those who have to advise travellers regarding the risks they might encounter when visiting other countries. The information is detailed and therefore not for the casual traveller who does not venture far afield. However, for the adventurous among us, it makes interesting armchair reading as well as providing practical information covering, in addition to vaccination requirements, some health risks to which travellers may be subject including environmental effects, risks from food and drink, sexually transmitted diseases, and hazards from insects and animals; geographical distribution health hazards to travellers in Africa, the Americas, Asia, Europe, and Oceania; precautions against certain diseases and injuries.

Helpful Organisations

A number of voluntary organisations will help and advise on holidays; these are listed in Section 9.

Country by Country

The following list includes details of access guides and other facilities where they are known. The leading address given in each country is the one, to the best of our knowledge, to apply to for general information. We make every effort to check these entries but inevitably foreign addresses are more difficult to keep up to date with. We suggest you also try the various countries' national tourist offices.

AUSTRALIA

ACROD Limited, PO Box 60 Curtin ACT 2605, Canberra (Tel: 062–82 4333).
ACROD have told us that they are definitely the right place to contact for more information for disabled holidaymakers visiting Australia and that they will provide any specific information about access, transport, medical treatment, services, etc on request. They also distribute two books – free by surface mail if requested well ahead of time or by airmail with an invoice. The books are: *Accessibility guide for disabled travellers to tourist attractions in Australia* and *Accommodation for disabled travellers in Australia*. ACROD will also be glad to send you a list of access guides. These publications are not available directly from ACROD but details are given in the list. Areas covered in the access guides include: Sydney, Adelaide, Victoria, Fleurieu, the Geelong and the

Barwon region, Perth, Alice Springs, Lismore, and Melbourne.

The list mentioned above includes the addresses of five agencies which will arrange holidays for disabled people. We mention these for your interest but we have not been able, in the time available, to check these for ourselves. All other addresses throughout the Directory are checked at source.

(a) Ros Langford, Assist Personnel Services, PO Box 83, Lara VIC 3212.
(b) Maureen Allen, Crossways Travel, Wesley Centre, 210 Pitt Street, Sydney NSW 2000.
(c) Heather Russell, Cumalong Tours, PO Box 223, Rozelle NSW 2039.
(d) Meryl Bolin, TAL Tours, GPO Box 4550, Sydney NSW 2001.
(e) Patricia McGinley, Tardis Travel, 884 Beaufort Street, Inglewood WA 6052.

Medical treatment on holiday
Proof of UK residence (e.g. UK passport or NHS medical card) and temporary entry permit. Free: hospital treatment. You must pay for: treatment at some doctors' surgeries; prescribed medicines; ambulance travel. N.B. You will need to enrol at a local Medicare office but this can be done after you get treatment. Some doctors' charges may be partially refunded by the Medicare scheme. You will need to claim at the local office before leaving.

AUSTRIA

Austrian National Tourist Office, 30 Saint George Street, London W1R OAL (Tel: 01–629 0461).

Hotels Guide for Disabled Persons. A photostat copy of a guide in German listing hotels, guest houses, and pensions and describing in detail accessibility to the various parts of the establishments. Available from the address above.

Anglo-Austrian Society
46 Queen Anne's Gate, Westminster, London SW1H 9AU (Tel: 01–222 0366).

The Anglo-Austrian Society links the British organisation PHAB (Physically Handicapped/Able-Bodied) and the AKN (Alternativgemeinschaft Körperbehinderter und Nichtbehinderter) – both having similar aims and activities. AKN runs holiday courses in Austria, to which British young people, able-bodied and physically handicapped are invited.

Courses are run on PHAB lines with activity and study groups – for example music, drama, photography, woodwork and crafts etc. There is also a programme of local visits and excursions to places of interest. Costs are kept to a minimum. They are also subsidised by grants from the Youth Exchange Centre (British Council), the Austrian Ministry of Education, and the Anglo-Austrian Society's Otto Harpner Fund. A typical holiday in 1988 cost £240 per person.

A hotel guide for handicapped travellers is on file at: Verband der Querschnittgelahmten Osterreichs, A–8144 Tobelbad, Styria.

A special hotel guide for disabled visitors to Vienna is available from: Verband der Querschnittgelahmten Osterreichs, Brigittenauer Lände 42, 1200 Wien.

A very neat little book described as a *City Map of Salzburg for handicapped people* provides very useful information in English, German, and Italian. Rather than being a map the book is a list of services in Salzburg giving clear details by means of signs and symbols showing accessibility to public buildings (places of interest, shops, restaurants, hotels, cafés, theatres, churches) – parking, entrance (whether steps or railings), lifts if any, and other details.

Available from: Osterreichischer Zivilinvalidenverband, Landesgruppe Salzburg, A–5020, Haunspergstrasse 39.

Orange Badge scheme, reciprocal arrangements, *see* page 198.

Medical treatment on holiday
Citizens of the United Kingdom who require urgent medical treatment as hospital in-patients while in Austria can normally obtain this free on the same terms as Austrian nationals. Admission to a public hospital is arranged by the local social insurance offices (Gebietskrankenkasse fur Arbeiten und Angestellten) on production of a UK passport.

BELGIUM (EEC)

Croix-Rouge de Belgique, Departement C.E.P.I.A.T.H., 1 rue Joseph Stallaert, bte 8, 1060 Brussels (Tel: (010 32 2) 647 10 10 ext. 316). The Belgian Red Cross Society has published a booklet listing (in French and Flemish) information on town halls, cultural buildings, sports clubs, churches, hotels, restaurants, shops, banks, and hospitals. They also have official guides on accessibility. Please send 100 Belgian francs for postage.

Belgian National Tourist Office
38 Dover Street, London W1X 3RB (Tel: 01–499 5379).

Hotels This general guide to accommodation, available from the Tourist Office, also lists many hotels which are accessible to disabled visitors in all parts of Belgium.

Distantlink Ltd
London House – Suite 16, 266 Fulham Road, London SW10 9EL (Tel: 01–351 7292).

Two well equipped holiday centres in Belgium also have rooms suitable for disabled guests. These are *De Ceder* near the old Flemish city of Ghent in northern Belgium and *Les Rièzes et Les Sars* in the French-speaking southern province of Namur.

Both offer an entertainment programme and there are extensive sporting facilities (indoor pool, tennis, petanque, jogging, badminton, etc.) plus skiing, in winter, from the door of *Les Rièzes*. We are informed that both centres provide a comprehensive medical service – you will need your form E111 (*see* page 175).

Belgian National Railways
22–25a Sackville Street, London W1X 1DE (Tel: 01–734 1491).
A number of facilities are available on Belgian Railways for handicapped travellers and these are described in the booklet written in French *accueille les handicapés*. Details of facilities may be obtained by writing to the above address. A list of stations will be supplied giving details of available services at each station and information will be given on the availablity of wheelchairs.

Medical treatment on holiday
You will need to produce your E111 document (*see* page 175). You will have to pay for treatment but about 75 per cent of charges are refunded by the Belgian Sickness Insurance Fund.
Further information about refunds, etc., may be obtained from: Regional offices of the Auxiliary Fund for Sickness and Invalidity Insurance (Caisse auxiliare d'assurance maladie-invalidité) usually located in each provincial capital. (*See* leaflet SA 41, details on page 175).
Orange Badge scheme, reciprocal arrangements, *see* page 198.

BENELUX (EEC)
Michelin Red Guide to Benelux. Uses the wheelchair access symbol. Available from: Michelin Tyres plc, Tourism Department, Davy House, Lyon Road, Harrow, Middlesex HA1 2DQ (Tel: 01– 861 2121).

BERMUDA
Bermuda Tourism, B.C.B. Ltd,
6 Burnsall Street, London SW3 3ST (Tel: 01–734 8813).
The *Access Guide to Bermuda for the Handicapped Traveller* is available from this office, together with lots of sun-soaked brochures. Also available an information sheet *Handicapped Visitors – Facilities in Bermuda* (1980). In addition, there is a paper entitled *Handicapped Travellers can be Comfortable in Bermuda* which goes into useful details in a nice, informal way.

Medical treatment on holiday
No reimbursement can be made of any medical expenses you incur in Bermuda and full costs will have to be paid.

CANADA
Canadian Paraplegic Association
520 Sutherland Drive, Toronto, Ontario M4G 3V9 (Tel: (010 1 416) 422 5640).
The Association will respond to travel questions about Canada or refer to the appropriate source.

Canadian Rehabilitation Council for the Disabled
Suite 2110, One Yonge Street, Toronto M5E 1E5 (Tel: (010 1 416) 862 0340).

A useful travel guide for people with disabilities affecting mobility, hearing, and sight is available from CRCD *Handi-Travel: A Resource Book for Disabled and Elderly Travellers* by Cinnie Noble. The book contains information on the travel industry, planning and preparation, holidaying by car, and provides special tips for travellers with diabetes, epilepsy, respiratory conditions and those on dialysis. Available in English and French price: $9.95 (cdn) plus $2 postage.
Dryden: A Guide for the Physically Disabled and the Elderly in the Dryden Area. Available for $1 postage free from Len Loteck, Dryden Handicapped Association, Inc, c/o 3–117 St. Charles Street, Dryden P8N 1L5.
Durham: Access Guide for the Disabled – Durham Region (1979). Available free from Ontario March of Dimes, c/o Civic Auditorium Complex, 141 Thornton Road South, Oshawa, Ontario L1J 5Y1.
Guelph: An Accessibility Guidebook of Guelph (1988). Available free from Guelph Services for the Physically Disabled, 53 Speedvale Avenue West, Guelph, Ontario N1H 1J6.
Accessibility Guide: Halifax/Dartmouth and Metropolitan Area (1984). Available free from the

Canadian Paraplegic Association, 5599 Fenwick Street, Halifax, Nova Scotia B3H 1R2.
Montreal: Access Montreal (1982). Available from the Junior League Office, 366 Victoria Avenue, Montreal H3Z 2N4.

The Ontario guides we mentioned in the last edition of the Directory are now out of print and it is intended, in the future, that information for disabled travellers should be integrated into general guides. In the meantime it is recommended that travellers with special needs should contact the Customer Sales and Service Division of the Ministry of Tourism and Recreation stating explicitly the services they need. The Division has indicated it will be glad to provide individual assistance. The full address is: Customer Sales and Service Division, Ministry of Tourism and Recreation, Tourism Marketing Branch, 77 Bloor Street West, 9th Floor, Toronto M7A 2R9.
Ottawa: Accessibility Guide of Ottawa-Carleton. Available from the Disabled Persons' Community Resources, 1400 Clyde Avenue, Suite 222, Nepean, Ontario K2G 3J2. Price: $1.50 for postage to disabled persons; price $5 plus $1.50 postage to non-disabled persons.
St. John's: Access: St. John's Region (1982). Available free from The Hub, PO Box 13788, St. John's, Newfoundland A1B 4G3.
Winnipeg: Easy Winnipeg Wheeling. Available from the Canadian Paraplegic Association, 825 Sherbrook Street, Winnipeg, Manitoba R3A 1M5.

Medical treatment on holiday
No reimbursement can be made of any medical expenses you incur in Canada and all costs will have to be paid.

DENMARK (EEC)
National Association for Disabled People (Landsforeningen af Vanføre), Hans Knudsens Plads 1 A 1, DK–2100 København Ø (Tel: (010 45) 01–29 35 55).
This organisation will provide information and advice.

Danish Tourist Board
Sceptre House, 169 Regent Street, London W1R 8PY (Tel: 01–734 2637).
The Board will provide information on special facilities to travellers with disabilities. It also supplies a manual to travel agents covering a great deal of information including general travel details, transport, accommodation, places of interest and a range of useful information. It would be worth asking your travel agent to consult this.

Medical treatment on holiday
(Excluding the Faroe Islands.) You will need to produce your UK passport. (E111 needed only if you are not a UK or a Danish national.) Free: hospital treatment arranged by a doctor (in an emergency you ask the hospital authorities to arrange free treatment); medical treatment given by a doctor registered with the Danish Public Health Service. You need to pay for: dental treatment given by a dentist registered with the Danish Public Health Service; some prescribed medicines available at reduced cost by showing your passport to the chemist. N.B. Before you leave Denmark apply to the Kommunens socialog sundhedsforvaltning with receipts for any payments made. Medical costs, part of dental costs and part of costs of prescribed medicines will be refunded. Information from: National Security Office (Sikringsstyrelsen) AEbelogade 1, Post Box 2566, 2100 Copenhagen.

Orange Badge scheme, reciprocal arrangements, *see* page 198.

FINLAND
Finnish Tourist Board
66 Haymarket, London SW1Y 4RF (Tel: 01–839 4048).
The FTB welcomes enquiries about holidays in Finland by disabled holidaymakers.

Medical treatment on holiday
You will need to produce a UK passport. Free: consultation at a health centre. You will need to pay for: hospital treatment; dental treatment; ambulance travel; prescribed medicines. N.B. Some charges may be partially refunded by the Finnish Sickness Insurance Institution. You will need to claim at a local office before leaving.

Orange Badge scheme, reciprocal arrangements, *see* page 198.

FRANCE (EEC)
Access Tourisme Service
15 rue du 11 Novembre, 45 130 Charsonville, Meung sur Loire (Tel: 38 74 23 17).
This organisation provides a service for disabled people including organising special tours in France, reserving suitable hotels, etc. and hiring cars with hand controls as well as minibuses.

Comité National Français de Liaison pour la Réadaptation des Handicapés,
38 Boulevard Raspail, 75007 Paris (Tel: (010 33 1) 45 48 90 13).
The department of Service Vacances et Echanges

Internationaux provides information concerning holiday camps, handicamps, or any kind of holidays for handicapped people.

Publications include: *Informations sur les Vacances et Loisirs*; *Guide des autoroutes à l'usage des personnes à mobilité réduite*; and *Vacances pour personnes handicapées: sejours sportifs et centres de vacances*.

French Government Tourist Office
178 Piccadilly, London W1V OAL (Tel: 01–491 7622).
The office has a special information sheet *Disabled Visitors to France* and will advise and help as far as possible. They have regional lists of hotels with rooms accessible to disabled visitors marked with an 'H' or the international wheelchair sign.

Motorail services on French railways – SNCF.

There are no special services but if you contact Motorail in advance they will be glad to offer help with boarding and alighting. Contact Motorail, 179 Piccadilly, London W1V 0BA. (Tel: 01–409 3518).
Cote d'Azur – for help and information on holidays in the South of France *see* Vakantie en Handicap (the Holiday and Handicap Association) page 189.

Access guides
The following guides are available from: RADAR, 25 Mortimer Street, London W1N 8AB (Tel: 01–637 5400). Prices include postage.
Access in Paris (1985) price: £3; *Access in Brittany* (1978) price: 35p; *Access in the Loire* (1978) price: 35p.
See also details of the book *Access at the Channel Ports*, page 191.
Michelin Red Guide to France uses the wheelchair access symbol. Available from: Michelin Tyres plc, Tourism Department, Davy House, Lyon Road, Harrow, Middlesex HA1 2DQ (Tel: 01–861 2121). Price: £9 post free.
Michelin Red Guide to Paris uses the wheelchair access symbol. Available as above. Price: £2 post free.

Où ferons-nous étape? This guide provides very simple access information to hotels throughout France as well some hotels in other European countries as well as a few African countries. It is available from: Association des Paralysés de France, 22 rue Du Pere Guerin, 75013 Paris (Tel: 45 80 82 40). Price: 70 francs.
Information for Disabled Visitors to Seine-Mari-

time, France. The purpose of this guide by Nicola Blois is to include information which will make a journey to this part of France more interesting and less fraught with problems for people with limited mobility. It is written for those who use wheelchairs all the time and for those who can stand or can walk for only short distances, but cannot manage flights of stairs. Details are given of parking, accessibility to buildings, pedestrianised streets, etc.

The places and their facilities are listed alphabetically. Three towns of great tourist interest in neighbouring Calvados are within a day's visit and are listed after those in Seine-Maritime. This is not a travel guide describing places of interest and giving hours of opening and entrance costs. Such information would need to be sought in a normal tourist guide. Available from: The Advisory Section, Education Department, County Hall, Glenfield, Leicester LE3 8RF (Tel: Leicester (0533) 871313).

Cottage Holidays in Rural France
VFB (Vacances Franco–Britanniques Ltd), 1 St. Margaret's Terrace, Cheltenham, Gloucestershire GL50 4DT (Tel: Cheltenham (0242) 580187 (brochures), 526338 (reservations).
Looking through the brochure is almost a holiday in itself. If you enjoy France and fancy tucking yourself away in a rural idyll, this might be just right for you. An access symbol is included against certain of the properties as a guide that they may be more suitable than others for those with access problems but the company says 'we prefer to discuss by telephone or letter the requirements of any particular enquirer before the booking is made; some requirements can vary so widely, and we may have on file rather more detailed information than could be included in a brochure.'
Prices vary considerably depending on location, season, mode of travel, etc. A price list will be sent with the brochure.

Medical treatment on holiday
You will need to produce E111 document – for details *see* page 175. You will need to pay for hospital treatment; dental treatment; other medical care; prescribed medicines. N.B. 70–80 per cent of the charges are refunded by the French Sickness Insurance Office.
Orange Badge scheme, reciprocal arrangement, *see* page 198.

GERMANY (EEC)

Bundesarbeitsgemeinschaft Hilfe für Behinderte e V

Kirchfeldstrasse 149, 4 Düsseldorf 1, West Germany (Tel: 010 492 11 3100623). Publishes *Ferienführer der Bundesarbeitsgemeinschaft Hilfe fur Behinderte*. A very comprehensive and helpful guide to hotels and guest houses throughout West Germany giving detailed information on the accommodation and on the surroundings. Details are also given to accommodation in 20 West German cities in *Ferienführer*. An English version of the guide is available free.

The Postillion

Contact: Miss Lore Herold, Löwenstrasse 12, 2000 Hamburg 20, West Germany (Tel: (010 49 40) 462184).
This is a worldwide contact circle to bring people who may be lonely into contact with each other. They also have a Hamburg Tourist Service for handicapped people. They will arrange accommodation, sightseeing tours, etc. When enquiring, please include an International Postal Reply coupon.

German National Tourist Office

61 Conduit Street, London W1R OEN (Tel: 01–734 2600).
Apart from general literature the office has an information sheet for disabled visitors and a leaflet *Autobahn Service für Behinderte* which gives a guide to the services available on German motorways for disabled people. In German, but the map has an English and French key and is easy to understand for non-German speakers.

The GNTO will also supply addresses to obtain access guides to the following towns: Aachen, Andernach, Bad Oeynhausen, Bonn, Coburg, Cologne, Darmstadt, Dortmund, Dusseldorf, Erlangen, Essen, Frankfurt/M, Freiburg, Hamburg, Heidelberg, Heilbronn, Herten, Kaiserslautern, Kiel, Koblenz, Krefeld, Ludwigshafen, Marburg, Munich, Neckargemund, Neuwied, Oldenburg, Saarbrucken, Solingen, Stuttgart, Tübingen.

The German Automobile Club (ADAC) publishes a camping guide (in German only) which includes the access symbol for those camp sites where there are special lavatories for disabled people. It is available from: Allgemeiner Deutscher Automobil-Club e.V, AM Westpark 8, 8000 Munich 70.

Michelin Red Guide to Germany. Uses the wheelchair access symbol. Available from: Michelin Tyres plc, Tourism Department, Davy House, Lyon Road, Harrow, Middlesex HA1 2DQ (Tel: 01–861 2121). Price: £11.50 post free.

Airports in Germany

A useful little booklet *Informationen für behinderte Fluggaste* is available in German containing information about facilities for disabled air travellers at all main airports in the Federal Republic of Germany. It is available from: Arbeitsgemeinschaft Deutscher Verkehrsflughäfen (Adv), 7000 Stuttgart 23, Federal Republic of Germany.

Medical treatment on holiday

You will need to produce E111 document – *see* page 175. Free: dental treatment; medical treatment. You will need to pay for: prescribed medicines; hospital treatment.

Orange Badge scheme, reciprocal arrangements for details *see* page 198.

GUERNSEY

Access guide available from: RADAR, 25 Mortimer Street, London W1N 8AB (Tel: 01–637 5400). Price: 20p for postage only.

Medical treatment on holiday

Treatment under the National Health Service is available only to people in the UK. Arrangements have been made, however, to enable persons from the UK who spend less than 3 months in the Islands in any one year to receive certain kinds of treatment in Jersey or Guernsey whether or not they are employed. In Guernsey and Alderney the following free services are provided: general practitioner and hospital treatment including drugs. When required outside hospital a prescription charge is made for drugs; physiotherapy treatment and the services of district nurses provided that each case is referred by a local medical practitioner; ophthalmic and dental treatment in a case of emergency only; conveyance of patients within Guernsey. There is no out-patient or casualty department at the Guernsey general hospital. In the event of a patient being ill and having to be transferred to the mainland, the States Insurance Authority may, in the first instance, meet the cost of the travelling expenses involved. The Authority may, however, seek recovery of those expenses from the patient. No reimbursement can be made of any medical expenses you incur in the Channel Islands.

HONG KONG

Hong Kong Tourist Association

125 Pall Mall, London SW1Y 5DA (Tel: 01–930 4775).
A Guide for Physically Handicapped Visitors to

Hong Kong is available free. This guide gives access and general information on hotels, restaurants, churches, transport, places of interest, and recreational activities. We understand the information is regularly updated.

Medical treatment on holiday
You will need to produce your NHS medical card and your passport. Free: In-patient treatment in general wards of public hospitals. Casualty services at certain listed hospitals and clinics. Emergency dental treatment at certain Government dental clinics. You will need to pay for: attendances at Government hospital out-patient and specialist clinics. Meals supplied to in-patients. Supply of appliances and prostheses.

IRELAND (REPUBLIC OF) (EEC)

Irish Tourist Board
Ireland House, 150 New Bond Street, London W1Y OAQ (Tel: 01–493 3201).
The ITB welcomes enquiries from disabled visitors to Ireland. They have an information sheet *Accommodation for the Disabled* to be used alongside the official *Guide to Accommodation* price: £2 including postage.

Medical treatment on holiday
No documents needed. Free: All medical and dental treatment. (The local Health Board will arrange for a consultation with a public health service doctor or dentist.) Hospital treatment arranged by a doctor in a public ward of a health service hospital. Prescribed medicines. N.B. You would need to make it clear to the doctor, dentist or hospital authorities that you wish to be treated under the European Community's social security regulations. You may be asked to complete a simple statement.

Orange Badge scheme – the concessions open under the Orange Badge scheme to residents in Northern Ireland are also open to Orange Badge holders from Great Britain.

ISRAEL

Israel Government Tourist Office
18 Great Marlborough Street, London W1V 1AF (Tel: 01–434 3651).
The Tourist Office will be glad to advise disabled travellers on their visits to Israel.

A very useful publication is *Access in Israel: A Guide for the Disabled and for those who have problems getting around*. Compiled in 1980 it still has a great deal of relevant information. It is available from RADAR, 25 Mortimer Street,

London W1N 8AB (Tel: 01–637 5400). Price: 40p postage only.

Palex Tours
Department for people with special needs, 59 Haatzmaut Road, Haifa (Tel: 04–524254).
This travel and tourism firm arranges tour programmes of 10 and 14 days suitable for individuals and for groups of disabled people. Palex works in cooperation with and under the supervision of The Roof Organisation for People with Disabilities in Israel.

El Al Israel Airlines Ltd
193 Regent Street, London W1R 8BS (Tel: 01–437 9277).
This airline has an information sheet *Facilities for Handicapped Persons Travelling by El Al*. There is also a somewhat out-of-date (1981) but none the less helpful leaflet *The Experience of Israel for the Disabled*. For further information contact Don Hulbert at the above address.

Medical treatment on holiday
No reimbursement can be made of any medical expenses you incur in Israel.

ITALY (EEC)

Italian State Tourist Office,
1 Princes Street, London W1R 8AY (Tel: 01–408 1254).
The Tourist Office states in its guide *Italy Travellers Handbook* that a number of tour operators specialise in holidays for disabled visitors and they will be glad to supply a list to enquirers.

Michelin Red Guide to Italy uses the wheelchair symbol to denote those places considered accessible to some degree to disabled people. Available from: Michelin Tyres plc, Tourism Department, Davy House, Lyon Road, Harrow, Middlesex HA1 2DQ (Tel: 01–861 2121). Price: £9.95 post free.

Project Phoenix Trust Fund – Overseas Study Tours for the Disabled
68 Rochfords, Coffee Hall, Milton Keynes MK6 5DJ.
The Trust has compiled pocket booklets on Rome and Florence (1983). The information is based on actual experience, and does not contain lists of hotels (unless they are personally known to the Trust). It is therefore selective information based on what study groups have done (and what they were unable to do), what they have seen and why they went to see it. The information will be of

181

interest to those holidaymakers who want something more than just sitting on a beach. The booklets cost £2.50 inclusive of postage.

Centro Studie Consulenza Invalidi,
Via Gozzadini 7, 20148 Milano (Tel: (010 392) 4045485).
This organisation is concerned with providing information for disabled people concerning aids, laws, education, etc. They will also supply information on holidays and have a leaflet (in Italian only) *Turismo – Vacanze per Disabile.* The letters in answer to our enquiries are always most warm.

Orange Badge scheme
The official guide from the tourist office says 'Disabled people wishing to drive their vehicle to Italy must have their Orange Badge well displayed to be able to obtain parking facilities granted to disabled drivers.' *See* also page 198.

Medical treatment on holiday
You will need to produce document E111 (for details *see* page 175). Free: hospital treatment, dental treatment, other medical treatment. You must pay for: prescribed medicines.

JERSEY

Access in Jersey – a guide for those who have problems getting around. Available free from Jersey Tourism, Weighbridge, St. Helier (Tel: Jersey (0534) 78000).
Holidays for kidney patients on dialysis *see* page 187.

Medical treatment on holiday
Treatment under the National Health Service is available only to people in the UK. Arrangements have been made, however, to enable persons from the UK who spend less than 3 months in the Islands in any one year to receive certain kinds of treatment in Jersey whether or not they are employed. The following free services are provided: hospital in-patient treatment; hospital out-patient and casualty treatment; conveyance of patients by ambulance within Jersey. In the event of a patient being ill and having to be transferred to the mainland, the States Insurance Authority may, in the first instance, meet the cost of the travelling expenses involved. The Authority may, however, seek recovery of those expenses from the patient. No reimbursement can be made of any medical expenses you incur in the Channel Islands.

LUXEMBOURG (EEC)
Tourist Office, 1010 Luxembourg, PO Box 1001,

Luxembourg (Tel: (010 352) 48 79 99) and 36–37 Piccadilly, London W1V 9PA (Tel: 01–434 2800). An attractive range of literature makes this small mountain country seem very inviting. A general guide to the Grand Duchy of Luxembourg and a colourful leaflet on camping includes the wheelchair access symbol. There is also a brochure listing hotels, auberges, restaurants, and pensions which includes the access symbol showing bedrooms accessible to physically handicapped guests. The Tourist Office is planning to extend the wheelchair access symbol to several other brochures.

Medical treatment on holiday
You will need to produce document E111 (for details *see* page 175). Free: hospital treatment. What you must pay for: dental treatment, other medical treatment, prescribed medicines. NB There can be a partial refund of charges by the Luxembourg Sickness Insurance Office.
 Orange Badge scheme – for reciprocal arrangements *see* page 198.

MALTA
Physically Handicapped Rehabilitation Fund
Rehabilitation Centre, Corradino, Paolo, Malta (Tel: (010 356) 227518).
Organises exchange visits with groups of physically handicapped people in the UK and other countries. The Fund also provides the loan of wheelchairs and other walking aids to handicapped tourists visiting the island. In addition, the Fund will advise handicapped tourists of hotels and accessibility to places of interest.

Medical treatment on holiday
You will need to produce your passport or tourist permit. Free: emergency treatment in a Government hospital. You will need to pay for: non-Government hospital treatment, treatment at a doctor's surgery, and prescribed medicines.

NEPAL
For details of trekking and exploring holidays *see* Adventure Trekking page 187.

THE NETHERLANDS (EEC)
The Netherlands abounds with facilities for handicapped travellers, for instance campsites which are so designed as to be accessible to wheelchair users, and where integration is automatically accepted. In addition there is a wealth of other accommodation from holiday bungalows and caravans to four-star hotels. Intending travellers are strongly recommended to contact The Netherlands Board

of Tourism, 25–28 Buckingham Gate, London SW1E 6LD (Tel: 01–630 0451), who have all this information at their fingertips, and are very ready to give advice.

In addition, a condensed guide in English is available free from the Board of Tourism which provides useful information for handicapped visitors on hotels, campsites, hostels, restaurants, places of interest, yacht harbours, horse riding, boat trips, fishing sites, swimming facilities, filling stations with adapted toilets, and travelling facilities for disabled people by rail, plane, taxi or touring car. The book has been compiled by ANWB (the Royal Dutch Touring Association), the Dutch sister organisation of the Automobile Association, and the Netherlands Society for Rehabilitation, Stichting Dienstverleners Gehandicapten (SDG), Postbus 222, 3500 AE, Oude Gracht 136 (Tel: (010 31) 30 33 11 21). The ANWB address is: Postbus 93200, 2509 BA, Den Haag (Tel: 070 14 71 47).

Travelling by train in the Netherlands

Netherlands Railways, 25–28 Buckingham Gate, London SW1E 6LD (Tel: 01–630 1735). Travelling by train in the Netherlands is made as easy as possible, and the following facilities are available.

1. If applied for in time, assistance will be given, where possible, at stations of departure, changing and arrival by a member of the railway staff. This assistance may also be given when changing to other forms of connecting public transport.
2. Those whose handicap makes it difficult to buy a ticket at the ticket window can obtain a ticket from the guard in the train without extra cost.
3. A wheelchair or other 'invalid' conveyance is transported free of charge.
4. At many stations a Red Cross wheelchair is available free of charge.
5. At all main stations and many other stations a movable ramp is available free of charge.
6. The assistance mentioned under 1 and 5 can be applied for on working days between 8 a.m. and 4 p.m., telephone (010 31 30) 33 12 53. Written applications can be addressed to NV Nederlandse Spoorwegen, Dienst van Exploitatie, Afd 6, Postbus 2025, 3500 HA Utrecht. Assistance has to be applied for at least 24 hours in advance, before 12 noon. Applications for Saturday, Sunday, and Monday have to be made on Friday before 12 noon. If no application for help has been made in

advance, usually no assistance by railway personnel can be given. For those who require assistance on their journey because of their handicap, an application can be made for a (female or male) Red Cross helper. Applications can be sent to the Netherlands Red Cross, Postbus 28120, Leeghwaterplen 27, 2502 KC, s-Gravenhage (Tel: (010 31 70) 846868). No charge is made for this help, but the fare and expenses of the helper will be charged.

Travelling by plane in the Netherlands
At Schiphol Airport necessary assistance will be given to handicapped passengers. When you book it is necessary to state your handicap. Adapted lavatories are available at the airport. If you need more specific information you could ask for the brochure *Schiphol's Helping Hands*, a publication of NV Luchthaven Schiphol, External Relations Department (Tel: (020) 517 24 77).

Motoring in the Netherlands
Seriously disabled visitors in the Netherlands may apply for a parking badge (well in advance of the journey) to Ministerie van Verkeer & Waterstaat, Koningskade 4, Den Haag. A fee would be charged for any medical examination which it was felt necessary to carry out. Orange Badges supplied in the UK are also valid in the Netherlands. *See* also page 198.

Camping and Caravanning in the Netherlands – *see* Vakantie en Handicap (Holiday and Handicap Association) page 189.

Medical treatment on holiday
You will need to produce document E111 (*see* page 175 for details). Free: hospital treatment, other medical treatment. You will need to pay for: dental treatment and for prescribed medicines.

NORWAY

Norges Handikapforbund
Nils Hansens Vei 2, Oslo 6 (Tel: (010 472) 64 86 10).
The Norwegian Association of the Disabled has a *Travel Guide for the Disabled* which provides information on access regarding hotels, campsites and tourist sites as well as public transport including railway stations, airports, and taxis. Price: N.kr. 58 plus postage.

Norwegian Tourist Board
20 Pall Mall, London SW1Y 5NE (Tel: 01–839 6255).

The Board can supply all the usual tourist information including a general guide to holidays in Norway with lots of useful information. It also has a hotel guide which includes the wheelchair access symbol for accommodation considered to have barrier-free facilities for holidaymakers using wheelchairs.

Travelling by train in Norway

Norwegian State Railway – specially designed coach for disabled persons. NSR have, for some years now, operated a railway coach which has been specially designed to provide facilities on long-distance trains to better suit the needs of disabled people. The coach contains a compartment for stretcher cases and a compartment specially adapted to take two wheelchairs by the window by removing the normal seating. Double sliding doors provide good access from the corridor.

Close to this compartment there is a toilet fully accessible by wheelchair. The coach is also provided with a transport chair which can be used when travellers with restricted mobility wish to be moved to an ordinary coach. The loading of wheelchairs into coaches has always been a problem; in this case the difficulty is solved by means of two lifting platforms which make it possible to wheel the chair into the luggage compartment and thence into the disabled person's compartment. The lifting platforms are easy to operate and are capable of lifting 250 kg. NSR have also introduced sleeping cars with compartments together with toilet facilities suitable for wheelchair users.

Coaches are operating between Oslo and Bergen, Oslo and Trondheim, Oslo and Stavanger, Trondheim and Bodo. Further information may be obtained from Norwegian State Railways Travel Bureau, Stortingsgata 28, Oslo 1, Norway (Tel: (010 47 2) 42 94 60).

Medical treatment on holiday

You will need to show a UK passport. Free: hospital in-patient treatment, ambulance travel. You will need to pay for: other hospital treatment, treatment at a doctor's surgery, dental treatment (except extractions), prescribed medicines. NB Some charges may be partially refunded by the Norwegian social insurance scheme. You must obtain receipts for payment and then claim at the social insurance office of the district where treatment is obtained before you leave Norway.

PORTUGAL (EEC)

Portuguese National Tourist Office

1–5 New Bond Street, London W1Y ONP (Tel: 01–493 3873).

The tourist office will be glad to send you general guidelines together with a sheet *Information for the Disabled* which lists hotels they have been informed are in some way accessible. They are mainly deluxe or first-class hotels. You would, of course, have to contact the hotels direct to ask for more information.

Winterlagos and Winterluz

J. & R. Turnbull, 21B West Street, Blandford Forum, Dorset DT11 7AW (Tel: Blandford (0258) 55082); and J. & R. Turnbull, Luz Ocean Club, Praia da Luz, 8600 Lagos, Algarve, Portugal.

Winterlagos is a small travel scheme set up specifically for the benefit of wheelchair users who have been reluctant to travel abroad because of uncertainty about general arrangements and facilities. It provides the opportunity for a winter holiday and takes advantage of low season rates.

Based on the old sea port of Lagos in the Algarve, Winterlagos will provide for a return flight from Gatwick including transfer to a minibus from Faro airport. Accommodation in Lagos will be in one of the principal hotels. Bed, breakfast and evening meal will be accounted for, and we are assured that all these hotels have accessible en-suite bathrooms and toilets, lifts to all floors, cafés and restaurants, balconies and swimming pools. Also included will be the use of the firm's minibus for some sightseeing excursions and evenings out.

Winterluz is a similar holiday but it differs in that the accommodation is in four two-person studio-style cottages set in a private park in the Algarvian fishing village of Praia da Luz, about 4 km from Lagos. It has its own swimming pool, bar, and café and is only about 30 metres from the beach.

Self-catering holidays can also be arranged using similar services surrounding the other holidays.

Guia Turistico Lisboa. In Portuguese and English, this guide briefly describes the accessibility or the difficulties of banks, railway stations, post offices, restaurants, hotels, and places of interest. Available from: Centro de Documentacao E Informacao Tecnica do Secretariado Nacional de Reabilitação, Av. Conde Valbom, 63–2, 1000 Lisboa (Tel: 76 10 81).

Medical treatment on holiday

You will need to produce your UK passport. Free: in-patient treatment in the general ward of an official hospital. You will need to pay for: medical consultation at an official health centre, prescribed medicines, dental treatment. NB You will need to make it clear that you wish to be treated under the EC social security regulations.

Orange Badge scheme – for reciprocal arrangements *see* page 198.

SPAIN (EEC)

Coordinadora Estatal de Minusvalidos Fisicos de Espana
c/o Eugenio Salazar, 2, 28002 Madrid (Tel: 413 80 01).

This organisation has produced *Guia de Hoteles espagñoles adaptados*. It is in Spanish and lists hotels, apartments, motels, hostels, and pensions throughout Spain which have special facilities. Each entry is graded by stars, and facilities such as lifts, bars, swimming pools, etc. are listed.

Majorca – the British Kidney Patients Association has a Holiday Dialysis Centre at Cala Mayor – for details *see* page 187.

Medical treatment on holiday
You will need to produce the document E111 (for details *see* page 175). Free: hospital treatment, other medical treatment. You will have to pay for: prescribed medicines, dental treatment. N.B. In most holiday resorts, only a limited service is available under the Spanish scheme. To get free treatment under the state scheme, you must follow the instructions issued with the E111. If you have to pay for a consultation or a hospital stay, the costs will rarely be refunded.

Parking
For brief information *see* page 198.

SWEDEN

Swedish National Tourist Office
3 Cork Street, London W1X 1HA (Tel: 01–437 5816).

The Tourist Office produces two publications. *Hotels in Sweden* marks with an 'H' those hotels which have special rooms with facilities for handicapped people. These rooms have especially large doors, no doorsteps, handles in the bathrooms and are integrated with the other rooms in the hotel. There are also lifts and easy access from street level. A fact-sheet is also available containing holiday information for disabled people.

Svenska Turistföreningen
Box 25, Besoksadress Vasagatan 48 101 20 Stockholm (Tel: (010 46 8) 790 31 00).

This organisation will provide a range of tourist information about hostels and travel in Sweden. *The Swedish Youth Hostels Handbook* describes which hostels are suitable for disabled people, in Swedish. In the international handbook, vol. 1, the Swedish hostels are described which are suitable for users of wheelchairs.

Medical treatment on holiday
You will need to produce a UK passport. Free: hospital in-patient treatment (including medicines), dental treatment for children. You will need to pay for: hospital out-patient treatment, other medical treatment, prescribed medicines (except for certain chronic conditions), ambulance travel. N.B. Travelling expenses to hospital may be partially refunded.

Orange Badge scheme – for reciprocal arrangements *see* page 198.

SWITZERLAND

Swiss National Tourist Office
Swiss Centre, New Coventry Street, London W1V 8EE (Tel: 01– 734 1921).

The Tourist Office has a very helpful guide *Swiss Hotel Guide for the Disabled*. Written in German, French, and English this gives information on accommodation throughout Switzerland indicating precisely those premises considered suitable for:
(a) wheelchair users;
(b) those who are severely handicapped in walking; and
(c) those who are slightly handicapped in walking.
Information is given on spas, climatic conditions and on the general facilities of the accommodation listed including sporting activities.

Schweiz Arbeitsgemeinschaft für Körperbehinderte (SAK) and Mobility International Switzerland
Postfach 129, 8032 Zurich, Switzerland (Tel: (010 41 1) 251 04 97).

The following guides are available: *Swiss holiday guide for the Handicapped throughout Switzerland; Motel Guide with Youth Hostels and Camping Places*. Additional information on barrier-free restaurants and toilets on the Swiss highways. Both guides have explanations in Italian, French, and English.
Holidays for the Handicapped. This brochure appears every year and contains:
(a) tips for the independent traveller through Switzerland and abroad;
(b) aids to plan holidays;
(c) organised holiday camps for handicapped children and adults; and

(d) organised holidays for adults abroad.

An excellent series of 20 pocket guides to the main cities of Switzerland – *City Guides* in which five symbols are used to denote varying degrees of accessibility. These are explained in German, French, Italian, and English.

The *Swiss Youth Hostel Guide* has a splendid map and gives full details of youth hostels including where they are accessible to wheelchair travellers. Available from: Swiss Youth Hostel Federation, Postfach 265, Engestrasse 9, CH – 3000 Bern 26 (Tel: 031 24 55 03).

Medical treatment on holiday

No reimbursement can be made of any medical expenses you incur in Switzerland.

Orange Badge scheme – for reciprocal arrangements *see* page 198.

TIBET

For trekking and adventure holidays *see* Adventure Trekking page 187.

UNITED STATES

USA Travel Information Centre

22 Sackville Street, London W1X 2EA (Tel: 01–439 7433).

The Centre has available *The United States Welcomes the Handicapped Visitor* guide. The guide is also available in Braille and on cassette. All are free.

Unfortunately a number of the access guides we listed in the last edition of this directory have been discontinued. We give details of those remaining below.

Los Angeles: Around Town with Ease. Available for $2 from Junior League of Los Angeles, Farmers Market, Third & Fairfax, Los Angeles, Ca 90036.

Access Washington: A Guide to Metropolitan Washington for the Physically Disabled. The information is published in six booklets: *Stadiums, Auditoriums, Recreation; Hotels/Motels; Restaurants; Theatre & Stage, Sites of Interest; Malls & Department Stores, Museums & Galleries, Libraries; Thought You'd Like To Know.* Each booklet is priced at $0.75. The complete set of booklets costs $3.75 plus $0.39 postage.

The Wheelchair Traveller. A directory of over 6,000 listings from the 50 US States, plus Canada, Mexico, Puerto Rico and more. For details *see* page 192.

Rehabilitation Gazette

Gazette International Networking Institute, 4502 Maryland Avenue, St. Louis, Missouri 63108 (Tel: 010 1 314 361 0475).

The *Rehabilitation Gazette* serves as an international clearing house of information on independent living for all persons with disabilities and co-ordinator of support groups and information for ventilator users and persons with the late effects of polio.

Gini Laurie, the inspiring and marvellously enthusiastic editor of the *Gazette* writes to us in her usually helpful way on travelling within the United States; 'Regular *Gazette* readers will have no trouble finding congenial disabled persons in the United States since all the many vignettes and profiles include the names and addresses. I would suggest picking a congenial-sounding person in the location wanted and writing for assistance with holidaying in the area. Americans are hospitable!' Gini also says she will be happy to help regular readers. She will be glad to help respirator (ventilator) users whom she will put in touch with other respirator users and equipment representatives all over the country. To become a subscriber to the *Rehabilitation Gazette, International Ventilator News, or Polio Network News,* write to Gini for details of subscription rates.

Medical treatment on holiday

Full costs will have to be paid – be warned! Armed with medical insurance, you will be safe from the very high charges made by medical and nursing services.

YUGOSLAVIA

Yugotours Limited

Chesham House, 150 Regent Street, London W1R 6BB (Tel: 01–734 7321).

This organisation is always very glad to help disabled people plan holidays in Yugoslavia, with their extensive knowledge of the country. They pointed out to us that 'unfortunately there are no hotels in Yugoslavia totally suitable for disabled/wheelchair clients, however we do have a list of hotels which are more suitable for disabled people, together with very detailed hotel information regarding lifts, steps, area, etc.' They will be glad to supply further information.

Medical treatment on holiday

You will need to produce your UK passport. Free: hospital treatment, some dental treatment, other medical treatment. You will need to pay for: prescribed medicines.

Interest and Specialist Holiday Organisations

Adventure Trekking
40 Queens Park Court, Edinburgh EH8 7DX (Tel: 031–661 1959).

This organisation specialises in adventure trekking in Nepal and Tibet. Working alongside experienced Sherpa guides, they will give you a very personal service, and the opportunity to experience a small-scale expedition in very remarkable countryside. In addition to treks and overland journeys, mountaineering expeditions, river rafting, research trips, jungle safaris, religious retreats, cultural shows and sight-seeing can also be arranged. The firm specialises in organising trips for individuals, families, small groups and women's groups. They welcome enquiries from those over 60 or people with disabilities. One of the organisers has a limited knowledge of British Sign Language.

The organisers are two women who have both travelled extensively and led treks in Nepal and India. Benedetta Gaetani is multilingual, a photographer, and very keen runner, and hill-walker – she has studied in Khatmandu. June Campbell trained as a nurse and set up Adventure Trekking with Benedetta. She worked with Tibetan refugee communities for many years and speaks fluent Tibetan. Nima Phuty Sherpa is an experienced organiser and Sherpa guide. Her extensive local knowledge is a valuable contribution to the enjoyment of holidays.

The British Ski Club for the Disabled
See details in Section 11, page 219.

Boswell and Johnson Travel Ltd
2nd Floor, International House, 82–86 Deansgate, Manchester M3 2ER (Tel: 061–832 1673).

Boswell and Johnson, the holiday tour operators and travel company, have formed a special Travel Club providing travel and holiday arrangements for disabled persons, under Sean O'Shea who is himself disabled. You may join the club at a cost of £3 per annum per family. This will be refunded on the first booking through the club. In addition, the second and subsequent holidays booked in any one year will attract a 5 per cent discount for every member of the party.

Club members will receive three newsletters a year containing information and articles of special interest to the disabled traveller. There is also holiday insurance designed specially for the disabled traveller available to members of the club.

The British Kidney Patient Association
Bordon, Hampshire (Tel: (042 03) 2021).

The BKPA has three Holiday Dialysis Centres – one in Sussex (for details *see* Section 9), and two abroad – in Jersey and Majorca. The Centre in Jersey is at the Holiday Village which looks out over Portelet Bay in the southernmost part of the island, four miles from St Helier. Dialysis is carried out each morning Sunday to Friday. The duration of dialysis is normally five hours. Patients need to complete and return an application form signed by the Senior Sister on the Renal Unit before treatment can be offered at the Centre. BKPA say it is important to first contact them before booking a holiday to see whether or not there is a dialysis vacancy.

For holiday insurance BKPA recommend contacting A. M. Marrs (P.G.) Ltd – for details *see* page 174.

Hertz Rent-a-car grant 25 per cent discount to all BKPA members. Discount vouchers are available from BKPA headquarters.

In Majorca, the Centre is at Cala Mayor, a small resort just three miles west of Palma. Dialysis is carried out on Monday, Wednesday, and Friday, mornings and afternoons. The duration of dialysis is five hours. Patients need to complete and return an application form, signed by their doctor, before treatment can be offered at the Centre. BKPA say it is important to first contact them before booking a holiday to see whether or not there is a dialysis vacancy.

Details of accommodation can be obtained from any travel agent. For holiday insurance BKPA recommend contacting A. M. Marrs (P.G.) Ltd – for details *see* page 174.

Camping
See details in Section 9, page 155.

Carefree Holidays Ltd
64 Florence Road, Northampton NN1 4NA (Tel: Northampton (0604) 34301/30382).

This firm provides holidays for the retired and for people with special needs in a wide range of carefully selected hotels and holiday centres which offer easy access for those who are elderly and for those with mobility problems. Accommodation is at ground floor level or serviced by a lift which in most instances is suitable for a person using a wheelchair. The accommodation chosen has not been designed for elderly people or for those who have mobility problems and there are usually no special aids or adaptations, but helpers will be on hand to provide practical support.

Folding wheelchairs can be conveyed on all of the holidays at no extra cost but if you use or will need a wheelchair during your holiday and are travelling alone you will be charged a supplement of 20 per cent of the holiday cost to cover the costs of taking the extra helpers required.

Carefree Helpers accompany each group to provide practical support for the whole group and not to any one individual, except in an emergency. The helpers will assist with luggage, room arrangements, excursions and give general advice and assistance including helping with wheelchairs although a supplementary helping charge will be made for unescorted wheelchair users.

The Central Bureau
Seymour Mews House, Seymour Mews, London W1H 9PE (Tel: 01–486 5101).
The Central Bureau is the national office responsible for the provision of information and advice on all forms of educational visits and exchanges. It administers the Language Assistant Scheme, Teacher and Exchange Scheme, School and Class Linking Schemes, Short Courses and a programme of international services to further higher and continuing education. Projects and schemes are run on an integrated basis whenever possible, encouraging opportunities where disabled people can mix freely and as a right with able-bodied people. With files on over 4,000 organisations operating in the field of educational travel worldwide, the Central Bureau's information and enquiry services respond to the needs of the educational field. Over 20,000 individual enquiries on opportunities available for work, travel, and study abroad are received and answered each year. Much of this information is incorporated in the Central Bureau's carefully researched, comprehensive publications: *see also* Books and Publications, page 191.

Youth Exchange Centre
Address as for Central Bureau above.
The YEC is jointly sponsored by the British Council and the Central Bureau. It was established in 1985 to promote youth exchanges between the UK and other countries. It has responsibility for the development, implementation and evaluation of policy governing youth exchanges and for advice on this to the Government. A network of regional committees has been established to promote youth exchanges and to develop local training and advisory support.

The YEC offers information, advice and grant aid to youth groups organising youth exchanges.

Broadly speaking a youth exchange is defined as a group (no larger than 25) of young people (14–25 years old) visiting or hosting a similar group from another country to take part in a programme of joint activities over a period of one to four weeks. Financial assistance is not available for touristic holidays. Youth exchanges involving participants with disabilities are eligible for YEC funding in the usual way. More flexible criteria are employed when awarding grants under the Special Fund for Disabled Youth Groups, which has been established to encourage participation by young people with disabilities. Further details available from the Development Officer.

Chalfont Line Holidays – for disabled people and their friends
4 Medway Parade, Perivale, Middlesex UB6 8HA (Tel: 01–997 3799).
This company seeks to provide integrated holidays which are barrier free and worry free. They have their own specialised coaches and on each holiday they provide a tour manager.

Disabled people are invited to bring a companion and members of the family are also encouraged to participate in these holidays.

Holidays have been arranged for destinations in the United Kingdom, Spain, Switzerland, Holland, France, and the United States.

Evergreen Travel Service Inc.
19505L 44th Avenue West, Lynnwood, Washington 98036, USA (Tel: (010 1 206) 776 1184).
While the group holidays arranged by this company, in the persons of Betty and Jack Hoffman, are mostly intended for holidaymakers in the United States, nevertheless they would be glad to welcome others on their tours where this is geographically possible. For instance, British people could join a European tour, by joining the group at a convenient airport. Their 'Wings on Wheels Tours' make exciting reading (though the tours may sound expensive). Betty and Jack personally accompany the tours and would welcome enquiries from Directory readers. They point out that when people from the United Kingdom go on their tours and join them in Europe, they have a decided advantage because of the airfares.

Holiday Care Service
2 Old Bank Chambers, Station Road, Horley, Surrey RH6 9HW (Tel: Horley (0293) 774535).
The Service has established a central clearing house of information on holiday opportunities for disabled people. For further details *see* page 163.

Intervac (International Home Exchange)
6 Siddals Lane, Allestree, Derby DE3 2DY (Tel: Derby (0332) 558931).
Each year Intervac publishes three Holiday Directories. Your details are listed in one of these and you receive all three books as they are published. Those offering accommodation which may be suitable for disabled people, are indicated by the use of the access symbol. Holidays are arranged by contacting other members by 'phone or letter. The Intervac international code helps to reduce language problems, although most members, in any case, speak some English. Annual membership, listed or unlisted £27.

The Les Evans Fund for Sick and Handicapped Children
183a St Mary's Lane, Upminster, Essex (Tel: Upminster (040 22) 22920).
Free holidays abroad are made available to children aged 8 to 15 years suffering severe illness and/or disability. Applicants are accepted and their holidays granted in accordance with medical priority. The Fund aims to provide 'the holiday of a lifetime'. A doctor and nurses accompany the children. Parents or guardians are only required to provide conveyance of the child to and from the airport.

Mobility International
228 Borough High Street, London SE1 1JX (Tel: 01–403 5688).
Mobility International exists to encourage the integration of handicapped with non-handicapped people by arranging international projects of wide appeal, which vary from youth festivals and activity programmes, where the accent is on leisure, sport and culture, to more professional conferences and seminars on specific themes. Mobility International has helped several thousand people to travel to join their projects or by giving advice to those who wish to travel alone.

Mobility International publishes *Mobility International News* packed with details of worldwide organisations and travel. Annual subscription is £4.

MPH Travel Club
12 Saxon Street, Dover CT17 9RT (Tel: Dover (0304) 210788).
The MPH Travel Club offers holidays for small and large groups of disabled people (mentally or physically) in the UK and to most parts of the world (especially Europe). Family and individual holidays are also available using your own tran-

sport plus a limited number of departures by coach equipped with a wheelchair lift.

If individuals wish to travel without family or friends on a 'public service tour' every effort will be made by MPH to find a suitable companion, but travel costs will have to be paid for the companion.

Project Phoenix Trust – Overseas Study Tours for the Disabled
68 Rochfords, Coffee Hall, Milton Keynes MK6 5DJ.
The Trust organises group study tours and interest holidays for adults of mixed physical abilities who want to share a common interest, say art or history, and who want to make this the focal point of their holiday. It is for those who enjoy learning something new in company with other like-minded people. For many disabled people it could be impossible to arrange this on their own. They may need some physical help to make the visit possible.

Most groups number between 24 – 30 people, with a ratio of one/two able-bodied helpers to one handicapped participant. All the visits are accompanied by a group leader, at least one tutor, and two SRNs in addition to other assistants.

Stichting Vakantie en Handicap (Holiday and Handicap Association)
Hulpdienst Côte d'Azur (Assistance Service), BP 62, 83480 Puget-sur-Argens, France (Tel: 94 45 60 95).
This association offers people with a physical disability and who need extra care and attention the sort of help they need to have an independent holiday abroad. There is help in arranging the holiday as well as assistance on the spot for holidays at the Côte d'Azur in the South of France and in the Netherlands. At the Côte d'Azur they can help with the hiring out of adapted caravans, letting of apartments, hiring of adapted cars, water sports facilities, etc. In the Netherlands there can be help with hiring of adapted campers and caravans. Brochures are available on the Côte d'Azur and Campers.

Threshold Travel
PO Box 25, Wythenshawe, Manchester M23 9JB (Tel: 061–905 1144).
This firm provides European and worldwide holidays especially chosen for physically handicapped people travelling with families and friends.

Holidays include: independent holidays and group holidays. A glossy brochure describes facilities available and locations. Applicants are required to state the nature of their disability in the

189

booking form and to give the name and address of their doctor.

Uphill Ski Club
See page 219.

Winged Fellowship Trust
Angel House, Pentonville Road, London N1 9XD
(Tel: 01–833 2594).
The Trust provides holidays for severely physically disabled people and welcomes those who have additional problems such as incontinence and speech defects – people who have difficulty in finding holiday accommodation. As well as holidays in the UK (described in Section 9), the Trust now offers a broad range of holidays abroad. Volunteers provide a one-to-one service and companionship. A nurse also accompanies groups travelling in the Fellowship's own bus.

Workcamps (Quaker)
See page 159 in Section 9 for information.

Young Disabled on Holiday
See page 166.

PILGRIMAGES TO LOURDES

Across Trust
Crown House, Morden, Surrey SM4 5EW (Tel: 01–540 3879).
The Across Trust has especially designed and equipped coaches, named the Across Jumbulances, and with these vehicles the Trust has been able to realise its objective to provide suitable transport for the severely handicapped and seriously ill person to go on pilgrimage to Lourdes or on holidays through Europe. Travellers can be lying down, if necessary, or wheelchair users.

Catholic Touring Association Ltd
122 Coombe Lane, London SW20 0BA (Tel: 01–947 6991).
The Association organises large diocesan pilgrimages to Lourdes which always cater for sick and disabled people belonging to a particular diocese. In addition, they arrange travel for individuals providing they have someone to attend to them at all times where this is necessary. People who are very disabled (needing to travel lying down) would need to be attached to one of the big pilgrimages where they travel by train in ambulance cars and are under full medical supervision the whole time.

HCPT (Handicapped Children's Pilgrimage Trust) and Hosanna House Trust
100A High Street, Banstead, Surrey SM7 2RB (Tel: Burgh Heath (0737) 353311).

HCPT takes approximately 2,500 children (usually between the ages of 7 and 18) on the annual pilgrimage in the week following Easter. The groups stay in the Lourdes hotels to enable the handicapped children to lead as full a life as possible in Lourdes. Parents are encouraged to make a contribution to the cost where possible.

In addition, handicapped adults may stay at Hosanna House near Lourdes from Easter to November. Weekly groups of 50 (in the spring of 1989 a new building will double this number) including helpers fly from Gatwick or Manchester airports.

General Holidays

Association of British Travel Agents
55–57 Newman Street, London W1P 4AH (Tel: 01–637 2444).
The travel industry generally is becoming more aware of the needs of disabled travellers, and travel agents are beginning to pay more attention to the wishes of their disabled clients by providing specialist information where required. You would be well advised to seek out those agents who are members of ABTA and who conform to a common code of practice. In the event of difficulties and if the agent has proved unco-operative over a complaint, you may then approach ABTA, who will offer free conciliation facilities.

Best Western Hotels International
26 Kew Road, Richmond, Surrey TW9 2NA (Tel: 01–940 9766).
The hotels within the Best Western organisation are, in the main, independently owned and run, meaning that hotels have to apply to join and have to maintain certain standards. Their glossy brochures show hotels throughout the UK and abroad. Among the welter of symbols indicating facilities are two wheelchair symbols, one showing access for wheelchairs in all areas and the other showing access for wheelchairs in some areas.

Cosmos Air plc
Cosmos House, Bromley Common, Bromley, Kent BR2 9LX (Tel:01–464 3444).
This company will advise individual disabled clients on the suitability of the hotels featured.

Villa Connections
55 Rathbone Place. Oxford Street, London W1P 1AB (Tel: 01–631 3199/3170).
This organisation provides furnished villas and apartments for holidays in Europe, the Americas, Far East, Near East, Australia and New Zealand.

We have been assured by the firm that they are happy to provide facilities for handicapped holidaymakers. Each individual enquiry is judged on its merits and costed accordingly.

Holiday Inns

A guide to their hotels is available listing those in the UK and abroad with special facilities. Each hotel has a room (if possible on the ground floor) with access facilities incorporating a bathroom, and including helpful details such as handrails, low mirrors, etc. Information available from: Holiday Inns, 10–12 New College Parade, Finchley Road, London NW3 5EP (Tel: 01–722 7755 central booking).

Horizon

Broadway, Edgbaston Five Ways, Birmingham B15 1BB (Tel: 021–643 2727).
This is the head office Agency Support department and it has plenty of information of help to disabled holidaymakers. Clients are invited to contact them direct.

Thomson Holidays

Greater London House, Hampstead Road, London NW1 7SD (Tel: 01–387 9697 – ext. 4242 for Client Services department).
Thomson say they want to make it easy for everyone to go abroad on holiday, regardless of limited mobility or other handicap. Disabled holidaymakers are invited to call the Client Services Department to speak with a skilled representative who can give you advice on suitable accommodation or travel arrangements. Given sufficient advance notice, Thomsons will be happy to carry collapsible wheelchairs on any of their flights.

Books and Publications

See also Access Guides listed under Country by Country.

AA Travellers' Guide for the Disabled – where to go, where to stay. As well as information for travellers in the UK (for details *see* Section 9, page 167), the guide includes information on travelling abroad and details of overseas organisations, and facilities for disabled people on French motorways. There are also six tours of Europe which have been specifically designed for accompanied disabled people who wish either to include a short tour of a specific area in their itinerary, or to use them as the basis for a motoring holiday. The section also includes details of recommended hotel accommodation. There is now also a feature on travelling in the United States.

The guide is available free to AA members, but otherwise costs £2.95. Published by and available from the Automobile Association, Fanum House, Basingstoke, Hampshire RG21 2EA (Tel: Basingstoke (0256) 20123).

Access at the Channel Ports a guide for disabled people. By Gordon Couch and David Barrett. This guide provides detailed information about the ports on both sides of the Channel and the ferry services which travel between them. The guide is essential for anyone who wants to avoid long walks or steps, or to know where there are suitable lavatories. The guide provides detailed and clearly presented information about access on the ships and at the various ports. Details include access to passenger terminal buildings, location of wheelchair accessible lavatories, accessibility of cabins and boarding arrangements. Price: £2.75 including postage. Available from: RADAR, 25 Mortimer Street, London W1N 8AB (Tel: 01–637 5400).

Around and About Travel. This is described as a newsletter for the physically challenged traveller and is published bi-monthly. It has some interesting articles for the international traveller with mobility problems. It is available from: 931 Shoreline Drive, San Mateo, CA 94404, USA (Tel: (415) 573 7998).

The Central Bureau

Seymour Mews House, Seymour Mews, London W1H 9PE (Tel: 01–486 5101).
1. *Working Holidays.* An authoritative annual guide to thousands of short-term paid and voluntary jobs available throughout the year in Britain and over 100 other countries. A marvellously challenging book opening up opportunities for the adventurous to turn their hand to a wide variety of jobs around the world, from archaeology to farmwork. There are opportunities to repair windmills in France; crew a yacht round the Greek islands; take people trekking in Norway; build trails in the tropical rain forests of Costa Rica; restore Welsh railway engines; work on an archeological dig in Monserrat; teach English to foreigners in Britain or to Japanese in Japan; and help run community projects and children's playschemes all over Europe. Full details are given on the type of work involved and the salary, board and accommodation provided, as well as comprehensive practical information on work and residence permits, travel, useful publications and how to advertise for a

job abroad. The symbols B, D, and PH are used to denote organisations prepared to consider applications from visually/hearing impaired or physically handicapped people. Price: £4.80 plus 70p postage.

2. *Volunteer Work* A guide to voluntary work and service with information on over 100 organisations recruiting volunteers for medium- and long-term projects in 153 countries worldwide. Information on each volunteer-sending agency covers its origins, background, general orientation and philosophy, countries of operation, projects, personal qualities and qualifications/skills required, length and terms of service, orientation/debriefing provided, and relevant literature. There is also detailed practical advice on selecting an agency, preparation and training, understanding development, medical requirements, travel, advisory bodies and help for returning volunteers. The symbol HVC is used to denote where handicapped volunteers are considered, based on the degree of handicap and the project concerned. Price: £3 plus 55p postage.

3. *Home from Home*. A new guide to international homestays, termstays, and exchange visits, with information on over 80 bona fide organisations arranging stays in 40 countries in Europe and around the world. Profiles on each organisation detail their status, be it charitable or commercial, the areas for stays, ages catered for, where opportunities are open to individuals, families or groups, the length and dates of stays, if any prior language knowledge is required, opportunities for language tuition, the arrangements for escorted travel, insurance provision and the costs involved. There is also authoritative practical information dealing with preparation and travel, and what to expect as a visitor or as a host family. Those organisations able to accept handicapped people are clearly marked. Price: £3.50 plus 45p postage.

Directory of Youth Exchange Programmes. This directory is a storehouse of information on international organisations promoting youth travel as well as a very full listing of opportunities to travel to very many different countries, from Afghanistan to Zimbabwe. Each entry describes the organisation arranging the programme, the type of programme and the language used, areas covered, etc. Those working with handicapped people are

indicated. Facilities for disabled visitors are not described, so it would be important to check on these. The Directory is available from: UNESCO, Youth Division, 7 Place de Fontenoy, 75700 Paris, France.

Good Hotel Guide. Published by the Consumers Association, PO Box 44, Hertford SG14 1SH. Lists hotels in the UK and Western Europe and uses the wheelchair symbol.

Holidays and Travel Abroad. This guide provides information on facilities in over 40 countries. Details include air and sea transport, accessible hotels, wheelchair hire, insurance requirements, and contact addresses. It also lists access guides appropriate to particular countries.

Available from: W. H. Smith & Son Ltd, price £2 or direct from the publishers (75p postage), RADAR, 25 Mortimer Street, London W1N 8AB (Tel: 01–637 5400).

Michelin Guide to the Main Cities of Europe. This guide includes the access symbol for cities in France, Benelux countries, Italy, and Germany. Available from Michelin Tyres plc, Tourism Department, Davy House, Lyon Road, Harrow, Middlesex HA1 2DQ (Tel: 01–861 2121). Price: £7.75.

Motoring and Mobility for Disabled People by Ann Darnbrough and Derek Kinrade. The book intended mainly for motorists in the UK also includes a chapter on holiday motoring, giving information on ferries, Motorail, hovercraft services, toll concessions. For details of the book *see* page 151.

Travel for the Disabled – a handbook of travel resources and 500 worldwide access guides. This guide is full of detailed and easy to understand information for those with disabilities. Travel books, magazines, and guides to parks, camping grounds and special camps, are noted throughout, as well as helpful hints for travelling by air, bus, car, cruise ship and train. It is very useful also to have so many access guides listed.

The book can be purchased direct from the publisher Twin Peaks Press, PO Box 8097, Portland, USA. Price: $9.95 plus $1.50 shipping.

The Wheelchair Traveller by Douglass Annand. This is a directory of over 6,000 listings from the 50 US States, plus Canada, Mexico, Puerto Rico and more. Lists accessible hotels, motels, restaurants and sightseeing attractions that can be enjoyed by handicapped travellers. This guide was compiled by a paraplegic who has travelled extensively. Price: $8.25 including postage and packing. Available from The Wheelchair Traveller, Ball Hill Road, Milford, NH 03055, USA.

World Hotel Directory. Published by Longman Group UK Ltd, 64 West Gate House, The High, Harlow, Essex CM20 1NE. Price: £45. The book should also be available in libraries. It lists mainly four- and five-star hotels and gives indication for wheelchair access.

Youth Exchange Centre
Address as for the Central Bureau above.
The Centre publishes *HELP! Guidelines on International Youth Exchange* a regularly updated guide for all those who are organising an exchange project or visit abroad for young people. It combines practical information with discussion of the overall aims of undertaking an international project, e.g.: preparing the group; fund raising; travel planning; passports and visas; emergencies while abroad; involving young disabled people; and evaluation of a youth exchange. Price: £5.

Camping and Caravanning

For further information *see* Section 9, page 155. See also page 189, this Section for information on camping and caravanning in the Netherlands and on the Côte d'Azur – Vakantie en Handicap (Holiday and Handicap Association).

Rail Travel

Railway travel abroad can be a hazardous business for those people with mobility problems. It needs to be remembered that most continental trains are very high up from the platform and there are steep steps to climb. Also disabled people who cannot travel in passenger coaches are usually not allowed to travel in the guard's van.

See under Belgium, the Netherlands, and Norway for special railway services in those countries.

Motorail in France – no special facilities are available but we are assured that they will be glad to give help with boarding and alighting if advance notice is given. Contact: Motorail, 179 Piccadilly, London W1V 0BA (Tel: 01– 409 3518).

Air Travel

Airlines require disabled people to contact them well in advance of their journey, in order that any necessary special arrangements may be organised. Depending on the severity of the disability, the airline may require a 'medical certificate of fitness

for air travel' to be completed by the traveller's doctor. Not all airlines want this, and it is important to check at the time of booking. For those having 'a longstanding and stable medical condition' it is possible to obtain a FREMEC (Frequent Travellers Medical Card) from any IATA airline. The application form, which must be signed by your GP, is obtainable through travel agencies. Having this card, which is valid for varying lengths of time (depending on the individual's circumstances) saves obtaining regular medical clearance for those who often travel by air.

It is worth noting that folding wheelchairs are carried on aeroplanes free of weight restrictions. Some airlines will allow disabled people to stay in their wheelchairs, arranging a space near the rear of the plane. One of the most striking improvements in air travel for severely disabled people has been the introduction by some airlines of on-board wheelchairs and removable arm-rests to make boarding, landing and movement within the aircraft easier for people with walking difficulties.

Airport information booklets including details of the special facilities available to the disabled traveller at BAA plc airports, may be obtained free of charge from Public Relations departments: Heathrow 01–745 7224; Gatwick (0293) 503096; Stansted – Bishops Stortford (0279) 502385. Ring Glasgow 041–848 4294 for the booklet covering Glasgow, Edinburgh, Prestwick, and Aberdeen airports.

For any further information on BAA publications contact BAA plc, Corporate Office, 130 Wilton Road, London SW1V lLQ (Tel: 01–834 9449).

Cardiff–Wales Airport has a booklet *Advice for Disabled Passengers.* Further details from Cardiff–Wales Airport, Cardiff CF6 9BD (Tel: Rhoose (0446) 711111).

Teesside Airport Authority's leaflet *Disabled Passengers' Guide to Teesside Airport and Hotel* is available free of charge from the Airport Director, Teesside Airport, Darlington, Co. Durham DL2 1LU (Tel: Dinsdale (0325) 332811).

Personal Toilet on Long Flights Contains useful information on this difficult problem, including: use of cabin toilet; alternative methods (body worn appliances, urinals, temporary catheterisation, protective garments, medication, restricted intake before flight); cleanliness and smell; defecation; helpful organisations; and details of useful publications. Available from the Disabled Living

Foundation, 380–384 Harrow Road, London W9 2HU (Tel: 01–289 6111). Price: £1.

Directory of Airline Facilities for Disabled People. Entries are listed alphabetically for the major airlines operating within and to and from the UK. For each airline there is a summary of its policies and practices with regard to: booking and seat allocation; boarding arrangements for passengers who cannot walk; what will be accessible to them in the aircraft; and in-flight arrangements. Produced by Access to the Skies in conjunction with RADAR, 25 Mortimer Street, London W1N 8AB (Tel: 01–637 5400). Please send 25p for postage.

Care in the Air – Advice for Handicapped Passengers. This little booklet very encouragingly starts out by pointing out that British Airways carries around 65,000 handicapped passengers every year – two-thirds of them using wheelchairs. It goes on to provide a practical guide to air travel discussing prior preparations, fares (blind persons are often entitled to special concessions on UK domestic routes), arrival at the airport, facilities at the airport, boarding, on-flight facilities including toilet arrangements, leaving the aircraft, etc. Available free from the Air Transport Users Committee, 129 Kingsway, London WC2B 6NN (Tel: 01–242 3882).

Heathrow Airbus Service for disabled passengers
All the buses on Airbus route A1 have been equipped with special lifts and space for two wheelchair passengers. Airbus A1 runs every 20 minutes daily between Victoria Station and the airport (Terminal 4 and Terminals 1, 2, 3), via Hyde Park Corner and Cromwell Road. First buses leave at 6.30 a.m. and the service continues until about 10.30 p.m. (10.00 p.m. on Sundays).

Airbus A2, which runs approximately half-hourly between Euston and Heathrow, has buses similarly adapted.

Further details from: London Regional Transport, Unit for Disabled Passengers, 55 Broadway, London SW1H OBD (Tel: 01–227 3312).

Travel-Care
This social work agency which provides help at Heathrow and Gatwick airports is an independent charity based at both airports, although each is run independently from the other. At Heathrow, there are five members of staff plus a group of volunteers who provide escort duties. The price per escort being £5 with this sum being waived in exceptional circumstances. (Tel: 01–745 7496). Open Monday to Friday 9 a.m. – 6 p.m. Saturday 9.30 a.m. to 4.30

p.m. There is also a social worker on call out of office hours. Use the telephone number above to gain access to the answerphone which will then provide a referral telephone number.

The Travel-Care service at Gatwick airport has a similar service. (Tel: Gatwick (0293) 504283). Hours: Monday to Friday 9.30 a.m.–4.30 p.m.; Saturdays 9.30 a.m.–5.30 p.m.; Sundays by arrangement.

Motoring

CAR FERRY CONCESSIONS
Many car ferry companies offer some measure of facilities, including financial concessions to disabled drivers whose cars have been adapted to suit their particular needs.

We give brief details below, but we would strongly recommend you send for a copy of the book *Access at the Channel Ports* which gives very full information on the ferry services, although this is not necessarily up to date (*see* page 191).

We divide the companies into two distinct groups:

Group 1 – those allowing eligible vehicles free passage (though some are now charging wharfage and harbour charges which were previously borne by the company).
Group 2 – those allowing various discounts in respect of eligible vehicles.

NOTE: We mention only the principal ferries. There are, in addition, many small ferry services within the British Isles, some of which provide concessions.

As you will see, the concessions normally apply to the eligible vehicle and represent either a total or partial reduction in charges. So far as we know there is only one exception, that of a Scottish ferry which allows discounts on passenger fares, otherwise driver and passenger fares are paid at normal rates.

In order to qualify for the concessionary rates all but one of the ferry companies (the exception is Sealink which has special arrangements) require drivers to be authorised by either the Disabled Drivers Association (DDA) or the Disabled Drivers Motor Club (DDMC) or the Disabled Motorists Federation (DMF). Full details of these clubs are given in Section 8.

Group 1. The following ferries carry eligible vehicles free of charge, subject to authorisation as shown above. However, some are now charging wharfage and harbour charges. These charges are made by Sealink and by B + I Line.

Sealink, P & O European Ferries, B + I Line, North Sea Ferries, Olau-Line (UK) Ltd, Brittany Ferries. See below for further details.

Sealink UK Limited
Disabled drivers' vehicles are no longer carried totally free – a port tax/administration charge is applicable on each route. It is not necessary for the disabled person to be a member of the DDA, the DDMC or the DMF to obtain the available concessions. You should send for an application form to Sealink UK Ltd, PO Box 29, London SW1V 1JX (Tel: 01–834 8122). The form has to be signed by a director of a local authority social services or social work department who must certify that the applicant is a severely disabled driver. You are asked to make sure that you apply well in advance of your journey so that all documentary procedures can be completed smoothly.

With prior notification, Sealink will help disabled passengers and disabled drivers as much as possible.

Routes to: France, Holland, Isle of Wight, Ireland, and Isle of Man.

P & O European Ferries
Channel House, Channel View Road, Dover, Kent CT17 9TJ (Tel: Dover (0304) 203388 reservations).
Concessions are available through membership of the DDMC, DDA or the DMF (see above).

All the ships are said to be accessible for disabled passengers in wheelchairs. Vehicles can, with prior notification, be parked near the service lifts and a steward will operate these as required. These lifts reach all decks on board the ships. There is ramped access to the car deck and to the main upper deck. There are sills of up to 4 inches to enter cabins, lavatories, and to move between lounges and outer decks. Entrances to all cabins are at least 22½ inches wide as are lavatory cubicles.

Wheelchairs are carried on all vessels. Prior notification will ensure that help is made available to disabled passengers whenever possible.

Most ships have washbasin facilities suitable for wheelchair users. Routes are: Dover/Calais, Dover/Zeebrugge, Dover/Boulogne, Dover/Ostend, Felixstowe/Zeebrugge, Portsmouth/Le Havre, Portsmouth/Cherbourg, and Cairnryan/Larne. Some deluxe cabins with lavatories are available on certain routes but there are no cabin facilities on the Dover/Calais route. There is no

pre-bookable seating accommodation on the Dover/Boulogne and Dover/Ostend services.

B + I Line
Reliance House, Water Street, Liverpool L2 8TP (Tel: 051–227 3131).
Concessions through membership of DMF, DDMC or DDA.

Vehicles are no longer carried totally free. A charge of £11 per vehicle is made, in each direction to cover wharfage and harbour charges previously borne by B + I Line.

These concessions do not apply July 3–September 5 on Fridays, Saturdays, Sundays, and Mondays.

The Liverpool terminal has good access, with lavatory cubicle doorways of at least 26 inches. With regard to the ships B + I Line themselves say 'Our MVs *Leinster* and *Connacht* are very modern and are equipped with lifts from the car deck to the upper decks on the ship. However, the best method of obtaining assistance is to let the company know in advance of travel and there is no problem for us to advise our operational people at the ferryport who will readily offer assistance as necessary. Certain cabins on the MVs Leinster and Connacht are especially equipped for handicapped persons, with adjacent toilets, etc.'

Routes between: Liverpool/Dublin; Holyhead/Dublin; Fishguard/Rosslare.

North Sea Ferries
King George Dock, Hedon Road, Hull HU9 5QA (Tel: direct reservations Hull (0482) 795141/712424).
Concessions through membership of DDA, DDMC or DMF (*see* page 142).

With prior notification, the company will help disabled passengers and drivers as much as possible.

Routes between: Hull and Rotterdam/Zeebrugge.

Olau-Line (UK) Ltd
Sheerness, Kent ME12 1SN (Tel: Sheerness (0795) 666666).
Concessions through membership of DDMC, DDA or DMF (*see* page 142).

In both ships operating on the route, the *Olau Britannia* and the *Olau Hollandia*, service lifts operate from the car deck to all other decks. The public facilities on board have level access. Lavatory and cabin doorways are 24½ inches. There are wheelchairs on board the ships and at the terminal at Sheerness, which is itself accessible. With prior notification, the company will help disabled passengers and drivers as much as possible.

Routes between: Sheerness and Vlissingen (Flushing).

Brittany Ferries
Brittany Centre, Wharf Road, Portsmouth PO2 8RU (Tel: Portsmouth (0705) 827701) and Millbay Docks, Plymouth PL1 3EW (Tel: Plymouth (0752) 221321).

Concessions through membership of DMF, DDMC or DDA (see page 142).

With prior notification, the company will help disabled passengers and drivers.

Routes between: Plymouth and Roscoff; Portsmouth and St. Malo; Plymouth and Santander; and Portsmouth and Caen.

Group 2. The following shipping lines are among those offering varying discounts mostly ranging from 20 to 50 per cent off the cost of carrying the car of a disabled person. In addition, many of the Scottish island and other national ferry services offer concessions. It is always worth enquiring before launching forth.

Isle of Man Steam Packet Company Ltd,
Imperial Buildings, Douglas, Isle of Man (Tel: reservations Douglas (0624) 72468).

This company offers DDA, DDMC or DMF members having specially adapted cars a reduction of 50 per cent off the standard car tariff.

The company operates a roll-on roll-off passenger car ferry service from Heysham throughout the year with their vessel *Tynwald*. Special arrangements must be made in advance on this service.

During the summer season, the vessels *Lady of Mann* and *Monas Queen* operate the services from Fleetwood, Liverpool, Stranraer, Belfast, and Dublin. There is access to the passenger accommodation from the car deck via a series of ramps. We are assured this makes the handling of wheelchairs a simple operation.

The company says that its officers will comply wherever possible with special requests from disabled drivers. Advance booking is essential.

P & O Ferries
PO Box 5, P & O Ferries Terminal, Jamieson's Quay, Aberdeen AB9 8DL (Tel: Aberdeen (0224) 589111).

On the following Scottish routes 50 per cent discount is available off the cost of carrying a car. Overnight ferries now have cabins specially de-signed to suit the needs of disabled passengers. Charges are the normal rates.

Routes between: Aberdeen/Lerwick; Aberdeen/Orkney; Scrabster/ Stromness.

DFDS Seaways
Parkston Quay, Harwich CO12 4QG (Tel: enquiries Harwich (0255) 552000).

Concessions through membership of DDMC, DMF or DDA and through Travellers Club Ltd. Members are entitled to free transport of their car providing it is under 1.85 m in height. A confirmation letter will be required from the organisation to confirm membership.

Information Sheet 1 is available which describes very clearly the facilities on board the various ships including accessibility to cabins, showers, and toilets. With prior notification the company will do all they can to help disabled passengers.

Routes between: Harwich/Newcastle and Esbjerg; Newcastle/Gothenburg; Harwich/Gothenburg; Copenhagen/Oslo. There are lifts in Gothenburg, Harwich (platforms 2 and 3) and Esbjerg (from the platform). In Harwich and Esbjerg the lifts are operated by the staff only, and extra assistance is necessary. There is an escalator from checkpoint to the finger in Harwich. Contact the Port Office for further details and assistance.

Caledonian MacBrayne Limited
The Ferry Terminal, Gourock PA19 1QP (Tel: Gourock (0475) 33755).

This firm offers travel at half the normal car single fare for the single journey to motorists (driver or passenger) who present a membership card of the Disabled Drivers Association, mobility allowance book, or VED disc exemption certificate.

It is not easy for people in wheelchairs to move around some ships but the good news is that the new vessels *Isle of Arran* and *Hebridean Isles* are fitted with lifts between decks, capable of conveying passengers in wheelchairs. We are also assured that ships' personnel are only too willing at all times to give physical assistance to handicapped and disabled people.

Routes between: Gourock/Dunoon; Wemyss Bay/Rothesay; Colintraive/Rhubodach; Largs Cumbrae Slip (for Milllport); Ardrossan/Brodick; Claonaig/Lochranza; Tayinloan/Gigha; Kennacraig/Port Ellen/Port Askaig; Oban/Craignure; Oban/Colonsay; Oban/Lismore; Oban/Coll/Tiree; Lochaline/Fishnish; Oban/Castlebay/Lochboisdale; Mallaig/Armadale; Kyle of Lochalsh/Kyleakin; Uig/Tarbert/Lochmaddy; Ullapool/Stornaway.

Red Funnel Group

12 Bugle Street, Southampton SO9 4LJ (Tel: Southampton (0703) 333042).
DDMC, DDA, and DMF members' cars are conveyed at half price on the Red Funnel route between Southampton and Cowes on the Isle of Wight. Motorists must produce a current membership card when making application to the Red Funnel office.

Fred Olsen Travel

Victoria Plaza, 111 Buckingham Palace Road, London SW1W OSP (Tel: 01–828 7000 (administration); 01–630 0033 (reservations)).
With prior notification, the company will help disabled drivers and passengers as much as possible – at terminals and on board ships.

Concessions apply to the periods 1 January–19 June and 18 August–31 December. A 50 per cent reduction will be made on the disabled person's passenger cabin accommodation. Anyone sharing the cabin will pay the full passenger cost. Four cabins have special facilities for disabled passengers.

HOVERCRAFT SERVICES

This is an alternative to the ferry services and can be used by private cars as well as coach and rail operators. Unfortunately, the service is somewhat more vulnerable to weather conditions than ferry services.

Hoverspeed

Dover International Hoverport, Kent CT17 9TG (Tel: Dover (0304) 240101)
There is good access throughout the newly designed terminal. Lavatory cubicle doorways are 26 inches. A specially adapted and accessible unisex lavatory is situated in the departure lounge. There are five steps up to the seating area on the Hovercraft but, if prior notice is given by telephoning the Hoverport Duty Office, wheelchairs may be taken on to the car deck and staff will assist the passenger to a seat. The lavatories on board are not accessible to people using wheelchairs. At Calais, the lavatory cubicle doorways are 27 inches wide.

Reservations: London 01–554 7061; Birmingham 021–236 2190; Manchester 061–228 1321; Dover (0304) 240241. Prior notification of any special requirements is needed by the company when they will do all they can to help. Postal reservations: Hoverspeed Limited, Freepost Dover, Kent CT17 9BR.

TAKING YOUR INVALID TRICYCLE ABROAD

Your three-wheeler may be taken outside the UK for the purpose of holiday travel and for no longer than 31 days, only to the Republic of Ireland or certain countries on the continent of Europe. It is necessary first to have the formal permission of the Department of Health and Social Security. It is advisable to give six weeks' notice to enable insurance arrangements to be made. Similarly, users on the mainland of Great Britain must obtain permission from the Department to take their three-wheeler to Northern Ireland.

The insurers make no charge for the extended cover necessary which includes accident damage and fire and theft. You will be responsible for arranging with the insurers the added cover, however, once permission to take your three-wheeler abroad has been been granted by the DHSS. You will also be liable to meet the cost of all repairs to the three-wheeler whilst abroad and for having it returned to your home address if for any reason you cannot complete your journey in it. If the vehicle has not been checked recently, you must arrange, through the manager of your Disablement Services Centre, for it to be inspected by an approved repairer before you start your journey. In the event of an accident abroad you would also be required to pay the first £10 of any claim. The insurers will issue an International Motor Insurance Card (Green Card), the production of which is necessary in most continental countries, and must be obtained before the start of a journey.

To start the official procedure you should contact in England and Wales: Department of Health and Social Security, Disablement Services Branch, Government Buildings, Warbreck Hill Road, Blackpool, Lancashire FY2 0UZ. In Scotland: Scottish Home and Health Department, Room 29E, St. Andrew's House, Edinburgh EH1 3DE.

Coach Travel

Greyhound Lines, International Sales

14–16 Cockspur Street, London SW1 (Tel: 01–839 5591).
This firm offers a Helping Hand service for handicapped people which is exceptionally considerate in the provision it makes for disabled travellers in the United States and Canada. Where a disabled person requires the assistance of a companion, on production of a medical certificate, only one ticket will be charged; an imaginative range of facilities and services is also offered.

Emergency Travel

The St John Ambulance Aeromedical Services
1 Grosvenor Crescent, London SW1X 7EF (Tel: 01–235 4633) (24-hour service); emergency 01–730 0318).

Provides volunteer medical practitioners and qualified nurses specially trained in in-flight care who also have the necessary aeromedical equipment. They will escort sick and injured people by air to and from any part of the world. This voluntary service is available to any company, organisation or private individual. It is able, at short notice, to provide qualified Aeromedical attendants to escort patients travelling on scheduled flights and, when necessary, to arrange the charter and the equipping of aircraft as air ambulances ranging from light aircraft to executive jets. In addition to escorting patients by air the service will, if necessary, undertake all the booking arrangements and supply an ambulance to or from the airport.

The St John Aeromedical Attendants are all volunteers who do not charge or receive any fees for their services. The cost of their return fare on scheduled flights, their expenses incurred in travelling to and from the United Kingdom and any overnight accommodation and incidental expenses and, in the case of chartered aircraft, the cost of chartering, are the responsibility of the patient, her/his agents or the person requesting the service. Further information from the Director, St. John Aeromedical Services.

ORANGE BADGE AND RECIPROCAL SCHEMES

Reciprocal arrangements with European countries
Since December 1981, holders of Orange Badges who visit some European countries which provide parking concessions for their own disabled citizens may take advantage of the concessions made by the host country by displaying their Orange Badge. The concessions vary from one country to another, but they usually allow for an extension of the time limit where waiting is restricted and an entitlement to use special parking places reserved for disabled people.

Apart from the UK, 12 countries are participating. They are Austria, Belgium, Denmark, Finland, France, West Germany, Italy, Luxembourg, Netherlands, Portugal, Sweden, and Switzerland. (While Spain does not have a reciprocal scheme, nevertheless limited information on parking arrangements is included in the list below.) The concessions available in Northern Ireland under their Orange Badge scheme are also open to Orange Badge holders from Great Britain. However, in many towns there are security zones where vehicles cannot be left unattended. For full information consult the local motoring organisations or the police. In addition to the countries mentioned, Jersey and Guernsey also recognise our badge.

It should be noted that in some countries responsibility for introducing the concessions rests with individual local authorities so that they may not be generally available. In such cases badge holders should enquire locally, as they should whenever they are in any doubt as to their entitlement. Moreover, as in this country, the arrangements apply only to badge holders themselves and the concessions are not for the benefit of able-bodied friends or relatives. Non-entitled people who seek to take advantage of the concessions in Europe by wrongfully displaying an Orange Badge will be liable to whatever penalties apply for unlawful parking in the country in question.

A summary of the parking concessions available to disabled people in each country is given below. Queries about these arrangements may be sent to the Department of Transport, Room C10/13A, 2 Marsham Street, London SW1P 3EB (Tel: 01–212 5252).

Pictorial representation (in colour) of the signs used in the various countries listed below is given in our book *Motoring and Mobility for Disabled People* for details *see* page 151.

Austria
The Austrian scheme of parking concessions allows badge holders to park without time limit where indicated and they may stop (even where double parked) where the sign is displayed.

A sign is also used to indicate that badge holders may park in a pedestrian zone when loading and unloading is permitted. In addition, the authorities may set aside special parking places for disabled people's vehicles near such places as hospitals and public service facilities for the care of disabled people.

Belgium
Special parking places are reserved for disabled people. These are indicated by a sign with the addition of the international symbol.

Badge holders may also park without time limit where parking time is otherwise restricted:
(a) by road signs
(b) in 'blue' zones
(c) by parking meters (most local authorities do not require badge holders to pay at meters).
Under no circumstances are badge holders al-

lowed to park in places where parking is prohibited.

Denmark

Badge holders are allowed to park for up to one hour where a shorter time limit applies to other motorists and unlimited parking is permitted where a time limit of one hour or longer would otherwise apply.

Finland

Finnish badge holders are allowed to park in places where parking is prohibited by road signs and they will be exempt from parking charges. Unfortunately, as far as we know, concessions have not yet been extended to include disabled visitors. It would be worth making enquiries when you book a holiday what the present situation is.

France

Responsibility for parking concessions in built-up areas rests with local mayors and not central or regional authorities. Apart from reserved parking places for disabled people (indicated by the international symbol) there is no formal system of concessions in operation although it is understood that, in practice, a good deal of latitude is given since the police have instructions to show consideration where parking by a disabled person is concerned.

In some towns or cities, such as Paris, disabled people are allowed to park at meter bays and pay only the initial charge.

West Germany

Badge holders are allowed to park:
(a) for a maximum of three hours where indicated (the time of arrival must be shown on a parking disc);
(b) beyond the permitted time in certain areas;
(c) beyond the permitted time where a sign is displayed with an additional panel restricting parking time;
(d) during the permitted periods for loading and unloading in pedestrian zones; and
(e) without charge or time limit at parking meters, unless other parking facilities are available within a reasonable distance.

Reserved parking places for disabled people are also provided; these are indicated by a sign including the international symbol or in exceptional cases where the symbol is marked on the highway.

Italy

Responsibility for the concessions rests with the local authorities. In general, public transport is given priority in town centres and private cars may be banned, but the authorities are required to take special measures to allow badge holders to take their vehicles into social, cultural, and recreational activity areas as well as to their work places.

Reserved parking bays are provided, indicated by signs with the international symbol (a small number of spaces are reserved for particular vehicles and in such cases the sign will show the appropriate registration number).

Luxembourg

In most urban areas reserved parking places are provided and indicated by signs including the international symbol. Generally speaking, however, badge holders are not allowed to exceed the parking time limit.

Netherlands

Badge holders are entitled to the following concessions:
(a) the use of a car park set aside for disabled people (the parking place must be signed and there is no time limit);
(b) indefinite parking in blue zones;
(c) indefinite parking at places marked with a sign in conjunction with an additional panel stating parking time;
(d) parking at places marked with signs for a maximum of two hours.

A disabled person's parking disc must be used. Concession (d) does not apply where other parking facilities exist within a reasonable distance. An extension of this time limit, particularly after 6 p.m. is being considered.

Portugal

Parking places are reserved for badge holders' vehicles. These are indicated by signs with the international symbol.

Badge holders are not allowed to park in places where parking is prohibited by a general regulation or a specific sign.

Spain

Spain cannot be included among those countries participating in reciprocal arrangements as there is no national system of parking concessions. Most large towns and cities operate their own individual schemes, but types of badges used and the concessions provided are not standardised. It is understood, however, that consideration would be shown to disabled badge holders from other countries.

Sweden

Badge holders are allowed to park:

(a) for three hours where parking is banned or allowed only for a shorter period;

(b) for a period of 24 hours where a time limit of three hours or more is in force;

(c) at reserved parking spaces, indicated by signs with the international symbol.

In general, parking charges must be paid although there may be local exemptions.

NOTE: Concessions have not, as far as we know, yet been extended to include disabled visitors – however it would be worth making enquiries to find out the latest position.

Switzerland

Badge holders are allowed to park:

(a) without time limit at parking places where time limits are in force or within a blue or red zone;

(b) without time limit at parking meters on payment of the minimum charge;

(c) where parking is otherwise banned, provided no obstruction or danger is caused and that no other parking spaces are available. Parking is not allowed where *stopping* is prohibited; and

(d) at reserved parking places indicated by a sign including the international symbol.

SECTION 11

ARTS, SPORTS AND LEISURE

For many of us, it is the activities we pursue in our spare time that add an extra meaning to our lives. Those numerous enterprises we pursue entirely voluntarily give us opportunities to express ourselves in a way denied to us in other aspects of our lives. We can be creative in a thousand different ways by following a hobby or a sport or a simple recreation of our choice either in our own homes or outside.

In this section we describe a wide range of arts, sports, and leisure activities which can be pursued by disabled people who need a special aid or facility to be able to enjoy and pursue a particular inclination. From chess to flying, from basketball to music there are organisations and groups of enthusiasts happy to help you overcome any particular difficulties.

Let's start at home where local authorities are empowered by the Chronically Sick and Disabled Persons Act 1970 to help disabled people who are resident in their areas to enjoy a wide range of recreational activities. For instance, they may provide or help people to obtain radio, television or similar leisure facilities. They may also provide lectures, games, outings, and many other leisure pursuits including social and youth clubs. Many local authorities operate a travelling library service which will call regularly at the homes of those who are unable to visit libraries.

The arrangements differ considerably from area to area but it is certainly worth making full enquiries as to the opportunities in your own locality. We would urge that you never be put off too easily if your own particular interests appear not to be provided for. This may merely be the result of a lack of demand; for instance almost any subject can be covered by an evening class when that need is demonstrated. Our experience is that requests from disabled people are often received with more than usual consideration. Nor should it be forgotten that many voluntary organisations provide recreational activities, while specialist sporting

and hobby clubs will often go out of their way to welcome and help a disabled person.

In addition, many sports centres and outdoor pursuits centres provide opportunities for disabled people to participate in their programmes. Many sports centres now run sports clubs especially for disabled people, and the local centre manager should be approached for details.

The British Sports Association for the Disabled will also be glad to provide information on local facilities and the local BSAD representative would be glad to offer individual advice.

For details of holiday courses on a wide variety of subjects, *see* Section 9.

Amateur Radio

The Radio Amateur Invalid and Blind Club
Secretary: Cathy Clark, 9 Conigre, Chinnor, Oxfordshire OX9 4JY.
The Club was founded in 1954 as a self-help organisation to enable blind and handicapped people to pool their knowledge, skills and spare radio components and to benefit from each other's experience. Over the years the Club has grown considerably, and has links with similar organisations, both in this country and abroad. Membership is by a normal subscription to *Radial*, the Club newsletter.

Members wishing to obtain their transmitting licences are helped in their studies by local amateurs and clubs. Cassettes are available for the use of blind members, and Morse code lessons are also taped. Local members undertake to keep equipment serviceable and advise members.
Radial is issued eight times a year at a minimum annual subscription of £2. It contains news of and from members and articles on many subjects. Also available on cassette.

The Radio Society of Great Britain
Lambda House, Cranborne Road, Potters Bar,

Hertfordshire EN6 3JE (Tel: Potters Bar (0707) 59015).
The national society of radio amateurs in the United Kingdom. Members of the RSGB receive the monthly edition of *Radio Communication* and are provided with information on technical matters and on the various activities and events of concern to amateurs. There are regional and area representatives who can provide advice on the hobby and also supply information on local club meetings.

Angling

People with a wide range of disabilities are able to enjoy angling. The different types of angling and the range of techniques available provide a spread of options to suit individual needs and tastes. The three forms of angling – coarse fishing, game fishing (salmon and trout) and sea fishing can be enjoyed from bank or shoreline, landing stages, piers or boats. Special facilities, if needed, can be provided in all these situations.

For further information *see* NAC below. *See also* the publication *Water Sports for the Disabled*. *See also* Section 9, Interest and Specialist Holidays.

Handicapped Anglers Trust
29 Ironlatch Avenue, St. Leonards-on-Sea, East Sussex TN38 9JE (Tel: Hastings (0424) 427931).
The aim of the Trust is to encourage and assist mentally and physically disabled people to participate in the sport of angling. Most of the work of HAT is concerned with the research, development and production of special aids and equipment. They are producing a special boat known as the Allenard Wheelyboat and this is a main priority. There are 21 of these craft around the country. The Trust believes there is an immediate need for at least 100 such craft in Great Britain. The hull is of double-skinned aluminium, filled with closed cell polystyrene. The deck is flat and there is a bow that can be lowered so that a wheelchair user can go aboard, row or motor without having to leave a wheelchair or be lifted. The unsinkable craft is also of considerable benefit to others with mobility difficulties. Each one costs, fully equipped, in the region of £1,500. There are other items that need development, these are not always a commercial proposition and without the assistance of the Trust would not be produced.

The *Wheelyboat Guide* is available on receipt of 25p for postage and packing.

National Anglers' Council
11 Cowgate, Peterborough PE1 1LZ (Tel: Peterborough (0733) 54084).
The NAC Committee for Disabled Anglers has obtained information on fishing venues suitable for disabled anglers. These are in separate sheets in county order, with details of officials to contact, species of fish, parking and shelter facilities. The sheets and much useful data on equipment, etc can be obtained from the NAC offices upon receipt of a stamped addressed envelope.

Committee for the Promotion of Angling for the Disabled
Tom Mackenzie, 17 Nicholson Street, Edinburgh EH8 9BE (Tel: 031-667 2288 – daytime Monday to Saturday).
Aims to develop angling facilities for disabled people in Scotland. A member of the Committee has designed a purpose-built seat and gantry. Anyone who would like to make use of special angling facilities is invited to contact the Committee. There are some concessionary rates available on various lochs and rivers in Scotland.

The Committee, together with the Scottish Sports Association for the Disabled (*see* page 226) has provided an access guide to fishing areas describing a range of information of concern to disabled fisherpeople including whether a special gantry is available.

Archery

The Grand National Archery Society
National Agricultural Centre, Stoneleigh, Kenilworth, Warwickshire (Tel: Coventry (0203) 23907).
For information on national activities contact the Secretary.

Archery for Disabled People
7 New Street, Shefford, Bedfordshire SG17 5BW.
This is part of the Grand National Archery Society and aims to help those disabled people who are keen to take up the sport and also to provide solutions experienced by existing archers. Help can be given with release aids, special adaptations and where to seek tuition. A new archery round was initiated in 1981, The Elizabethan, specifically for the novice and severely disabled person. For further information, physically disabled people should contact the National Coordinator, John Burgess, at the above address – please enclose a 4 in × 9 in s.a.e.

The British Sports Association for the Disabled

have published a book *Archery* by Alf Webb available from them at Harvey Road, Aylesbury, Buckinghamshire HP21 9PP (Tel: Aylesbury (0296) 27889). Price: £1.75 including postage and packing.

Arts

For information on Music *see* page 214.

Artists with Disabilities

Primarily a support group for people with disabilities who practise the arts including painting, drawing, sculpture, drama, music, and writing. They have organised a festival of artists with disabilities and a number of exhibitions. Four members have exhibited together at the People's Gallery in London under the title of *No Need for Glass*.

Contact: Keith Armstrong, 22 Seymour House, Church Way, Somers Town, London NW1. Please send an s.a.e. with any enquiry. The Group may also be contacted c/o Housmans Bookshop, 5 Caledonian Road, Kings Cross, London N1. Send s.a.e with enquiry.

Arts Council Directory

Arts and Disability Organisations and Projects Arts Council, 105 Piccadilly, London W1V OAU (Tel: 01–629 9495).

This directory of organisations, with addresses and telephone numbers, and in some cases brief descriptions of roles, is intended both as a contact list and a guide to the range of activity in the field of arts and disability. Details included are for both national and local organisations concerned directly with arts and disability as well as of general disability organisations and of sources of funds. The directory is available free.

Arts for Disabled People in Wales

Channel View Leisure Centre, Jim Driscoll Way, The Marl, Grangetown, Cardiff CF1 7NF (Tel: Cardiff (0222) 377885).

This is aimed to provide the widest possible range of arts opportunities for people with disabilities, so they may achieve a new degree of skill in the arts and an enhanced opportunity to exercise genuine personal choice, a greater ability for self-advocacy together with an added pleasure in life.

ADPW's strategy is to do this by working in partnership with statutory authorities, voluntary bodies and to establish initiatives in the community. The key to this, they believe, is to raise awareness of the value of arts activities and to develop training programmes so that arts provision becomes the norm rather than the exception.

Artsline

5 Crowndale Road, Camden, London NW1 1TU (Tel: 01–388 2227).

Artsline is London's free information and advice service for disabled people on arts and entertainment. They have access information on arts venues of every type in London including details on steps, ramps, lifts, rails, lavatory facilities, wheelchair spaces, parking, transport, hearing loops, provision for guide dogs, availability of food and any other information you may require to enable you to enjoy the arts in London. Artsline can also give you full information on 'what's on' in all the arts in London.

Disability Arts in London is Artsline's monthly listings and arts magazine. It is free to disabled users and has news, views, pictures, and features by and about disabled artists in London. The magazine, like Artsline itself, is run by disabled people. As well as print it is available on tape. There is also a booklet/tape for disabled children and their parents or carers on what London has to offer them by way of arts and leisure.

In addition, Artsline can also tell you about classes, workshops and adult education courses in various art forms either for beginners or for those who are more experienced.

Telephone lines are open for calls between 10 a.m. and 4 p.m. Monday to Friday and 10 a.m. and 2 p.m on Saturday. An answerphone is available for the rest of the time to record enquiries which will be dealt with the following day. Letters are also welcome.

Artlink

Edinburgh and the Lothians 4 Forth Street, Edinburgh EH1 3LD (Tel: 031–556 6350/557 3490).

Artlink runs a variety of participatory arts projects for physically and mentally handicapped people in hospitals, training centres, schools and residential homes in Edinburgh and the Lothians. An Artlink access guide *Venues* to arts and historic venues in Edinburgh and the Lothians is available.

They also run an information and access advisory service, and an escort scheme with volunteer drivers to encourage people to attend and take part in arts events.

Trust Fund for the Training of Handicapped Children in Arts and Crafts

94 Claremount Road, Wallasey, Merseyside L45 6UE.

The objects of the Trust are to encourage and to help financially the arts and crafts education and the artistic development and training of mentally and/or physically handicapped children (usually under the age of 18 years), as individuals or through various special schools and organisations. The size of grants varies according to requirements and loans may be arranged in certain circumstances. Assistance is given for capital expenditure on equipment, running costs, tuition, materials, educational courses, etc. Applications, stating specific needs and estimates, must be made in writing.

Conquest – The Society for Art for the Physically Handicapped
3 Beverley Close, Ewell, Epsom, Surrey KT17 3HB (Tel: 01–393 6102/6690).
Conquest aims to encourage physically handicapped adults to take up and pursue artistic, creative activity. For this purpose groups have been formed and a magazine and pamphlets produced. In addition, exhibitions are held, talks are given and information is available.

The Creative Tree
Gina Levete, who draws on her extensive experience to compile this illustrated, practical guide provides advice on how to set up art, dance, drama, and music programmes for disabled and disadvantaged people. The text is supplemented by an *International Directory of Ideas* with addresses and brief analyses of nearly 1,000 projects worldwide. Published by: Michael Russell (Publishing) Ltd, The Chantry, Wilton, Salisbury, Wiltshire SP2 OJU. Price: £7.95 including postage.

Crypt
Forum Workspace, Stirling Road, Chichester, West Sussex PO19 2EN (Tel: Chichester (0243) 786064).
Crypt aims to provide opportunities for young people who are physically disabled to develop their creative potential in group homes in a community setting. The students will have demonstrated their potential in an arts related subject and will be keen to explore creativity further while experiencing a measure of independence in the community. CRYPT serves as a bridge (for one to three years) between an institution and independent living where possible. Personal development in artistic and social skills is strongly encouraged. CRYPT believes that disability need not be a handicap and that expression through the arts can be a liberating experience.
There are currently three projects at: Brackle-

sham/West Sussex; Newham/London; and Nottingham.
Membership subscription is £3. There is also a newsletter.

Fair Play
Campaign for Equal Opportunities in the Arts for People with Disabilities, 1 Thorpe Close, London W10 5XL (Tel: 01–960 9245).
This is a lobby organisation working towards equal training and employment opportunities in the performing and recorded arts, film, television, video, and radio for people with disabilities.

Help Yourself to the Arts
This is a handbook giving detailed information on the facilities offered by a wide range of venues in the counties of Derbyshire, Leicestershire, Nottinghamshire, Northamptonshire, and also in Milton Keynes. Details of access for those who are mobility, visually or hearing impaired are very clear. Available free on receipt of an s.a.e. (A4 size or larger – 17p in stamps) from East Midlands Arts, Mountfields Houses, Forest Road, Loughborough, Leicestershire LE11 3HU (Tel: Loughborough (0509) 218292).

Phoenix
The Editor, 10 Woad Lane, Great Coates, Grimsby DN37 9NH.
Phoenix is a quarterly magazine by and for disabled people who are also interested in the arts. It contains a mixture of fiction, poetry, prose, reviews, illustrations, literary criticism, a television column, and articles on the disability movement.
Contributions for publication of all types are welcomed. There is a small payment for those items used. Phoenix is available by subscription only: £4 for four issues; on cassette £9.45 for four issues. A sample issue will be sent for £1.

Shape
1 Thorpe Close, London W10 5XL (Tel: 01–960 9245).
Shape (London) is an organisation which develops the arts with, by and for people with physical, mental or sensory disabilities, elderly people and people recovering from mental illness, through participation in arts activities and events. Shape organises workshops in varied locations such as day centres, hospitals, hostels and community centres. Shape also organises training courses for artists and staff, and tours performances and exhibitions. In addition, it provides information and advice to a wide range of individuals and organisations, and liaises with other arts and disability

bodies to establish joint projects and initiatives. (For details of the Shape London Ticket Scheme *see* page 207).

Since its inception, other organisations with similar aims have been formed independently around the country. These are collectively known as *The Shape Network*. These are as follows:

Shape East, c/o Eastern Arts, Cherry Hinton Hall, Cambridge CB1 4DW.

East Midlands Shape, New Farm, Walton-by-Kimcote, Lutterworth, Leicestershire LE17 5RL

Artlink for Lincolnshire and Humberside, Humberside Leisure Services, Central Library, Albion Street, Hull HU1 3TF.

Artability (South East), Cooper Hut, Thomas Delarue School, Shipbourne Road, Tonbridge, Kent TN11 9NR.

Arts Integration Merseyside, c/o DRU, Mount Vernon Green, Hall Lane, Liverpool L7 8TF.

Shape Up North, 191 Bellevue Road, Leeds LS3 1HG.

North West Shape, The Green Prefab, Back of Shawgrove School, Cavendish Road, West Didsbury, Manchester M20 8JR.

Northern Shape, Todd's Nook Centre, Monday Crescent, Newcastle upon Tyne NE4 5BD.

Southern Artlink, 125 Walton Street, Oxford OX2 6AH.

Artshare South West, Exeter and Devon Arts Centre, Bradninch Place, Gandy Street, Exeter EX4 3LS.

Artlink, 17a Hanover Street, Newcastle-under-Lyme, Staffordshire ST5 1HD.

Solent Artlink, Hornpipe Community Arts Centre, 143 Kingston Road, Portsmouth.

Affiliated to the network:

Artlink Edinburgh and The Lothians, 4 Forth Street, Edinburgh EH1 3LD.

Project Ability, 37 Otago Street, Glasgow G12 8JJ.

Scottish Council on Disability Committee on Arts for Scotland, Princes House, 5 Shandwick Place, Edinburgh EH2 4RG.

Arts for Disabled People in Wales, Channel View, Jim Driscoll Way, The Marl, Grangetown, Cardiff CF1 7NF.

Athletics

Athletics by Moira Gallagher. This book is published by the British Sports Association for the Disabled. Chapters include: Athletics for all Disabilities; The Rules of Athletics and How to Officiate; Organising an Athletic Meeting; Athletics Awards to Young Athletes. Price: £1.75 including postage and packing. Available from BSAD, Stoke Mandeville, Harvey Road, Aylesbury, Buckinghamshire HP21 9PP.

Basketball

The Great Britain Wheelchair Basketball Association
Tony Sainsbury, 76 Leicester Road, Failsworth, Manchester M35 OQP (Tel: 061– 682 9521).
The Association is the governing body of wheelchair basketball in Great Britain. The aim of the Association is to promote and encourage the game, particularly through its various leagues and competitions. The National League is made up of a First Division and regional divisions playing matches between October and April each year. Playing membership is open to those 'who have a severe permanent physical disability of one or both lower extremities which excludes their participation in the regular game of basketball'. The Association encourages all levels of the sport organising coaching and tournaments for youngsters; the age limit for the Senior National League is a minimum of 14 years. Teams are available for international championships and Olympic Games at senior women's and men's levels. There are also mixed teams with women and men playing together.

Billiards and Snooker

While, because of the regulation height of the tables, there are obvious difficulties in playing these games from a wheelchair, some disabled people can overcome this handicap. From another point of view, wheelchairs benefit from the fact that it is necessary to have considerable space around the table to handle the long cues. For details of snooker playing by disabled people contact the British Sports Association for the Disabled, Stoke Mandeville, Harvey Road, Aylesbury, Buckinghamshire HP21 8PP (Tel: Aylesbury (0296) 27889).

Billiards and Snooker Control Council
Coronet House, Queen Street, Leeds LS1 2TN (Tel: Leeds (0532) 440586).
The Council is responsible for the organisation and running of all national billiards and snooker events for non-professional players. It jointly sponsors the Billiards and Snooker Foundation and as such administers a national coaching scheme.

Board Games

Some of the most popular games, such as Scrabble, Mastermind, backgammon, chess, and draughts are available in specially adapted versions which make them suitable for blind and partially sighted players, as well as remaining suitable for sighted players. Details from the Royal National Institute for the Blind, 224 Great Portland Street, London W1N 6AA (Tel: 01–388 1266).

John Slade, 170 Cambridge Road, Seven Kings, Ilford, Essex IG3 8NA (Tel: 01–599 4256), has both redesigned board games and devised new ones with playing pieces which are both visual and tactile. He has produced an explanatory leaflet. These board games are available from RNIB.

WAVES
Corscombe, nr. Dorchester, Dorset DT2 0NU (Tel: Corscombe (093 589) 248).
The company manufactures and supplies a variety of magnetic board games at prices from £3.40 to £18.12. These include some dual purpose boards, which have on the reverse the relatively unfamiliar but absorbing game, Nine Men's Morris (mentioned by Shakespeare).

Boating

See also Section 9 Sailing and cruising holidays. Useful guidance is included in the publication *Water Sports for the Disabled see* page 229.

Bowling

There can be problems taking wheelchairs on to outdoor bowling greens. Ramps are necessary to get on to the green and unfortunately these cannot be standardised as the drop varies. Then the green itself may be damaged by the wheels. However, these difficulties can be overcome and some clubs welcome disabled members in wheelchairs. Indoor clubs pose fewer problems. For further information contact the British Sports Association for the Disabled (*see* page 224) who will put you in touch with the nearest BSAD Development Officer.

The English National Association of Visually Handicapped Bowlers
Secretary: Geoff Rawlinson, 11 Wordsworth Road, Clevedon, Avon BS21 6PQ (Tel: Bristol (0272) 875969).
The Association has some 300 members many of whom belong to the 29 member clubs which are situated throughout the UK. The aim is to promote bowls and set up clubs and tournaments for visually handicapped women and men. There is a small annual subscription fee.

Northern Ireland Association of Visually Handicapped Bowling Clubs
Stewart Quin, Dufferin Cottage, 157a Groomsport Road, Bangor, Co. Down, Northern Ireland BT20 5PQ (Tel: Bangor (0247) 454704).

Camping

See details of camping holidays in Section 9.

Canoeing

See also Section 9 *Interest and Specialist Holidays*

British Canoe Union
Flexel House, 45–47 High Street, Addlestone, Weybridge KT15 1JV (Tel: Weybridge (0932) 41341).
Canoeing is a sport in which it is possible for people with certain disabilities to take part, very often at a standard comparable to an average canoe club member and occasionally to a far higher standard. The British Canoe Union considers that disabled people should be encouraged to play an active part as normal members of the sport. However, there are several groups which make special provision for disabled people, and many kayaks and canoes which are eminently suited or can be easily adapted for special needs. The BCU will give advice on all of these aspects. They also have a publication *A Guide to Canoeing with Disabled Persons* by Geoff Smedley, price: £2.
Useful guidance for disabled canoeists is contained in the publication *Water Sports for the Disabled*. *See also* Spastics Society, page 229.

Chess

British Chess Federation
9a Grand Parade, St. Leonards-on-Sea, East Sussex TN38 ODD (Tel: Hastings (0424) 442500). The British Federation is an 'umbrella' organisation to which is affiliated a multitude of local chess clubs and specialist societies. The Federation carries information on chess by correspondence.

British Postal Chess Federation
Secretary: Malcolm Peltz, 14 Linden End, Aylesbury, Buckinghamshire HP21 7NA.
Membership of the British Postal Chess Federation is open to British groups which organise correspondence chess and to individuals as Vice-Presidents (VPs). Associations, clubs, etc pay an annual fee based on their active correspondence

chess playing membership. The official journal of the Federation *Information Circular* is sent to members. This publication contains details of all games played by British players in the CC Olympiads, European CC Team Championship, North Atlantic Team Tournament and international friendly matches as well as many of the games played in the British championships.

The annual subscription for a BPCF Vice-President is £5. This includes receiving the *BPCF Information Circular*. This is also available to non-members at £2 for a year's subscription of four issues. Sample copies are available for 50p (stamps acceptable).

A booklet *Correspondence Chess* is available describing the Federation's activities.

British Correspondence Chess Society (affiliated to the BPCF above).
M. Corrigan, 12 Oakhurst Rise, Charlton Kings, Cheltenham, Gloucestershire GL52 6JU.
The Society organises tournaments, matches and competitions for players of all strengths including beginners. The BCCS provides entry to national and international correspondence chess events. Membership includes the free bi-monthly magazine *Chess Post* which includes articles and news and has information on games and results. Annual subscription £7.50.

Braille Chess Association
Stan Lovell, 7 Coldwell Square, Cross Gate, Leeds LS15 7AB.
The Association offers its members a wide variety of services, including participation in international team and individual championships; postal chess in Braille and on cassette; over the board chess against sighted teams; discussion groups on tape; publications of the BCA *Gazette* in Braille or on tape; a cassette tape service of chess books and other chess publications (small copying charge on members' own tapes); a library of Braille chess books; the sale of a Braille book *The ABC of Chess*. Annual subscription is £4 or pro rata. There is one year's free membership to those under 18.

Friedreich's Ataxia Group Postal Chess Club
Organiser: R. G. Hughes, 4 Lambs Hill Close, Thornton, Blackpool, Lancashire FY5 5JS.
The chess club is open to all members of FAG, for whom there are no fees.

Magnetic Chess, Draughts or Checkers with Boards
Details from: WAVES, Corscombe, nr Dor-chester, Dorset DT2 0NU (Tel: Corscombe (093 589) 248).

Cinemas and Theatres in London

Shape (London) Ticket Scheme
1 Thorpe Close, London W10 5XL (Tel: 01–960 9245).
This scheme arranges reduced ticket prices for a wide range of events in London's theatres, concert halls, arts centres, museums, and galleries. The scheme's free booking service takes full account of particular access, seating requirements, and special needs of people with disabilities, and can organise volunteer drivers and escorts for ticket scheme members who cannot use regular transport or would like someone to accompany them.

Membership is open to all people with disabilities within the Greater London Area.
See also Artsline (page 203) which helps make art and entertainment more accessible in London by providing information about what's on and about facilities (or lack of them!).

Cookery

Cookery for Handicapped People by James Hargreaves. This cookbook is specifically designed for the use of mentally handicapped people. The aim is to encourage school-leavers and adults alike to learn how to fend for themselves independently in the community by preparing and cooking simple meals. James Hargreaves developed this book as a result of two years' trial and error experiments in a special school. He wanted his pupils to be able not merely to cook simple dishes, but to follow a recipe and produce a range of meals that would provide an interesting and varied diet. Few of the youngsters could read well, but most of them could learn to recognise some words and relate them to specific items, and they soon mastered the basic skills necessary for working safely and competently in the kitchen.

The imaginative recipes included in this special large-format book were all evolved through trial and error with the pupils themselves and have been formulated with a minimum of written words – some sequences having none at all. Only a rudimentary knowledge of numbers is required and weighing skills are unnecessary. The assumption is that the child or adult is reasonably strong and physically co-ordinated and able to make a cup of tea and a sandwich. The book is intended for parents and teachers.

Published by the Souvenir Press Ltd, Department J.H., 43 Great Russell Street, London

WC1B 3PA. Price: £8.95 plus £1 postage and packing.

Cycling

See also Section 9 for cycling holidays.

Tandem Club
25 Hendred Way, Abingdon, Oxfordshire OX14 2AN.

The Club has 4,000 members and exists to encourage tandem cycling by sending a bi-monthly magazine to all full members, by providing a comprehensive spare parts service and technical advice, by organising day runs and touring weekends and by running both open and club trials.

The Club has a liaison officer for handicapped members who is glad to offer help to blind, partially sighted people or those with, say, balancing problems or only one leg. The annual subscription of £7 covers up to two people (one full and one joint member).

Cyclists' Touring Club
Cottrell House, 69 Meadrow, Godalming, Surrey GU7 3HS (Tel: Godalming (048 68) 7217).
The Club would be glad to explore ways in which handicapped people could take part in local cycling activities. If anyone would like to discuss such opportunities, we have been assured, he or she will receive every assistance. The club produces a talking magazine for blind or partially sighted members.

Dance

See also Glissade below.

Amici Dance Theatre Company
Faith Wilson, 123 Tottenham Court Road, London W1P 9HN (Tel: 01–388 8782/8706).
Amici is an integrated company of blind, mentally handicapped and able-bodied dance students. All of the participants have studied creative dance for several years with the choreographer Wolfgang Stange. Since studying at the London School of Contemporary Dance, Berliner Wolfgang Stange has taught and run creative movement workshops with groups of mentally handicapped or physically disabled people and psychiatric patients in hospitals, day centres and adult education groups throughout the UK and in Austria, Hong Kong, New Zealand, and Sri Lanka.

No Handicap to Dance: Creative Improvisation for People with Handicaps by Gina Levete. Published by Souvenir Press, 43 Great Russell Street, London WC1B 3PA (Tel: 01–580 9307).

The author shows how people with even severe physical and mental disability can take part in dance, creative improvisation, music and movement if they are encouraged to respond to music and ideas in their own way. Gina Levete describes in detail method classes and workshops that she has used with her own classes of children and adults, showing the immeasurable benefits they can bring to people whose lives are confined by handicap or institutional restrictions. Price: £6.95.

Drama

BBC Television Play Synopses
Printed by the BBC and distributed by RNID free of charge to deaf people to help them follow TV series transmitted by the BBC. Apply to The Royal National Institute for the Deaf, 105 Gower Street, London WC1E 6AH (Tel: 01–387 8033).

Glissade Dance/Theatre
c/o Lynn Legge, 10 Masefield Crescent, Cowplain, Portsmouth, Hampshire PO8 8JS (Tel: Portsmouth (0705) 261985); and Ian Fuller, 4a Henley Road, Southsea, Hampshire PO4 OHS (Tel: Portsmouth (0705) 739032).
Glissade is a performance orientated arts organisation, running weekly workshops in dance and drama and taking part in arts awareness training. Disabled people and able-bodied people work together as an integrated team with each member being expected to play a full part in putting on a performance and learning at least one additional skill.

Graeae Theatre Company
The Diorama, 14 Peto Place, London NW1 4DT (Tel: 01–935 5588).
Graeae is Britain's only full-time company of disabled actors. They undertake national tours, theatre-in-education work (mainly in London) and run training courses for disabled performers.

If you are interested in considering joining Graeae then you should keep in touch and you will be informed when auditions are taking place.

Path Productions
38a Duncan Terrace, London N1 8AL (Tel: 01–359 7866).
A theatre company integrating performers with and without disabilities (physical and mental). There are two productions a year (January and July) at the Jeanetta Cochrane Theatre, London WC1 as well as monthly workshops on various aspects of theatre and performing arts at the Abbey Community Centre, London SW1.

All interest in any area is welcomed by PATH. For further details contact the Administrator, Sophie Kingshill.

Disability, Theatre and Education by Richard Tomlinson. Published by Souvenir Press, 43 Great Russell Street, London WC1B 3PA (Tel: 01–580 9307).

The author describes, from his own experience, the essential factors for setting up a company of professional standard (he had been involved with setting up the Graeae Theatre Company), and discusses the work of other companies now being formed throughout the country. He shows how theatre work in workshops and schools can be used to bring disabled people more fully into the community, and how material can be adapted from existing scripts as well as written specially for the occasion. Price paperback £4.95; hardback £7.95 plus 56p and 80p respectively for postage.

Drama for Mentally Handicapped Children by Ann B. McClintock. Published by Souvenir Press, 43 Great Russell Street, London WC1B 3PA (Tel: 01–580 9307).

This book describes lesson plans which may be used by parents and non-specialists. It will, therefore, have a use throughout the child's everyday life and will enable parents to prepare him or her for a forthcoming event, as well as continuing the developmental work of the school.

For details of the Shape ticket scheme for Londoners *see* page 207.

Farming in the City

National Federation of City Farms
The Old Vicarage, 66 Fraser Street, Windmill Hill, Bedminster, Bristol BS3 4LY (Tel: Bristol (0272) 660663).

All City Farms and Community Garden Projects hope to incorporate facilities for disabled people. Cardiff City Farm, for instance, has a greenhouse which has facilities for gardeners in wheelchairs. Windmill City Farm in Bristol is building a garden for disabled people and has a 'Rumpus Room' (a soft adventure play area) designed for handicapped children of all ages, as well as for able-bodied under sevens.

The Federation suggests that individuals contact their nearest City Farm to find out the extent of such facilities and how much they can be involved. Your local library should know of any nearby City Farm or the Federation would be glad to tell you. They have a leaflet describing the concept of City Farms and listing them. Membership is open to voluntary organisations, charities, and individuals.

Fencing

Wheelchair Fencing Association
Leslie Veale, 14 Kingsley Park Grove, Sheffield S11 9HL (Tel: Sheffield (0742) 362194).

The WFA co-ordinates and assists the development of wheelchair fencing activities throughout Great Britain and is affiliated to the Amateur Fencing Association of Great Britain. They can supply information on local clubs, coaches, copies of the rules for fencing, plans for chair stabilising frames (£1 per set), and general information on the sport. Membership is £2 per annum. Associate membership for able bodied people is £1 per annum.

Flying

Contact: Dawn Marler, 28 Addenbroke Drive, Wylde Green, Sutton Coldfield, West Midlands B73 5PY (Tel: 021–355 4384).

Anyone interested in learning to fly should contact Dawn Marler who will do her best to advise you and to put you in touch with a suitable school of flying in your area. Dawn can also advise on any controls which may be needed. A number of severely disabled people are now happily flying.

International Air Tattoo Flying Scholarships for Disabled People
Building 1108, Royal Air Force, Fairford, Gloucestershire GL7 4DL (Tel: Cirencester (0285) 713300).

Candidates must be between the ages of 17 and 40 years and must be registered disabled. They must be able to attend and accept residential accommodation at an approved flying school without the aid of an attendant. The course lasts approximately 42 days. Candidates must be able to communicate easily, hear and understand written and verbal instruction. He/she must also have enough mobility to get in and out of a standard training aircraft unaided and be able to operate all the flying controls and aircraft systems safely. Some medical conditions will automatically exclude candidates from consideration. These include: epilepsy, profound deafness, quadriplegia, mental illness, chronic heart disease, and serious visual defects.

Up to nine scholarships are awarded annually with two reserve candidates. Candidates who have been nominated as reserves are automatically considered for the following year's scholarships, without further application. Assistance is given with travelling expenses where necessary.

Application forms for scholarships in any year have to be returned by 31 January.

Football

See the book *Sport and Recreation for Disabled People*

Gardening and Horticulture

See also Section 9 *Field Studies and Outdoor Pursuits*

The Alpine Garden Society
Lye End Link, St. John's, Woking, Surrey GU21 1SW.
For all who are interested in rock gardening and alpine plants. The Society offers: a quarterly bulletin; a list of some 4,000 species of seeds; shows for exhibitions; local groups; and tours to overseas mountain resorts under the guidance of expert leaders. Single membership is £10 per year (family £12).

Federation to Promote Horticulture for Disabled People
The Drove, Gillingham, Dorset (Tel: Gillingham (074 76) 2369/2242).
The Federation aims to identify the benefits which can be gained by disabled people from out-of-doors pursuits and to influence all concerned to recognise those benefits and to provide solutions to the problems that arise.

The Federation is a forum through which the many organisations and individuals involved in outdoor activities for disabled people keep in touch. To this end courses, conferences, and meetings are arranged. Papers presented at these activities are published as annual proceedings.

Membership for those interested in or concerned with the promotion of horticulture and land use for disabled people is available at an annual fee of £7.50.

The Garden Club
Membership Secretary: Marjorie Haines, Church Cottage, Headcorn, Kent TN27 9NP (Tel: Headcorn (0622) 890467).
A nationwide body affiliated to the Gardens for the Disabled Trust. It aims to encourage gardening by disabled people both for enjoyment and as a therapy. Members receive a quarterly newsletter and there is a comprehensive advisory service on gardening with a disability. Grants are made for the adaptation, planning and equipment of disabled members' gardens, including the provision of suitable tools. Applications for grants must be supported by the local social services department. The Club is building up local representation so that local groups can be formed as needed.

Membership is open to any disabled person who enjoys gardening of any kind, from tending a bedside pot plant to managing a large garden. Individual membership is £2 a year. Life membership is £15. Membership for institutions is £5 a year. Able-bodied and disabled members are also sought to act as local advisers/helpers/representatives in all areas.

Gardens for the Disabled Trust
Address as for *The Garden Club* above.
Gives practical help with gardening for disabled people, with special interest in gardens which are cared for by a group such as hospitals, special schools, centres and so on. The Trust will consider a grant towards the suitable adaptation of equipment, raising of flower beds and so on.

Garden Research Department
Mary Marlborough Lodge, Nuffield Orthopaedic Centre, Headington, Oxford OX3 7LD (Tel: Oxford (0865) 64811).
The Centre will give advice and information on all aspects of gardening for disabled people and it is here that experiments and research are undertaken to continue to find the best possible ways of helping disabled gardeners to enjoy their hobby. The department will be glad to answer written enquiries but please enclose an s.a.e.

Gardening. One of the books in the series *Equipment for the Disabled*, containing the following sections: garden design; garden tools: forks, spades, hoes, rakes, tool handles, pruners, secateurs, flower gatherers, lawnmowers, lawn shears and edgers; hanging baskets; wildlife; greenhouses and accessories; plant propagation; indoor gardening; hand tools; safety; gardening for profit; gardening for food; gardening for blind people; buying wisely; clubs for disabled gardeners; sources of information; select bibliography.

Price: £3.95 plus 75p postage and packing. You are requested to send your cheque with your order making cheques payable to Oxfordshire Health Authority.

The Royal Horticultural Society
Vincent Square, London SW1P 2PE (Tel: 01–834 4333).

The RHS welcomes disabled gardeners. If you are keen to learn more about the delights of horticulture many evening classes are of a very high standard and include the general examination of the RHS. If you prefer to study at home, the RHS would be glad to advise you as to which correspondence schools are prepared to teach the subject by post. The RHS also has a garden at Wisley, Surrey where they have erected a garden for disabled people which includes many helpful ideas. A useful publication list is available. For details of the garden, write to The Director, Royal Horticultural Society Garden, Wisley, Woking, Surrey GU23 6QB.

The Society for Horticultural Therapy
Goulds Ground, Vallis Way, Frome, Somerset BA11 3DW (Tel: Frome (0373) 64782).
Horticultural Therapy is an organisation which offers practical help, through its services, to disabled gardeners and those who work with them. It publishes a most imaginative magazine *Growth Point*, which sets a very high standard in magazine publication. It includes articles and information of interest to the small-scale gardener and the professional horticulturist both in this country and abroad. The layout of interestingly organised print, spiced with pictures, cartoons and other graphics makes it a joy to read.
HT offers the following services.
1. *Project development* provides specialist staff to help plan and develop work on sites which may be managed by an NHS hospital, a social service department or a voluntary organisation.
2. *Land Use Volunteers* (LUVs) are qualified or experienced young horticulturists. They can help a project by providing enthusiastic and competent help for up to 12 months as long as the project can supply board, lodging and pocket money.
3. *The HT Training Service* runs one-day and in-house Study Days for professional carers and horticulturists working with disadvantaged people. These provide insights into the therapeutic opportunities of horticulture and provide practical information and training in horticultural techniques.
4. *Information service.* This provides a wide range of information either as a direct answer or by linking up the enquirer with other sources of information. A series of information sheets and special papers is available. The service also runs workshops for groups

throughout the country. Demonstration Gardens are run in inner city centres on a full-time basis to provide practical support and workshop facilities for groups and individuals.
5. *Membership service* provides a range of benefits to disabled gardeners and those who work with them. Subscription rates £10 p.a. (£7.50 for registered disabled people).

VISUALLY IMPAIRED GARDENERS
RNIB's booklet *Gardening without sight* by Kathleen Fleet for visually impaired gardeners who enjoy growing flowers or vegetables in their garden, allotment or indoors is available free in print, Braille or on tape. Contact the Royal National Institute for the Blind, 224 Great Portland Street, London W1N 6AA for details.
Come Gardening magazine and the *Cassette Library for Blind Gardeners* An annual subscription of £1 covers receipt of the *Come Gardening* magazine each quarter and use at any time of the Cassette Library for Blind Gardeners. Cheques and postal orders should be made payable to *Come Gardening* and should be sent to: Kathleen Fleet, 48 Tolcarne Drive, Pinner, Middlesex HA5 2DQ (Tel: 01–868 4026). When writing you are asked to supply your own name and address in block capitals and not to send cassettes as you will be given full particulars about these in reply to your subscription.
Come Gardening is circulated quarterly in Braille and on C90 cassette. The Braille copies are small-sized volumes and the taped copies require only one cassette. The cassette copies are on loan so must be returned each quarter. Subscribers should state whether they wish to receive Braille or cassette copies. Slow Braille readers often find that their speed in touch reading can be helped by having both Braille and taped copies. In addition, the Moon branch of the RNIB prints Moon copies.
Every reader, whether taking Braille or taped copies, can have free access to all the Cassette Library for Blind Gardeners recordings at any time, but to obtain copies of these additional recordings magazine readers must send their own cassettes. A library catalogue list will be supplied to every subscriber and additions to the Library anounced in the *Come Gardening* magazine. Catalogue lists are sent in Braille to Braille readers and in typescript to those who receive the magazine on tape. Anyone wishing to have a cassette copy of the list can send a C60 cassette to the Library Service, the address of which is given in the magazine. The magazine consists of short articles

about all aspects of gardening, so readers will be able to find something for individual use and personal interest in every issue. The contents contain answers to readers' questions, news of recent products and ideas for helping gardeners without sight. Communication with readers is considered to be of great importance, as the magazine articles are based on their requests.

The Cassette Library for Blind Gardeners – the existing master tapes in the Library cover a wide range of gardening subjects and include Royal Horticultural Society Handbooks and other small specialist booklets. Library recordings are chosen as supplements to the magazine.

The library points out that certain simple rules must be observed by subscribers, for example poor quality cassettes cannot be accepted for making copies as they damage the equipment.

GARDEN TOOLS FOR DISABLED PEOPLE

A wide range of tools is available on mail order and in garden shops. A few of these have been designed for people with disabilities while many others are simply designed to make gardening a lot easier for the great numbers of people with physical frailties who otherwise would not be able to indulge themselves in this absorbing hobby. The Society for Horticultural Therapy (*see* above) has information on all aspects of making gardening easier.

GARDENING BOOKS AND PUBLICATIONS

Gardening is for Everyone: A Week-by-Week Guide for People with Handicaps By Audrey Cloet and Chris Underhill, published by Souvenir Press. In this imaginative and detailed guide keen would-be gardeners will find a host of ideas for every week of the year, and within the scope of those whose mobility may be restricted. Designed with beginners in mind, it explains every technique with text and clear drawings, showing how to grow potatoes in containers, how to create a garden indoors, how and when to sow and plant, and how to make decorative pictures from pressed flowers, seedheads and grasses. Price: £4.95 paperback plus 50p postage and packing. Available from Horticultural Therapy, Goulds Ground, Vallis Way, Frome, Somerset BA11 3DW.

Gardens of England and Wales. The booklet gives details of 2,400 private gardens open to the public for a small admission fee on certain days of the year. It gives the access symbol for those gardens considered to be manageable, in whole or in part, by visitors in wheelchairs. It can be obtained from

many booksellers price £1.50 or £2.25 direct from National Gardens Scheme, 57 Lower Belgrave Street, London SW1W OLR (Tel: 01–730 0359).

Golf

See also Section 9, Multi-Activity Adventure Centre.

Society of One-Armed Golfers Don Reid, 11 Coldwell Lane, Felling, Tyne and Wear NE10 9EX (Tel: 091 469 4742).

The Society holds regular meetings. Apart from a week-long annual championship, weekend and one-day events are organised by regional convenors in England, Scotland, and Ireland. Members pay an annual subscription of £3 and there is provision for junior members (under 18) at 50p.

HANDBELL RINGING

Handbell Ringers of Great Britain
36 Kensington Drive, Bury, Lancashire BL8 2DE (Tel: 061–764 0604).

The Society's aim is to promote the art of handbell tune ringing, and to achieve this aim arranges events bringing together handbell ringers. Seven regional associations promote local events and issue newsletters. The national magazine *Reverberations* is published bi-annually. Annual subscription is £2.

Mayola Music Ltd
205 High Street, Clapham Village, Bedfordshire MK41 6AJ (Tel: Bedford (0234) 62474).

This firm publishes a book *Handbell People* which includes amongst its 'people' those who are physically disabled, blind, deaf or mentally handicapped, providing helpful information on how to assist people with different needs enjoy handbell and handchime ringing. Price: £1 plus 30p postage. They also publish a free catalogue of handbell music and will also supply new handbells and handchimes.

Handicrafts

Fred Aldous Ltd
PO Box 135, 37 Lever Street, Manchester M60 1UX (Tel: 061–236 2477).

This firm will be glad to send you a catalogue selling masses of DIY items for the home handicraft enthusiast. Pewter and copper, enamelling, jewellery accessories, flower making, handbag handles, lampshade materials and so on. In fact, the firm handles all those little things it is usually so difficult to buy.

Bradley Inkle Looms
82 North Lane, East Preston, Sussex BN16 1HE (Tel: Rustington (0903) 770108).
A table inkle loom is available which is relatively easy to use, even for those with limited movements. Each one is hand made and the design has been perfected for simplicity and ease of operation so that even those who are partially sighted can cope. The usual table model costs £18.50 plus carriage.
Inkle Weaving: A Comprehensive Manual has been written by Lavinia Bradley and published by Routledge & Kegan Paul Ltd (1982). Price: £6.50 plus 50p for postage. The manual shows how to use the loom to its full potential.

Dingle Hill Products
Mid Cowden, Comrie, Perthshire PH6 2HU (Tel: Comrie (0764) 70667).
Some disabled people have found that they have had to give up spinning because disablement prevented their pedalling a traditional spinning wheel. There are also many who have not considered spinning as an occupation or hobby due to disablement.

This firm has developed the Dingle Hill Spinner which is powered by a small electric motor enabling anyone with more-or-less normal manual dexterity to spin, and derive the same satisfaction as when using a normal spinning wheel. We are assured that the Spinner has been tested by two well-known spinning instructors both of whom are said to be delighted with its action and have recommended it for use by disabled people. The Dingle Hill Spinner is only £55 against £95 for their traditional foot operated wheel, plus £4 postage and packing. It measures only 11 in × 8 in × 6 in and is very light.

Craftsman's Mark Limited
Tone Dale Mill, Wellington, Somerset TA21 OAW (Tel: Wellington (082 347) 7266).
This firm supplies undyed woollen yarns in natural colours specially designed for the use of handweavers, also plain cotton, jute, sisal and natural linen. For samples and details of prices apply to the firm.

Dressmaking for the Disabled by E. E. Rogers and B. M. Stevens. Published by the British Association of Occupational Therapists.
A guide to adapting paper patterns to individual physical disabilities.
Available from: Haigh & Hochland Ltd, International University Booksellers, The Precinct Centre, Oxford Road, Manchester M13 9QA (Tel: 061 273 4156). Price: 80p.

Knitting and Crochet with One Hand by Mary Konior. Published by Philip & Tacey Ltd, North Way, Andover, Hampshire SP10 5BA (Tel: Andover (0264) 332171). Price: £3 including postage and packing.
This ringbound and large print book describes in a few pages how to master the intricacies of knitting and crochet with one hand. It also describes how to do basic Tunisian crochet which is a cross between knitting and crochet and is apparently easier to manage than either.

Jigsaws

The British Jigsaw Puzzle Library
Old Homend, Stretton, Grandison, Ledbury, Herefordshire HR8 2TW (Tel: Trumpet (053 183) 462).
This is a lending library and puzzles are exchanged by post. All the puzzles are wooden without guide pictures and have varying numbers of pieces. Subscription rates on request and on receipt of an sae.

Judo

British Judo Association
16 Upper Woburn Place. London WC1H 9QH (Tel: 01–387 9340).
The BJA is the official governing body for judo in Great Britain, and it has formed a working party to take into account the needs of disabled people interested in the sport.

Anyone interested in membership or in learning judo or a group requiring a coach at either national, area or local level or requiring any other information, should contact the chairperson of the working party at the above address.

Modelling

British Model Soldier Society
David Pearce, 22 Lynwood Road, London W5 1JJ (Tel: 01–998 5230).
The Society has a number of groups throughout the country and publishes a quarterly bulletin and eight newsletters. The subscription for adults is £7, for young people under 17, £3.

Model Railways

The Model Railway Club
Keen House, 4 Calshot Street, London N1 9DA.
The Club was founded in 1910 and is thus, we are told, the oldest model railway society in the world.

Purpose-built club rooms were opened at Keen House in 1960 and weekly meetings are held there on Thursday evenings. In addition, there are occasional Saturday afternoon meetings organised in conjunction with some of the 140 or so clubs affiliated to The Model Railway Club. A bimonthly bulletin is distributed to members and affiliated clubs. A most important feature of the Club's activities is the building and exhibiting of model railways and currently the club has projects in 'O' gauge, 'S' gauge, 'OO' gauge, and 'N' gauge. These provide scope for members to produce items of rolling stock, buildings and scenic features, as well as to build its baseboards and install track and the necessary electrical wiring.

The Model Railway Club is the organiser of the annual IMREX International Model Railway Exhibition held each Easter at the Royal Horticultural Halls, Westminster, London. Subscription for adults living or working within 35 miles of London is £15 and £7.50 for others. Junior rates are half those for adults.

Mountaineering

A Man and his Mountains
Hey! Hey! Hey! we're going to make it. Norman Croucher's love of mountains did not leave him when he lost his legs below the knees in a railway accident. With tin legs and crutches, Norman has climbed in South America, China, Peru, East Africa, and Europe. However, this is no tale of simple heroism, it is a story of a man's passion for mountains against all the odds. Love of mountains and their challenge and respect for the men and women who share the adversities and the triumphs, as well as heroism and determination are what makes this book a wonderful read. The illustrations are great too. Published by: William Heinemann Ltd, 10 Upper Grosvenor Street, London W1X 9PA (Tel: 01–493 4141). Price: £9.95.

Motorcycling

The British Wheelchair Motorcycle Association
Andy Strong, 16 Tippets Mead, Tawney Croft, Bracknell, Berkshire RG12 1FH.
The BWMA is mostly for enthusiasts who want to keep on motorbike riding after becoming disabled. Members have a range of bikes, including the Suzuki ATI. They will be glad to advise on any adaptations necessary to enable a disabled person to drive – these may include hand gear changes and footplates instead of pegs. Motor bikes will need to

be balanced with a side car which can also carry the wheelchair. A number of members are enthusiastic racers.

Music

See also Section 9 Holiday Courses.

Association of Professional Music Therapists
68 Pierce Lane, Fulbourn, Cambridgeshire CB1 5DI.
Music therapists' training takes four years and they are now recognised by the health service. They work with people who have a wide variety of clinical problems such as lack of physical coordination, emotional disturbance, language delay and disorder, severe depression, sensory impairment, etc. Music therapists learn to communicate with their client, finding the musical idiom with which to reach, support and develop whatever potential there is.

British Society for Music Therapy
Guildhall School of Music and Drama, Barbican, London EC2Y 8DT (Tel: 01–368 8879).
Membership is open to all who can further the Society's object, which is to promote the use and development of music therapy in treatment, education, rehabilitation and training of children and adults suffering from emotional, physical or mental handicap. The BSMT publishes papers, available to the general public, and a Journal and Bulletin to members. It also holds conferences, regional and members' meetings and workshops.

Council for Music in Hospitals
Sylvia Lindsay, 340 Lower Road, Little Bookham, Surrey KT23 4EE (Tel: Bookham (0372) 58264).
The Council arranges more than 1,500 performances a year in hospitals, homes, hospices, training centres, etc. throughout Great Britain. The concerts are given by carefully selected professional musicians and cater for a wide range of musical tastes. Programmes include shortened versions of well-known operas, song and instrumental recitals, old time music and community singing, and even music from China, Mexico and flamenco dancing. CMH aims through a flexible repertoire to involve their audience in the music and thereby provide a musical experience in which all can share.

Disabled Living Foundation
380–384 Harrow Road, London W9 2HU (Tel: 01–289 6111).
The Disabled Living Foundation has a Music Advisory Service which is available to disabled

people, whatever their age or disability, and to all those involved with them.

Twenty-two resource papers are available covering a wide range of information, including: piano music for one hand; music for partially sighted people; musical activities for emotionally and behaviourally disturbed children; working in music with disabled people and training available; and sources of possible grants and funding. A full list of publications is available – please enclose an s.a.e.

The Music Advisory Service is studying the role of music in terminal care; the effects of dyslexia (specific learning difficulties) on reading and writing music; music and deaf people (this covers all degrees of deafness).

The Equipment Centre at the DLF includes an exhibition of musical instruments and photographs; and a large collection of books relating to music and disabled people is held in the library. Visits to either of these can be arranged by the Music Adviser.

A free newsletter, *Music News* is produced twice a year detailing current developments and events throughout the UK. Anyone wishing to be added to the mailing list or wanting further information should contact the Music adviser.

Royal National Institute for the Blind
224 Great Portland Street, London W1N 6AA (Tel: 01–388 1266).
The RNIB has a free music catalogue in Braille.

BOOKS AND PUBLICATIONS

British Music Education Yearbook. Information is, primarily, for those intending musicians with a physical or mental handicap; for able-bodied people wishing to pursue a career in music therapy. There are contact addresses for organisations, associations, etc. specialising in music for disabled people. Price: £8.95.

British Music Yearbook. As well as a wide range of information this Yearbook includes a section describing organisations concerned with disabled people. Price: £10.95.

Both Yearbooks are published by Rhinegold Publishing Limited, 241 Shaftesbury Avenue. London WC2H 8EH (Tel: 01–240 5749 – book sales).

Music for Mentally Handicapped People. by Miriam Wood. Published by Souvenir Press, 43 Great Russell Street, London WC1B 3PA (Tel: 01–580 9307).

This book explains how even a non-musician can organise a music programme for a child at home or for a group of pupils in school. Those who have never learnt to play an instrument are coaxed into picking out notes and chords on the piano or guitar, or using one of the mechanical instruments available to those who really cannot play.

Nature Study

See also Section 9 Field Studies.
See also Fieldfare Trust page 225.

The Country Landowners' Association Charitable Trust
16 Belgrave Square, London SW1X 8PQ (Tel: 01–235 0511).
The CLA trust was founded with the main purpose of encouraging and helping landowners to provide facilities on their land for those who are physically or mentally disabled to enjoy sport and recreation. A number of projects supported have included nature trails, bird-watching, rides, self-catering farm holidays, and an indoor riding school. The second edition of *Guide to Countryside Recreation for Disabled People* has been published – price: £1.

RSPB Reserves for the Disabled
The Royal Society for the Protection of Birds, The Lodge, Sandy, Bedfordshire SG19 2DL (Tel: Sandy (0767) 80551).
This leaflet lists reserves suitable for disabled visitors and highlights the facilities available to make your visit both easy and interesting. These include wide surfaced pathways and nature trails, special boardwalks, rest benches, toilet facilities, birdwatching hides and information centres which are accessible to people in wheelchairs.

At one reserve, Radipole Lake in Weymouth, Dorset the Society has provided listening posts and a tap-rail to help blind or partially-sighted people appreciate the wildlife they cannot see. There is an audio-loop in the visitor centre for those who are hearing impaired.

The RSPB now owns or manages more than 121 reserves throughout the UK covering about 142,000 acres of woods, heaths, marshes, lakes, cliffs, moors and meadows throughout the UK. So far 26 of the reserves have been adapted to cater for disabled visitors.

For a free copy of the leaflet send a stamp to the address above.

Members receive the beautiful colour magazine *Birds* quarterly, have free entry to reserves and are encouraged to join local groups whose activities include talks and film shows, bird-watching outings and fund-raising events. Disabled members are welcome. Subscription £12 – reduced on application by older people.

National Trust Properties
Guides are available which include information on those properties which are accessible to disabled visitors. *See* Section 16 for details.

Informal Countryside Recreation for Disabled People (1981). Number 15 of an advisory series published by the Countryside Commission. This book aims to provide countryside recreation site managers and providers with the advice and ideas which will help them to encourage disabled people to enjoy the countryside. The book first looks at the nature of disability relating to those who are mobility impaired, those with a loss of sensory perception and those with a mental handicap.

Advice is given on diversional and other requirements which need to be followed if common features such as car parks, footpaths, lavatories, gates and stiles are to be usable by disabled people. Other parts deal with recreation in the countryside and the problems of transport.

There is also a useful list of addresses and interesting lists of plants with aromatic foliage, plants with highly fragrant or scented flowers, and trees and shrubs with ornamental bark or twigs. The book is available free from the Countryside Commission, John Dower House, Crescent Place, Cheltenham, Gloucestershire GL50 3RA (Tel: Cheltenham (0242) 521381).

Painting and the Arts

See Arts page 203.
See also General Study Courses Section 9.

Parascending

British Association of Parascending Clubs
18 Talbot Lane, Leicester LE1 4LR (Tel: Leicester (0533) 530318).
This Association encourages parascending by disabled people. If you are interested in having a go the central office will give you the name of the most suitable club within that region. A special harness and seat arrangement has been designed. Beneath the seat a 'D' ring, centrally mounted, locates in a standard quick release fitting mounted on the wheelchair and operated by a cable/lever on the wheelchair handle, thus enabling the seat to separate from the wheelchair during launch.

Photography

Photography for the Disabled
190 Secrett House, Ham Close, Ham, Richmond, Surrey (Tel: 01–948 2342).
This organisation develops special equipment for disabled photographers. It is possible to obtain cameras where the shutters can be clicked by a mouth- operated pneumatic shutter or an adapted camera to fit on to a wheelchair. Other innovations can also be made for operation.

Playing Cards

Waddingtons
Castle Gate, Oulton, Leeds LS26 8HG (Tel: Leeds (0532) 826195).
Waddingtons produce 'Easy to See' playing cards (stock no. 33281) and these should be readily available in the shops. However, while Waddingtons do not offer a mail order service if anybody has difficulty getting the cards they will be glad to send them. Price in the shops should be about £2.

Royal National Institute for the Blind
224 Great Portland Street, London W1N 6AA (Tel: 01–388 1266).
The RNIB has large print playing cards available at £1.80; £1.20 concessionary rate to partially sighted people.

Playing card holder
Designed for the use of players with only the use of one hand, and it is free standing on a table. A privacy screen is incorporated into the bench of the holder to prevent other players seeing the cards or the order into which they are arranged.

For further details contact: D. C. Williams, 170 Lytham Road, Warton, nr Preston, Lancashire PR4 1AH. (Tel: Spreckleton (0772) 633732).

Poetry

The Poetry Society
National Poetry Centre, 21 Earls Court Square, London SW5 (Tel: 01–373 7861).
The Society exists for anyone interested in writing, reading or listening to poetry. It aims to make poetry available to as many people as possible through the channels of voice, print and personal creativity. Members receive copies of the *Poetry Review* and are entitled to half-price admission to events which take place at the National Poetry Centre. These include the Thursday night 'Poets-in-Person' readings and different workshops. Occasional festivals are held throughout the year.

The bookshop specialises in poetry from the

small and independent presses, and there is a mail-order catalogue for distribution to members.

The Society administers a programme of 'Poets in Schools', and verse speaking examinations. It also organises several poetry competitions, some for members only.

Annual membership: London £15; country £12; associate/student members £10; life £250; corporate/affiliate £9.

Puppetry

Puppetry for Mentally Handicapped People by Caroline Astell-Burt. Published by Souvenir Press, 43 Great Russell Street, London WC1B 3PA (Tel: 01–580 9307).

The author describes the special contribution puppetry can make to the lives of mentally handicapped people, helping them to act and speak for themselves through the medium of the puppet and providing the excitement and stimulation of theatre.

Intended for use by parents, teachers, therapists and care staff, the book explains how to make puppets of all kinds, from simple sock puppets to elaborate marionettes, and how to perform with them in play and learning situations. Price: £4.95 paperback; £6.95 hardback plus postage.

Quadball

British Quadball Association
3 Butterfield Crescent, Swanwick, Derbyshire DE55 1BA.

Quadball is a team game for quadriplegic players sometimes known as wheelchair rugby. There are some seven teams in the UK and it is hoped there will be a National Quadball Championship Tournament. For further details of the BQA write to the chairperson Trevor Murray at the above address.

Radio and Television

British Wireless for the Blind Fund
224 Great Portland Street, London W1N 6AA (Tel: 01–388 1266).

Radios are available on free 'permanent' loan to registered blind persons aged 16 or over. Distributed on behalf of the BWBF by the local voluntary organisation for the blind, or social services department.

Wireless for the Bedridden
81b Corbets Tey Road, Upminster, Essex RM14 2AJ (Tel: Upminster (040 22) 50051).

This organisation aims to provide, on free loan, radio and television sets to disabled people who

are housebound and in financial need. The radios are high quality mains and battery sets. The colour televisions are rented from a leading rental company and the society can help with the purchase of the first licence. Black and white televisions are purchased and help can be provided with the licence in cases of special need.

Royal National Institute for the Deaf
105 Gower Street, London WC1E 6AH (Tel: 01–387 8033).

The RNID produces a comprehensive leaflet describing aids for listening to radio and television, with a list of manufacturers.

Reading

If you are interested in reading and have mobility problems, getting to a good bookshop (particularly one that is accessible) often presents a real problem; you therefore may have little opportunity to browse and buy the books you really want. We describe below just three firms who will supply books of your choice.

The Armchair Book Service
The Cleuch, Twynholm, Kirkcudbright, Scotland DG6 4SD (Tel: Twynholm (055 76) 215).

The Armchair Book Service offers postal book service to customers in the United Kingdom and overseas who do not have access to a good British bookshop. The partners are both experienced booksellers who aim to give a helpful personal service to their customers. Their main business is in new rather than second-hand books, but any available book can be supplied to order.

There are normally no fees other than onward postage. Within the UK the Service uses the Post-a-Book service when this method proves cheaper than normal post. Special requests, however, which involve more than normal research may be charged at cost.

The Service operates six days a week, but by mail order only. There is no retail shop. Telephone enquiries are welcome at any reasonable hour, including the cheap period after 6 p.m. Monday to Friday and all day on Saturday.

Dillons Bookshops
This company has a number of bookshops around the country, the largest being: Dillons Bookstore, 82 Gower Street, London WC1E 6EQ (Tel: 01–636 1577). The shop is very accessible with ramps and lifts, and stocks 150,000 different titles in 52 specialist sections covering subjects of academic

and general interest. There are also large station-ery, art materials and music departments including sheet music as well as records, tapes and compact discs. Mail order is also available from this address.

The Good Book Guide
Braithwaite & Taylor Limited, 91 Great Russell Street, London WC1V 3PS (Tel: 01–580 8466).
The imaginative and straightforward consumer advice offered by *The Good Book Guide* – through its colour, illustrated publications – makes brows-ing at home possible. In each issue of the *Guide* some 500 new hardback and paperback books are objectively and concisely reviewed by professional book reviewers in over 20 different subject areas. All of these books are available through their 24 hour dispatch service. They have extended their service, firstly through their consumer book, *The Good Book Guide to Children's Books,* and se-condly *Bookpost*, a method through which *any* book currently in print can be ordered through the *Guide*. A complimentary copy of the *Guide* and full information about its services can be obtained from: The Good Book Guide, Braithwaite & Taylor Limited, 91 Great Russell Street, London WC1V 3PS (Tel: 01–580 8466).

Royal National Institute for the Blind
224 Great Portland Street, London W1N 6AA (Tel: 01–388 1266).
The RNIB has a leaflet *Magazines* giving details of magazines available in Braille and on tape.

Riding

See also Section 9.

Riding for the Disabled Association
Avenue R, National Agricultural Centre, Kenil-worth, Warwickshire CV8 2LY (Tel: Coventry (0203) 56107).
Each of the 550 groups throughout the UK consists of an organiser, secretary, riding instructor, usually a physiotherapist and some 30 helpers. Basically the riding is free but where schools are concerned, and individuals can afford it, contri-butions are welcomed.

Riding for the Mentally Handicapped
Published by MENCAP – The Royal Society for Mentally Handicapped Children and Adults, 123 Golden Lane, London EC1Y 0RT.

Sailing

See also Section 9 for information on sailing holi-days.

Useful guidance for disabled sailors is contained in the publication *Water Sports for the Disabled*. For details *see* page 229.

RYA Seamanship Foundation
RYA House, Romsey Road, Eastleigh, Hamp-shire SO5 4YA (Tel: Eastleigh (0703) 629962).
The Foundation's aims are:
(a) to improve the knowledge and seamanship of yachtsmen/women and other pleasure-boat owners by better training;
(b) to provide opportunities for young people, especially those from deprived areas, to bene-fit from activities directly connected with sail-ing and the sea;
(c) to organise courses and to provide special equipment to enable handicapped people to learn to sail and afterwards to participate on equal terms with able-bodied people; and
(d) to promote research into the design of craft and equipment with a view to improving safety and efficiency.

They Said We Couldn't Do It
Edited by John Chartress this book is a well-illustrated and marvellously descriptive account of how individual sailors have overcome their handi-caps to enjoy 'messing about in boats'. In among these accounts we learn of the wide variety of solutions found to overcome specific problems. Also included are details of instructional tech-niques. It concludes by saying that sailing is fun and that is what this book is all about. Available from RYA as above. Price £1.

Skiing

Back-Up
c/o The British Ski Federation, 118 Eaton Square, London SW1W 9AF (Tel: 01– 874 8974/1980).
The main aim of Back-Up is to facilitate sporting and recreational pursuits for spinally injured people. The first project is to provide holidays in the Alps for groups of spinally injured people. The cost of the holiday is £500 per person. The long term aim is to have a purpose-built centre in the Alps, which will be used for both winter and summer holidays, allowing people to try out a whole range of sports and leisure pursuits in a secure and caring environment.

Back-Up have designed special toboggans for the artificial slopes in the UK and would like these toboggans to be made available on all dry slopes in the UK. The cost of each is £900. Each spinally injured person may require adaptations to the toboggan which can increase the cost.

Back-Up are also now running outdoor pursuits courses in conjunction with the Calvert Trust, Keswick (for details of the Trust *see* page 153).

Annual subscription is £10 for individuals and £100 for company membership.

The British Ski Club for the Disabled
Corton House, Corton, nr Warminster, Wiltshire (Tel: Warminster (0985) 50321).
The Club was formed to provide skiing facilities for disabled people. It is affiliated to the English Ski Council, the Ski Club of Great Britain and the British Sports Association for the Disabled.

Special training is often necessary and facilities and equipment have to be suitable if the maximum benefit and proficiency is to be achieved. The Club has sessions at ski centres in Britain and acts as an information and advisory centre to all interested in cross country (Nordic), downhill (Alpine) skiing, sledging and skating as well as being responsible for training teams to compete in national competitions. Teams are also trained to compete in the Winter Sports for the Disabled. Skiing holidays are arranged annually.

Instructors and guides are always required, so the Club welcomes and needs able-bodied members willing to qualify. Membership per annum: individuals £7; family £10; affiliation £12.

The English Ski Council
6th Floor, Area Library Building, The Precinct, Halesowen, West Midlands B63 4AJ (Tel: 021–501 2314).
The Council publishes a booklet about teaching skiing to disabled people entitled *National Handicapped Coaching Supplement to Ski Teaching.* This is available free.

The Uphill Ski Club
12 Park Crescent, London W1N 4EQ (Tel: 01–636 1989).
This is an independent club affiliated to the Spastics Society which takes people with cerebral palsy as well as those with other disabilities on winter sports holidays. Equipment is available to compensate for the user's disabilities and to enhance their abilities. Paraplegics, being unable to use their lower limbs, usually ski on short skis and a pair of outriggers, the skis often being tied together to prevent the 'splits'. Hemiplegics have difficulty in exerting equal pressure on both skis and particularly in unweighting the spastic limb. Some hemiplegic skiers therefore use a short ski on their weakened leg and a standard length ski and outrigger on their good side.

National Handicapped Skiers Association
Harlow Ski School, Harlow Sportcentre, Hammarskjold Road, Harlow, Essex CM20 2JF (Tel: Harlow (0279) 21792).
The Association has been formed to co-ordinate, in conjunction with the English Ski Council, a structured system of courses for instructors to teach disabled people to ski, to provide suitable facilities, and to develop appropriate aids, as well as to integrate disabled skiers with other skiers. The NHSA does not run holidays.

Specialist equipment is needed for many disabled skiers. The Association supplies outriggers, which help to give balance, to people throughout the UK. They have also purchased two paraskis, specially designed sledges with braking and steering mechanism to enable paraplegics to ski unaided, and are developing their own monoski (also used by paraplegics, with outriggers). A booklet about teaching skiing to disabled people is distributed by the English Ski Council, 4th Floor, Area Library Building Precinct, Halesowen, West Midlands B63 4AJ (Tel: 021–501 2314).

Subscription to belong to the NHSA is £5.00.

Sub-Aqua Sports

The British Sub-Aqua Club
16 Upper Woburn Place. London WC1H OQW (Tel: 01–387 9302).
While the BSAC does not actively recruit disabled persons as members, it gives its branches every encouragement to accept and train them as divers where the branches are prepared to do so. The Club has published a comprehensive set of guidance notes for the use of branches wishing to train disabled people, and for the disabled members themselves. Copies of these notes are available from BSAC at £1 a copy.

The Club has a co-ordinator on its National Diving Committee who is responsible for giving advice on diving for disabled people and he/she too can be contacted via BSAC.

Scottish Sub-Aqua Club
The Sports Centre, 22 Academy Street, Shettleston, Glasgow G32 9AA. (Tel: 041–763 0612).
The governing body of sports diving in Scotland. Physically disabled people are generally welcome to join, subject to the approval of the club's medical advisers and the nature of their disability.

Swimming

The baths managers of many swimming pools

make special provision for disabled people, either for organised groups by allocating special times, or to individuals by making general facilities accessible. Further details of local facilities are available direct from the local swimming pools, or from area officers of the British Sports Association for the Disabled (*see* page 224).

Amateur Swimming Association
Swimming for the Disabled, c/o Harold Fern House, Derby Square, Loughborough, Leicester LE11 0AL (Tel: Loughborough (0509) 230431).

Association of Swimming Therapy
Secretary: Ted Cowen, 4 Oak Street, Shrewsbury, Shropshire SY3 7RH (Tel: Shrewsbury (0743) 4393).
The Association aims to teach safety, and happy swimming in the water, regardless of the severity of handicap, provided that medical approval is given. It encourages handicapped people to take part in swimming and water recreation, the formation of swimming clubs and swimming competitions. A team of lecturers is always prepared to advise, help or train in any area on request. Instructors and helpers are trained within their clubs.

The AST works through regional associations to which local clubs can affiliate and on whose experience, advice and instructor training they can call. Audiovisual slide programmes on techniques for handling handicapped people in water can be purchased, and three films are available on hire. The AST can also arrange insurance cover granting indemnity to AST members against liability for bodily injury to third parties or accidental damage to property.

A publication is available, *Swimming for the Disabled*, covering safety in dressing room and at bathside, as well as in the water; the four stages through which a learner must work – adjustment to water, rotations, buoyancy and balance, propulsion; games to develop expertise and aid progress; and how to form and operate a swimming club. There is also a section describing in layperson's terms the various disabilities which can be encountered by an instructor working with disabled people. Published by EP Publishing Ltd. Price: £4.95. For further details write to AST enclosing an s.a.e.

National Association of Swimming Clubs for the Handicapped
Rosemary Leeson, 219 Preston Drove, Brighton BN1 6FL (Tel: Brighton (0273) 559470).

The Association acts as a co-ordinating body for member organisations. It encourages, promotes and develops swimming among handicapped people.

The following booklets are available:

Register of Swimming Clubs for Handicapped People, price £1.
Teaching Disabled People to Swim:
  Part 1 – *Disabilities*, price 25p;
  Part 2 – *Balance, Buoyancy and Propulsion*, price 25p;
  Part 3 – *Pupil and Teacher*, price 25p.

Tennis

The Scottish Lawn Tennis Association
Ian Woodcraft, 12 Melville Crescent, Edinburgh EH3 7LU (Tel: 031–225 1284).
Wheelchair tennis can be played on normal tennis courts and some clubs make facilities available for this. Short tennis may also be an interesting game for those in wheelchairs. As the name implies, Short tennis is simply tennis on a smaller scale. All that is needed is an oversize foam ball which travels through the air and bounces lower and more slowly, therefore allowing more time to play the strokes. It is played on a badminton court so no longer does the court seem enormous with tennis balls bouncing around your ears at high speeds and with no real chance of reaching angled shots.

Ian Woodcraft will be glad to give information to any disabled person who is interested in playing on normal size tennis courts or who would like to try short tennis. He is familiar with clubs, not only in Scotland, but also throughout the UK.

Theatres in London

See Shape ticket scheme for London. *See also* Artsline page 207 for details about access, etc.

Toys and Play

Play Matters – The National Toy Libraries Association
68 Churchway, London NW1 1LT (Tel: 01–387 9592).
The Association is the parent body for over 1,000 toy libraries in the United Kingdom, many of which lend toys to handicapped children for recreational use and to develop skills. As well as giving advice on how to set up and run a toy library, it maintains links at the national level with therapists, psychologists, teachers and researchers; with toy manufacturers, art colleges and

toy designers; with children's societies and be-tween the toy libraries themselves.

Information and guidance on toys and play is passed on to members through *ARK* which is published four times a year, also through small conferences and a wide selection of booklets. A permanent display of toys at Churchway can be viewed by appointment.

In 1981, the Association merged with ACTIVE, which promotes a do-it-yourself approach to leisure, learning and communication aids for severely handicapped children and adults. (For further details of ACTIVE *see* page 57).

Membership of Play Matters costs £13.00 per year for toy libraries, ACTIVE groups or individuals.

There are a number of Play Matters publications and we describe very briefly just five below.

The Good Toy Guide (1986). A guide to over 700 widely available toys designed to help parents, teachers, therapists and all those concerned with children and play to choose toys discriminately. All toys have been play-tested by children under the supervision of Play Matters' professionally qualified Advisory Panel. Each toy has a detailed description, measurements, price guide and BBB (Best Bought Between) age banding which gives guidance on the best time to buy for maximum play value. Price: £1.75 (£1.50 to members).

(The Good Toy Guide is to be replaced shortly by a new annual publication, *What Toy?* maga-zine, price £1.75.)

Hear & Say. Written by a speech therapist and an audiologist to help parents and anyone concerned with children with language problems. There are many suggestions of toys to buy, how to use them and points to bear in mind when playing with a hearing impaired child. Price: £2.75 (£2.25 to members).

Look & Touch. Written for children with visual handicaps. Price: £1.40.

Mucky Play. Lots of ideas for sand and water play. This publication was written by a former Advisory Panel member who is a therapist and a psycho-logist. Price: £1.25 (£1.05 to members).

Do It Yourself. Ideas and suggestions for DIY toys, ranging from simple, cheap ideas that could be made by schools, youth or voluntary groups to more complex designs for proficient needle-workers and carpenters. It includes designs to meet the special needs of handicapped people. Price: £3.60 (£3.05 to members).

Handicapped Persons Research Unit (HPRU)
Newcastle upon Tyne Polytechnic, 1 Coach Lane, Coach Lane Campus, Newcastle upon Tyne (Tel: Newcastle upon Tyne 091–2358 211).
A *Playaids Catalogue* is available as a result of a national exhibition of playthings and other aids organised by HPRU in 1982. It contains illustrated descriptions of over 150 items suitable for handi-capped children. The ideas range from variations on existing playaids and innovative ideas to unique designs made from throwaway materials. Price: £3 including postage and packing.

STEPS – Sequal Toy Educational Postal Service
Paul Hames, 17 Sutton Close, Torquay, Devon TQ2 8LL (Tel: Torquay (0803) 34288 (home); (0803) 36621 (office).
STEPS is a free service (run entirely by volun-teers), to help handicapped children of all ages, who are unable to benefit from a toy library-type source. STEPS offers a three year project, during which time they supply each child with a total of 12 toys (average cost £30 each toy including the switch). The aim is to meet a child's individual needs. An assessment of the child's needs is made, mainly to determine any degree of co-ordinated movement, which if a switching device can be found, can be harnessed to one of the adapted toys. The toys are catalogued for six different stages of development.

Toy Aids Projects
Lodbourne Farmhouse, Lodbourne Green, Gill-ingham, Dorset SP8 4EH (Tel: Gillingham (074 76) 2256).
Makes available some battery-operated remote-controlled toys, with specially enlarged switches suitable for handicapped children who would find ordinary controls difficult to operate. The toys are adapted by handicapped people and are sold at normal retail prices.

Play for the Handicapped Child by Joan Hill. Price: £1 including postage and packing from the Education Department, Wiltshire County Coun-cil, County Hall, Trowbridge BA14 8JB (Tel: Trowbridge (022 14) 3641).
This short booklet is addressed to parents of handicapped children: How does play help? How do I decide the kind of play my child needs? Of particular interest are the development charts which follow the main text. Here, types of play for five different stages of development between birth and six years are suggested, although these ages

relate to the stage of development reached by a child, not his/her chronological age.

BOOKS ON TOYS AND PLAY

Easy to Make Toys for Your Handicapped Child by Don Caston.
The author provides detailed instructions for making 60 imaginative toys that will aid development and skills. They are all considered to be within the scope of the beginner. Price: £5.95.

Let's Make Toys by Roy McConkey and Dorothy M. Jeffree.
The book discusses the role of toys in play and the importance of having the right toy. There is a chapter on choosing toys and then there are guidelines on the tools and materials you will need for making junk toys, wooden ones and some with electrical components in them. Price: £7.95.

Let Me Play by Dorothy M. Jeffree, Roy McConkey and Simon Hewson.
A programme of games devised to encourage motor and sensory skills, intellect, imagination and social confidence in severely handicapped children. The authors have recognised that in handicapped children the spontaneous wish to play often needs to be encouraged. The book helps teachers and parents to introduce the experience of play and to build on it from basic exploratory games to quite complex perceptual discriminatory, manipulative and memory games.

All three books are available from Souvenir Press, 43 Great Russell Street, London WC1B 3PA (Tel: 01–580 9307).

Water Skiing

British Disabled Water Ski Association
The Tony Edge Centre, 18 Greville Park Avenue, Ashstead, Surrey KT21 2QS (Tel: Ashstead (0322) 73046).
This specialised club was formed to help disabled people to water ski. The Southern Region of the Association has its own training centre based in a restored quarry site at Wraysbury near Staines. A Northern Region has now been formed and courses are run around the country.

Wheelchair Dancing

National Wheelchair Dance Association
National Chairperson: Dorothy Liddell, 15 Knightsridge Road, Dechmont, West Lothian EH52 6LT. (Tel: 050 681 392 (home); 031 661 1212 (business)).

In 1984, it was decided to split the Association into four autonomous regions as below. A newsletter linking the regions is issued quarterly. Wheelchair dance festivals are held regularly. Besides the home festivals there are international festivals with teams from the continent competing with winners from the home festivals. Besides set dances – known as championship dances, there are novelty sections where dances are made to a team's own choice of music. There is also ballroom and disco dancing.

Information on the WDA, tapes and dance instructions, may be obtained through the regional secretaries. A starter kit of simple dances has been compiled by Derek Hinton, Chairperson of Southern England comprising dance instructions and music cassette and this is available from the England South Secretary. Price: £2 to cover postage and tape.

Regional secretaries of the WDA:

Scottish region: Jim Thomson, c/o Scottish Council for Spastics, New Trinity Centre, 7a Loaning Road, Edinburgh EH7 6JE (Tel: 031 661 1212).
Welsh region: Vicky Lewis, Ysgol Erwr Delyn, Penarth CF6 1WR.
England North region: D.A. Phillips, 70 Cherwell Road, Westhoughton, Bolton BL5 3TX (Tel: (0942) 815193 (home); 061 945 4170 (business)).
England South region: Mrs J.M. Boyle, 30 Templer Road, Paignton TQ3 1EL (Tel: Paignton (0803) 522138).

Writing

National Association of Disabled Writers
British Section of the International Association of Disabled Dissident Writers, 18 Spring Grove, Harrogate, North Yorkshire HG1 2HS.
This is described as a Human Rights organisation having the aim of freedom of thought, enquiry and expression. They publish a bi-monthly *International Newsletter* and maintain links with similar organisations in other countries.

Membership is £5 per year to those who can afford it and free to those writers who cannot.

Readers'/Writers' Guide to Periodicals in the Disability Field, published in June 1987 by the Committee to Promote Writing in Disability Studies, chaired by Professor Joseph L. Baird of the English Department, Kent State University, Ohio.
The Guide provides a listing of English language

periodicals dealing with the experience of disability. The latest edition of the Guide is updated, enlarged and now international in scope. It is described as being 'an introduction to the state-of-the-art in disability publications: the politics, problems, and progress of those working to provide an outlet for quality literature and art by and about persons with disabilities'.

It is available from: Phoenix, 10 Woad Lane, Great Coates, Grimsby DN37 9NH (Tel: Grimsby (0472) 883040).

The Writers' and Artists' Yearbook is published by A. & C. Black (Publishers) Ltd, Howard Road, Eaton Socon, Huntingdon, Cambridgeshire PE19 3EZ (Tel: Huntingdon (0480) 212666).
This reference book (available in paperback, price £5.95 plus £1.55 postage and packing – 1988 edition) has an extensive list of journals and magazines both in this country and abroad, together with other useful information about publishers, copyright, etc. The details about journals and magazines include the type and length of articles or stories which are normally published.

Yoga

Yoga for Health Foundation
Ickwell Bury, nr Biggleswade, Bedfordshire SG18 9EF (Tel: Northill (076 727) 271).
The practice of yoga has special advantages for disabled people, developing control of movements and of breathing, and ameliorating the effects of some physical disabilities.

Yoga for the Disabled. A practical self-help guide, including yoga exercises, which when combined with breathing and the technique of relaxation explained in the book, will lead to greater health and a more positive outlook on life. The book is for people who use wheelchairs as well as those who can walk.
Price: £3.99 plus 50p postage and packing. Available from the Yoga for Health Foundation as above.

Sports Associations and Others

Back-Up
Sports for spinally injured men and women *see* page 218.

British Amputee Sports Association
Harvey Road, Aylesbury, Buckinghamshire HP21 9PP
BASA is an organisation promoting, co-ordinating and developing sport for those who are without

part or all of a limb or limbs, from any cause – accident, illness, or from birth. BASA encourages amputees to explore new activities, as well as developing existing talents; to compete with each other and with able-bodied persons; to achieve improved health, fitness and confidence through sporting activities; to provide opportunities for the exchange of ideas leading to the physical and psychological benefits of companionship and achievement.

Teams are selected to represent Great Britain at international events in swimming, volleyball, athletics, air-weapons, table tennis, weightlifting, etc. Other regular activities include archery, badminton, snooker, and bowls.

Contact is maintained with amputees enjoying squash, football, basketball, sub-aqua swimming, diving, wind-surfing, mountain climbing, canoeing, cycling, flying, gliding, horse riding, darts, tennis, water-skiing, snow skiing, golf, fishing, fencing, judo, karate, yachting, rowing, parachuting, marathon, motor and motor-cycle racing, parachuting, etc.

Supporters are welcome as associate members. Information is provided to members through a regular newsletter.

British Association for Sporting and Recreational Activities of the Blind
Julie Whiting, 158 Bell Lane, Byfield, Daventry, Northamptonshire NN11 6US (Tel: Daventry (0327) 62214).
This national organisation keeps members in touch with sporting and recreational activities arranged for blind people in the United Kingdom and abroad. The quarterly magazine *Participation* is available on tape and in print. Individual membership subscription is £2 a year; organisation fee according to size.

British Deaf Sports Council
R. Haythornthwaite, Office Suite No. 1, 54 Boroughgate, Otley LS21 1AE (Tel: Otley (0943) 462917 voice; 850081 vistel).
BDSC organises sporting activities locally, regionally, nationally, and internationally. The Council is involved in promoting a wide range of sports.

Through its affiliation with the CISS (International Committee of Sports for the Deaf) the Council sends British representative teams to European and World Games every four years. The BDSC is keen to point out, however, that it is not an elitist body but is concerned that all deaf people are catered for – from a local game of dominoes to promoting world-class competitors.

More detailed information may be obtained by contacting your Regional Office (Regional Officers are themselves deaf). Addresses are available from the above address.

British Paraplegic Sports Society
Ludwig Guttmann Sports Centre for the Disabled, Harvey Road, Aylesbury, Buckinghamshire HP21 8PP (Tel: Aylesbury (0296) 84848).
The BPSS is the governing body of sport for those who are spinal cord paralysed (paraplegics and tetraplegics). It is responsible for organising the annual National Stoke Mandeville Games Federation and the annual International Stoke Mandeville Games.

The BPSS maintains and administers the Ludwig Guttmann Sports Centre for the Disabled which provides extensive sporting residential facilities for disabled sportspeople for training and leisure as well as for competitive events. In accordance with the objects of the BPSS, the integration of disabled people with their able-bodied fellows is encouraged by extending Club membership of the Centre to able-bodied sports enthusiasts. We understand that this is the only sports centre in Great Britain that is able to offer specially built residential accommodation together with comprehensive sports facilities for disabled people.

The Centre includes a large sports hall, swimming pool, indoor bowls green, halls for table tennis, fencing, weight-lifting and snooker.

The British Sports Association for the Disabled
Hayward House, Barnard Crescent, Aylesbury, Buckinghamshire HP21 9PP (Tel: Aylesbury (0296) 27889).
The BSAD exists to bring the joys of sport and physical recreation to people, young and old, with many different kinds of disability, who may not have thought they could experience them. The BSAD helps to inform statutory and voluntary agencies of what is already done in many sports and activities for disabled people and what still needs to be done. The BSAD is recognised by the Government and the Sports Council as the co-ordinating body for all types of sport for all types of disablement and its aims are:
(a) to encourage, promote and develop sport and recreation amongst disabled people and so enable them to compete with each other and with able-bodied people;
(b) to endeavour to secure the provision and improvement of facilities for sport and re-creation for disabled people by the government and local authorities;
(c) to tell disabled people of the benefits of re-creation through sport.
The BSAD has representatives throughout the country organising regional sport, and these agents are always glad to advise and instruct, and will arrange talks and lectures to clubs.

Support is given to local authorities and other bodies to form new sports clubs for disabled people to encourage integration into existing able-bodied sports clubs. For further details and advice on aids and equipment for sporting activities write direct to the above address.

CP-ISRA (The Cerebral Palsy International Sports and Recreational Association)
Secretary General: Dr. A.A. van Schaveren, c/o Heijenoordseweg 5, 6813 GG Arnhem, The Netherlands (Tel: (0) 8306 – 22593/ (0) 85 – 526726).
CP-ISRA encourages the development of sporting and recreational activities - whether in the framework of competition or not – by persons with a disability e.g. brain damage or related conditions. The Association organises and gives support to international events in sporting and recreational activities or to related events.

To participate in national or international CP-ISRA events, CP athletes should be in membership through an organisational body in their own country.

General Information
The three organisations below provide information services which include extensive resource material on sports and general recreational activities, details of relevant aids and publications.

Disabled Living Foundation
380–384 Harrow Road, London W9 2HU (Tel: 01–289 6111).

Scottish Council on Disability
Information Department, 5 Shandwick Place, Edinburgh EH2 4RG (Tel: 031–229 8632).

Northern Ireland Council on Disability
2 Annadale Avenue, Belfast BT7 3JR (Tel: Belfast (0232) 640011/649555).
A publication is available free: *Sport and Leisure Opportunities for the Disabled in Northern Ireland*. This lists the wide range of voluntary organisations concerned with sport and leisure opportunities, as well as leisure centres, swimming pools, universities and colleges of further education, education

and library boards, health and social service addresses and finally the addresses of secretaries of governing bodies of sport in Northern Ireland from aeromodelling to cycling and darts to yoga.

Wales
See Welsh Sports Association for the Disabled, page 228.

The Duke of Edinburgh's Award
5 Prince of Wales Terrace, Kensington, London W8 5PG (Tel: 01-937 5205).
This award scheme involves service, expeditions, skills and physical recreation, and welcomes the participation of physically handicapped young people (aged 14 to 25). Provision is made where necessary for appropriate adjustments to accommodate their individual handicaps. The Award's *Guide for the Handicapped* gives details of these and is available from all Award offices. The criteria for entry are that young people will gain something from participating in Award activities and will not suffer physical deterioration in the process. Further information from the Adviser for the Handicapped.

EXTEND (Exercise Training for the Elderly and/or Disabled)
3 The Boulevard, Sheringham, Norfolk NR26 8LJ (Tel: Sheringham (0263) 822479).
EXTEND is an organisation run in association with the Women's League of Health and Beauty. It aims to improve the health and vitality and mobility and thus the quality of life of elderly and mentally or physically disabled people through recreational movement. With help from government, local authorities and other sources, EXTEND is actively promoting special training and encouraging the setting up of local classes in various parts of the country. With any enquiries, please send an s.a.e.

The Fieldfare Trust
67a The Wicker, Sheffield S3 8HT (Tel: Sheffield (0742) 701668).
The Trust organises activities and events for handicapped and disadvantaged people to enjoy the countryside. These tend to be special events that can stimulate other agencies to open up more of the countryside and the experiences it has to offer to the wider community. New ideas and initiatives can be supported and developed in this way and a greater awareness created of the needs and capabilities of disabled people in the countryside.
  The Fieldfare team consists of disabled and able-bodied people with a professional approach and commitment to the countryside and everyone's right to enjoy it. The Trust operates in the North of England from the Peak District to the Scottish border.

Friends for the Young Deaf
FYD Communication Centre, East Court Mansion, Council Offices, College Lane, East Grinstead, Sussex RH19 3LT (Tel: East Grinstead (0342) 23444 voice; 21488 teleprinter).
Among its activities (*see* also page 229), FYD has continued to develop the Communication Through Sport project. A wide variety of sporting and leisure events is organised, including training courses, coaching courses, water sports, tennis, badminton, squash, and camping weekends, drama, drawing and painting classes, etc.
  FYD liaises with CCPR (Central Council for Physical Recreation) to promote among young deaf people the CCPR community sports leaders award. The young people may then be encouraged to progress further and obtain qualified coaching awards.

The Girl Guides Association
17–19 Buckingham Palace Road, London SW1W OPT (Tel: 01-834 6242).
As far as possible girls with handicaps are encouraged to join their local Brownie, Guide or Ranger Unit and to participate fully in all Guiding activities. There are also Units attached to schools and residential homes.

HAPA (Handicapped Adventure Playground Association)
HAPA Office, Fulham Palace, Bishops Avenue, London SW6 6EA (Tel: 01–736 4443).
HAPA has built and equipped five adventure playgrounds which are for the use of physically, mentally or otherwise handicapped children and young people. Brothers and sisters may join in during school holidays. Playgrounds are in Chelsea, Wandsworth, Islingon, Fulham, and Lambeth and HAPA are always pleased to advise others wishing to establish similar schemes.

International Blind Sports Association
Secretary General Bjorn Eklund, c/o SHIF, Idrottens Hus, S–123 87 FARSTA, Sweden (Tel: 8–7136 000).
The Association publishes the quarterly periodical *Blind Sports International*. It is supplied free of charge and is available in English, French, German, and Spanish. It provides very precise information on the various sporting events played at

international level. This is essential information for serious sportspeople.

MENCAP – Royal Society for Mentally Handicapped Children and Adults
MENCAP Centre, 123 Golden Lane, London EC1Y ORT (Tel: 01–253 9433).
MENCAP has a list of publications concerned with sport for mentally handicapped people.

The Society's National Federation of Gateway Clubs provides facilities throughout the UK giving mentally handicapped people the opportunity to take part in a varied range of leisure activities. Some clubs take their members rambling, fell walking, rock climbing, horse riding and canoeing. Others concentrate on team sports like football and rounders, and on athletics and swimming. There are facilities for painting, craftwork, music and dancing, drama and various indoor games.

PHAB (Physically Handicapped and Able-Bodied)
Tavistock House North, Tavistock Square, London WC1H 9HX (Tel: 01–388 1963).
Through over 500 PHAB clubs throughout the UK, this organisation seeks to extend the opportunities for physically handicapped people to enjoy a wide range of leisure and recreational activities alongside and with able-bodied members. Holiday courses are run on such subjects as art, pottery, crafts, music, drama, photography, sailing, riding, swimming, and canoeing.

REMAP (Rehabilitation Engineering Movement Advisory Panels)
25 Mortimer Street, London W1N 8AB (Tel: 01–637 5400).
Local REMAP panels of voluntary engineers, occupational therapists, etc. are much concerned with aids to assist in leisure activities. Local panels have helped disabled people to enjoy playing musical instruments, to take part in sporting activities and to engage in a wide range of leisure opportunities with the aids that have been custom made for individuals. Aids have been devised to help a climber with a weak hand by designing an ice-axe specially strengthened to take the holding straps and the vital cross-piece; to help individuals to play snooker; to make it possible for a man in a wheelchair to go on smoking his pipe when he could no longer hold it safely. Extra large chess pieces have been made, and a life-long player of the French Horn has been enabled to continue playing despite muscular deterioration which was preventing her from supporting the weight of the instrument.

For further details of how REMAP works *see* Section 3.

Royal National Institute for the Blind
224 Great Portland Street, London W1N 6AA (Tel: 01–388 1266).
The RNIB would be glad to advise blind and partially sighted people how they take up or continue to enjoy a broad range of sporting and leisure activities. The RNIB links up with other organisations for activity holidays and other events. For further information contact the Sports and Recreation Officer.

Scottish Spinal Cord Injury Association
(Formerly Scottish Paraplegic Association)
Executive Officer: Maggy Jones, 5 Shandwick Place, Edinburgh EH2 4RG (Tel: 031–228 3827).
Aims to help spinal cord injured people in Scotland back to an active life in the community. The Association has an information and welfare service. It has two specially adapted holiday cottages in Irvine. There is also an active sports programme at local, national and international level in competitive sports and information can be given on a wide range of recreational activities.

Scottish Sports Association for the Disabled
The Administrator, Fife Sports Institute, Viewfield Road, Glenrothes, Fife KY6 2RA (Tel: Glenrothes (0592) 771700).
The SSAD, the co-ordinating body for all sport for all disabled people in Scotland, can offer a comprehensive specialist advice service on most aspects of participation in sport and recreation by people with disabilities. The Association has the services of a full-time officer who has at his disposal a large range of films, videos, books and information, and experience which can be made available to any group, club, organisation, governing body of sport or statutory agency wishing to include disabled people in its activities.

Additionally, SSAD operates a number of branches throughout Scotland, some with full-time officers who can be contacted to provide more local advice and information.

Scottish Sports Council
1 St. Colme Street, Edinburgh EH3 6AA (Tel: 031–225 8411).
The Scottish Council is the national agency responsible for encouraging the development of sport and physical recreation among the public at large in Scotland, for fostering the provision of

facilities and for promoting the attainment of high standards. The Council employs a Development Officer, Ron Stuart, for sport and physical recreation for disabled people. He works closely with the Scottish Sports Association for the Disabled.

The Scout Association
Programme and Training Department, Gilwell Park, Chingford, London E4 7QW (Tel: 01–524 5246).
There is provision within The Scout Association for the full integration of handicapped young people with able-bodied people in normal Beaver Scout Colonies (6–8 years), Cub Scout Packs (8–10½ years), Scout Troops (10½–15½ years) and Venture Scout Units (15½–20 years). Literature is available describing special support.

SPAC (Stoke Paraplegic Athletic Club)
SPAC is a club run by paraplegics and tetraplegics for paras and tetras of all ages. Based at the Stoke Mandeville Sports Stadium for the Disabled, the club meets at weekends and there is accommodation on Saturday nights. Since it was founded in 1966, SPAC has fielded many representatives for the British teams competing at home and abroad and in keeping with its tradition is keen to welcome new members. Anyone interested in finding out more should contact: Tommy Taylor, 17 Glynleigh Drive, Polegate, East Sussex BN26 6LU (Tel: Polegate (032 12) 3232).

Spastics Society
Leisure Services Officer, Stephenson House, Brunel Centre, Bletchley, Milton Keynes MK2 2EW (Tel: Milton Keynes (0908) 643277).
The Spastics Society organises a number of competitive sporting events in different parts of the country, such as swimming galas and athletics meetings. The Society is also responsible for the selection of teams to compete at international level as there is now a well-established structure for competition at this level.
   The Society is also able to provide advice on a wide range of leisure activities through its contacts with established sport and leisure organisations.

See also Churchtown Farm Field Studies, Lanlivery, Cornwall, where courses are provided in adventure pursuits, including sailing, pony trekking, and a wide variety of leisure activities such as photography, brass rubbing, stone polishing and bird-watching. Details in Section 9.

The Sports Council
16 Upper Woburn Place, London WC1H OQP (Tel: 01–388 1277).
Through its headquarters, nine regional offices, six national centres and the many agencies in the field, the Sports Council seeks to provide increasing opportunities for disabled people to take part in the activity of their choice at top international or at recreational level, either integrated into community sport or in separate clubs. The staff are always prepared to provide details of local facilities and contacts with other organisations at local or national level.

The Sports Council for Northern Ireland
House of Sport, Upper Malone Road, Belfast BT9 5LA (Tel: Belfast (0232) 381222).

Sports Council for Wales
National Sports Centre for Wales, Sophia Gardens, Cardiff CF1 9SW (Tel: Cardiff (0222) 397571).
The Sports Council has set up the 'Welsh Committee on Sport for the Disabled'. The Committee acts as a forum for the development of sport for disabled people in Wales. It has been established to: promote and encourage sports and recreation for disabled people in Wales; prepare athletes to represent Wales in national competitions; organise and govern competition sport within the boundaries of the Association; promote and encourage the raising of standards at all levels of sport for disabled people; encourage the organisers of competitions to present the sport in the best way possible; represent the views of its membership at both national and international level; develop links and promote integration with able-bodied sports.

United Kingdom Sports Association for People with Mental Handicap
First Floor, Unit 9, Longlands Industrial Estate, Milner Way, Ossett WF5 9JN (Tel: Wakefield (0924) 280027).
The Association has in membership voluntary, statutory and professional organisations concerned. Its prime aim is to co-ordinate the work of its member organisations, to provide a national forum, to represent the UK internationally and to develop the training of leaders and coaches. Its regional structure has the same boundaries as the British Sports Association for the Disabled.

Voluntary Council for Handicapped Children
8 Wakley Street, London EC1V 7QE (Tel: 01–278 9441).

The Council produces a number of fact-sheets including the following on leisure pursuits: *Water Sports for Handicapped Children* price: 30p; *Play and Toys for Handicapped Children* price: 50p; *Art, Music and Drama and the Handicapped Child* price: 60p.

Welsh Sports Association for the Disabled
This body is the main contact for sport in Wales. WSAD has three regional organising committees: in north, west and south-east Wales. For further information contact the Secretary: Barbara Woodgate, 4 Ffordd-y-Bryn, Mochdre, Colwyn Bay, Clwyd LL28 5DA (Tel: Colwyn Bay (0492) 47897).

Books and Publications

RNIB Aids and Games. An illustrated catalogue produced by and available in large print and Braille from the Royal National Institute for the Blind, 224 Great Portland Street, London W1N 6AA (Tel: 01–388 1266).

European Charter for Sport for All: Disabled Persons. This charter was drafted by a group of experts set up by the Committee for the Development of Sport. Published by the Council of Europe and available from HMSO Publications Centre, 51 Nine Elms Lane, London SW8 5DR (Tel: 01–211 5656).

Give Us the Chance by Kay Latto. A guide to sport and physical activities with mentally handicapped people. The book gives general guidance on teaching methods, choosing an activity and making the most of available outdoor activities. It also gives examples of all types of sport and physical activities that can be undertaken by mentally handicapped people and includes useful hints on teaching and how the activities can be adapted. Published by the Disabled Living Foundation and available from: Haigh & Hochland Ltd, International University Booksellers, The Precinct Centre, Oxford Road, Manchester M13 9QA (Tel: 061–273 4156. Price: £9.50.

Joining In – Integrated Sport and Leisure for Disabled People. In this booklet, Norman Croucher discusses the question of the integration of disabled and able-bodied people in sporting activities and provides useful information on angling, camping, croquet, darts, canoeing, flying, skiing, and rock climbing. *See also* Norman Croucher's book describing his experiences as a mountaineer, page 214, and his book *Outdoor Pursuits* below.

Joining In is available from: The Disabilities Study Unit, Wildhanger, Amberley, Arundel, West Sussex BN18 9NR. Price: £1 to be sent with order.

Outdoor Pursuits for Disabled People by Norman Croucher. The author has scaled Mont Blanc, the Matterhorn, and many other mountains in distant parts of the world on his two metal legs, and is a considerable encouragement to all other would-be sportspeople. (*See also* his book describing his mountaineering experiences on page 214). This guide is intended to encourage people, with whatever type of disability, to experiment with outdoor pursuits they had thought beyond their abilities. The information covers a wide range of sports and there are useful appendices listing helpful organisations, etc.

Published by: Woodhead-Faulkner, Fitzwilliam House, 32 Trumpington Street, Cambridge CB2 1QY, in association with the Disabled Living Foundation. Price: £10.95.

Outdoor Adventure for Handicapped People by Mike Cotton. Published by Souvenir Press, 43 Great Russell Street, London WC1B 3PA (Tel: 01–580 9307).
This approach to the world of outdoor activities shows that sailing, canoeing, rock climbing, caving and tobogganing are well within the capabilities of handicapped people, under the correct supervision.

Each chapter is written by an expert in the field, who provides all the necessary practical information and advice for those who would like to organise expeditions for their students or children. Details are given for each activity on safety precautions, clothing and equipment, together with advice on how to teach people with specific disabilities and how to encourage feelings of confidence and independence. Price: £7.95.

Out of Doors with Handicapped People by Mike Cotton. Published by: Souvenir Press, 43 Great Russell Street, London WC1B 3PA (Tel: 01–580 9307).
As a result of the author's years of experience he is able to outline a wide range of projects that can be enjoyed by people without the full use of their limbs, both in city and country environments. Bird-watching, pond studies, and fishing are combined with more energetic pursuits like visiting a farm and camping. price: £5.95.

Spectator's Access Guide by Peter Lawton. Published by and available from: RADAR, 25 Mortimer Street, London W1N 8AB (Tel: 01–637 5400).

A 368-page guide for people with disabilities who take a keen interest in watching live sport. It is an updated version of the access guide *Sports and Leisure*.

The guide consists of regional sections divided into sporting headings such as cricket, horse racing, league football, motor racing, and swimming. There is also a 'special national centres' heading which covers indoor athletics, rowing, show jumping, and tennis – over 250 venues are mentioned.

Essential information for the disabled spectator is listed under each sporting venue, for example details of car parking and access to lavatories. Information about viewing facilities for ambulant disabled people, those in wheelchairs, and people who are partially sighted or hard of hearing is also given. This could include details about on-site commentary or special sections for spectators who are in wheelchairs.

Price: £3 including postage and packing.

Sport and Leisure for Visually Handicapped People is available from: Education and Leisure Division, the Royal National Institute for the Blind, 224 Great Portman Street, London W1N 6AA (Tel: 01-388 1266). Price: £6 including postage and packing.

The guide aims to summarise the information and advice available to visually handicapped people, who are already interested in sport and leisure activities and also to stimulate interest in others. It provides useful information on many activities, from archery to wrestling, and has an extensive contact address list. It is expected there will be a Braille edition in 1989.

Sports and Recreation Provision for Disabled People. Edited by Neil Thompson and written by a team of experts brought together by the Disabled Living Foundation, the Sports Council and other organisations, this book is intended for architects and all those involved in the commissioning, design, construction and management of sports and leisure facilities. General guidance is given on policy together with practical examples of detailed design in both sports or leisure buildings and outdoor recreation facilities. From indoor dry sports or swimming pools, to nature trails, angling or camping, the book provides expert advice and illustrates practical examples which meet the general and specific needs of disabled sports participants.

Available from: The Architectural Press, 9 Queen Anne's Gate, London SW1H 9BY. Price: £14.95.

Water Sports for the Disabled (1983). This book, produced by the British Sports Association for the Disabled gives essential advice to disabled participants in all types of water sports. Available from: A. & C. Black, Howard Road, Eaton Socon, Huntingdon, Cambridgeshire PE19 3EZ (Tel: Huntingdon (0480) 212666). Price: £9.95 plus £1.49 postage and packing.

Water Sports and Epilepsy
A pamphlet written by Norman Croucher aimed at encouraging and helping people with epilepsy to enjoy more water sports and to enjoy them more fully. Price: 50p. Available from: the Disabilities Study Unit, Wildhanger, Amberley, Arundel, West Sussex BN18 9NR.

Wheelchair Sports by Ray Clark and illustrated with photographs. This is a practical guide to sports techniques for disabled people in such sports as shot-put, discus, javelin, wheelchair racing, and slalom. It gives details of training programmes involved.

Price: £12.50 plus £1.50 postage and packing. Available from the publishers: Woodhead-Faulkner (Publishers) Ltd, 32 Trumpington Street, Cambridge CB2 1QY (Tel: Cambridge (0223) 66733).

SEX AND PERSONAL RELATIONSHIPS

Ignorance is not bliss, and at last we are coming to an understanding of the vital importance sexual pleasure and love-making have for all our lives. The need for physical closeness to other beings is, after all, as natural as breathing. As we grow up we learn to put a distance between ourselves and others, and there are periods when there is just no one near. But as sexual expression and warmth and closeness can be the well-spring of some of our greatest happinesses, so its frustration can lead to the most profound and unremitting misery.

For people with disabilities sexual problems may well be compounded by physical difficulties. It may not be possible to have spontaneous love-making when careful preparations have to be made and our partners may find this as hard as we do. For partners it can be hard to combine the roles of nurse and lover. However, many of these problems can be overcome given a little practical advice and by the exercise of imagination and tolerance between partners.

Disability can affect our sexual activities in a number of different ways, either directly or indirectly. There is a direct effect when the spinal cord is damaged and nerves passing to the sexual organs are affected. If messages from the brain intended to stimulate sexual responsiveness are not able to travel effectively all the way down the spinal cord until they reach the sexual organs, then depending on the severity of the damage, the functions and the feelings of those organs will be affected to a greater or lesser degree. This would impair, for instance, those with spinal injuries through accidents or those with multiple sclerosis – a disease of the nervous system where the sheaths surrounding nerves in the brain and spinal cord are damaged, thus affecting the function of the nerves involved, or people with spina bifida whose spinal cord has not fully developed. Men with diabetes may have problems with their erections either because the nerves have become diseased and do not function properly or because the blood vessels may have become narrowed as a result of diabetes.

Indirect effects may include: incontinence; pain (which if prolonged will naturally diminish the sex drive, and is especially liable to affect people with arthritis); fear of further physical damage, for instance, after a hip replacement operation or after a heart attack; lack of body control as occurs with spasms; fear of inducing fits in those with epilepsy.

For some, intercourse is not possible or only rarely attainable, but it can be a great mistake to see the goal of intercourse as the only reason for making love – it is, in fact, only a part of our sexual activity. Gentle and prolonged love-making with no 'goal' necessarily in sight, where sexual activity is less of a tumultuous release and more of a prolonged sharing can bring wonderful and satisfying experiences to the couple willing to experiment in this way.

We all know how easily love lives can go stale with the same old boring routine and it is only by being imaginative and varied in our activities that we can ensure this does not happen to us. Finding new ways to enjoy sexual activities can be very rewarding and is marvellous for releasing inhibitions. Willingness to experiment can be a great asset for everyone and especially for anyone with limited movement. Different positions padded up with pillows, prolonged caressing massage, oral sex, masturbation, varying the surroundings, warm shared baths and showers, gently lit beds in a cosy room with drinks at hand can all add a new dimension and be especially helpful to people whose bodies have parts which do not respond in the way they would wish.

Orgasm for some people can be elusive and sometimes physically unattainable, although we know of spinally injured people who can induce a state of high mental excitement during love-making, reaching what they describe as psychological climax even though the physical process of orgasm has been damaged or blocked altogether. One man described this clearly when he said 'Orgasm goes on between my ears not between my legs.'

This is only possible, of course, for those who experienced climaxes before their accidents or disability and who have the imaginative ability to practise a deep recall of the excitement of their previous orgasmic experiences.

Others who have difficulty reaching climax may be affected by drugs they are taking (in this case, they would be wise to talk to their doctor to see whether the medication can be changed), while in other people it is the disease or condition which will not allow them to attain orgasm or, in men, stops them from having erections. It may be easier to come to terms with the difficulties and to build up alternative love-making activities if you have a full understanding of your own situation. Men will need to learn whether their lack of erections stems from permanent physical causes or from a purely psychological impotence arising after a period of ill-health, which, given suitable treatment and help from an understanding partner, may be only temporary. (*See also* information on impotence page 234.)

We would urge people experiencing difficulties to seek help. SPOD (*see* page 233) would be glad to help and may be able to recommend someone you can talk to locally. In the following pages we describe a few books and publications you may find helpful, as well as organisations and agencies. Somewhere in all this information there may be some answer to the quest for your own fulfilment.

Sex need not be disabled, it only feels like it when practical (and psychological) difficulties remain unsolved.

Helpful Organisations

We list below organisations which provide specialist services and also some of the general organisations which have indicated they would be glad to help with questions on sexuality whenever they can. It is not possible to list all of these; for instance, some local branches of Relate, the National Marriage Guidance Council are accessible to people in wheelchairs and also have counsellors who have an understanding of special needs.

Action for Research into Multiple Sclerosis (ARMS)
4a Chapel Hill, Stansted, Essex CM24 8AG (Tel: Bishops Stortford (0279) 815553).
ARMS Telephone Counselling Service:
England and Wales – 01–222 3123 (London); 021–476 4229 (West Midlands).
Scotland – 041–637 2262 (Glasgow).
ARMS runs a very good 24-hour counselling ser-

vice with trained counsellors who know about MS from personal experience. They are there to listen to any problems concerning MS and will be glad to help with sexual problems, while also helping callers cope with their distress, fears, and anger. From their own experience the counsellors can offer hope for the future.

British Pregnancy Advisory Service
Head office: Austy Manor, Wootton Wawen, Solihull, West Midlands B95 6BX (Tel: Henley-in-Arden (056 42) 3225).
A non-profit-making charitable trust which offers help, information and counselling for any problems connected with pregnancy, contraception, infertility or sexuality. At some of its branches a special counselling service for disabled people with sexual problems is available.

Brook Centres
Central office: 153a East Street, London SE17 2SD (Tel: 01–708 1234/1390).
The Centres welcome disabled people, but only their Centres in London (as above); Coventry and Warwickshire Hospital, Stoney Stanton Road, Coventry (Tel: Coventry (0203) 412627); and Edinburgh: 2 Lower Gilmore Place, Edinburgh EH3 9NY (Tel: 031–229 5320) are accessible. The Centres offer a contraception service (including routine screening); pregnancy testing, diagnosis and counselling (including, where appropriate, referral to NHS or voluntary charitable agencies for further advice and/or help with motherhood, adoption or abortion); counselling for emotional or sexual problems; advice on sex education courses and speakers.

DISCERN
94 Mansfield Road, Nottingham NG1 3HD (Tel: Nottingham (0602) 588043).
DISCERN was set up by a group of professional people who in the course of their work had encountered many disabled people who were experiencing sexual problems. These counsellors are willing to work with individuals, couples and groups. Although DISCERN is based in Nottingham, and prefers counselling its clients face-to-face, it is happy to provide a national telephone service. Anyone requesting the service DISCERN offers should contact any member of the team between 2 p.m. and 8 p.m. Monday to Thursday.

Disdate
56 Devizes Avenue, Bedford MK41 8QT (Tel: Bedford (0234) 40643).
This is basically a penfriend/dating agency for

disabled, lonely and understanding people and was founded by a disabled person. The life registration fee is £8 to cover advertising, printing and other expenses. This covers a minimum of three introductions – more if you are not satisfied. For further details contact Bruce Brown.

The Family Planning Association and The Family Planning Information Service
27–35 Mortimer Street, London W1N 7RJ (Tel: 01 636 7866).
The Family Planning Information Service was set up to ensure that people know about and use the free NHS family planning facilities. An extensive range of free leaflets, posters, and information sheets can be obtained from the FPIS office. There are also telephone and mail enquiry services, a walk in information bureau and a library.

There are 11 regional offices which act as information and activity centres for the whole of the country. Details of all these and other services are available from the address above.

Family Planning Service at Home
NHS domiciliary family planning services operate in a number of areas – though this is a very limited service. If you are seeking birth control advice and services and have difficulty in reaching a clinic, arrangements could be made for the domiciliary service to visit you. Your social worker or family doctor could advise about this or you could contact your local family planning clinic (in the telephone book under Family Planning).

Gemma
For details of this organisation for disabled lesbians *see* page 299.

Handidate
The Wellington Centre, 52 Chevallier Street, Ipswich, Suffolk IP1 2PB (Tel: Ipswich (0473) 226950).
Handidate is a friendship agency designed principally for people with disabilities (whether inherited or acquired). It has been designed and is being run by a young man with cerebral palsy – Conrad Packwood. A nationwide register has been compiled of people who wish to extend their circle of friends. Handidate aims to help people of all disabilities to enjoy a fuller social life, from friendship and companionship to life-long partnership. If you are interested, a form will be sent to you for you to describe yourself and your interests and preferences.

There are two types of membership:
1. Full membership (includes penfriend intro-

ductions). The fee is £25 per year and it is expected that four candidates' details will be sent to you during this period. In addition, your name may be sent to any number of other Handidate members.
2. Penfriend membership only:
The fee is £2.00 per introduction.

Muscular Dystrophy Group of Great Britain and Northern Ireland
Nattrass House, 35 Macaulay Road, London SW4 0QP (Tel: 01–720 8055).
The Group has 12 Family Care Officers throughout the UK to advise people with muscular dystrophy and their carers. The Information Officer at the above address will be happy to put you in touch and to answer general queries. She can also provide details of the nearest genetic counselling centre. Two leaflets are produced: *Inheritance and the Muscular Dystrophies*, providing a brief summary of the complex genetics of these conditions; and *Carrier Detection and Pre-Natal Diagnosis of Inherited Dystrophies*.

For further details of the Group *see* page 311.

The Outsiders Club
Box 4ZB, London W1A 4ZB (Tel: 01–499 0900).
This is an independent group which aims to rescue others who have become emotionally stranded, and help each other find partners to love.

People who have been discarded by society, 'loners', chronically shy people, people who were born, or have become, disabled or disfigured, people suffering phobias, those weakened by illness – everyone is welcome to join. At non-threatening events and over the telephone, they help each other to build up their confidence, go out on dates and hopefully find the kind of partner they are looking for.

To most people, emotional stability and sexual satisfaction are essential for them to function properly in their work or socially. The Outsiders Club hopes that it will contribute to making its members happier and better able to function. It has found that some members cheer up so dramatically that even their disabilities are lessened; speech is improved and depressions are lifted.

The Club provides a system in which people can meet each other. People get together who have similar difficulties, offering each other comfort and practical help. They can swap ideas on how to cope with shared handicaps; shy people can team together to go out and enjoy themselves; those who are lonely can offer each other company.

There are hundreds of members in the Club,

living all over the country and abroad too, but it tries to keep small, so that it can be responsive to each member as he or she joins. Sexual tastes are not questioned or condemned; members are encouraged to become relaxed about themselves and uninhibited. The Club runs a postal library of books on emotional, personal and sexual topics and lends book-tapes and erotic tapes to blind members. Every member receives listings, a booklet of practical suggestions (*see* page 240) and details of contacts as well as newsletters about forthcoming events and parties. Blind people receive all this on tape.

A charity has been formed to operate alongside the Outsiders Club, the Social Habilitation and Integration Trust for Disabled People. The aims include: to help people who are handicapped in any way make happy and fulfilling relationships; to help counter loneliness or emotional isolation felt by some people with handicaps.

Relate: National Marriage Guidance
Herbert Gray College, Little Church Street, Rugby CV21 3AP (Tel: Rugby (0788) 73241).
Relate services are available to all, of any age, of either sex, in any circumstances, who are worried about personal relationships, regardless of whether they are married or not. It can be a couple or a woman or man alone.

Counselling normally takes place in Relate premises, some of which are accessible. Sessions are usually arranged weekly to last for an hour, free from interruptions, for as long as is necessary for clients to talk through their problems. If there is a sexual problem as distinct from purely a relationship problem, it may be appropriate, with the client's agreement, to seek the help of one of Relate's Sexual Dysfunction Clinics.

There is no obligatory charge for counselling help, but naturally Relate as a voluntary organisation, hopes that clients will contribute to the cost of the work and this is something the counsellor will discuss with you.

Relate operates in England, Wales and Northern Ireland. It is independent and is not attached to any sectarian, denominational or cultural institution. There are now over 500 counselling centres throughout the country, with a total complement of more than 1,750 counsellors. Some counsellors have specialist knowledge of disability where this is needed.

To make an appointment, telephone, write or call in to your local Relate office. Telephone numbers and addresses for Relate are listed in telephone directories under 'Marriage Guidance'.

Scottish Marriage Guidance Council
26 Frederick Street, Edinburgh EH2 2JR (Tel: 031–225 5006).
The SMGC is constitutionally separate from Relate, but close working links are maintained. It operates in a similar way and has virtually the same objectives. In addition, sex therapy is available in Aberdeen, Edinburgh, and Glasgow.

Spinal Injuries Association
76 St James's Lane, London N10 3DF (Tel: 01–444 2121).
The SIA has a marvellously refreshing attitude to its members and this is best reflected in its newsletter, which deals practically and imaginatively with all aspects of living with a disability. In contrast to many other magazines in the field of disability, it is, above all, reader responsive, and indeed, its readers set the tone by writing frankly and fully of their difficulties and of their achievements. Sexual matters, artificial insemination, pregnancy and parenthood, management of incontinence and all other matters of daily living are discussed regularly and fully.

The Welfare Service, with a 24-hour answerphone for members, aims to provide friendly counsel and advice, to help solve problems (including those of a personal and sexual nature), sometimes by putting people in touch with other individuals or organisations. For further details of SIA *see* page 331.

SPOD: Association to Aid the Sexual and Personal Relationships of Disabled People
286 Camden Road, London N7 OBJ (Tel: 01–607 8851).
SPOD provides information on disability and sexuality, including a range of publications (*see* page 242). SPOD has a countrywide network of counsellors and can usually put disabled people in touch with a counsellor near to their home. SPOD also organises a range of study days and workshops on various aspects of sexuality.

Voluntary Council for Handicapped Children
National Children's Bureau, 8 Wakley Street, London EC1V 7QE (Tel: 01–278 9441).
The Council provides a number of information sheets. One of these entitled *The Sexual Needs of Handicapped Young People*, lists useful organisations and relevant publications and films. For further details of the Council's work *see* page 334.

Impotence and Disability

Impotence – the persistent inability to initiate or maintain an erection satisfactory for sexual intercourse. Such a condition, arising as a result of disability, can have a devastating effect on a man at any time but perhaps all the more so when he has led a satisfactory sex life up until the time an acquired disability makes erections difficult or impossible to attain. If he has a sexual partner then there will need to be a good deal of readjustment if they are to maintain a happy relationship. However, many such couples have so adjusted and lead fulfilling emotional and sexual lives each giving and receiving pleasure. (In the introduction to this section we write more fully on this aspect.)

Until fairly recently, it was thought that most, if not all, impotence was due to psychological causes, now it is recognised that probably half of all impotent men have an underlying physical cause for the problem. Certain drugs prescribed for high blood pressure or for other conditions, and some tranquillisers and anti-depressants may also cause impotence as a side effect. If you feel this might be the case it is important to discuss the matter with your doctor who may be able to restrict the dosage or substitute another form of treatment.

Other causes of impotence include genital diseases, prostate problems, hormonal disorders, surgery or accident affecting the spinal cord, and sometimes other long-term conditions like diabetes and multiple sclerosis.

Erection and ejaculation are complicated processes involving several different mechanisms – including the endocrine, circulatory, and nervous systems, so any disability which affects these actions will clearly affect the ability to have an erection. In an initial assessment of impotence, where the cause is not obvious, a doctor will seek evidence of possible hormone deficiency, and the blood supply to the feet will be examined to see if there is any evidence of blood vessel disease. After this initial assessment the doctor will have some idea of the likely cause of the problem and will then advise on any further investigations that are necessary. These might include a measure of the male sex hormone in the blood stream, an estimation of the blood to the penis by one of several different methods, and possibly a test to determine the ability of the nerves to conduct impulses normally.

When the person has been fully assessed possible treatments are then discussed with both him and any partner. Impotence is a problem which affects two people, and it is most important before proceeding to treatment that both partners are involved.

Erections may be seen in terms of the reflex as well as the psychological aspect. Reflex ejaculation can be triggered by vibratory means. If the nerve supply is intact then this may work. One method of testing whether reflex ejaculation can be stimulated is to scratch the soles of the feet. If the hips flex, then the necessary nerve pathway is likely to be intact.

There are drugs which can induce erections. One of these is Papaverine. Professor Giles Brindley has developed the technique of injecting this drug (or sometimes other drugs) into the base of the penis. The amount to be injected needs to be carefully established by trial and error under expert supervision, although subsequently the injection can be self-administered. After a few minutes, if the dose is correct, an erection will occur lasting between 30 minutes and 4 hours due to the drug relaxing the smooth muscle thereby preventing blood from leaving the penis. Professor Brindley has reported good results with the self-application of Papaverine for inducing an erection of up to 2 hours' duration. As the technique is new it is not yet without problems and must, at least initially, be closely supervised by an expert. For example, if too much Papaverine is injected, an erection lasting many hours may result which can damage the erectile mechanism. In these circumstances an antidote must be injected into the base of the penis. The longest the procedure has been in regular use is 4 years (1988), so little is known, as yet, about the long term effects. It is possible that injecting into the same area over a period of time may cause tissue damage. A maximum frequency of use of once fortnightly is recommended.

Another technique surrounds the various semi-rigid and inflatable penile prostheses. One such is the Finney prosthesis which consists of a pair of semi-rigid rods with a conical tip for better fitting and a tail which can be trimmed to the correct size. The major problem with all such implants is the risk of infection sometimes necessitating further corrective surgery or removal of the implant. Counselling is considered vital both before and after the procedure in order to establish that both partners want to go ahead and have realistic expectations. Sometimes, while the man himself may be relatively happy with the outcome, his partner may disagree.

The Correctaid 'Condom'

A new product from America has been designed to

produce an erection without surgery or drugs. Developed by Frank Gerow, professor of plastic surgery at Baylor College of Medicine in Houston, Texas, the Correctaid is a shaped condom of soft transparent silicone rubber with an incorporated tube, which by means of a vacuum causes the penis to expand and fill the device thus maintaining an erection (for details *see* page 237).

Fertility in men with spinal injuries
A range of techniques is available to enable men with spinal injuries to ejaculate. Sometimes ejaculation during intercourse is possible and a pregnancy is achieved. However, where this is not possible ejaculation may be achieved using vibrators or with electro-techniques, and the semen stored. If a good sample is obtained, it is frozen to permit repeated insemination. If semen is of low quality it can now be artificially improved by laboratory techniques which filter out the most viable and motile spermatozoa.

Readers seeking further information are recommended to contact their doctors or specialist consultants who may be able to help or may refer you to an impotence clinic. Some of the information above was extracted from an article in the Spinal Injuries Association Newsletter, August 1987 which was reporting on a meeting held at Stoke Mandeville hospital on 'The Sexual Aspects of Spinal Cord Injury'. This was organised by the International Medical Society of Paraplegia. We are grateful to the Spinal Injuries Association for permission to use this material. We would recommend that readers with spinal cord injury should contact SIA for further information.

Management of Continence and Sexuality

Incontinence refers to a loss or a weakening of control of the bladder or bowel, or of both. There can be any number of causes of incontinence which may be temporary or permanent. These may include temporary illness, childbirth, local conditions affecting the bladder or womb including infections, complications of artery disease, or disease or injury of the spinal cord.

The management of continence is improving all the time. This is not to say that it is ever easy, but a greater understanding and awareness of the individual needs of people who suffer in this way and an understanding of the universality of the problem have led to the development of techniques of management and the production of more acceptable equipment.

At the same time there is an increasing recogn-

ition of the sexual needs and aspirations of disabled people and the difficulties, in sheer practical terms, which incontinence can pose. There is no simple answer and it is vital that the disabled person should seek professional help and advice in this matter as much can be done to bring the problems within manageable limits. With proper diagnosis and management techniques it has been found that only a small proportion of people need to use appliances on a long-term basis. In seeking help it is important to persist even if the first doctor or nurse approached does not provide the advice needed. The general practitioner and/or consultant should be prepared to help not only in better overall management of a continence problem but also with regard to its relevance to sexual activity. A District Nurse will advise you and will arrange supplies of pads, gloves, catheters, etc. It is worth noting that attached to some District General Hospitals are Urological Assessment Clinics, with sophisticated equipment for diagnosis. The importance of seeking medical advice before adopting any particular procedure cannot be emphasised too strongly.

Fluid intake
While an adequate overall intake of fluids must be maintained (it is vital as a means of combating infection) it is often possible to regulate this to fit in with sexual activity.

Control exercises
In some cases of urinary incontinence a great deal can be done to improve the condition by a programme of simple physical exercises. This mostly applies in the case of stress incontinence where it may be possible gradually to strengthen the appropriate muscles. Stress in this context is a purely physical condition, when a slight leakage occurs during some minor exertion such as sneezing, laughing or coughing. Suitable exercises are described in Dorothy Mandelstam's book *Incontinence: a guide to understanding and management* (*see* page 239).

Emptying the bladder
Some people are able to use what is known as the Credé method to make sure the bladder is totally empty at a particular time. This involves taking a deep breath, folding arms across the abdominal area and bending forward at the waist to increase the pressure in the lower abdominal area. Another method known as 'percussion' is simply banging the abdomen with palm or fist. (This can be very

frustrating if it does not work and is not worth the trouble of persisting for too long!).

Emptying the bowel

Maintaining a regular bowel programme is the best protection against accidents; however, a degree of flexibility in routine can be achieved where this is needed to fit in with a personal lifestyle. The frequency of bowel movement varies considerably from person to person – commonly once a day, sometimes twice a week, with some people reporting once weekly evacuation with no visible ill effects. For those people using suppositories, a suppository inserter can be a great help.

Equipment

There is a wide variety of equipment on the market. The best possible advice, combined with trial and error, should usually determine the most appropriate equipment for individual needs. The Disabled Living Foundation has a fairly comprehensive list of continence aids. Their continence adviser will be glad to answer queries (*see* Section 3 for details).

Intermittent or self-catheterisation

In the past few years this system of regularly emptying the bladder has gained a wider acceptance and indeed has been found preferable where retention of residual urine is a problem. Intermittent self-catheterisation is a clean, non-sterile method of introducing a catheter into the bladder every two to four hours, depending on the doctor's guidance and individual requirements.

Cleanliness, smell and continence

This is perhaps the biggest single problem and causes the most distress to the disabled person and their partner – however, much can be done to eliminate odour as far as possible. Since problems of odour arise as soon as urine or faeces are exposed to the air, it is essential that any wet or soiled articles are dealt with as soon as possible. A neutralising deodorant will help in this respect. One example is Nilodor. A drop or two can be used in appliances, commode pans, urinals and on protective padding, bed linen, carpets, etc. It is available from chemists. It is worth remembering that while it is necessary to avoid smell, fresh urine is in no way harmful.

Considering Genetics

For those of us who, rightly or wrongly, are worried about passing on a handicap to our children, the study of human genetics provides an opportunity to consider carefully our own, our family's and our partner's inheritance before we decide whether or not to have children. We can seek guidance as to whether in our own particular coupling there is any risk of producing a handicapped child.

Genetic counselling

Genetic counselling consists essentially in giving as accurate information as possible, to the extent that knowledge permits, on the risks of transmission of inherited or partly-inherited conditions.

By advising us about any potential risks, a genetic counsellor will clarify our options, and then, by giving us the information we need, will enable us to make up our minds on this complicated issue. We may decide to plan a family of our own despite any risks there may be, but being aware of the dangers, we will be ready to seek early medical help for a handicapped infant if necessary. Alternatively, should an unwanted pregnancy occur, we may wish to seek a termination.

Where a male partner has a serious disease, some women may wish to consider artificial insemination by a donor (advice and information is available from the Family Planning Association and from the British Pregnancy Advisory Service).

Genetic counsellors are not there to tell us what to do, but should be prepared to present us with the fullest understanding of any disease risk, its implications, and the options available. We will then need to talk and think the issues through, and the doctor should be prepared to stand back to let us make our own informed decisions. Neither an outsider's religious beliefs, which may encourage acceptance of the birth of a child (whether handicapped or not), nor the beliefs of a doctor concerned with eugenics who might strongly discourage a couple from having a handicapped child, should be allowed to interfere.

Your doctor should know of the nearest Genetic Advisory Centre. These are also listed in the booklet *Human Genetics* (for details *see* page 238). Unfortunately this booklet was printed in 1972 so is likely to be somewhat out of date.

Pre-natal diagnosis

A number of diseases and abnormalities can be detected by a simple test in pregnancy, although there would be little point in undergoing this procedure unless you were prepared to seek termination of the pregnancy if the foetus was found to be abnormal. It is now possible to determine the sex of a foetus. This may have practical application where the mother is a carrier for a sex-related condition and there is a one in two risk of a son being affected but no direct risk to a daughter except, of course, that the daughter may pass the disease on to any sons she may have.

The Maternity Alliance, a charity concerned with improving Britain's maternity services, wants screening for spina bifida available for all women, and screening for Down's Syndrome to all women over 35. At present these services are patchy throughout the health authorities. (*See* details of their report page 239.)

Aids and Equipment

The use of sex aids is frowned on by many people. The manner of their selling does not help. The sleazy shops and the off-putting (for some people) brochures confirm the feelings that they can be no part of a 'normal' relationship. But within reason, and provided inhibitions can be overcome, an introduction to the use of sex aids can transform people's relationships. Quite apart from their potential for harmless fun in bed, many such aids can be positively helpful in overcoming sexual problems and have a special place where disability has adversely affected sexual function and sensation.

Blakoe Ltd
229 Putney Bridge Road, London SW15 2PY (Tel: 01–870 0971).
This firm produces a range of sex aids and, bearing in mind the consideration that there are still many people who feel that the use of artificial aids to achieve sexual satisfaction is unnatural, Blakoe have carefully chosen to market those aids which they consider have a purpose in a therapeutic sense, and none is included purely because it contributes to eroticism. It is claimed that all assist the natural processes of the sex act and so contribute towards attaining satisfactory and happy relationships. Among the aids available, which are tailored to individual requirements, are for women: clitoral and vaginal stimulators; for men: erection promoters and penis supports and substitutes. It is stressed, however, that the use of these appliances should follow medical and psychological examination to identify causes of any problems (*see The Blakoe Manual of Mechanotherapy* below).

Genesis Medical Ltd
Freepost 24, London W1E 5HP (Tel: 01–434 2864).
The Correctaid is a shaped condom of soft transparent silicone rubber with an incorporated tube which is designed to produce an erection which can be maintained. The penis is introduced into the open end and then the air is drawn out through the tube to create a vacuum which gently draws the penis into the sheath and causes it to expand and fill the device. With the erect penis filling the Correctaid, the tube is closed and wrapped loosely out of the way around the base of the device. Wearing the Correctaid like a condom with the vacuum intact keeps the penis erect. Price: £240.

Harmony (Bulkcourt) Ltd
41 Cross Street, Manchester 2 (Tel: 061–834 2934).
This mail order company is sensitive to people with sexual problems and supplies prosthetics to the National Health Service and various medical groups. Its catalogues, though explicit, offer useful explanations. Discounts are available to disabled customers.

The William Merritt Disabled Living Centre
St Mary's Hospital, Green Hill Road, Armley, Leeds LS12 3QE (Tel: Leeds (0532) 793140).
The Centre has a small display of sex aids and manufacturers' catalogues. These aids can be ordered direct from the Centre on the client's behalf. Counselling is not available, but there is a referral system to other agencies for clients who require this.

SPOD
286 Camden Road, London N7 0BJ (Tel: 01–607 8851.
SPOD would be glad to advise on aids and equipment (*see* page 233).

Books and Publications

There are so many publications dealing with the subjects of sex and family relationships that it would be impossible to list them here; therefore only specialist books relating to disablement and sexuality have been included. However, for further reading, Relate and the Family Planning Association publish lists of books they can supply by well-known authors, covering a wide variety of views and offering information, advice and encouragement to each of us in whatever particular dilemma or situation we find ourselves.

Association to Combat Huntington's Chorea
34a Station Road, Hinckley, Leicestershire LE10 1AP (Tel: Hinckley (0455) 615558).
There are a number of helpful publications including the following.
Facing Huntington's Chorea: a Handbook for Families and Friends, which describes the disease and its effects and carefully illustrates the inheritance factors. Every child born to a parent with

Huntington's Chorea (the symptoms of which do not usually appear until mid-life) has a 50 per cent chance of inheriting the defective gene and therefore of developing the disease in later life. Price: 75p plus postage.

Tomorrow's Child? A leaflet discussing the problems of and alternatives to parenthood in a Huntington's Chorea family. Free on receipt of a self-addressed envelope.

What is HC? A comprehensive question-and-answer leaflet on Huntington's Chorea. Free on receipt of a self-addressed envelope.

Telling the Children. A Fact Sheet discussing the problems and suggesting some possibilities.

Sexual Problems. A Fact Sheet discussing these problems in Huntington's Chorea.

A full literature list is available on request.

The Blakoe Manual of Mechanotherapy: A concept in the treatment of sexual dysfunction is written by the makers of Blakoe sexual aids and is intended mainly for members of the medical profession. It discusses very briefly some of the reasons for physical and psychological sexual problems and naturally goes on to recommend use of the firm's sexual aids where these would be suitable. Published by Medical Division, Blakoe Ltd, 229 Putney Bridge Road, London SW15 2PY (Tel: 01–870 0971).

Entitled to Love: the Sexual and Emotional Needs of the Handicapped by Dr Wendy Greengross. Available from Relate: National Marriage Guidance, Herbert Gray College, Little Church Street, Rugby CV21 3AP (Tel: Rugby (0788) 73241) price: £2.90 including postage and packing.

The author sets out to challenge at all levels the widely accepted view that people with disabilities do not, or should not, have sexual feelings. This is not a handbook on sex, but a discussion weaving understanding and concern into readable patterns. She makes the point that we all have to take emotional risks and being over-protective to people with disabilities is never kind and may often be cruel.

Dr Greengross goes on to discuss the problems of handicapped people in institutions (e.g. having little privacy), as well as the problems of staff who may find difficulty in coming to terms with the sexual needs of those in their care. She deals with sex education and the sexual problems of the adolescent, and also makes a plea that couples, where movements are restricted, should be ready to consider experimentation to widen the scope of their love-making.

Genetic Counselling in Mental Handicap by Brian Kirman. Published by the Royal Society for Mentally Handicapped Children and Adults (MENCAP). Available from the MENCAP Bookshop, 123 Golden Lane, London EC1Y ORT. Price: 50p plus 25p postage.

Brief, but informative, explanation of the nature of genetic counselling, why it is necessary, what it involves, and ethical considerations.

The Genetics of Down's Syndrome (An Account for Parents) by M. Crawford. Written to give parents a reasonably detailed explanation of chromosomal abnormalities. This pamphlet is available from Down's Syndrome Association, 12/13 Clapham Common South Side, London SW4 7AA (Tel: 01–720 0008). Price: £1.70 including postage and packing. A range of leaflets is also available on all aspects of Down's Syndrome.

Handicapped Married Couples by Michael and Ann Craft. This is an excellent and moving account of 40 mentally handicapped couples as discovered through the authors' careful analysis of a survey carried out by them. Dr Craft is a consultant psychiatrist and Mrs Craft is a social worker. The idea that mentally handicapped men and women are capable of normal sexual feelings, and are entitled to express these, has until recently been totally unacceptable to all but an enlightened few. Michael and Ann Craft have now published the evidence showing that marriage between mentally handicapped people, under the right conditions, has a high chance of success and should be encouraged rather than forbidden.

Published by Routledge & Kegan Paul Ltd. Price: £11.95. Available from: MENCAP Bookshop, 123 Golden Lane, London EC1Y ORT.

Human Genetics. This is a helpful booklet prepared by the DHSS. It is concerned with the medical implications of human genetics and in particular the role of genetic counselling. It is presented in a simplified form and gives the bare outline of the subject only. The main types of inheritance: dominant, recessive (including the implications of marriage between blood relatives), sex linked (X-linked) are explained and some examples given. Also discussed are conditions due to chromosomal abnormalities and those with partial and complex inheritance. While this booklet is primarily intended to alert doctors to the problem of genetic disease in the community and to the number of persons who would find genetic counselling of benefit, and therefore presumes a knowledge of medical terms, it could well be of interest to those who are concerned about possible genetic problems within their own families. A list of Genetic Advisory Centres is also included but as the booklet was produced in 1972 this may be somewhat out of date.

The booklet is available free from the Department of Health and Social Security, Room B1305, Hannibal House, Elephant and Castle, London SE1 6TE.

Images of Ourselves edited by Jo Campling 1981. Published by Routledge & Kegan Paul plc, 11 New Fetter Lane, London EC4P 4EE (Tel: 01–583 9855). Price: £5.95.

Brief lives of 24 disabled women who talk very frankly about themselves. They range from adolescence to old age and their disabilities are various. We learn very clearly how these women have coped with living with their disabilities and the attitudes they have encountered. Thus, the themes of relationships, sexuality, motherhood, education, employment and the practical problems of daily life emerge in a personal and essentially real way. These women are not conventional characters, they have a determination and sense of individuality which would make their standards hard to reach. Nevertheless, many women readers will have a happy time identifying with the intimate details of coping with and enjoying life. This is a provocative and stimulating book.

Incontinence – A guide to understanding and management by Dorothy Mandelstam, published by the Disabled Living Foundation. The book sets out clearly and simply, the basic causes of incontinence, how they affect different people and how these different causes can be treated. It also contains information about a whole range of appliances and special clothing which help the management of incontinence when it cannot be cured.

Available from: Haigh & Hochland Ltd, International University Booksellers, The Precinct Centre, Oxford Road, Manchester M13 9QA (Tel: 061–273 4156). Price: £4 including postage and packing.

Living with a Colostomy by Margaret Schindler. Published by Thorsons Publishers Ltd, Denington Estate, Wellingborough, Northamptonshire NN8 2RQ (Tel: Wellingborough (0933) 440033). Price: £5.50 including postage and packing.

This book is written to provide reassuring advice on returning to normal life after a colostomy operation. It gives guidance on diet, appliances, travel and personal relationships. The discussion on sexuality comes alive through the words of people who have had colostomies themselves. They are a source of considerable encouragement in the way they tell of their experiences.

Just one story will give the flavour – the author describes her visit to a 50-year-old patient who was very unhappy on her return home from hospital.

'I took with me for this visit a very young looking 70-year-old friend who is a colostomist as well as having a mastectomy, and blessed with a delicious sense of humour. When we arrived we found that the patient and her husband were very distressed because they had been told when they asked about their sex life "that at 50 they would have to forget all about that kind of thing". My 70-year-old friend said "Well, I don't know about you, but twice a week is just about right for me." '

Living with Paraplegia by Michael Rogers. Available from booksellers or in case of difficulty from the publisher, Faber & Faber Ltd, 3 Queen Square, London WC1N 3AU. Price: £5.95. The author, who is himself paralysed, maintains that since patients treated by modern methods in specialised centres can now usually look forward to a normal lifespan, they must learn a new way of living if they are to enjoy a worthwhile existence. The author discusses, with the benefit of personal experience, the information necessary and the mental adjustments to be made when returning to the community. He includes a wide range of information and has chapters on sexuality and the psychological aspects of paraplegia.

Marriage, Sex and Arthritis. Produced by the Arthritis and Rheumatism Council, 41 Eagle Street, London WC1R 4AR (Tel: 01–405 8572). Price: 20p for postage only. A short, clearly written booklet containing information on sex, family planning, pregnancy, childbirth and inheritance of arthritis.

The Maternity Alliance report of a survey *It all depends where you live* by Catherine Boyd. This report is available from the Alliance at 309 Kentish Town Road, London NW5 2TJ. Price: £1.50 plus 20p postage and packing. This study is aimed at informing women of what screening facilities are available and persuading district authorities to adopt comprehensive and uniform policies.

Multiple Sclerosis: a Self-Help Guide to its Management by Judy Graham. Published by: Thorsons Publishers Ltd, Denington Estate, Wellingborough, Northamptonshire NN8 2RQ (Tel:

Wellingborough (0933) 440033). Price: £4.95 plus 55p postage.

There has been very little information of a practical nature available to people with MS. The matter of diets has been dealt with in a piecemeal way, but it has always been very difficult for those with MS to get hold of facts. This is a complete lifestyle book of inestimable value to individuals who want to run their own lives and want to try regimes or diets which may not have been fully proved to improve the health of people with MS, but which have nevertheless been shown to be of benefit to many people.

Naturally, the author writes about relationships and sex, woven in as they should be in her recommendations for managing MS and for establishing a pattern for more satisfactory living. The book also includes a chapter on childbirth.

Practical Suggestions. An Outsiders Club booklet available from: Box 4ZB, London W1A 4ZB (Tel: 01–499 0900). This booklet is positively jam-packed with advice and practical suggestions on meeting and keeping partners. All the questions we ask ourselves but mostly do not dare to express are here brought out into the open with suggestions on how to cope with the problems. There are sections on home truths; the problems of meeting people; other people's attitudes; our attitudes to ourselves; physical barriers; feeling trapped in a situation; establishing a sexual and social identity. Also included are lots of addresses for sources of help and useful organisations. Available to members of the Outsiders Club.

Personally Speaking – the lives of women with spinal cord injury (provisional title). A new book due to be published early in 1989. Further details from the Spinal Injuries Association, 76 St. James's Lane, Muswell Hill, London N10 (Tel: 01–444 2121).

The Sex Directory by Ann Darnbrough and Derek Kinrade. Published by Woodhead-Faulkner Ltd, Fitzwilliam House, 32 Trumpington Street, Cambridge CB2 1QY (Tel: Cambridge (0223) 66733). Price: £19.95 plus £2.50 postage and packing.

This is a guide to sexual problems and where to go for help. In the first part of the book it describes the sort of problems people encounter and provides information on the national agencies (some with local branches) offering help and advice. Subjects cover: family planning; abortion; genetic counselling; infertility; menstruation; menopause; sexual abuse; venereal diseases; AIDS; sex in later life; sex aids; homosexuality; transvestism and transsexuality; sex law. There is also a chapter devoted to disability and sexuality although disabled people, like anyone else, will find useful information in other chapters as well.

The second part of the book lists, county by county, local agencies and individual counsellors providing a range of services to assist people with sexual problems. Where they have special experience of helping disabled people this is indicated.

Sex Education for Young People with a Physical Disability by Mary Davies. Available from: SPOD, 286 Camden Road, London N7 0BJ (Tel: 01–607 8851). Price: £2. This is an illustrated guide for parents and teachers. It looks at the fears and worries of adolescents with a physical disability concerning sexual and personal relationships and the effect of physical disabilities on sexual function. The subjects of menstruation and incontinence are discussed. The author leads readers to consider their attitudes towards masturbation and sexuality generally in disabled young people. An appendix provides a simple table of the effects of various disabilities on sexual function.

Sex and the Handicapped Child by Wendy Greengross. Published by Relate: National Marriage Guidance (1980). Erection, masturbation, homosexuality and contraception present particular problems to the parents of handicapped children. Yet there is little help available. This book examines the reasons for this and suggests positive ways of helping. It ends with two useful lists, one of helpful reading, the other of helping organisations for disabled people. Available from: SPOD, 286 Camden Road, London N7 0BJ (Tel: 01–607 8851). Price: £1.20 including postage and packing.

Sex and the Mentally Handicapped by Ann and Michael Craft. Written for professionals and parents caring specifically for mentally handicapped people – the authors look at many of the questions, anxieties and fears raised by the sexuality of this group. They examine myths and misconceptions, and offer guidelines for those wishing to plan health and sex education programmes for mentally handicapped youngsters and adults, including a review of the audiovisual resources available. They give the results of their research into marriages where one or both partners are mentally handicapped, and conclude that, with adequate counselling and support, a partnership can relieve much tension and loneliness and also enrich the quality of life enjoyed by handicapped people.

Published by Routledge & Kegan Paul Ltd. Available from bookshops and from SPOD, 286 Camden Road, London N7 0BJ (Tel: 01–607 8851). Price: £5.25 including postage and packing.

Sex for Young People with Spina Bifida or Cerebral Palsy. This is a wonderfully straightforward book with sensitive line drawings by Liz McQuiston which illustrate the text perfectly. The illustrations are helpfully explicit without being too clinical. In addition, there are some delightful drawings showing the joy of loving and coupling where the lines of bodies merge in a manner which would be difficult to portray so gracefully in photographs.

Essentially this is a book for the young and uninitiated and for their parents. It explains carefully all those aspects of growing up which disabled youngsters may well find perplexing, cut off as they so often are from the sort of contact and communication their able-bodied peers take for granted. There are full descriptions of the bodies of men and women and their functions including how conception takes place and how a baby grows. Worries about having a handicapped baby and genetic counselling are also discussed. There is helpful advice on menstruation and coping with incontinence in order to be able to enjoy sex. There are brief references to abortion and sterilisation and useful information about some of the methods of contraception. Masturbation is discussed and reassurance given about this very natural form of sexuality. Homosexuality is also mentioned along with the very mixed-up emotions most teenagers have with regard to their feelings for their own and the opposite sex. Finally there is a useful dictionary of terms and some helpful names and addresses and a brief list of further reading. We would warmly recommend this book to young disabled people who are seeking to understand their own sexuality. While written specifically for those with spina bifida and cerebral palsy it would be a useful book for those with different handicaps.

Available from the Association for Spina Bifida and Hydrocephalus, 22 Upper Woburn Place, London WC1H OEP. Price: £1.50 including postage and packing.

Sexual Adjustment: a Guide for the Spinal Cord Injured. Published by Accent Special Publications, Box 700, Bloomington, Illinois 61702, USA. Price: US $4.95 plus US $1.15 shipping. While written mainly about sexual adjustment for the paraplegic male, this book offers useful inform-

ation to individuals with other physical disabilities as well.

Sexual Aspects of Social Work by Bill Stewart. Aims to help social workers, towards a better understanding of the sexual aspects of their work. One chapter specifically relates to the sexual problems experienced by handicapped people. Published by: Woodhead-Faulkner Ltd, Fitzwilliam House, 32 Trumpington Street, Cambridge CB2 1QY. Price: £17.95 plus postage and packing.

Sexuality and Disability by Inger Nordqvist. Published by The Swedish Institute for the Handicapped, Box 303, S–161 26 Bromma, Sweden. Price: 35 Swedish krona. The book aims to dispel many myths while at the same time providing some basic knowledge to make it easier to tackle questions of sexuality and disability. It is designed as a simple, general and easy-to-understand training manual that can be used in staff training courses, adult study circles and other educational settings. The target groups are nursing teachers, student nurses, teachers and students at schools that have contact with disabled people.

Sexuality and Multiple Sclerosis by Michael Barrett of the MS Society of Canada. Reprinted by SPOD, 186 Camden Road, London N7 0BJ (Tel: 01–607 8851). It is free of charge.

This booklet describes itself as an 'exploration of sexual possibilities, expectations and concerns and of ways to communicate them'. As such, it has a warm and encouraging way of discussing sexuality and of helping people with MS to cope with the frustrations, tensions and fatigue which all too often characterise the condition. The author emphasises the need to discover and use imaginative ways of love-making to enhance sexual activity which may otherwise be restricted.

Sexuality and the Physically Handicapped: an Introduction for Counsellors. Available from SPOD, 186 Camden Road, London N7 OBJ (Tel: 01–607 8851). Price: £2 including postage and packing.

Many professionals are reluctant to consider problems in the personal and sexual relationships of disabled people as part of their concern. This can be because they do not have relevant information easily available to them.

The aim of this booklet is to provide information on various disabilities, outlining possible implications for sexual and personal relationships. Subjects considered include: masturbation, sex aids, drugs and their possible effects on sex, incontinence and, to help the reader gain further information, a resource list and a list of helpful organisations.

So You're Paralysed . . . by Bernadette Fallon. This book has been written for newly paralysed people and their families, and, while it is intended for those who have sustained injury, it would be helpful to all who have a degree of paralysis however caused. The approach is sensitive but down to earth and aims to help people who find themselves in the bewildering position where responsibility for the most intimate bodily functions seems to have been handed over to medical staff. Sex is just one of the subjects covered in this book; it takes its place, as of course it should, with all the other physical (and mental) functions of life. The revised and updated edition (1987) is available from the Spinal Injuries Association, 76 St. James's Lane, London N10 3DF. Price: £4 plus 50p postage and packing.

It has been translated into Dutch, Greek, French, Italian, and Spanish.

SPOD advisory leaflets
All 25p each and available from SPOD, 186 Camden Road, London N7 OBJ (Tel: 01–607 8851).
1. *SPOD is . . .*
2. *Physical Handicap and Sexual Intercourse: Positions*
3. *Physical Handicap and Sexual Intercourse: Methods and Techniques*
4. *Aids to Sex for the Physically Handicapped*
5. *Sex for the Severely Handicapped*
6. *Mentally Handicapped People and Sex*
7. *Your Handicapped Child and Sex*
8. *Your Disabled Partner and Sex*
9. *Physically Handicapped People and Contraception*
10. *Sex and the Person with an Ostomy*
SPOD also has a range of resource lists which give details of books, papers, films, tapes, etc. on particular subjects. These are listed below and may be obtained by sending 25p for each list.
1. Arthritic Disorders
2. Attitudes towards Sex and Disabled People
3. Disabled People and Marriage
4. Elderly People
5. Multiple Sclerosis
6. Sexual Concerns of Disabled Women
7. Sexuality and the Heart Patient
8. Sexuality and Mastectomy
9. Sex Education for the Mentally Handicapped

10. Sex Education for the Physically Handicapped
11. Spinal Injury
12. Sexuality and Visual Impairment
13. Films on Sexuality and Disability
14. Audiovisual Materials on Sexuality and Mental Handicap
15. Professional Workers/Training and Sexuality.
SPOD has a number of Information Sheets. These are 25p each and are as follows:
1. Male Fertility after Spinal Injury
2. Resuming Sex Activity after a Heart Attack
3. Sex Aids
4. Incontinence and Sex
5. Sex and Arthritis
6. Positions for Sex for either Men or Women suffering from Arthritis
7. Drugs and Sex.

Toward Intimacy: Family Planning and Sexuality Concerns of Physically Disabled Women by The Task Force on Concerns of Physically Disabled Women, edited by Susan Shaul, Jane Bogle and others. The booklet is dedicated to exploring the various relationships within a disabled woman's life. It explores a woman's relationship to her body and how this image affects her personally and her relationship with others. A major section is devoted to a thorough exploration of sexuality as it relates to specific disabilities, and there is a detailed investigation of contraceptives. Menstruation, masturbation and the many forms of sexually related disease are covered. Also included are discussions of the important relationships with parents and health care practitioners. The booklet contains personal statements of disabled women discussing their own experiences including the joys and frustrations of sexuality and disability. This sensitively illustrated manual acknowledges the unique concerns of disabled women and provides the reader with the comfort of sharing other disabled women's similar experiences.

Published by Human Sciences Press, 3 Henrietta Street, London WC2E 8LU (Tel: 01–240 0856). Price: £5.00.

The Wheelchair Child by Philippa Russell. This book contains a thoughtful consideration of the developmental sexual and emotional problems associated with disability. For further details *see* page 344.

SECTION 13

LEGISLATION AFFECTING DISABLED PEOPLE

To an unthinking recipient of any of our many national welfare benefits it might appear that authority is inspired by a touching benevolence and is devoted to charitable purposes and good works. In fact, of course, every aspect of professional social welfare in this country rests firmly upon parliamentary legislation. A basic knowledge of such legislation is indispensible in two respects:

(a) to ascertain the extent to which benefits and services should be available.
(b) to enable disabled people to secure those benefits and services to which they are entitled.

We therefore make no apology for the fact that this chapter is heavy going. It is not, of course, intended to be an exact statement of the law. Our summaries and interpretations of the statutes are intended as a guide. We have avoided altogether the complex legislation on which tax reliefs, and social security and National Insurance benefits are based, preferring to rely on the practical explanations of the working arrangements given in Section 2, Financial Benefits and Allowances.

There is little doubt that, while the voluntary sector will continue to have an important role, any major advances in provision for disabled people, whether to protect their rights as citizens or to afford the practical and financial help which they need to overcome disadvantage, must come through either new or amended legislation.

Access

REPRESENTATION OF THE PEOPLE ACT 1983

Section 18

This concerns the responsibility of local authorities in England and Wales to provide 'such reasonable facilities for voting [in Parliamentary elections] as are practical in the circumstances and, *in particular they shall, so far as is reasonable and practicable, designate as polling stations only places which are accessible to electors who are disabled*'.

NOTE: The words in italics were inserted by the Representation of the People Act 1985.

THE BUILDING (DISABLED PEOPLE) REGULATIONS 1987 (SI 1987 No.1445)

This Statutory Instrument added, from 14 December 1987, a new Part M to the main Building Regulations 1985 (SI 1985 No.1065). This requires 'reasonable provision' to be made to enable disabled people (see below) to gain access to certain premises, and to those parts of those premises to which it is 'reasonable to provide access'. Official guidelines on how to meet the requirements of Part M were published in an Approved Document on 23 November 1987. The premises concerned are new shops, offices, factories (within the meaning of section 175 of the Factories Act 1961), schools or other educational establishments and any other premises to which the public are admitted. In the case of shops and offices, the requirements apply to the whole premises, but in the other cases the regulations apply only to so much of the premises as is on the storey of the building which contains its principal entrance.

The main points in the guidance are as follows.

1. A lift should be provided to any storey in a two storey building where the upper floor is more than 280 square metres and in a three (or more) storey building where the upper floor space is more than 200 square metres.
2. If sanitary conveniences are provided in such buildings, the regulations also require that 'reasonable provision' shall be made for disabled people.
3. The regulations also require that where relevant premises contain audience or spectator seating, 'reasonable provision' shall be made to accommodate disabled people. Guidance is that where the seating is fixed or arranged in tiers, the number of spaces provided for wheelchair users should be six or 1/100th of the total seats available to the public, whichever is the greater.

In addition to the provisions concerning new buildings, the 1987 regulations affect the main 1985 Regulations by extending the meaning of a 'material alteration', so that when a building is altered or extended, access and facilities for disabled people are not adversely affected.

For the purposes of the regulations, disabled people are defined as people with a physical impairment which limits their ability to walk, and people who need to use a wheelchair for mobility.

The regulations do not cover alterations and extensions (unlike separate regulations for Scotland) and the Department of the Environment has acknowledged that the regulations are not comprehensive. The DOE says that this will only be possible when guidance is available on means of escape for disabled people from all public buildings.

See also the access provisions in sections 4, 5, 6, 8, 8A and 8B of the Chronically Sick and Disabled Persons Act 1970 under the heading Statutory Services, and the reference therein to section 6 of the Disabled Persons Act 1981. The Building Regulations are intended to supplement and not to diminish these provisions.

Education

EDUCATION ACT 1944 (ENGLAND AND WALES ONLY)
(AS AMENDED)

Section 8

This requires that schools to be provided by local education authorities (LEAs) must be 'sufficient in number, character, and equipment to afford all pupils opportunities for education offering such variety of instruction and training as may be desirable in view of their different ages, abilities and aptitudes'. In particular, section 8(1) (b) requires that there shall be sufficient schools 'for providing secondary education, that is to say full-time education, suitable to the requirements of senior pupils'. These are defined by section 114 as pupils who have reached the age of 12 but not the age of 19. This means that local education authorities have a duty to provide for young people up to and including the age of 18. Such education may be provided in school or in an establishment for further education.

Later in the same section, among the duties to which the LEAs must have particular regard is 'the need for securing that special educational provision is made for pupils with special educational needs'.

Taken together, these provisions mean that local education authorities are required by law to provide education for pupils with special educational needs up to and including the age of 18, where this is wanted.

Section 36

This section imposes a duty on the parent of every child of compulsory school age to cause him/her to receive efficient full-time education suitable to his/her age, ability and aptitude, and to any special educational needs the child may have, either by regular attendance at school or otherwise.

Section 37

This deals with the arrangements for making school attendance orders to secure education for a child suitable to his/her age, ability or aptitude or to his/her special educational needs.

Section 55

Local education authorities are required to make transport arrangements to facilitate the attendance of pupils at school, county colleges or further education classes free of charge; if such transport is not provided, the authority must pay (wholly or partly as it thinks fit) reasonable travelling expenses.

Section 56

This provides that if a local education authority is satisfied that because of 'extraordinary' circumstances, a child or young person cannot attend a suitable school to receive either primary or secondary education, it has the power (subject to the Secretary of State's approval) to make special arrangements for education otherwise than at school. Or, if the authority is satisfied that it is impracticable for the pupil to receive full-time education, it may (if the Secretary of State approves) arrange for education similar in other respects, but less than full-time.

EDUCATION (MISCELLANEOUS PROVISIONS) ACT 1953
(ENGLAND AND WALES ONLY)

Section 6

This section empowers local education authorities, with the approval of the Secretary of State for Education, to arrange the provision of primary or secondary education for pupils to be at non-maintained schools.

Where education is so provided, or is provided under the Education Act 1981 (*see* page 246), the authority is responsible for the payment of the whole of the fees in three defined cases. These include:

(a) where because of a shortage of reasonably convenient schools, education suitable to the pupil's age, ability and aptitude, and special educational needs he/she may have cannot be provided by the local education authority except at a school which is not maintained by that or another authority; and

(b) where the authority is satisfied that the pupil has special educational needs and that it is expedient in his/her interests that the required special educational provision should be made for the pupil at a school not maintained by it or another LEA.

If, further, the authority is satisfied that residence at the school is necessary in order that the pupil should receive education suitable to his/her age, ability, aptitude and to any special educational needs he/she may have, it will also pay for the cost of board and lodging.

EDUCATION (HANDICAPPED CHILDREN) ACT 1970

The Act provided (in England and Wales) for the discontinuance of classifying handicapped children as being unsuitable for education at school. 'No further use' was to be made of the powers under section 57 of the Education Act 1944 for classifying children suffering from mental disability as children unsuitable for education at school. Local health authorities were relieved of their powers and their duty to make arrangements for training such children.

Comparative Scottish legislation, the Education (Mentally Handicapped Children) Act 1974, similarly gave education authorities responsibility for the education of children previously categorised as ineducable and untrainable.

Similar provision in Northern Ireland came only on 1st April 1987 by The Education (Northern Ireland) Order 1987 (SI 1987 No.167). Children who would previously have been determined as unsuitable for education are now the responsibility of the Education Service, and boards are required to secure appropriate special educational provision for them. Other changes are largely based on the Education Act 1981 (*see* below).

EDUCATION ACT 1980 (ENGLAND AND WALES ONLY)

Section 8

A wide range of information is required to be provided by local education authorities. Regulations made under the Act (The Education (School Information) Regulations 1981 – SI 1981 No. 630 as amended by SI 1983/41) set out in detail the information to be provided by English and Welsh authorities. This includes, by Schedule 1, Part II the authorities' detailed arrangements and policies in relation to:

(a) the identification and assessment of children with special educational needs and the involvement of parents in that process;

(b) the provision made in county, voluntary and special schools maintained by them for pupils with special educational needs and the use made by them of special schools maintained by other authorities;

(c) special educational provision otherwise than at school.

The authorities' arrangements and policies as respects the use of non-maintained special schools and of independent schools providing wholly or mainly for pupils with special educational needs. The arrangements for parents who consider that their child may have special educational needs to obtain advice and further information.

The authorities' general arrangements and policies in respect of transport to and from maintained and non-maintained special schools and such independent schools as are mentioned above.

The arrangements for parents to obtain the information set out in Schedule 2 of the Regulations (details of individual schools including special curricula and other arrangements made for particular classes or descriptions of pupil including those with special educational needs) in the case of special schools used by the authority which are maintained by them or other authorities.

Changes in respect of any matter mentioned in this Part which have been determined to be made after the start of the school year to which the information relates.

Schedule 2, paragraph 4 of the Regulations indicates that information relating to special education is to be published in two ways:

> By copies being available for distribution without charge to parents *on request* [our italics], and for reference by parents and others at the offices of the relevant local education authority;
> By copies being available for reference by parents and other persons:
> (i) at every school maintained by the authority; and
> (ii) at the public libraries in the area of that authority.

EDUCATION ACT 1981 (ENGLAND AND WALES ONLY)

This Act is based on the proposals of the Warnock Report, *Special Needs in Education* (1978). It replaced the previous system of 'ascertainment' – assignment to a particular category of handicap based on medical assessment – by a new concept of certain children having special educational needs of whom a small percentage require 'careful multi-professional assessment to reveal the totality of their special educational needs'.

Throughout the Act, by Section 114(1) of the Education Act 1944, references to 'parent' include a guardian and every person who has the actual custody of the child or young person. Where a child is in the care of a local authority, it will be for the Director of Social Services to involve the child's natural parent according to the circumstances of each case.

References in our text to Regulations refer to the Education (Special Educational Needs) Regulations 1983 (SI 1983 No. 29). Department of Education and Science Circular 1/83 to local education authorities considers the implications of the Act and its procedural application.

Section 1

Defines 'special educational needs' in terms of learning difficulties which call for 'special educational provision'. A child is deemed to have a learning difficulty if:

(a) he has significantly greater difficulty in learning than the majority of children of his age; or

(b) he has a disability which either prevents or hinders him from making use of educational facilities of a kind generally provided in schools, within the area of the local authority concerned, for children of his age; or

(c) he is under the age of five and is (or would be if special educational provision were not made for him) likely to fall within paragraph (a) or (b) when over that age.

However, special educational provision can vary with circumstances: if the child is under 2 years of age, it can be any kind of educational provision, but in relation to a child of 2 years or over it means provision which is additional to, or otherwise different from, the educational provision made generally for children of the same age in schools maintained by the local education authority concerned.

NOTE: A child is not taken as having 'learning difficulties' simply because the language taught is foreign to that which has at any time been spoken in the child's home.

Section 2

(1) and (4): These sub-paragraphs amend section 8(2) of the Education Act 1944 to require local education authorities, in securing the availability of schools for their areas, to have regard to the needs of pupils requiring special educational provision and obliges authorities to keep their arrangements for special educational provision under review.

(2) and (3): In subsequent sections, the Act lays down formal procedures for the assessment of certain children (in practice, those with severe or complex learning difficulties) whose needs are, or probably are, such as to require local education authorities to determine their special educational provisions and to have the protection of a Statement. Section 2(2) and (3) require that where an authority arranges special educational provision for a child who is the subject of a Statement, it is to secure that the child is educated in an ordinary school, provided that the views of the child's parent have been taken into account. However, this provision is made subject to the arrangements being compatible with:

(a) the child receiving the special education provision he requires;

(b) the provision of efficient education for the children with whom he will be educated; and

(c) the efficient use of resources.

NOTE: While undoubtedly there will be children for whom integration would be the wrong solution, these clauses unfortunately provide ample scope for local education authorities to evade the main purposes of the Act.

(5): Duties are also imposed by this section which are intended to secure that individual county and voluntary schools, and maintained nursery schools, are conducted in a way which will meet the special educational needs of their pupils.

Section 3

Empowers local authorities, if satisfied that it would be inappropriate for special educational provision (or part of that provision) required for a child with special educational needs to be made in a school, to arrange, after consultation with the child's parent, for it to be made elsewhere.

Sections 4 and 5

These sections deal with the duty of local education authorities to identify and assess children aged 2 or more for whom they are responsible and who have special educational needs which call for the authority to determine the special educational provision that should be made for them. DES Circular 1/83, paragraphs 13/16 offers guidance on the children who should be so identified. In practice, they will be children broadly corresponding to those who would have been 'ascertained' under earlier legislation as falling into a category requiring special educational treatment. As a preliminary to assessment, the local education authority must notify the child's parent:

(a) that it proposes to make an assessment;
(b) of the procedure to be followed in making it;
(c) of the name of the local education authority officer from whom further information may be obtained; and
(d) of the right to make representations and submit written evidence to the authority within a specified period (not less than 29 days).

A copy of the notification must also be sent to the local social services department and district health authority.

Circular 1/83 goes further. It indicates that the serving of a formal notice under section 5 should not be the first indication to a parent that a child has learning difficulties, and that, before a notice is served, 'every possible effort' should be made to effect initial contact between teacher, or any other professional making the referral. and the child's parent. There is also a right to information. Section 5(3) of the Act provides that parents should be informed of the procedures to be followed in assessment, and given the name of an officer of the authority from whom further information can be obtained.

After the expiry of the specified period, the authority shall, if it considers it appropriate after taking parental views into account, proceed to assess the educational needs of the child concerned, first notifying the parent in writing of its decision and the reasons for making it. Alternatively, if having notified a proposal to assess, the local education authority decides not to proceed with assessment, it must notify this decision to the parent in writing. The assessment procedures are set out in Schedule 1, Part 1 of the Act and in regulations made thereunder.

Where a local education authority proposes to make an assessment, it is empowered to serve a notice on the child's parent to require the child's attendance at a stated time and place for examination. Parents must, however, also be informed of their right to attend the examination, and to submit any information they wish.

Under Regulation 4, in order to make an assessment, local education authorities must seek

educational, medical and psychological advice and any other advice which they consider desirable. The authority must provide the person whose advice is being sought with any parental representations or evidence submitted by or at the request of the parent. The adviser may consult others, and must give his/her advice in writing. Regulations 5, 6 and 7 specify from whom educational, medical and psychological advice may properly be taken. DES Circular 1/83 offers guidance on the approach to be adopted by professional advisers and indicates that the main focus should be on the child rather than on his/her disability, and that the assessment of special educational needs (which must be seen as a continuing process) is not an end in itself, but a means of arriving at a better understanding of a child's learning difficulties for the practical purpose of providing a guide to his/her education and a basis against which to monitor progress. Where a child has moved from one education area to another, Regulation 12 allows such advice to be obtained from the old authority.

In making an assessment, the local education authority is required (by Regulation 8) to take a number of matters into account, *viz:*

(a) any representations made by the child's parent;
(b) any evidence submitted by or at the request of that parent;
(c) the advice obtained under Regulation 4; and
(d) any information relating to the health or welfare of the child from any district health authority or social services department.

DES Circular 1/83 adds: 'In looking at the child as a whole person, the involvement of the child's parents is essential. Assessment should be seen as a partnership between teachers, professionals and parents.' Close relations should be established and maintained with parents, 'and can only be helped by frankness and openness on all sides'. Moreover, 'the feelings and perceptions of the child concerned should be taken into account.'

If, having made an assessment, the local education authority concludes that it does not have to determine special educational provision, it must notify the parent of his or her right to appeal to the Secretary of State for Education, who may, if he thinks fit, direct the local education authority to reconsider its decision.

Section 6

Empowers local education authorities, with the consent of a parent, to assess the special educational needs of children *under* the age of 2, and requires authorities to do so at the parent's request.

An assessment under this section can be made in whatever manner the local education authority considers appropriate, whereupon it may 'make a Statement' of the child's special educational needs and thereafter maintain that statement as it considers appropriate.

Section 7
Where an assessment has been made under section 5, local education authorities are required to make and maintain a statement of special educational needs for any child determined as requiring special educational provision. Thereupon, it is a duty of the local education authority to arrange that the specified provision is made, unless a parent has made suitable arrangements.

The factors in making this decision will vary from area to area, depending on the range of provision which is normally available to the authority, but the Secretary of State for Education has indicated that he expects local education authorities to afford the protection of a statement to all children who have 'severe or complex learning difficulties which require the provision of extra resources in ordinary schools and in all cases where the child is placed in a special unit attached to an ordinary school, a special school, a non-maintained special school or an independent school approved for the purpose'.

Form and Content of Statements
In addition to setting out special educational needs (section 7(1)), Statements must, by Regulation 10:
(a) specify the special educational provision (in terms of facilities and equipment, staffing arrangements, curriculum or otherwise) which the local education authority considers appropriate to meet the child's special educational needs.
(b) without prejudice to the generality of (a) above, specify either
 (i) the type of school which the local education authority considers would be appropriate for the child and, if it considers that a particular school would be so appropriate the name of that school, or
 (ii) if they consider it appropriate that the child should be provided with education otherwise than at school, particulars of what they consider appropriate;
(c) specify any additional non-educational provision:

(i) which, unless proposed to be made available by the local education authority, they are satisfied will be made available by a district health authority or social services department or some other body, and
(ii) of which in their opinion advantage should be taken if the child is properly to benefit from the special educational provision specifed at (a) and (b) above; and
(d) set out the representations, evidence, advice and information taken into consideration in pursuance of Regulation 8.
A model form of statement is appended to the Regulations.

Parental Rights
Before making a statement of a child's special educational needs, the local education authority must serve the parent with a copy of the proposed statement and a written explanation of the right to:
(a) make representations about the content of the proposed statement;
(b) require a meeting to discuss the proposed statement. If, having required and attended such a meeting, a parent disagrees with any part of the assessment, there is an additional right, within a specified period, to require the local education authority to arrange further meetings as they consider will enable the parent to discuss the professional advice on which the proposed statement is based in so far as it is relevant to the disagreed matters, either with the person who gave the advice or with another person who is, in the opinion of the authority, appropriate to discuss it with the parent.
After considering a parent's representations, the local education authority may take any one of three courses. They may:
(a) make a statement as originally proposed;
(b) make a statement in a modified form;
(c) determine not to make a statement.
Again, this decision must be notified in writing to the parent. If a statement is made, the local education authority must provide the parent with a copy and a written notice advising a right of appeal (*see* section 8 following) and the name of the person to whom application can be made for information and advice about the child's special educational needs.

Review
Statements must be reviewed at least annually (Schedule 1, paragraph 5). DES Circular 1/83,

paragraph 55 offers guidance and recommends the involvement of parents.

Reassessment
A reassessment will, in practice, normally be appropriate if and when there has been a significant change in the circumstances of the child, and may arise as a result of a review or in response to a parental request. Where a local education authority maintains a statement for a child whose educational needs have not been assessed since a date prior to him/her reaching the age of 12½, then those needs must be reassessed within one year of the child reaching the age of 13½, Regulation 9 (*see also* section 9 below).

Confidentiality
Statements are confidential to prescribed persons. Regulation 11 places restrictions on disclosure without parental consent except in limited, specified circumstances, and requires that they be kept, so far as is reasonably practical, secure from access by unauthorised persons.

Amendment or cessation
Before it amends or ceases to maintain a statement, a local education authority must notify parents in writing, advising them of their right to make representations within 15 days. Local education authorities must consider any such representations and inform parents in writing of their subsequent decision (this does not apply where statements are lapsed because a child ceases to be a responsibility of a local education authority, nor to amendments which arise from the making, amendment or revocation of a school attendance order) (Schedule 1, paragraph 6.)

Section 8
Provides for parents to appeal to appeal committees constituted under the Education Act 1980, against what is being proposed by way of special educational provision. Such committees may require authorities to reconsider their decisions, and there is a final right of appeal to the Secretary of State for Education.

Section 9
Enables parents to request that the special educational needs of their children be assessed.

Where no statement has been made under section 7, such a request must be met unless it is in the opinion of the local education authority, unreasonable. If a section 7 statement is being maintained, a request for an assessment must also be complied with if an assessment has not been made

in the six months prior to the request, unless the authority is satisfied that an assessment would be inappropriate.

Section 10
Requires District Health Authorities to inform parents and the appropriate local education authority when they consider that a child under the age of 5 has special educational needs.

Comparative Scottish legislation is contained in the Education (Scotland) Act 1980, Sections 60–65 (as substituted by the Education (Scotland) Act 1981, section 4) and the Education (Scotland) Act 1981, section 3.

Up to the time of writing, no similar legislation has been introduced in Northern Ireland, though there is pressure that urgent steps should be taken to remedy this disparity.

Guides
A Guide to the 1981 Education Act (RADAR), price 45p inc. p&p: intended for voluntary organisations and parents.
Assessment Under the 1981 Education Act (RADAR), price 45p inc. p&p.
Appeals under the Education Act 1981 (RADAR), price 45p inc. p&p.
Summary of Education Act 1981 (Advisory Centre for Education), price £1.50.
Special Education Handbook (Advisory Centre for Education), price £3: explains the 1981 Education Act for parents of children with special needs.
Under 5s with Special Needs (Advisory Centre for Education), price £2.50: a second guide to the 1981 Education Act which is specifically aimed at the parents of pre-school children.
Summary of Regulations accompanying the 1981 Education Act, and the Circular of Guidance from the Department of Education and Science to local education authorities (Centre for the Study of Integration in Education), price 20p.

Employment

DISABLED PERSONS (EMPLOYMENT) ACT 1944
(DOES NOT APPLY IN NORTHERN IRELAND)

This Act defines a 'disabled person' as one 'who on account of injury, disease (including a physical or mental condition arising from imperfect development of any organ), or congenital deformity, is substantially handicapped in obtaining or keeping employment, or in undertaking work on his own account, of a kind which apart from that injury, disease or deformity would be suited to his age, experience and qualifications' (section 1).

There are four main provisions of the Act.

1. To set up a Register of 'disabled persons', in consultation with 'District Advisory Committees', the Secretary of State for Employment is empowered to regulate the conditions of entry to, retention on and disqualification or withdrawal from the Register. The aim is 'to secure that the fact that a person's name is in the Register will afford reasonable assurance of his being a person capable of entering into and keeping employment, or of undertaking work on his own account'.

2. An employer who normally has or even temporarily has a workforce of 20 or more must, subject to certain exceptions, give employment to a quota (i.e. a proportion of his total staff wherever employed – staff who work less than 10 hours a week are disregarded; staff who work from 10 to 30 hours a week are treated as one half) of registered disabled persons (currently 3 per cent). The proportion may be 'standard' or (and this is rarely used in practice) 'special' (for specified types of work) or a combination of the two, and the percentages are set by Ministerial Order.

   There are two restrictions upon employers.

   (a) If, when a vacancy occurs, an employer who is subject to the quota scheme is below that quota or if taking on an unregistered person would bring him below the quota, then he must not engage or offer to engage an unregistered person, unless he obtains a permit to do so *or* the prospective employee is entitled to employment under an Act of Parliament. (Permits might be issued if, for example, the vacancy was unsuitable for a disabled person, or it could be demonstrated that no disabled person was available to fill it.)

   (b) An employer who is and could remain subject to the quota scheme must not discharge a registered person if he is below his quota or if to do so would bring him below his quota, unless there is reasonable cause. Penalties are prescribed for breach of these restrictions, but there is provision for referral to an advisory committee and for representations by the employer before prosecution is considered (sections 9–10).

3. The Secretary of State for Employment may designate certain categories of employment so as to reserve further entry into them for registered disabled persons. (Rarely used in practice. Only car park attendants and electric lift operators are designated at present.) It is an offence for an employer to engage, offer to engage, or transfer an unregistered person for such work unless he obtains a permit to do so or the prospective employee is entitled to employment under an Act of Parliament (section 12).

4. The Secretary of State for Employment may provide special facilities for the employment of persons so seriously disabled as to be unable to obtain normal employment or to sustain a business of their own in competition with able-bodied people (section 15).

Guide
Employers' Guide to Disabilities by Melvyn Kettle and Bert Massie, published by Woodhead-Faulkner (Publishers) Ltd, Fitzwilliam House, 32 Trumpington Street, Cambridge CB2 1QY, 1986, price £17.95 plus £2 postage and packing.

NOTE: An official interpretation of the Act may be obtained from the Department of Employment.

DISABLED PERSONS (EMPLOYMENT) ACT 1958 (AS AMENDED) (DOES NOT APPLY IN NORTHERN IRELAND)

This Act amends the 1944 Act of the same name in two main respects.

1. It allows a registered disabled person to have his name removed from the Register on written application (Section 2).

2. It imposes a duty upon local authorities to provide the facilities referred to in section 15 of the 1944 Act (*i.e.* 'sheltered' employment) for registered disabled persons resident in their areas, to such an extent as the Secretary of State for Employment may direct (it also *empowers* local authorities to provide such facilities for non-residents) (section 3).

EMPLOYMENT AND TRAINING ACT 1973 (AS AMENDED) (SECTIONS 2 AND 12 MENTIONED BELOW DO NOT EXTEND TO NORTHERN IRELAND)

A Commission established by the Act (now known as the Manpower Services Commission) is charged with a duty to make such arrangements as it considers appropriate to assist persons to select, transfer, obtain and retain employment suitable for their ages and *capacities* (section 2). Section 12 makes it clear that this includes consideration of physical handicap, and requires the Commission in such cases to give preference to disabled people, of either sex, who have served whole-time in the armed forces, merchant navy or mercantile marine, in line with section 16 of the Disabled Persons (Employment) Act 1944 (as amended by the Armed Forces Act 1981, Schedule 5).

It is unlawful for the MSC to discriminate against women or on racial grounds in providing courses or other facilities (Sex Discrimination Act 1975 and Race Relations Act 1976 as amended by the Employment and Training Act 1981).

COMPANIES ACT 1985

Section 235(5) and Schedule 7, Part III require that directors' reports for companies where the average number of persons employed in each week during the financial year exceeded 250 shall contain a statement describing such policy as the company has applied during its financial year:

(a) for giving full and fair consideration to applications for employment by the company made by disabled persons, having regard to their particular aptitudes and abilities;

(b) for continuing the employment of, and for arranging appropriate training for, employees of the company who have become disabled persons during the period when they were employed by the company; and

(c) otherwise for the training, career development and promotion of disabled persons employed by the company.

Comparative legislation for Northern Ireland became effective on 28 February 1983.

The Regulations do not apply to nationalised industries, health authorities, local government or the Civil Service, but Department of Environment Circular 28/81 states 'the government are concerned that public sector employers should publish similar statements about their policies, and authorities are asked to make arrangements to do so'. We would suggest that disabled people seeking, or in employment in the public sector should ask their personnel sections for any such statements.

Housing and Rates

CHRONICALLY SICK AND DISABLED PERSONS ACT 1970

Section 2(1)(e)

This section concerns the provision of assistance to disabled people in arranging for home adaptations. *See* under the heading Statutory Services in this section.

Section 3

This section concerns the responsiblity of local housing authorities towards disabled people. *See*

under the heading Statutory Services in this section.

LAND COMPENSATION ACT 1973

Section 45

Compensation for compulsory requisition of a dwelling constructed or substantially modified to meet the needs of a disabled person shall, if the person whose interest is acquired so elects, be assessed 'as if the dwelling were land which is devoted to a purpose of such a nature that there is no general demand or market for that purpose'. The effect of this provision is to allow the assessment of compensation to be made under section 5(5) of the Land Compensation Act 1961 on the basis 'of the reasonable cost of equivalent reinstatement' rather than the normal basis of section 5(2), *viz.* 'the amount which the land if sold in the open market by a willing seller might be expected to realise'.

RATING (DISABLED PERSONS) ACT 1978
(AS AMENDED BY THE RATES ACT 1984 AND THE LOCAL GOVERNMENT, PLANNING AND LAND ACT 1980)

Section 1

This section provides for a rebate of rates in respect of certain *hereditaments* (broadly, property) situated in England and Wales possessing special facilities (which are prescribed) required for meeting the needs of a resident disabled person. As well as facilities within a home, the section extends to garages, carports or land used (other than temporarily) to accommodate a vehicle used by and required for meeting the needs of a disabled person.

A 'disabled person' is defined as anybody who is blind, deaf or dumb or who suffers from mental disorder of any description or who is substantially and permanently handicapped by illness, injury or congenital deformity or any other disability for the time being prescribed for the purposes of section 29(1) of the National Assistance Act 1948.

'Required for meeting the needs' is also carefully defined as being essential or of major importance to the well-being of the disabled person because of the nature and extent of that person's disability.

A resident disabled person includes one who is 'usually' resident in the hereditament.

The rebate may be allowed to either the disabled person himself, if he is the occupier of the property of if he pays all or any of the rent, or to anybody who belongs to the same household as the disabled person, who, similarly, is the occupier or pays all or any of the rent of the property.

Section 2
Provides for rebates of rates for institutions for disabled people in England and Wales.

Section 3
Procedures for application and appeal in England and Wales. The rating authority is given the right to determine the 'rebate period'. Application must be made by the entitled person (*see* section 1) to the rating authority. Appeal against refusal or against a decision as to whether the hereditament is used wholly, partly or predominantly for qualifying purposes, may be made to the county court.

Schedule 1
Provides for the determination of the amount of rebate under section 1.

Section 4
Comparative legislation to section 1, applicable in Scotland. This is broadly similar, but there are differences in the way the rebate is assessed (Schedule 1 does not apply).

Section 5
Provides for rebates of rates for institutions for disabled people in Scotland.

Section 6
Comparative legislation to section 3, applicable in Scotland. Broadly similar, save that appeals are the province of the sheriff.

A general outline of the rebate scheme is given in section 4 of this Directory, House and Home.
  Relief is determined in accordance with Table 13.1.

Table 13.1   Rate relief in England, Scotland and Wales

Item	Description	England and Wales Rebate is equal to the rates that would be chargeable on the property for the rebate period if its rateable value were:	Scotland Rebate is calculated as follows:
(a)	A property which includes a room (other than a bathroom or lavatory) predominantly used (whether for therapy or other purposes) by and required for meeting the needs of a resident disabled person (*see* Note 1).	£30 (*see* Note 2).	So much of the rates chargeable on the property for the rebate period as is attributable to the special facility (*see* Note 3).
(b)	A property which includes an additional bathroom or lavatory which is required for meeting the needs of a resident disabled person (*see* Note 1).	(i) £20 where the facility is a bathroom (*see* Note 2). (ii) £10 where the facility is a lavatory (*see* Note 2).	As item (a) above.
(c)	A property which includes a heating installation to provide, in two or more rooms, heating which is required for meeting the needs of a resident disabled person (*see* Note 1).	So much only as is attributable to the heating installation (*see* Note 3).	As item (a) above.
(d)	A property which includes any other facility which is required for meeting the needs of a resident disabled person (*see* Note 1), e.g. a lift or escalator.	So much only as is attributable to the facility (*see* Note 3).	As item (a) above.
(e)	A property which includes floor space to permit the use of a wheelchair used by and required for meeting the needs of a resident disabled person (*see* Note 1).	£30 (*see* Note 2).	The rates that would be chargeable on the special facility for the rebate period if its rateable value were £30 (*see* Note 2).
(f)	A property which includes a garage, carport or land used (other than temporarily) to accommodate a vehicle used by and required for meeting the needs of a disabled person (*see* Note 1).	*Either*: 1 (i) £25 where the facility is a garage (*see* Note 2); (ii) £15 where the facility is a carport (*see* Note 2);	As item (a) above.

Table 13.1 contd   Rate relief in England, Scotland and Wales

Item	Description	England and Wales Rebate is equal to the rates that would be chargeable on the property for the rebate period if its rateable value were:	Scotland Rebate is calculated as follows:
		(iii) £5 where the facility is land (*see* Note 2). *Or*: 2 (If the applicant so elects.) So much of its rateable value as is attributable to the garage, carport or land (*see* Note 3). If, however, the garage, carport or land is also used for other purposes, the rating authority has discretion to reduce any rebate under this alternative proportionately or by any lesser amount.	
(g)	Property which consists of a garage, carport or land used (other than temporarily) to accommodate a vehicle used by and required for meeting the needs of a disabled person (*see* Note 1).	*Either*: 1 (i) £25 where the facility is a garage (*see* Note 2); (ii) £15 where the facility is a carport (*see* Note 2); (iii) £5 where the facility is land (*see* Note 2). *Or*: 2 (If the applicant so elects.) The rates chargeable on the property for the rebate period. If, however, the garage, carport or land is used for other purposes, the rating authority has discretion to reduce any rebate under this alternative proportionately or by any lesser amount.	As item (a) above.

NOTE:
1. 'Required for meeting the needs of', 'resident' and 'disabled person' are all clearly defined (*see* page 251).
2. The Secretary of State may by order vary any of these amounts.
3. The amount attributed must be certified by the valuation officer (in Scotland, the assessor). There is a right of appeal.
4. Where the property qualifies for rebate for only part of a rebate period, the rating authority has discretion to reduce any rebate proportionately or by a lesser amount.
5. In England and Wales, in respect of items (a), (b) or (f), if the valuation officer certifies that no part of the rateable value of the property is attributable to the room which is predominantly used by the disabled person, the additional bathroom or lavatory or, as the case may be, the garage, carport or land used for accommodating the vehicle, the rebate is nil.

RATES AMENDMENT (NORTHERN IRELAND) ORDER 1979
Extends to Northern Ireland similar provisions to those of the Rating (Disabled Persons) Act 1978. However, relief is not fixed; in all cases the District Valuer has to certify the value of any qualifying facility.

HOUSING ACT 1985

Sections 8 to 10
These sections set out the main powers and duties of local housing authorities. Under section 8, a local housing authority has a duty to consider housing conditions in its district and the needs of the district with respect to the provision of further housing accommodation. In discharging this duty, the authority must, by the Chronically Sick and Disabled Persons Act 1970, section 3(1), have regard to the special needs of chronically sick or disabled persons. These same sections allow, among other things, the direct funding of council house adaptations. In this there is an overlap with social services authorities, which also have, by section 2(e) of the Chronically Sick and Disabled Persons Act 1970 (*see* heading Statutory Services) a duty, where they are satisfied as to need, to make

arrangements for housing adaptations. To clarify this dual responsibility, a joint DOE/DHSS circular was issued in 1978, *Adaptations of housing for people who are physically handicapped*. The following extracts are taken from paragraphs 5 and 6 of that circular:

> Responsibility for identifying, assessing and advising on the housing needs of individual disabled people, including the need for adaptation of their homes, should remain with social services authorities, in collaboration with health authorities.

> The Secretaries of State accordingly now ask that . . . all housing authorities accept responsibility for work involving structural modification of the dwellings owned or managed by them and that responsibility for non-structural features, and the provision of aids and equipment, should rest with social services authorities (or as appropriate health authorities).

Annex 1 to the Circular presents a list of items that can be regarded as structural features which, when provided for a disabled person in council housing, can be funded by the housing authority.

Grant Aid

Part XV of this Act deals with the financial assistance available towards works of improvement, repair and conversion. A general explanation is given in Section 4, House and Home. The Act makes special provision for disabled people in a number of places, and provides for home improvement grants. There are two kinds of grant: intermediate and improvement, and different rules apply to each.

1. *Intermediate Grants* (sections 474/482)
   These cover:
   (a) works required for the improvement of a dwelling by the provision of standard amenities (namely a fixed bath or shower, a washbasin, a sink, hot and cold water supply and a w.c.) which it lacks; *or*
   (b) works required for the provision of a dwelling for a disabled occupant of any standard amenity where an existing amenity of the same description is not readily accessible to him/her, by reason of his/her disability.
   Intermediate grants are available at 75 per cent of the eligible expense, but this can be increased to 90 per cent if the local authority considers that the applicant could not meet his/her share of the work without undue hardship. Guidelines issued by the Department of the Environment (Circular 21/80) make it clear that 'very sympathetic consideration should be given to any applicant whose principal source of income consists of a state retirement or disability pension'. The eligible expense is the cost of the work required for the provision of a standard amenity or the relevant expense limit (*see* Section 4, House and Home) whichever is the lower.

The local authority must award an intermediate grant if the application fulfils the conditions. Where an application is made for an intermediate grant, the grant may also be given for works of repair or replacement needed to put the dwelling into a state of reasonable repair. It may, however, be more advantageous for a disabled person to apply for an improvement rather than an intermediate grant, because the eligible expense limits for improvement grants are higher.

A local authority may entertain a grant application only if the following conditions are met.
(a) The applicant has the necessary title to the dwelling, i.e. has freehold or leasehold interest with at least five years unexpired, or is a tenant as defined in Section 463(3) of the Act.
(b) The applicant must provide a certificate of future occupation. An owner-occupier would have to certify that the dwelling would be occupied for a period of five years by the applicant and members of his/her household or a member of his/her family. A landlord would have to certify that for a period of five years the dwelling would be let or available for letting as a residence and not for a holiday, to a person other than a member of his/her family.

2. *Improvement Grants* (sections 467/473)
   These are discretionary grants for works to provide a dwelling by the conversion of a house or other building or for the improvement of a dwelling, except as are wholly covered by (1) above. By section 518(3) 'improvement' in relation to a dwelling for a disabled occupant includes the doing of works required for making it suitable for his/her accommodation, welfare or employment.

   Local authorities can approve grants in such circumstances as they see fit. They are able to approve grant aid up to a maximum of 75 per cent (or 90 per cent for those in hardship) of the eligible expense. The current eligible expense limits are £13,800 in Greater London and £10,200 elsewhere. Much larger sums are potentially available by way of improvement grants than intermediate grants, but only at the discretion of the local authority concerned.

Improvement grants for owner-occupiers are normally confined to dwellings with rateable values which fall below prescribed limits. However, these limits do not apply where the application is made in respect of a dwelling for a disabled occupant and it appears to the local authority that the works are needed to meet a requirement arising from the particular disability from which the disabled occupant suffers. Moreover, DOE Circular 36/81 advises that where a second or subsequent grant is sought for the adaptation of a dwelling for a disabled occupant, authorities should treat such applications as though no previous grant had been made when calculating the amount of grant to be approved.

Improvement and intermediate grants are normally given only in respect of buildings erected or provided up to and including 2 October 1961, but, subject to the overriding directions of the Secretary of State, local authorities have discretion to allow grants for dwellings built after that date 'if they consider it appropriate to do so'. In fact, the Secretary of State has given directions which enable authorities to consider such discretionary action in the case of dwellings for disabled people. Grants are not, however, available to enable works of adaptation to be carried out to dwellings under construction.

Grants for Council Tenants

Home improvement grants are available for secure tenants under section 463 of the Act. In the case of a council tenant, a local authority cannot be a party to the contracting of grant-aided adaptation works, but may arrange for some other person or body to act as agent on behalf of a disabled person. Where a council tenant receives a grant, the social services authority may, at its discretion, meet all or part of the applicant's share of the cost under the powers provided by section 2 of the Chronically Sick and Disabled Persons Act 1970.

Definitions

Section 518 of the Act contains the following definitions:

'*Disabled occupant*' means a disabled person for whose benefit it is proposed to carry out any of the relevant works.

'*Disabled person*' means:

(a) any person who is registered in pursuance of arrangements made under section 29(1) of the National Assistance Act 1948; or

(b) any other person for whose welfare arrangements have been made under that provision or, in the opinion of the welfare authority, might be made under it.

'*Dwelling for a disabled occupant*' means a dwelling which:

(a) is a disabled occupant's only or main residence when an application for a grant in respect of it is made; or

(b) is likely in the opinion of the local housing authority to become a disabled occupant's only or main residence within a reasonable period after the completion of the relevant works.

Dialysis Adaptations

District Health Authorities are responsible for any necessary adaptations directly related to the installation of home dialysis equipment (DOE Circular 59/78, paragraph 21). In exceptional circumstances, a local authority may use its discretion to approve an improvement grant for work required to adapt or provide a room to house such equipment where they consider that such an adaptation is needed to make the house suitable for the accommodation or welfare of a disabled person.

Building Regulations

Where in the course of adapting a house for a disabled person, modifications are made to the structure of the dwelling, the works undertaken must comply with the requirements of the Building Regulations 1985. Normally, approval will not be required for the ramping of a dwelling entrance, the replacement of kitchen or bathroom fixtures or fittings or the installation of a stairlift, but might need to be obtained for the relocation of kitchen or bathroom fixtures or the installation of a vertical home lift. In cases of doubt, advice should be sought from the building control officer of the local housing authority.

Right to Buy

This Act also confers the right to buy tenanted properties in prescribed circumstances. By *section 120* and *Schedule 5*, however, this right does not arise, if:

(a) the dwelling-house has features which are substantially different from those of ordinary dwelling-houses and are designed to make it suitable for occupation by physically disabled people, *and* either

   (i) it has had those features since it was constructed, or where it was provided by means of the conversion of a building, since it was so provided, or

   (ii) it is one of a group of dwelling-houses which it is the practice of the landlord to let for occupation by physically disabled people, and a social service or special facilities are provided in close proximity to the group of dwelling-houses wholly or partly to assist those people;

(b) the landlord or a predecessor of the landlord has carried out one or more of the following alterations to make the dwelling-house suitable for occupation by physically disabled people,

   (i) the provision of not less than 7.5 square metres of additional floor space,

   (ii) the provision of an additional bathroom or shower-room,

   (iii) the installation of a vertical lift;

(c) the dwelling-house is one of a group of dwelling-houses which it is the practice of the landlord to let for occupation by people who are suffering or have suffered from a mental disorder, and a social service or special facilities are provided wholly to assist those people.

HOUSING ASSOCIATION ACT 1985

This Act confers powers to the Housing Corporation, acting as agent for the Secretary of State for the Environment, to make grants to housing associations for approved purposes. Among other things, it allows a housing association to fund adaptations for disabled people who live in dwellings owned by the association. As with housing authorities, these powers overlap with those of social services authorities and the position is similar. Paragraph 12 of DOE Circular 59/78 (*Adaptations of housing for people who are physically handicapped*) reads:

> The general provisions of this circular relating to the adaptation of existing local authority housing are equally applicable to housing associations.

Under Housing Corporation procedures, housing associations must seek the advice of social services authorities on the type of adaptation needed. Housing Corporation Circular 16/86 introduced a streamlined procedure for project approval.

DRAINAGE RATES (DISABLED PERSONS) ACT 1986

Where a rate rebate has been allowed under sections 1 or 2 of the Rating (Disabled Persons) Act 1978, there is corresponding proportional relief in respect of any drainage rates made by the relevant internal drainage board.

BUILDING (DISABLED PEOPLE) REGULATIONS 1987

See heading Access.

Marriage

MARRIAGE ACT 1983

Enables marriages of people who are:

(a) housebound; or

(b) detained (other than short-term) under the Mental Health Act 1983

to be solemnised, in England and Wales, at their usual place of residence.

NOTE: This legislation follows Article 12 of the European Convention on Human Rights.

Mental Health/Mental Handicap

MENTAL HEALTH ACT 1983

This Act concerns the reception, care and treatment of 'mentally disordered patients', the movement of their property and other related matters. The main provisions are as follows:

Part I: definition of four conditions: 'mental disorder', 'severe mental impairment', 'mental impairment' and 'psychopathic disorder'.

Part II: provision for compulsory admission to hospital and for guardianship, the position of patients who are subject to detention or guardianship, the duration of such detention or guardianship, and the procedures for discharge. Sections 26 to 30 concern the function of relatives of patients.

Part III: patients involved in criminal proceedings or under sentence.

Part IV: the need for consent to treatment, and the permitted exceptions (Sections 62–63).

Part V: the continuance of Mental Health Review Tribunals to deal with applications and references by and in respect of patients under the provisions of the Act.

Part VI: the removal and return of patients.

Part VII: the management of property and the affairs of patients, (as amended by the Public Trustees and Administration of Funds Act 1986)

Part VIII: the functions of local authorities and the Secretary of State.

The Act has only limited application to Northern Ireland (*see* section 128). In Scotland, see also the Mental Health (Scotland) Act 1984, a few sections of which apply to England and Wales.

The above is only a basic outline of this extremely complex legislation. Those concerned may wish to read either the Act itself or the following guides:

Compulsory Detention in Hospital (wallchart) (MIND, 1983) £1.20
The Court of Protection (MIND, 1983) £1.95
Mental Health Act Manual (MIND, 1983) £16.75
The Mental Health Act 1983 – An Outline Guide (MIND) 20p
Mental Health: Tribunal Procedure (MIND, 1984) £11.95
A Place of Safety (MIND, 1987) a research report £2.25
A Practical Guide to Mental Health Law (MIND, 1983) £2.95
Proper Channels (MIND, 1987) a guide to complaining about medical treatment £2.90
Scots Law and the Mentally Handicapped (Scottish Society for the Mentally Handicapped, 1984) £3.50.

POLICE AND CRIMINAL EVIDENCE ACT 1984

Section 77

If, in a trial on indictment, the case against the accused depends wholly or substantially on a confession he/she has made and the court is satisfied:
(a) that that person is mentally handicapped; and
(b) that the confession was not made in the presence of an independent person;
then the jury must be warned that, because of these circumstances, there is a special need for caution before convicting in reliance on the confession.

In the case of a summary trial, in these circumstances, the court must treat the case as one in which there is a special need for caution before convicting the accused on the basis of his/her confession.

For these purposes, a mentally handicapped person means someone who is in a state of 'arrested or incomplete development of mind which includes significant impairment of intelligence and social functioning'. An 'independent person' does not include a police officer or anyone employed for, or engaged on, police purposes.

The Act is the subject of a 'Code of Practice for the Detention, Treatment and Questioning of Persons by the Police' (Code DTQ). This extends protection to mentally ill as well as mentally handicapped people, and requires special consideration if it appears possible, or an officer is told, that a person may be so affected, in the absence of clear evidence to the contrary (para. 1.3). Someone who is mentally ill or mentally handicapped is described as a person 'at risk', and it is ruled that he/she must not be interviewed in the absence of an 'appropriate adult' (i.e. the independent person mentioned in the Act itself) (para. 13). The only exception to this rule is where an officer of the rank of superintendent or above considers that delay will involve an immediate risk of harm to persons or serious loss of or damage to property (Annex C).

See also articles 'Confessions and the Mentally Ill' in the *Law Society Gazette*, 3 September 1986, and 'Confessions, Cautions, Experts and the Subnormal' (*sic*) in the *New Law Journal*, 28 August 1987.

SEX LAW

Guide
The Law and the Sexuality of People with a Mental Handicap edited by D. Carson (Southampton University Law Faculty, 1987), price £4 plus 51p postage and packing.

Mobility and Motoring

ROAD TRAFFIC ACT 1972 (as amended by the Road Traffic Act 1974)

With Regulations, this Act, among other things, sets out the conditions of holding a driving licence. In the United Kingdom, you must hold a licence before driving most categories of vehicle on the road. The licence may be 'provisional' if you are learning to drive, or 'full' if you have passed a test of competence to drive. The minimum age for driving a car is 17, but this is reduced to 16 if the vehicle concerned is an 'invalid carriage'. (*Invalid carriage* is defined in section 190(5) as a mechanically propelled vehicle with an unladen weight not more than 254 kg (5 cwt) which is specially designed and constructed, not merely adapted, for the use of a person suffering from some physical defect or disability, and used solely by that person. For the purposes of Part II of the Act, however – relating to the licensing of drivers – the maximum weight is increased to 508 kg (10 cwt) by the Motor Vehicles (Driving Licences) Regulations 1981. Certain kinds of invalid carriage, however, are treated as not being motor vehicles and are wholly outside the licensing provisions – (*see* page 25). The minimum age is likewise reduced to 16 if the driver is in receipt of mobility allowance.

Sections 87 and 87A
With Regulations made thereunder (The Motor Vehicle (Driving Licences) Regulations 1987, SI 1987 No. 1378, and in particular Regulation 24) these sections contain powers to refuse, revoke or limit a licence to people suffering from certain disabilities, referred to as being either 'relevant' or 'prospective'.

'Relevant disabilities' are broadly as follows:
1. Epilepsy.
2. Severe mental handicap.
3. Liability to sudden attacks of disabling giddiness or fainting resulting from:
    (a) any disorder or defect of the heart, as a result of which the person concerned has a device implanted in his/her body (commonly called a cardiac pacemaker) designed to correct the disorder or defect (but see item 3 below);
    (b) any other cause.
4. Inability to read in good daylight (with the aid of glasses if worn) a registration mark fixed to a motor vehicle at a distance of 20.5 metres where the letters and figures are 79.4 mm high. Less stringent standards apply for a licence restricted to Group K vehicles only i.e. mowing machines or pedestrian-controlled vehicles).
5. Any other disability likely to cause the driving of a vehicle to be a source of danger to the public.

'Prospective' disabilities are those which, by virtue of their intermittent or progressive nature or otherwise, may in time become 'relevant' as described above.

Notification of a disability
Applicants for licences are under a legal obligation to declare a disability (either relevant or prospective) as required by the appropriate section of the licence application form.

A licence holder is similarly required by law to inform the Licensing Centre 'forthwith' if during the currency of a licence he/she becomes aware that he/she is suffering from a relevant or prospective disability not previously disclosed or if a

previously notified disability becomes worse. The notification is required in writing and should advise the nature and extent of the disability. Failure to notify without reasonable excuse is an offence under section 170 of the Road Traffic Act 1972.

Temporary disabilities (those reasonably expected to last less than three months) which the licence holder has not previously suffered are outside this obligation. A licence must, in law, be refused or revoked if the applicant or licence holder is suffering from a relevant disability (as previously defined) unless the disability is one of the following.
1. A disability which is not progressive in nature and which consists solely of any one or more of the following:
    (a) the absence of one or more limbs;
    (b) the deformity of one or more limbs;
    (c) the loss of use (including a deficiency of limb movement or power) of one or more limbs.
    (Reference to a limb includes reference to a part of a limb.)
    Provided in this case either that the application is for a provisional licence or, if a driving test has been passed at any time it does not appear that the disability has arisen or become worse since that time or was, for whatever reason, not disclosed at that time.
2. Epilepsy which in a particular case is appropriately controlled.
    The applicant must satisfy the conditions that:
    (a) he/she has been free from any epileptic attack during the period of two years immediately preceding the date when the licence is to have effect (or, if not, that he/she has had such attacks only whilst asleep during a period of *three years* immediately preceding the date when the licence is to have effect); and
    (b) the driving of a vehicle by him/her in pursuance of the licence is not likely to be a source of danger to the public.
3. Any disorder or defect of the heart, which has been controlled by implanting a cardiac pacemaker (see 3 (a) of the list of relevant disabilities above. The applicant must satisfy the conditions that:
    (a) his/her driving of a vehicle in pursuance of the licence is not likely to be a source of danger to the public; and
    (b) he/she has made adequate arrangements to receive regular medical supervision by a cardiologist throughout the period of the

licence, and is conforming to those arrangements.

Where a disability is such as not to necessitate refusal or revocation of a driving licence, any licence issued may nevertheless be restricted in duration and/or the description of vehicles which may be driven. Such restrictions are typically worded: 'Entitled to drive . . . with all controls so fitted that they can be correctly and conveniently operated with/without/despite (followed by a description of disability, e.g. loss of left leg).'

Because some disabled drivers overcome their disabilities more successfully than others it is not considered practicable to specify what adaptations if any, are required. The restriction on driving licences is, in fact, so worded that it places the onus on the driver to ensure that the practical effect of his/her disability does not affect the safe control of his/her vehicle. It is for the licence holder to decide in the light of this what, if any, adaptations are required. Essentially, he/she must be satisfied that if stopped by a police officer it could be demonstrated that the terms of the licence were being met. (An explanatory leaflet is issued with all restricted licences.)

Disabled people whose full licence authorises them to drive only an invalid carriage or vehicle of special construction or design are not entitled to drive any other type of vehicle. If they wish to drive a vehicle of a type not covered by their full licence they should contact the Licensing Centre about amending their licence.

NOTE: It is important to be aware that it is an offence under section 5 of this Act to drive or attempt to drive a motor vehicle on a road or other public place if 'unfit to drive through drink or drugs'. Conviction carries an automatic disqualification from driving. An offence could arise from normal and prescribed use of a medicine, if thereby a driver was so affected as to be unfit to drive.

There is a separate offence of being 'in charge' of a motor vehicle on the road or other public place when unfit to drive through drink or drugs. You would not be regarded as in charge of a vehicle if you could prove that the circumstances were such that there was no likelihood of you driving while you remained unfit to drive, but clearly this could be difficult to establish.

Licences for 'trike' drivers who change to a standard car
The law does not permit the grant of a full licence to drive a car unless:
(a) the applicant can satisfy the Secretary of State that he has held a licence, valid within the last ten years, for the class of vehicle for which he/she is applying; or
(b) the applicant has passed a driving test for the

relevant class of vehicle(s) within the last ten years; or
(c) the applicant can satisfy the Secretary of State that he/she has held an appropriate licence valid within the last ten years which was issued in Northern Ireland, the Isle of Man or the Channel Islands.

If a 'trike' driver is not thus entitled to a full licence for the vehicles he/she now wishes to drive, he/she would have to apply for provisional entitlement to be added to his or her Group J licence in order to take the appropriate driving test. Such applications would, of course, be subject to medical enquiries. However, no fee is payable for either the restoration of previous entitlement or the addition of provisional entitlement.

Vehicles which can be driven without a licence
By the Chronically Sick and Disabled Persons Act 1970, section 20, as amended by the Road Traffic Act 1972, Schedule 7, an invalid carriage which complies with the use of Invalid Carriages on Highways Regulations 1970 (SI 1970 No. 1391) and which is being used in accordance with the conditions prescribed by those Regulations, is exempted from a number of statutory requirements. For this purpose, an invalid carriage is defined as a vehicle, whether mechanically propelled or not, constructed or adapted for use for the carriage of one person, being a person suffering from some physical defect or disability. The invalid carriage must comply with the following conditions.
1. The vehicle must not exceed 250 lb unladen weight.
2. If mechanically propelled, it must be so constructed as to be incapable of exceeding four m.p.h. on the level under its own power.
3. If mechanically propelled, it must have brakes which comply with the current regulations.
4. When used during the hours of darkness, it must have a front light, rear light and rear reflectors.

In the case of an invalid carriage which fulfils all these conditions the following provisions are applicable.
1. No statutory provision prohibiting or restricting the use of footways shall prohibit or restrict the use of that vehicle on a footway.
2. If the vehicle is mechanically propelled it shall be treated for the purposes of the Road Traffic Regulations Act 1967 and the Road Traffic Act 1972 as not being a motor vehicle.
3. Whether or not the vehicle is mechanically

propelled, it shall be exempted from the requirements of sections 68 to 81 of the Road Traffic Act 1972 (relating to lighting).
Such vehicles are not liable to vehicle excise duty and need not be registered.

NOTE: The invalid tricycle, or 'trike', is of course outside this exemption. Nor does it fall into the classification of 'invalid carriage' in section 190(5) of the Road Traffic Act 1972 (*see* page 257) or the identical definition in section 253(5) of the Road Traffic Act 1960. It is, therefore, subject to all normal legislation relating to motor vehicles, but equally is not prohibited from motorways or subject to speed restriction.

MOTOR VEHICLES (WEARING OF SEAT BELTS) REGULATIONS 1982 AND MOTOR VEHICLES (WEARING OF SEAT BELTS BY CHILDREN) REGULATIONS 1982

These Regulations are made under the Road Traffic Act 1972, as amended by the Transport Act 1981. Since 31 January 1983, they have required seat belts to be worn by anyone aged 14 or more when travelling, as driver or passenger, in the front seats of certain vehicles, i.e.:

cars and three-wheeled vehicles (weighing 408 kilograms or more unladen) with not more than 12 passenger seats, made after 30 June 1964 and first registered after 31 December 1964 (usually C or later number plates);

light vans (with an unladen weight not exceeding 1,525 kilograms or a laden weight of 3,500 kilograms) made after 31 August 1966 and registered on or after 31 March 1967 (usually E or later number plates),

three-wheeled motor vehicles (exceeding 255 kilograms unladen weight) made after 28 February 1970 and first registered after 31 August 1970 (usually fitted J or later number plates); and

any vehicle which has belts fitted (although not required by law) because of the use being made of the vehicle.

The seat belt must comply to standards prescribed by regulations both as regards the belt itself and its anchorage, but the normal requirements are somewhat relaxed for vehicles specially constructed or adapted for physically disabled people. Nevertheless, such special seat belts must be worn, and if you are using a vehicle fitted with the normal design of seat belt, you will have to wear this unless exempted in one of the ways described below.

There is also a responsibility upon drivers to ensure that children under 14 do not ride in a front seat of any vehicle covered by the adult regulations unless they are wearing a seat belt or are in an approved child restraint. (Further guidance is given in a free leaflet *Child Safety in Cars* available from your local road safety officer or from the Department of Transport, Distribution, Building No. 3, Victoria Road, South Ruislip, Middlesex, HA4 0NZ.

Exemptions
You do not have to wear a seat belt in the following circumstances.

If you are sitting in a middle front seat (e.g. a bench seat) and two passengers (including yourself) are sitting in front. (When the passenger in a middle front seat is a child under 14, exemption applies only if there is no belt fitted to the child's seat and *all* other front and back seats are occupied.)

If you are driving a vehicle and carrying out a manoeuvre which includes reversing.

If you have a valid medical exemption certificate (*see* below) (also applies to children).

If you are making a local delivery or collection round using a vehicle constructed or adapted for that purpose.

If your seat belt has become defective on your journey or previously and you have already arranged to have the belt repaired or replaced.

If your inertia reel seat belt has, for the moment, locked because your vehicle is or has been on a steep incline. But you will have to put the belt on as soon as the mechanism has unlocked.

If you are a qualified driver and you are supervising a learner driver who is carrying out a manoeuvre which includes reversing.

If you are the driver of a taxi which is being used for seeking hire or answering a call for hire or carrying a passenger for hire. (You will only be exempt if you carry the plate showing your vehicle is licensed as a taxi.)

If you are the driver of a private hire car vehicle which is being used to carry a passenger for hire. (You will only be exempt if you carry the plate showing that your vehicle is licensed as a private hire car vehicle or that it is licensed at the hackney carriage rate under the Vehicles (Excise) Act 1971.)

If you are riding in a vehicle and you are looking into or repairing a mechanical fault. You will only be exempt if the vehicle is on trade plates.

These are the main exemptions to the law. Others are only for people in special jobs and in certain circumstances, for example the police.

The exemption which is significant for disabled people is contained in Regulations 5(d) and requires the holding of a statutory form of certificate, signed by a registered medical practitioner, to the effect that it is inadvisable on medical grounds to wear a seat belt. If, as the holder of such a certificate, you are told by a police officer that you may be prosecuted for a seat belt offence (maximum penalty £50) and cannot produce the certificate then and there, you need to do so within five days to establish your exemption from the law.

NOTE: Disability does not, of course, mean that you will be automatically entitled to exemption from seat belt regulations. Indeed, it seems likely that most disabled people who are fit to drive will also be fit to wear a seat belt, and that it will normally be in their best interests to do so. A number of seat belt adaptations are now available which make it possible to adjust seat belts better to accommodate any physical difficulties.

THE DISABLED PERSONS (BADGES FOR MOTOR VEHICLES) REGULATIONS 1982

These Regulations are made in pursuance of Section 21 of the Chronically Sick and Disabled Persons Act 1970, and are generally known as the Orange Badge Scheme. For a general description of the arrangements *see* Section 8 of this Directory.

THE ROAD TRAFFIC REGULATION ACT 1984

This Act concerns the regulation of road traffic, including parking restrictions.

Section 105

Allows exemption from wheel clamping under section 104 if a current disabled person's badge is displayed on the vehicle concerned.

If, however, the vehicle was not being used either by the badge holder or under the special provisions for institutional use (Chronically Sick and Disabled Persons Act 1970, section 21(4)) *and* was not being used in circumstances where a disabled person's concession would be available to a disabled person's vehicle, then the person guilty of the illegal parking would be guilty of a further offence under section 105(5).

Section 117

By this section, a person who is guilty of an offence under the Act is guilty of a further offence if at the same time he was wrongfully using a disabled person's badge in circumstances where one of the concessions in favour of disabled people would have been available to a disabled person's vehicle.

TRANSPORT ACT 1985

Section 18

Exempts from PSV operator and driver licensing requirements vehicles being used under a permit granted under section 19 or 22 of the Act and the driving of any vehicles when it is so used. Section 19 allows the grant of a permit to vehicles which are adapted to carry more than eight but less than 16 passengers (small bus) or more than 16 passengers (large bus). A large bus permit can be granted to anybody who assists and co-ordinates the activities of bodies concerned with education, religion, social welfare, or other activities for the benefit of the community. Small bus permits can be granted to anybody concerned with any of these same activities or with recreation.

Use of a small or large bus, and exemption from the PSV licensing requirements is subject to requirements that the bus is:
(a) being used by a body which has been granted a permit;
(b) not being used to carry members of the general public, nor with a view to profit, nor incidentally to an activity which is carried on with a view to profit;
(c) being used in every respect in accordance with any conditions attached to the permit; or
(d) not being used in contravention of any regulations made under Section 21 of the Act.

Section 57(2)

Adds a new paragraph 9A to the Transport Act 1968, sub-paragraph (5) of which empowers passenger transport authorities, among other things, to formulate policies to describe measures to be taken by the area executive to promote the convenience of the public (*including persons who are elderly or disabled*) in using the available public passenger transport services (whether subsidised or not).

Section 63(6)

Conveys parallel powers to non-metropolitan county councils in England and Wales (or regional or islands councils in Scotland) in areas other than Passenger Transport Areas.

Section 93

Empowers local authorities acting either singly or together, to establish a travel concession scheme for journeys on public transport by:
(a) men over 65 and women over 60;
(b) people whose age does not exceed 16;
(c) people over 16 but not exceeding 18 who are in full-time education;

(d) people so blind as to be unable to perform any work for which sight is essential;

(e) people suffering from any disability, or injury which in the opinion of the authority (or authorities) seriously impairs their ability to walk;

(f) such other classes of persons as the Secretary of State may by order specify (at the time of writing no such order has been made).

The scheme may apply to journeys:

(a) between places in the principal area covered by the scheme;

(b) between such places and places outside but in the vicinity of that area; or

(c) between places outside but in the vicinity of that area.

The principal area can be the area of the local authority (or authorities) concerned, or a specified area within that area.

Section 106(1)

Empowers transport authorities, individually or together, to make grants towards the cost of providing, maintaining or improving:

(a) any vehicle, equipment or other facilities provided wholly or mainly for the purpose of facilitating travel by members of the public who are disabled; or

(b) any equipment or other facilities specifically designed or adapted for that purpose which are incorporated in any vehicle, equipment or other facilities not provided wholly or mainly for that purpose.

Section 125

Concerns the establishment of The Disabled Persons Transport Advisory Committee, its membership, and terms of reference. The Secretary of State is enjoined, so far as is reasonably practicable, to secure that at all times at least half of the committee are people who are themselves disabled. Schedule 5 sets out provisions for the administration and constitutional basis of the Committee.

Guides

Motoring and Mobility for Disabled People (RADAR, Ann Darnbrough & Derek Kinrade, 1988).

Epilepsy and the Law (leaflet, National Society for Epilepsy).

Driving Licences: Driving and Epilepsy (Academic Press, 1983)

Personal Injury

Guide

Disability and Compensation Claims by P.Noble, B.Hellyer and E.Fanshawe (Sweet & Maxwell, Spon (Booksellers) Ltd., North Way, Andover, Hampshire SP10 5BE (Tel: Andover (0264) 62141), Oct. 1986), price £5.95. Said to be the first systematic guide to expense claims in a personal injuries action.

Residential Nursing Homes

REGISTERED HOMES ACT 1984

Consolidates previous legislation on homes for residential care, nursing, and mental nursing. Requires registration of such homes, and empowers the Secretary of State to make regulations as to their conduct (Sections 16 – 26). Regulations have been made as follows:

SI 1984 No. 1345: The Residential Care Homes Regulations 1984

SI 1984 No. 1578: The Nursing Homes and Mental Nursing Homes Regulations 1984.

Guides

New Law Journal, June 1985, pp. 615–617.

Home Life, a Code of Practice for Residential Care (Centre for Policy on Ageing, 1984).

Registration and Inspection of Nursing Homes – A Handbook for Health Authorities (National Association of Health Authorities in England and Wales, 1985).

Statutory Services

NATIONAL ASSISTANCE ACT 1948 (AS AMENDED BY LOCAL GOVERNMENT ACT 1972)

Section 29

This section of the Act deals with the promotion of the welfare of handicapped persons by local authorities. A local authority may, with the approval of the Secretary of State, and to such extent as the Secretary of State may direct, in respect of people ordinarily resident in the area of the authority, make arrangements for promoting the welfare of 'persons who are blind, deaf or dumb, or who suffer from mental disorder of any description and other persons who are substantially and permanently handicapped by illness, injury or congenital deformity or such other disabilities as may be prescribed by the Secretary of State'.

The arrangements which authorities may make include:

(a) advice on available services to those concerned;
(b) instruction in ways of overcoming the effects of disabilities;
(c) provision of workshops and hostels for handicapped workers*;
(d) provision of work for handicapped persons*;
(e) assistance in the disposal of the produce of such work;
(f) provision of recreational facilities;
(g) compilation and maintenance of a register of handicapped persons.

* But see Disabled Persons (Employment) Act 1958.

Section 30
Allows local authorities to use certain voluntary organisations for disabled people's welfare as their agents in making the above arrangements.

CHRONICALLY SICK AND DISABLED PERSONS ACT 1970 (AS AMENDED)

Section 1
Local authorities must:
(a) take steps to inform themselves of the numbers and needs of disabled persons (as defined in section 29 of the National Insurance Act 1948) in their areas;
(b) publish information as to the services they provide under Section 29 of the National Assistance Act 1948, but only 'from time to time at such times and in such manner as they consider appropriate' (*but see* (c) below);
(c) ensure that disabled people (as defined in section 29 of the National Assistance Act 1948) who use any of the services provided under section 29 of the National Assistance Act 1948 are informed of any other service provided by the authority (whether under section 29 or otherwise) which in the opinion of the authority is relevant to their needs and of any service provided by any other authority or organisation which in the opinion of the authority is so relevant and of which particulars are in the authority's possession. (This takes account of amendments introduced by section 9 of the Disabled Persons (Services, Consultation and Representation) Act 1986).

Section 2
Where a local authority which acts under the said section 29 is satisfied that in order to meet the needs of a disabled person (as defined in section

29) resident in its area it must make arrangements for any or all of the matters set out below, then it is duty bound, under the general guidance of the Secretary of State, to do so.
1. The provision of practical assistance for that person in his home.
2. The provision for that person of, or assistance to that person in obtaining, wireless, television, library or similar recreational facilities.
3. The provision for that person of lectures, games, outings or other recreational facilities outside his home or assistance to that person in taking advantage of educational facilities available to him.
4. The provision for that person of facilities for, or assistance in, travelling to and from his home for the purpose of participating in any services provided under arrangements made by the approval of the authority, in any services provided otherwise than as aforesaid which are similar to services which could be provided under such arrangements.
5. The provision of assistance for that person in arranging for the carrying out of any works of adaptation in his home or the provision of any additional facilities designed to secure his greater safety, comfort or convenience.

NOTE: Advice on the effect of this paragraph is given in the Joint Circular *The Chronically Sick and Disabled Persons Act 1970* (DHSS Circular 12/70). Paragraph 7 of the circular reads:

The duty requires the authority to assess the requirements of individuals determined by them to be substantially and permanently handicapped as to their needs in these matters. If they are satisfied that an individual is in need in any (or all) of these matters, they are to make arrangements that are appropriate to his or her case. The task of assessment should be undertaken as a normal part of the authority's social work service, i.e. it should be an occasion for considering all relevant needs and not merely those to which the Section refers; and a judgement whether these needs or others are of prior importance should be drawn from a complete and not a partial picture of the situation.
6. Facilitating the taking of holidays by that person, whether at holiday homes or otherwise and whether provided under arrangements made by the authority or otherwise.
7. The provision of meals for that person whether in his home or elsewhere.
8. The provision for that person of, or assistance to that person in obtaining, a telephone and

any special equipment necessary to enable him to use a telephone.

Section 3

A local housing authority in discharging its duty under section 10 of the Housing Act 1985 (to consider housing conditions and the need for further housing accommodation in its district) must have regard to the special needs of chronically sick or disabled people.

Sections 4, 5, 6, 8, 8A and 8B

Require that in providing buildings open to the public, provision must be made for the needs of disabled visitors in the external and internal means of access and in any parking facilities or lavatories. Similarly, where lavatories are provided for the public by local authorities, or under local authority notice in buildings such as hotels, restaurants and theatres, account must be taken of the needs of disabled people. Comparable requirements apply to universities, colleges, schools and further education institutions and to new office, shop, railway or factory premises. All such provision is required only 'in so far as it is in the circumstances both practicable and reasonable' (*but see* Note to Section 6 of the Disabled Persons Act 1981 on page 266).

A new section 8B was added by section 7 of the Disabled Persons Act 1981, requiring the Secretary of State to report to Parliament on his proposals for ensuring the improvement of means of access to buildings and premises referred to in sections 4, 8 and 8A of the 1970 Act, to public lavatories, to lavatories in places used or to be used for entertainment, exhibitions or sporting events to which the public is admitted, to places selling food and drink for consumption on the premises and to betting offices.

Section 7 (substituted by section 5 of the Disabled Persons Act 1981)

Requires that where any provision required by or under sections 4, 5, 6, 8 or 8A of the Act is made at buildings or premises:
(a) a notice or sign indicating that provision is made for disabled people must be displayed outside; and
(b) signs must be displayed inside to show both the route to and location of such provision.
Lavatories provided elsewhere than in a building, and not in themselves buildings, must also carry a notice as at (a).
Where parking is provided for disabled people under section 4, notices or signs must be displayed

indicating an appropriate route for disabled people between the parking place and the related building or premises.

Sections 9, 10 and 12, 15 and 23

Provide for disabled persons or those experienced in working with disabled persons to serve on advisory bodies and local authority committees wherever possible.

Section 16

Requires the National Advisory Council of the Disabled Persons (Employment) Act 1944 to provide for the training of those who train or find employment for disabled people.

Sections 17 and 18

Requires the Secretary of State to use his best endeavours to secure that, as far as practicable, disabled and long-term patients under the age of 65 are not cared for in any part of the hospital which is normally used, wholly or mainly, for the elderly (65 plus) and to present an annual statement to Parliament in this regard. Local authorities are required to supply statistics about the numbers of disabled persons under 65 in old people's homes.

Section 20

Wheelchairs, etc., whether or not motorised, may be used on footpaths, bridle paths and pavements and do not have to carry lights in these circumstances.

Section 21

Covers the issue of orange badges by local authorities for motor vehicles 'driven by, or used for the carriage of, disabled persons'.

Comparative legislation was enacted by Northern Ireland on 31 July 1978 through the Chronically Sick and Disabled Persons (NI) Act 1978. This is broadly similar to the preceding legislation.

Guides

Joint Circular, *The Chronically Sick and Disabled Persons Act 1970* (DHSS Circular 12/70, MHLG Circular 65/70).
Chronically Sick and Disabled Persons Act 1970 (Disabilities Studies Unit, price 13p inc. postage and packing, available from RADAR).
Getting the best out of your Act Spastics Society and others, 1986) free (send s.a.e. to Spastics Society; Braille or tape versions from RNIB).
The Chronically Sick and Disabled Persons Act 1970 – A Guide to Affiliated Clubs and Groups (The British Association of the Hard of Hearing, 1984).

264

LOCAL AUTHORITY SOCIAL SERVICES ACT 1970 (AS AMENDED)

This Act requires every local authority to establish a social services committee to deal with (amongst other things) the following provisions.

1. Provision of residential accommodation for the aged, infirm, etc. (National Assistance Act 1948, sections 21 and 27).
2. Welfare of persons who are blind, deaf, dumb, or otherwise handicapped or are suffering from mental disorder; use of voluntary organisations for administering welfare schemes (National Assistance Act 1948, sections 29 and 30).
3. Registering charities for disabled people (for purposes of their raising funds) (National Assistance Act 1948, section 41).
4. Provision of facilities to enable disabled persons to be employed or work under special conditions (Disabled Persons (Employment) Act 1958, section 3).
5. Welfare and accommodation of 'mentally disordered persons' (Mental Health Act 1959, sections 8 and 9, and the Registered Homes Act 1984 as far as it applies to mental nursing homes).
6. Home-help and laundry facilities (National Health Service Act 1977, Schedule 8).
7. Promotion of welfare of old people (Health Services and Public Health Act 1968, section 45).
8. Financial and other assistance to voluntary organisations (Health Services and Public Health Act 1968, section 65).
9. Obtaining information as to the need for, and publishing information as to, the existence of certain welfare services (Chronically Sick and Disabled Persons Act 1970, section 1).
10. Provision of welfare services (Chronically Sick and Disabled Persons Act 1970, section 2).

LOCAL GOVERNMENT ACT 1972

Section 195 (2)
Provides for consultation by district councils in non-metropolitan counties with respect to the nature and extent of the accommodation needed for people who, because of infirmity or disability, need accommodation of a special character.

CHRONICALLY SICK AND DISABLED PERSONS (AMENDMENT) ACT 1976

Inserts a new section 8A into the Chronically Sick and Disabled Persons Act 1970 (*see* page 263).

NATIONAL HEALTH SERVICE ACT 1977

Section 5(2)(a)
Under this section, the Secretary of State *may* 'provide invalid carriages* for persons appearing to him to be suffering from severe physical defect or disability and, at the request of such a person, may provide for him a vehicle other than an invalid carriage'. By Schedule 2 of the Act, the Secretary of State also has power, in respect of any such invalid carriage or vehicle so provided or which belongs to any person such as is mentioned in section 5(2)(a), on such terms and subject to such conditions as he may determine:
(a) to adapt it so as to make it suitable for the circumstances of that person;
(b) to maintain and repair it;
(c) to insure it and pay the vehicle excise duty;
(d) to provide a structure in which it may be kept, and to provide all necessary materials and works to that purpose;
(e) make payments by way of grant towards costs incurred by any such person as is mentioned in section 5(2)(a) in respect of:
    (i) taking action under (a) to (d) above;
    (ii) the purchase of fuel for the vehicle (so far as the cost of the purchase is attributable to the excise duty thereon);
    (iii) taking instruction in driving the vehicle.

* Defined as 'a mechanically propelled vehicle specially designed and constructed (not merely adapted) for the use of a person suffering some physical defect or disability and used solely by such a person'. In practice, no vehicles are now issued to new applicants.

Section 8, paragraph 3
Lays a *duty* on local social services authorities to provide or arrange to provide 'on such a scale as is adequate for the needs of their area, home-help for households where such help is required in a variety of circumstances, including situations where help is needed because of the presence of a person who is suffering from illness, lying-in, an expectant mother, aged, or *handicapped as a result of having suffered from illness or by congenital deformity*' (our italics).

Section 21
Prescribes certain functions as exercisable by local social services authorities. These include home-help and laundry facilities.

Every such authority also has the *power* (not the duty) to provide or arrange for the provision of laundry facilities for households for which home-help is being, or can be, provided under this sub-paragraph.

DISABLED PERSONS ACT 1981

This Act amends and inserts provisions into various other Acts aimed at ensuring that better provision is made for the needs of disabled people using highways, buildings and other public places.

Section 1

Inserts a new section 175A into the Highways Act 1980 (also serves as a new section 27A to the Roads (Scotland) Act 1970). The new section requires statutory authorities responsible for highways to consider the needs of disabled or blind people when carrying out, in a street, works which may impede their mobility. Specific attention is drawn to the placing of lamp-posts, bollards, traffic signs, apparatus or other permanent obstructions, and to the proper protection of 'holes in the road', be they temporary or permanent.

Highway authorities are also directed to have regard to the needs of disabled people when considering the desirability of providing ramps at appropriate places between carriageways and footways.

Section 3

Inserts new sections 29A and 29B into the Town and Country Planning Act 1971. These concern grants of planning permission in respect of premises covered by sections 4 to 8A of the Chronically Sick and Disabled Persons Act 1970 (see page 264) and require attention to be drawn to the relevant provisions of that Act and either the British Standards Institution Code of Practice BS 5810: 1979 (Access for the Disabled to Buildings) or Design Note 18 (Access for the Physically Disabled to Educational Buildings) as appropriate.

NOTE: Design Note 18 is relevant only in England and Wales. It is of lesser scope than BS 5810:1979 and fails to meet the requirements of disabled staff or disabled visitors. In Scotland, BS 5810 applies equally to educational buildings as to other premises.

Section 4

Amends section 20 of the Local Government (Miscellaneous Provisions) Act 1976 by the insertion of three new sub-sections 11, 12 and 13, designed to ensure that when a notice is served to provide, maintain, keep clean or make available 'sanitary appliances' at a place of entertainment, attention is drawn to sections 6(1) and 7 of the Chronically Sick and Disabled Persons Act 1970 and to the British Standards Institution Code of Practice BS 5810:1979 (Access for the Disabled to Buildings).

Section 5

Substitutes a new section 7 in the Chronically Sick and Disabled Persons Act 1970 (see page 264).

Section 6 (England and Wales only)

Further amends the Chronically Sick and Disabled Persons Act 1970, sections 4(1), 5(1), 6(1), 8(1) and 8A(1), from a date to be announced. The words 'in so far as it is in the circumstances both practicable and reasonable' would be deleted in favour of a requirement of 'appropriate provision' in accordance with British Standards Institution Code of Practice BS 5810:1979 (Access for the Disabled to Buildings) or Design Note 18 (Access for the Physically Disabled to Educational Buildings), unless it can be shown to the satisfaction of a body appointed by the Secretary of State, that 'in the circumstances it is either not practicable to make such provision or not reasonable that such provision should be made'.

NOTE: The difference may appear slight, but the amendment, if brought into force, would both specify the kind of provision required and make non-provision exceptional and subject to the satisfaction of an expert body. However, at the time of writing, it is uncertain whether Section 6 will be brought into effect, given the incorporation of access provisions into the Building Regulations (see heading Access on page 243).

Section 7

Inserts a new Section 8B into the Chronically Sick and Disabled Persons Act 1970 (see page 264).

NOTE: Guidance on the implementation of the Disabled Persons Act 1981 is contained in Department of Health and Social Security Circular to local authorities, LAC (82) 5.

Comparative Northern Irish legislation is contained in the Disabled Persons (Northern Ireland) Order 1982 (SI 1982 No. 1535).

HEALTH AND SOCIAL SERVICES AND SOCIAL SECURITY ADJUDICATION ACT 1983

Section 17

Concerns charges for local authority services provided under Section 29 of the National Assistance Act 1948 (see page 262). Section 17(3) reads:

If a person:
  (a) avails himself of a service to which this section applies and,
  (b) satisfies the authority providing the service that his means are insufficient for it to be reasonably practicable for him to pay for the service which he would otherwise be obliged to pay for it, the authority shall not require him to pay more for it than it appears to them that it is reasonably practicable for him to pay.

DISABLED PERSONS (SERVICES, CONSULTATION AND REPRESENTATION) ACT 1986

NOTE: Sections 4 (except paragraph (b)), 8(1), 9 and 10 implemented 1 April 1987; Sections 5 and 6 implemented 1 February 1988; Remaining sections (at the time of writing) have not yet been implemented.

The Government has made it clear that it will not be possible to implement those provisions which carry significant resource implications until such time as the necessary resources can be made available.

In the following summary those parts of the Act not yet in force as indicated above are in italics.

Section 1
Provides for the appointment by or on behalf of disabled persons or authorised representatives for the purposes of the Act. The Secretary of State is empowered to make regulations concerning such appointments.

It seems likely that such regulations will provide for local authorities to appoint a representative if it appears to them that the disabled person, because of any mental or physical incapacity, cannot do so and, in the case of disabled children, for parents or guardians to appoint themselves or some other person, or for local authorities to make an appointment if the child is in care.

Section 2
Places a duty on a local authority, at the request of a disabled person to allow his/her authorised representative to act on his/her behalf, to accompany him/her to meetings to discuss the provision for social services and to make available to the representatives information that the disabled person is entitled to receive. But the authority need not allow attendance at meetings by, or supply information to, representatives if it is satisfied that to do so would be likely to be harmful to the interests of the disabled person, having regard to that person's wishes. Where a disabled person is residing in hospital, Part III accommodation, a residential care home, accommodation provided by a voluntary organisation in a place specified by a guardian under the Mental Health Act of 1983 (1984 in Scotland), the disabled person or authorised representative may, at any reasonable time, visit him/her there and interview him/her in private.

Section 3
Requires local authorities, when assessing a disabled person's needs for social services, to provide an opportunity for that person or his/her representative to make representation as to those needs.

They must also provide, on request, in writing, a statement of services they intend to provide (or not to provide) and the basis on which the assessment is to be made. The section also provides for further representations and for the implementation of its provisions in cases where the disabled person cannot communicate, or be communicated with, by reason of any mental or physical incapacity.

Section 4
When required by a disabled person, *an authorised representative*, or a carer (as described in section 8), a local authority is required to decide whether the needs of the disabled person concerned call for the provision of any of the welfare services under the Chronically Sick and Disabled Persons Act 1970, (*see* page 263).

Section 5 (England and Wales only)
Concerns children who have special education needs and who are the subject of a statement under section 7 of the Education Act 1981 (*see* page 248) and provides that local education authorities shall determine, upon the occasion of the first review or reassessment (whichever is the earlier) of the child's special educational needs following his/her 14th birthday, whether or not the child is a disabled person. If so, and the child is leaving special education, the local authority must carry out (unless requested not to do so by the parent or guardian – or the child if he/she has reached the age of 16) an assessment of the needs of the person in question.

Section 6
Requires local education authorities to keep under review the dates when disabled children are expected to leave full-time education and, for the purpose of section 5, to notify social services departments eight months in advance; social services departments on receiving such notification are required within five months to carry out an assessment of the young person's need for services.

Section 7
Requires health authorities to make arrangements, before discharge of people leaving hospital who have received in-patient treatment for mental disorder for a continuous period of at least six months, for an assessment of their need for services under the National Health Service Act 1977 (in Scotland, 1978), unless required by the person concerned not to do so. Local authorities are similarly required to arrange for assessment of

needs for services under any of the welfare enactments, unless requested by the person concerned not to do so.

Section 8

Requires social services departments, when assessing the needs of a disabled person who is cared for by another person (who is not an employee of the statutory services) to have regard to the carer's ability to provide that care on a regular basis. *If the carer cannot communicate or be communicated with because of a mental or physical incapacity, then the authority must provide such services as are necessary to ensure that it is properly informed as to the ability of the carer to continue to provide care.*

Section 9

Extends section 1 of the Chronically Sick and Disabled Persons Act 1970 to inform anyone receiving social services about all other services provided by the authority, and of services provided by any other authority or organisation that may be considered relevant to that person's needs.

Section 10

Provides that where under any enactment it is desired to appoint or co-opt to a council, committee, etc., a person with special knowledge of the needs of disabled people, there will be prior consultation with appropriate organisations of disabled people.

Section 11

Requires the Secretary of State to report annually to Parliament about the development in the community of health and social services for mentally ill or mentally handicapped people, on the number of people being treated for mental illness or mental handicap as in-patients in NHS hospitals, and on any other matter he/she considers appropriate.

Guides

Disabled Persons (Services, Consultation and Representation) Act 1986 – A Guide to the Act (MIND/RADAR), price 40p inc. postage and packing, available from RADAR.

Voting

REPRESENTATION OF THE PEOPLE ACT 1983

Section 19(1)(c)

Exempts from the normal rule that voting at a Parliamentary election shall be in person, those unable or likely to be unable because of blindness or any other physical incapacity either to get to the polling station, or, if able to go, to vote unaided. Section 19(4) allows any such person to vote by post if he/she applies to be treated as an absent voter and provides an address in the United Kingdom to which a ballot paper is to be sent for the purpose.

Section 19(1)(f)

Affords a similar exemption to anyone who is a voluntary patient in a mental hospital (i.e. is not liable to be detained there by law). A procedure is prescribed under rules set out in Section 7(4) for such a person to make a declaration (called 'a patient's declaration') if able to do so without assistance. Such a declaration would be made to secure registration in the Register of Electors. Any person so registered, not being a service voter or eligible to vote by proxy, can also vote by post as above.

Sections 32(1)(c) and (e) and 32(4)

These sections have parallel provisions for local elections.

Further Information

CANS, The Citizens' Advice Notes Service of the National Council for Voluntary Organisations provides details of current social and industrial legislation. Subjects covered include: education, employment, health and welfare, housing, social security and transport. The main body of information is presented in a loose-leaf binder. This is updated by three supplements in each subscription year (1 April to 31 March). Available from NCVO, 26 Bedford Square, London WC1B 3HU.

The Spastics Society, 12 Park Crescent, London, W1N 4EQ
Campaigns (Research and Resources) Department
The Spastics Society aims to ensure that local and national policy makers take full account of the needs and aspirations of people with disabilities. The department keeps a watchful eye on the process of legislation and, where necessary, presses for adequate provision for people with disabilities to be included.

Fact-sheets and briefing papers clarifying some of the more complex issues affecting disabled people are available free from the Campaigns Department upon request. These include information on government policy making, help available in the employment field, a fact sheet on VAT and a guide to benefits.

SECTION 14

CONTACT, TAPE, BRAILLE, MOON TYPE AND LARGE PRINT ORGANISATIONS

In this Section you will find information about the following.
1. Contact organisations.
2. Organisations concerned with publications on tape.
3. Organisations concerned with publications in braille and Moon type.
4. Organisations concerned with publications in large print.
5. Organisations concerned with publications on floppy disc.
6. Organisations/individuals offering recording services.
   (a) on tape.
   (b) in Braille.
7. Organisations offering other tape services.

See also Section 2, Financial Benefits and Allowances for details of postal concessions.

Our coverage is selective rather than comprehensive. For detailed information about tape publications, reading services and clubs, we recommend the *TNAUK Guide to Tape Services for the Handicapped, see* Talking Newspaper Association of the United Kingdom on page 274, and for information concerning equivalent publications, organisations and services in braille, Moon type or large print, contact the Royal National Institute for the Blind, *see* page 275.

Contact Organisations

Braille Correspondence Club
Linda Watts, Special Unit Blind, Social Services Department, Civic Centre, Newcastle upon Tyne NE1 8PA.
This club links braillists both in the United Kingdom and abroad. Anyone interested should contact the above address, giving personal details including interests and standard of Braille.

Correspondence Care and Support Group
Lisa Rowe, PO Box 81, Sunderland, Tyne and Wear SR6 9PA
The above group was formed in 1984 and now has a

membership of over 250, some of them in Australia and Canada and one in France. Ages range from 10 to 97! The group is intended to benefit those who are lonely, ill, disabled or housebound, the founder herself being disabled.

On joining, a new member is sent a list of all members' names, addresses and interests, and there is also a tape section for those who prefer to send recorded messages. Members pay a minimum of £3 a year to help with postage and printing. For further details please send a large s.a.e. to the above address.

Disabled Christians' Fellowship
50 Clare Road, Kingswood, Bristol BS15 1PJ (Tel: Bristol (0272) 616141).
The Fellowship is an evangelical and interdemoninational organisation with branches in many areas of the British Isles. Members receive a monthly magazine, *The Vital Link*, and can, if they wish, be linked with other members for correspondence. If there is a local branch in your area, you would be able to attend meetings (usually monthly) for which transport is normally provided. Many branches also have friends who can visit those who are housebound. A number of DCF holiday weeks are arranged each year, and there is a special 'Teens and Twenties' section of the Fellowship. From time to time, opportunities arise for disabled Christians to share their faith as members of a team conducting services or missions.

Friends by Post
Mrs Ilse Salomon, 6 Bollin Court, Macclesfield Road, Wilmslow, Cheshire SK9 2AP (Tel: Wilmslow (0625) 527044).
Friends by Post aims at finding letter-writing friends for those who have no one to talk to. Its leaflets explain that it links like-minded people for a regular weekly or fortnightly letter exchange. It also offers hints on how to transform a letter exchange between strangers into a written conversation between friends. There is no charge except for an s.a.e. when requesting the explanatory leaflet.

Handidate

Conrad Packwood, The Wellington Centre, 52 Chevalier Street, Ipswich, Suffolk IP1 2PB.

Handidate is a computerised penfriend and dating agency. It can match people up by area, age and hobbies. The service is open to anyone whether old, young, able-bodied or physically or mentally handicapped.

Full membership costs £25 for one year, and for that you are given four names and addresses. Your name and address will similarly be passed on to many others who may contact you. The charge for those who want a pen-friend only is £2.

Inter-Nations Friendship Circle

Mr T. L. Simmons, 30A Wellington Parade, Blackfen Road, Sidcup, Kent DA15 9NF.

A pen-friendship organisation with members all over the world. Friends of the INFC receive a list of members each year.

Penfriends World-wide

June Maughan, 60 Ellesmere Road, Benwell, Newcastle upon Tyne NE4 8TS (Tel: 091–2736732).

This correspondence club was formed in 1977 and is open to anyone. A number of members correspond by cassette tape. More visually handicapped and physically disabled people would be welcomed, and can be put in touch with a pen-friend in a similar age group or with similar interests. Your name can also be included for one free listing in the quarterly magazine, *World Messenger*. This service is free to visually handicapped and physically disabled people, but a stamp for reply would be appreciated. Mrs Maughan would like you to mention *Directory for Disabled People* when writing.

Brenda Perridge

8 Dukes Close, North Weald, Epping, Essex CM16 6DA.

Correspondence groups are arranged linking people of similar age or with interests in common, either in writing or by cassette. Please send 25p plus s.a.e. for a complete listing. A magazine, *One*, is also available at £1.80 a year (please send three large s.a.e.s).

The Postillion

Miss Lore Herold, Lowenstr.12, 2000 Hamburg 20, West Germany (Tel: (010 49 40) 46 21 84).

A worldwide contact circle for handicapped, ill or lonely people. The organisation has been active since 1975 and has contacts in Germany, Austria, Switzerland, England, America, Canada, New Zealand, Africa, Sri Lanka and Indonesia. Some of the contacts have resulted in marriage. A newsletter is published every two months, and this includes details of all new contacts. Membership is free, but applicants are asked to send an international postal reply coupon with their letter.

Surrey Tapes for the Handicapped Association

Mrs Jean Woodiwiss, 34 Tudor Close, Cheam, Surrey.

This Association circulates 60-minute cassettes among members. It could be described as a talking family circle and is intended for housebound people or those who have difficulty in communicating with others because of their isolation.

Tape Programmes for the Blind

Maurice Chambers, 'Kingsmead', Blackfirs Lane, Marston Green, Solihull, West Midlands B37 7JE (Tel: 021–779 3202).

As well as offering cassettes from a library of recorded material, Tape Programmes for the Blind links a growing circle of people who keep contact by round-robin conversation tapes. Mr Chambers is a former RAF squadron leader and is particularly interested to hear from any ex-service personnel who are visually handicapped. There is no subscription, but donations are always welcome.

Wider Horizons

Mr A. B. Fletcher, 'Westbrook', Back Lane, Malvern, Worcestershire WR14 2HJ.

In addition to publishing a magazine containing the work of members, 'Wider Horizons' aims to promote wider interests, new friendships and the exchange of information and views between members. Efforts are made to link up members by correspondence or cassette with others having similar interests, or through 'special interest' folder groups. There is an annual subscription of £3, but for those on limited incomes this is reduced to whatever can be afforded, with a minimum of £2.

World-wide Tapetalk

Charles Towers, 35 The Gardens, West Harrow, Middlesex HA1 4HE.

This organisation aims to promote, through the exchange of tape recordings (cassette or open-reel), contacts and friendships between people of all nationalities, able-bodied or disabled – no distinction is made. On joining, members receive the latest, comprehensive *Tape Station Directory*, together with a personal tape station identification card, hints on successful tape-talking, and a magazine, *Sound Advice*. Annual membership costs £5 and there is an additional enrolment fee of £1.00.

Organisations concerned with Publications on Tape

COMMERCIAL SERVICES

By far the widest range of tape cassettes is that provided commercially. Such cassettes cover varied interests and are readily available to mail order. Many public lending libraries now include tape cassettes on their shelves.

Some of the best guides to the vast amount of available material are provided by General Gramophone Publications Ltd., 177–179 Kenton Road, Harrow, Middlesex HA3 0HA (Tel: 01–907 4476), *viz*:

Gramophone, a monthly magazine founded in 1923, price £1.10;
Gramophone Classical Catalogue, quarterly £2.50 (£3.15 by post);
Gramophone Popular Catalogue, quarterly £3 (£3.55 by post);
Gramophone Spoken Word Catalogue, annual £2.75 (£3.06 by post);
Gramophone Recommended Recordings, £1.50 (£1.77 by post).

The following firms offer mail order services.

Chivers Press Publishers
93–100 Locksbrook Road, Bath, Avon BA1 3HB (Tel: Bath (0225) 335336).
Chivers pioneered complete and unabridged books on tape. A complete reference catalogue of spoken-word audio cassettes contains over 6,000 titles, covering a wide range of interests for all ages. As well as fiction, poetry, prose and plays (particularly strong on Shakespeare), there is an extensive choice of non-fiction titles: including biographies, great events, great composers, philosophy, religion, education, vocational training and health. There are readings in six foreign languages: French, German, Greek, Latin, Russian and Spanish, courses in forty languages from Africaans to Welsh, plus English as a foreign language, and a series of sound recordings of nature, wildlife, steam and diesel locomotives, and of BBC sound effects. Prices (excluding VAT) range from as little as £1.05 (in the children's section) to £439 (a complete, cased, de-luxe dramatised Bible on 80 cassettes). Chivers own audio books are recorded in combinations of four, six or eight C60/90 cassettes costing £18.95, £22.95, and £27.50 (all excluding VAT) respectively. The children's section offers un-abridged contemporary stories for youngsters on two or three cassettes (£8.65 to £11.25 plus VAT).

Cover to Cover Cassettes Ltd
Dene House, Lockeridge, Marlborough, Wiltshire SN8 4EQ (Tel: Marlborough (0672) 86495). A good range of 'classics' and children's books. Example price (including VAT) *Far From the Madding Crowd*, 11 cassettes, £28.

Eloquent Reels
Alhampton, Castle Cary, Somerset BA4 6PZ (Tel: Ditcheat (074 986) 593).
'Classics' of literature, each book adapted to six hour length on four cassettes complete in a good-looking binder. Price (including VAT) £12.95.

ISIS Audio Books
55 St Thomas' Street, Oxford OX1 1JG (Tel: Oxford (0865) 250333).
Thirty-six books are published each year on cassette. All are complete and unabridged, and often read by the authors themselves. Each month's output consists of one non-fiction, one fiction and one Barbara Cartland romance. The editorial direction of the audio books reflects that of the ISIS large print list (*see* page 276). Prices (excluding VAT) £18.95 (4 cassettes) to £27.50 (8 cassettes).

Soundings Ltd
Essell House, 48 Roxburgh Terrace, Whitley Bay, Tyne and Wear NE26 1DS (Tel: 091–253 4155).
Romance, general fiction, Western, mystery, non-fiction titles. Prices (excluding VAT) from £8.50 (2 cassettes) to £26.99 (8 cassettes). Five new titles each month.

TalkTapes
13 Croftdown Road, London NW5 1EL (Tel: 01–485 9981).
A very wide range of educational, spoken word and entertainment recordings on standard compact cassettes (and music on cassette, LP and compact disc).
The general catalogue covers poetry, drama, fiction, critical studies, English and foreign languages, religion, science, business studies, radio comedy etc. from leading audio publishers. Many additional special lists provide more detailed subject listings.

All items are for sale by mail order only and on cash with order terms (no loan service). Please send two 13p stamps for catalogue and full details of service. Special terms to organisations.

Visionaid Systems
The Old School, The Green, Ruddington, Nottinghamshire NG11 6HH (Tel: Nottingham (0602) 847879).
A large range of books: general fiction, humour, autobiography, adventure, mystery, romance, science fiction, horror, Western; also some plays, poetry, short stories and children's titles. Prices (excluding VAT) from £3.99 (1 cassette children's story) to £27.50 (8 cassettes).

VOLUNTARY SERVICES

Taped Books

British Library of Tape Recordings for Hospital Patients
12 Lant Street, London SE1 1QH (Tel: 01–407 9417).
Operates a scheme to provide taped books for patients in hospitals.

Calibre
Aylesbury, Buckinghamshire HP22 5AN (Tel: Aylesbury (0296) 432339 and 81211).
Calibre is a lending library of books on standard compact cassettes for anyone who cannot read printed books either through poor sight or through difficulty in handling or reading. Calibre has around 3,000 recorded titles read by professionals, including 500 children's books. All books are unabridged and cover the full range of fiction and non-fiction.

Members use their own cassette recorders, and receive book cassettes by post. There is also a free quarterly cassette magazine, with Calibre news, book reviews and articles of general interest. Through the magazine, members can contact each other, make friends and form clubs. No subscription is charged for ordinary membership (though donations are always needed). Applications should be accompanied with a doctor's certificate confirming that you are unable to read printed books in the ordinary way.

National Library for the Handicapped Child
University of London Institute of Education, 20 Bedford Way, London WC1H 0AL (Tel: 01–636 1500, ext. 599; after hours 01–255 1363).
For details of this library, *see* Section 15, Helpful Organisations. The stock includes books on tape, video, filmstrip and slides.

National Listening Library (Talking Books for the Handicapped)
12 Lant Street, London SE1 1QR (Tel: 01–407 9417).
This charity provides a postal library of books recorded on long-playing cassettes for handicapped people who are unable to read a book for reasons other than blindness.

There is a long list of books covering a wide range of interests, including books for children. Members are asked to contribute £15 a year towards the costs of the service.

RNIB Student Tape Library
See Section 6, Further Education.

RNIB Talking Book Service
Mount Pleasant, Wembley, Middlesex HA0 1RR (Tel: 01–903 6666).
Has over six thousand titles for leisure reading recorded on special six-track cassettes. RNIB's Technical and Consumer Services Division, of which the Talking Book Service is part, records over 2,000 new items a year.

Membership is open to anyone who is registered as blind with their local authority or to any other visually handicapped person who can provide a certificate from a consultant ophthalmologist, ophthalmic optician or family doctor that the applicant has defective reading vision (N12 or worse with spectacles). There is an annual subscription (including hire of playback machine) which is often paid by local social services departments or societies for blind people.

Taped Magazines, Newspapers and other material

Alternative Talking Newspapers Collective
c/o Neil Harvey, Flat 7, 19 Lee Terrace, Blackheath, London SE3 9TF (Tel: 01–318 2002).
The collective was formed by a group of blind and partially sighted people to campaign about the lack of left wing and feminist material available to them. They have done the positive (and important) thing of making a broad range of alternative material available. This includes a tape magazine, *Left Out*, a digest of the left presses, a lot of gay material, dissident poetry, and the Manifesto of the Green Party.

Birmingham Tapes for the Handicapped Association
Derek L. Hunt, 20 Middleton Hall Road, Kings Norton, Birmingham B30 1BY (Tel: 021–459 4874).
The Association sends out a regular monthly magazine on tape cassette all over the British Isles and overseas on a round-robin basis. Its contents include stories, poems, news, interviews and music. There is a 50p registration fee on joining, plus a membership fee of £1 payable annually. A free tape library service is now available to members.

The Blind Centre for Northern Ireland
70 North Road, Belfast BT5 5NJ (Tel: Belfast (0232) 654366).
The Blind Centre provides information through its

tape magazines on free C90 cassettes. *Soundvision Ulster* is distributed throughout the Province, in Eire and to others now living in Great Britain. The magazine is sent monthly to over 900 recipients, and deals with sport, cooking, drama, yoga and an Ulster news round-up. This service has now been in existence for ten years.

Disability Now
This is the excellent newspaper published by The Spastics Society (*see* page 330) that is available on tape and, at the time of writing, free. Contact Gayle Mooney on 01–636 5020, ext 244.

Global Radio
48 Mayfair Avenue, Loose, Maidstone, Kent (Tel: Maidstone (0622) 53122).
This organisation produces two sound magazines: *Fanfaire*, of general interest, and *Pure Hi Fi*, about equipment, compact discs and records. Blank professional cassette tapes and Ampex open-reel recording tape are available at discounted prices. Membership subscription for blind or disabled people £2 a year.

In Touch Bulletin
BBC, Broadcasting House, London W1A 1AA.
The BBC's *In Touch* quarterly bulletin is available to blind or partially sighted people or to anyone concerned either professionally or voluntarily with their welfare. It is, of course, a mine of information on all matters of interest to visually handicapped people. It is available on tape for £1 a year from Tape Recording Services for the Blind, 48 Fairfax Road, Farnborough, Hampshire GU14 8JP (alternatively, print and Braille versions are free – *see* Appendix A and page 275 respectively).

The Multiple Sclerosis Society of Great Britain and Northern Ireland
25 Effie Road, Fulham, London SW6 1EE (Tel: 01–736 6267).
The Society's quarterly journal, *MS News* and monthly information bulletin, *MSS Bulletin* (summarised over a three month period) are both available in tape cassette versions. *MS News* is available in this format to all members who have difficulty in reading, through vision impairment or other physical disabilities. The tape version of *MSS Bulletin* is available for the same subscription as the printed version.

Muriel Braddick Foundation (incorporating Tapes for the Handicapped Association).
14 Teign Street, Teignmouth, South Devon (Tel: Teignmouth (062 67) 6214).

The Foundation seeks to enrich the lives of housebound and isolated handicapped people by providing specially prepared cassette tapes directed to the specific tastes and interests of the recipient. For those who do not possess cassette recorders, and who are unable to provide them for themselves or with the assistance of social services departments, the Foundation provides easily handled machines on a free loan basis. These may be either battery or mains operated.
The organisation has a number of county branches and publishes a magazine, *Focus* (20p per copy plus postage and packing). The normal membership fee is not less that £2 per annum (which includes *Focus*), but no charge is made to disabled people.

National Music for the Blind
Radio Churchtown
Radio Camelot
The Guiding Star
2 High Park Road, Southport PR9 7QL (Southport (0704) 28010).
These services, operating from the same address, provide respectively:
(a) tapes of music, plays, stories and documentaries;
(b) tape programmes of nostalgic content;
(c) tape programmes of outdoor interviews; and
(d) extracts from national newspapers on tape, with record requests.

National Tape Magazine for the Blind
Lilac Cottage, Moorhouses, New Bolingbroke, near Boston, Lincolnshire PE22 7JL (Tel: Coningsby (0526) 42918).
NTM was formed in 1976 in an effort to keep visually handicapped people in touch with developments in services, aids, etc. A tape magazine is sent out at monthly intervals (except August) and this is supplemented by a weekly library service of features which are too long for the magazine tape. The editor, W. F. Cox, is himself blind. Subscription: magazine, £2.50 per annum; library service, £3 per annum.

Sequal News
Mark Hansford, 19 Shalford Road, Billericay, Essex CM11 2EG.
A taped version of the quarterly magazine of Sequal (*see* page 328) is available from this address.

Soundaround
74 Glentham Road, Barnes, London SW13 9JJ (Tel: 01–741 3332).
Launched in 1975, *Soundaround* is a national news

magazine for visually handicapped people, produced monthly on compact cassette. It now reaches up to 35,000 listeners throughout the world. The editor, Nigel Verbeek, is himself blind. He brings together a fascinating combination of news, views, letters, hobbies, pen-pals, features and celebrity spots. Above all, the magazine is in tune with its listeners and the issues which affect them. *Soundaround* is available free to visually handicapped people.

The Talking Newspaper Association of the UK
90 High Street, Heathfield, East Sussex TN21 8JD (Tel: Heathfield (043 52) 6102).

The Association has voluntary groups in over 500 areas in the United Kingdom which produce tape versions of local newspapers for distribution to visually and physically handicapped people in their areas. The Association itself produces tape versions of over 100 national newspapers and magazines, each of which is available against an annual subscription of £7. TNAUK will send details of your nearest Talking Newspaper and a list of national papers and magazines on tape.

The Association publishes the *TNAUK Guide to Tape Services for the Handicapped*, which is widely acclaimed as an invaluable work of reference. Costing £3.50 including postage and packing, the Guide has:

listings of local and national newspapers and magazines on tape;
health information tapes;
educational and professional information on tape;
tape libraries;
reading services;
sources of religious material on tape;
special interest tape sources;
tape magazines and clubs; and
indexes of material on tape (by title, subject and county).

Tape Recording Service for the Blind
48 Fairfax Road, Farnborough, Hampshire GU14 8JP (Tel: Farnborough (0252) 547943).

This Service (*see* page 277) keeps certain material in readiness for copying or supply. This includes holiday phrase language courses in foreign languages (French, German, Italian and Spanish), touch-typing, and Braille; three magazines, *viz: New Beacon*, the monthly journal of the RNIB, *In Touch*, the quarterly bulletin of the BBC, and *En Passant*, a monthly magazine for blind chess enthusiasts; a catalogue of books issued by the British Talking Book Service; and a wide selection of Marks and Spencer cookery books. Send an s.a.e. for further details.

Religious Subjects on Tape

Bible Society
Publishing Division, Stonehill Green, Westlea, Swindon SN5 7DG (Tel: Swindon (0793) 617381).

The Society produces the *New Testament and Psalms (Good News Bible)* on 23 cassettes, sold individually or as a complete set in a presentation case. Also available is the *Authorised Version of the Holy Bible* in 15 volumes each containing four cassettes. Prices available on application to the Customer Services Department. A 50 per cent discount is available to registered visually handicapped people.

One
8 Dukes Close, North Weald, Epping, Essex CM16 6DA.

A four-monthly Christian magazine with articles, book reviews, tape and pen friends, tape library etc. Price £1.80 plus three large stamped addressed envelopes per year.

Torch Trust for the Blind
Torch House, Hallaton, Market Harborough, Leicestershire LE16 8UJ (Tel: Hallaton (085 889) 301).

The Trust provides Christian literature in various forms, including compact cassettes. Lending library facilities and a range of magazines are free to registered blind or partially sighted people, but there is a nominal charge for some of the literature. *See also* Section 15, Helpful Organisations.

World-wide Evangelical Tape Fellowship
Mr and Mrs Thomas, 'Kuriakos', 21 Herbrand Road, Bedford MK42 0SD.

The Fellowship has an extensive library of tape cassettes relating to the Christian religion, including Bible studies, church services, music and books. These tapes are available to members on free loan. Further tapes are circulated at regular intervals throughout the year, and members are encouraged to correspond, by tape or letter, on a personal basis.

Membership is restricted to people who are 'sincere believers in the Christian faith' who must adhere to an 11-point fundamentalist 'Declaration of Faith' prescribed by the Fellowship. There is no subscription charge.

Organisations Concerned with Publications in Braille or Moon Type

Although Braille and Moon type have both been around for many years (Moon since 1847, and Braille even longer), it is, of course, Braille which has come to be accepted most widely. Nevertheless, Moon does survive; it is relatively easy to learn, and with the introduction of the Moon-writer, it has found new popularity.

BOOKS IN BRAILLE AND MOON TYPE

National Library for the Blind
Cromwell Road, Bredbury, Stockport SK6 2SG (Tel: 061–494 0217).

The Library, founded in 1882, provides reading of all kinds free of charge in Braille (including music), Moon and large print. Braille and Moon are lent post free to individual readers; large print through public libraries.

In 1986/7 it served some 5,000 readers and issued 205,663 volumes of embossed books, from a stock of about a third of a million volumes. About 800 of these readers are outside the United Kingdom.

RNIB Technical and Consumer Services Division
Braille House, 338–346 Goswell Road, London EC1V 7JE (Tel: 01–837 9921).
Among other services, this RNIB Division has a Braille lending library. Though much smaller than the National Library for the Blind, it is particularly valuable to those who need material for school or college. It has 7,000 titles in Braille, and recorded 5,000 issues in 1986/7. New material can be commissioned on behalf of a customer.

Scottish Braille Press
Craigmillar Park, Edinburgh EH16 5NB (Tel: 031–662 4445).
SBP has a catalogue of Braille books with over 200 titles. The range in each section is inevitably limited, but includes education, fiction (adult and juvenile), foreign languages, gardening, general interest, homecrafts, health, music and musical literature, poetry and religion. Prices range from £1.80 to £5.50 per volume, but there are some concessions, including a discount of 90 (yes, 90!) per cent to individual blind people ordinarily resident in Great Britain and Northern Ireland.

In addition to these main services, in some areas there are small libraries run by local societies for blind people, mostly, however, lending books provided by the National Library. It is also possible to purchase Braille books from the NLB, as well as from the RNIB at 224 Great Portland Street, London W1N 6AA and the Scottish Braille Press, Craigmillar Park, Edinburgh EH16 5NB.

MAGAZINES AND NEWSPAPERS IN BRAILLE AND MOON TYPE

In Touch Bulletin
BBC, Broadcasting House, London W1A 1AA.
The BBC's *In Touch* quarterly bulletin is available to blind or partially sighted people or to anyone concerned either professionally or voluntarily with the welfare of visually handicapped people. It is, of course, a mine of information on all matters of interest to visually handicapped people. It is available in Braille free of charge from Scottish Braille Press, Craigmillar Park, Edinburgh EH16 5NB. Enquiries about the Moon version should be made to the Moon Branch of the RNIB, Holmesdale Road, Reigate, Surrey RH2 0BA. (Alternatively, there are print and taped versions – *see* Appendix A and page 273 respectively.)

RNIB Technical and Consumer Services
Braille House, 338–346 Goswell Road, London EC1V 7JE (Tel: 01–837 9921).
Among other services, RNIB makes available a large number of magazines in Braille. Subjects include: news and current affairs, radio and television, home and family, teenagers' and children's interests, law and professional matters, religion, recreation, and blind welfare.

Scottish Braille Press
Craigmillar Park, Edinburgh EH16 5NB (Tel: 031–662 4445).
As well as printing magazines in Braille for over 20 organisations, SBP publishes three weekly and three monthly magazines which are available on annual subscription (not subject to discount).

RELIGIOUS SUBJECTS IN BRAILLE AND MOON TYPE

Bible Society
Publishing Division, Stonehill Green, Westlea, Swindon, SN5 7DG (Tel: Swindon (0793) 617381).
The Society offers the scriptures in Braille (*Good News Bible* and *Authorised Version*). For details and prices, contact Customer Services Department at the above address and ask for *Catalogue of Scriptures for the Visually Handicapped*.

Torch Trust for the Blind
Torch House, Hallaton, Market Harborough, Leicestershire LE16 8UJ (Tel: Hallaton (085 889) 301).
The Trust provides Christian literature in various forms, including Braille and Moon type. Lending

library facilities and a range of magazines are free to registered blind or partially sighted people, but there is a nominal charge for some of the literature. *See also* Section 15, Helpful Organisations.

Publications in Large Print

COMMERCIAL BOOKS

W.H.Allen (Publishers)
44 Hill Street, London W1X 8LB (Tel: 01–493 6777).
Crescent series: fiction, non-fiction, biography, romance, thrillers. Prices £7.95 to £10.95.

Chivers Press Publishers
93–100 Locksbrook Road, Bath, Avon BA1 3HB (Tel: Bath (0225) 335336).
 Chivers carries a large stock of large print books with regular additions. The range is wide, but with the emphasis on fiction. The Windsor selection features best-selling novels by John le Carre, Jeffrey Archer, Danielle Steel and Robert Ludlum; New Portway concentrates on quality fiction and country books; Atlantic has romances, westerns and mysteries from England and America; and Lythway publishes a wide range of popular fiction and non-fiction. Prices range from £7.25 to £10.95. Some Atlantic titles are available in softcover at £4.95. Chivers also carry American imports from G. K. Hall and John Curley Associates. They also have an extensive children's large print section in the Lythway range. Designed for the partially-sighted child and the reluctant reader, the books are attractively produced, often using the original cover artwork and inside illustrations. They range in price from £6.95 to £7.95.

Clio Press Ltd
55 St Thomas' Street, Oxford OX1 1JG (Tel: Oxford (0865) 250333).
ISIS series: predominantly non-fiction (autobiographies, biographies, travelogues, self-help books, poetry, hymns and drama). Fiction titles are 'classics' and contemporary. 60 new titles are produced annually. In addition, 20 US titles (*Landmark*) are published by ISIS. A special feature of the ISIS list is the availability of reference books: a dictionary, thesaurus, atlas, medical dictionary, retirement guides and teach-yourself-chess. Prices from £3.25 to £24.95 (a world atlas).
 Under Clio's *Windrush* imprint, a series of children's books is published with 24 new titles annually. In addition, 24 US titles (*Cornerstone*) are published by *Windrush*. Prices from £6.95 to £40 (*The Nardia Chronicles* in seven volumes).

Ulverscroft Large Print Books Ltd
The Green, Bradgate Road, Anstey, Leicester LE7 7FU (Tel: Leicester (0533) 364325).
Ulverscroft pioneered large print nearly 25 years ago. The 1988 catalogue contains titles published in the Ulverscroft, Charnwood, and Linford (softcover) series, offering a wide range of reading, which is always being enlarged. The emphasis is on fiction, including adventure and suspense, mystery, romance and Westerns, as well as a range of 'classics'. Non-fiction titles include *The Little Oxford Dictionary*, a cookery book and stories of personal experiences (we noticed, in particular, Norman Croucher's *High Hopes*). Finally, there is a 'religious and inspirational' section. Prices ordinarily range from £4.50 to £9.95, with exceptions such as the dictionary (£14.95) and *War and Peace* (£25, 5 volumes).

VOLUNTARY

National Library for the Blind
Cromwell Road, Bredbury, Stockport SK6 2SG (Tel: 061–494 0217).
 The Library, founded in 1882, provides reading of all kinds free of charge in Braille (including music), Moon and large print. Large print (Austin books) are made available through public libraries. The series, launched in 1966, has concentrated on less-popular titles which might not otherwise have appeared in large print.

National Library for the Handicapped Child
University of London Institute of Education, 20 Bedford Way, London WC1H 0AL (Tel: 01–636 1500, ext.599; after hours 01–255 1363).
For details of this library, *see* Section 15, Helpful Organisations. The stock includes large print books.
 In addition to these specific sources, commercially produced large print books are, of course, widely available in public and hospital libraries.

MAGAZINE IN LARGE PRINT

Partially Sighted Society
206 Great Portland Street, London W1N 6AA (Tel: 01–387 8840).
The Society's magazine, *Oculus*, is sent out bi-monthly to members, in large print, and contains items of interest to people with visual impairment. The magazine can be supplied to non-members for £3 per annum.

RELIGIOUS SUBJECTS IN LARGE PRINT

Bible Society
Stonehill Green, Westlea, Swindon SN5 7DG
(Tel: Swindon (0793) 617381).
The Society offers 25 per cent discount on large
print Bibles for those who are registered as visually
handicapped.

Torch Trust for the Blind
Torch House, Hallaton, Market Harborough,
Leicestershire LE16 8UJ (Tel: Hallaton (085 889)
301).
The Trust provides Christian literature in various
forms, including large print. Lending library facilities and a range of magazines are free to registered
blind or partially sighted people, but there is a
nominal charge for some of the literature. *See also*
Section 15, Helpful Organisations.

Organisations Concerned with Publications on Floppy Discs

COMMERCIAL

Information Education Ltd
Unit 33, Enterprise Centre, Bedford Street,
Stoke-on-Trent ST1 4PZ (Tel: Stoke-on-Trent
(0782) 281643).
This company publishes a range of 'Viewbooks' on
discs for users of microcomputers. The standard
Viewbooks are aimed at the 16–19 age range for
study purposes for GCSE, 'A' level and first year
degree courses, but the latest publications include
a story for children aged 7 to 11 which, it is hoped,
will be the first of many such discs. Also of
particular interest is the *Viewbook Dictionary* –
the latest edition of the *Oxford Children's Dictionary* – and, for people who wish to keep work on
disc in an organised way, the *Viewbook Author*
which contains the shell programme on which all
Viewbooks are based. This is a content-free disc
that allows the user to keep work within the
Viewbook format, so that it can be arranged
and accessed rapidly in the same way as
Viewbooks.

We found the Viewbook remarkably easy to
use. Simple alternative 'next-move' instructions
appear beneath the text and this allows users – who
need have had no previous experience of computers – to move quickly to any page. Books are
laid out in the normal format, with numbered
pages, contents, indexing and cross references.

Two of the benefits of the Viewbooks are that
they can readily be used by physically handicapped
people who might have difficulty in handling a

conventional book, and that access at any desired
point is much quicker and more flexible than is the
case with a tape recording. If necessary, control of
the keyboard can be facilitated through a dual
switching system or a Perkins brailler. For visually
handicapped users, output is possible through
enlarged type on the screen or enlarged print on an
attached printer. Users with no sight can access the
text by using a speech synthesiser, and print it out
in Grade 2 Braille using a translator and embosser.
The publishers say that they are negotiating with
several publishers to produce Viewbook editions
of many existing books for use by physically or
visually handicapped readers.

All standard Viewbooks are £17 plus VAT. This
price includes a licence for the authorised user to
make up to 20 copies to be used on the same
premises. The *Viewbook Dictionary* costs £35 plus
VAT and also comes with the licence. The *Viewbook Author* costs between £49 and £99 plus VAT,
depending on the microcomputer concerned.
Special software facilities for disabled people are,
of course, at extra cost.

The number of discs per Viewbook depends on
the hardware used. Further details from the above
address.

Organisations/Individuals offering Recording Services

TAPE SERVICES

We give below details of some of the main services.
A fuller listing can be found in the *TNAUK Guide
to Tape Services for the Handicapped* (Talking
Newspaper Association UK, 90 High Street,
Heathfield, East Sussex TN21 8JD), price £3.50,
which is available in large or standard print.

ADA Reading Services
6 Dalewood Rise, Laverstock, Salisbury, Wiltshire SP1 1SF (Tel: Salisbury (0722) 26987).
A family service which will always do its best to
help visually handicapped people. Requests
should be accompanied by sufficient tape cassettes
and a self-addressed label for return.

Confederation of Tape Information Services
c/o The RNIB Tape Service, Project Office, 79
High Street, Tarporley, Cheshire CW6 0AB (Tel:
Tarporley (082 93) 2115).
The umbrella body for 23 organisations and
individuals who are actively providing tape recording services. It has started a newsletter, *On Track*,
in tape, Braille and large print versions, which it is
hoped to publish quarterly. This has information

on equipment and organisations and is free to members. The Confederation has also published *A Guide for Readers*, a basic guide for people who are setting up a tape recording service.

Membership subscription: organisations £12; individuals £2.

RNIB Technical and Consumer Services Division
Braille House, 338–346 Goswell Road, London EC1V 7JE (Tel: 01–837 9921).
As well as pre-recorded material, a recording service offers a fast response, including almost any academic subject at any level. If you want to use the RNIB's extensive tape services, or information about them, the Customer Services team can help. They can also tell you where and how to get other tape services in the United Kingdom.

Tape Recording Service for the Blind
48 Fairfax Road, Farnborough, Hampshire GU14 8JP (Tel: Farnborough (0252) 547943).
The Service will record for visually handicapped people any printed material other than party political or religious work (except by special arrangement). Fiction will be accepted only if it is required for personal study or is not available in current libraries. As well as conventional cassettes, there are limited facilities for APH four track work (please phone in advance). All requests should be accompanied by a self-addressed envelope for return and, if possible, sufficient tape cassettes. Personal or confidential papers are given special attention. Except for the cost of supplying cassettes when requested, the service is free, though voluntary donations are welcome.

Certain material is kept in readiness for copying or supply (*see* page 274).

BRAILLE SERVICES

RNIB Technical and Consumer Services Division
Braille House, 338–346 Goswell Road, London EC1V 7JE (Tel: 01–837 9921).
Has facilities to provide a huge range of Braille items. As well as a library, a specialist transcription service is able to handle almost anything, from academic work to individual bank statements. In addition, RNIB is always looking for better ways to help teach people to read Braille. If you want any Braille services or information about them,

the Customer Services team can help. They can also tell you where and how to get other Braille services in the United Kingdom.

LARGE PRINT SERVICES

The Partially Sighted Society
206 Great Portland Street, London W1N 6AA (Tel: 01–387 8840) operates a large print printing service in Doncaster and will quote for any item which anybody wants printing. There is also an enlarging service at Doncaster which, subject to copyright agreement, can undertake the enlargement of such things as newspaper and journal articles, knitting patterns and examination papers. Single copy work is made using special process camera equipment and, provided the print definition of the original is good, the enlarged copy is often better. Enhanced contrast is obtained from the intense white background of the enlargement. Prices on request. For either service apply to Queen's Road, Doncaster, South Yorks DN1 2NX.

OTHER TAPE SERVICES

Hagger Electronics
Spirella Building, Bridge Road, Letchworth, Hertfordshire SG6 4ET (Tel: Letchworth (0462) 677331).
Successors to the Audio Reading Trust in supplying and servicing the American Printing House variable speed, four-track recorder, which has tone indexing and allows for eight hours recording on a C105 cassette. It also accepts standard cassettes and those recorded in the US Library of Congress format, essential for students wishing to join *Recording for the Blind Inc.*, 215 East 58th Street, New York, NY 10022, USA.

This cassette recorder also enables visually handicapped school children to assimilate information more rapidly and improves retention of the material. The multi-track facility allows for questions recorded by a teacher to be answered by a pupil without any danger of obliterating the original recording.

Hagger Electronics also supply good quality cassettes with tactile markings to indicate tape length and side. Please send s.a.e. for price list and further details.

HELPFUL ORGANISATIONS

Organisations of or for disabled people are numerous and various in character; some are concerned with a single disability, while others provide services over a wide range; some exist for a single purpose while others are multi-functional. They do not always fall easily into specific categories and the arrangement which we have adopted for this section is a simple alphabetical listing by name. If, however, you do not know in advance the name of the organisation which may be able to help you, you will find, as part of the alphabetical list, functional headings with a listing of the relevant organisations. A simple example is 'Autism: *See* National Autistic Society'. If there is no listing for an unusual disease which concerns you, see the heading *Rare Diseases*.

It is impossible in a Directory such as this to give detailed information in relation to specific disabilities without running into several volumes.

But relevant organisations can usually offer this kind of expertise, as well as helpful advice, counselling or support. We would urge readers not to try to struggle alone; there is help, but only you can make your needs known, and that is part of the way towards finding a solution.

Access Committees for England, Northern Ireland, Scotland, and Wales
See Section 16

Action Against Allergy (AAA)
43 The Downs, London SW20 8HG (Tel: 01–947 5082)
An association to study the role of modern foods, chemicals and biological materials in the causation of the allergic illnesses increasingly affecting people in the western world. Send s.a.e. for further information, recommended reading and general help.

Action for Dysphasic Adults
Northcote House, 37a Royal Street, London SE1 7LL (Tel: 01–261 9572).
Dysphasia is a communication handicap resulting from the loss or impairment of speech and language after stroke or head injury.

The charity provides information and advice to people with dysphasia and their carers, and aims to create greater awareness among professional groups and the general public of the nature of dysphasia and the needs of dysphasic adults. A further objective is to facilitate and extend long-term and, where possible, intensive rehabilitation in association with speech therapy services.

Publications and materials available from ADA include free booklets written for the families and carers of people with dysphasia, identity cards for those with speech and language impairment, educational videos for sale or hire, posters and books.

Action Research for the Crippled Child
Vincent House, North Parade, Horsham, West Sussex RH12 2DA (Tel: Horsham (0403) 210406). Promotes and supports medical research into all aspects of crippling diseases regardless of cause. Current emphasis is on prevention, especially in the child, but ways of alleviating the effects of an existing handicap in all age groups are included.

A magazine, *Action Research*, produced three times a year for a non-medical readership, describes the latest developments in medical research projects which the charity supports.

The charity also administers the Snowdon Award Scheme, which provides grants to help disabled young people in higher education.

Action for the Victims of Medical Accidents (AVMA)
24 Southwark Street, London SE1 1TY (Tel: 01–403 4744).
A charity which helps those who believe they may have suffered a medical accident to assess what has happened to them. If negligence is a possibility, it will put victims in touch with solicitors, and solicitors with medical experts.

As well as assisting with personal cases, AVMA

is addressing the whole problem of medical accidents and is working to change the attitude of health carers towards victims and to change the system for compensating victims and ensuring the accountability of health carers.

In the meantime, although there is no wish to promote unnecessary legislation, AVMA seeks to make it easier for ordinary people to pursue necessary litigation to which they have a right.

AVMA does not have a membership, but publishes newsletters and other information. Any person or organisation making a donation will be placed on the mailing list.

Ad Lib
7 Comber House, Comber Grove, Camberwell, London SE5 (Tel: 01–703 0717).
Ad Lib works throughout the country to create a greater awareness of disability within the community, and is directed towards both able-bodied and disabled people. The aims of the project are three-fold.
1. To improve general public awareness of the needs and abilities of disabled people,
2. To improve support amongst people with disabilities.
3. To improve the level of provision for people with disabilities.
Ad Lib offers practical research services, participative workshops, advice and consultancy, and help in setting up support networks for people with disabilities to share experiences and gain mutual support. The training on offer is tailored to suit the needs of individuals and groups. It is of general relevance and of particular interest to anyone who has an involvement in disability, whether a disabled person, friend, carer, volunteer or professional worker. 'Closed' self-advocacy sessions may be held specifically to help disabled people to recognise and explore in a supportive environment the issues which affect them. 'Open' disability awareness training gives participants the opportunity to challenge many of the myths surrounding disability and to make positive, practical changes to their work. Training courses may be residential or non-residential, in blocks according to the needs of the participants.

Consultancy or research projects may be commissioned by voluntary or statutory groups. This may involve investigating the specific concerns of an organisation (e.g. examining its employment practices), or may be wider-scale (e.g. examining the delivery of a community service to people with disabilities), or it may involve producing an activity/resource pack for a group (e.g. increasing access to the group's activities).

Advisory services
Most organisations within this section offer advisory services related to their own activities, but for general advisory services, *see* Citizens' Advice Bureau Service and DIAL UK.

Advocacy
See National Citizen Advocacy.

Age Concern England (National Old People's Welfare Council)
Bernard Sunley House, 60 Pitcairn Road, Mitcham, Surrey CR4 3LL (Tel: 01– 640 5431).
A national organisation established to promote the welfare of old people. Over 1,300 independent local groups provide a wide range of services. The Age Concern movement also campaigns on issues of concern to elderly people. Age Concern England provides central co-ordination and information services. The wide variety of publications includes *Your Rights*.

Age Concern Scotland
33 Castle Street, Edinburgh EH2 3DN (Tel: 031 225 5000).
Age Concern Scotland aims to improve services for older people and campaign on their behalf. A network of over 200 local groups provide practical services and friendships for older people in Scotland. Age Concern Scotland co-ordinates these groups and brings together in membership many national organisations as well as individuals. Recent publications include *Residential Care: Is It For Me?* There is a bi-monthly newsletter, *Adage*.

Albino Fellowship
16 Ronaldshaw Park, Ayr KA7 2TJ (Tel: Ayr (0292) 262584).
The characteristic colouring of albinos – white or very fair hair and pink and white skin – is caused by pigment deficiency. Albinos are particularly sensitive to light and are likely to have low visual acuity and other eye problems. It is a comparatively rare condition affecting roughly one in 20,000 of the population.

Founded in 1976, the Albino Fellowship offers support and information to albinos directly and works to dispel the widespread ignorance concerning the condition and its effects.

An important feature of the Fellowship, particularly for parents of a recently-born albino baby, is the introduction to other parents (or an older albino) living in the same area, who has already experienced the problems and can relieve natural fears and can advise on subjects such as exposure to light, clothing, sun-glasses and spectacles. Authoritative advice is also available to members meeting with obstruction or other difficulties at school or in employment. Information on these and other matters is disseminated through the *Newsletter* and at the annual meeting, as well as occasional open meetings.

Allergy
See Action Against Allergy

The Alternative Centre
College House, Wrights Lane, Kensington, London W8 5SH (Tel: Psoriasis helpline 01–351 2726; Eczema helpline 01–938 2645).
This Centre offers practical advice and emotional support to those looking for help in coping with the problems of psoriasis and eczema present in their daily lives. A self-help guide, *Living with Psoriasis*, by Sandra Gibbons, is available, price £5.95 including postage and packing.

Alzheimer's Disease Society
Bank Buildings, Fulham Broadway, London SW6 1EP (Tel: 01–381 3177).
Alzheimer's disease is a condition which causes intellectual disturbance by damaging some of the cells in the brain. The cause is unknown, and the treatment is, at present, limited to amelioration of its effects.

The Society, founded in 1979, aims to give support to families by linking them through membership; to provide information about the disease and available aids; to ensure that adequate nursing care is available when it becomes necessary; and to promote research and the education of the general public. A newsletter is published; meetings and symposia are arranged.

The ADS has a network of relatives' self-help groups and contact people throughout the United Kingdom. There are over 120 branches and a number of day centres and sitting services. Recommended subscription £5 per annum.

The Amnesia Association (AMNASS)
25 Prebend Gardens, London W4 1TN (Tel: 01–747 0039).
This charity was founded in 1986 following the screening of the memorable Channel 4 documentary, *Prisoner of Consciousness*. This both heightened public awareness and understanding of the problems of amnesia and convinced carers that there was an opportunity to achieve better provision for sufferers.

AMNASS works for the provision of a range of appropriate care facilities which at present are virtually non-existent. It seeks to provide support to families of those affected by amnesia by offering information and advice. It may also be possible to form local groups of interested people. A further priority is to promote awareness of amnesia and the distress and suffering which it causes. Finally, AMNASS aims to encourage research into the causes, diagnosis and management of amnesia and to make the useful results of such research more widely known.

AMNASS publishes a newsletter, *Recall*, which demonstrates an approach which is positive, sensitive to the views of the membership, and instructive to others.

Amputees
See British Limbless Ex-service Men's Association; National Association for Limbless Disabled; and Reach.

Angelman Syndrome Support Group
15 Place Crescent, Waterlooville, Portsmouth, Hampshire PO7 5UR.
Angelman Syndrome is a rare condition affecting children. The Support Group has studied a number of case histories and has found that up to the age of six months the development of most of the children affected appeared to be normal; it was only in later assessments that developmental delay became apparent. Convulsions in some children started between nine months and three years of age, but their severity and frequency varied widely. The general abilities of the children are also varied: the most advanced can feed themselves, walk, are bladder or toilet trained and can say a few words. The concentration span in most cases seems very short, which in turn restricts understanding. All the children attend special schools.

There is very little written information on the syndrome, and the information given to parents by the medical profession is very limited and appears to be uncoordinated.

The Support Group was set up in April 1986 after many families requested a need for support and information. Its principal aims are to:
(a) promote a better understanding of AS for both families and the medical profession;
(b) remove the feeling of isolation from parents by keeping in regular contact;

(c) assist any future AS children and their families; and

(d) encourage greater medical research into this syndrome.

Ankylosing Spondylitis
See National Ankylosing Spondylitis Society.

Anorexic Family Aid (AFA)
Sackville Place, 44 Magdalen Street, Norwich, Norfolk NR3 1JE (Tel: Norwich (0603) 621414). Anorexia Nervosa is a serious illness of deliberate self-starvation with profound psychiatric and physical implications. Although the symptoms are found in men and women of all ages, the disease is most common in adolescent girls and young women.

AFA was founded in 1976 to help all those concerned with Anorexia and Bulimia Nervosa, especially the families of those affected. A national information centre was set up in 1984 in response to nationwide enquiries and requests for help. The Centre does not offer treatment but encourages full use of the available medical services. The information given includes the names of recognised professionals who are active in the treatment of anorexia and bulimia nervosa.

Membership of AFA provides:
(a) information about treatment available in each area of the country;
(b) telephone and postal support;
(c) guidelines giving helpful suggestions on many aspects of these disorders;
(d) a bi-monthly newsletter; and
(e) a booklist.
Services provided by AFA include:
(a) posters and fact sheets;
(b) information packs;
(c) a list of speakers;
(d) a journal, *The British Review of Bulimia and Anorexia* (annual subscription £10);
(e) workshops and conferences for professionals.
A self-help group meets in Norwich.

Annual membership £5; life membership £25; overseas membership £10.

ANTS (Ann's Neurological Trust Society)
Jocelyn Lodge, Keythorpe, Tugby, Leicester LE7 9XJ (Tel: Tugby (053 756) 244).
Syringomyelia is a chronic progressive disease of the nervous system characterised by the development of a cavity (syrinx) within the spinal cord or the lower part of the brain. The effects are variable. The commonest symptoms are pain, curvature of the spine, disruptions of joints, loss of feeling in the limbs (particularly loss of ability to feel heat, cold and pain sensations), and wasting, weakness and clumsiness of the limbs. In the late stage of the most severe varieties of the disorder, swallowing or breathing may be affected and a proportion of those affected may have to use a wheelchair. The disease is less common than multiple sclerosis, but does have certain similarities. For instance, it may show itself in early adult life, it affects both sensation and muscle power, it is sometimes spasmodic in its deterioration, the precise clinical course cannot be forecast and its cause or causes are largely unknown. Early diagnosis is the key to successful treatment.

The primary task of ANTS is to raise funds for research. In addition, a self-help group has been set up to:
(a) offer support and reassurance to anyone who has this disorder or whose relatives are affected by it;
(b) give advice where possible on how to cope with the everyday difficulties experienced by those affected;
(c) provide a means of communication between those affected; and
(d) publicise the disorder (because of its rarity many doctors have little knowledge of the condition).
A newsletter, *Antics*, is published.

Arachnoiditis Self-help Group
PO Box 81, Sunderland, Tyne and Wear SR6 9PA. Despite this being a rare disease, this group has over 30 members and new contacts are continuing to make themselves known. Enquirers receive information about the disease, together with a list of contact names and addresses.

ARMS (Action for Research into Multiple Sclerosis)
4A Chapel Hill, Stansted, Essex CM24 8AG (Tel: Bishop's Stortford (0279) 815553)
Counselling: England and Wales 01–222 3123 or 021–476 4229 Scotland 041–637 2262
ARMS is a vigorous organisation run by people with personal experience of multiple sclerosis providing information to others who suffer from multiple sclerosis. Its Newsletter is particularly good: direct, relevant, informative and non-patronising. The organisation manages a research programme with projects at hospitals, universities and centres in the UK, has 60 therapy centres and offers a 24-hour counselling service.

Nearly all ARMS publications are available on cassette. A catalogue is available from Sue Webster and Derek Hasted, 1 Passfield Walk, West Leigh, Havant, Hampshire PO9 5QG.

Arthritis Care
6 Grosvenor Crescent, London SW1X 7ER (Tel: 01–235 0902).
The Association caters for the social and welfare needs of rheumatism and arthritis sufferers. It has over 400 branches throughout the United Kingdom (including Northern Ireland) which hold regular social meetings.

The Association administers four specially adapted holiday centres and a residential home with nursing care. A welfare department advises on a variety of subjects, e.g. holidays, transport and equipment for use at home, and publishes a quarterly newspaper, *Arthritis News*.

Arthritis and Rheumatism Council
41 Eagle Street, London WC1R 4AR (Tel: 01–405 8572).
The Council aims to inspire and encourage medical research into the causes and cure of arthritis and rheumatism, ensure that the beneficial results of the research are made available to sufferers as quickly as possible and raise the funds necessary for the research to continue. It publishes

a quarterly magazine called *Arthritis Research Today* which can be obtained for a nominal annual subscription and contains many short articles on interesting aspects of medical research and arthritis.

Arthrogryposis
See TAG.

ASBAH
See Association for Spina Bifida and Hydrocephalus.

Assistance Dogs for Disabled People
23 Slipper Road, Emsworth, Hampshire PO10 8BS (Tel: Emsworth (0243) 375723); also at 1 Harris Street, Fleetwood, Lancashire FY7 6QX (Tel: Fleetwood (03917) 5547).
At the time of writing, ADDP is at the project stage. Building on work done in the USA and Holland, ADDP will breed and train dogs to help disabled people. Assistance dogs can react to commands to perform many of the tasks that the disabled owner cannot do without help – e.g. operating light switches and lift buttons, opening and closing doors and retrieving articles. Recipients have to be carefully selected and will be

required to attend an intensive training course with the dogs.

Association for All Speech Impaired Children (AFASIC)

347 Central Markets, Smithfield, London EC1A 9NH (Tel: 01–236 3632/6487).

AFASIC is an association of parents and professionals which seeks to draw to the attention of the public and local and central government the special needs of children and young people with specific speech and language disorders. The Association believes that regular speech therapy and education by specially trained teachers (preferably in a language unit attached to an ordinary school) are essential if these children are to achieve their potential and to participate fully in society.

AFASIC provides an advice and information service, fund raises for mobile speech therapy clinics and organises activity week holidays for the children. It campaigns for more language units attached to ordinary schools and improved speech therapy services, runs courses and symposia and was instrumental in setting up the first training course for teachers of language disordered children. It is currently investigating the field of employment training for speech and language disordered young people. The Association has a network of 27 regional groups and 15 area correspondents. A newsletter is published for members.

Association of Carers

See Carers National Association

Association to Combat Huntington's Chorea

34a Station Road, Hinckley, Leicestershire LE10 1AP (Tel: Hinckley (0455) 615558). Family services: 108 Battersea High Street, London SW11 3HP (Tel: 01–223 7000).

The United Kingdom National Association – Combat – was founded in 1971 and devotes its energies to promoting and supporting research; identifying areas of special need; minimising the effects of the disease in any possible way; educating and influencing professional and the general public into an awareness of the realities of the condition; sustaining and comforting those who suffer; providing and running a holiday and short-term care home for patients; developing a branch network for local needs; providing specialised aid and counselling; carrying out clinical trials of aids and appliances applicable to the disease; initiating social research intended to improve the quality of life of HC families; publishing and distributing appropriate literature; and raising funds so that this disease can finally be eradicated.

Association of Crossroads Care Attendant Schemes Ltd

10 Regent Place, Rugby, Warwickshire CV21 2PN (Tel: Rugby (0788) 73653).

This scheme became a national organisation in April 1977. It represents a bold, imaginative (though totally practical) and much needed strategy to improve the care of disabled people within the community. The scheme's primary objective is to relieve stress in the families or carers of disabled people and to avoid their admission to hospital or residential care should a breakdown or other failure occur in the household. To achieve this objective the Association promotes the establishment of domiciliary support services in local areas, managed by local committees and staffed by 'care attendants' who are paid for their time and provided with appropriate training. Attendants are not professional people, but act rather as substitute relatives, providing care in a homely and friendly way, in a manner to which the disabled person is accustomed. An important aspect of an attendant's work is that attendance is provided on a flexible basis, if necessary outside what are considered normal working hours. The Association emphasises that such teams supplement and complement, not replace, existing statutory services and work closely with them, striving for the highest possible standards of care.

Many physically handicapped people are able to live at home only because of the support they get from other people – friends, housekeepers or relatives. Those who care for disabled people in this way are often under great strain themselves and the support provided by care attendants can make all the difference. Equally, if for any reason a breakdown occurs in normal support, the help of a care attendant, for a few hours a week, can fill the gap and save the situation.

In addition to the main office, there are seven regional offices and a Scottish office. Details of these and of places where the scheme operates are available from the above address. A useful publications list is also available free on request.

Association of Disabled Professionals

The Stables, 73 Pound Road, Banstead, Surrey SM7 2HU (Tel: Burgh Heath (0737) 352366).

The Association is a self-help group seeking to improve the rehabilitation of disabled people. Members can help other members with advice on education/training and employment problems.

Publishes an occasional *Newsletter* and a quarterly *House Bulletin*.

Association of Parents of Vaccine Damaged Children
2 Church Street, Shipston-on-Stour, Warwickshire CV36 4AP (Tel: Shipston- on-Stour (0608) 61595).
Represents, through parents, those children who have suffered handicaps as a result of vaccination, and campaigns for state provision for them.

Association of Professions for Mentally Handicapped People
Greytree Lodge, Second Avenue, Ross on Wye, Herefordshire HR9 7HT (Tel: Ross on Wye (0989) 62630).
APMH was founded in 1973 to promote the general welfare of mentally handicapped people and their families, by encouraging high standards of care and development, by facilitating co-operation and the sharing of knowledge among professional workers, by offering a unified professional view on the strategies of mental handicap and by educating the public to accept, understand and respect mentally handicapped people.

The Association now embraces over 40 different professions in the fields of health, education, social service and voluntary services. It is consulted by government departments, has held regular congresses and workshops and has published a number of relevant reports and papers.

Association for Research into Restricted Growth
c/o Pamela Rutt, 61 Lady Walk, Maple Cross, Rickmansworth, Herts WD3 2YZ (Tel: Rickmansworth (0923) 770759).
Since its foundation in 1970, the Association has been concerned chiefly to provide, through *ARRG News*, meetings and conventions, a forum for communication among people of restricted growth. It thus brings together people with common problems and needs, providing opportunities for social contact and discussion.

The Family Affairs Committee makes available advice, support and counselling for parents of affected children. Information is available on the practical implications of living with restricted growth, clothing, home adaptations, employment etc.

The Association has established a regional panel of specialists to whom GPs can refer people for medical advice. Publications include *The Layman's Guide to Restricted Growth* and *Coping with Restricted Growth*.

Association for Spina Bifida and Hydrocephalus (ASBAH)
22 Upper Woburn Place, London WC1H 0EP (Tel: 01–388 1382).
Northern Ireland Association: Long Eaves, 24 Tulleywiggan Road, Cookstown, Co.Tyrone (Tel: Cookstown (064 87) 62290).
ASBAH is a welfare and research organisation and has almost 80 local associations in England, Wales and Northern Ireland.(Scotland has its own Association (*see* page 328)). It provides information, advisory and welfare services and practical assistance, and supports the work of the local associations. Some areas are served by fieldworkers, and there is an activity and short-term care centre in Ilkley, Yorkshire. ASBAH also sponsors research into the causes of spina bifida and hydrocephalus, and publishes a bi-monthly magazine *LINK*.

LIFT, a group for young members (13 to 25 years) within the Association has information on social and leisure activities, a quarterly free newsletter and training programmes on personal care and social independence.

BACUP (British Association of Cancer United Patients and their families and friends)
121/123 Charterhouse Street, London EC1M 6AA (Tel: administration 01–608 1785; cancer information service 01–608 1661)
This organisation was set up to provide information and support to cancer patients, their families and friends, health professionals and the general public. A team of experienced cancer nurses answer telephone and written enquiries on all aspects of cancer care. BACUP provides booklets and leaflets on the main types of cancer and on the emotional and practical problems of coping with the disease. *BACUP News*, published three times a year, is sent on request to those who have sought BACUP's help.

The Behcet's Syndrome Society
20 The Green, Whiston, Rotherham, South Yorkshire S60 4JD (Tel: Rotherham (0709) 362653 or York (0904) 37310).
Behcet's Syndrome is a rare condition characterised by inflammation of the blood vessels supplying the central nervous system, the results of which can affect neurological function. Its effects can be very alarming, but fortunately problems usually clear up of their own accord or respond to treatment, and seldom lead to serious disability.

The Society provides a contact and support system for those affected and their families, and financial aid in cases of hardship caused by the syndrome. It is setting up an information network among the medical profession, and is promoting research into the disorder. All members receive a general guide, and more detailed explanatory leaflets are available on request. The Society also issues newsletters from time to time.

Contact addresses of those members who agree to waive the normal rule of confidentiality are supplied to other members on request, usually on a relatively local basis. Membership costs £5 a year, but this is not compulsory and anyone with the syndrome is automatically a member.

Bereavement
See Compassionate Friends.

Blindness and Partial Sight
See: Guide Dogs for the Blind Association; Jewish Blind Society; London Association for the Blind; National Association for Deaf-Blind and Rubella Handicapped; National Deaf-Blind Helpers League; National Federation of the Blind of the United Kingdom; National League of the Blind and Disabled; National Library for the Blind; Optical Information Council; Partially Sighted Society; Royal Commonwealth Society for the Blind; Royal National Institute for the Blind; St. Dunstan's.

Bobath Centre
5 Netherhall Gardens, London NW3 5RN (Tel: 01–435 3895).
The Centre provides physiotherapy, occupational therapy, speech therapy and medical advice for children with cerebral palsy and related neurological disorders. No charge is made to British children for this service (up to age 18 years). A letter of referral from a consultant paediatrician, together with a medical history, is required before an appointment can be considered. The Centre also provides physiotherapy for adult stroke patients and head injury sufferers. This service is charged for and details are available on request. A letter of referral, with medical history, from a consultant (or in some cases a general practitioner) is also required. The Centre is non-residential.

Brain Injury
See British Institute for Brain Injured Children.

Breakthrough Trust: Deaf-Hearing Integration
Charles W. Gillett Centre, Selly Oak Colleges, Birmingham B29 6LE (Tel: 021– 472 6447 (voice); 021–471 1001 (Vistel)).
Promotes a variety of projects, activities and cul-

tural pursuits which in a natural way brings deaf and hearing people, children and adults, into harmonious contact with each other through practical self-help ventures, e.g. Total Communication Workshops, Information Service, social activities, integration weekends, holiday projects and activities for deaf and additionally handicapped deaf children and young people, and telecommunication services for deaf people. The centre has a resources room with an extensive library and a working display of special equipment concerned with deafness.

The Trust's Roughmoor Centre at Shaw, Swindon, Wiltshire SN5 9PW (Tel: Swindon (0793) 771021) offers the use of its farmhouse accommodation for a variety of projects including integration projects for deaf and hearing children, families, young people and deaf people with additional handicaps. Advice and information on deafness is offered to local people and groups.

The Breast Care and Mastectomy Association of Great Britain
26 Harrison Street, London WC1 8JG (Tel: 01–837 0908).
This Association was formed in 1973 and aims to complement medical and nursing care by providing information and support to women before and after all kinds of breast surgery. Literature is available free, and a nationwide network of volunteers offers any woman the chance to talk to another and to gain reassurance and confidence.

British Association of Cancer United Patients
See BACUP.

British Association of the Hard of Hearing
7–11 Armstrong Road, London W3 7JL (Tel: 01–743 1110 (voice); 01–743 1492 (Vistel)).
BAHOH is a national organisation for those who have lost all or part of their hearing after acquiring normal speech and language and who communicate via a hearing aid and/or lipreading (sign language is rarely used in BAHOH). It was founded in 1947 by hard of hearing people who continue to guide its policies and know the problems associated with hearing loss from personal experience.

BAHOH has 230 social clubs throughout the United Kingdom, organises social gatherings on a national and regional basis, and arranges holidays some of which have been abroad. It co-operates with statutory and voluntary bodies to advance measures to prevent and cure deafness and to secure the provision of better services for hard of hearing people. It has a range of relevant publications, including a quarterly magazine *Hark* (annual subscription £3).

British Association of Myasthenics
9 Potters Drive, Hopton, Great Yarmouth, Norfolk NR31 9RW (Tel: Lowestoft (0502) 731904). The Association seeks to help families and social workers to know more about this rare disease. Chapters have been and are being established, and quarterly bulletins are issued. Purposes include contact, welfare, education, publicity and, by fund raising, the support of research in conjunction with the Muscular Dystrophy Group.

British Council of Organisations of Disabled People
St. Mary's Church, Greenlaw Street, Woolwich, London SE18 5AR (Tel: 01–854 7289). BCODP was established in 1981 to act as a co-ordinating forum for organisations of (i.e. controlled by) disabled people. Its main purpose is to provide a forum for the exchange of information, ideas and views, with the object of enabling disabled people to develop and express their own needs and to take collective action. The Council is keen to promote and establish local grassroots organisations of disabled people and to work towards active participation of disabled people in securing equal and full social integration.

Member organisations are equally represented on BCODP and membership is open to any group in which disabled people have at least 51 per cent control on its executive/management committee, and a clause to ensure this in its constitution.

BCODP is the national constituent member of Disabled People's International which has consultative status to the United Nations on issues concerning disabled people.

The British Deaf Association
38 Victoria Place, Carlisle CA1 1HU (Tel: Carlisle (0228) 48844 (voice); (0228) 28719 (Vistel)). The Association has local branches throughout the country. It organises a variety of group activities for deaf people, and is able to advise individuals and parents on development and education. Special holidays for deaf and elderly people are arranged, with financial assistance in suitable cases. The Association also organises courses for school leavers, outdoor and adventure courses for young deaf people, and an annual summer school and short special interest courses for all age groups. Educational material (including sign lan-

guage video tapes) and a monthly news magazine are available. Publications list on request.

British Diabetic Association
10 Queen Anne Street, London W1M 0BD (Tel: 01–323 1531).

BDA seeks to safeguard the interests of diabetics and provides information and advice. It raises money for research and organises holidays for diabetics of all ages. A bi-monthly magazine *Balance* is sent free to all members and is available at newsagents; cassette versions are provided for people registered as blind. A wide range of literature is produced, and a series of four VHS video films is available covering all aspects of diabetes.

British Dyslexia Association
Church Lane, Peppard, Oxon RG9 5JN (Tel: Reading (0734) 668271/2).

The Association represents and co-ordinates the activities of local Dyslexia Associations. It co-operates with the Department of Education and Science and with local education authorities. Corporate members are involved in research, assessment and teaching. The Association provides counselling and advice to parents and other people in obtaining remedial help for those who are handicapped by dyslexia.

British Epilepsy Association
Anstey House, 40 Hanover Square, Leeds LS3 1BE (Tel: Leeds (0532) 439393). Also: 142 Whitchurch Road, Cardiff CF4 3NA (Tel: Cardiff (0222) 628744) and The Old Postgraduate Medical Centre, Belfast City Hospital, Lisburn Road, Belfast BT9 7AB (Tel: Belfast (0232) 248414), and regional offices in Birmingham, Leeds, London and Reading.

The Association, which was founded in 1950, offers a range of services under the following categories.
1. Social Work: providing professional advice and counselling services to individuals, families and employers.
2. Education: *see* Section 5.
3. Information: providing information and practical advice on coping with epilepsy and the problems it brings in everyday life – the family, the home, mobility, employment and education.
4. Representation: attending appeal and industrial tribunals for people with epilepsy.
5. Action Groups: establishing a nationwide network of self-help action groups which provide support and advice at local level.

6. Holidays: consideration of requests for welfare grants to assist with holidays.
7. Newsletter: producing a quarterly newsletter *Epilepsy Now!*.

British Heart Foundation

102 Gloucester Place, London W1H 4DH (Tel: 01–935 0185).

Primarily a medical research charity working in the field of cardiovascular disease. Activities include provision of Heart Research Series leaflets and a range of other advisory leaflets free of charge to heart patients and their families. No funds are available for welfare or rehabilitation grants to individuals.

The British Institute for Brain Injured Children

Knowle Hall, Knowle, Bridgwater, Somerset TA7 8PJ (Bridgwater (0278) 684060).

The Institute's role is to teach parents of brain injured children programmes of stimulation therapy which are carried out by the parents in their own homes, under the guidance of the Institute's staff. Families are offered an initial assessment for their children, followed by regular re-assessment appointments and additional in-patient therapy for children with specific breathing problems.

British Institute of Mental Handicap

Wolverhampton Road, Kidderminster, Worcestershire DY10 3PP (Tel: Kidderminster (0562) 850251).

The BIMH aims to raise standards of treatment, care and management of mentally handicapped people both in hospital and in the community. An Information and Resource Centre answers queries on all aspects of mental handicap. Conferences and workshops are organised on a national basis. Publications include a quarterly journal, *Mental Handicap*, a quarterly collection of topical articles under the title *Mental Handicap Bulletin*, and a monthly *Current Awareness Service* devoted to the latest books and articles in the field, and books on various aspects of mental handicap.

Individual membership, which includes *Mental Handicap,* and entitles the member to reduced charges at BIMH conferences and discounts on publications, costs £14 per annum and is open to anyone. Details of other forms of membership are available on request.

British Kidney Patient Association

Bordon, Hampshire (Tel: Bordon (04203) 2021/22).

Gives advice and help to sufferers and raises funds. Seeks to extend the donation of kidneys by healthy people. Provides holidays for dialysis patients in holiday centres on the West Sussex coast, and on the islands of Jersey and Mallorca. Membership is open to all kidney patients at a fee of £1 for life membership. This entitles them and their immediate family to financial help.

British Legion

See Royal British Legion.

British Limbless Ex-service Men's Association

Frankland Moore House, 185–187 High Road, Chadwell Heath, Essex RM6 6NA (Tel: 01–590 1124).

Has local branches. Advises on pensions, employment and welfare matters. Safeguards the interests of members and runs two residential convalescent homes. Publishes a magazine *Blesmag*.

British Nursing Association (a Nestor-BNA company)

North Place, 82 Great North Road, Hatfield, Hertfordshire AL9 5PL (Tel: Hatfield (07072) 63544).

With 100 branches in England, Scotland and Wales, BNA provides fully qualified nurses and also carers or auxiliaries to private patients for care in their own homes. As well as specialised care, the company offers twilight visits and 'sleeper' duties for those who need only limited assistance, and escort services for patients who cannot travel alone. BNA say that, in particular, they recognise that disabled people should not miss out on a social life because of lack of help, and that their services, such as escort duties and twilight visits, which are adapted to the individual's needs, can provide increased freedom, while costs are often met by attendance allowances.

A nurse or carer (male or female) can be provided for any period from one to 24 hours a day. BNA has a national branch network and is able to respond at short notice seven days a week round the clock to cover routine and emergency needs. Contact the above address or see Yellow Pages for your nearest local branch.

British Polio Fellowship

Bell Close, West End Road, Ruislip, Middlesex HA4 6LP (Tel: Ruislip (0895) 675515).

Has local branches. Encourages mutual support, service and recreation. Provides personal welfare and advisory services and aims at rehabilitation through training. The Fellowship has a residential/holiday establishment as well as self-catering accommodation (a bungalow, holiday flat and a holiday caravan). Publishes *The Bulletin*, a bi-monthly newspaper.

British Retinitis Pigmentosa Society
Greens Norton Court, Greens Norton, Towcester, Northamptonshire NN12 8BS (Tel: Towcester (0327) 53276).
Retinitis Pigmentosa (RP) refers to a group of hereditary diseases of the retina, in which the light sensitive tissue of the eye slowly degenerates, progressively restricting vision.

BRPS, formed in 1975, aims chiefly to counsel, support and encourage those who have RP and to pursue measures towards finding the cause, effective treatment and cure of the disease. It further seeks to increase public awareness of RP, and to co-operate with government, statutory and relevant voluntary organisations and professional workers, nationally and internationally. It will continue to press for more government-funded research as well as raising money on its own account for this purpose.

The Society has a branch structure covering over two thousand members, and provides a regular flow of information relating to the disease.

British Sports Association for the Disabled
See Section 11, Sports and Leisure.

British Tinnitus Association
c/o The Royal National Institute for the Deaf, 105 Gower Street, London WC1E 6AH (Tel: 01–387 8033).
Subjective tinnitus is an extremely common complaint affecting a large number of people with normal hearing as well as those with varying degrees of hearing impairment. Very small abnormalities in the hearing nerve can generate sounds, inaudible to other people, but which can take the form of a great variety of ringing, whistling, buzzing or other complicated sounds which plague the affected person.

The BTA was formed in July 1979 to bring together sufferers and other interested people for discussion of problems, experiences and any matters of mutual interest that might help to relieve suffering in day-to-day living. There are now just over 100 local self-help groups throughout the country. The Association also seeks to enlist financial and other support, sympathy and understanding from the general public, and to bring pressure to bear on MPs and other relevant persons and organisations to encourage the channelling of funds into the relief and cure of tinnitus.

The Association conveys information to members through the *BTA Newsletter*, published four times a year in the magazine *Soundbarrier*, and issued by the RNID. Much basic information, including a section on tinnitus maskers and their availability both commercially and through the NHS and an authoritative article on tinnitus research and current treatment, is available in the BTA's *Information Booklet*, obtainable on request.

Brittle Bone Society
Unit 4, Block 20, Carlunie Road, Dunsinane Industrial Estate, Dundee DD2 3QT (Tel: Dundee (0382) 817771).
The Society seeks to promote research into the causes, inheritance and treatment of Osteogenesis Imperfecta and similar disorders, characterised by excessive fragility of the bones. It also provides advice, contacts, encouragement and practical help for those affected and their relatives, and raises funds for research.

Broadcasting Support Services
252 Western Avenue, London W3 6XJ (Tel: 01–992 5522).
BSS provides follow-up services for viewers and listeners. This may be in the form of leaflets available from its PO Box 7 and PO Box 4000 addresses or from telephone helplines open after a particular programme. BSS specialises in providing back-up to broadcasts/programmes concerned with education, health, disability, leisure, welfare rights and emotional issues. It has access to many information services and compiles data bases on national and local sources of help which it uses to put viewers and listeners in touch with voluntary organisations and support groups.

Bulimia Nervosa
See Anorexic Family Aid.

The Campaign for Mentally Handicapped People
12A Maddox Street, London W1R 9PL (Tel: 01–491 0727).
Established as an independent group in 1971, CMH campaigns for greater integration of mentally handicapped people in ordinary society and for the abolition of specialist subnormality hospitals. It collects and disseminates information to evaluate needs and to promote improvements in provision.

Conferences and meetings are organised, and a quarterly newsletter is published. Other publications include policy statements, discussion and enquiry papers, conference reports, evidence to government bodies, and specialist studies. These

are available from CMH Publications at 5 Kentings, Comberton, Cambridgeshire CB3 7DT.

CMH membership costs £10 per annum for
individuals, £25 per annum for organisations.

Cancer
See below and BACUP, Leukaemia Care Society,
Leukaemia Research Fund, Marie Curie Memorial Foundation, Women's National Cancer Control Campaign.

Cancer After Care and Rehabilitation Society
21 Zetland Road, Bristol BS6 7AH (Tel: day
Bristol (0272) 427419; evening Bristol (0272)
691868).
This Society, founded in 1971, now has over 40
branches and is still growing. It does not offer
medical advice, but tries to overcome the emotional stress, fear, depression and aggression
which commonly affect people with cancer, and to
help families to cope. This may simply be by being
prepared to listen, or by providing information or
practical support. Many members are, from their
own experience, able to understand the traumas
associated with the disease and the problems which
arise. As well as the local branches, a phone-link
system allows people with the same/similar type of
cancer to contact each other.

The Society has a holiday chalet at Hemsby,
near Great Yarmouth.

CancerLink
46 Pentonville Road, London N1 9HF (Tel: 01–
833 2451).
CancerLink was founded in 1982 by a group of
people with personal and professional experience
of cancer. It grew out of the perception that there
was not enough support available for people affected by cancer.

An information service provides information
about all aspects of cancer, by telephone or letter.
Nurses in this service also offer support and help to
clarify the enquirers' options, enabling them to
make informed decisions.

CancerLink's Groups Support Service acts as a
resource to cancer support and self-help groups
throughout Britain. There are about 250 of these
groups; new ones are starting all the time. These
groups are developing different ways of supporting
people affected by cancer. The Groups Support
Service works with these groups, providing an
information exchange, training and support, and
also helps people to set up new groups.

Publications include guides to useful organisations and groups, guidance on home care, and a
quarterly newsletter, *Link Up* (£2 per annum). A
video film on breast cancer is also available
(£12.50).

Cancer Relief Macmillan Fund (National Society for Cancer Relief)
Anchor House, 15/19 Britten Street, London SW3
3TZ (Tel: 01–351 7811).
Cancer Relief, founded in 1911, provides services
in the following areas.
1. Home visits by Macmillan nurses to provide
    pain relief to people with cancer and emo-
    tional support to them and their families.
    Contact the above address through your GP.
2. Continuing care homes providing specialist in-
    patient and day care.
3. Cash grants to people with cancer and their
    families to relieve them of the stress caused by
    heavy bills. Apply through social service de-
    partments, your community nurse, health
    visitor or hospital social worker, or contact
    Cancer Care's Patient Grants Department
    direct.
4. An education programme to train doctors and
    nurses in the new skills of pain relief.

Cardiac Spare Parts Trust
2 High Street, Olney, Buckinghamshire MK46
4BB
A support trust for those who have undergone or
who require heart surgery, and for those with
pacemakers. Founded in 1969 by heart patients,
the Trust seeks to assist patients prior to their
operation, to provide any help required afterwards, to raise funds for cardiac research equipment, and to give advice in these areas.

Carers
See Association of Crossroads Care Attendant
Schemes, Carers National Association, Home
Care Support, Special Care Agency.

CARE (Cottage and Rural Enterprises Ltd)
9A Weir Road, Kibworth, Leicester LE8 0LQ
(Tel: Kibworth (053 753) 3225).
CARE is an organisation which aims to care for
mentally handicapped adults of both sexes in vil-
lage communities where they can work and live as
normal a life as possible. 'Villages' exist at East
Anstey (North Devon), Petworth (West Sussex),
Leicester, Samlesbury (near Preston, Lancashire),
Sevenoaks (Kent), Ponteland (Newcastle upon
Tyne) and Ironbridge (Shropshire).

Residents of mixed handicaps and abilities live
in cottage units for up to 14 people, and work in
pottery, agriculture, horticulture, printing,

woodwork and craft workshops. The aim is to provide necessary care, support and guidance and the opportunity to realise expectations of a useful, secure and enjoyable life.

CARE raises its own funds to meet capital costs, while the day-to-day expenses are largely met by fees paid by the residents' home local authorities and DHSS grants.

Carers National Association
29 Chilworth Mews, London W2 3RG (Tel: 01–724 7776) and Lilac House, Medway Homes, Balfour Road, Rochester, Kent (Tel: Medway (0634) 813981).
Two organisations have come together to form the Carers National Association. The two were known as: the Association of Carers; and the National Council for Carers and their Elderly Dependants.
  The aims are:
(a) to encourage carers to make known their own needs;
(b) to develop appropriate support for carers;
(c) to provide information and advice for carers; and
(d) to bring the needs of carers to the attention of government and other policy makers.

Catholic Handicapped Fellowship
2 The Villas, Hare Law, Stanley, Co.Durham DH9 8DQ (Tel: Stanley (0207) 34379).
This Fellowship stresses the difficulty of providing both for the spiritual and special physical needs of handicapped children and the need for parents to have a 'friendly hand'. Organised in independent Diocesan Fellowships in Roman Catholic dioceses in England, each Fellowship has its own order of priorities, but there is a general pattern in all – family care, meetings and activities for children and parents, social activities, holidays and pilgrimages, religious instruction and help in taking handicapped people to Mass.

Central Bureau for Educational Visits and Exchanges
See Section 10, Holidays Abroad.

Centre on Environment for the Handicapped
See Section 4, House and Home.

Centre for Policy on Ageing
25–31 Ironmonger Row, London EC1V 3QP (Tel: 01–253 1787).
CPA issues a range of publications intended to be of practical help to professionals concerned with direct services/policies for older people. Some publications are intended to provide a regular

monitoring of current research, publications and events; others provide analysis of policy and practice in given fields. A publications list is available.

Centres for Independent Living
See Section 4, House and Home.

Cerebral Palsy
See Bobath Centre, Scottish Council for Spastics, Spastics Society.

Charcot-Marie-Tooth Disease
See CMT International.

Chest, Heart and Stroke Association
Tavistock House North, Tavistock Square, London WC1H 9JE (Tel: 01–387 3012).
Also: 21 Dublin Road, Belfast BT2 7FJ (Tel: Belfast (0232) 320184), and 65 North Castle Street, Edinburgh EH2 3LT (Tel: 031–225 6527).
CHSA works to prevent chest, heart and stroke illnesses and helps people who suffer from them. It offers advice and welfare services, publishes many helpful booklets, leaflets and films (list available), sponsors research into chest disease and strokes, and can refer enquirers to local stroke clubs and schemes.

Child Growth Foundation
2 Mayfield Avenue, London W4 1PW (Tel: 01–994 7625 or 01–995 0257).
This Foundation works for children who either do not grow or who grow too much. It was registered in 1976 to help to maintain the services of 21 Growth Centres caring for such children.
  It aims to:
(a) raise money to support growth specialists and institutions caring for children with growth disorders, and to promote research into disorders hitherto untreatable;
(b) promote awareness of growth and its potential problems in the public in general and the medical profession in particular; and
(c) maintain a membership and register of families of children with growth disorders so that they may both help each other locally and the Foundation's objectives nationally.
Monthly seminars have been held for members of the medical profession, and the Foundation has published, among other things, *A Child's Guide to Child Growth*, price £3 (send A4 s.a.e.)

Child Poverty Action Group
4th Floor, 1–5 Bath Street, London EC1V 9PY (Tel: 01–253 3406).
CPAG promotes the relief of poverty among children and families. Although not directly concerned

with disablement, CPAG's work on spreading information about poverty can help the cause of those with disabilities in hardship. Numerous publications include the *National Welfare Benefits Handbook* and the *Rights Guide to Non Means-Tested Social Security Benefits* (annual guides to the welfare benefits system). CPAG members get a range of publications in return for their subscriptions. Write to CPAG for more information.

Children's Society (Church of England's Children's Society)
Edward Rudolf House, Margery Street, London WC1X 0JL (Tel: 01–837 4299).
The Society provides help and support to families through family and day care centres and community and neighbourhood centres. Many of the Society's homefinding teams specialise in placing children with special needs. Specific services for disabled people include: residential centres, holiday schemes, respite care, further education and training, and community support. For further information about the Society's services, please contact the Social Work Director at the above address.

Chiropody
See The Society of Chiropodists.

Church Action on Disability
Charisma Cottage, Drewsteignton, Exeter EX6 6QR (Tel: Drewsteignton (0647) 21259).
This is a programme supported by the major Christian denominations in England which seeks to create the necessary resources, both written and personal, to increase awareness, amongst Christian congregations, of people with disabilities, and to encourage action within Christian congregations to create access in its widest sense to buildings, worship and ministry through physical action and change of attitudes.

Launched in July 1987, it is designed initially as a three-year campaign. Voluntary regional officers will co-ordinate a network of voluntary area and local contacts to speak to church congregations and other groups, encouraging them to consider the issues involved and to take action where appropriate. A magazine, *All People*, is published quarterly, the issue of which is included in the £5 annual membership subscription.

Citizens' Advice Bureau Service
Administration: National Association of Citizens' Advice Bureaux (NACAB), 115/123 Pentonville Road, London N1 9LZ (Tel: 01–833 2181).
Local Citizens' Advice Bureaux (CABx) provide information and advice, free of charge, on every subject. There are over 1,000 CAB outlets in the UK, and in 1986/7 they dealt with 6.8 million enquiries. 80 per cent of these enquiries related to social security and welfare benefit problems, money matters including debt and credit, housing and consumer complaints, and employment and legal tangles. Over half the bureaux offer sessions with local solicitors in attendance, and one third have qualified accountants on hand. Fifteen per cent have specialist debt counsellors, but all CAB workers are trained to deal with money problems. All bureaux also have a community information system which includes everything from the address of the nearest library or tax office to details of local self-help groups and the names of local solicitors. As well as giving you information and advice, the CAB will write or telephone on your behalf, if you wish.

CAB is an independent organisation – not part of local or central government – and does not support any one political party. Ninety per cent of its workers are volunteers who go through an extensive training programme lasting up to one year. A few CABx have specific disability advice workers but generally CABx do not specialise in this field. Many of the matters dealt with by CABx are, however, as relevant to disabled people as to anyone else and the CAB information system does have a number of items centring on the needs of disabled people. CABx also have extensive information on local support groups, social service contacts etc.

Consult your telephone directory or local library for the address and telephone number of your nearest CAB. If necessary, please check that the CAB office is accessible before you go; many are not.

CLAPA (Cleft Lip and Palate Association)
1 Eastwood Gardens, Kenton, Newcastle upon Tyne NE3 3DQ (Tel: Tyneside (091) 2859396).
One in every 700 infants in Britain is born with a cleft lip or palate. It is a source of great personal distress to the child and the parents.

CLAPA believes that there are many positive things which can and should be done to help alleviate this distress. It comprises parents and professionals from a variety of disciplines: plastic surgeons, dental specialists, psychologists, speech therapists and social workers, all linked by experience or vocation to a particular understanding of the needs and treatment, from infancy through to adulthood, of those affected, and jointly concerned to help such individuals look better, speak better and adjust better.

CLAPA aims to give counselling and support to parents, encourage and support relevant research, conduct educational seminars, publish and distribute educational material and provide an informal link between parents and professionals. There are over 30 local groups, and a newsletter and advisory literature is published.

Cleft Lip and Palate Association
See above.

CMT International (Charcot-Marie Tooth Disease/ Peroneal Muscular Atrophy International Association Inc.)
73 Watson Close, Upavon, Pewsey, Wilts SN9 6AF (Tel: Durington Walls (0980) 630025).
Charcot-Marie-Tooth Disease (also known as peroneal muscular atrophy) is a little known hereditary disease which is characterised by degeneration of the motor nerves which stimulate muscles. The muscles slowly atrophy through lack of use, resulting in weakness in the feet, lower legs, hands and forearms. The disease can persist through three, four or even five generations.

CMT International is a support group drawn from people who themselves have CMT, assisted in many cases by relatives and friends. It was founded in Canada in 1984, and established in the UK in 1986. Well over 200 families are already in membership in this country. A bi-monthly newsletter is issued, plus newsletters from Canada which are more medically based. Advice or simply the opportunity to 'talk things over' is offered, and local groups are being set up in various parts of the country.

CMT International also assists in research, both financially and in providing the opportunity for further study among those affected.

Colitis
See National Association for Colitis and Crohn's Disease.

College of Health
2 Marylebone Road, London NW1 4DX (Tel: 01–935 3251).
The College publishes a quarterly magazine, *Self-Health*, which covers the prevention of ill health, self-care when ill, finding the best treatment, making the best use of conventional health services and learning more about alternative medicine. *Self-Health*, says the College, is independent and accepts no advertising, so that it is free from commercial pressures and can therefore provide un-

biased and honest information. Subscribers (£10 a year) are encouraged to put forward their own views, and can take advantage of an information service. Another service can put you in touch with any one of 1,200 self-help and voluntary organisations.

College of Speech Therapists
Harold Poster House, 6 Lechmere Road, London NW2 5BU (Tel: 01–459 8521/2/3).
The College has a number of pamphlets for sale to parents and relatives. Details, with prices, will be sent in response to an s.a.e. The College will also advise the location of qualified speech therapists who operate independently of the NHS.

Colostomy Welfare Group
38–39 Eccleston Square, London SW1V 1PB (Tel: 01–828 5175).
The Group seeks to help people through the anxiety before and after colostomy operations by giving a free advisory service and providing all patients with the opportunity to meet and talk to an ex-patient who is well rehabilitated, and who has been trained to give help, relief and comfort to others facing the same experience.

Combat
See Association to Combat Huntington's Chorea.

Communication Handicaps
See Vocal.

Communilink Private Speech Therapy Referral Service
4 Woodstock Road, London NW11 8ER (Tel: 01–458 8585).
Communilink provides direct contact with qualified speech therapists in private practice nationwide when help is required on a private basis for a speech, language or voice disorder, e.g. a stammer, delayed or disordered speech, stroke, head injuries after an accident.

Community Service Volunteers
See Section 7, Employment.

The Compassionate Friends
6 Denmark Street, Bristol BS1 5DQ (Tel: Bristol (0272) 292778).
This organisation was founded in Coventry in 1969. It is now a nationwide organisation of bereaved parents, who have themselves experienced heartbreak, loneliness and social isolation and who seek to help other bereaved parents. While religious or philosophical beliefs are helpful to

some bereaved parents, CP has no religious affiliation.

Initial contact with bereaved parents is in the form of a leaflet giving a local contact address. If this link is taken up, the parents will be put in touch with others in similar circumstances, and contact will be made by visits, telephone calls, letters or small meetings. A quarterly newsletter is also distributed to all members, initially free of charge. CP has a wide range of literature and operates a postal library.

Contact a Family
16 Strutton Ground, Victoria, London SW1P 2HP (Tel: 01–222 2695/3969).

Contact a Family aims to promote the formation of local self-help groups of families who share the problem of having a child with special needs who lives at home. Parents thus have the chance to meet socially, exchange ideas and give each other practical help, mutual support and understanding.

Membership of a group gives parents a better opportunity to press collectively for improved services and to express their common needs. Families are encouraged to organise services themselves with the help of volunteers and in some cases full time community workers. Family events such as holiday play schemes, baby-sitting, swimming clubs and family holidays are the sort of activities arranged through *Share an Idea* newsletter.

Contact a Family now links its own and independent self-help groups nationwide and runs a telephone service – *Contact Line* – to link up families. Training days are held for parents and self-help groups. A video film and set of guidelines for the formation of a group are available.

The Cornelia de Lange Syndrome Foundation
46 Victoria Street, Staple Hill, Bristol BS16 5JS (Tel: Bristol (0272) 573046).
CdLS is a rare condition that affects approximately 1 in 30,000 children. The children affected are small for their age and have some degree of mental and/or physical handicap. The syndrome varies in severity and appears to strike at random with no known cause. It is, however, highly unlikely to affect subsequent children. At present, the only way of detecting the condition before birth is a fetoscope test, which is done at 17½ weeks.

The CdLS Foundation has approximately 80 families in the United Kingdom and 500 in the USA. Most of the children affected are living at home with their families, leading full and happy lives. Younger children attend special nursery or opportunity groups, older ones attend special schools or day care centres. For most families, the worst problem is the feeling of isolation after being told that their child has a rare handicap. The CdLS Foundation was set up by parents for parents, and the *Reaching Out* newsletter is its main way of keeping in touch. Annual conventions are organised and families are free to contact each other as and when they choose. Some families, whose children have died, are willing to share their experiences with others in the same situation.

Council for the Advancement of Communication with Deaf People
Pelaw House, School of Education, University of Durham DH1 1TA (Tel: 091– 384 3611).
CACDP is comprised of deaf and hearing representatives from national organisations concerned with deafness. Its purpose is to improve communication between deaf and hearing people – and thus advance the welfare, status and opportunities for those who are deaf in a hearing world. This aim is achieved by the development of training and examination in communication skills as a stimulus to learning and a measure of ability and by administering a register of qualified interpreters.

Most of those who undergo training and examinations developed by CACDP are hearing people who wish to communicate with those who are deaf. They may be neighbours, relatives or workmates or they may be involved with deaf people as social workers, teachers or aspiring interpreters.

CACDP, apart from approving curricula and arranging examinations, provides training courses and financial support for new courses in certain circumstances – especially where such training would not otherwise take place. Where possible, it encourages development of training by Colleges of Further and Higher Education reserving for itself the primary function of an examining body.

CACDP does not advocate one method of communication in preference to another, but seeks to meet the needs of all who are deaf. It has developed training schemes and examinations in sign communication skills, lip speaking, and communicating with deaf-blind persons.

Counsel and Care for the Elderly
Twyman House, 16 Bonny Street, London NW1 9LR (Tel: 01-485 1550).
This charity offers an information and advice service to elderly people and those concerned with their care. Grants are made for nursing care at home and in nursing homes.

Crohn's Disease
See National Association for Colitis and Crohn's Disease.

Crossroads Care Attendant Schemes
See Association of Crossroads Care Attendant Schemes.

CRYPT (Creative Young People Together)
See Section 6, Further Education.

Cystic Fibrosis Research Trust
5 Blyth Road, Bromley, Kent BR1 3RS (Tel: 01–464 7211)
Also: 39 Hope Street, Glasgow G2 6AE (Tel: 041–226 4244), and Anchor Lodge, Cultra, County Down (Tel: Holywood (023 17) 3178), and 5 Ystrad Close, Johnstown, Carmarthen SA31 3PE (Tel: Carmarthen (0267) 237943).
Cystic Fibrosis (CF) is an inherited disease affecting the lungs and digestive system, which threatens the lives of many thousands of children in this country from birth onwards.

The Cystic Fibrosis Research Trust was founded in 1964 to finance research to find a cure and, in the meantime, to improve treatment, to help and advise parents, to educate the public, and to promote earlier diagnosis in young children. The Trust is currently funding over 50 major research projects. There are over 280 branches and local groups throughout the UK. The Trust also publishes a wide range of relevant literature, a quarterly magazine *Cystic Fibrosis News*, and a newspaper, *CFNOW*.

Cystic Hygroma and Haemangioma Support Group
Villa Fontane, Church Road, Worth, Crawley, West Sussex RH10 4RS (Tel: Crawley (0293) 885901).
Cystic Hygroma is a growth which probably results from faulty development of the lymphatic system before birth. More than half of all cases affect the head and neck, and although the growth is benign there may be problems with feeding and breathing.

This support group aims to link parents of children who are affected by these rare conditions. It publishes an information booklet on the conditions and a newsletter (three times a year). The Group is co-operating with Professor Smithells, a geneticist, in a survey to try to establish possible causes of cystic hygroma.

Deafness
See Hearing Impairment

Depressives Associated
PO Box 5, Castle Town, Portland, Dorset DT5 1BQ.
This organisation offers the following help:
1. Information to help you to understand what depression is, the problems associated with it and how other people have learned to cope. A quarterly newsletter contains up-to-date information, helpful suggestions and other information designed to help you to gain a measure of relief and understanding. There is also a selection of booklets and fact-sheets covering subjects frequently asked about.
2. Understanding, personal replies. The Association says that when you register with it you will no longer feel isolated and shut off from others. They too have experienced the misery which depression can bring, whether as ex-sufferers or as relatives of a sufferer.
3. Hope. The Association says that it can show you that depression can be overcome and that you need not fear it.
4. Contact and friendship. One of the aims of the Association is to help people to establish small self-help groups. Wherever possible it will put you in touch with one. If there is no group near to you, the Association will endeavour to put you in touch with others locally who have previously made contact, which may eventually form the basis for a new group.
Membership (including the newsletter) costs £5 a year.

Diabetes
See below and British Diabetic Association.

Diabetes Foundation
177a Tennison Road, London SE25 5NF (Tel: 01–656 5467).
This organisation was formed in 1982 and the main aims are as follows:
1. To fund research into the causes and complications of diabetes, including blindness, heart and kidney disease, gangrene; while the primary objective of the Foundation will be to find a cure for diabetes.
2. To provide a programme of public awareness and education.
3. To raise funds to supplement hospitals with equipment and other help required for diabetic care.
4. To represent the interests of all diabetics in the United Kingdom.
The Foundation issues an interesting quarterly magazine *Diabetic Life*, for the understanding of

diabetes, with regular mailings to members of the most recent progress in diabetic research work. In addition, The Foundation has a panel of doctors and allied members of the medical profession who are able to give general help and advice to diabetics and especially the parents of diabetic children.

A 24-hour telephone helpline is operated on the above number to give non-medical advice, with co-ordinators appointed throughout the country as local contacts. The annual membership subscription is £3.50 (£2 for pensioners).

DIAL UK (National Association of Disablement Information and Advice Lines)

Victoria Buildings, 117 High Street, Clay Cross, Chesterfield, Derbyshire S45 9DZ (Tel: Chesterfield (0246) 250055).

The first Disablement Information and Advice Line (DIAL) was set up early in 1977. DIALs are autonomous local associations of people with personal experience of disability with the primary aim of providing information for other disabled people or those concerned with disability. DIALs prefer to give information direct to disabled people and thus to enable them to help themselves, although they can, where necessary, refer people on to back-up services such as advocacy or supportive counselling. DIALs therefore work in close co-operation with other services who can meet a special need, and can provide open access to relevant specialist information and appropriate local services. Although disability is not a necessary qualification to provide such a service, it has been found that it often breaks down the barriers between caller and information provider and affords shared experiences which encourage communication. The National Association, formed in 1980, unites, supports and represents local groups throughout Britain, as well as providing training opportunities for DIAL volunteers.

The Disability Alliance

25 Denmark Street, London WC2 8NJ (Tel: 01–240 0806).

The Disability Alliance is a federation of over 90 organisations of and for people with disabilities who have joined together to press for the introduction of a comprehensive income scheme for disabled people, replacing the existing patchwork of social security benefits with a rational system based on severity of disability alone.

A sister organisation, the Disability Alliance Educational and Research Association, publishes yearly The Disability Rights Handbook, which has become recognised as one of the most authoritative guides to welfare benefits (the 12th edition (87/88) costs £3). The Association also runs a Welfare Rights Information Service which will give free advice and information on social security matters to advisers. Individuals are requested to try their local agencies first and ask them to make contact where there are still problems. The Service operates three days a week (unfortunately variable) and enquiries can be made from 2 to 4.30pm, or, of course, in writing.

The Alliance seeks to encourage the take-up of existing benefits by those entitled to them and presses for improvements in the way they are operated. A publications list, which includes a number of research pamphlets concerned with the financial implications of disability, is available on request.

Disabilities Study Unit

Wildhanger, Amberley, Arundel, West Sussex BN18 9NR (Tel: Bury (079 881) 406).

The objects of the Disabilities Study Unit are the relief of disabled people generally, whether of individuals or of groups, and in particular for the conduct or promotion of research or studies into the needs of disabled people in their living conditions, and ways of relieving these needs, and the application and publication of the result of such research and studies for the benefit of disabled people.

To these ends, the DSU is willing to undertake projects submitted to it, but the Unit's financial resources are strictly limited and projects from outside the unit will normally also have to be funded from outside. The DSU is a non-profit-distributing organisation and all projects are costed on this basis.

The DSU has already produced a number of notable publications in the field of disability, including a directory of sports centres in England and Wales with their facilities for disabled people, a collection of essays under the title Disability – Legislation and Practice, One of the Family, a booklet for brothers and sisters of children with handicaps, Loneliness – The Other Handicap, Water Sports and Epilepsy and Sex Education for the Physically Handicapped.

Disabled Against Animal Research and Exploitation

22 The Severn, Grange Estate, Daventry, Northamptonshire NN11 4QR (Tel: Daventry (0327) 71568).

This is a national organisation supported by the

British Union for the Abolition of Vivisection. Many of its members are themselves disabled or represent a disabled person as a family member or close friend. As such, they see a parallel between the frustration and anger frequently imposed by the constraints of disability and the pain of an animal who is held by force and manipulated in animal experimentation. DAARE repudiates attempts to justify the abuse of animals as necessary to further research into the cause and cure of disabling conditions.

Disabled Drivers' Association
See Section 8, Mobility and Motoring.

Disabled Drivers' Motor Club Ltd
See Section 8, Mobility and Motoring.

Disabled Living Foundation
380–384 Harrow Road, London W9 2HU (Tel: 01–289 6111).
The DLF is a charitable trust concerned with all disabilities (mental, physical and sensory). It works to help disabled people in those aspects of ordinary life which present special problems and difficulties. Its activities include an excellent information service, a permanent collection of aids and equipment of all kinds, and incontinence and clothing advisory specialists. It has made special studies concerned with music, employment, further education, and the problems of those with partial sight. Fuller details of the Foundation's services and of its many helpful publications are given in Section 3, Aids and Equipment.

Disabled Living Services
Redbank House, 4 St Chad's Street, Manchester M8 8QA (Tel: 061–832 3678).
An independent voluntary organisation providing services for physically disabled people and their families. It provides a welfare counselling service, a volunteer befriending scheme and a craft teaching service, and manages the regional Disabled Living Centre (see Section 3, Aids and Equipment).

Disabled People's International
Box 36033, S–100 71 Stockholm, Sweden.
This international coalition of consumer organisations of disabled people was conceived in Winnipeg, Canada at the 1980 World Congress of Rehabilitation International. In 1981, the First World Congress of Disabled People's International in Singapore formally established the organisation and elected its first World Council. Organisations of disabled people from more than 50 countries were represented at this founding congress, and similar organisations from 30 countries now have formal representation on the World Council. DPI has consultative status or its equivalent with the major United Nations bodies and agencies, and has affiliations in more than 80 nations. DPI has five regions: Africa, Asia, Europe, Latin America and North America. The representative for Europe, who is also vice-chairperson of DPI, is Ann Marif Saebones, c/o DPI Europe at the above address.

Disablement Income Group (DIG)
Millmead Business Centre, Millmead Road, London N17 9QU (Tel: 01–801 8013).
Also: ECAS House, 28–30 Howden Street, Edinburgh EH8 9HW (031–667 0249).
DIG is a national charity, with 40 local branches, which aims to promote the financial welfare of disabled people in the United Kingdom. Publications include a quarterly membership newspaper, a twice-yearly journal, *Progress,* and a directory. DIG operates an advisory service, undertakes research and advocates reforms in the social security system, including the introduction of a national disability income.

Disfigurement
See Society of Skin Camouflage and Disfigurement Therapy.

Distressed Gentlefolk's Aid Association
Vicarage Gate House, Vicarage Gate, London W8 4AQ (Tel: 01–229 9341).
DGAA provides financial help, clothing, comforts and holidays in suitable cases. It runs 13 nursing/residential homes.

Dogs for the assistance of disabled people
See below and Assistance Dogs for Disabled People, Hearing Dogs for the Deaf, Pet Concern.

Dogs for the Disabled
Brook House, 1 Lower Ladyes Hills, Kenilworth, Warwickshire CV8 2GN (Tel: Kenilworth (0926) 59726).
A charity devoted to the provision, free of charge, of dogs (chosen from those which are lost, abandoned or unwanted), which are specially trained to:
(a) perform tasks which disabled people (other than those suffering from blindness and deafness), find it difficult or impossible to perform themselves; and
(b) assist in seeking help when an emergency arises.

Down's Syndrome
See below and Scottish Down's Syndrome Association.

Down's Syndrome Association
12–13 Clapham Common Southside, London SW4 7AA (Tel: 01–720 0008).
The Association gives practical support, advice and objective information to children and adults with Down's Syndrome.

Dr Barnado's
Tanners Lane, Barkingside, Ilford, Essex IG6 1QG (Tel: 01–550 8822).
Barnado's aims to provide and develop, in consultation with statutory authorities and other agencies, selected services for children in need and their families. Residential work provides for children who are handicapped physically, mentally and emotionally. Field social work projects include highly concentrated efforts to find homes for 'hard to place' children; sustained programmes for the training of social work volunteers; support projects for those who are bereaved and for one-parent families. Day care centres for pre-school children, for the non-school attenders and for unemployed youth are available. Holiday play schemes are in operation and also holiday placements for mentally handicapped children. The services are operated on a devolved divisional basis (eight divisions).

Dyslexia
See British Dyslexia Association, Scottish Dyslexia Association.

Dysphasia
See Action for Dysphasic Adults.

Dystrophic Epidermolysis Bullosa Research Association (DEBRA)
Suite 4, 1 King's Road, Crowthorne, Berkshire RG11 7BG (Tel: Crowthorne (0344) 771961).
Epidermolysis Bullosa is the name given to a group of non infectious diseases running in families and characterised by blistering and shearing of the skin on trivial injury. The blisters may be filled with clear fluid or with blood and cell fluid. It can vary from a relatively mild disorder to a severely mutilating and sometimes fatal disease. The exact cause is not yet known. The disease is quite rare, but is known to affect well over 2,000 people in Britain.
    DEBRA is a self-help organisation which offers friendship and support to parents and those affected. The Association promotes research into the cause, nature, treatment and cure of this disease,

offers a contact service to members, and funds a clinical nurse specialist at the Hospital for Sick Children, Great Ormond Street. A range of advisory literature is published which includes a bibliography of Epidermolysis Bullosa.

Eczema
See The Alternative Centre, National Eczema Society.

Educational Visits and Exchanges
See Central Bureau for Educational Visits and Exchanges.

Electronic Aids for the Blind
28 Crofton Road, Orpington, Kent BR6 8DU (Tel: 01–709 1186 – office hours).
EAB began its work in 1978 as a national charity operating voluntarily to provide electronic equipment and services at low cost or no cost to blind and visually impaired people, and to ensure that the training in the use of such equipment was carried out properly. Particular concerns have included education, employment, mobility and social needs at home. The emphasis in EAB's work is to help specially selected people who will be able effectively to use and exploit advanced equipment which is not normally available from social services departments or other charities whose efforts are directed to the generality of blind people. Funds do not at present match the needs of those who could benefit from EAB's help, and the organisation has therefore currently embarked on an ambitious development plan aimed at raising the scale of its activities.

Epidermolysis Bullosa
See Dystrophic Epidermolysis Bullosa Research Association.

Epilepsy
See British Epilepsy Association, National Society for Epilepsy, Scottish Epilepsy Association.

Ex-services Mental Welfare Society
Broadway House, The Broadway, Wimbledon, SW19 1RL (Tel: 01–543 6333).
    A specialist organisation concerned with the welfare of those ex-servicemen and women from all ranks of HM Forces and the Merchant Navy who suffer from psychiatric disabilities, more particularly those with active or long regular service. The Society operates throughout the UK and Eire, with headquarters in London, and offices in Manchester and Glasgow. Great emphasis is placed on domiciliary visiting, and the closest liaison is maintained with mental hospitals. The

Society runs convalescent homes, a hostel for single men, cottages for married people and their families, and a veterans' home. Application to the General Secretary.

The Family Welfare Association
501–505 Kingsland Road, London E8 4AU (Tel: 01 254 6251).
An independent social work charity providing a professional counselling service to individuals and families in need, through nine FWA social work centres in London, one in Milton Keynes and one in Northampton. FWA also offers training programmes for social workers, and publishes annually *Guide to Social Services* and *Charities Digest*.

The Foundation for Communication for the Disabled
25 High Street, Woking, Surrey GU21 1BW (Tel: Woking (04862) 27848).
This charity has been set up to find ways in which new technology can help disabled people to communicate, usually by enabling them to produce text.

The Foundation's approach is to take advantage of existing mass produced, portable equipment, which can be modified as necessary to meet the needs of disabled people. The Foundation offers a free assessment and back-up service and, where necessary, technical manuals are rewritten in non-technical language.

At the time of writing, systems are supplied based on four portable devices: Microwriter; Microscribe; NEC lap-held computer; and Psion Organiser. They can be used with printers, voice synthesisers, TV displays and enlarged text displays.

People with visual, speech, hearing, physical and certain learning difficulties have been helped.

Friedreich's Ataxia Group
The Common, Cranleigh, Surrey GU6 8SB (Tel: Cranleigh (0483) 272741).
The Group works to raise money for research into the cause and treatment of Friedreich's Ataxia, a crippling disease of childhood. It also maintains a small welfare fund to help sufferers and their families. It publishes a quarterly newsletter, an information folder and other literature useful to sufferers, their families, social workers, etc., and has for free loan a 25 minutes, 16mm colour, optical sound film.

Friends for the Young Deaf Trust
East Court Mansion, Council Offices, College Lane, East Grinstead, Sussex RH19 3LT (Tel: East Grinstead (0342) 23444).
This Trust was established in 1967. It promotes the general welfare of deaf people, especially the deaf child and school-leaver. FYD addresses itself to the needs of deaf children and young deaf people in the community, where they can often experience severe isolation. FYD's aim is to encourage their self-esteem, self-confidence and independence.

The combined office and resource centre at East Grinstead organises a wide range of educational and recreational activities. It provides, for Sussex, Surrey, Kent and London, a focal source of information and point of contact both for those affected and those wishing to help them.

A research project, *Deaf-fax,* concerned with the development of electronic aids for people with impaired hearing and/or speech is linked to similar developments in Europe.

Gay Men's Disabled Group
c/o Gay's the Word, 66 Marchmont Street, London WC1N 1AB.
Aims to provide close support for gay men with disabilities and to bring them and gay men without disabilities together; to make gay groups and society at large more aware of the needs of disabled people; and to further gay liberation and the liberation of people with disabilities.

A newsletter is produced about four times a year and includes a pen-friend/contact section. This operates on a box number system and all correspondence is treated as strictly confidential. From time to time throughout the year, meetings of the Group are held; these vary quite a bit – some are social, some discussion groups and so on. The newsletter is available on tape, and a tape library of gay fiction is available to members only. Correspondence can also be in Braille or by tape.

Annual membership £5 (£2.50 for OAPs, students and the unwaged).

Gemma
BM Box 5700, London WC1N 3XX.
Gemma is a group for disabled/able-bodied homosexual women aiming to lessen the isolation of those whose disability hinders appropriate relationships and access to homosexually orientated literature. The group stresses that it is not a dating agency, nor a ghetto of disabled lesbians, nor even a counselling service; simply a group of friends with some understanding through personal experience providing a bridge into a wider friendship

circle, which includes pen-friendships, meetings and socials.

A quarterly newsletter is available on tape.

Gingerbread
35 Wellington Street, London WC2E 7BN (Tel: 01–240 0953).
An association with over 300 local self-help groups in England and Wales which seeks to encourage and promote the interests of lone parents and their children. This includes those who are divorced, separated, widowed, unmarried or for other reasons are having to care for their families on their own. Groups provide a number of activities including meetings, outings, advice on emotional and practical problems such as housing, access and welfare benefits, and they campaign for a better quality of life for all one-parent families. There is a wide range of literature, including a magazine *Ginger*. Details of local group contacts are available from the national office.

The Girl Guides Association
See Section 11, Sports and Leisure.

Glaucoma
See International Glaucoma Association.

GLAD – Greater London Association for Disabled People
336 Brixton Road, London SW9 7AA (Tel: 01–274 0107).
GLAD is a London-wide voluntary organisation which supports a network of borough disablement associations. GLAD works on a variety of policy issues including transport, disability in ethnic communities, and disability awareness training. It also answers enquiries on disability issues in London and produces *Guides to Information*.

GRACE (Mrs Gould's Residential Advisory Centre for the Elderly)
PO Box 71, Cobham, Surrey KT11 2JR (Tel: Cobham (0932) 62928/65765).
GRACE co-ordinates information about nursing homes, privately run residences and some hotels and guest houses, all of which are regularly visited by GRACE staff. Offers advice regarding available accommodation to suit the individual needs of clients, whether for permanent or short-stay residence and with or without nursing care. To defray some of the cost a registration fee is charged, which is returnable if accommodation is secured in one of the residences suggested by GRACE.

Property of a kind handled by estate agents, and self-catering accommodation, are not covered.

The service covers 25 counties of England south of a line from Norfolk to Hereford and Worcester, but excludes London.

Greater London Association for Disabled People
See GLAD.

Growth
See Child Growth Foundation.

The Guide Dogs for the Blind Association
Alexandra House, 9 Park Street, Windsor, Berkshire (Tel: Windsor (0753) 855711).
The Association provides dogs and training in their use for registered blind people aged 18 and over. Its work has expanded considerably in recent years: there are now nine training centres and nearly 4,000 guide dog owners. Over 600 owner and dog 'units' are trained each year.

Guild of Aid for Gentlepeople
10 St Christopher's Place, London W1M 6HY (Tel: 01–935 0641).
The Guild's aim is to make grants and special gifts to gentlefolk in distress as a result of old age, disability or misfortunes not of their making. Applications to be made to the Secretary.

Haemangioma
See Cystic Hygroma.

Haemophilia Society
123 Westminster Bridge Road, London SE1 7HR (Tel: 01–928 2020).
Advice and information are available through various publications or in response to enquiries. The Society seeks to promote and protect the interests of people with haemophilia and to represent their special needs to government and local authorities, both generally and in specific cases. Currently this applies to problems arising from the contamination of their life-saving blood products with HIV and hepatitis and problems arising from AIDS. Financial help is given in suitable cases. Local groups provide social fellowship, and raise funds for research.

Handicapped Adventure Playgrounds Association (HAPA)
See Section 11, Sports and Leisure.

Handicapped Persons Research Unit
Newcastle upon Tyne Polytechnic, 1 Coach Lane, Coach Lane Campus, Newcastle upon Tyne NE7 7TW (Tel: Newcastle upon Tyne (091) 2358211).
An interdisciplinary research and consultancy unit concerned with realistic problems as they occur in the field of handicap. To this end it undertakes

professional and postgraduate research into a wide range of subjects concerned with mentally and physically handicapped people. Many research reports have been published including the *Directory of Non-Medical Research relating to Handicapped People* (1987).

The Unit offers information services on two databases: BARD and BARDSOFT, which are described in Section 3, Aids and Equipment.

Headway (National Head Injuries Association)
200 Mansfield Road, Nottingham NG1 3HX (Tel: Nottingham (0602) 622382).
A voluntary organisation which seeks to provide support for head injury patients and their families in the problems they have to face. Self-help support groups allow people involved to meet with each other.

A list of information booklets and leaflets for patients, families and professionals is available.

Health
See Action for the Victims of Medical Accidents, College of Health, Health Education Authority, The Healthcall Directory, Healthline, Help for Health, National Association of Leagues of Hospital Friends, Patients' Association.

Health Education Authority
Hamilton House, Mabledon Place, London WC1H 9TX (Tel:01–631 0930).
The HEA was set up by government to lead and support health promotion in England. It took over the responsibilities of the former Health Education Council on 1st April 1987, and will, from an early date, assume responsibility for public health education on AIDS.

The Authority will plan and promote the national programmes of health education, carry out research and assist in the development of local programmes in co-operation with the NHS, local authorities, professional organisations, voluntary bodies, industry and commerce, having previously taken over the health promotional activities of the DHSS and the work of the Central Council for Health Education.

The HEA has an information service on all health-related matters, and maintains an excellent library and resources centre. A free publications catalogue lists and illustrates the many leaflets and posters which are available, and resource lists can be provided on a variety of subjects including one under the title *Handicap*.

The Healthcall Directory (Air Call Medical Services Ltd)
Ashton House, 403 Silbury Boulevard, Central Milton Keynes, Buckinghamshire.
Healthcall is a confidential telephone service, operating 24 hours a day, which gives free (apart from the cost of the call) medical information. There are over 300 tapes from which to choose, each on a separate telephone number. Connection is promised within 20 seconds. Tapes vary in duration from approximately two to seven minutes, and you should be aware that calls are charged not at the ordinary rate but at British Telecom's M rate (at the time of writing 22 pence per minute cheap rate (6 p.m. to 8 a.m.) or 35 pence per minute peak rate (8 a.m. to 6 p.m.).

The dental topics have been written by members of the British Dental Association. All other topics have been written and produced by a team of doctors and specialists and are approved by the Royal College of General Practitioners. The tapes are not intended as a cure-all. If after listening to a tape you are still concerned about a problem, or if you suffer from any persistent symptoms, you are advised to consult your doctor as soon as possible. The library is extensive and includes tapes on several disabling conditions. For a free directory call 0898 600 600.

Healthline
18 Victoria Park Square, London E2 9PF (Tel: Healthline tapes 01–980 4848; office 01–980 6263).
Healthline, a confidential telephone service, gives free (apart from the cost of the call) information on health matters by playing taped messages over the phone. Calls are charged at the ordinary rate. There are nearly 250 topics to choose from, and the tapes, most of which last between three and seven minutes, have been written and approved by medical experts. The tapes explain particular health problems and give information about causes, symptoms and treatment. There is also advice on self-help, but invariably it is made clear when you should consult a doctor. Many of the tapes include details of self-help groups and other organisations to contact for further information and help. The tapes cover a wide range of subjects including women's health, disability, alternative medicine, emotional and sexual matters, as well as many general health problems. The section on disability includes tapes on the services available to blind people; adaptations to your home; things to make life easier.

To use the service phone 01–980 4848 between 2

p.m. and 10 p.m. any day of the week. The operator will play you the tape of your choice. It is useful to have a pen and paper handy to note down the names and addresses of organisations you may wish to contact.

For a free copy of the Healthline directory listing all the tapes available, send an s.a.e. to Healthline, PO Box 499, London E2 9PU.

Hearing Dogs for the Deaf

Little Close, Lower Icknield Way, Lewknor, Oxfordshire OX9 5RY (Tel: Kingston Blount (0844) 53898).

In Great Britain, one in five of the population has a significant hearing loss. The Hearing Dogs for the Deaf scheme has been in operation since 1982. Its aim is to train dogs to act as 'hearing ears' for deaf people by responding to everyday sounds. Since the scheme started, a number of dogs have been successfully placed and have proved their worth as hearing companions. With the continuing progress and expansion of the programme, the training of many more dogs is planned.

Potential owners are carefully selected. They must be severely or profoundly deaf, and also have the desire and ability to look after a dog properly. An experienced counsellor evaluates the application and is involved in familiarising owners-to-be with their dogs. A skilful dog trainer chooses a dog to suit the needs and wishes of the person concerned. Dogs of high intelligence and friendly disposition, showing keen responses to sound and a willingness to please, are selected.

The dog is then trained to respond to the sounds chosen by the new dog owner, such as a knock on the door, a whistling kettle, or an alarm clock. A dog can even be trained to fetch a deaf mother when her baby cries.

A home-like environment is used for the training, which takes about four months to complete. The counsellor makes pre- and post-placement visits to ensure that the dog and the new owner are suited, happy and working well together. Applicants are dealt with equally and in strict rotation. Owners will receive assistance in the care and support of their dogs, with free veterinary check-ups and vaccinations.

Hearing Impairment

See British Association of the Hard of Hearing, British Deaf Association, Council for the Advancement of Communication with Deaf People, Link – the British Centre for Deafened People, National Association for Deaf-Blind and Rubella Handicapped, National Deaf-Blind Helpers League, National Deaf Children's Society, Royal Association in Aid of the Deaf and Dumb, Royal National Institute for the Deaf, Sympathetic Hearing Scheme.

Heart Disease

See British Heart Foundation, Cardiac Spare Parts Club, Chest Heart and Stroke Association.

Help the Aged

St James's Walk, London EC1R 0BE (Tel: 01–253 0253).

Help the Aged is a national charity dedicated to improving the quality of life of elderly people in need of help in the UK and overseas. This aid is pursued by the raising and granting of funds towards community-based projects, housing and overseas aid.

In the United Kingdom, Help the Aged works to combat elderly people's loneliness and isolation by funding and supporting: minibuses; day centres; day hospitals; research; development and education; a network of sheltered housing schemes and residential care homes including the unique Gifted Housing Plan; 24-hour emergency alarm systems and advice on how to obtain them.

The charity also publishes a wide range of information sheets and advice leaflets for elderly people, and operates a first line advice service.

Help for Health Information Service

Grant Building, Southampton General Hospital, Southampton SO9 4XY (Tel: Southampton (0703) 777222 ext.3753; Southampton (0703) 779091 (24-hour Ansaphone)).

A resource centre of information to enable patients to understand health problems, to look after themselves and to make full use of the help available from statutory and voluntary sources. Although primarily a local service, Help for Health has an extensive database and will deal with enquiries from elsewhere. It is widely respected for its expertise.

Help for Health provides an enquiry service by telephone, letter or personal visit. The centre keeps addresses of voluntary organisations and self-help groups, both national and regional, and has a large collection of relevant literature. It publishes a regular newsletter, a wide range of information sheets and handbooks on a number of topics, including epilepsy, multiple sclerosis, stroke, schizophrenia and Parkinson's disease.

Help for Health's information officer Robert Gann has written *The Health Information Handbook: Resources for Self-care* (see Appendix A), which describes the Help for Health Project and similar services in the UK and abroad, and gives practical advice on setting up a collection of health information.

Hodgkin's Disease Association
PO Box 275, Haddenham, Aylesbury, Buckinghamshire HP17 8JJ (Tel: Haddenham (0844) 291500, 7 p.m. to 10 p.m. or answerphone).
This is a self-help group providing emotional support and information for people with Hodgkin's Disease and Non Hodgkin's Lymphoma and their families. The Association has a helpline and publishes relevant literature and has a network of helpers with experience of lymphomas, to whom enquirers may be linked if they wish.
Membership subscription £2 a year.

Home Care Support (HCS)
382 Hillcross Avenue, Morden, Surrey SM4 4EX (Tel: 01–542 0348).
HCS is a licensed carers' agency which aims to provide reliable, responsible and friendly caring staff, enabling those who are caring for handicapped children or elderly people to have a break. Not all staff supplied are nurses, but all have nursing training or experience and are competent in caring for people in their homes.
Carers will undertake such tasks as cooking and shopping, or will act as companions, but do not undertake heavy domestic cleaning duties. Hours are flexible, and the service can be daily, evenings or weekends. A sleep-in service at night on a long or short-term basis can also be arranged.
All requests for help are carefully assessed so that the client's needs are met. A free advisory service to families enabling them to choose the best care for their particular needs is offered.
Details of charges on request.

Home and School Council
81 Rustlings Road, Sheffield S11 7AB (Tel: Sheffield (0742) 662467).
Aims to encourage the spread of good practice in home and school relationships.

Horticultural Therapy
See Section 11, Sports and Leisure.

Huntington's Chorea
See Association to Combat Huntington's Chorea.

Hydrocephalus
See Association for Spina Bifida and Hydrocephalus, Scottish Spina Bifida Association.

Hyperactive Children's Support Group
71 Whyke Lane, Chichester, W. Sussex PO19 2LD.
The HACSG was formed in 1977 to help and support (other than financially) hyperactive children and their families. It encourages the formation of local groups where parents may get together for mutual support and understanding. It aims to persuade the medical profession and the health and education authorities to take more interest in the day-to-day problems of hyperactive children and adolescents, to promote urgent research into the causes, treatment and management of hyperactivity, to press for its early and proper diagnosis, and to disseminate information to all interested people.
While recognising various causes of hyperactivity, the Group is particularly concerned to explore sensitivity to chemical food additives and to offer advice on basic diet. Journals are published three times a year. The membership fee is £6.50, which includes a diet/information handbook.

Hypertropic Pyloric Stenosis
See Pyloric Stenosis Society.

The Ileostomy Association of Great Britain and Ireland
Amblehurst House, Chobham, Woking, Surrey GU24 8PZ (Tel: Chobham (099 05) 8277).
IA was formed in 1956 as a mutual support association by a group of people with ileostomies. The primary aim has always been to help others facing ileostomy surgery to return to a fully active and normal life as soon as possible. There are over 60 branches in Great Britain – including three in Wales, three in Scotland, one in Northern Ireland and one in the Republic of Ireland. There are also honorary officers who provide a range of advisory services. A quarterly journal is sent free of charge to all members, and local meetings are arranged at which the latest ileostomy equipment and skincare preparations are displayed.

Impaired Lives Insurance Bureau
The Old Barn, Stoke Green, near Stoke Poges, Buckinghamshire SL2 4HN (Tel: Slough (0753) 25064).
This Bureau specialises exclusively in advice on insurance matters to people with impairments, and offers to assist 'in the placement of their insurance requirements at the most favourable terms'. It is linked with a number of leading life, pension and health insurance companies who are prepared to consider those who are in less than perfect health.

You will be asked to complete a proposal form and to send an initial fee of £35 to cover the cost of a medical report (from your own GP) and the Bureau's administration costs. Your proposal form will be passed to the Bureau's doctor, who will write to your GP requesting a report. If it proves to be impossible to provide you with a quotation (something which is said to be unlikely), your fee, except for your own doctor's fee, will be refunded. The service is confidential and you will not be visited except at your specific request, nor subjected to unwanted telephone calls.

Independent Development Council for People with Mental Handicap

126 Albert Street, London NW1 7NF (Tel: 01–267 6111).

The Council was set up in 1981 at the instigation of leading organisations working in the field of mental handicap to promote nationally the development of appropriate services for people with mental handicap and their families.

The Council offers independent advice to relevant government departments and other concerned bodies on policies, good practices, and necessary national and local action.

In pursuing its objectives, the Council is guided by the belief that services for mentally handicapped people should affirm and enhance their dignity, self-respect and individuality, pay due regard to their views and wishes, assist them to lead as normal a life as possible and to share in and contribute to community and family life.

Infantile Hypercalcaemia Parents Association (incorporating Williams Syndrome)

Mulberry Cottage, 37 Mulberry Green, Old Harlow, Essex (Tel: Harlow (0279) 27214).

The IHCPA has been set up to help parents of children with William's Syndrome/Infantile Hypercalcaemia, by providing information about the condition, putting parents in touch with each other, enabling their children to meet, acquiring background information to assist research, and stimulating interest, particularly among the medical profession, in the condition. A record of affected children is maintained.

The Infantile Hypercalcaemia Foundation, a separate charity, is initiating research into this very complex disease.

Information Services

Virtually all of the organisations listed in this section provide information to some extent. Those which concentrate on the provision of general information and advice are the Citizens' Advice Bureau Service, DIAL UK, the Disability Alliance Educational and Research Association, the Disabled Living Foundation, the Northern Ireland Information Service, the Scottish Council on Disability Information Service and the Wales Council for the Disabled Information Service,

Insurance

See Impaired Lives Insurance Bureau.

International Glaucoma Association

King's College Hospital, Denmark Hill, London SE5 9RS (Tel: 01–274 6222, ext 2466 – Mondays and Thursdays only).

The patient-based IGA aims to encourage general awareness and understanding of glaucoma, thus improving the chance of early diagnosis as well as providing and stimulating increased resources for a high standard of management for glaucoma patients.

The IGA holds discussion forums, answers written enquiries (s.a.e. please) and helps to support important clinical research.

Free information booklet sent on request. Members receive twice yearly newsletters and invitations to meetings. Membership is open to all.

Intestinal Disorders

See National Society for Children with Intestinal Disorders.

The In Touch Scheme

10 Norman Road, Sale, Cheshire M33 3DF (Tel: 061–962 4441).

This scheme (not to be confused with the BBC's *In Touch* programme/book for blind people) provides contacts for parents of children who have rare physical disorders or are mentally handicapped. Membership has increased steadily since the scheme was set up in 1968 and contacts are facilitated both in response to specific requests and through a newsletter which is published three times a year. A useful handbook of addresses for parents with a handicapped child is available (revised, enlarged 3rd edition, 60 pages, price £2.90).

Because the membership is both national and international, it it often possible to link families who have children affected by rare handicap conditions. Annual subscription: £2 for parents (optional); £5 for professionals and groups.

Intractable Pain Society

Association of Anaesthetists, 9 Bedford Square, London WC1B 3RA.

This is a Society for those doctors concerned with

the treatment of chronic pain in the United Kingdom and Ireland. It exists to enable experience to be exchanged and advice to be given concerning methods and research as to the best methods of treatment. While referrals to pain relief clinics can only be made by members of the medical profession, information concerning the location of clinics can be obtained from the Honorary Secretary.

Invalid Children's Aid Nationwide (ICAN)

Allen Graham House, 198 City Road, London EC1V 2PH (Tel: 01–608 2462).
Provides free help and advice for parents of children with special needs. This is given through its information service which deals with general enquiries, its secretary for schools who will advise on educational problems, and its social work service, which operates in parts of London and Surrey. ICAN runs four residential schools – three for children with speech and language disorders, and one for severe asthmatics. They also have a publications list, with particular emphasis on speech and language disorders.

See also Section 5, Education.

Invalids at Home Trust

17 Lapstone Gardens, Kenton, Harrow HA3 0EB (Tel: 01–907 1706).
The Trust provides financial help to individual people living at home who are either substantially handicapped or severely long-term ill, either to meet the heavy additional costs of living at home or to cope with emergencies.

Assistance can be provided for almost any expense which has to be met by the handicapped person living at home and which is not covered by statutory provision, with the exception of medical treatment, telephone rental and call charges (except where Social Services are paying the rental). Priority is given for items directly related to needs which arise from disability or illness, and which help to ensure disabled people's safety, comfort and independence, or help them to earn a living. Televisions can only be considered if the person is isolated and housebound.

Jennifer Macaulay Trust for Spinal Muscular Atrophy

11 Ashtree Close, Wellesbourne, Warwickshire (Tel: Stratford-upon-Avon (0789) 842377).
Spinal Muscular Atrophy (SMA) is a severe genetic physical handicap in which damage of anterior horn cells in the spine causes muscle deterioration. In its severer forms it is fatal. An acute form, known as Werdnig-Hoffman disease affects new born babies and is usually fatal within the first two years.

The Trust has been established as a support group for those affected and their families, and offers the chance to talk to others in similar situations. A quarterly newsletter and other information is published, and an annual conference is organised each September.

The Trust also aims to raise awareness of SMA and to support current research being sponsored by the Muscular Dystrophy Group.

Jewish Blind Society

211 Golders Green Road, London NW11 9DN (Tel: 01–458 3282).
This is the national social work agency for Jewish blind and partially sighted people. Its services include the teaching of mobility and daily living skills, and it has two integrated day centres, afternoon clubs, residential and holiday homes, and a communication department which includes a tape library, Braille and large print publications.

The Society is extending its work to disabled people within the age range from leaving school to retirement and is occasionally able to offer financial assistance.

Jewish Welfare Board

221 Golders Green Road, London NW11 9DW (Tel: 01–458 3282).
The JWB is the largest Jewish social work agency. It concentrates its work on those who are very old or mentally-ill, and their families, but undertakes some work with other client groups in partnership with smaller welfare organisations. The Board has three social work teams based at Redbridge, Hackney and Edgware.

JWB's major resources are 11 homes for elderly people, one mental after-care hostel, one rehabilitation hostel for mentally handicapped people, and several group homes for both mentally ill and mentally handicapped people. It also runs four day centres for elderly people suffering from mental illness.

John Grooms Association for the Disabled

10 Gloucester Drive, London N4 2LP (Tel: 01–802 7272).
This well established association has grown rapidly in recent years and now has 35 projects in England and Wales: residential homes for severely disabled people at London, Norwich and Southend; as-

sessment flats; work projects at Edgware and Hertfordshire; elderly people's accommodation; two seaside hotels, 18 self catering units and subsidised hotel accommodation in London providing holidays for disabled people; a housing association which has 19 schemes under management or planned; work overseas; an information service which includes films.

Kidney Disease
See British Kidney Patients' Association, National Federation of Kidney Patients' Associations, Renal Society.

King's Fund Centre
126 Albert Street, London NW1 7NF (Tel: 01–267 6111).
This Centre is maintained by the King Edward's Hospital Fund for London, an independent charity which seeks to encourage good practice and innovations in health care through research, experiment, education and direct grants.

The Centre houses modern conference and library facilities, and provides a base for the Fund's focus on health services development. The objective is to support innovations in the NHS and related organisations, to learn from successful experiments, and to encourage the uptake of new ideas and good practice in health care.

One focus of the Centre's work is long-term community care, an aspect of which is the development of services which better meet the needs of people with mental handicap, physical handicap, psychiatric problems or simply growing older.

The extensive library can be used by anyone interested in health services, and there is a parallel information service for those who are unable to visit the Centre. Books are not available for loan, but selected lists of references can be provided.

In 1986, the King's Fund established an Institute to provide independent health policy analysis, and more recently has also set up an 'Informal Caring Programme' to improve public recognition of and provide information for people who look after relatives or friends who cannot, through disability, illness or old age, manage at home without help. An 'Informal Caring Support Unit' seeks, in various ways, to stimulate, through statutory and voluntary agencies, an exchange of information and ideas on how to improve support for carers. Guides for carers and training programmes for professionals in the health and social services (both statutory and voluntary) have been developed.

The Lady Hoare Trust for Physically Disabled Children
7 North Street, Midhurst, West Sussex GU29 9DJ (Tel: Midhurst (073 081) 3696).
The Trust provides a nationwide team of professional social workers who will visit families with a physically handicapped child, assess need and provide casework support. Under certain circumstances small grants are sometimes made.

L'Arche UK
14 London Road, Beccles, Suffolk NR34 9NH (Tel: Beccles (0502) 715329).
Since 1964, L'Arche has established over 70 communities in various parts of the world where mentally handicapped people live and work together with non-handicapped assistants. The organisation aims to provide a home and to develop self-respect, independence, spiritual values and a sense of being useful. Wherever possible, handicapped members are encouraged to work in open employment. In the United Kingdom there are communities in Bognor Regis, Inverness, Kent, Lambeth (London) and Liverpool. Admissions, when vacancies become available, are normally arranged through local social services departments. Films and publications list available.

Laryngectomy
See National Association of Laryngectomee Clubs.

Laurence-Moon-Beidl Syndrome
Although there is no separate organisation representing those affected by this condition, the British Retinitis Pigmentosa Society (*see* page 289) will endeavour to advise on visual problems, the present state of research, provide information on special equipment, and put enquirers in touch with others who are similarly affected.

Leonard Cheshire Foundation
26–29 Maunsel Street, London SW1P 2QN (Tel: 01–828 1822).
The Foundation runs 77 residential homes in the United Kingdom mainly for severely physically handicapped men and women of all ages. Of these, one caters for mentally handicapped adults, one for mentally handicapped children, and three offer a half-way-house for patients discharged from long-stay psychiatric hospitals who need time to acquire sufficient confidence before living independently in the community. The Foundation has also set up 23 Family Support Services in England, offering part-time help to disabled people living in their own homes. In addition, it has recently opened a country house hotel for disabled people

on the Royal Sandringham Estate in Norfolk.

Overseas, the Foundation runs 147 residential homes for mentally and physically handicapped men, women and children in 45 countries.

The Foundation publishes a quarterly journal, *The Cheshire Smile*.

Leukaemia Care Society
PO Box 82, Exeter, Devon EX2 5DP (Tel: Exeter (0392) 218514).
The Society provides personal support, counselling and financial assistance to leukaemia sufferers and their families. Holidays are available in the Society's caravans.

Leukaemia Research Fund
43 Great Ormond Street, London WC1N 3JJ (Tel: 01–405 0101).
Apart from its major role of raising funds for research, this organisation runs an information service and has published a number of booklets on leukaemia and allied blood diseases for patients and their families, covering the nature of the diseases, symptoms, diagnoses, treatments and the outlook for the future.

Link – The British Centre for Deafened People
19 Hartfield Road, Eastbourne, East Sussex BN21 2AR (Tel: Eastbourne (0323) 638230).
Link provides residential courses for adults who have become deafened, together with members of the family. Payment including travelling expenses may be met by social services, health authorities or voluntary sources.

Link – The Neurofibromatosis Association
1 The Alders, Hanworth, Middlesex TW13 6NU.
Neurofibromatosis (nf) is a genetic disorder affecting roughly 1 in 3,000 people, although only some 10 to 20 per cent of those affected will ever need medical treatment for the condition. Nf is still poorly understood and many milder cases remain undiagnosed. It can, however, be progressive during lifetime and in its severest form can have very serious physical and mental effects.

Link is a national association with emergent local groups. It seeks to provide mutual support, linking sufferers with each other as well as with the medical profession. It provides information on nf and promotes awareness and understanding of the problems encountered in the disorder. Finally, it sponsors medical research into the treatment, prevention and cure of nf.

A newsletter is published four times a year, and fact sheets are available. The membership subscription is £3 per annum.

Liver disease
See The Michael McGough Foundation against Liver Disease in Children.

London Association for the Blind
14–16 Verney Road, London SE16 3DZ (Tel: 01–732 8771).
The Association operates nationally. It has hotels at Bognor Regis and Weston-super-Mare providing holidays for registered blind and partially sighted people, their families and escorts, at which guide dogs can be accommodated; two homes in Surrey for elderly blind and partially sighted men and women, 54 warden-supervised flats in Epsom, Surrey for single and married blind people; and residential accommodation in south-east London for working blind people. The Association also provides sheltered employment in a modern factory in south-east London for work in PVC welding.

Grants in the form of annuities and lump sum payments are given in appropriate cases to registered blind or registered partially sighted men, women and children. Applications can be made either through a social worker, local organisation for blind people, or other impartial organisation.

Lowe's Syndrome Association
29 Gleneagles Drive, Penwortham, Preston PR1 0JT.
Also known as the Oculo-Cerebro-Renal (eye-brain-kidney) Syndrome, this rare genetic condition affects males and results in multiple handicaps.

The Association, which was established in 1983, is an international, voluntary organisation made up of parents, medical and educational professionals, friends, relatives and others concerned about this condition. Its primary aims are to foster communication among families, to provide medical and educational information, to promote a better understanding of Lowe's Syndrome and the potential of those affected, and to encourage research. So far, only nine affected families in the UK are known to the Association. They are in regular contact for mutual support.

A newsletter, *On the Beam*, is published three times a year, and various relevant publications (from the USA) are available. Membership is open to all at a subscription of $13 a year.

Marfan Association
51 Kynaston Avenue, Thornton Heath, Surrey CR4 7BZ.
Marfan Syndrome is a rare (1 in 10,000), mostly

inherited disorder of the connective tissue, which affects many organ systems including skeleton, eyes, lungs, heart and blood vessels. By far the most serious of these is the heart system, and it is vitally important that those affected are examined at regular intervals throughout their lives.

The Marfan Association was formed in 1984 out of concern at the lack of knowledge available and support given to those affected by this condition. Support groups have been set up throughout the country to help to educate and support those affected and their families, and to ensure that the medical profession generally is kept informed of any steps forward in research and treatment.

For further information, contact the Support Group Co-ordinator, Di Rust, 70 Greenways, Courtmoor, Fleet, Hampshire GU13 9XD (Tel: Fleet (0252) 617908). If you require medical information, contact Dr. Anne Child, The Marfan Association, Department of Histopathology, St George's Hospital Medical School, Cranmer Terrace, Tooting, London SW17 0RE (Tel: 01–672 1255).

The Maria Scleroderma Therapy Trust

4 Newbury Court, Newbury, Gillingham, Dorset SP8 4QX (Tel: Gillingham (07 476) 4448).

Scleroderma is characterised by thickening of the deeper inner layer of the skin, causing leathery induration, followed by atrophy and pigmentation. Finger tips are particularly affected early on. Typically, when exposed to cold air or water, the fingers blanch or mottle, become numb and tingle. This is Raynauds phenomenon (see page 323), though there are many causes of Raynauds other than scleroderma. Sometimes the tissue thickening affects the gullet causing some difficulty in swallowing. Other parts of the body can be affected; the intestines and lungs are commonly affected. Different patterns of scleroderma have different names. In some the skin alone is affected (morphoea), in others skin is only one of several organs involved (systemic scleroderma). The cause is uncertain, and whilst a number of drugs are used in treatment, the results are variable.

The Trust, which operates nationally, was formed in 1977. Its long-term objectives are broadly to further research, publishing useful findings, to provide therapy and to raise the money necessary to start and maintain a special clinic for those affected. In the meantime, the Trust is able to link people together. It holds annual seminar/ workshops where people with scleroderma can learn how better to cope and live with the disease.

Regular newsletters are published and there is an informative booklet about the condition.

Membership currently numbers nearly 500 people with scleroderma. There is no set membership fee.

Marie Curie Memorial Foundation

28 Belgrave Square, London SW1X 8QG (Tel: 01–235 3325).

The Foundation is concerned with the welfare of cancer patients. Its nationwide services include 11 residential nursing homes (431 beds), day and night domiciliary nurses, welfare needs in kind, advice and helpful leaflets on care and aspects of the cancer problem, and a research institute. Information freely available from the above address.

Mastectomy

See The Breast Care and Mastectomy Association of Great Britain.

Medic-alert Foundation

11–13 Clifton Terrace, London N4 3JP (Tel: 01–263 8597).

The Foundation provides a service to people with unseen medical problems. They wear a warning emblem to alert anyone who may attend them in circumstances which preclude normal communication. A central reference office, able to provide more detailed information, is on call round the clock. It is available by reverse call charge from anywhere in the world.

MENCAP – The Royal Society for Mentally Handicapped Children and Adults

123 Golden Lane, London EC1Y 0RT (Tel: 01–253 9433).

MENCAP operates in England, Wales and Northern Ireland and provides a wide range of services for mentally handicapped people, their families and the professionals who work for them. The Society has consistently worked to improve provision for mentally handicapped children and adults by seeking to persuade local authorities and central government to provide desperately needed services. Over the years, it has mounted pioneer demonstration projects to point the way ahead and to show that mentally handicapped children and young people can be trained to expand their capabilities, go out to work, earn their own living and make a real contribution to the community where they live and work.

It is above all an organisation of parents. Over 550 local societies run pre-school play groups, nurseries, hostels and clubs, backed up by eight divisional offices which undertake welfare counselling and liaison with statutory authorities. The following services are provided.

1. For mentally handicapped people:
   (a) two social training units providing a bridge between school and the outside world;
   (b) holidays, many of them for the very severely handicapped;
   (c) facilities for leisure activities through the National Federation of Gateway Clubs (these are now nation-wide with over 40,000 members who enjoy sports, handicrafts, outings and other activities);
   (d) four residential homes for very severely handicapped children;
   (e) a Trustee Visitor's Service which provides personal visits for mentally handicapped people after the death of their parents;
   (f) Pathway, a work training scheme.
2. For parents:
   (a) a welfare visiting scheme run by local society voluntary visitors;
   (b) a welfare and counselling service;
   (c) help and support through a nationwide network of divisional offices;
   (d) books, pamphlets and leaflets on all aspects of mental handicap;
   (e) a quarterly magazine *Parents Voice*;
   (f) a monthly newspaper *Mencap News*;
   (g) advice and information;
3. For professionals:
   (a) a specialist information service;
   (b) conferences, seminars, in-service and day-release courses;
   (c) publication of a quarterly *Journal of Mental Deficiency Research*.

MENCAP has an extensive publications list, and many books are on display at Golden Lane. Particularly valuable is an information pack *Welfare and Legal Communications*, issued three times a year to keep parents and advisers up to date with developments affecting mentally handicapped people. This is available by subscription only and costs £8 a year.

An entirely different organisation, The Scottish Society for the Mentally Handicapped, operates in Scotland.

The Meningitis Trust
Fern House, Bath Road, Stroud, Gloucestershire GL5 3TJ (Tel: Stroud (04536) 71738/39/30).
Meningitis is an infection of the Meninges, the layer of membrane between the brain and the skull.

The Meningitis Trust was set up in 1985 by concerned parents as the result of the meningitis outbreak in the Stroud area. It exists to:
(a) raise money to fund research;
(b) provide information; and
(c) support those affected and their families.

It has a network of small support groups throughout England and Wales, and through its Stroud office it provides a 24-hour helpline.

Mental After Care Association
Bainbridge House, Bainbridge Street, London WC1A 1HP (Tel: 01–436 6194).
The Association provides homes and hostels, long- and short-stay, for adults recovering from mental illness under the care of trained staff.

Mental Handicap
See Association of Professions for Mentally Handicapped People, British Institute of Mental Handicap, The Campaign for Mentally Handicapped People, CARE, Independent Development Council for People with Mental Handicap, L'Arche UK, MENCAP, Scottish Society for the Mentally Handicapped.

Mental Health
See Ex-Services Mental Welfare Society, Mental Aftercare Association, MIND, Psychiatric Rehabilitation Association, Richmond Fellowship, Scottish Association for Mental Health.

Metabolic Diseases
See Research Trust for Metabolic Diseases in Children.

The Michael McGough Foundation Against Liver Disease in Children
PO Box 494, Western Avenue, London W3 0SH (Tel: 01–992 3400).
There are over 100 conditions which can lead to liver disease in children which may result in fatal cirrhosis or cause damage to other organs of the body.

The Foundation is the only national charity dedicated to the eradication of liver disease in children. It aims to:
(a) create a greater awareness of the problem of childhood liver disease;
(b) raise funds to promote research into causes and cures;
(c) provide emotional support for families.

Formed in April 1980, the Foundation now has a network of support groups throughout the country, and it facilitates contacts between families of children affected. A newsletter and information about liver diseases in children is published.

Microcephaly Support Group
17 Tennyson Rise, East Grinstead, West Sussex
RH19 1SQ.
This Group offers support/contact for families who
have microcephalic children.

MIND (National Association for Mental Health)
22 Harley Street, London W1N 2ED (Tel: 01–637
0741).
Also five regional offices, including:
    Wales: 23 St Mary Street, Cardiff CF1 2AA
(Tel: Cardiff (0222) 395123).
MIND runs an advice service which offers advice,
referrals and short-term help to patients and their
families; also an information service for both mental health professionals and the general public.
    MIND has pioneered a variety of community-
based projects and presently aims to support
people in the community who would otherwise be
in psychiatric hospitals
    MIND also runs a legal and welfare rights
service to protect the rights of patients and mental
health workers and to press for changes in the law.
It also provides a mental health review tribunal
service.
    In the community, MIND supports and co-
ordinates approximately 200 local mental health
associations and organises regional meetings and
conferences.
    MIND aims to stimulate research, and keeps up
sustained pressure for improvements in the mental
health services, putting forward practical proposals and submitting evidence to government
committees and enquiries. It provides a wide range
of publications on all aspects of mental health (a
list is available), and also publishes a bi-monthly
magazine called *Open Mind* and a series of fact
sheets on mental illness, mental handicap, manic
depression and schizophrenia.
    A holiday list will be provided free on receipt of
a large s.a.e.

Mobility Information Service
See Section 8, Mobility and Motoring.

Motability
See Section 8, Mobility and Motoring.

Motor Neurone Disease
See below and Scottish Motor Neurone Disease
Association.

Motor Neurone Disease Association
61 Derngate, Northampton NN1 1UE (Tel: Northampton (0604) 250505).
Motor neurone disease, often shortened to MND,

is the name given to a group of diseases in which
the nerve cells located in the brain and spinal cord,
which control the muscles of movement, are slowly
destroyed. With no nerves to control them, the
muscles gradually weaken and waste away and
weakness affects the arms and legs and the throat
and chest, resulting in difficulties in movement,
speech, swallowing and breathing.
    The cause of MND is unknown. It does not
affect the sense or the intellect and the person
affected is able to think, reason and experience
emotion at all stages of the disease. The onset of
the disease usually comes after the age of 40, but
there have been cases as young as 20. The average
course for the disease might be four years, though
there are some people who have lived with MND
for 20 years.
    The Association aims to provide moral support
to those affected by MND and their families; to
provide financial help where this is needed to
obtain special equipment not readily available
from the usual caring agencies; to collect and
spread information about the disease; and to foster
interest in and provide funds for further research.
There are local groups in various parts of the
country, and there are a number of paid Regional
Care Advisers who are in touch with and advise
professionals and people with MND and their
families.

Mucopolysaccharide Diseases
See Society for Mucopolysaccharide Diseases.

Multiple Sclerosis
See below and ARMS.

*Multiple Sclerosis Society of Great Britain and
Northern Ireland*
25 Effie Road, London SW6 1EE (Tel: 01–736
6267).
Also Northern Ireland: 34 Annadale Avenue,
Belfast BT7 3JJ (Tel: Belfast (0232) 644914); and
Scotland: Association of Scottish Branches, 27
Castle Street, Edinburgh EH2 3DN (Tel: 031–225
3600).
The Society promotes research into the cause and
cure of MS; its many local branches spearhead the
raising of funds and are also the primary means of
bringing welfare, advice, encouragement, help
with holidays, special equipment etc., and a wide
range of social activities to members, according to
local needs. The Effie Road office provides back-
up information and welfare services.

MS Crack is the younger members' arm of the

Society and helps them to meet their particular needs through self-help groups within the parent branches.

The Society publishes a quarterly magazine *MS News* and a monthly bulletin which incorporates news for MS Crack members. They are also available on cassette, both on a quarterly basis.

Muscular Dystrophy Group of Great Britain and Northern Ireland

Nattrass House, 35 Macaulay Road, London SW4 0QP (Tel: 01–720 8055).
Primarily a medical research charity, the Group's secondary (though no less important objective) is concerned with services to those affected by muscular dystrophy. An information officer, based at the above address, is able to advise on a wide range of subjects including how those with a neuromuscular illness may best use available statutory and voluntary facilities. Literature about muscular dystrophy and the allied neuromuscular diseases is available, and a monthly newsletter and quarterly journal are published.

The Group currently has 12 family care officers based in neuromuscular centres throughout the United Kingdom, and there are approximately 400 local branches and representatives providing an informal supportive network to those with neuromuscular disorders.

Myalgic Encephalomyelitis Association

PO Box 8, Stanford-le-Hope, Essex SS17 8EX (Tel: Stanford-le-Hope (0375) 642466).
The Association was formed in 1978. It offers support to those affected by this debilitating and capricious disease. It promotes research to try to establish a diagnostic test and to effect a cure, and works to make people aware of the disease and its effects. A major object is to pass on information obtained from the medical profession.

Myasthenia

See British Association of Myasthenics.

National Ankylosing Spondylitis Society

6 Grosvenor Crescent, London SW1X 7ER (Tel: 01–235 9585).
Ankylosing spondylitis (AS) is a painful condition of the spine and associated joints.

The Society's prime objects are research into the causes of AS, the relief of suffering and the education of those affected and the public. Cassette tapes of beneficial exercises are available. The Society promotes the welfare of people affected by

AS, and deals with individual enquiries. Support groups are also being formed. A free 17 page *Guidebook for Patients* can be obtained from the Society.

National Association for Colitis and Crohn's Disease

98A London Road, St Albans, Hertfordshire AL1 1NX.
Crohn's Disease affects the intestinal tract causing inflammation of the bowel wall. It can affect any part of the tract from mouth to anus, but is most common in the lower part of the small intestine (ileum) or part or all of the colon, or both. The inflammation causes swelling and thickening of the bowel wall, painful ulcerations and diarrhoea with mucus and bleeding in some cases. Sometimes the thickening of the wall causes obstruction, with vomiting and constipation.

Ulcerative Colitis is an inflammatory disease in which the inner lining layer of the colon becomes inflamed causing ulcers and producing excess mucus, with bleeding, pain and diarrhoea.

Information booklets and bi-annual newsletters are published. These are free to members, but limited to people suffering from inflammatory bowel diseases, their families and friends. Research projects are funded. There is a membership of 8,500 with 40 area groups throughout Great Britain.

National Association of Laryngectomee Clubs

4th floor, 39 Eccleston Square, London SW1V 1PB (Tel: 01–834 2857).
Many of those who have undergone surgical removal of the larynx find it extremely difficult to master the technique of producing alternative speech from the oesophagus. The result is often a retreat from communication into loneliness. In an attempt to meet this problem, laryngectomee clubs have been formed in many areas, in association with speech therapy clinics. Members meet regularly to try out their new voice techniques and give and receive confidence and fluency in a congenial, sympathetic and social atmosphere. The Association encourages the formation and affiliation of clubs, and collects, co-ordinates and disseminates information concerning the rehabilitation of members. It advises on the availability of speech aids and medical supplies, demonstrates speech aids and lectures on mouth to neck resuscitation on request of professional bodies. Arrangements can also be made for an experienced

oesophageal speaker to visit pre- and post-operative patients.

The National Association of Leagues of Hospital Friends

2nd Floor, Fairfax House, Causton Road, Colchester, Essex CO1 1RJ (Tel: Colchester (0206) 761227).

Membership is open to all Leagues of Hospital Friends and to other bodies whose objects are in general to provide care and relief for patients and former patients in hospitals in the United Kingdom or in the community, who are sick, convalescent, disabled, handicapped, infirm or in need of financial assistance, and to assist generally in charitable work within hospitals or care institutions. It is an entirely volunteer movement and has about 470,000 members in 1,360 Leagues of Friends who give their services, time, talent and money to the cause. Currently some £15 million is raised each year. The function of the National Association is to provide a support and advice centre for its members and to co-ordinate certain matters for the entirely autonomous individual Leagues of Friends. The function also embraces the role of catalyst for change, and the production of a quarterly magazine *The Hospital Friend*.

National Association for Limbless Disabled

31 The Mall, Ealing, London W5 2PX (Tel: 01–579 1758/9).

Founded in 1981, the Association aims to relieve and promote the rehabilitation of people who have suffered the loss of a limb or part of a limb.

Membership is open, from age 16, to those who have lost one or both legs, or one or both arms, or hands or feet. An advisory service seeks to ensure that members receive their proper entitlements under existing legislation and to assist needy dependants wherever possible. The Association also seeks to help members to secure suitable employment, to combat discrimination and to provide opportunities for a better, fuller social life for its members.

The Association works to facilitate the sharing of knowledge and experience to help all limbless members of the community, and co-operates with other organisations and government departments to improve services, including advances in the design and fitting of artificial limbs.

Membership fees: ordinary member £2 per annum; honorary/associate member £3.50 per annum. The membership fee includes the cost of a quarterly magazine.

National Association for the Relief of Paget's Disease

413 Middleton Road, Middleton, Manchester M24 4QZ.

Paget's Disease involves thinning of bone followed by unregulated new bone formation. It is quite common in the older age groups and in a small proportion of cases can be progressive, leading to pain, deformity and other associated disabilities. The disease is now being diagnosed in younger sufferers.

The Association was founded in 1973 to raise funds for research and to increase public awareness of the disease. It has subsequently helped to fund a number of important research projects, and has established branches in various parts of the country. Members are regularly kept in touch with progress and new ideas about treatment.

National Association for the Welfare of Children in Hospital

Argyle House, 29–31 Euston Road, London NW1 2SD (Tel: 01–833 2041).

NAWCH helps children in hospital and their parents. It supplies books, leaflets and relevant information. Local groups offer practical help. Publications and reports are also made available to professionals, and a journal is issued three times a year. Subscription £10 a year.

National Autistic Society

276 Willesden Lane, London NW2 5RB (Tel: 01–451 3844).

Runs an advisory and information service. Publishes literature on the education and management of autistic children, and a quarterly periodical *Communication*. With affiliated regional societies, the NAS provides special schools and residential services for adults in various parts of the United Kingdom, and organises courses, conferences and seminars.

National Back Pain Association

Grundy House, 31–33 Park Road, Teddington, Middlesex TW11 0AB (Tel: 01–977 5474/5).

Back pain affects four out of five people at some time during their lives.

The Association raises funds for research into the causes and treatment of back pain. It seeks to help prevent damage by teaching people to use their bodies sensibly, and encourages the formation of local branches to help disseminate useful information and provide neighbourly help to sufferers. The Association also publishes a quarterly magazine *Talk Back*, available on subscription, and various literature on back pain and ways of lifting (send large s.a.e.), but regrets that it cannot deal with enquirers' specific complaints.

National Bureau for Students with Disabilities
See Section 6, Further Education and Training.

The National Childbirth Trust
9 Queensborough Terrace, Bayswater, London W2 3TB (Tel: 01–221 3833).
The Trust offers parent-to-parent support through a national contact register of parents with disabilities. Antenatal classes, specialised help with breast feeding, postnatal support and friendship are available through a network of over 300 branches and groups. Helpful leaflets, including *Resource List for Parents with Disabilities: pregnancy, birth and early parenthood* are available. The NCT magazine *New Generation* and some leaflets can be provided on tape.

National Children's Bureau
8 Wakley Street, London EC1V 7QE (Tel: 01–278 9441).
A voluntary and independent organisation concerned widely with children's needs in the family, school and society, and their all-round development and well-being. Membership includes statutory and voluntary organisations as well as individuals.

The Bureau has four basic aims: to make existing knowledge on children's development and needs readily available through its information service, library and numerous publications; to improve communication and co-operation between education, medical and social workers and between statutory and voluntary services; to evaluate existing services and encourage new developments; to contribute to new knowledge and to assist others wishing to do so.

The Bureau also undertakes an extensive research programme and its information service and library handles about 6,000 enquiries a year. The Voluntary Council for Handicapped Children (*see* page 334) was established and operates under its aegis.

The Bureau's booklist is impressive and includes works on the social, emotional and educational adjustment associated with various specific forms of handicap affecting children.

National Children's Home
85 Highbury Park, London N5 1UD (Tel: 01–226 2033).

NCH operates over 150 projects in the United Kingdom, and works in Jamaica and the Eastern Caribbean. Projects range through a variety of residential provision for children and young people, independence units, schools for children with learning difficulties, extended education units, units for mentally handicapped children, a school for physically handicapped children, family centres, community projects, telephone and face-to-face counselling and intermediate treatment.

For further information write to the Director of Social Work at the above address enclosing a large s.a.e.

National Citizen Advocacy
2 St Paul's Road, London N1 2QR (Tel: 01–359 8289).
Citizen advocacy provides the opportunity for residents of hospitals for people with learning difficulties who are without relatives or regular visitors to have an advocate: an ordinary citizen who forms a partnership with a person on a one-to-one basis and helps them to express their wishes to staff or relatives. Training is given to prepare prospective advocates for this special role, including information on legal rights, services and benefits available to people with learning difficulties.

NCA promotes the development of citizen advocacy in England and Wales. It provides help and support to people setting up citizen advocacy schemes, and can provide details on request of CA schemes currently operating in the United Kingdom.

National Council for Carers and their Elderly Dependants
see Carers National Association

National Council for One Parent Families
255 Kentish Town Road, London NW5 2LX (Tel: 01–267 1361).
The Council gives free, confidential advice and practical help (including representation at tribunals) to lone parents and single, pregnant women, publishes informative pamphlets and booklets, and presses the needs of one-parent families and their children to the government, local authorities and society in general.

National Council for Voluntary Organisations
26 Bedford Square, London WC1B 3HU (Tel: 01–636 4066).
NCVO is a national resource centre providing advisory and information services for voluntary organisations. It represents the voluntary sector to

government and other sections of society and attempts to promote new forms of voluntary social action.

About 550 voluntary organisations are in membership – including many of those representing or working on behalf of disabled people – and some 200 local development agencies. All member organisations in the disability field come together in the Health and Handicaps Group which meets quarterly to discuss specialist issues.

Advice and information on such matters as charity law, tax affairs, fund raising, management, publishing, and relations with government departments and local authorities is available, usually without charge, to all voluntary organisations, local or national, whether members or not. NCVO is particularly pleased to hear from new or would-be voluntary organisations.

Several units may be of particular interest to disability groups: for example, the Inner Cities Unit, which advises voluntary bodies on how to make the most of Urban Programme funds; and the Community Schemes Unit, which does the same for the Department of Employment's training and temporary employment programmes. A Community Health Initiatives Resource Unit began work in July 1983.

NCVO, as the Bedford Square Press, has a range of relevant publications. A catalogue is available from the Sales Manager, Bedford Square Press at the above address. Titles include *The Voluntary Agencies Directory* (*see* Appendix A).

National Deaf-Blind Helpers' League
18 Rainbow Court, Paston Ridings, Peterborough PE4 6UP (Tel: Peterborough (0733) 73511).

The League offers hope and encoragement to deaf-blind people, bringing them together through regional group activities, rallies and *The Rainbow*, a quarterly magazine available in Braille, Moon type and ordinary print. The League also provides private self-contained flats for deaf-blind people capable of running their own homes, and a small guest house and short stay centre where deaf-blind people are encouraged towards re-integration into the community. Help is given as and where needed.

National Deaf/Blind and Rubella Association
See Sense.

National Deaf Children's Society
45 Hereford Road, London W2 5AH (Tel: voice 01–229 9272; Vistel 01–229) 1891).
The Society's main aims are: to stress the need for

early diagnosis; to press for the provision of adequate education for all deaf children; to explore the whole field of suitable employment for deaf school-leavers; to publicise the needs of deaf children; to assist in the training of teachers and other staff to care for deaf children in and out of school.

Activities include: advice to parents, both directly and through literature, on the education and employment of their deaf children; bursaries to student teachers; assistance with publication of books for deaf children; consideration of medical and technical research projects in the field of deafness in children; provision of grants, holidays and special equipment; welfare counselling of parents of deaf children.

See also Section 3: Aids and Equipment for details of the Society's Technology Information Centre in Birmingham.

National Eczema Society
Tavistock House North, Tavistock Square, London WC1H 9SR (Tel: 01–388 4097).
The Society was formed in 1975 to act as an information centre and mutual support organisation for those affected by eczema, their families and others concerned with their welfare. The Society now has branches and groups of members throughout much of the British Isles. Its publications include a quarterly magazine, *Exchange* and two leaflets, *What is the National Eczema Society* and *Eczema Hints and Facts*, all free to members. The Society acts as a source of information on eczema for the public and the news media, producing many leaflets and four particularly valuable information packs concerned with eczema in relation to babies, children, teenagers (16+) and adults, price £2 including postage and packing.

In addition, funds are raised for research into the causes and treatment of the condition.

The National Federation of the Blind of the United Kingdom
Unity House, Smyth Street, Westgate, Wakefield WF1 1ER (Tel: Wakefield (0924) 377012).
Founded in 1947, the NFB is a nationwide organisation of, and fully controlled by, visually handicapped people who believe that no one understands their problems better than themselves. It provides a collective means by which blind and partially sighted individuals can effectively bring their views to bear on the development of services which affect them. Co-operation is actively sought with government departments and local authorities, and members of the organisation are frequently invited to discuss policy with these bodies.

The Federation is also a member of the World Blind Union and the European Blind Union. It is also affiliated to, and takes an active part in, the British Council of Organisations of Disabled People.

NFB is working to achieve a number of important objectives:

(a) Integrated education for visually handicapped children in ordinary schools, with all necessary support;

(b) A guaranteed right to work for disabled people in general, and blind and partially sighted people in particular;

(c) The creation of a safer and better planned environment where people can move about without fear of being molested, and with emphasis on unobstructed footways, road safety, and colour contrasting to help the partially sighted;

(d) Improved public transport with audible information, and travel concessions;

(e) A handicap allowance which, as far as blind people are concerned, would compensate for the extra expense incurred through blindness;

(f) Better social services that are sensitive and responsive to the special needs of disabled people;

(g) Improvement of the NHS, with particular emphasis on the special needs of the visually handicapped;

(h) Greater participation by visually handicapped people in the administration of their own welfare services, by means of increased representation of organisations of visually handicapped people on all relevant bodies;

(i) A better understanding between sighted and visually handicapped people with a view to achieving meaningful integration in all spheres of life.

The NFB can already point to many notable achievements in pursuit of these aims.

The NFB is organised in branches located throughout the United Kingdom, including one which operates by post for those who are not within easy reach of a local branch. Policy is decided by an Annual Delegate Conference, and implemented by an executive council. None of the Federation's officers are paid.

The NFB can give guidance on education, rehabilitation, training and employment, as well as advice on day-to-day problems related to blindness. It also helps its members to live a normal life by assisting with the purchase of special aids. It produces a quarterly magazine *Viewpoint*, in Braille, ink print and on compact cassette. This is issued free to all members in the medium of their choice, and is available to anyone else for a small annual subscription.

National Federation of Kidney Patients' Associations

Acorn Lodge, Woodsetts, Worksop, Nottinghamshire S81 8AT (Tel: Worksop (0909) 562703).

The NFKPA was formed in 1978 to provide a strong, well-informed voice for kidney patients. The Federation is devoted to the welfare of kidney patients by using personal experiences to help fellow sufferers, encouraging self-help by advice and information, through personal contact, quarterly newsletter and annual conference.

The Federation produces informative leaflets for kidney patients, professionals and support staff, and campaigns at local and national level for better treatment facilities.

There are 40 member organisations throughout the UK whose activities include the purchase of kidney machines and other life-saving equipment, provision of holiday facilities and practical help for kidney patients and their families.

National Information Forum

c/o Disabled Living Foundation, 380–384 Harrow Road, London W9 2HU (Tel: 01–289 2791).

The Forum was set up in 1981 to:

(a) encourage the provision of information to people with disabilities and their carers, by every appropriate means;

(b) carry out research into the most effective means of delivering such information;

(c) raise awareness, particularly in the caring professions and voluntary organisations, of the importance of information and of the responsibility for providing it;

(d) provide training in the skills of providing information.

The Forum has organised seminars for GPs and for paramedical and nursing professionals; devised and produced a video training pack, *The Need to Know*, aimed at professionals; compiled a guide to sources of information; designed and distributed a model leaflet for local authorities who need to give advice about local services; persuaded British Telecom to include a page of information compiled by the Forum to be included in all editions of Yellow Pages.

The Forum is particularly concerned to bridge the gap between those who provide information and those who need it. As the 1987 winner of the

Which? Jubilee Award and with additional funding from the Cripplegate Foundation, it is carrying out a practical project in Islington to test new ways of conveying information. A report on its findings will be published.

The Forum also offers training seminars for professionals in the health and social services and in voluntary organisations. Future projects, subject to funding, will include pioneering ways of providing clear, practical information for people with disabilities leaving hospital, and those involved in their care; providing a basic information pack for local voluntary organisations; publishing a regular bulletin describing practical examples of good practice which could be more widely adopted; and producing and distributing a basic information guide for doctors.

The National League of the Blind and Disabled
2 Tenterden Road, London N17 8BE (Tel: 01–808 6030).
A trade union of blind and disabled people formed in 1899 and affiliated to the TUC since 1902. Membership is open to any registered blind, partially sighted or seeing disabled person of either sex over the age of 16.

Broadly, the objects of the League are to secure improvements in education and the economic and social conditions of blind and disabled people. Of particular help to many members over the years has been the provision of legal assistance in a variety of circumstances, notably in relation to accidents at work, and, more often, accidents outside work such as falling into unguarded holes.

There are 60 branches of the League in various parts of Great Britain, and a membership of around 3,500. A challenging and well-produced printed journal *The Advocate* and a Braille journal *The Horizon* are issued quarterly (free to members).

The National Library for the Handicapped Child
University of London Institute of Education, 20 Bedford Way, London WC1H 0AL (Tel: 01–636 1500, ext.599; after hours 01–255 1363).
The library assists both children and adults by offering a wide range of preselected books and non-book materials which are interesting and suitable for children who are having difficulty in learning to read, or in reading what is currently available to them. In addition, the Library displays not only books, but also a number of pieces of equipment designed to help print-handicapped children to enjoy reading.

The Library shelves hold picture books for young children and older children, fiction for all levels of understanding and reading experience, non-fiction, large print books, and extra large picture books. It also has books on tape, video, filmstrip and slides.

For adults there is a wide range of reference materials. The stock includes books on specific reading handicaps and the teaching of children who are hearing impaired, visually impaired, mentally handicapped or physically disabled. There are books to stimulate a child's reading, and some to help the parent understand the child's disability.

The Library also has all the equipment necessary to enable a visitor to experience the freedom offered by computer software. There are also special toys and reading aids designed to help the child's ability to communicate.

In addition to a printed catalogue of its own holdings, the Library has a small publishing programme in conjunction with commercial companies. The titles produced so far are short photographic books covering specific social skills. The Library also encourages commercial publishers in the United Kingdom to consider the needs of the disabled child, in particular those with reading disabilities.

Children, their parents, teachers and others involved in work with children who have special educational needs are welcome to visit the Library and use the facilities. The Library is open Monday to Friday from 10 a.m. to 5 p.m.

The National Osteoporosis Society
Barton Meade House, PO Box 10, Radstock, Bath BA3 3YB (Tel: Radstock (0761) 32472).
Osteoporosis is the name given to a condition in which the bones have become porous and brittle as a result of calcium deficiency. It affects one in forty men and one in four women, particularly after the menopause, when calcium is lost more rapidly. Typically, bones may break easily. Those in the spine may become compressed, causing loss of height. Eventually, they may fracture and collapse causing the curve of the spine sometimes described as 'dowager's hump'.

The NOS offers (free to members): information about osteoporosis, regular newsletters, and in some areas the opportunity to join local groups. The Society also seeks to increase public awareness of the prevalence and the serious effects of this bone disease, to encourage the medical profession, the government and relevant organisations to work towards improved methods of prevention and treatment, and to assist appropriate research.

Ordinary membership £5 a year (please send s.a.e.); medical/health care professionals £10.

National Reye's Syndrome Foundation of the United Kingdom
15 Nicholas Gardens, Pyrford, Woking, Surrey GU22 8SD (Tel: Byfleet (093 23) 46843).
Reye's Syndrome is an acute disorder which affects children from infancy onwards when they seem to be recovering from a viral illness like influenza, chicken pox or diarrhoea. The child has a change of personality or becomes drowsy or unconscious and develops frequent or persistent vomiting. Abnormal accumulations of fat develop in the liver and some other organs of the body, along with a severe increase of pressure in the brain. Early diagnosis is vital. The cause is unknown, but a number of studies suggest a possible link between the development of Reye's Syndrome and the use of Aspirin (acetyl salicylate acid) which may aggravate the condition.

The Foundation was formed to provide funds for research into the cause, treatment, cure and prevention of Reye's Syndrome, to inform both the public and medical communities, and to provide support for parents whose children have been affected by the syndrome.

The Foundation publishes a leaflet, *Your Child and Reye's Syndrome: The Facts and the Dangers*, giving information about symptoms and what to do if they develop.

National Schizophrenia Fellowship
78 Victoria Road, Surbiton, Surrey KT6 4NS (Tel:01–390 3651).
Schizophrenia is a common and often disabling form of illness which affects around one in 100 people in Britain at some time during their lives. It tends to isolate those affected from others, and can make it hard or impossible for them to hold down a job, or to live independently. It affects men and women of all races and all walks of life and often begins in early adulthood, making it difficult to marry and raise a family. It makes people more prone to stress, and quite ordinary problems can make the illness worse. The condition is commonly misunderstood. It is not having a 'split personality', nor 'being in two minds' about something, but it is characterised by a disintegration of thought processes, of contact with reality and emotional response. Those affected commonly have delusions, hearing voices that no one else can hear or thinking that their actions and thoughts are con-

trolled from 'outside'. They will often withdraw from social contact, lose energy and neglect themselves.

NSF is the largest support group in Britain for schizophrenia and related problems, with over 5,000 members. It supports carers, relatives and those affected by schizophrenia. New members can be put in touch with others in a similar position through a network of more than 100 local groups. The Fellowship also offers information and advice, and deals with more than 5,000 calls and letters a year. Local voluntary group leaders are also trained to give advice, and some local groups provide special advice services. All members receive a newsletter, *NSF News*, four times a year.

In addition to its services for members, the NSF campaigns for better services, presses for more research funding, organises relevant conferences and meetings, and publishes leaflets and reports (list available on request).

Individual or family membership costs £10 a year, but this can be waived, wholly or partially, for people on state benefits or similarly low income.

National Society for Children with Intestinal Disorders (NASCID)
39 The Ridings, Bishop's Stortford, Hertfordshire CM23 4EH (Tel: Bishops's Stortford (0279) 505482).
A small number of children suffer from small bowel failure as a result of disease or surgical resection of their intestines. As a consequence, many such children receive long-term intravenous feeding or enteral feeding by nasogastric tube. Indeed many of them are kept alive solely by these methods.

NASCID was started in January 1986 to act as a self-help group for the parents of children so affected. It aims:
(a) to offer support to parents;
(b) to raise funds for research and other purposes; and
(c) to keep up to date with new medical and scientific techniques.
NASCID cannot offer medical advice on the condition of any individual child.

The National Society for Epilepsy
Chalfont Centre for Epilepsy, Chalfont St Peter, Gerrards Cross, Buckinghamshire SL9 0RJ (Tel: Chalfont St Giles (024 07) 3991).
This centre provides long-term residential care for 350 adults, and short-term accommodation for 45

317

adults for observation, assessment and drug control. The emphasis is on rehabilitation, and employment is provided for those whose condition necessitates long-term accommodation.

The Education and Information Service also offers lectures and literature to those involved in the professional management of epilepsy, as well as to people with epilepsy and their families.

The National Society for Phenylketonuria and Allied Disorders

26 Towngate Grove, Mirfield, West Yorkshire.
The Society is run by parents. It makes available a leaflet giving basic information about phenylketonuria and has published a number of booklets of dietary information/recipes. A quarterly newsletter keeps members up to date, and contacts for mutual advice and support are encouraged. An annual holiday conference and regional day conferences are organised. Annual subscription for voting members is £2; membership is otherwise free.

National Women's Register

245 Warwick Road, Solihull, West Midlands B92 7AH (Tel: 021–706 1101).
NWR offers women of all ages with enquiring minds the opportunity to meet in each other's homes to participate in stimulating and wide-ranging discussion, leading to friendship and activities. Disabled women are welcome.

Network for the Handicapped

16 Princeton Street, London WC1R 4BB (Tel: see below).
Network is a free Law and Advisory Centre for disabled and handicapped people and their families. It was formed out of a group of families with handicapped children called *Kith and Kids*. They combined with solicitors and barristers who were willing to work voluntarily, and Network has been running since 1976.

Problems dealt with arise from all Social Security benefits such as attendance allowance, mobility allowance, vaccine damage payment claims etc., the Chronically Sick and Disabled Persons Act 1970, the Disabled Persons (Services, Consultation and Representation) Act 1986, housing, patients' rights, consumer rights, wills, trusts and settlements, charity law, education, all aspects of Social Security legislation and many others.

Network is open to anyone who is disabled or to a parent, guardian or relative of a disabled person who falls within the categories catered for under the Mental Health Act 1983 or the Chronically

Sick and Disabled Persons Act 1970, or any organisation directly involved in this field.

Network has a residential solicitor, a secretary/co-ordinator and a secretary/social worker. Disabled people can be visited in their homes within the Greater London area if they are housebound. There is also a back-up service of volunteer lawyers and advisers, some of whom have been working with them since 1976. Some of the lawyers are themselves disabled.

Appointments can be made by ringing Helen Berent on 01–831 8031 or 01–831 7740; advice may be given by telephone or letter. It is essential to make an appointment if you want to see the solicitor or adviser in person. The Centre is open Mondays to Fridays from 10 a.m. to 5 p.m. approx.

Neurofibromatosis

See Link – The Neurofibromatosis Association.

NICOD (formally The Northern Ireland Council for Orthopaedic Development)

2nd floor, 7 Donegall Square West, Belfast BT1 6JD (Tel: Belfast (0232) 328378).
A voluntary organisation working in Northern Ireland to help those who are physically handicapped with conditions such as cerebral palsy, spina bifida, and muscular dystrophy to lead a full life.

NICOD is affiliated to and works very closely with The Spastics Society, and carries out the equivalent of its work in Northern Ireland. In addition, NICOD liaises closely with the Northern Ireland Association for Spina Bifida and Hydrocephalus.

The Council provides advice clinics for the treatment of all physically handicapped children from birth to 16 years old. These are situated at Belfast, Erne, Londonderry and Omagh. Treatment is given by physiotherapists, occupational therapists and speech therapists, and parents are made aware of the importance of correct handling and positioning of their child at home. Advice and information is given on a variety of subjects, all aimed at helping parents to cope better with the problems associated with young physically handicapped children.

NICOD also provides a work centre at Balmoral (Belfast) for disabled school leavers, and a residential hostel in Belfast so that moderately handicapped young people from country areas can attend the work centre or obtain suitable employment in the area.

A residential hostel is also available for severely physically handicapped people in Belfast. Fees are charged for residential accommodation, but sponsorship can be arranged through Health Boards. All other services are provided free to the handicapped person.

Northern Ireland Council on Disability

2 Annadale Avenue, Belfast BT7 3JR (Tel: Belfast (0232) 491011).

NICD is an independent voluntary organisation representing every aspect of disability and providing a means of consultation and joint action for organisations and individuals working for the well-being of people with disabilities. With over 100 member organisations, the Council provides specialist information, training and support services, including a transport service. A development unit is concerned with issues including education, access to the built environment, employment and training, housing, recreation, and creating an awareness of the special needs of people with disabilities. The Council's staff will help with advice on setting up new groups, charitable status, writing constitutions, and media contact. The fast-growing Council is active in identifying needs and issues affecting disabled people and those who care for them, and lobbying on issues of concern. It publishes a quarterly magazine *Disability Today*, which aims to promote debate on such issues in a Northern Ireland context.

The NICD Information Office receives over 6,000 enquiries annually, from people with disabilities, their families, carers and those professionally involved with their well-being. Information about mobility, housing, educational rights, employment, benefits and support services is available by telephone, personal appointment or through NICD publications.

The Information Service is open from 10 a.m. until 4 p.m. Monday to Friday.

In addition to making referrals, the Service can, through its welfare rights advice workers, negotiate on behalf of callers, advise on appeal tribunals, and take cases to Commissioner's level.

Training is available, for example on disability benefits, on request and in co-ordination with other organisations.

Northern Ireland Polio Fellowship

475 Antrim Road, Belfast BT15 3BP (Tel: Belfast (0232) 749857).

Independent of the British Polio Fellowship, the NIPF aims to provide a better life for disabled people, and to give mutual help and encouragement to those disabled by polio.

Oculo-Cerebro-Renal Syndrome

See Lowe's Syndrome.

Oesophageal Atresia

See TOFS.

The Officers' Association

48 Pall Mall, London SW1Y 5JY (Tel: 01-930 0125).

Also Scotland: New Haig House, Logie Green Road, Edinburgh EH7 4HQ (Tel: 031-557 2782).

The Association exists to relieve distress among those who have held a commission in HM Forces, and their widows and dependants, and to aid and promote the interests of all such persons. Apart from giving financial help in appropriate cases, the Association can advise on the best method of finding accommodation for the elderly and sick in long-stay residential care and nursing homes and short-stay convalescence homes. In addition, the Association co-operates with the Housing Association for Officers' Families which provides housing for disabled officers and their families. Ex-officers are also eligible to be considered for flats belonging to the Royal British Legion Housing Association.

Ollier's Disease Self-help Group

Bridge House, 45 Baring Road, Beaconsfield, Buckinghamshire HP9 2NF (Tel: Beaconsfield (049 46) 3301).

Ollier's Disease is a very rare condition which leads to shortening and distortion of limbs and for which there is no known cure.

The Group facilitates contact and support of those with first-hand experience of the disease. It seeks to generate support within the medical profession, and raises funds for research. A newsletter is published (at present only annually).

Old people

See Age Concern England, Age Concern Scotland, Centre for Policy on Ageing, Counsel and Care for the Elderly, Help the Aged, Pensioners Link.

One Parent Families

See National Council for One Parent Families.

Optical Information Council

Temple Chambers, Temple Avenue, London EC4Y 0DT (Tel: 01-353 3556).

The Council publishes a number of free leaflets giving information on the help available for the visual problems of the partially sighted, the use of low-visual aids, and methods of protecting the eyes against glare.

Orthopaedic Development
See NICOD.

Osteogenesis Imperfecta
See Brittle Bone Society.

Osteoporosis
See The National Osteoporosis Society.

Outset
Drake House, 18 Creekside, London SE8 3DZ
(Tel: 01–692 7141).
Outset is a national charity which works to improve the quality of life for people with disabilities.

It has a specialist research team which has carried out identification surveys and undertaken research about housing design, access to services and facilities and informal care in the community. The Disability Information Unit has a comprehensive databank providing current statistics on the difficulties and aspirations of the disabled population.

Outset ITec provides training in basic computer literacy skills for young people, and Outset's Hammersmith and Fulham Project provides information technology training. The Employment Development Unit stimulates employment initiatives creating new opportunities for people with disabilities. Outset also runs office services agencies employing disabled people and has a sheltered placement scheme.

Paget's Disease
See National Association for the Relief of Paget's Disease.

Parents for Children
222 Camden High Street, London NW1 8QR (Tel: 01–485 7526).
This is an adoption agency specialising in the placement of both older children and children with mental and physical disabilities. Families who live within a 100-mile radius of London are welcome to enquire about becoming adoptive parents. Most local authority social services departments are also happy to hear from prospective adopters who will consider a child with a disability.

Parkinson's Disease Society of the UK
36 Portland Place, London W1N 3DG (Tel: 01–323 1174).
Parkinson's Disease is a slowly progressive deterioration of certain cells at the base of the brain. The main symptoms are muscular rigidity, tremor, and difficulties with movements like walking, swinging the arms, talking, writing, blinking, swallowing etc. The symptoms as a whole may be mild, but they generally increase gradually over the years, though the rate of deterioration can be appreciably affected by treatment. The cause is not definitely known.

The Society provides an information and advice service at headquarters and through approximately 160 local branches around the country. Particular attention is given to problems of daily living for Parkinsonians and their families. The Society raises funds for research and publishes a helpful quarterly *Newsletter* and other literature. A Welfare Education Officer assists professionals with training courses, seminars, etc.

Partially Sighted Society
206 Great Portland Street, London W1N 6AA (Tel: 01–387 8840), or Dean Clarke House, Southern Hay East, Exeter EX1 1PE (Tel: Exeter (0392) 210656.
The Society offers assistance to all people with impaired vision. Its services include: information and advice; publications, including a bi-monthly magazine *Oculus* in large print; a special printing and enlargement service; and aids to vision. The Society has over 20 local branches in the United Kingdom offering direct support and contact. Nationally, the Society represents the interests of partially sighted people to government bodies and other organisations. It organises conferences, runs exhibitions and displays, and contributes to the training of specialist workers. It maintains working committees in specific areas such as education, employment and mobility, and has access to special advisers on topics such as low vision aids and lighting. Membership is open to all.

Patients' Association
Room 33, 18 Charing Cross Road, London WC2H 0HR (Tel: 01–240 0671).
An independent advisory service for patients, which also aims to represent and further their interests, and to make sure they are treated as people. It campaigns for improvements in the NHS, and produces a number of information leaflets, for example on the legal rights of patients, changing one's doctor, going into hospital, and using the NHS. *See* Section 1 for details.

Pensioners' Link
17 Balfe Street, London N1 9EB (Tel: 01– 278 5501/2/3/4).
An organisation which strives to enable pensioners to link up with each other, to lead full and active ives and to maintain their independence in old age. It helps to set up pensioner groups (e.g.

reminiscence, ethnic, household groups) and runs projects dealing with issues such as welfare rights, health education, outings, heating and draught-proofing. There is also a thriving Older Women's Project. Workers also visit housebound, isolated people, helping out with odd jobs and in some cases with decorating. The organisation operates in 11 London boroughs and has 15 centres.

People First
126 Albert Street, London NW1 7NF (Tel: 01–267 6111).
People First started in America in the early seventies and was taken up in Britain in 1984. It is a self-advocacy organisation for people in adult training centres, social education centres, hostels, hospitals, group homes, youth clubs, colleges and in schools for 16s and older. Members assert the right to speak and take responsibility for themselves. They point out that it is degrading that people speak for you, treating you like a child, and that there are people who haven't been given a chance because of this. People First also seeks to break down barriers, to get rid of unwanted labels and to educate people to this end. A newsletter is published and regular meetings held in which members talk over ideas and problem solving. Membership costs £1 a year.

Peroneal Muscular Atrophy
See CMT International.

Pet Concern
Animal Welfare Trust, Tyler's Way, Watford Bypass, Watford, Hertfordshire WD2 8HQ (Tel: 01–950 8215 or 01950 0177).
Pet Concern was established in 1979 to care for the pets of elderly people during hospital treatment or convalescence. If within easy reach of the Trust's London or Birmingham rescue centres, dogs may be boarded at £1.25 a day and cats at 80p a day.

PHAB (Physically Handicapped and Able-Bodied)
Tavistock House North, Tavistock Square, London WC1H 9HX (Tel: 01–388 1963).
Also Northern Ireland: 76 University Street, Belfast BT7 1HE (Tel: Belfast (0232) 325506).
This is a United Kingdom organisation concerned with the integration of people with and without physical disabilities, largely through leisure activities. The central office can supply information about the seven divisional and regional offices in the United Kingdom. There are now over 500 clubs throughout the United Kingdom in which those with and without disabilities share on an equal basis; those who are able-bodied are enrolled as full members rather than as 'helpers'. The clubs provide a setting in which barriers can be overcome and relationships established through the sharing of varied activities, one result of which is to give people with disabilities the necessary confidence to take their full place in the community alongside their able-bodied peers.

The training of club leaders is an important aspect of PHAB's work, and a home-based distance learning pack is available alongside the courses which are arranged in different parts of the United Kingdom. In addition to supporting and developing clubs and groups, PHAB arranges residential courses in this country and abroad for people of all ages and for families. The PHAB International Federation, which will link together about 12 countries, is due to be launched during 1988.

Phenylketonuria
See National Society for Phenylketonuria and Allied Disorders.

The Phobics Society
4 Cheltenham Road, Chorlton-cum-Hardy, Manchester M21 1QN (Tel: 061–881 1937).
Founded in 1970, the Phobics Society is dedicated to promoting the relief and rehabilitation of those affected by agoraphobia and other phobic illnesses. It offers immediate advice and understanding to those who seek help, and tries to convince them that they have a well-documented illness which can be treated and overcome.

There are now some 4,500 members, and branches have been formed in various parts of the United Kingdom, allowing phobics to discuss their problems and exchange views. The Society maintains contact with members through a regular newsletter. Annual membership £3.

Play Matters (The Toy Libraries Association)
See Section 11, Sports and Leisure.

Polio
See British Polio Fellowship, Northern Ireland Polio Fellowship.

Prader-Willi Syndrome Association (UK)
30 Follett Drive, Abbots Langley, Hertfordshire WD5 0LP (Tel: Watford (0923) 674543).
Prader-Willi Syndrome is a complex, uncommon condition affecting males and females in roughly equal proportions from birth onwards. Its characteristics include uncontrollable appetite (from about age 2), poor muscle tone and balance,

learning difficulties, lack of normal sexual development, emotional instability and lack of maturity.

The Association was founded in 1981 and is run primarily by parents of those affected in conjunction with medical specialists. The Association aims to provide support for parents and carers, to promote knowledge and awareness of the syndrome among the medical professions and the public, and to improve the quality of care given to Prader-Willi people. Information leaflets, handbooks, medical texts and papers are all made readily available. The Association actively promotes medical research by funding specific projects and seminars. Regional groups within the Association work locally raising funds, spreading awareness of the syndrome, and providing local support for individual members.

A newsletter (approximately quarterly) and information sheets are published. Membership subscription £5 per family or member.

Professional Classes Aid Council
10 St Christopher's Place, London W1M 6HY (Tel: 01–935 0641).
The Council exists to help professional people and their dependants in times of distress by means of continuing grants and special gifts. Applications to the Secretary.

Psoriasis
See below and The Alternative Centre.

The Psoriasis Association
7 Milton Street, Northampton NN2 7JG (Tel: Northampton (0604) 711129).
The Association collects funds for and promotes research, seeks to advance education, public acceptance and understanding, and provides information and a point of social contact for those affected by this skin condition. It publishes a tri-annual newsletter. A slide set, *The Social Effects of Psoriasis*, is available from Graves Medical Audiovisual Library (*see* page 345).

Psychiatric Rehabilitation Association
The Groupwork Centre, 21a Kingsland High Street, London E8 2JS (Tel: 01–254 9753).
The purpose of the Association is to stimulate patients towards greater initiative and awareness of their environment and society. It prepares and encourages them to return and re-adapt to their community. At the same time, the Association attempts to improve attitudes towards the mentally ill and promotes practical measures and research for preventing and combating mental distress within the community. The Association pioneers community care projects and includes among its many services, day centres, evening centres, industrial units, group homes and evening restaurant clubs, with a special emphasis on the needs of the isolated patient. The Association has concentrated for many years on the development of research programmes to study social problems associated with mental illness, and to assess methods and standards of rehabilitation required.

PRA has produced a number of teaching aids for community care: in particular, tape/slide programmes on groupwork, day centres, industrial education units and residential care, which are used in conjunction with a manual, *An Aid to Community Care*.

PRA Aids for the Handicapped Ltd, a separate company, produces aids for disabled people.

Pyloric Stenosis Society
28 Shaftesbury Avenue, Chandler's Ford, Hampshire SO5 3BS (Tel: Eastleigh (0703) 265231).
Pyloric Stenosis is a condition found in young babies (and very occasionally in adults) where the exit of the stomach, called pylorus, is narrowed and food is prevented from entering the intestine. This causes vomiting which can be severe and can lead to dehydration. Although a simple operation can put things right, lack of understanding can cause great anxiety. The Society offers counselling and will send factual information.

Queen Elizabeth's Foundation for the Disabled
Leatherhead, Surrey KT22 0BN (Tel: Oxshott (037 284) 2204).
The Foundation runs four units.
1. Banstead Place, Park Road, Banstead, Surrey SM7 3EE (Tel: Burgh Heath (073 73) 356222). A centre for total assessment (educational, social, medical, and vocational) of physically handicapped young people (16 to 20+) leading to placement. There is also a mobility centre which offers information and assessment on outdoor mobility to disabled people of all ages (see Section 8, Mobility and Motoring for details).
2. Queen Elizabeth's Training College. Provides further education and training for young people over the age of 16.
3. Dorincourt, Oaklawn Road, Leatherhead, Surrey KT22 0BT (Tel: Oxshott (037 284) 2599). Comprises a sheltered workshop (Dorincourt Industries), a hostel for people from 16 to late middle-age, and an arts centre offering a significant programme of activity as

a realistic and satisfying alternative to paid employment.

4. Lulworth Court, Chalkwell Esplanade, West-cliff-on-Sea, Essex SS0 8JQ (Tel: Southend-on-Sea (0702) 347818). A holiday and convalescent home for severely disabled men and women (16 upwards). Enquiries to Leatherhead headquarters.

Rare Diseases

If the disease which concerns you is not specifically listed in this section, it may be possible to locate a support group or to make contact with those similarly affected through either the In Touch Scheme (page 304) or Share-a-Care (page 329).

The Rathbone Society

1st floor, Princess House, 105/107 Princess Street, Manchester M1 6DD (Tel: 061–236 5358).

The organisation, which has been developed from Elfrida Rathbone's ideals of 70 years ago, helps those young people who as 'slow learners' are unable to achieve a level of education that is essential if they are to be able to cope with life. In addition to its 17 training workshops, Rathbone has a wide range of supporting centres primarily working with those who, for a variety of reasons, are educationally handicapped.

The Society also has some 120 local branches which provide facilities such as community projects, work and leisure programmes, parental guidance and hostels. While some of this work is undertaken by volunteers, the Society now also employs a large number of professional staff.

Raynaud's Association

112 Crewe Road, Alsager, Cheshire ST7 2JA (Tel: Alsager (093 63) 2776).

Raynaud's Phenomenon (or Syndrome) is a distressing condition in which blood is prevented from reaching the fingers and toes. People who are severely affected are constantly in pain. Ulcerations form on fingers and toes, which may become gangrenous and can require amputation. Many sufferers are seriously disabled. There is, as yet, no cure.

A number of relevant publications are available and the Association issues regular newsletters giving details of treatments which may alleviate the symptoms, and news of research. A Trust has been set up to raise funds for research, and a research unit at King's College Hospital Medical School in London is working to discover causes as well as ways of alleviating the pain.

The Association also facilitates communication between those affected. It is hoped that by contacting each other, and discussing symptoms, treatments and tips found to be helpful, members may gain support and comfort. Membership fee £4.

Reach – The Association for Children with Artificial Arms

7 Farmington Road, Benhall, Cheltenham GL51 6AG (Tel: Cheltenham (0242) 36552).

Reach is a society of parents of children with missing hands or arms. It aims to secure the best possible services and provision for such children; to gather and distribute information about new developments in artificial arms; to support parents of affected children (especially when they are first faced with the problem) and to establish links between them; and to encourage research and the development of artificial arm technology.

Reading Difficulties

See National Library for the Handicapped Child.

Renal Society

41 Mutton Place, London NW1 8DF. (Tel: 01–485 9775)

The Society aims to give encouragement to kidney patients whose treatment is diet alone and who do not belong to a renal unit. Contacts can be made through a periodic newsletter.

Responaut

Pen-Glyn, Beedon Hill, Beedon, Newbury, Berkshire.

This is the title of a periodical by, for and about respirator-aided and other gadget aided people.

Restricted Growth

See Association for Research into Restricted Growth, and Child Growth Foundation.

Retinitis Pigmentosa

See British Retinitis Pigmentosa Society.

Rett Syndrome

See UK Rett Syndrome Association.

Reye's Syndrome

See National Reye's Syndrome Foundation of the United Kingdom.

Richmond Fellowship

8 Addison Road, London W14 8DL (Tel: 01–603 6373).

The Fellowship provides residential short-term and long-term therapeutic care for people who have suffered or are on the verge of a nervous breakdown in 50 therapeutic communities and group homes throughout England, Wales and

Scotland. The College runs courses for members of the caring professions and others who wish to gain skills in counselling and group work.

Royal Association in Aid of the Deaf and Dumb
27 Old Oak Road, London W3 7HN (Tel: 01–743 6187).
Operative in Greater London, Essex, Surrey and Kent, the Association provides trained staff to act as interpreters and to advise and help with everyday problems. Its services include: special churches; social clubs and recreational facilities; specialist social services for deaf patients in hospitals for mentally ill and mentally handicapped people, and for blind-deaf people.

The Royal Association for Disability and Rehabilitation (RADAR)
25 Mortimer Street, London W1N 8AB (Tel: 01–637 5400).
RADAR acts as a co-ordinating body for the voluntary groups serving disabled people, and is able to provide information on relevant subjects. It seeks generally to investigate the causes and problems of disablement and to promote measures to eliminate or alleviate them. It is particularly active in promoting better access to public buildings and has published a number of Access Guides. RADAR also produces a helpful publications list, two first-class holiday guides (Britain and abroad), a quarterly journal *Contact* and a monthly *Bulletin*.

The Royal British Legion
48 Pall Mall, London SW1Y 5JY.
With over 800,000 members in 3,500 branches, the Legion works for the welfare of ex-service people and their dependants. Each branch has a service committee of voluntary social workers.

The Legion provides financial assistance in cases of need; a pensions service for claims on behalf of those suffering from disabilities attributable to service in the Forces, and on behalf of widows; residential homes for the elderly and incapacitated; rest homes; and holidays for severely disabled people. The Legion is the largest independent employer of disabled people in the United Kingdom and has a range of industries and retraining schemes. At the Legion village in Kent there is a treatment, rehabilitation and assessment centre for disabled people.

The Royal British Legion Housing Association, which is self-supporting, has built 11,500 flats of sheltered accommodation for the elderly, some of which are suitable for disabled people.

Royal Commonwealth Society for the Blind
Commonwealth House, Haywards Heath, West Sussex RH16 3AZ (Tel: Haywards Heath (0444) 412424).
The Society promotes and co-ordinates education, training, rehabilitation, employment and welfare of blind people in developing countries of the Commonwealth, and implements programmes for the prevention and cure of blindness.

The Royal National Institute for the Blind (RNIB)
224 Great Portland Street, London W1N 6AA (Tel: 01–388 1266).
RNIB works for the better education, training, rehabilitation, employment and general welfare of Britain's blind people. It runs schools, training colleges, two rehabilitation centres, homes for elderly blind people and hotels for holidays. It sells specially adapted goods, publishes Braille and Moon books and magazines, and provides services for producing individual items in Braille, Moon and on tape. RNIB runs Braille and tape libraries and a Talking Book library. It helps blind people find commercial and professional jobs and funds research into the prevention of blindness. It publishes a monthly magazine, *New Beacon*, in print and Braille, and also publishes leaflets and information sheets on blindness and services for blind people.

The Royal National Institute for the Deaf (RNID)
105 Gower Street, London WC1E 6AH (Tel: 01–387 8033).
The Institute promotes the prevention and mitigation of deafness, and seeks to ensure the welfare of all hearing-impaired people. Its range of special services for deaf and deaf-blind people includes vocational training, rehabilitation and longer-term residential support. RNID offers comprehensive advisory, information and library services and carries out research in both medical and scientific spheres. It also provides a wide range of technical development to assist deaf people in their everyday lives.

Royal Society for Mentally Handicapped Children and Adults
See MENCAP.

RTMDC (Research Trust for Metabolic Diseases in Children)
9 Arnold Street, Nantwich, Cheshire CW5 5QB (Tel: Nantwich (0270) 629782).
Metabolic diseases are most generally described as inherited biochemical genetic disorders or inborn errors of metabolism. There are hundreds of such

diseases. A few are well known and are catered for by other major charities, e.g., diabetes, cystic fibrosis and muscular dystrophy. The vast majoriy, when named, mean nothing to most people, yet many of these inborn errors lead to severe physical and/or mental handicap and in all cases the conditions are degenerative.

RTMDC was founded in 1981 and has three basic aims:
(a) to promote research;
(b) to educate the public; and
(c) to act as a parent support group.
This last aim is a very important aspect of the Trust's work, because many families of children with these conditions have previously felt very isolated, with nowhere to turn for support.

RTMDC runs a completely confidential parent-contact service, and holds an annual parents' conference.

Rubella
See Sense – The National Deaf-Blind and Rubella Association.

St Dunstan's
191 Old Marylebone Road, London NW1 5QN (Tel: 01–723 5021).
Founded in 1915, this organisation continues to help men and women blinded in war or peacetime service in the forces or who become blind in later years because of injuries sustained during such service. At Ian Fraser House, Ovingdean, East Sussex, a complete welfare service is provided and extra-site facilities are available to rehabilitate and train men and women for employment, or if this is not possible because of age or ill health, to help them adjust for blindness and to develop new interests. After training is completed, arrangements are made for placement and settlement, the provision of any necessary equipment and continuing support. The aim is not to shelter them in a 'home', but to put them back in the everyday world of the sighted community.

St Dunstan's is always ready to consider individual financial needs; grants and allowances can be made to meet special problems, and other financial benefits are awarded automatically in appropriate circumstances. St Dunstan's estate department resolves many housing difficulties, purchasing suitable properties to rent for members or helping them to buy their own home with the help of a special mortgage scheme. The mortgage is at advantageous rates and is provided without the usual building society criteria.

A monthly magazine in letterpress, Braille or on tape cassette is published for members.

The Salvation Army Association for the Handicapped
101 Queen Victoria Street, London EC4P 4EP (Tel: 01–236 5222).
The aim of the Association is to provide spiritual fellowship, advisory and practical help to Salvationists and adherents. A monthly newsletter circulates for the exchange of news between members and to provide general information. It has a youth supplement. Blind and partially sighted members can receive the newsletter on tape.

Fellowship meetings are held four times a year at various places in the United Kingdom, and a week-long music school is run for both able-bodied and disabled people every year.

The Samaritans
For administrative purposes only: 17 Uxbridge Road, Slough SL1 1SN (Tel: Slough (0753) 32713).
The Samaritans, founded in 1953 to help the suicidal and the despairing, have 182 branches in the British Isles. Samaritans are ordinary people from all walks of life who devote part of their spare time to help people in distress. They are carefully chosen and prepared, and work under the guidance of a volunteer director. The branches can be contacted at any hour of the day or night by telephone, or by personal visit any day or evening. Some people also contact by letter, and a few are visited, when it seems particularly necessary, at their own homes. The service is absolutely confidential and free. The telephone numbers and addresses of local branches are in telephone directories.

Not all branches are wheelchair accessible, nor is the service specifically orientated towards disability: the Samaritan's focus is on the level of distress or despair rather than on specific questions posed.

The Schizophrenia Association of Great Britain
Bryn Hyfryd, The Crescent, Bangor, Gwynedd (Tel: Bangor (0248) 354048/6703791).
When founded in 1970, the Association was concerned only with the problems of schizophrenia. It now tries to help all people with psychiatric problems, whatever their diagnoses. A twice-yearly newsletter and other helpful information keeps members informed of developments in the field.

To try to dispel the stigma attached to schizophrenia, the Association holds conferences, symposia, lectures, and publishes books and leaflets. Research projects are financed, including a major investigation of the biochemical cause of schizophrenia at the University College of North Wales. The Association is presently seeking funding for an Institute of Biochemical Psychiatry in Bangor.

Membership costs £5. Please send a large s.a.e. for papers and an application form.

Scleroderma
See The Maria Scleroderma Therapy Trust.

The Scoliosis Association (UK)
380–384 Harrow Road, London W9 2HU (Tel: 01–289 5652).

Scoliosis (or lateral curvature of the spine) can occur at any time between birth and maturity, and affects roughly two per cent of secondary-school-aged children. It almost never develops in adults. If untreated, it may lead to severe deformity and lung damage, with serious consequences.

SAUK is an independent national organisation which aims to promote information about the condition, and also to act as a channel through which people with scoliosis, and especially parents of children with scoliosis, can find and talk to those who have had the same experience.

A quarterly newsletter is produced containing news, views, ideas, book reviews and information on all aspects of scoliosis.

There is no charge for membership.

Scottish Association for Mental Health
40 Shandwick Place, Edinburgh EH2 4RT (Tel: 031 225 4446).

SAMH is the only national Scottish organisation concerned with the development of services relating to mental illness and mental health, and with education and the promotion of mental health. It has developed a strategy based on three components.

1. The development of services and facilities within the voluntary sector. SAMH acts as a catalyst, a source of advice and information and as a direct instigator of action, working particularly through a network of local associations.
2. Co-operation with the statutory sector services in health, social work, housing and related fields, bringing together the statutory and voluntary services and influencing the allocation of resources and systems of planning in order that an *appropriate* mental health

care service may emerge. In this context, SAMH acts as an intermediary, able to press, advise and challenge.
3. The promotion of, and contribution to, educational initiatives towards both the public and those providing services, aimed at giving a fundamental new impetus to the change in attitudes within society towards mental illness and to the recognition of the dignity and value of each individual and the quality of his/her life. The Association also develops education and action using its experience and understanding of mental illness and society to promote positive mental health.

Scottish Council on Disability
5 Shandwick Place, Edinburgh EH2 4RG (Tel: 031–229 8632).

The Council provides a means of consultation and joint action among voluntary and statutory organisations in Scotland on such topics as employment, access and mobility. It runs a Mobile Advice Centre and a comprehensive information service in Scotland similar to that provided by the Disabled Living Foundation in England (for details see Section 3, Aids and Equipment).

The Council's publications list offers a wide range of books for sale, and an excellent bi-monthly newsletter is published. There is also an extensive library open to students and visitors.

National Committees have been set up on the arts, access and mobility.

Scottish Council for Spastics
22 Corstorphine Road, Edinburgh EH12 6HP (Tel: 031–337 9876).

The Council is responsible, within Scotland, for the care, treatment, education and employment of some 2,000 children and adults who are affected by cerebral palsy or allied conditions.

With the co-operation of statutory and local authorities, the Council operates three schools at Edinburgh, Lanark and Corseford. It also runs the New Trinity Centre in Edinburgh, which provides sheltered employment in laundry, metalwork, woodwork and gardening, as well as occupational training and work centre activities and a 'special needs' unit. There are facilities for assessment, further education, remedial work and speech therapy.

The well-equipped Scottish Spastics Work Centre in Glasgow has facilities for further education, while on the same estate the Council operates a day centre for severely handicapped adults.

The Council also provides residential accommodation for adults in Paisley and near Erskine.

The Upper Springland complex in Perth provides semi-independent flatlets for disabled people, as well as offering respite care and holiday accommodation.

Various forms of therapy are provided from an out-patients department in Edinburgh and a mobile therapy unit which operates from Paisley. Both these units offer a home visiting service.

Scottish Down's Syndrome Association
54 Shandwick Place, Edinburgh EH2 4RT (Tel: 031–226 2420). This is an independent organisation which sponsors local parent/child self-help groups, supports research into Down's Syndrome, provides a counselling service for new parents of Down's babies and for families with educational/social difficulties. There is a specialist information service for members, and appropriate material is published. The Association promotes and supports a housing association for adult Down's persons, and holds seminars and conferences. Membership fees are £3 per annum.

Scottish Dyslexia Association
45 Millig Street, Helensburgh G84 9PN (Tel: Helensburgh (0436) 5907).
This is a voluntary association for the study and treatment of dyslexia, with branches in Dundee, Edinburgh, Fife, Girvan, Glasgow and Perth. The associations in Dundee (Tayside), Edinburgh and Glasgow all offer both assessment and teaching services, as well as a free advisory service. Tayside, in addition, has a resources centre for teaching aids and a lending library service for members.

The Scottish Dyslexia Association is separate from the British Dyslexia Association, but maintains close contact. It acts as a clearing house for enquiries and as a co-ordinating organisation for the various dyslexia associations in Scotland.

Scottish Epilepsy Association
48 Govan Road, Glasgow G51 1JL (Tel: 041–427 4911).
The Association provides information and advice centres, extensive casework services and a combined workshop/work centre/training centre. It oversees and encourages parents' groups, organises conferences and arranges lectures. Regional branches have been established in Strathclyde, Tayside, Grampian, Central, Shetlands and The Borders regions.

The Scottish Health Education Group
Health Education Centre, Woodburn House, Canaan Lane, Edinburgh EH10 4SG (Tel: 031–447 8044).
The Group applies a vigorous health education policy across Scotland. Its objective is to improve the lifestyle of the population in relation to health. The programme's concerns include alcohol, smoking, immunisation, dental health, mental health, and the elderly. The Group aims to help each individual to make the best possible choice for optimum health and well being.

Scottish Motor Neurone Disease Association
Rooms 11/12, 136 Ingram Street, Glasgow G1 1EJ (Tel: 041– 552 0507).
The SMNDA was set up in 1981 primarily to raise money for research. It is not part of the English Motor Neurone Disease Association, but parallel with it, maintaining friendly contacts. A patient-care officer visits those affected, giving advice on allowances etc., and informs the Association where there are needs not met by other welfare services. A variety of aids has been provided in cases of proven need, and the Association will represent people suffering from motor neurone disease in problems over local authority services, e.g. the need for ground floor accommodation.

Scottish Society for the Mentally Handicapped
13 Elmbank Street, Glasgow G2 4QA (Tel: 041–226 4541).
The Society's work parallels that of MENCAP, which does not operate in Scotland. It is a parent-based organisation and is concerned with all aspects of the welfare of mentally handicapped people and their families. At present there are over 80 branches throughout Scotland and these provide a variety of services, including social clubs, holiday facilities and day centres.

At a national level, the Society provides information and short-term care, and is concerned with obtaining better services in Scotland and in improving public attitudes. Two of its major concerns are housing and employment. It established the Key Housing Association in 1977 to provide supported accommodation for moderately handicapped adults, and is in the process of setting up a new project to develop small-scale housing facilities for those who are more severely or profoundly handicapped.

The Society is a sponsor of the sheltered placements scheme and also runs a number of riding schemes providing opportunities for recreation and skills training. Recently, the Society has funded a new Chair in Learning Difficulties at St Andrews University and has sponsored research.

Scottish Spina Bifida Association

190 Queensferry Road, Edinburgh EH4 2BW (Tel: 031–332 0743).

The Association helps families in Scotland having the care of someone with spina bifida or hydrocephalus, by providing advice, information and assistance with a view to helping those affected attain their full potential. There are nine branches where members can meet each other and take part in various recreational activities.

Training weekends are organised from time to time, and the Association's publications include a national newsletter, issued five times a year. Young adults have their own regular magazine, *Contact.*

Scottish Spinal Cord Injury Association

Princes House, 5 Shandwick Place, Edinburgh EH2 4RG (Tel: 031–228 3827).

SSCIA helps people who have suffered damage to their spinal cord through birth, injury or disease, assisting them to return to an active life in the community. Members are kept informed through a journal and newsletter, and there is an information service on such matters as benefits, transport, housing, holidays and equipment. Support is offered through a counselling and welfare service, as well as a mutual-help Link Scheme operating between members. Sports events are organised, and members are shown new ways of taking part in old sports. There are also some wheelhouse holiday cottages.

The SSCIA works with the Spinal Injuries Association in those matters which relate to the United Kingdom as a whole. It acts as a pressure group to improve services and facilities for spinal cord injured people, and represents the interests of members to government departments, health boards and hospitals. The Association also works to increase public awareness of the problems of severe disability, and encourages research into the treatment of spinal injury.

Sense – The National Deaf/Blind and Rubella Association

311 Gray's Inn Road, London WC1X 8PT (Tel: 01–278 1005).

Sense provides advice and support to deaf-blind and Rubella handicapped children, their families and professionals in the field, both from the London office and through regional branches. Information and guidance is available on benefits, education provision, community placements, aids and equipment. A quarterly newsletter, *Talking Sense*, is published to members.

The Family Advisory service offers counselling guidance, support and advice to families, mainly those with pre-school children, through visits to their homes or, in some cases, at centres at Ealing and in the Midlands.

The family centre at Sense-in-Midlands has 36 places for further education students, conferences and courses for professionals working with the deaf-blind and an expanded adult support service.

The Manor House in Market Deeping provides assessment, residential care and training for deaf-blind adolescent and young adults. Individual programmes include communication skills. Sense-in-Scotland runs a similar centre called Overbridge.

Sense is also in the forefront of the campaign to increase uptake of Rubella vaccination and therefore reduce the incidence of Congenital Rubella Syndrome.

Sequal

Ddol Hir, Glyn Ceiriog, Llangollen, Clwyd LL20 7NP (Tel: Oswestry (0691) 72331).

This organisation provides communication aids of all kinds for severely physically disabled people. Electronic aids and microcomputers of all kinds provide the basis for the supply of equipment, with special emphasis placed on the inputs and activators. Two welfare officers cover the British Isles for the assessment of members, and the organisation is run by a voluntary group of severely disabled people who themselves make full use of new technology to remain independent. There is an information back-up to members on all aspects of disability.

A general interest magazine, *Sequal News*, is published quarterly. A taped version is also available and can be obtained by writing to Mark Hansford, 19 Shalford Road, Billericay, Essex CM11 2EG.

Membership costs £5 a year or £20 for life.

Shaftesbury Society

Shaftesbury House, 2A Amity Grove, London SW20 0LH (Tel: 01–946 6635).

The Society maintains four residential schools for physically disabled children (one of which has an extended education unit), one further education centre, and four homes for young men and women suffering with muscular dystrophy and allied neuromuscular disorders. Clubs and holiday centres are provided for physically handicapped people. In London, mission centres practise Christian social work.

An expanding housing association provides sheltered housing schemes in the south of England, with special facilities for disabled people, and there is a holiday centre for elderly and disabled people at Dovercourt.

The Society publishes *The Shaftesbury Review* annually in April.

Shape
9 Fitzroy Square, London W1P 6AE (Tel: 01–388 9622/9744).

An arts organisation working with and for all kinds of disadvantaged people through creative activities. *See* Section 11, Sports and Leisure for details.

Share A Care
8 Cornmarket, Faringdon, Oxfordshire.

This organisation keeps a national register of people who have rare diseases to enable those who share similar problems to contact each other and gain mutual support. It also keeps an extensive list of support and self-help groups which are suggested, if appropriate. It operates only by post, does not provide information about individual diseases, and realistically points out that some diseases are indeed rare and that quite a few people remain unmatched. If writing, an s.a.e. is appreciated.

Sickle Cell Society
Green Lodge, Barretts Green Road, London NW10 7AP (Tel: 01961 7795).

The Society has two main aims: to give help and support to affected families, and to inform the public and health professionals about the problems of sickle cell disease. The Society has produced a leaflet, *Sickle Cell Anaemia, Sickle Cell Trait* which is available free of charge, a report, *Sickle Cell Disease – The Need for Improved Services* (80p), and a guide for families, *A Handbook on Sickle Cell Disease* (£1). In addition to giving information, the Society supports families through home visits and, through a welfare fund, provides financial assistance when it is needed. Please send an s.a.e. if seeking further information.

Skin Camouflage
See Society of Skin Camouflage.

Skin Problems
See above and The Alternative Centre.

Socialist Disability Action Group
c/o National League of the Blind and Disabled, 2 Tenterden Road, London N17 8BE (Tel: 01–808 6030).

Inaugurated in 1983, the Group welcomes into membership both individual members (over 15) and affiliated organisations. The Group recognises that there are people with physical, sensory and mental impairments, who are disabled by *society* from full participation in the social, economic and cultural life of the community. It therefore aims to encourage the political expression of such people, within the context of Socialist ideals, in order that they may gain control in directing every aspect of their lives. It also seeks to initiate and participate in campaigns on all issues affecting disabled people.

Individual membership fee £3 a year (£1 if unwaged).

The Society for Mucopolysaccharide Diseases
30 Westwood Drive, Little Chalfont, Buckinghamshire (Tel: Little Chalfont (024 04) 2789).

The Society has three main aims.
1. To act as a support group for families of children and young adults suffering from any one of the seven Mucopolysaccharide diseases. Families in similar circumstances are put in touch with one another for their mutual benefit.
2. To stimulate public awareness of these diseases and the plight of affected families.
3. To raise funds to help further research into MPS and to provide group holidays for MPS sufferers and their immediate families.

Parent contact is maintained by telephone and letter, and a quarterly newsletter is published (free to affected families and available to professionals and other interested people for an annual subscription of £5 (UK), £10 (overseas)).

Society of Skin Camouflage and Disfigurement Therapy
52 Crossgate, Cupar, Fife, Scotland KY15 5HS (Tel: Cupar (0334) 55746, Monday to Friday 9 a.m. – 4.30 p.m.; Auchtermuchty (0337) 7281, all week 6 a.m. – 8 p.m.).

The Society is concerned with educating society into accepting disfigured people rather than regarding them as strange or threatening. Through discussion, counselling and self-help it also seeks to create a better understanding of how to overcome the problems and fears associated with disfigurement.

The Society strongly recommends that the parents of a disfigured child should seek its guidance at the earliest opportunity. The Society publishes a journal, *Skin Deep Bulletin*, and holds a free weekly NHS Disfigurement Guidance and Skin Camouflage Clinic at Perth Royal Infirmary.

It also promotes and undertakes research, lectures and educational projects, and is helping to set up neighbourhood contacts throughout the United Kingdom. The Society's advice can often be of help in compensation or insurance claims which include disfigurement. Doreen Trust, founder of the Society, has written *Skin Deep* (1977), and *Overcoming Disfigurement* (1986). Advice and guidance sheets are available on a wide range of relevant topics, and the Society provides a *Disfigurement Handbook* free of charge in response to an A5 s.a.e.

Sole-Mates
46 Gordon Road, London E4 6BU (Tel: 01–524 2423).
This voluntary organisation helps people who have different sized feet by, wherever possible, partnering them with someone who takes reverse shoe sizes to themselves. Over 2,500 people are on the Sole-Mates register to date. The organisation also caters for people who need only one shoe. Some pairs of 'odd' shoes in a variety of styles can be purchased from stock.

A free advisory service includes a list of relevant suppliers and services. Registration fee for the partnership scheme costs £2.50. S.a.e. with all enquiries, please.

The Spastics Society
12 Park Crescent, London W1N 4EQ (Tel: 01–636 5020).
The Society has extensive facilities for the assessment, treatment, training and education of children and adults with cerebral palsy. It was founded in 1952 by a group of parents who were concerned about the neglected needs of their disabled children.

The Society runs 56 establishments, including 13 residential schools, further education establishments, 33 residential centres and 11 employment units. In addition, 187 affiliated local groups throughout England and Wales run a further 65 establishments to help people with cerebral palsy in their own localities. These include workshops, day centres and holiday bungalows.

The Society has also established a special scheme in Milton Keynes to provide independent living for up to 45 handicapped people along the lines of the Fokus Development in Sweden. The specially adapted flats are part of a regular housing estate, but with help on hand from a skilled care staff. An integral part of this scheme is a professional workshop where graduates work on computer technology.

The Society runs a library and bookshop, and a substantial list of the publications that are available can be obtained on application from: The Librarian at the above address. The Society's monthly newsletter, *Disability Now*, is obtainable from The Circulation Supervisor, also at Park Crescent, on free distribution.

The Society also operates a number of special services.

1. *Family Help Unit:* the East Anglia Family Health Unit in Bury St Edmunds, Suffolk, provides expert care for 15 children with cerebral palsy, many of whom may be mentally retarded, between the ages of 2 and 16. It also operates two mother and baby units where a mother can stay with her handicapped child to learn how to cope with the problems of caring for him or her. Day care facilities are also offered.

2. *Family Services and Assessment Centre*: this centre at 16 Fitzroy Square, London W1P 5HQ (Tel: 01–387 9571) offers expert advisory and counselling services to people with cerebral palsy and their families. Children, adolescents and adults are assessed by a small panel of professional staff in a pleasant environment so that advice may be offered on the many problems to be faced. There is accommodation available to the families of children, or to cerebrally palsied people visiting for an assessment. People with disabilities who may wish to stay in London overnight or for a short holiday can be accommodated when there are vacancies though those who need personal care are invited to bring a helper with them.

3. *Social Work Service*: also based at Fitzroy Square, the Society offers a network of social work services throughout England and Wales. Appointments for home visits or for assessments can be arranged.

Special Care Agency
Kiln Bolton House, Upper Basildon, Reading, Berks RG8 8TB (Tel: Upper Basildon (0491) 671842).
This agency endeavours to find and provide help in the home for people with special needs caused by disability. It works on a non-profit-making basis, and fees are kept as low as possible. The agency aims to be a sympathetic listener to people's problems, and may be able to link them with others or with professional help of which they may not be aware.

Speech Impairment/Therapy
See Association for all Speech Impaired Children; Centre for Clinical Communication Studies; College of Speech Therapists, Communilink.

Spina Bifida and Hydrocephalus
See Association for Spina Bifida and Hydrocephalus, Scottish Spina Bifida Association.

Spinal Cord Injury
See below and Scottish Spinal Cord Injury Association.

Spinal Injuries Association
76 St James's Lane, London N10 3DF (Tel: 01–444 2121).
The SIA is run by wheelchair users and their friends for paraplegics and tetraplegics and their families, and aims to help individuals to achieve their own goals, bring about the best medical care and rehabilitation, and stimulate scientific research into paraplegia.

The SIA provides information on all aspects of paraplegia to spinal cord injured people, their families and everyone concerned with their welfare. It motivates members to set and meet objectives in such areas as education, home adaptations, wheelchair living, self-help aids and personal care.

The SIA Welfare Service maintains up-to-date information on all aspects of independent living. As well as advising on rights, and helping individuals to get the best out of local services, SIA is actively involved in projects to widen the choice of housing available to members. There is also a Link Scheme which introduces newly paralysed people to more experienced members. The SIA is committed to the idea of peer counselling, and is actively engaged in encouraging training for this so that members can benefit from the skill and experience of others. The Welfare Service offers counselling, support, encouragement and advice.

The SIA also seeks to develop communication between statutory and voluntary bodies on mobility, access, employment, integration and other problems common to all disability groups. It is consulted by government and has advised on the design of new spinal units.

The Association has two seven-berth *Kingfisher* narrowboats controllable from a wheelchair, and holiday caravans in Sussex and Ile d'Oleron, France; these can be booked for active family holidays. SIA has published a number of relevant books and leaflets and publishes a quarterly newsletter which is one of the best of its kind, is packed full of practical and useful ideas, and serves as a very lively forum for members. Membership is open to all.

Spinal Muscular Atrophy
See Jennifer Macaulay Trust.

SPOD (The Association to Aid the Sexual and Personal Relationships of Disabled People)
See Section 12, Sex and Personal Relationships.

Sue Ryder Foundation
Cavendish, Suffolk CO10 8AY (Tel: Glemsford (0787) 280252).
The Foundation has 20 homes in the United Kingdom. One is a holiday/short-stay home for handicapped and elderly people, and patients with Huntington's Chorea, while other homes are for handicapped and elderly people, the continuing care of cancer patients and mentally ill people. Domiciliary visiting is also undertaken from several of the Foundation's homes.

The Foundation is also active in a number of overseas countries.

The Sympathetic Hearing Scheme
7/11 Armstrong Road, London W3 7JL (Tel: 01–740 4447).
This is a scheme organised and administered by the British Association of the Hard of Hearing. More than one person in seven has a hearing impairment of some kind. The Sympathetic Hearing Scheme has been introduced to help them to lead easier lives. It also aims to help anyone who works with the public by providing a basic training in communicating with hearing impaired people.

The Scheme utilises the 'ear' symbol which has been adopted by interested groups worldwide. The aim is that a sticker showing the symbol will be displayed wherever someone is available to take a little trouble to serve a deaf or hard of hearing person when asked.

Anyone who has problems hearing can obtain a plastic card with the 'ear' symbol to show when they need help. With a short basic training, hearing people can deal, simply and effectively, with anyone who shows the card.

A leaflet which includes basic guidelines is available.

Syringomyelia
See ANTS (Ann's Neurological Trust Society).

Tadworth Court Trust
Tadworth Court Children's Hospital, Tadworth, Surrey KT20 5RU (Tel: Burgh Heath (073 73) 57171).

The Trust provides a number of services for children and their families:

1. High quality medical facilities for children with cystic fibrosis and others with chronic conditions who may require nursing care and medical treatment.
2. Short-term respite care for handicapped and chronically sick children in response to requests from social services and local authority departments.
3. Specialised hospice care for children who are terminally ill, including those with degenerative conditions; and support services for their families.
4. A head injury rehabilitation service for children.
5. Physiotherapy, speech therapy, recreational therapy and hydrotherapy for all children, irrespective of why they are at Tadworth Court.
6. Education at an independent residential school specialising in the provision of education for profoundly multi-handicapped children.

TAG: The Arthrogryposis Group
Witts End, Ghyll Road, Scotby, Carlisle, Cumbria CA4 8BT (Tel: Carlisle (0228) 72553).
Arthrogryposis Multiplex Congenita (AMC) refers to a group of conditions in which multiple joint deformities are present at birth. These are not caused by any true bone abnormalities, but are due to contractures of the soft tissues surrounding the joint. Rigidity of the ligaments, tendons and muscles hold the limb in a characteristic posture. The condition may affect all the joints or only one or two, and the limbs may similarly be affected. AMC is fortunately very rare, affecting about one in 56,000 births. It is not genetically inherited and is not progressive. Most arthrogrypotics achieve a degree of independent mobility and go on to lead useful lives with normal or near-normal life expectancy.

TAG has existed as an informal body since 1981, and is now established as a support group for the families of arthrogrypotic children and adults. The Group aims to create a greater awareness of this rare condition both with the medical profession and the public. Steps have been taken towards gathering a more complete body of information regarding arthrogryposis and a research fund has been established. A newsletter is issued three times a year, and the Group holds an annual conference for members and interested professions each September.

Tay-Sachs and Allied Diseases Association
17 Sydney Road, Barkingside, Ilford, Essex (Tel: 01–550 8989).
Tay-Sachs is an inherited disorder caused by the absence of a vital enzyme, resulting in the destruction of the nervous system. It is always fatal; to date there is no cure. A Tay-Sachs baby develops normally for the first few months; then a relentless deterioration of mental and physical abilities begins. Death is inevitable, usually by the age of 2½ years.

The Tay-Sachs Association was set up for the advancement of education and relief of suffering from Tay-Sachs and allied diseases, to promote screening to detect such diseases wherever possible, and to publicise the fact that screening facilities are available. When possible, it provides financial assistance to sufferers and their families, and makes available leaflets giving information about the disease and addresses where screening is carried out.

Terrence Higgins Trust
BM Aids, London WC1N 3XX (Helpline – Tel: voice (3 – 10 p.m. every day) 01– 242 1010, Vistel (7 – 10 p.m. every day) 01–405 2463).
One of the leading voluntary organisations concerned with the problems associated with infection or the risk of infection by human immunodeficiency viruses (HIV) and, in some cases, the development of AIDS.

Special groups take referrals from the telephone Helpline. Services include support groups, 'buddies' for those who have actually developed AIDS, groups for people who are HIV antibody positive, advice on legal and drug matters, counselling, and the provision of relevant information and legal advice.

The Trust has an extensive library of books, articles and papers concerned with AIDS and the preliminary infection, and distributes information widely.

The Thistle Foundation
27A Walker Street, Edinburgh EH3 7HX (Tel: 031–225 7282).
This Foundation offers physically disabled men and women an alternative to life in hospital. At its one location in the south-east suburbs of Edinburgh, there are over 100 purpose-built family houses (one member of the family must be disabled) and a hostel for 22 single disabled adults. A

respite care unit offers short stay accommodation to physically disabled people on a regular basis, thereby giving relatives a break from continual caring. Medical, physiotherapy, occupational therapy and nursing services are provided, together with extensive recreational facilities. In the houses, the aim is to maintain the integrity of the family unit in spite of disability. In the hostel, residents are encouraged to live full and independent lives.

Tinnitus
See British Tinnitus Association.

TOFS Support Group
124 Park Road, Chesterfield, Derbyshire S40 2LG (Tel: Chesterfield (0246) 37996).
About one in 3,000 babies are born with oesophageal atresia and/or tracheo-oesophageal fistula, the trachea (windpipe) and oesophagus (food pipe) not having divided properly.

TOFS Support Group began in 1982, and now operates nationally, promoting contact between TOF families, providing advice and information, and raising funds for research and special hospital equipment. A national conference is held every two years, and in some areas local meetings are organised. A monthly newsletter, *Chew*, is published.

Tourette Syndrome Association
734 High Road, Goodmayes, Ilford, Essex IG3 8SX (Tel: 01–599 1826).
The Association aims to help those who suffer from Gilles de la Tourette Syndrome, and their families, and to give them support. It seeks to reduce the estimated 7– to 14–year delay between the onset of symptoms, correct diagnosis and appropriate treatment, and to promote research. A newsletter is circulated, and information is provided about the syndrome and the educational needs of students with its associated learning difficulties.

Toy Libraries
See Section 11, Sports and Leisure.

Tracheo Oesophageal Fistula
See TOFS.

Tuberous Sclerosis Association of Great Britain
Little Barnsley Farm, Catshill, Bromsgrove, Worcestershire B61 0NQ (Tel: Bromsgrove (0527) 71898).
The Association was formed in 1977 to act as a mutual self-help group for families concerned with the disease, to promote information about the condition and to support research. Parents keep in contact through correspondence, magazines, an annual meeting and newsletters. Information leaflets, a parents' contact letter and reports on the talks on tuberous sclerosis are available from the Secretary.

UK Rett Syndrome Association
14 Alfred Close, Chatham, Kent ME4 5EE (Tel: (0634) 828992).
Rett Syndrome is a rare neurological disorder which affects only girls. At present, its diagnosis depends upon the recognition of regression in behaviour and some physical changes, usually after nine months of age, after an apparently normal development. There is usually a reduction in the rate of head growth, with loss of manipulative ability in particular. This is replaced by characteristic hand-wringing movements, usually by the age of four years, and often while still quite young. There is an incidence rate of approximately one in 15,000 female births

The Association was founded in April 1985 as an informal parents' support group, but since then it has been developed into an organisation with a membership of over 100, including parents and interested medical personnel.

Its aims are to:
(a) offer parent support, friendship and practical help to those families and carers who have a child affected by Rett Syndrome; and
(b) help to influence professionals in the fields of education, treatment, diagnosis, care and understanding of this very distressing and rare brain disorder.

The Association keeps in touch with its members by means of a quarterly newsletter and regular meetings. However, much of its work is on an individual basis.

All funds raised over and above the costs of the day-to-day running of the Association are put into welfare and research funds within the Collegiate House Trust.

Urostomy Association (formerly Urinary Conduit Association)
'Buckland', Beaumont Park, Danbury, Essex CM3 4DE (Tel: Danbury (024 541) 4294).
The UA was formed in 1971 to help people before and after surgery resulting in a urinary diversion/ileal conduit. Advice can be given about appliances, housing, work situations, sexual problems etc. to assist confident resumption of normal activities.

There are 22 branches in various parts of Great

Britain, and the Association arranges visits both at home and in hospital. The UA Journal is published twice yearly and provides a forum for the exchange of views and ideas.

Research into urinary conditions and the development of equipment is supported. Annual subscription £4.

Usher's Syndrome
This is one of the conditions associated with retinitis pigmentosa. Queries should be addressed to the British Retinitis Pigmentosa Society.

VOCAL (Voluntary Organisations Communication and Language)
336 Brixton Road, London SW9 7AA (Tel: 01–274 4029).
VOCAL brings together 28 voluntary organisations active in the field of communication handicaps and is the central organisation offering specific guidance on communication problems.

It provides support and link services for people with speech and language disorders; it works closely with the speech therapy profession to increase awareness and understanding of communication problems; it is building links with other professions and highlighting the urgent need for better facilities and speech therapy services; and it is establishing research projects so that effective speech therapy programmes can be made available to anyone who requires such help.

Voluntary Council for Handicapped Children
National Children's Bureau, 8 Wakley Street, London EC1V 7QE (Tel: 01–278 9441).
The Council provides information to parents and professionals on all aspects of childhood disability and on services for handicapped children and their families. It holds regular seminars and workshops and has a range of information material including booklists, fact sheets and the free parents' booklet, *Help Starts Here: for parents of children with special needs (an introduction to the intricacies of the welfare state)*.

Wales Council for the Disabled (Cynsor Cymru i'r Anabl)
Caerbragdy Industrial Estate, Bedwas Road,

Caerphilly, Mid Glamorgan CF8 3SL (Tel: Caerphilly (0222) 887325).
The national co-ordinating body for disabled people living in Wales. It seeks to translate the general concern for disabled people into positive action on their behalf, and to further their full integration into society. The Council provides a forum for consultation amongst and co-operation between voluntary, professional and statutory organisations. It makes representations to local and central government, and comments on proposed legislation on all matters affecting disabled people. It provides information on facilities and amenities for disabled people in Wales, and publishes a helpful guide for disabled visitors and a newsletter at regular intervals.

Werdnig-Hoffman Disease
See Jennifer Macaulay Trust.

Williams Syndrome
See Infantile Hypercalcaemia.

Wireless for the Bedridden
81b Corbets Tey Road, Upminster, Essex RM14 2AY (Tel: Upminster (040 22) 50051).
Provides, on free loan, radio and TV sets to needy invalids and the aged poor. Maintenance is covered, and in some cases the licence fee.

Women's National Cancer Control Campaign
1 South Audley Street, London W1Y 5DQ (Tel: 01–499 7532/4).
The Campaign is concerned with measures for the prevention and early detection of women's cancers, particularly of the cervix and of the breast. Leaflets are available on request with s.a.e.

Women's Royal Voluntary Service
234 Stockwell Road, London SW9 9SP (Tel: 01–733 3388).
The WRVS, in addition to its other services for the community, provides care and practical help for the needs of disabled people of all ages, working in co-operation with local authority social services departments. Any disabled person in need of help or advice can contact their local WRVS office (listed in your telephone directory) or the Organiser, WRVS, Welfare for the Disabled, at the above address.

SECTION 16

ACCESS

This new section in the Directory largely describes access guides. Many of these, unfortunately, are very limited in their access information and refer only to access by people in wheelchairs into the building. Only a few refer to access to the services and facilities within buildings, not only to wheelchair users, but also to those who are visually or hearing impaired.

If you are visiting somewhere described as 'accessible', it will often be necessary to prepare for your visit by asking direct questions in advance.

Some legislation is available to back up demands for accessibility in buildings used by the public. (For details *see* Access in Section 13.) It was the Chronically Sick and Disabled Persons Act 1970 which first legislated on access, requiring that in buildings open to the public, provision must be made for the needs of disabled visitors in the external and internal means of access, and in any parking facilities or lavatories.

Part M of the Building Regulations (covering new buildings) now requires that new shops and offices of any number of floors should be accessible. Part M also covers the 'principal entrance storey' of other buildings used by the public. The Regulations now indicate too that alterations and extensions to existing accessible buildings should not make them less accessible.

It is necessary to keep on campaigning for safe crossings, dropped kerbs, parking facilities as well as accessibility to and within buildings.

Transport Access

For details of access surrounding cars, trains, and planes *see* Section 8.

Access Committees

Access Committee for England
35 Great Smith Street, London SW1P 3BJ (Tel: 01–222 7980).
The Committee was formed in 1984 to achieve an accessible environment for people with physical, sensory or mental disablement. Its aim is to work towards the removal of the physical and attitudinal barriers which prevent full participation in the life of society.

Services include information and advice, and design guidance. A quarterly newsletter *Access Action* is produced and a number of other publications including the useful guide to the work of local access groups *Working Together for Access*. Published by the Centre on Environment for the Handicapped on behalf of the Access Committee for England 1985. Price: £3 including post and packing.

The guide contains sections under the following headings.
1. What is an access group? – defining the tasks, organisation and publicity.
2. Access groups in action – profiles of six access groups.
3. Planning – how planning applications are dealt with and how access groups can influence the planning process.
4. Building Regulations – guidance on Part T which required access and facilities for disabled people in certain new buildings under the Fourth Amendment to the Building Regulations 1976. (These have now been overtaken by Part M which is described in Section 13)
5. Fire and means of escape – outlines the relevant legislation and considers the role of the fire officer.
6. Who's who in the local authority? – Building links with the people who matter in local authorities.
7. How the Access Committee for England can help.
8. Legislation, references and organisations.

Access Committee for Wales
Wales Council for the Disabled, Caerbragdy Industrial Estate, Bedwas Road, Caerphilly, Mid Glamorgan CF8 3SL (Tel: (0222) 887325). The Access Officer is Carol Thomas.

The Committee is setting up local access groups throughout Wales. It also compiles reports on access issues and provides advice to local authorities, architects and individuals.

Committee on Access for Scotland
Scottish Council on Disability, 55 Shandwick Place, Edinburgh EH2 4RG (Tel: 031 229 8632).

Local access panels have been set up around Scotland – the aim is to have one in every district. An Access and Development Officer has been appointed.

Northern Ireland Regional Access Committee
2 Annadale Avenue, Belfast B77 3JH (Tel: Belfast (0232) 640011). The Access Officer is Michael Delahunt.

There are a number of local groups and posters and fact sheets are available.

Centre on Environment for the Handicapped
35 Great Smith Street, London SW1P 3BJ (Tel: 01–222 7980).This organisation is committed to the shaping of environments which cater for everyone – including disabled people. They also work closely with the Access Committee for England. For further details of CEH *see* Section 4.

CEH produce a range of publications including the following on access matters.

Reading Plans by Stephen Thorpe (1986). A layperson's guide to the interpretation of architects' drawings. Price: £3.50.

Designing for People with Sensory Impairments by Stephen Thorpe (1986). A companion publication to *Access for Disabled People: Design guidance notes for developers*. The booklet provides clear guidance in the form of technical drawings and supporting text on: External features; Internal Features; Management; Sensory impairment; and Legislation. It is intended for architects, planners, developers, building owners, and managers on how to meet the needs of people with sensory impairments in public buildings and spaces. Price: £2.

Access for Disabled People (1985). Design guidance notes for developers by Stephen Thorpe. This is a series of sheets with drawings and explanatory notes including sections on: What plans are for; Dimensions and scales; Measuring areas and using a scale rule; Doors and doorways; Thresholds; Ramps, staircases and lifts; Lavatories; Symbols; Legislation; and a useful bibliography.

Access Fact Sheet by Stephen Thorpe (1985). This is in A3 poster format and is based on BS5810:1979 Code of Practice for Access for disabled people to buildings. Drawings and text provide technical guidance on access to and within new and existing buildings, with additional information and recommendations. Price £1.

British Standards

British Standards Institution
2 Park Street, London W1A 2BS (Tel: 01–629 9000).

Code of Practice for Access for the Disabled to Buildings (BS 5810: 1979). Price: £19.10 (£7.64 to members).

A high price for 16 pages! But this is the authoritative statement of 'appropriate provisions' for disabled people and is called up as such by both the Disabled Persons Act 1981 and the Local Government (Miscellaneous Provisions) (Scotland) Act 1981.

The Code details the basic architectural provisions that need to be incorporated for use by disabled people, including those dependent on wheelchairs and those with hearing or sight impairments. It incorporates design recommendations for dropped kerbs; level, ramped and stepped approaches to buildings; entrance doors and lobbies; and sets out criteria for internal planning, including changes of level, auditoria, lifts, doors, passageways, lobbies and staircases. There is a section on lavatories and another on general design recommendations, including car parking, approaches, floor and wall surfaces, handrails, doors, switches and controls, induction loops and telephones.

Finally, the now familiar access symbol is illustrated for display in buildings where provision for disabled people conforms to the Standard.

The following British Standards are referred to: BS 5395: Code of Practice for stairs, ladders, and walkways; BS 5619: Design of Housing for the Convenience of Disabled People (*see Section 4*); BS 2655: Lifts, escalators, passenger conveyors and paternosters; BS 5655: Lifts and service lifts.

Access Data Sheets
These have been produced by RADAR and give extracts from BS 5810: 1979 (see above). Each of the eight sheets sets out clearly extracts of specific recommendations from the Code as follows:
1. Approach to buildings.
2. Doors.
3. Internal circulation areas.

4. Lifts.
5. Internal staircases.
6. Lavatories.
7. Auditoria, etc.
8. Induction loop systems.

Available from RADAR, 25 Mortimer Street, London W1N 8AB (Tel: 01–637 5400). Price: 45p a set of eight including postage and packing.

Accessible Lavatories

The National Key Scheme provides disabled people with keys to special lavatories throughout the country. Keys may be obtained from your local Social Services Department or, in case of difficulty, enquiries about the scheme should be sent to RADAR, 25 Mortimer Street, London W1N 8AB (Tel: 01–637 5400). Also available from RADAR an Information sheet (13p for postage); NKS List and a key – list of lavatories fitted with the NKS lock for disabled people in the UK. Price: £2.50; NKS list only, 50p.

Toilet Guide 1988 – A Guide to Public Toilets in Scotland Accessible to People in Wheelchairs. This guide has been compiled with information supplied by District Councils and includes National Key Scheme (NKS) toilets where advised. It includes information on whether there is an attendant available and whether male or female; whether it is unisex or segregated; and details of parking.

Available from: Information Department, Scottish Council on Disability, Princes House, 5 Shandwick Place, Edinburgh EH2 4RG (Tel: 031–229 8632). Price: £1.00.

A-Z Guides
Geographers' A-Z Map Company Ltd, Vestry Road, Sevenoaks, Kent TN14 5EP (Tel: Sevenoaks (0732) 451152).

This company are now including details of Public Toilets for Disabled People in their maps as they are updated. Those already giving this information include: A-Z Sheffield; A-Z Stoke-on-Trent; Barnsley Town Plan; Cambridge Town Plan; Chesterfield Town Plan; Doncaster Town Plan; Rotherham Town Plan; Stoke-on-Trent Town Plan.

Tourist Board Guides and Other Facilities

For details of these guides giving access information to both accommodation and to places of interest *see* Section 9.

Travel for the Disabled This is a handbook of travel

resources and 500 worldwide access guides. For details *see* page 192 Section 10.

Access (1983) This pamphlet is produced by the Disabled Living Foundation, 380 – 384 Harrow Road, London W9 2HU Tel: 01–289 6111. Although this is now somewhat out of date it has some useful information and suggests ways in which people can help as well as discussing design features to be considered.

Servicecall Systems Ltd
Millford Lane, Bakewell, Derbyshire DE4 1DX (Tel: Bakewell (0629 81) 2422).

Servicecall consists of a transmitter (used by the disabled person to summon assistance) and a receiver and extension box. The receiver is mounted on the window of, say, banks, petrol stations, shops, etc. Servicecall has been sponsored by BP Oil who together with other petrol companies, we are assured, have committed themselves to putting hundreds of receivers into their stations. Transmitters will also be available for sale at selected stations. Another commitment has, we understand, been made by Barclays Bank and the Halifax Building Society to consider favourably installing a receiver wherever they are asked to do so by a disabled customer. Other shops and services may also be responsive to such a request.

The transmitter is hand held and when aimed and pressed will send a signal up to approximately 40 metres and further in dull conditions or at night. It fits in a pocket and works through glass. With each transmitter is sent a supply of this leaflet for you to give to those places where you get or would like service.

Price: transmitter £24; receiver £58; extension box £10.

County/Town/City Access Guides

We list below access guides to various areas. First those guides available from RADAR then guides available from elsewhere.

The following are available from RADAR, 25 Mortimer Street, London W1N 8AB Tel: 01–637 5400.

	Price inc p&p
ENGLAND	
Berkshire	
Newbury 1985	40p
Reading 1986	20p
Buckinghamshire	
Milton Keynes 1983	85p

County Durham	
Chester-le-Street 1986	25p
Cumbria	
Kendal 1984	45p
Dorset	
Poole Town Shopping Centre 1986	£1.00
Bournemouth *see below*	
Essex	
Essex Visitors Guide 1987	20p
Gloucestershire	
Gloucester 1986	20p
Greater London	
Access in London 1984	£2.50
Haringey 1984	90p
(*See also* London access guides below)	
Hereford and Worcester	
Redditch 1984	50p
Hertfordshire	
Where Shall We Go? 1985/6	60p
Watford Access Information 1985/6	25p
Kent	
Dover 1984	55p
Thanet	50p
Lancashire	
Blackpool	20p
Lincolnshire	
Spalding 1986	20p
Norfolk	
Great Yarmouth 1986	40p
King's Lynn	70p
Northumberland	
Berwick-upon-Tweed 1986	£1.20
Surrey	
Guildford 1983	45p
Sussex	
Access Arun 1988	£2.55
Arun/Adur Districts, The Downs and Worthing 1983	80p
Chichester District/Bognor Regis	80p
Crawley/Horsham and area 1983	80p
Mid Sussex	80p
Warwickshire	
Nuneaton, Bedworth & Bulkington 1983	45p
Bridlington 1987	30p
Yorkshire	
Harrogate 1983	70p
Leeds & District 1983	£1.34
Sheffield (5th edition) 1984	55p
Wakefield 1986	£1.00
York 1986	£1.00
(Doncaster and Huddersfield *see below*)	
SCOTLAND	
Annan 1983	35p
Edinburgh/Lothian 1984	£1.20
(*See also* below)	
WALES	
Cardiff 1987	30p
(*See also* below)	
Isle of Man	
Isle of Man 1985	45p
Channel Islands	
Guernsey	20p
Jersey	20p
(*See also* Section 10)	
FRANCE	
Access in Paris 1985	£3.00
Brittany 1978	35p
Loire 1978	35p
(*See also* Section 10)	
ISRAEL	
Access in Israel 1980	40p
(*See also* Section 10)	

Additional guides for England are as follows:

Cambridgeshire	
Access Booklet for Peterborough	Free
Available from: Social Services Department, Touthill Close, City Road, Peterborough	
Cumbria	
Kendal – a Brief Guide for Disabled Visitors. Available from: Leisure Services Department, South Lakeland District Council, 47/51 Highgate, Kendal LA9 4ED	Free
Devon	
Guide to Torbay for Disabled Persons 1984	Free
Available from: Torbay Tourist Board, Carlton Chambers, Vaughan Parade, Torquay TQ2 5JG	
Dorset	
Bournemouth and surrounding area – Facilities for the Disabled Visitor 1987	Free
Available from: Tourist Information Centre, Westover Road, Bournemouth BH1 2BU	
(Poole *see above*)	
Greater London	
The Wheelchair Guide to London 1984	£1.00
Available from: London Central YMCA, 112 Great Russell Street, London WC1B 3NQ	
Access to the Underground	70p
Large Print Central London Bus Map	Free
Underground – Large Print Map	Free
The three above publications are available	

from: London Regional Transport, 55
Broadway, London SW1H 0BD
(*See also* London access guides above)
Royal Parks and Palaces   Free
Information which includes details of
accessibility (though this is limited) relating
to the Tower of London; Hampton Court
Palace; Kensington Palace; Kew Palace and
Queen's Cottage; and Banqueting House,
Whitehall is available from the Department
of the Environment, (Royal Parks and
Palaces), 2 Marsham Street, London SW1.
Restaurant Switchboard provides free
information and advice on eating out in the
London area and will give information on
accessibility. Tel: 01–888–8080 9 a.m. –
8 p.m. Monday to Saturday.

Hampshire
An Access Guide to Winchester   Free
Available from: Winchester Group for
Disabled People, 4 Grayshott Close,
Winchester SO22 6JA

Isle of Wight
Guide to the Isle of Wight for the Disabled   85p
Available from: IOW Community Services
Council, Mount Pleasant Road, Newport,
IOW.

Staffordshire
Uttoxeter for the Disabled   Free
Available from: Town Hall, High Street,
Uttoxeter.

Yorkshire
Access Guide to Doncaster 1984   Free
Available from: Doncaster Council for the
Disabled, 95 Thorne Road, Doncaster
DN1 2JT
Huddersfield Access Guide 1988   Free
Available from: Access for All, Welfare
Centre, Zetland Street, Huddersfield
HD1 2RA
(Harrogate, Leeds, Sheffield, Wakefield,
York *see above*)

ENGLAND – MISCELLANEOUS GUIDES

Brewers' Society Pub Facility Symbols
42 Portman Square, London W1H OBB (Tel: 01–
946 0115 for further details from ACE the agency
acting for the Brewers' Society).

New symbols, including the access symbol, are
being shown on pubs in many parts of England. It
is hoped the symbols will also be used in Scotland
and Wales in due course. The symbols relate to the
availability of a 'Family Room', a table service
restaurant, a pub garden, bar food service, accommodation; also whether the pub has any historic interest. Facilities for disabled people will
have been independently ratified by an expert and
will provide a level or ramped route leading from
the car park to a main door of the pub; a level or
ramped entrance leading into a main assembly
area of the pub; a level or suitably ramped route
from the assembly area to where the disabled
person is able to order, by visiting the appropriate
servery/ies, the total choice of drink and food
items on sale; unimpeded access to suitable WC
provision.

Church Action on Disability
Charisma Cottage, Drewsteignton, Exeter EX6
6QR (Tel: Drewsteignton (0647) 21259).
This is a programme supported by the major
Christian denominations in England which seeks
to create the necessary resources, both written and
personal, to achieve the following stated aims:
1. To achieve awareness amongst Christian congregations of people with disabilities so that
they may participate in worship, service, and
ministry and be enabled to make their contribution to the life of the church.
2. To encourage action within Christian congregations to create access in its widest sense to
buildings, worship and ministry through
physical action and change of attitudes.
Launched in July 1987, it is designed as a 3-year
campaign in the first instance. Voluntary regional
officers have been appointed who will co-ordinate
the work of a network of voluntary area and more
local contact people in speaking to church congregations and other groups, encouraging them to
consider the issues involved and to take action
where appropriate.

A magazine *All People* is published, quarterly
issues of which are included in the £5 annual
membership subscription.

English Heritage Guide
Published by English Heritage, Historic Buildings
and Monuments Commission for England, 15/17
Great Marlborough Street, London W1V 1AF
(Tel: 01–734 6010).

This guide describes over 350 historic buildings
to visit throughout England – Roman forts and
Norman castles, prehistoric monuments and windmills, medieval abbeys and stately homes. Sites are
listed county-by-county, with full details of opening arrangements, locations and facilities. There
are maps of every county, many illustrations, and a
full alphabetical site index.

The book uses the wheelchair symbol to denote

that a reasonable amount of the monument or building may be enjoyed by visitors in wheelchairs. In addition, English Heritage will also supply a list of properties in their care with more details of accessibility for all people with mobility difficulties – number of steps, distance from car park, provision of seats, condition of paths, exposure of sites, etc. Price: £1.95.

Forestry Commission
231 Corstorphine Road, Edinburgh EH12 7AT (Tel: 031–334 0303).
Accessible facilities for disabled visitors are provided on Forestry Commission land, including lavatory, car parking, and suitable paths for wheelchairs. Contact the local office or write for the *Forestry Commission Address and Telephone Directory*. This does not provide details of facilities but it will provide you with the names of people to contact in different parts of the country.

National Federation of City Farms
The Old Vicarage, 66 Fraser Street, Windmill Hill, Bedminster, Bristol BS3 4LY (Tel: Bristol (0272) 660663).
All City Farms have some facilities for disabled people and the Federation actively encourages this. For details of any in your locality contact the Federation. For details of any special facilities contact the local farm direct. They also publish a very interesting quarterly magazine *City Farmer*: this is for community gardeners as well as for city farmers. The magazine is well illustrated and a fascinating read. Price: 65p a copy.

The National Trust Handbook (England, Wales and Northern Ireland)
36 Queen Anne's Gate, London SW1H 9AS (Tel: 01–222 9251).
There are many properties listed which indicate their suitability for wheelchair users. One symbol indicates that one or more wheelchairs are available for visitors' use, another symbol indicates that visitors are welcomed in their own wheelchairs, but there are none for hire. Free admission will be given to any individual necessarily accompanying a disabled or visually handicapped person to any Trust property. Most properties now admit guide dogs for the blind, unless otherwise stated in the individual entries in the booklet. Additional information is given on such items as accessibility of lavatories, availability of Braille guide books, lifts, special nature trails, etc.
Price: £2.95 plus 30p postage but issued free to National Trust members.

The National Trust – Facilities for Disabled and Handicapped Visitors. This annual booklet should be used alongside the above National Trust Handbook for members and visitors alike. The facilities booklet is available free on receipt of a self-addressed label, stamped with minimum postage.

WALES
See also guides available from RADAR above.

Welsh Heritage
The responsibility for historic buildings and monuments in Wales is with Cadw whose address is: 9th Floor, Brunel House, Fitzallan Road, Cardiff CF2 1UY. Contact them for further details including accessibility.

Forestry Commission
Victoria House, Victoria Terrace, Aberystwyth, Dyfed SY23 2DQ (Tel: Aberystwyth (0970) 612367).
For details of accessibility and other facilities contact the appropriate Forest District Office Manager direct. Names and addresses of these are given in the booklet *Forestry Commission Address and Telephone Directory*.

National Federation of City Farms
The Old Vicarage, 66 Fraser Street, Windmill Hill, Bedminster, Bristol BS3 4LY (Tel: Bristol (0272) 660663).
All City Farms have some facilities for disabled people and the Federation will be glad to send you a list of farms whom you can then contact direct. In Wales there is one called Cardiff City Farm, Sloper Road, Grangetown, Cardiff CF1 8AB (Tel: Cardiff (0222) 384360). The Federation publish a most interesting quarterly magazine, price 65p a copy.

The National Trust Handbook (England, Wales, and Northern Ireland) see above for details.

Disabled Visitors Guide
Arfon Borough Council, Town Hall, Bangor, Gwynedd LL57 2RE (Tel: 370666). This guide includes information on some of the places of interest in North Wales as well as local information relating to Gwynedd.

Clwyd Association for the Disabled
CVSC Offices, Station Road, Ruthin, Clwyd LL15 1BP (Tel: Ruthin (082 42) 2441/3805)).
CAFD have produced three guides (all 1983): 1. Colwyn District; 2. Alyn and Deeside; 3. Glyndwr.

Reservoir Recreation – with special interest to the

disabled This booklet has been produced by Welsh Water, Cambrian Way, Brecon, Powys LD3 7HP (Tel: Brecon (0874) 3181). Information is given on facilities at all the reservoirs in the Northern Division, South Eastern Division, and the South Western Division in Wales. It is an attractively designed booklet and is nicely descriptive of the areas.

SCOTLAND

See also guides available from RADAR above.

Scottish heritage
The responsibility for historic buildings and monuments in Scotland is with the Historic Buildings and Ancient Monuments Directorate, Scottish Development Department, 20 Brandon Street, Edinburgh EH3 5RA.
  Contact them for further details including accessibility.

Forestry Commission
231 Corstorphine Road, Edinburgh EH12 7AT (Tel: 031–334 0303).
For details of accessibility and facilities contact the appropriate Forest District Office Manager. Details of these are given in the booklet *Forestry Commission Address and Telephone Directory.*

National Federation of City Farms
The Old Vicarage, 66 Fraser Street, Windmill Hill, Bedminster, Bristol BS3 4LY (Tel: Bristol (0272) 660663).
All City Farms have some facilities for disabled people. The Federation will be glad to send you a list and you can then contact the ones of your choice direct.
  The Federation publishes a most interesting quarterly magazine costing 65p a copy.

Access for the Disabled – A Guide to Dundee Available from: D. Halkerston, 6 Rockfield Crescent, Dundee DD2 1JE. Price: £2.00. This guide provides details of shops, banks, hotels, entertainment and leisure facilities, medical services, places of interest, places of worship, public offices, and restaurants and cafes. It also has a section on transport and travel.

Orkney Isles – Access & Information Guide for People with Disabilities (1987). Available from: Voluntary Services Orkney, Quest Buildings, Albert Street, Kirkwall, Orkney KW15 1HL (Tel: Kirkwall (0856) 2897). This 176 page guide to shops, offices, services, and all places used by the general public on the islands is available free.

Aberdeen Tourist Board
St. Nicholas House, Aberdeen AB9 1DE (Tel: Aberdeen (0224) 632727).
At the time of writing (1988) a new edition of *Aberdeen for the Disabled* is being prepared.

Artlink Edinburgh and the Lothians
4 Forth Street, Edinburgh EH1 3LD (Tel: 031–556 6350/557 3490).
Artlink runs an information and access advisory service, and an escort scheme with volunteer drivers to encourage people to attend and take part in arts events. An Artlink access guide *Venues* to arts and historic places in Edinburgh and the Lothians is available.

The National Trust for Scotland Guide to over 100 Properties Available from the Trust at 5 Charlotte Square, Edinburgh EH2 4DU (Tel: 031–226 5922). Price: 80p plus 20p postage and packing. This book includes information on Trust properties giving details of visiting arrangements and indicating those properties which are practicable for wheelchairs.
  Also available is a free leaflet on *Information about Trust Properties for Disabled Visitors* Send 18p s.a.e. for a copy.

For A' the Folk Available free of charge from the Directorate of Scottish Services, Argyle House, 3 Lady Lawson Street, Edinburgh EH3 9SD (Tel: 031–229 9191). This brochure to Scotland's national museums, galleries, and the National Library of Scotland describes facilities for disabled people in some detail.

APPENDIX A
SELECTED FURTHER INFORMATION

Selected publications that are specific to particular sections of this Directory are listed in those sections. Those which concern specific disabilities are too numerous to list: details of those which are best suited to your needs should be available from relevant organisations (*see* Section 15).

Important Publications Lists

Disabled Living Foundation
380–384 Harrow Road, London W9 2HU (Tel: 01–289 6111).
An extensive listing under the following subject headings: clothing; employment; housing and design of furniture and equipment; incontinence; music and the arts; physical recreation; visual handicap; general. The books themselves are available from Haigh and Hochland Ltd., International University Booksellers, The Precinct Centre, Oxford Road, Manchester M13 9QA (Tel: 061–273 4156).

Royal Association for Disability and Rehabilitation
25 Mortimer Street, London W1N 8AB (Tel: 01–637 5400)
This list covers: holidays and travel; sport and leisure; mobility; access and access guides; aids and adaptations; REMAP; education; employment; housing; legal and parliamentary; DHSS leaflets; communication aids for the speech impaired; reference books (specific disabilities and general).

Souvenir Press Ltd
43 Great Russell Street, London WC1B 3PA (Tel: 01–637 5711/2/3).
This publisher's Human Horizons series explores new ways of helping and developing the abilities of handicapped children and adults. The aim is to present material clearly, without technical jargon, and in a way which is easy to understand and to adapt at home or at school. There are now nearly 60 titles available. A complete catalogue is available from Souvenir Press.

Directories and Bibliographies

Bardsoft (Handicapped Persons Research Unit, Newcastle upon Tyne Polytechnic, 1 Coach Lane, Coach Lane Campus, Newcastle upon Tyne NE7 7TW (Tel: 091–235 8211)). A database containing information on over 2,000 computer software programmes for special needs, relating to over 40 types of microcomputer.

Charities Digest (Family Welfare Association, 501–503 Kingsland Road, London E8 4AU, 1988), price £8.95 including postage and packing. An annual reference guide to charities and benevolent institutions and the work they do.

Directory of Agencies for the Blind in the British Isles and Overseas (Royal National Institute for the Blind, 244 Great Portland Street, London W1N 6AA, 1988), price £5. The directory covers the national government and voluntary agencies concerned with blind people as well as regional and local associations, schools, ophthalmic hospitals, homes and hostels. It includes information about periodicals in Braille and Moon, and about publishers of large print material. It also lists organisations and sources of funds which can provide financial help to blind individuals, and a few self-help groups of professional blind workers.

Directory of Hospice Services (St Christopher's Hospice, 51–59 Lawrie Park Road, Sydenham, London SE26 6DZ, 1988), single copies free. Published annually, listing in-patient units, home care teams, Sue Ryder homes, hospital support teams, hospice projects and other useful addresses.

Directory of Non-Medical Research Relating to Handicapped People, Volume 4, by Jim Sandhu, Steven Richardson and Rosalyn Routledge (Handicapped Persons Research Unit, Newcastle upon Tyne Polytechnic, 1 Coach Lane, Coach Lane Campus, Newcastle upon Tyne NE7 7TW, 1987), price £15.00 including postage and packing. 485 pages. This volume of the Directory consists of over 600 detailed descriptions of non-medical research and design development projects in the handicap/disability field being undertaken in the United Kingdom, and is complementary to three earlier volumes. The projects cover such topics as: child development, education, post-school, recreation, health and social services, community and institutional care, rehabilitation and assessment. Access to information is through a descriptive contents list and subject, worker and institution indexes. Volume 5, which complements all previous volumes, should be out in 1988. By this time all entries will also be in the form of a database called BARDSEARCH.

Directory of Voluntary Organisations on Disability in Scotland (Scottish Council on Disability, 5 Shandwick Place, Edinburgh EH2 4RG, 1984), price £3.

Health Help '87/8 (National Council for Voluntary Organisations, 26 Bedford Square, London WC1B 3HU, 1987), price £2.95. Lists 700 organisations concerned with different disabilities and health problems.

Incontinence: Bibliography compiled by Philippa Lane in co-operation with Dorothy Mandelstam (Reedbooks Ltd for the DLF, 1981, available from Haigh and Hochland Ltd, International University Booksellers, The Precinct Centre, Oxford Road, Manchester M13 9QA), price £7 including postage and packing. Multi-disciplinary in approach and lists less easily found material concerned with practical management, as well as medical, surgical, social and psychological references.

Self-help and the Patient (Patients' Association, Room 33, 18 Charing Cross Road, London WC2H 0HR, 1986), price £2.95 including postage and packing. A directory of national organisations concerned with various diseases and handicaps.

The Self-Help Guide by Sally Knight and Robert Gann (Chapman and Hall, 11 New Fetter Lane, London EC4P 4EC, 1988), price £6.95. A directory of self-help organisations in the United Kingdom.

Useful Addresses for Parents with a Handicapped Child by Ann Worthington (In Touch, 10 Norman Road, Sale, Cheshire M33 3DF, 3rd edition, 1985), price £2.90 including postage and packing. 68 pages. Addresses of organisations, toys and play, aids and equipment, education, further education, long and short term care, holidays, finance and rights, publications.

Voluntary Agencies: The 1988 Directory (National Council for Voluntary Organisations, 26 Bedford Square, London WC1B 3HU, 1987), price £7.95, or by post from Harper and Row Distributors Ltd., Estover Road, Plymouth PL6 7PZ, price £8.95 including postage and packing. This edition has been revised and expanded to include some 1,600 leading voluntary agencies. Names and addresses are listed alphabetically, with summaries of aims and activities. Symbols indicate charitable status, local branches, use of volunteers, number of paid staff, size of organisation, trading companies and library/information room.

A list of useful addresses following the directory section includes professional and public advisory bodies which are relevant to the work of voluntary organisations. The index is classified according to the major subject interests.

Publications concerned generally with Disability and Related Issues

Caring at Home by Nancy Kohner (National Extension College, 18 Brooklands Avenue, Cambridge CB2 2HN, 1988), price £3.95 plus postage and packing. A handbook for people looking after someone at home who is handicapped, disabled, ill or frail. It covers a wide range of topics important to all carers including: health and local authority services; voluntary and community help; money and legal matters; time off; day-to-day caring skills; coping with feelings.

Coping with Disability by Peggy Jay (Disabled Living Foundation, 1984), price £9 including postage and packing, available from Haigh and Hochland Ltd., International University Booksellers, The Precinct Centre, Oxford Road, Manchester M13 9QA. Provides a great deal of practical information, backed up by extensive illustrations, designed to show disabled people how to get help from the health and social services, from voluntary organisations and others. It contains advice on how to make life easier in the home: how to get in and out of a bath and manage independently in the lavatory, how to cope with problems of clothes and dressing, cooking, eating, housework and laundry. There are sections on mobility, on keeping in touch, on getting out and about, and on pastimes and leisure activities.

The Health Information Handbook: Resources for Self Care by Robert Gann (Gower Publishing Group Ltd., Gower House, Croft Road, Aldershot, Hampshire GU11 3HR, 1986), price £20.45 including postage and packing. This handbook offers practical guidance to library services, advice services, voluntary and self-help groups of all kinds on the provision of health information to the public. It examines the need for information on health and illness, provides an overview of health information provision in the United Kingdom and gives an international perspective based on practices in the USA and Europe.

An important feature of the handbook is a section giving practical advice to those setting up health information services on how to make the right contacts, establish basic collections of publications and to organise this material for use.

The contents include: reponsibility for health; the informed patient; health information in the UK; health information in other countries; getting started – collecting and organising health information; index.

Taking a Break: A Guide for People Caring at Home (Kings Fund Informal Caring Programme, 1987), available from Taking a Break, Newcastle upon Tyne X, NE85 2AQ, price 60p including packing and postage (cheques and postal orders payable to King Edward's Hospital Fund for London; free to carers). A 36-page booklet of advice on arranging time off for carers, that is anyone who looks after a relative or friend who is elderly, ill or disabled. Based on carers' experiences, it offers practical information and advice which will help you and the person you look after to arrange a break. The contents include: descriptions of over 20 different types of break; information and advice on how to make practical arrangements; hints on coping with emotional worries and resolving practical problems; ideas for improving services for carers and the people they look after; an extensive list of useful contacts and national organisations.

The Wheelchair Child by Philippa Russell (Souvenir Press Ltd., 43 Great Russell Street, London WC1B 3PA, revised 1984), price £6.95 plus £1 postage and packing. This book covers problems from early childhood to young adulthood. The author, Senior Officer of the Voluntary Council for Handicapped Children, combines basic information on the main handicapping conditions, the medical and community services available to handicapped children, and practical advice on aids, appliances, home adaptations and financial grants, with a thoughtful consideration of the developmental and emotional problems attached to disability. As well as the special needs for education and leisure, she deals with problems of depression for child and parent, the difficulties of siblings, dependency, adolescence and sex; and, especially in relation to degenerative handicaps, the facing of early death.

Magazines and Periodicals

Accent on Living (Accent Special Publications, Box 700, Bloomington, Illinois 61701, USA), price to subscribers outside USA: $7.50 (1 year), $12 (2 years) or $16.50 (3 years). Although primarily written for American readers, this magazine for disabled people contains much that is of general interest and is extremely well produced. It is published quarterly, with over 18,000 paid subscribers in the USA and a few elsewhere. Accent has also produced a number of helpful booklets, including *Buyers Guide* (products for disabled people), price $10 and *Sexual Adjustment*, price $4.95. Add $1.15 per book for orders to be mailed outside USA.

Caring (incorporating *Handicapped Living*) (A. K.Morgan Publications Ltd., Stanley House, 9 West Street, Epsom, Surrey KT18 7RL), price 85p monthly or on subscription at £10.60 a year. A magazine which is described (January, 1988) as 'for the disabled, carers and the elderly'.

Disability Now edited by Mary Wilkinson (The Spastics Society, 12 Park Crescent, London W1N 4EQ), monthly, free on request. By no means restricted to the concerns of people with cerebral palsy, this newspaper sets a high journalistic standard, and is a mine of news and information. It would be difficult to praise it too highly. As well as normal print, there are tape versions (contact 01–636 5020 ext.244) and discs suitable for the 2 switch Amstrad CPC6128 and the BBC 'B' computers (contact 02407 4231).

Audio/Visual

Camera Talks Ltd
197 Botley Road, Oxford OX2 0HE (Tel: Oxford (0865) 726625).
This company produces and distributes an extensive range of audio visual aids, including slide sets, 35mm filmstrips, cassetted tapes, 16mm films, and related equipment. A catalogue is available arranged by subject headings which include physiotherapy, occupational therapy, mental health, social services, and care of the aged. All programmes are available on approval (sale or return). The majority are slide/tape, with the tape pulsed for synchronisation with the slides if used with an automatic projector. Printed commentaries are also available. Prices (at the time of writing): slides

and notes, £35 per part; cassetted tape commentary, £9.50. Programmes are also available for hire at £5 per part per week, including a box of slides, tape and notes.

Concord Video and Film Council Ltd
201 Felixstowe Road, Ipswich, Suffolk IP3 9BJ (Tel: Ipswich (0473) 726012).
This company makes available for hire and sale an extensive range of documentary films and video cassettes with special emphasis on social issues. It is registered as a charity and now has the largest educational film library in Britain. The programmes are selected primarily to promote discussion, for instruction and for training, many being used in the course of education or for training in the health service or social services. Many voluntary organisations have used Concord to distribute their films, in order to publicise their work and draw attention to the special needs of those people they exist to serve. The library includes numerous documentary films on handicapped children, on children in hospitals and institutions, on blindness and deafness, education, mental health, physical handicaps and rehabilitation.

A free brochure giving details of approximately 100 programmes dealing with disablement (both physical and mental) is available on request. A comprehensive catalogue and index of all films and video cassettes costs £1.50 plus £1 postage. Inclusion on mailing list to receive regular supplements is included without extra charge.

Graves Medical Audiovisual Library
Holly House, 220 New London Road, Chelmsford, Essex CM2 9BJ (Tel: Chelmsford (0245) 283351).
This library carries a large stock of tape-slide and video tape programmes available for hire or sale. They are mostly of professional medical interest, but some bear on disability in a more general way, with an extensive range of material relating to the care and understanding of mentally handicapped children and adults, including a number of tape/slide sets on sexual matters. Please apply for hire and sale prices.

The Mental Health Film Council
380–384 Harrow Road, London W9 2HU.
Has a catalogue of over 600 films and videos concerned with all aspects of mental health and disability, price £5 including postage and packing.

INDEX

NOTE: Page numbers in bold indicate main entries.